GCSE MATHS
LEVEL B

Jean Holderness

Causeway Press Ltd

Published by Causeway Press Ltd
P.O. Box 13, Ormskirk, Lancashire L39 5HP

First published 1994
Reprinted 1995

British Library Cataloguing-in-Publication Data.
A catalogue record for this book is available from the British Library.

ISBN 1-873929-15-3

The GCSE Maths Series
Available now:
GCSE Maths: Level A by Jean Holderness
GCSE Maths: Level B by Jean Holderness

To follow:
GCSE Maths: Level C by Jean Holderness

The Causeway Maths Series
Available now:
Causeway Maths 1 by David Alcorn
Causeway Maths 2 by David Alcorn
Causeway Maths 3 by Jean Holderness

To follow:
Causeway Maths 4 by Jean Holderness
Causeway Maths 5 by Jean Holderness
Causeway Maths 6 by Jean Holderness
Causeway Maths 7 by Jean Holderness

Other titles published by Causeway Press:
Mathematics: Levels 3 & 4 by David Alcorn
Mathematics: Level 5 by Jean Holderness
Mathematics: Level 6 by Jean Holderness
Mathematics: Level 7 by Jean Holderness
Mathematics: Level 8 by Jean Holderness
Mathematics: Levels 9 & 10 by Jean Holderness

GCSE Maths: Higher Level by Jean Holderness
GCSE Maths: Intermediate Level by Jean Holderness
GCSE Maths: Foundation Level by Jean Holderness
Pure Maths in Practice by Jean Holderness

Typeset and printed at Alden Press Limited,
Oxford and Northampton, Great Britain

Preface

This book is planned for use on a 2-year or a 1-year course leading to the Intermediate level papers of the GCSE. It is based on the syllabuses published for use in 1994, which are all linked with the National Curriculum programme of study and attainment targets for Key Stage 4.

Students will have been learning Mathematics from an early age, so they will have already met many of the topics in this book. The earlier chapters will help to revise and consolidate the work of former years. A good understanding of the basic topics, leading to a sense of achievement, will form a firm foundation to build on when progressing through the syllabus.

The order of the book has been carefully planned, although, of course, it need not be followed rigidly. To some extent it follows the order of the topics in the National Curriculum. Chapters contain a mixture of straightforward questions for students who need to master the techniques, and more varied questions for others to do. Each chapter ends with a practice test.

After every 5 chapters there is a miscellaneous section which includes an aural exercise; revision exercises, which could also be used as practice tests; and suggestions for activities to link with AT1, 'using and applying mathematics'. There are puzzle questions throughout the book. Also there are suggestions to students for study, revision and preparation for the examination.

I should like to thank my brother Jim, and all my family and friends who have given me support and encouragement while I have been writing this book. I should also like to thank all those teachers, and others, who have provided helpful comments on the previous GCSE series.

Thanks also go to those who have helped with the production of the book, Sue, Andrew, Mark, Maureen, Fred and the staff at Alden Multimedia and Alden Press. From Causeway Press I have had great support from Mike and everyone else, and especially from David, who has given me a great amount of practical help and encouragement over several months.

I hope that you find this book useful and interesting.

Jean Holderness

Acknowledgements

Artwork created electronically by
Mark Andrews [Quantum Graphics, Northampton]

Page design, cover and artwork
Susan and Andrew Allen

Copyright photographs
ACE/PHOTOTAKE (cover)
Andrew Allen
Jim Holderness

Contents

Topics for Activities (included in the miscellaneous sections)

To Tessa and Sam

Tables

Time

60 seconds = 1 minute	52 weeks = 1 year
60 minutes = 1 hour	365 days = 1 year
24 hours = 1 day	366 days = 1 leap year
7 days = 1 week	12 months = 1 year

The Metric System   **British Units**

Length

1000 mm = 1 m	12 inches = 1 foot
100 cm = 1 m	3 feet = 1 yard
1000 m = 1 km	1760 yards = 1 mile

Area

$100 \text{ mm}^2 = 1 \text{ cm}^2$	144 sq. inches = 1 sq. foot
$10\,000 \text{ cm}^2 = 1 \text{ m}^2$	9 sq. feet = 1 sq. yard
$1\,000\,000 \text{ m}^2 = 1 \text{ km}^2$	
$1 \text{ hectare} = 10\,000 \text{ m}^2$	1 acre = 4840 sq. yards
$100 \text{ hectares} = 1 \text{ km}^2$	640 acres = 1 sq. mile

Volume

$1000 \text{ mm}^3 = 1 \text{ cm}^3$	1728 cu. inches = 1 cu. foot
$1\,000\,000 \text{ cm}^3 = 1 \text{ m}^3$	27 cu. feet = 1 cu. yard

The Metric System	British Units

Weight

100 mg = 1 g	16 ounces = 1 pound
100 cg = 1 g	14 pounds = 1 stone
1000 g = 1 kg	112 pounds = 1 hundredweight
1000 kg = 1 tonne	8 stones = 1 hundredweight
	2240 pounds = 1 ton
	20 hundredweights = 1 ton

Capacity

1000 ml = 1 ℓ

100 cl = 1 ℓ

1000 ℓ = 1 kl

1 litre = 1000 cm^3

1 litre of water weighs 1 kg

1 cm^3 of water weighs 1 g

8 pints = 1 gallon

1 pint of water weighs $1\frac{1}{4}$ lb

1 gallon of water weighs 10 lb

To change to the metric system

Length

1 inch = 2.54 cm

1 foot = 30.48 cm

1 yard = 91.44 cm = 0.9144 m

1 mile = 1.609 km

Weight

1 oz = 28.35 g

1 lb = 453.6 g

1 ton = 1016 kg = 1.016 tonne

Capacity

1 pint = 0.568 litre

1 gallon = 4.546 litre

To change from the metric system

Length

1 cm = 0.394 in

1 m = 39.37 in = 1.094 yd

1 km = 1094 yd = 0.621 mile

Weight

1 kg = 2.205 lb

1 tonne = 0.984 ton

Capacity

1 litre = 1.76 pints = 0.220 gallons

To the student : 1

Learning mathematics

Maths is not a new subject since you have been learning it all your life, but in this book are all the topics you need to learn for the Intermediate level of the GCSE in Maths.

We hope that you will enjoy studying Maths. Just think of some of the ways in which Maths is linked with our lives, for example:
Shapes in the natural world involving symmetry, curves, spirals, etc.
Shapes in architecture and design.
Management of our money.
Understanding of diagrams, graphs and maps.
Ability to think logically, so as to plan ahead.
You can think of many more examples of how Maths is essential in today's world.

Learn to think for yourself. Do not rely on being told how to do everything. The more things you can work out for yourself the better you will do.

Try to discover things for yourself. Look for patterns in numbers and shapes. From a particular result, could you deduce a general formula ? As an example, suppose you have a spare moment waiting for a lesson to begin and you put your ruler down on your exercise book and draw lines on either side of it, then you move the ruler and cross the lines with two others, getting a shape in the middle. Now you can discover many things about that shape: What is it ? Are there any equal lines or angles, or any point or lines of symmetry ? What is the sum of the angles ? What is its area ? By altering the angle at which the lines cross can you get a different area ? What is the least possible area ? Can you draw a sketch graph of the relationship between angle and area ? If you add more lines to the drawing you can make more discoveries.

As you work through this book, try to learn the important facts and methods of each chapter. If you do not understand the main ideas, ask someone to help you, either your teacher, someone else in your class or anyone else who can explain them to you. But when you have to answer an unusual question, before you ask for help, try to use your own commonsense and reason it out.

If you work steadily you can gain a good grade in GCSE Mathematics.

How this book is arranged

There are 25 main chapters. At the beginning of each chapter there is a list of topics included in that chapter. Then there are main facts or methods followed by worked examples, and an exercise to give you practice. The last exercise in each chapter has more varied questions. You may do them at this stage or you may leave them to return to later to give you more revision practice. Finally, there is a test on the ideas of the chapter.

There should be no need to do every part of every question in an exercise. More questions, rather than fewer, have been included for those students who need them. As soon as you have understood a topic you could go on to something else. Use your time wisely so that you complete the syllabus. Learn the important facts, methods and formulae as you go along.

After every 5 chapters there is a Miscellaneous Section. This can be used at any time. It includes an aural practice exercise, revision questions and suggestions for activities or independent work.

There are puzzle questions fitted in at the ends of some chapters. Try some of these, and remember that some may have a catch in them ! Many puzzles do not form part of the examination course but they may be useful for independent work, and may suggest ideas for further investigation.

Now, get started and **enjoy your Maths**.

1 **Numbers**

The topics in this chapter include:

- multiplying and dividing mentally, and by using non-calculator methods,

- understanding and using terms such as prime, cube, square root and cube root,

- using index notation to express the powers of whole numbers,

- using the rules of indices for positive integer values,

- expressing positive integers as a product of prime numbers,

- generating sequences, exploring number patterns,

- using negative numbers.

Numbers

A calculator is an invaluable tool for saving time and doing accurate calculations, but there are basic arithmetical operations which you should be able to do mentally, quickly and accurately, and for which you should not waste time pressing calculator keys.

You may be asked to multiply and divide mentally in questions such as 80×0.2 and $600 \div 0.2$, so you will need to know the basic tables.

There will be many situations in your life when you need to work something out quickly and you will not have your calculator available. So make sure you are mentally alert.

To check your tables

On squared paper, or with columns drawn on lined paper, copy the chart at the top of the next page. You are going to fill in the results of multiplication, so the numbers in the first few squares down the first empty column are 12, 22, 10, 16, etc. You will work down each column in turn. Before you begin, note the time. You should complete the chart within 5 minutes. If you take longer, then repeat the exercise, using numbers in a different random order, until you improve. Then check the accuracy of your work, which should be completely correct.

X	2	8	6	9	4	11	3	7	5	12
6	12									
11	22									
5	10									
8	16									
12										
3										
10										
4										
9										
7										

Exercise 1.1

These questions are intended to improve your speed and accuracy so concentrate and do them quickly.

Write down the answers only in questions 1 to 7.

1. Work out, working downwards in columns.

8×7	$30 + 90$	$21 - 6$	6×12	$100 \div 5$
6×4	$8 + 7$	$30 \div 5$	6×0	$99 + 7$
20×1	11^2	30×20	$\sqrt{64}$	99×0
20×3	$56 \div 7$	$20 - 8$	13×1	12^2

2. Work out

$32 \div 4$	$27 \div 9$	$55 \div 5$	$72 \div 12$	$15 \div 5$
$42 \div 7$	$132 \div 11$	$72 \div 9$	$30 \div 6$	$49 \div 7$
$96 \div 12$	$60 \div 6$	$36 \div 3$	$77 \div 11$	$45 \div 5$
$56 \div 8$	$144 \div 12$	$35 \div 7$	$60 \div 5$	$81 \div 9$

3. What is the remainder when

    1 18 is divided by 5,   **4** 52 is divided by 4,
    2 39 is divided by 7,   **5** 100 is divided by 8 ?
    3 68 is divided by 11,

4. What must be added to

    1 8×7 to make 60,   **4** 7×11 to make 80,
    2 4×3 to make 20,   **5** 9×9 to make 100 ?
    3 5×9 to make 50,

5. Find the value of

1	$5 \times 3 \times 1$	**5**	$5000 \div 20$	**8**	$(8 \times 12) - (7 \times 12)$
2	$4 \times 2 \times 0$	**6**	$89 + 99$	**9**	$(6 \times 19) + (4 \times 19)$
3	$10^2 - 9^2$	**7**	$180 \div 5$	**10**	$\frac{2}{3}$ of 36 $+ \frac{1}{3}$ of 36
4	$10 \times 20 \times 40$				

6. **1** How many more 4's than 5's are there in 40?
    2 How many more 8's than 12's are there in 96?
    3 Find two consecutive numbers whose squares differ by 11.
    4 Find two consecutive numbers whose squares add up to 181.
    5 Find three consecutive numbers whose squares add up to 50.

7. **1** Find two numbers whose sum is 13 and whose product is 36.
    2 Find two numbers whose sum is 11 and whose product is 30.
    3 Find two numbers whose sum is 52 and whose product is 100.
    4 Find two numbers whose sum is 16 and whose product is 15.
    5 Find two numbers whose sum is 16 and whose product is 48.
    6 Find three numbers whose product is 36 and whose sum is 11.
    7 Find three numbers whose product is 60 and whose sum is 12.
    8 Find two numbers whose product is 72 and which differ by 1.
    9 Find two numbers whose product is 24 and which differ by 5.
    10 Find two numbers whose product is 77 and which differ by 4.

8. **1** Start from 100 and count down in 6's until you reach a number less than 10. What number is this?

    2 Start from 1, then 2, then 4, and double the number every time until you reach a number greater than 1000. What number is this?

    3 Start from 25 000 and keep dividing by 5 until you reach a number less than 10. What number is this?

    4 Start with 1 and keep adding 7's until you reach a number greater than 100. What number is this?

    5 Start from 0 and add 1, then 2, then 3, and so on until you reach a number greater than 100. What number is this?

9. **1** Write down any number between 1 and 10, multiply this by 3, then to the result add 8. Double this answer. Now subtract 3, multiply by 5, add 7. Subtract 2 and divide by 10. Add 17, divide by 3 and take away the number you started with. What is your answer?

    2 Write down any number between 1 and 10, add 3 and multiply the result by 6. Then subtract 12, divide by 3, multiply by 10. Add 5, divide by 5 and add 7. Subtract 12 then divide by the number you started with. What is your answer?

9. **3** Write down any number less than 5, double it and add 3. Square the result, add 3
      and divide by 4. Subtract 1 and multiply by 2. Subtract 4, divide by the number you
      started with, add 14 and halve the result. Take away the number you started with.
      What is your answer?

Some multiplication and division without using a calculator

Multiplying whole numbers by 10

$$7 \times 10 = 70$$
$$87 \times 10 = 870$$
$$987 \times 10 = 9870$$
$$980 \times 10 = 9800$$
$$900 \times 10 = 9000$$

The figures 7 units, 8 tens and 9 hundreds have all become ten times bigger by moving up one
place to become 7 tens, 8 hundreds and 9 thousands. 0's are used to fill the empty spaces.

Multiplying whole numbers by 100 or 1000

To multiply by 100 is simply the same as multiplying by 10 and then by 10 again, so the
numbers move up two places.
To multiply by 1000 is the same as multiplying by 10, by 10 again and then by 10 again, so the
numbers move up three places.

$$8 \times 100 = 800$$
$$78 \times 100 = 7800$$
$$678 \times 100 = 67\,800$$
$$5670 \times 100 = 567\,000$$
$$5000 \times 100 = 500\,000$$

$$23 \times 1000 = 23\,000$$
$$123 \times 1000 = 123\,000$$
$$4020 \times 1000 = 4\,020\,000$$

Multiplying whole numbers by 20, 30, 40, . . . , 200, 300, 400, . . . , 2000, 3000, 4000, . . .

$$
\begin{aligned}
70 \times 500 &= 7 \times 10 \times 5 \times 100 \\
&= 7 \times 5 \times 10 \times 100 \\
&= 35 \times 1000 \\
&= 35\,000
\end{aligned}
$$

$$
\begin{aligned}
800 \times 20 &= 8 \times 2 \times 1000 \\
&= 16\,000
\end{aligned}
$$

$$
\begin{aligned}
5000 \times 20 &= 5 \times 2 \times 10\,000 \\
&= 100\,000
\end{aligned}
$$

$$
\begin{aligned}
9000 \times 3000 &= 9 \times 3 \times 1\,000\,000 \\
&= 27\,000\,000
\end{aligned}
$$

Dividing whole numbers by 10, 100 or 1000

$9000 \div 10 = 900$
$6800 \div 10 = 680$
$6850 \div 10 = 685$

The figures have all become ten times smaller by moving down one place. 0's no longer needed disappear.

$\begin{aligned} 9\,300 \div 100 &= 93 \quad \text{(Moving down 2 places)} \\ 800 \div 100 &= 8 \\ 30\,000 \div 1000 &= 30 \quad \text{(Moving down 3 places)} \\ 34\,000 \div 1000 &= 34 \\ 534\,000 \div 1000 &= 534 \end{aligned}$

Dividing whole numbers by 20, 30, 40, . . . , 200, 300, 400, . . . , 2000, 3000, 4000, . . .

$6000 \div 30 = \dfrac{600\cancel{0}}{3\cancel{0}} = \dfrac{600}{3} = 200$

The 0's are crossed out because we are dividing both numbers by 10. (This can be called **cancelling**.)

What we are really doing is
$6000 \div 30 = (6000 \div 10) \div 3 = 600 \div 3 = 200$

$800 \div 400 = \dfrac{8\cancel{0}\cancel{0}}{4\cancel{0}\cancel{0}} = \dfrac{8}{4} = 2$

(We have divided both numbers by 10, and then by 10 again.)

$30\,000 \div 5000 = \dfrac{30\,\cancel{0}\cancel{0}\cancel{0}}{5\cancel{0}\cancel{0}\cancel{0}} = \dfrac{30}{5} = 6$

$7200 \div 60 = \dfrac{720\cancel{0}}{6\cancel{0}} = \dfrac{720}{6} = 120$

$3500 \div 700 = \dfrac{35\cancel{0}\cancel{0}}{7\cancel{0}\cancel{0}} = \dfrac{35}{7} = 5$

You can still use this method without writing anything down, if you have to do it in your head e.g. $40\,000 \div 800$ equals $400 \div 8$ which is 50, (mentally dividing by 100 first).

Long multiplication and long division

To multiply by a number between 10 and 100

Examples

1 328×46

First multiply 328 by 6, then 328 by 40, and add the results together.

$$\begin{array}{rr} & 328 \\ \times & \underline{46} \\ & 1968 \\ & \underline{13120} \\ & \underline{15088} \end{array}$$

← write down the 0 because this comes from multiplying by 10, then multiply 328 by 4.

or

$$\begin{array}{rr} & 328 \\ \times & \underline{46} \\ & 13120 \\ & \underline{1968} \\ & \underline{15088} \end{array}$$

if you prefer to multiply by 40 before you multiply by 6.

2 173×91

$$\begin{array}{rr} & 173 \\ \times & \underline{91} \\ & 173 \\ & \underline{15570} \\ & \underline{15743} \end{array} \qquad \text{or} \qquad \begin{array}{rr} & 173 \\ \times & \underline{91} \\ & 15570 \\ & \underline{173} \\ & \underline{15743} \end{array}$$

Normally you would use your calculator to do such questions but it is essential to know how to work out the answers yourself as you cannot always rely on having a calculator handy.

This method is called **long multiplication**. There are other methods of working and you can use any method you prefer as long as it gives the correct answer.

To divide by a number between 10 and 100

Examples

3 $826 \div 14$

First, 14 into 8 won't go.
14's into 82 goes 5 times. Put 5 in the answer above the 2 of 82.
Multiply 14 by 5 (=70) and write this under the 82.
Subtract 70 from 82 leaving 12.
Bring down the next figure, 6, making 126.
14's into 126 goes 9 times. Put 9 in the answer above the 6.
Multiply 14 by 9 (=126) and write this under the 126.
Subtracting leaves 0 so there is no remainder. The answer is 59.

$$\begin{array}{rl} & 59 \quad \text{Answer} \\ 14 & \overline{)826} \\ & \underline{70} \\ & 126 \\ & \underline{126} \\ & 0 \end{array}$$

The difficult part of such a question is deciding how many times 14 goes into 82 and into 126. You can do it the long way by working out the 14 times table until you get far enough:

$14 \times 1 = 14$, $14 \times 2 = 28$, $14 \times 3 = 42$, etc.

You could make a rough guess instead.

$14 \times 10 = 140$ so half of that, $14 \times 5 = \frac{1}{2}$ of $140 = 70$. Then $14 \times 6 = 70 + 14 = 84$, so 14 goes into 82 five times.

4 $988 \div 19$

$19\overline{)988}$ First, think of 19 as nearly 20.
                  How many 20's in 98. Nearly 5.
                  Check whether 19×5 is less than 98. Yes, it is, so the first part of the answer is a five.

$$\begin{array}{r} 5 \\ 19\overline{)988} \\ 95 \\ \hline 38 \end{array}$$

$19 \times 5 = 95$. Put the 5 above the 8 of 98, and 95 below 98, subtract 95 from 98 and put the 3 below. Bring down the next 8.

$$\begin{array}{r} 52 \ \text{Answer} \\ 19\overline{)988} \\ 95 \\ \hline 38 \\ 38 \\ \hline 0 \end{array}$$

How many 19's in 38 ? (How many 20's ?)
There are nearly 2 20's, and there are exactly 2 19's.
$19 \times 2 = 38$. Write 2 in the answer above the 8 of 38.
Write 38 below 38 and subtract, leaving 0 so there is no remainder.
The answer is 52.

5 Divide 919 by 24, giving the answer and the remainder.

$$\begin{array}{r} 38 \\ 24\overline{)919} \\ 72 \\ \hline 199 \\ 192 \\ \hline 7 \end{array}$$

Answer 38, remainder 7.

6 Divide 919 by 24, giving the answer correct to 1 decimal place.

$$
\begin{array}{r}
38.29 \\
24\overline{)919.00} \\
\underline{72} \\
199 \\
\underline{192} \\
7\,0 \\
\underline{4\,8} \\
2\,20 \\
\underline{2\,16} \\
4
\end{array}
$$

Answer so far 38.29 . . .
Answer correct to 1 decimal place $= 38.3$

Remember to put the decimal point in the answer. There is no need to show it in the working.

This method is called **long division**. There are other methods of working and you can use any method you prefer as long as it gives the correct answer.

Exercise 1.2

You should do these questions without using a calculator.

1.
1 28×10	**5** 400×2000	**8** 20×7000
2 710×100	**6** 8000×30	**9** 6000×50
3 903×1000	**7** 300×600	**10** 70×400
4 60×80		

2.
1 $7000 \div 10$	**5** $90\,000 \div 300$	**8** $20\,000 \div 50$
2 $30\,000 \div 100$	**6** $800 \div 40$	**9** $600 \div 300$
3 $6000 \div 1000$	**7** $6000 \div 200$	**10** $5000 \div 20$
4 $4000 \div 100$		

3.
1 804×45	**5** 397×54	**8** 703×15
2 457×19	**6** 216×66	**9** 989×73
3 673×92	**7** 525×62	**10** 140×87
4 144×68		

4.
1 $608 \div 16$	**5** $423 \div 47$	**8** $403 \div 31$
2 $438 \div 73$	**6** $522 \div 18$	**9** $374 \div 17$
3 $961 \div 31$	**7** $221 \div 13$	**10** $850 \div 25$
4 $378 \div 54$		

5. Work out the answers to these questions and also give the remainders.

1 $940 \div 18$	**4** $475 \div 31$
2 $572 \div 47$	**5** $358 \div 16$
3 $681 \div 54$	

6. Work out the answers to these questions giving them correct to 1 decimal place.

1	$980 \div 22$	**4**	$436 \div 15$
2	$608 \div 14$	**5**	$821 \div 27$
3	$759 \div 71$		

Index notation

5^2 (five squared) means 5×5 and equals 25.
4^3 (four cubed) means $4 \times 4 \times 4$ and equals 64.
10^6 (ten to the sixth) means $10 \times 10 \times 10 \times 10 \times 10 \times 10$ and equals $1\,000\,000$ (one million).

Square numbers are $1^2, 2^2, 3^2, 4^2, \ldots$ which worked out are 1, 4, 9, 16, $\ldots$

Cube numbers are $1^3, 2^3, 3^3, 4^3, \ldots$ which worked out are 1, 8, 27, 64, $\ldots$

Square roots

$\sqrt{49} = 7$ since $7^2 = 49$.

Cube roots

$\sqrt[3]{125} = 5$ since $5^3 = 125$.

Rules of indices

$3^2 \times 3^5 = 3 \times 3 \quad \times \quad 3 \times 3 \times 3 \times 3 \times 3 = 3^7$

This rule can be expressed generally as $a^m \times a^n = a^{m+n}$

$(4^5)^3 = 4^5 \times 4^5 \times 4^5 = 4^{15}$

This rule can be expressed generally as $(a^m)^n = a^{mn}$

$6^5 \div 6^3 = \dfrac{6 \times 6 \times 6 \times 6 \times 6}{6 \times 6 \times 6} = 6^2$

This rule can be expressed generally as $a^m \div a^n = a^{m-n}$, where $a \neq 0$.

(These rules have been used in cases where m and n are whole numbers, and in the third one, $m > n$. However, the rules are true for any values of m and n.)

$a^m \times a^n = a^{m+n}$

$(a^m)^n = a^{mn}$

$a^m \div a^n = a^{m-n}$

Prime Numbers and Factors

A prime number has no factors (except itself and 1). The first few prime numbers are 2, 3, 5, 7, 11, 13, 17, ...
Other numbers can be expressed in prime factors.

Example

1      $240 = 2 \times 120$
$\quad\quad = 2 \times 2 \times 60$
$\quad\quad = 2 \times 2 \times 2 \times 30$
$\quad\quad = 2 \times 2 \times 2 \times 2 \times 15$
$\quad\quad = 2 \times 2 \times 2 \times 2 \times 3 \times 5$
$\quad\quad = 2^4 \times 3 \times 5$

(A quicker way to split it up would be
$240 = 10 \times 24$
$\quad\quad = 2 \times 5 \times 4 \times 6$
$\quad\quad = 2 \times 5 \times 2 \times 2 \times 2 \times 3$
$\quad\quad = 2^4 \times 3 \times 5)$

Tests of divisibility

Divisibility by 2

If the units figure is even, i.e. 2, 4, 6, 8, 0, the number divides by 2.

Divisibility by 3

Add up the digits in the number, and if the answer is more than 9 you can add up the digits of that answer, and repeat until you get a 1-figure number. If this number divides by 3 then 3 is a factor of the original number.
For example, for 2841, $2 + 8 + 4 + 1 = 15$ (and $15 \rightarrow 1 + 5 = 6$). This divides by 3 so 3 is a factor of 2841.

(Also, if the 1-figure number is 9, the original number divides by 9.)

Divisibility by 5

If the units figure is 5 or 0 the number divides by 5.

Divisibility by 7

There is no simple test.

Divisibility by 11

Alternate figures add up to the same total or there is a difference of 11 (or 22, 33, . . .) between the totals.
For example, for 28413, alternate figures are 2, 4, 3 with total 9; and 8, 1 also with total 9; so the number is divisible by 11. For 616, the totals of alternate figures are 12 and 1. There is a difference of 11 so the number is divisible by 11.

Square numbers

If a number is expressed in prime factors and its indices are even it is a perfect square. Its square root can be found by dividing the indices by 2.

Example

2        $1936 = 2^4 \times 11^2$

         $\sqrt{1936} = 2^2 \times 11 = 4 \times 11 = 44$

Highest common factor (HCF)

This is the highest factor of two (or more) numbers.

Example

3   Find the HCF of 88 and 132.

         In prime factors, $88 = 2^3 \times 11$
         $132 = 2^2 \times 3 \times 11$
         Both numbers have a factor 2^2 and a factor 11.
         The HCF $= 2^2 \times 11 = 4 \times 11 = 44$.

Lowest common multiple (LCM)

This is the smallest number which is a multiple of two (or more) numbers.

Example

4   Find the LCM of 40 and 130.

         $40 = 2^3 \times 5$
         $130 = 2 \times 5 \times 13$
         Any multiple of 40 must include 2^3 and 5.
         Any multiple of 130 must include 2, 5 and 13.
         So the lowest common multiple must include 2^3, 5 and 13.
         The LCM $= 2^3 \times 5 \times 13 = 8 \times 5 \times 13 = 520$.

Exercise 1.3

1.   Which of these numbers are prime numbers?   21,   23,   25,   27,   29.

2.   What are the next two prime numbers after   **1**   30   **2**   80?

3. Find the values of

1	2^4	6	$2^3 \times 3^2$
2	7^3	7	$2^2 \times 5 \times 7$
3	10^5	8	$2^3 \times 11$
4	$\sqrt{121}$	9	$3^3 \times 10^2$
5	$\sqrt[3]{64}$	10	$2 \times 5^2 \times 13$

4. Express these numbers in prime factors.

1	48	4	60	7	70	10	100	13	121
2	99	5	180	8	96	11	39	14	81
3	52	6	24	9	64	12	80	15	150

5. Express these numbers in prime factors and hence find their square roots.

1	225	2	1764	3	1089	4	256	5	5625

6. Express these numbers in prime factors and hence find
   (1) their highest common factor,
   (2) their lowest common multiple.

1	28, 16	4	210, 630
2	10, 45	5	144, 216
3	66, 88		

7. Simplify, leaving in index form.

1	$3^2 \times 3^4$	6	$2^8 \div 2^5$
2	$5^6 \div 5^3$	7	$5^5 \div 5$
3	$7^3 \times 7^3 \times 7^2$	8	$\left(6^2\right)^3$
4	$\left(2^4\right)^5$	9	$\left(3^3\right)^6$
5	$3^8 \div 3^4$	10	$\left(5^4\right)^2$

8. From the numbers   8,   37,   50,   73,   81,   91,   360

   1 Which number is a square number?
   2 Which number is a cube number?
   3 Which two numbers are prime numbers?
   4 Which number is a multiple of 13?
   5 Which number is a factor of 72?
   6 Which number can be written in index form as $2^3 \times 3^2 \times 5$?
   7 Which number is equal to the sum of two other numbers in the list?
   8 Which number when divided by 9 leaves a remainder of 5?

9. Express 1728 in prime factors and hence find its cube root.

Sequences of numbers

Whole numbers $1, 2, 3, 4, \ldots$

Odd numbers $1, 3, 5, 7, \ldots$

Even numbers $2, 4, 6, 8, \ldots$

Multiples of 5. $5, 10, 15, 20, \ldots$

Prime numbers $2, 3, 5, 7, 11, \ldots$ (These do not follow a regular pattern, but apart from 2 and 5 they all have unit figures of 1, 3, 7 or 9.)

Square numbers $1, 4, 9, 16, \ldots$ from $1^2, 2^2, 3^2, 4^2, \ldots$

Triangular numbers $1, 3, 6, 10, 15, \ldots$ from $1, 1+2, 1+2+3, \ldots$

Fibonacci sequence $1, 1, 2, 3, 5, 8, 13, \ldots$ (Each number after the first two is found by adding the two preceding numbers.)

There are many other sequences of numbers.
If you have to identify a sequence and continue it, see if you can recognise anything special about it. Also look at the differences between successive terms.

e.g. 8, 17, 26, 35, ...
You might notice that the difference between successive numbers is always 9. You get the next term by adding on 9.
You might notice that the unit's figures go down in 1's and the ten's figures go up in 1's, so the next term is 44. This will give you terms up to 80, although the sequence continues beyond that.
You might notice that the digits add up to 8 each time.

e.g. 6, 12, 24, 48, 96, ...
The differences between successive terms are 6, 12, 24, 48. These are the same numbers as in the sequence, so the sequence is a doubling one. The next term is $96 \times 2 = 192$.

e.g. $\frac{1}{2}, \frac{1}{4}, \frac{1}{6}, \frac{1}{8}, \ldots$
These are fractions which are getting smaller. The numerators are all 1. The denominators in turn go 2, 4, 6, 8 so they increase by 2 each time and the next one is 10. So the next number in the sequence is $\frac{1}{10}$.

e.g. 2, 3, 5, 9, 17, 33, ...
The sequence is growing more and more rapidly and after 2 the numbers are all odd.
Investigate the differences between successive terms. They are 1, 2, 4, 8, 16. These are always doubled, the next difference is 32 and the next number in the sequence is $33 + 32 = 65$.

The sequence beginning $1, 2, 4, \ldots$

These three terms are not enough to give us sufficient information to identify which sequence it is.
It could be 1, 2, 4, 8, 16 ... or 1, 2, 4, 7, 11.
What are the rules for these sequences ?

Unless you know the rule, you need enough terms to identify the sequence.
Sometimes there is more than one possible sequence, but if one sequence is obvious, do not try
to find a more unlikely one.

Difference methods

Look at the sequence on the right.   2   5   10   17   26
Find the differences between consecutive terms.   3   5   7   9
Find the differences between those numbers.   2   2   2

Assuming that the 3rd row is a row of 2's, you can continue the middle row and use it to write
more terms in the sequence on the top row.

2   5   10   17   26 → 37 → 50 → 65 → 82

  3   5   7   9 → 11 → 13 → 15 → 17

    2   2   2   2   2   2   2

Here is another example.

2   3   7   14 → 24 → 37 → 53

  1   4   7 → 10 → 13 → 16

    3   3   3   3   3

Geometrical representation of sequences

Draw the next picture in each of these sequences.

1   **Square numbers**

    1   4   9   16

Draw the next picture in each of these sequences.

2 **Triangular numbers**

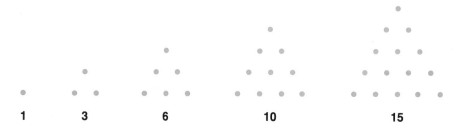

1   3   6   10   15

3 **Rectangular numbers**

Here the rectangle is 2 units longer than wide.

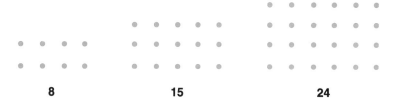

8   15   24

4 **Trapezium numbers**

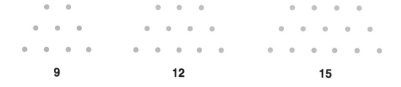

9   12   15

5 **Hexagonal numbers**

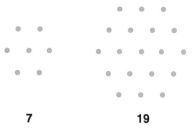

7   19

Exercise 1.4

1. Copy and continue these sequences for 3 more terms. Describe the rule for continuing the sequence in each case.

    1   4, 10, 16, 22, 28, ...   **6**   3, 4, 6, 9, 13, ...
    2   3, 6, 9, 12, 15, ...   **7**   3, 1, $\frac{1}{3}, \frac{1}{9}, \frac{1}{27}$, ...
    3   5, 10, 20, 40, 80, ...   **8**   3, 7, 15, 31, 63, ...
    4   3, 9, 27, 81, 243, ...   **9**   3, 8, 18, 38, 78, ...
    5   3, 0, −3, −6, −9, ...   **10** 1, 2, 6, 24, 120, ...

2. Write down the first 5 terms of these sequences. In each one, the first term is 12.

    1   Add 4 each time.
    2   Subtract 3 each time.
    3   Multiply by 5 each time.
    4   Divide by 2 each time.
    5   Add 1, then add 2, 3, 4, ...

3. Every term of these sequences is obtained from the sum of the previous two terms. Write down the next 3 terms of each one.

    1   1, 4, 5, ...   **4**   3, 1, 4, ...
    2   2, 8, 10, ...   **5**   3, 4, 7, ...
    3   0, 1, 1, ...

4. Continue these sequences for the next 3 terms, using the difference method.

    1   1, 5, 11, 19, 29, ...   **4**   4, 3, 12, 31, 60, ...
    2   2, 7, 13, 20, 28, ...   **5**   5, 10, 20, 35, 55, ...
    3   3, 5, 10, 18, 29, ...

5. What do you notice about the sum of any two consecutive triangular numbers ? Can you show why this is so, using a dots pattern ?

6. Write down the next 5 terms of the Fibonacci sequence
    1, 1, 2, 3, 5, 8, 13, ...
    Copy and complete this number pattern to the line beginning '10th term'.

    > 1st term × 3rd term − 1 = 1 × 2 − 1 = 1 = 1^2
    >
    > 2nd term × 4th term + 1 = 1 × 3 + 1 = 4 = 2^2
    >
    > 3rd term × 5th term − 1 = ...
    >
    > 4th term × 6th term + 1 = ...
    >
    > ...

    Comment on the pattern.

Using negative numbers

Addition and subtraction

Use your number line for counting up, when the sign is +, or down, when the sign is −.

Examples

$4 + 2 = 6$
Start at 4 and go up 2, getting to 6.

$4 - 7 = -3$
Start at 4 and go down 7, getting to −3.

$(-3) + 5 = 2$
Start at −3 and go up 5, getting to 2.

$(-3) + 1 = -2$
Start at −3 and go up 1, getting to −2.

$(-3) - 6 = -9$
Start at −3 and go down 6, getting to −9.

```
5 —
4 —
3 —
2 —
1 —
0 —
−1 —
−2 —
−3 —
−4 —
−5 —
```

Sometimes you may have to work out expressions such as $(-4) - (+3)$ or $5 - (-6)$. These are best done by changing the middle two signs into one according to rules.

> $+ +$ should be replaced by $+$
>
> $+ -$ or $- +$ should be replaced by $-$
>
> $- -$ should be replaced by $+$

So there are two stages to working out such questions.
If two signs follow each other, replace them by one sign.
Then use the number line to work out the answer.

Here are some examples:

$(-5) + (+1)$ Replace $+ +$ by $+$, which means 'go up'.
$= (-5) + 1$ Start at −5 and go up 1, getting to −4.
$= -4$

$(-5) - (+3)$ Replace $- +$ by $-$, which means 'go down'.
$= (-5) - 3$ Start at −5 and go down 3, getting to −8.
$= -8$

$5 + (-7)$ Replace $+ -$ by $-$, which means 'go down'.
$= 5 - 7$ Start at 5 and go down 7, getting to -2.
$= -2$

$5 - (-1)$ Replace $- -$ by $+$, which means 'go up'.
$= 5 + 1$ Start at 5 and go up 1, getting to 6.
$= 6$

Multiplication and division

$(+4) \times (+3)$ is the same as 4×3 and equals 12.

$(+4) \times (-3)$ is the same as $4 \times (-3)$ and equals -12.

$(-4) \times (-3)$ is the tricky one. It equals 12 (not -12).

$+$	$\times$	$+$	$=$	$+$
$+$	$\times$	$-$	$=$	$-$
$-$	$\times$	$-$	$=$	$+$

The rules for division follow those for multiplication, and are

$$(+12) \div (+3) = 4$$
$$(+12) \div (-3) = -4$$
$$(-12) \div (+3) = -4$$
$$(-12) \div (-3) = 4$$

$+$	$\div$	$+$	$=$	$+$
$+$	$\div$	$-$	$=$	$-$
$-$	$\div$	$+$	$=$	$-$
$-$	$\div$	$-$	$=$	$+$

If your calculator has a $\boxed{+/_-}$ key, then you can enter negative numbers, and you can do calculations with the calculator, although it is better just to use the rules and manage without the calculator.

e.g. For $(-4) + (-3)$ press $4\,\boxed{+/_-}\,\boxed{+}\,3\,\boxed{+/_-}\,\boxed{=}$ and you will get the answer -7.

For $(-4) - (-3)$ press $4\,\boxed{+/_-}\,\boxed{-}\,3\,\boxed{+/_-}\,\boxed{=}$ and you will get the answer -1.

For $(-4) \times (-3)$ press $4\,\boxed{+/_-}\,\boxed{\times}\,3\,\boxed{+/_-}\,\boxed{=}$ and you will get the answer 12.

For $(-12) \div (-3)$ press $12\,\boxed{+/_-}\,\boxed{\div}\,3\,\boxed{+/_-}\,\boxed{=}$ and you will get the answer 4.

Exercise 1.5

Work out the answers to these calculations.

1.
1	$4 + 3$	**8**	$(-1) + 11$	**15**	$(-8) + 0 + 4$
2	$4 - 1$	**9**	$(-8) - 1$	**16**	$(-12) + 6 - 2$
3	$(-2) + 1$	**10**	$(-5) + 8$	**17**	$3 - 1 - 5$
4	$2 - 8$	**11**	$(-7) + 6 + 1$	**18**	$(-2) - 5 + 3$
5	$(-3) + 3$	**12**	$2 - 5 + 4$	**19**	$6 - 1 - 5$
6	$(-4) - 4$	**13**	$10 - 5 + 6$	**20**	$(-5) + 4 + 2$
7	$9 - 12$	**14**	$(-1) + 6 - 3$		

Work out the answers to these calculations.

2. 1 $3 - (+4)$ 7 $0 - (+5)$
    2   $(-2) + (-5)$ 8 $(+4) - (-3)$
    3   $(-6) - 0$ 9 $(-5) + (+2)$
    4   $(+1) + (-1)$ 10 $(+7) - (+6)$
    5   $(-2) - (-4)$
    6   $(-6) + (+3)$ 12 $(-6) - (-3) - (+6)$

3. 1 $(-2) \times 8$ 7 $0 \times (-10)$
    2   $(-6) \times (-4)$ 8 $(-2) \times (-1)$
    3   $(+7) \times (-5)$ 9 $(-3) \times 3$
    4   $5 \times (-2)$ 10 $(-8) \times (-8)$
    5   $(-1) \times (-3)$ 11 $(-1) \times (+2)$
    6   $(-7) \times 0$ 12 $(-1) \times 1$

4. 1 $6 \div (-3)$ 7 $49 \div (-7)$
    2   $(-15) \div (+5)$ 8 $(-1) \div (+1)$
    3   $18 \div (-6)$ 9 $(-24) \div (-3)$
    4   $(-36) \div (-4)$ 10 $(+30) \div (+5)$
    5   $(-4) \div 4$ 11 $8 \div (-4)$
    6   $36 \div (-6)$ 12 $0 \div (-2)$

5. 1 $2 - 2\frac{1}{2}$ 6 $0 \times (-6)$
    2   $(-5)^2$ 7 $(-1) \times (-2) \times (-3)$
    3   $0 - 8$ 8 $(-12) \div (+12)$
    4   $(-1) \div (-1)$ 9 $3 \div (-6)$
    5   $(-1) + (+1)$ 10 $(-1)^3$

6. 1   If the temperature is $+3°$ and it falls by $10°$,
        what is the new temperature ?

    2   If the temperature is $-6°$, by how many degrees
        must it rise to become $+7°$?

    3   If the temperature is $+10°$ and it falls to $-5°$ overnight,
        through how many degrees has it fallen ?

    4   After rising 9 degrees the temperature is $+1°$.
        What was it originally ?

    5   After falling 4 degrees the temperature is $-9°$.
        What was it originally ?

Exercise 1.6 Applications

1.   From the numbers   8,   12,   16,   19,   20

   1   Which number is a prime number ?
   2   Which number is a square number ?
   3   Which number is a multiple of 5 ?
   4   Which number is a factor of 84 ?
   5   Which two numbers have a sum which is a square number ?
   6   Which two numbers have a sum which is a cube number ?

2.   Express 1080 in prime factors.
   If $1080 = 2^a \times 3^b \times 5^c$, state the values of a, b and c.
   State the smallest number by which 1080 must be multiplied to make a perfect square.

3.   Express in prime factors the numbers 378 and 441.
   Find
   1   the square root of 441,
   2   the highest common factor of 378 and 441,
   3   the lowest common multiple of 378 and 441, expressed in prime factors.

4.   Find the values of   **1** $\sqrt{25 \times 144}$ **2** $\sqrt{25 + 144}$ **3** $\sqrt{25} + \sqrt{144}$

5.   6 is called a **perfect number** because its factors are 1, 2, 3 and when you add them up
   their sum equals 6.
   12 has factors 1, 2, 3, 4, 6 and their sum equals 16, not 12, so 12 is not a perfect number.
   However, there is one other number less than 50 which is a perfect number.
   Which is it ?

6.   Copy and complete this number pattern.

   $142857 \times 1 = 142857$
   $142857 \times 5 =$
   $142857 \times 4 =$
   $142857 \times 6 =$
   $142857 \times 2 =$
   $142857 \times 3 =$

   What do you notice about the answers ?

7.   Copy and complete this magic square which uses
   numbers 1 to 16.
   All rows, columns and the main diagonals add up to 34.

			12
3	16		
15		14	

8. Extend this number pattern to 65^2.

    $$5^2 = 0 \times 10 + 25 = 25$$
    $$15^2 = 10 \times 20 + 25 = 225$$
    $$25^2 = 20 \times 30 + 25 = 625$$

    Use the pattern to find the value of 85^2.

9. Mrs Davies makes 200 soft toys. The material for
    each toy costs 48p. Other expenses amount to £50.
    She sells the toys for £1.95 each. What profit does
    she make ?

10. The weekly wages paid by a firm to 20 workmen total £2520. What will the weekly wages
    be if they employ two extra men, and pay them all at the same rate ?

11. If £9.10 is made up of equal numbers of 5p, 10p and 20p coins, how many coins are
    there ?

12. Give the next 4 terms in two possible sequences beginning 1, 3, 9, ... and say which rules
    you used to continue each sequence.

13. Copy and complete the table, of the number of lines needed to join 2, 3, 4, ... points.
    (The diagrams may help you to discover the pattern.)

Number of points	2	3	4	5	6	7	8	9	10
Number of lines needed	1	3	6						

2 points
1 line

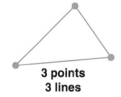

3 points
3 lines

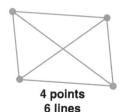

4 points
6 lines

5 points

14. Mr Bramwell has an agreement with his bank to overdraw money, that is, to spend more money than is in his account.

    1   If he has £300 in his account and writes a cheque for £450, by how much will his account be overdrawn ?

    2   If his account is overdrawn by £200 and he takes out another £60, by how much is he overdrawn now ?

    3   If his account is overdrawn by £150 and he puts £80 into the account, by how much is he overdrawn now ?

    4   If his account is overdrawn by £100 and he puts £130 into the account, by how much is his account in credit ?

15.

Steve is playing a computer game. To make the robot go to the right he presses the + key. To make the robot go to the left he presses the − key.

e.g. To get from $\boxed{-2}$ to $\boxed{0}$ he would press +2,

    to get from $\boxed{-1}$ to $\boxed{-3}$ he would press −2.

What must he press to move the robot

  1 from $\boxed{-3}$ to $\boxed{3}$,   **4** from $\boxed{2}$ to $\boxed{-2}$,

  2 from $\boxed{0}$ to $\boxed{3}$,   **5** from $\boxed{-2}$ to $\boxed{1}$?

  3 from $\boxed{1}$ to $\boxed{-1}$,

Where does the robot end up if

  6 it was at $\boxed{-1}$ and Steve pressed −2,   **9** it was at $\boxed{-2}$ and Steve pressed +4,

  7 it was at $\boxed{0}$ and Steve pressed +2,   **10** it was at $\boxed{-1}$ and Steve pressed +1 ?

  8 it was at $\boxed{3}$ and Steve pressed −6,

Practice test 1

1.   From the numbers 18, 19, 20, 23, 25, 27, write down

     1   the prime numbers,
     2   a square number,
     3   the numbers which are multiples of 3,
     4   a cube number,
     5   two numbers whose sum is 44.

2.   Express 360 and 405 in prime factors.
     Given that $360 \times 405 = 145\,800$, express $145\,800$ in prime factors.

3.   Expressed in prime factors two numbers are $7^2 \times 11^3 \times 13$ and $7^3 \times 11 \times 17$.
     Find, expressed in prime factors,
     1   the highest common factor of these numbers,
     2   the lowest common multiple of these numbers.

4.   Work out these calculations without using your calculator, and write down enough
     working to show that you have not used a calculator.

     1   72×18
     2   $896 \div 14$
     3   A wheel makes 2000 revolutions per minute. How long will it take to make $50\,000$
         revolutions ?

5.   Copy and continue this pattern to 27×37.

         $3 \times 37 = 111$
         $6 \times 37 = 222$
         $9 \times 37 = 333$

         $\ldots$

6.   Find the next 2 numbers in these sequences.

     1   6, 13, 20, 27, 34, ...   4   4, 5, 8, 13, 20, ...
     2   6, 2, −2, −6, −10, ...   5   64, 32, 16, 8, 4, ...
     3   4, 20, 100, 500, 2500, ...

7.   Say how many degrees the temperature has risen or fallen in the following cases.

     1   It was $+8°$ and is now $+11°$.   6   It was $+10°$ and is now $-17°$.
     2   It was $+6°$ and is now $-3°$.   7   It was $-8°$ and is now $+2°$.
     3   It was $-4°$ and is now $+2°$.   8   It was $-3°$ and is now $0°$.
     4   It was $-9°$ and is now $-7°$.   9   It was $+5°$ and is now $+1°$.
     5   It was $0°$ and is now $-6°$.   10 It was $-1°$ and is now $-4°$.

8.   Work out the answers to these calculations.

1	$(-5) - 3$	**5**	$(-6) + 8$	**8**	$(-7)^2$
2	$(+3) - (-6)$	**6**	$(-10) \div (-2)$	**9**	$(-9) \times 0$
3	$(-9) \times (-7)$	**7**	$0 - (-9)$	**10**	$(-2)^3$
4	$(-60) \div (+12)$				

PUZZLES

1.   A man has a wad of £5 notes numbered consecutively from 232426 to 232440. What is their total value ?

2.   What is the next letter in this sequence ?
     N   N   N   E   N   E   E   N   E   E   –   –   –

3.   How many squares can be formed by joining 4 of these points ?

4.   Copy this long division sum and fill in the missing figures.

```
            2 *
      * 3 )1 2 4 *
          * 6
          3 * *
          3 * *
```

5.   Down the corridor next to the school hall there are five classrooms, numbered from 1 to 5, and these are occupied by the five forms, 7A, 7B, 7C, 7D and 7E.
     7A is not in room 1, 7B is not in room 5, 7C is not in room 1 or room 5.
     7D is in a room with a lower number than 7B. 7C's room is not next to 7B's room.
     7E's room is not next to 7C's room. Which class is in room 1 ?

2 Angles and triangles

The topics in this chapter include:

- measuring and drawing angles,

- explaining and using properties associated with intersecting lines, parallel lines and triangles.

Angles

An angle is the amount of turning between two lines.

This is angle *ABC* (or $\angle ABC$) or angle *CBA*.
If there is no possibility of confusion it can be
called $\angle B$.

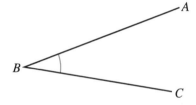

Angles can also be identified by small letters.
This angle is *b*.

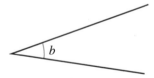

Measuring angles

1 complete turn or revolution is divided into 360°.

1 half-turn is 180°.

1 quarter-turn is 90°. This is also called a right angle.

The sign for a right angle is

Perpendicular lines are lines which meet each other at right angles.

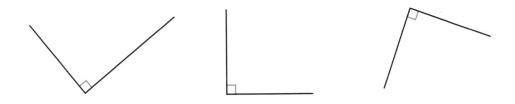

Types of angles

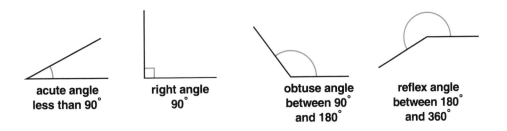

acute angle
less than 90°

right angle
90°

obtuse angle
between 90°
and 180°

reflex angle
between 180°
and 360°

Using a protractor

1   To measure an angle

(1)   Put the centre point of the protractor on the point of the angle.
(2)   Put the 0° line of the protractor on one of the lines of the angle.
(3)   Count round from 0° to read the size of the angle.
       If the 0° you are using is on the
       outside set of figures, use those
       figures, counting past 10°, 20°, 30°, etc.
       If the 0° you are using is on the
       inside set of figures, then you will
       use those figures.
       (Not all circular protractors are
       marked in the same way so yours
       may not be numbered like the one
       shown below.)

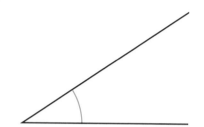

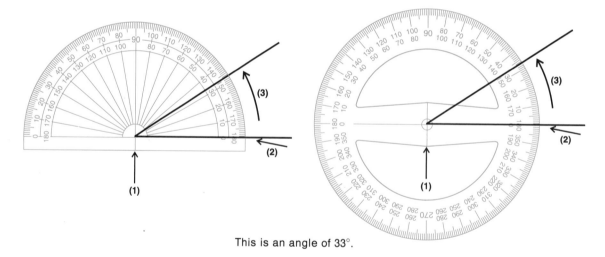

This is an angle of 33°.

Use the other 0° line if it is more convenient.

2   To draw an angle

Mark a point P on a line PQ, as shown.
At point P, using the line PQ, make an angle of 28°.

(1)   Put the centre point of the protractor on the point *P*.
(2)   Put the 0° line of the protractor on the line *PQ*.
(3)   Count round from 0° to 28°. Put a dot at 28°.
      (Decide from where 0° is, whether you are using the inside or the outside set of figures.)

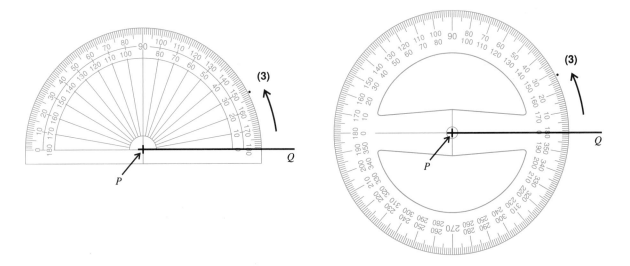

(4)   When you have removed the protractor, join the dot to point *P*.

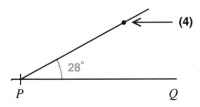

Exercise 2.1

1.   State whether these angles are acute, obtuse or reflex angles.

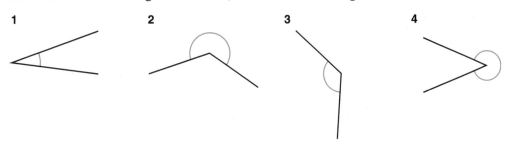

2.   Estimate the sizes of these angles, in degrees. Check your estimate by measuring with
      your protractor.

1   **2**   **3**

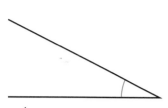
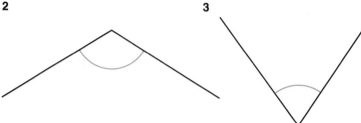

3.   Draw a line PQ of length 8 cm and at P make an angle QPR of
      1   37°   **2**   151°   **3**   72°

<h1>Calculations with angles</h1>

Angles at a point

These add up to 360°.

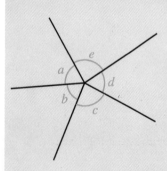

$a + b + c + d + e = 360°$

Adjacent angles (on a straight line)

These add up to 180°.

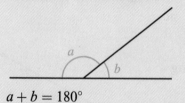

$a + b = 180°$

Vertically opposite angles

These are equal.

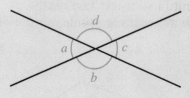

$a = c$

$b = d$

Parallel lines

Parallel lines are lines with the same direction. They remain the same distance apart, so never meet each other.

The sign for parallel lines is similar arrows on the lines.

The symbol // can be used for 'is parallel to'.

To draw parallel lines with a set-square

Example

Draw a line through C, parallel to AB.

Place the longest side of the set-square on AB so that, if possible, the set-square is placed over C.

Place a ruler along one of the other sides of the set-square.

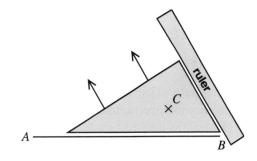

Keeping the ruler fixed, slide the set-square along the ruler until its longest side passes through C. Draw a line along this edge.

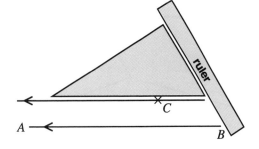

Practise drawing different parallel lines until you are sure that you can draw them correctly.

Calculations with angles and parallel lines

Corresponding angles

These are equal.

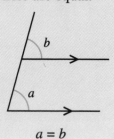

$$a = b$$

Alternate angles

These are equal.

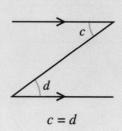

$$c = d$$

Interior angles

These add up to 180°.

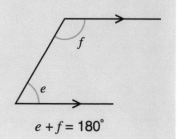

$$e + f = 180°$$

Example

Calculate the sizes of angles a, b, c and d.

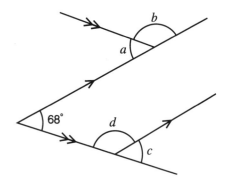

$a = 68°$	alternate angles
$b = 112°$	adjacent angles (to a)
$c = 68°$	corresponding angles
$d = 112°$	interior angles (or adjacent to c)

Exercise 2.2

1. Estimate the sizes of the marked angles, in degrees. Check your estimate by measuring with your protractor. Verify that the angles at a point add up to 360°, adjacent angles on a straight line add up to 180°, and vertically opposite angles are equal.

1

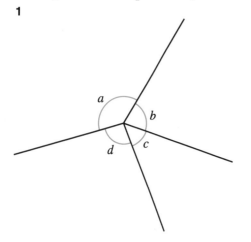

2

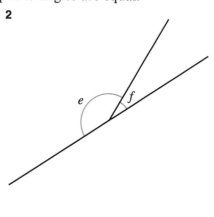

3

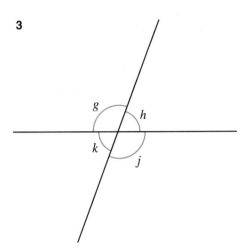

2.   Estimate the sizes of the marked angles, in degrees. Check your estimate by measuring with your protractor. Verify that corresponding angles are equal, alternate angles are equal and interior angles add up to 180°.

1

2

3

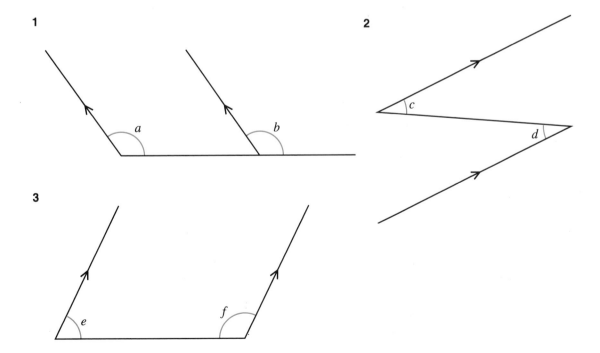

3. Calculate the sizes of angles a, b, c, d, e, f, g, h.
    Give the reasons.

1

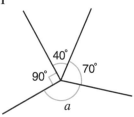

2

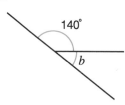

3

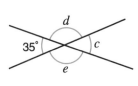

4

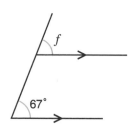

5

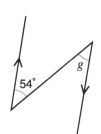

6

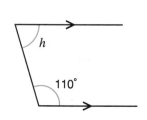

4. Calculate the sizes of angles a, b, c, d, e, f, g, h.

1

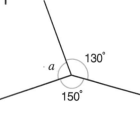

2

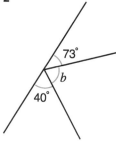

3

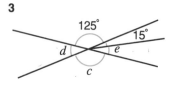

4

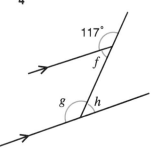

5.   Calculate the sizes of angles j, k, m, n, p, q.

1
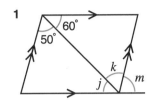

2
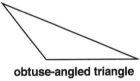

Triangles

Kinds of triangle

Angles in a triangle

No angle more than 90°

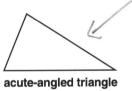

hypotenuse

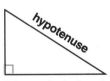

acute-angled triangle   right-angled triangle   obtuse-angled triangle

one angle larger than 90°

Sides in a triangle

$a + b + c = 180°$

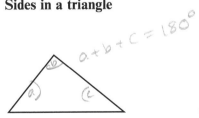

scalene triangle   isosceles triangle   equilateral triangle
(3 sides of different lengths) (two sides equal)   (all 3 sides equal)

(The sign for lines of equal length is similar small marks crossing the lines.)

Angle properties of a triangle

Angle sum of a triangle

The sum of the angles of a triangle is 180°.

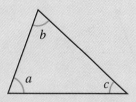

$$a + b + c = 180°$$

Exterior angle of a triangle

If a side is extended, the exterior angle is equal to the sum of the two opposite interior angles.

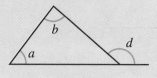

$$d = a + b$$

Isosceles triangle

The angles opposite the equal sides are equal.

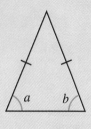

$$a = b$$

Equilateral triangle

All angles are 60°.

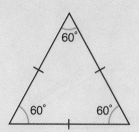

Symmetry

An isosceles triangle has one axis of symmetry.

 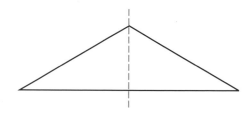

An equilateral triangle has 3 axes of symmetry.

An equilateral triangle has rotational symmetry of order 3.

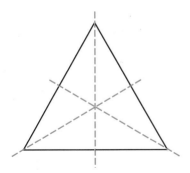

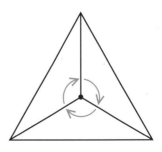

Example

Find the size of ∠ECB.

△ABC is isosceles, so $b = c$.
$b = 69°$ angle sum of △ $= 180°$
                     $180° - 42° = 138°$
                     $138° ÷ 2 = 69°$
$b = d$ alternate angles
$d = 69°$
i.e. ∠ECB $= 69°$

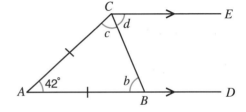

Exercise 2.3

1. Estimate the sizes of the angles in these triangles. Check your estimate by measuring with your protractor. Verify that the sum of the angles is 180°.

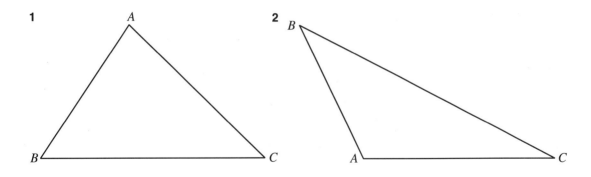

2. Estimate the sizes of the angles in these isosceles triangles. Check your estimate by
    measuring with your protractor. Verify that the angles opposite the equal sides are equal.

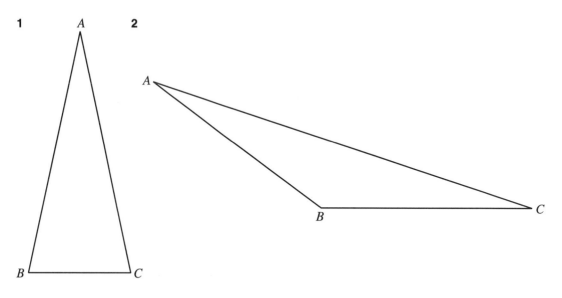

3. Calculate the sizes of the 3rd angles in these triangles.

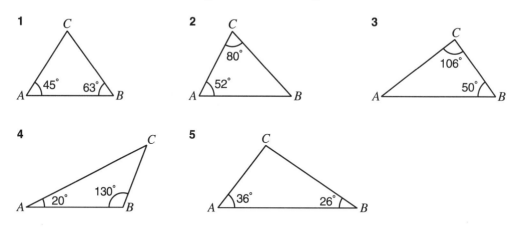

4. Calculate the sizes of angles *a*, *b*, *c*, *d*.

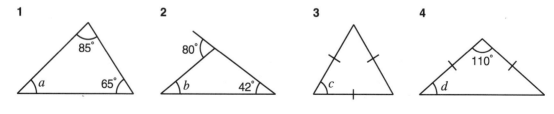

5. If $AB = AC$, which two angles are equal ?

Find the sizes of
1   $\angle ACD$,
2   $\angle CDA$,
3   $\angle DAB$,
4   $\angle BAC$.

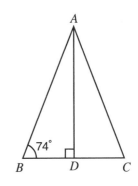

6. Calculate the sizes of
1   $\angle ACD$,
2   $\angle CDB$,
3   $\angle DBC$,
4   $\angle BCD$.

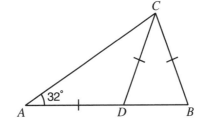

Constructing triangles

Follow the instructions and draw these triangles accurately.

1   To draw a triangle, given 1 side and 2 angles

Example

Draw a triangle ABC with $AB = 9$ cm,
$\angle A = 48°$ and $\angle B = 77°$.

Draw AB, 9 cm long.
Measure an angle of 48° at A and an angle of
77° at B. Continue these lines until they meet
at C.

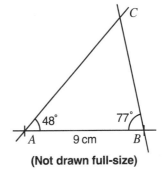

(Not drawn full-size)

(If a line AB has to be drawn to an accurate length it is useful to draw the line slightly
longer than needed and then mark A and B by small marks crossing the line.)

(If instead of being given the size of $\angle B$ you had been told that $\angle C = 55°$, you could have
calculated the size of $\angle B$, since the 3 angles of a triangle have a sum of 180°, and then
you could continue as above.)

2   To draw a triangle, given 2 sides and the angle included between these sides

Example

Draw a triangle ABC with $AB = 9$ cm, $\angle A = 49°$ and $AC = 7$ cm.

Draw AB, 9 cm long.
Measure an angle of 49° at A and measure off a distance of 7 cm along this angle line, to give the point C.
Join BC.

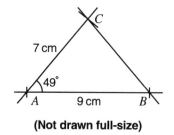

(Not drawn full-size)

3   To draw a triangle, given 3 sides

Example

Draw a triangle ABC with $AB = 9$ cm, $BC = 8$ cm and $AC = 7$ cm.

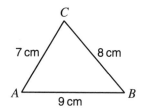

Draw AB, 9 cm long.
With compasses, centre A, radius 7 cm, draw an arc.
With centre B, radius 8 cm, draw an arc to cut the first arc at C.
Join AC and CB.

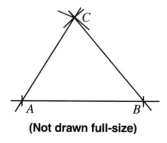

(Not drawn full-size)

4   To draw a triangle, given two sides and a non-included angle

Example

Draw a triangle ABC with $AB = 5$ cm, $\angle A = 50°$ and $BC = 6$ cm.

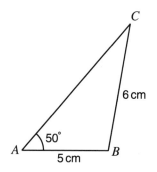

Draw AB, 5 cm long.
Measure an angle of 50° at A and extend this
angle line onwards.
With compasses, centre B, radius 6 cm, draw
an arc to cut the extended line at C.
Join BC.

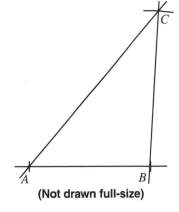

(Not drawn full-size)

(In some cases there could be two points where the arc meets the line, so there would be
two possible triangles of different shapes satisfying the given data.)

Exercise 2.4

Questions 1 to 5. Construct these triangles full-size.

1.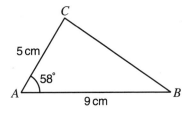

   Estimate the length of BC and the sizes of $\angle B$ and
   $\angle C$. Check your estimates by measurement.

2.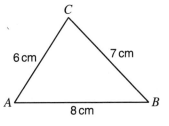

   Estimate the sizes of the angles A, B and C, and then
   check by measuring them with your protractor.

3.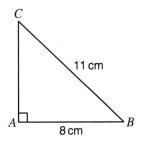

   Estimate the length of AC and the sizes of angles B
   and C. Check your estimates by measurement.

Questions 4 and 5. Construct these triangles full-size.

4.

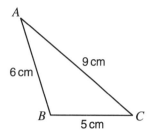

D is the mid-point of AB. Mark D on your diagram.
Through D draw a line parallel to BC. Let this line
cut AC at E.
Measure AE and EC.

5.

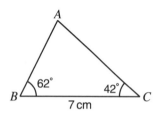

Through A draw a line parallel to BC, and through C
draw a line perpendicular to BC. Let these lines meet
at point D.
Measure AD and CD.

Exercise 2.5 Applications

1. **1** Through how many degrees does the hour hand
of a clock turn in 1 hour ?

   2 Through how many degrees does the hour hand
of a clock turn between 1 pm and 4.30 pm ?

   3 What is the size of the obtuse angle between
the hands of a clock at half-past two ?

2. Calculate the sizes of the angles marked with small letters.

1

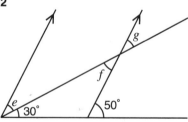

2

3

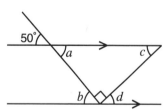

4

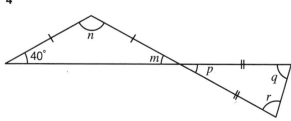

3.   Find the size of $\angle A$ and then find the value of x.

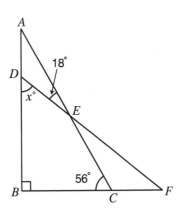

4.   In $\triangle ABC$, $AB = AC$, and the bisectors of
      $\angle B$ and $\angle C$ meet at I. (Bisectors of angles are
      lines which cut the angles in half.)

      Find the sizes of
      1    $\angle ABC$,
      2    $\angle IBC$,
      3    $\angle BIC$.

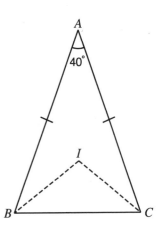

5.   In the diagram, $AB = AC$ and
      $\angle B$ is bisected by BD.

      Find the sizes of
      1    $\angle ABC$,
      2    $\angle BAD$,
      3    $\angle ADE$.

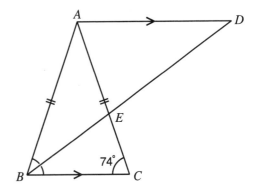

6.   Draw accurately a triangle ABC with $AB = 8$ cm, $\angle A = 56°$ and $\angle B = 64°$.
      From D, the mid-point of BC, draw a line parallel to BA, to meet AC at E. Join AD.
      Measure the angles ADE and EAD.

7.   Draw accurately a triangle ABC with $AB = 7$ cm, $\angle A = 90°$ and $BC = 10$ cm.
      Measure AC.

8. Draw accurately a triangle *ABC* with *AB* = *AC* = 7 cm and *BC* = 11 cm. Measure the angles of the triangle.
    Draw the line of symmetry of the triangle.

9. Make a rough copy of this map of Treasure Island and find the place where the treasure is hidden.

    'Halve the distance in a straight line from *A* to *B*, and from this halfway point proceed in a straight line at right angles to the line *AB* until you reach the river. Having crossed the river, march North to the coast. Here you will find a cave where the treasure lies hidden.'

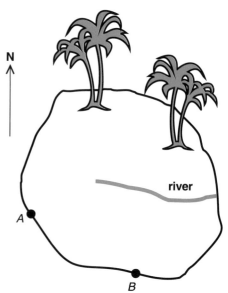

Practice test 2

In questions 1, 2, 3, calculate the sizes of the marked angles.

1.

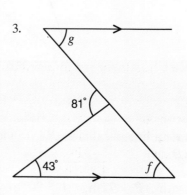

2.

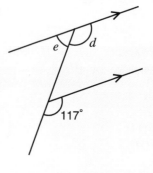

3.

4. If $AB = AC$, which two angles are equal ?

Find the sizes of $\angle ABC$, $\angle BCA$,
$\angle ACD$, $\angle CDB$, $\angle BCD$.

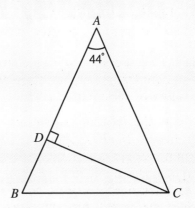

5. **1** Draw accurately an equilateral triangle ABC with all sides 7.4 cm long.
    2 Draw on the diagram all the axes of symmetry.
    3 Mark point O, the centre of rotational symmetry. What is the order of rotational symmetry ?

6. Construct triangle ABC with the measurements given.
    Measure $\angle A$.
    Draw the bisector of $\angle A$, meeting BC at D.
    Measure BD and DC.

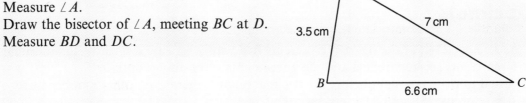

PUZZLE

6. Decode this bill. Each capital letter stands for a figure and each figure stands for the corresponding letter.

R	6480	at	LI pence each	UI
I	6489520	at	BI pence each	UI
L	372430	at	BN pence each	RP
L	3711430	at	C pence each	BN
				£ L.SE

3 Decimals, money and measures

> **The topics in this chapter include:**
>
> - calculating with decimals,
> - converting fractions to decimals,
> - approximating, using significant figures or decimal places,
> - using trial and improvement methods,
> - converting one metric unit to another,
> - using British units and knowing their rough metric equivalents.

Decimals

In the number 234.567 the figure 5 represents five-tenths because it is in the first decimal place, the 6 represents six-hundredths and the 7 represents seven-thousandths.
It is usual to write a nought before the decimal point if there is no other number there,
e.g. 0.51, not just .51, and 0.02, not just .02.

Working without a calculator

Addition, subtraction, easy multiplication and division

When adding, subtracting, or when multiplying or dividing by whole numbers, keep the figures in their correct positions relative to the decimal point.

Examples

1 $1.5 + 14.83$

$$
\begin{array}{r}
1.5 \\
+\ 14.83 \\
\hline
16.33
\end{array}
$$

2 $12.1 - 3.02$

$$
\begin{array}{r}
12.10 \\
-\ 3.02 \\
\hline
9.08
\end{array}
$$

3 12.6×4

$$\begin{array}{r} 12.6 \\ \times \quad 4 \\ \hline 50.4 \end{array}$$

4 $27.6 \div 8$

$$\begin{array}{r} 8\overline{)27.60} \\ \underline{3.45} \end{array}$$

Powers of 10

When multiplying by 10, 100, 1000, ... the numbers grow larger, so the figures move upwards (to the left), 1, 2, 3, ... places, assuming that the decimal point is fixed. Add 0's to fill any empty places between the figures and the decimal point.

Examples

5 $2.56 \times 10 = 25.6$
$3.5 \times 100 = 350$
$0.0041 \times 1000 = 4.1$

When dividing by 10, 100, 1000, ... the numbers become smaller, so the figures move downwards (to the right), 1, 2, 3, ... places, assuming that the decimal point is fixed. Add 0's to fill any empty places between the decimal point and the figures.

Examples

6 $31.8 \div 10 = 3.18$
$23 \div 100 = 0.23$
$5.6 \div 1000 = 0.0056$

To multiply by 20, multiply by 10 and then multiply that answer by 2. To divide by 20, divide by 10 and then divide that answer by 2.

Examples

7 $2.89 \times 20 = 28.9 \times 2 = 57.8$
$4.54 \div 20 = 0.454 \div 2 = 0.227$
$28.5 \times 30 = 285 \times 3 = 855$
$5.43 \times 40 = 54.3 \times 4 = 217.2$
$9.6 \div 80 = 0.96 \div 8 = 0.12$
$8.02 \times 200 = 802 \times 2 = 1604$
$648.6 \div 300 = 6.486 \div 3 = 2.162$
$3690 \div 900 = 36.9 \div 9 = 4.1$

Multiplication

To multiply two (or more) decimal numbers, first ignore the decimal points and multiply, then restore the decimals in the answer keeping as many decimal places in the answer as there were altogether in the question.

Examples

8 2.31×0.7 (3 decimal places altogether)
        $(231 \times 7 = 1617)$
        $2.31 \times 0.7 = 1.617$ (restoring 3 decimal places)

9 0.004×0.3 (4 decimal places)
        $(4 \times 3 = 12)$
        $0.004 \times 0.3 = 0.0012$ (including two 0's to restore 4 decimal places)

Division

Instead of dividing by a decimal, multiply both numerator and denominator by 10, 100, 1000, ... as necessary, to make the denominator into a whole number.

Examples

10 $0.07 \div 0.2 = \dfrac{0.07}{0.2} = \dfrac{0.7}{2}$ (multiplying both numerator and denominator by 10 to make 0.2 into 2)

$= 0.35$

11 $3.6 \div 0.04 = \dfrac{3.6}{0.04} = \dfrac{360}{4}$ (multiplying both numerator and denominator by 100 to make 0.04 into 4)

$= 90$

If the division is not exact, it will be necessary to stop after a suitable number of decimal places.

12   Find the value of $22 \div 7$, correct to 3 decimal places.

$7\,\overline{)22.0000}$
$\quad\ 3.1428$

Since the figure in the 4th decimal place is 8, the figure in the 3rd decimal place must be corrected up from 2 to 3.

$22 \div 7 = 3.143$, correct to 3 decimal places.

The rule for decimal places is:
Work to one more place than you need. If this extra figure is 5 or more, add 1 to the final figure of your answer.

Examples

13   3.2976 = 3.3   to 1 decimal place

                  = 3.30   to 2 decimal places

                  = 3.298   to 3 decimal places

      0.8692 = 0.9   to 1 decimal place

                  = 0.87   to 2 decimal places

                  = 0.869   to 3 decimal places

      0.0827 = 0.1   to 1 decimal place

                  = 0.08   to 2 decimal places

                  = 0.083   to 3 decimal places

    0.00426 = 0.004   to 3 decimal places

                = 0.0043   to 4 decimal places

Significant figures

2.51, 25 100 and 0.0251 all have 3 significant figures, that is figures not counting 0's at the beginning or end of the number.
However, 0's in the middle of a number are counted, so 2.01, 20 100 and 0.0201 also have all got 3 significant figures.

To write a number to less significant figures than it has, use similar rules to those for changing to less decimal places.

Examples

14   To 3 significant figures, 3 657 000 = 3 660 000

                                9483 = 9480

                              587.9 = 588

                              4.962 = 4.96

    To 2 significant figures, 3 657 000 = 3 700 000

                                9483 = 9500

                              587.9 = 590

                              4.962 = 5.0

Decimals in order of size

To compare 0.56 and 0.6, write 0.6 as 0.60 so that both numbers have the same number of decimal places.
Then 0.56 is 5 tenths and 6 hundredths, which is 56 hundredths, and 0.60 is 60 hundredths.
0.56 is smaller than 0.6.

To compare 0.24 and 0.231 write 0.24 as 0.240.
Then 0.240 is 240 thousandths, and 0.231 is 231 thousandths.
0.231 is smaller than 0.24.

To compare 0.77, 0.769 and 0.7, write all three numbers with 3 decimal places.
0.77 = 0.770 and this is 770 thousandths.
0.769 is 769 thousandths.
0.7 = 0.700 and this is 700 thousandths.
In order of size, smallest first, the numbers are 0.7, 0.769, 0.77.

To convert fractions into decimals

$\frac{3}{5}$ means $3 \div 5$ so you can do this calculation on your calculator, getting 0.6.

$\frac{5}{7}$ means $5 \div 7$ so you can do this calculation on your calculator.
The result is 0.7142... so you must correct this to a sensible number of decimal places.
If you need 2 decimal places, the next figure (in the 3rd decimal place) is 4 so you do not correct up.
$\frac{5}{7} = 0.71$, correct to 2 decimal places.

$\frac{7}{9} = 0.7777...$
The figure in the 3rd decimal place is 7 so you correct up the 2nd decimal place from 7 to 8.
$\frac{7}{9} = 0.78$, correct to 2 decimal places.

It is useful to turn fractions into decimals if you need to compare their sizes.

Example

15   Write $3\frac{3}{8}$, $3\frac{1}{3}$, $3\frac{2}{5}$ in order of size.

$3\frac{3}{8} = 3.375$
$3\frac{1}{3} = 3.333...$
$3\frac{2}{5} = 3.4$
In order of size, smallest first, they are $3\frac{1}{3}$, $3\frac{3}{8}$, $3\frac{2}{5}$.

Exercise 3.1

In this exercise, do not use your calculator, except for checking.

1. 1 $1.32 + 2.5 + 3.79$
    2 $5.87 + 1.03 + 0.1$
    3 $0.4 + 0.08 + 0.15$
    4 $9.99 + 0.03$
    5 $2.05 + 4.93 + 0.88$

2. 1 $21.03 - 0.07$
    2 $7.92 - 0.97$
    3 $0.5 - 0.13$
    4 $10 - 0.91$
    5 $5.82 + 2.19 - 3.13$

3. 1 3.87×4
    2 0.05×12
    3 0.8×7
    4 3.14×3
    5 1.92×5

4. 1 $3.88 \div 4$
    2 $0.056 \div 8$
    3 $0.8 \div 5$
    4 $19.8 \div 9$
    5 $35.4 \div 6$

5. 1 1.32×10
    2 2.5×100
    3 1.03×1000
    4 0.027×100
    5 3.1×20

6. 1 $3.79 \div 10$
    2 $0.15 \div 100$
    3 $21.3 \div 1000$
    4 $3.1 \div 1000$
    5 $3.4 \div 20$

7. 1 0.8×0.09
    2 0.05×0.06
    3 0.12×0.1
    4 0.9×0.7
    5 0.04×0.5

8. 1 If $314 \times 28 = 8792$, find 3.14×2.8
    2 If $57 \times 14 = 798$, find 0.57×0.14
    3 If $218 \times 91 = 19\,838$, find 21.8×9.1
    4 If $15 \times 16 = 240$, find 1.5×0.16
    5 If $31 \times 41 = 1271$, find 0.31×0.0041

9. 1 $15.6 \div 0.4$
    2 $2.49 \div 0.03$
    3 $21.7 \div 0.7$
    4 $270 \div 0.9$
    5 $0.032 \div 0.04$

10. Write as decimals

    1 $\frac{3}{4}$ 2 $\frac{2}{5}$ 3 $\frac{7}{10}$ 4 $\frac{37}{100}$ 5 $\frac{3}{5}$

11. Write these numbers correct to 3 decimal places.

    1 29.7122 2 1.62815 3 202.9157 4 4.6798 5 0.003527

12. Write the numbers of question 11 correct to 3 significant figures.

13. Write these numbers correct to 3 significant figures.

    1 $56\,752$ 2 82.9804 3 253.312 4 206.789 5 1000.5

Do not use your calculator, except for checking.

14.   Find the values of the following, correct to 2 decimal places.
       1 $20 \div 7$ **4** $8.74 \div 9$
       2 $15.5 \div 0.3$ **5** $0.91 \div 0.8$
       3 $0.052 \div 0.6$

15.   Write these fractions as decimals, correct to 2 decimal places.

       1 $\frac{2}{3}$ **2** $\frac{5}{7}$ **3** $\frac{4}{9}$ **4** $\frac{1}{6}$ **5** $\frac{8}{11}$

16.   Write these numbers in order of size, smallest first.
       0.8,   0.75,   0.81,   0.7   0.778.

17.   Write these numbers in order of size, smallest first.
       62.5,   63.7,   60.9,   62.49,   63.72.

18.   Write down any even number between 1 and 11. Add 1.83 and multiply the total by 5.
       Now subtract 10.9 and then divide by 10. Add 0.675 and double the result. Subtract the
       number you started with. What is your answer ?

Using your calculator

A calculator will save you time in doing routine calculations
but do not use it for simple arithmetic which you can do more
quickly in your head.

Scientific calculator

These instructions are for a scientific calculator.
With some calculators you may have to do some operations in a different way.

It is advisable to start every new calculation by pressing the $\boxed{C}$ key (for CLEAR), but you
may find that on your calculator this is unnecessary if you have just pressed the $\boxed{=}$ key.
This also works after pressing some of the other keys.

If your calculator does not seem to work in the ways shown here, read the instruction booklet
and try the examples shown there.

1.   When doing multiplication and division, it is better to multiply first and divide last if the
       division is not exact.
       e.g. For $\frac{2}{3}$ of 20, find $2 \times 20 \div 3$ instead of $2 \div 3 \times 20$.
       The answer is 13.333 ...

2. If the answer is not exact, or has several figures, then round it up to a sensible degree of accuracy.
    Usually 3 significant figures will be sufficient for a final numerical answer.

3. If you have a question involving addition or subtraction together with multiplication, the calculator will read it as if there were brackets round the multiplication part, and do that part first.
    e.g. $25.1 + 76.2 \times 0.3$ is read as $25.1 + (76.2 \times 0.3)$ and the answer is 47.96.

    Similar rules work with addition or subtraction together with division.
    The calculator will do the division first.
    e.g. $5.93 - 0.86 \div 0.4$ is read as $5.93 - (0.86 \div 0.4)$ and the answer is 3.78.

4. If there are brackets then the part in brackets is worked out first.
    e.g. $(25.1 + 76.2) \times 0.3$
    Use the bracket keys on your calculator, or instead, you can press 25.1 $\boxed{+}$ 76.2 $\boxed{=}$ $\boxed{\times}$ 0.3 $\boxed{=}$
    so that the calculator works out the addition before multiplying by 0.3.
    The answer is 30.39.

    For $(5.93 - 0.86) \div 0.4$, use the bracket keys or press 5.93 $\boxed{-}$ 0.86 $\boxed{=}$ $\boxed{\div}$ 0.4 $\boxed{=}$
    The answer is 12.675.
    $$\frac{5.93 - 0.86}{0.4}$$ is the same question, written in a different way.

5. **Using the memory**
    $$\frac{23.5 + 12.9}{18.1 - 6.9}$$
    First find $18.1 - 6.9$ and put the answer (11.2) in the memory.
    Then press 23.5 $\boxed{+}$ 12.9 $\boxed{=}$ $\boxed{\div}$ $\boxed{RM}$ $\boxed{=}$
    The answer is 3.25
    RM stands for 'recall memory'.

    Alternatively, you could find $(23.5 + 12.9) \div (18.1 - 6.9)$, using brackets.

6. **Checking calculator answers**
    It is easy to get a wrong answer from a calculator by pressing the wrong keys, so look at the answer and see if it seems to be about right.
    You could also do the calculation twice, possibly entering the numbers in reverse order, to see if you get the same result.

Check the size of the answer

$5813 + 1967$
The numbers are approximately 6000 and 2000.
The answer should be approximately $6000 + 2000 = 8000$.
(The exact answer is 7780.)

5813×2
The answer should be approximately $6000 \times 2 = 12\,000$.
(The exact answer is 11 626.)

$5813 - 1967$
The answer should be approximately $6000 - 2000 = 4000$.
(The exact answer is 3846.)

$5813 \div 2$
The answer should be approximately $6000 \div 2 = 3000$.
(The exact answer is 2906.5.)

Check the units figure

$5813 + 1967$
The units figures are 3 and 7.
$3 + 7 = 10$ so the units figure in the answer is 0.
(The answer is 7780.)

13×67
$3 \times 7 = 21$ so the units figure in the answer is 1.
(The answer is 871.)

$5813 - 1967$
You cannot use $3 - 7$ so use $13 - 7 = 6$ and the units figure in the answer is 6.
(The answer is 3846.)

(You cannot do a similar check for division.)

Check by doing the reverse operation

To check $5813 - 1967 = 3846$, do the calculation $3846 + 1967$ and you will get 5813.
To check $5813 \div 2 = 2906.5$, do the calculation 2906.5×2 and you will get 5813.
To check $\sqrt{121} = 11$, do the calculation 11×11 and you will get 121.

7. **Keys** $\boxed{\sqrt{\ }}$ $\boxed{x^2}$ $\boxed{y^x}$ $\boxed{\sqrt[3]{\ }}$

$\boxed{\sqrt{\ }}$ is the square root key. It must be pressed after the number.

So for $\sqrt{6}$ press 6 $\boxed{\sqrt{\ }}$ and you will get $2.4494 \ldots$

To 3 significant figures this is 2.45.

$\boxed{x^2}$ is the squaring key.

For 3.2^2 press 3.2 $\boxed{x^2}$ and you will get 10.24.

$\boxed{y^x}$ or $\boxed{x^y}$ is the key for getting cubes and other powers.

For 7^3 press 7 $\boxed{y^x}$ 3 $\boxed{=}$ and you will get 343.

For 2^6 press 2 $\boxed{y^x}$ 6 $\boxed{=}$ and you will get 64.

A different way to get 7^3 is to press 7 $\boxed{\times}$ $\boxed{x^2}$ $\boxed{=}$.

To get 8^4 press 8 $\boxed{x^2}$ $\boxed{x^2}$, and you will get 4096.

For cube roots, use the key $\boxed{\sqrt[3]{}}$.

For the cube root of 125 press 125 $\boxed{\sqrt[3]{}}$ and you will get 5.

If there is not a cube root key, use the inverse key to $\boxed{y^x}$.

This is marked $\boxed{\sqrt[x]{y}}$.

For the cube root of 125 press 125 $\boxed{\sqrt[x]{y}}$ 3 $\boxed{=}$ and you will get 5. (The 3 is to show that you want the **cube** root.)

The quickest way to get a fourth root is to press $\boxed{number}$ $\boxed{\sqrt{}}$ $\boxed{\sqrt{}}$ e.g. for $\sqrt[4]{256}$ press 256 $\boxed{\sqrt{}}$ $\boxed{\sqrt{}}$ and you will get 4.

8.   **To find the remainder in a division sum**

e.g. Divide 961 by 23 and give the answer and remainder.

On your calculator, $961 \div 23 = 41.7826\ldots$
From this, the whole number answer is 41.
Leaving the answer on your calculator, subtract 41 and press $\boxed{=}$.
This leaves $0.7826\ldots$
Multiply this decimal by 23 and it gives 18. This is the remainder.
Due to rounding errors on the calculator, instead of giving 18 exactly it might give something like 18.00000001 or 17.99999999. Count either of these as 18.

Money

Since there are 100 pence in £1, our money calculations use the decimal system.

£2 and 48 pence is £2.48
£3 and 5 pence is £3.05
£3 and 50 pence is £3.50. On a calculator this may be recorded as 3.5
Remember that this means £3.50, not £3.05.

Trial and improvement methods

Example

Suppose the $\sqrt[x]{y}$ button on your calculator is not working properly, or there is not that key on your calculator, and you need to find the cube root of 500, correct to 2 decimal places.

First make a list of cube numbers.

Number	Cube
1	$1^3 = 1 \times 1 \times 1 = 1$
2	$2^3 = 2 \times 2 \times 2 = 8$
3	27
4	64
5	125
6	216
7	343
8	512

You can stop at 8, because the cube root of 343 is 7, the cube root of 512 is 8, and so the cube root of 500 is somewhere between 7 and 8, and it seems to be nearer to 8 than to 7, because 500 is nearly up to 512.

So find the value of 7.7^3 (or 7.8^3 would do).
$7.7^3 = 7.7 \times 7.7 \times 7.7 = 456.5$; too small.
$7.8^3 = 474.6$; still too small.
$7.9^3 = 493.0$; still too small.
You already know that 8^3 is too big, so the number lies between 7.9 and 8.0.

$7.95^3 = 502.5$; too big.
Now you know that the number lies between 7.9 and 7.95.

$7.93^3 = 498.7$; too small.
$7.94^3 = 500.6$; too big.
So the number lies between 7.93 and 7.94.

Next try $7.935^3 = 499.6$, too small.
So the answer lies between 7.935 and 7.94, and therefore to 2 decimal places it is 7.94.

(Finally, borrow a calculator with a $\sqrt[x]{y}$ key which works. Press 500 $\sqrt[x]{y}$ 3 $=$ and it gives 7.93700526 so we can see that our answer is correct, to 2 decimal places.)

Exercise 3.2

1. Find the results of these calculations without using your calculator. Then repeat the questions using your calculator, making sure that you get the same results.

1 $\dfrac{5 \times 3}{2}$

2 $(6 - 2) \times 3$

3 $7 + (5 \times 4)$

4 $20 \div (3 + 2)$

5 $(5 \times 7) - 29$

6 $10^2 - 7^2$

7 $\dfrac{15 + 13}{4}$

8 $\frac{12}{4} + \frac{15}{3}$

9 $(12 \times 4) - (10 \times 3)$

10 $\sqrt{64} - \sqrt{36}$

2. By using approximate values, estimate answers for these calculations.
Then find the correct answers, using your calculator.

1 39×71

2 $377 \div 13$

3 73^2

4 $558 \div 31$

5 $\sqrt{118.81}$

6 $(4680 \times 18) - (490 \times 80)$

7 $\dfrac{84 \times 429}{12}$

8 $(53 \times 119) + (87 \times 181)$

9 $28^2 - 21 \times 18$

10 $2 \times 3.14 \times (17 + 32)$

3. Use your calculator to find answers to the following, correct to 3 significant figures.

1 $2 \times 3.14 \times 27$

2 $\dfrac{0.00211}{0.7 \times 19}$

3 $(81.8 + 1.82) \div 65.8$

4 $4 \times \pi \times 8.2^3$

5 $34.5 \div (16.3 - 10.02)$

6 $\sqrt[3]{0.0073}$

7 $\sqrt{32.1^2 + 45.5^2}$

8 $\dfrac{23.29 + 19.72}{15.21 - 5.93}$

4. Find the whole number answers and the remainders when

1 371 is divided by 12,

2 827 is divided by 23,

3 1024 is divided by 13,

4 7 is divided into 2000,

5 60 is divided into 400.

5. Mrs Martin spent £6.36 on meat and £3.84 on vegetables.
How much was this altogether ? What change did she get from a £20 note ?

6. What is the price of a bar of chocolate if 9 of them cost £2.16 ?

7. How many 19p stamps can be bought for £10, and how much change is there ?

8. Petrol costs 52.3p per litre. What is the cost of 30 litres ?

9. Mrs Rija buys 12 yards of curtain material at £4.65 per yard. What is the total cost ?

10. A shop's takings during the week were Monday £591.17, Tuesday £629.80, Wednesday £212.14, Thursday £859.75, Friday £905.22, Saturday £1028.60. What were the total takings for the week, to the nearest £1 ? The shopkeeper was hoping for total takings of £5000. How many £'s was he short of his target ?

11. Mr Rigby has a £20 voucher to spend at the garden centre. He decides to buy 4 bushes for £1.85 each and spend the rest on bulbs at 21p each. How many bulbs can he buy ?

Use trial and improvement methods to solve the problems in questions 12 to 15.

12. Two integers (positive whole numbers) have a product of 918. One number is 7 larger than the other one. Find the numbers.

13. The sum of the cubes of two consecutive integers is 3059. Find the numbers.

14. Find the square root of 600, correct to 2 decimal places, without using the square root key on your calculator.

15. Kevin thinks of a number. He finds that the square of the number added to 8 times the original number is 345. What is the original number ?

The metric system

Length

The main unit of length is called the **metre** (m).
One-thousandth part of a metre is a millimetre (mm).
One-hundredth part of a metre is a centimetre (cm).
One thousand metres is a kilometre (km).

i.e.   1000 mm = 1 m

       100 cm = 1 m   (so 10 mm = 1 cm)

       1000 m = 1 km

Weight

The main unit of weight is the **gram** (g).
One-thousandth part of a gram is a milligram (mg).
One-hundredth part of a gram is a centigram (cg).
One thousand grams is a kilogram (kg).
Since a kilogram is rather a small weight, a larger unit is often needed.
One thousand kilograms is a tonne, sometimes called a metric ton.

i.e.
$$1000\,\text{mg} = 1\,\text{g}$$
$$100\,\text{cg} = 1\,\text{g}$$
$$1000\,\text{g} = 1\,\text{kg}$$
$$1000\,\text{kg} = 1\,\text{tonne}$$

Capacity

The main unit of capacity is the **litre** (ℓ).
One-thousandth part of a litre is called a millilitre (ml).
One-hundredth part of a litre is called a centilitre (cl).
One thousand litres is a kilolitre (kl).

i.e.
$$1000\,\text{ml} = 1\,\ell$$
$$100\,\text{cl} = 1\,\ell$$
$$1000\,\ell = 1\,\text{kl}$$

$$1\,\text{litre} = 1000\,\text{cm}^3$$

It is useful to know that

1 millilitre of water weighs 1 gram.

1 litre of water weighs 1 kilogram.

To change from one unit to another

centimetres into millimetres

To change centimetres into millimetres multiply by 10, because 1 cm = 10 mm.
5 cm = 50 mm
6.2 cm = 62 mm

millimetres into centimetres

To change millimetres into centimetres divide by 10, because 10 mm = 1 cm.
30 mm = 3 cm
24 mm = 2.4 cm

metres into centimetres

1 m = 100 cm, so to change metres into cm multiply by 100.
3.2 m = 320 cm
5.61 m = 561 cm

centimetres into metres

100 cm = 1 m, so to change cm into metres divide by 100.
62 cm = 0.62 m
560 cm = 5.6 m

metres into millimetres

1 m = 1000 mm, so to change metres into mm multiply by 1000.
2 m = 2000 mm
1.5 m = 1500 mm
0.07 m = 70 mm

millimetres into metres

1000 mm = 1 m, so to change mm into metres divide by 1000.
2500 mm = 2.5 m
6 mm = 0.006 m

The methods are similar for changing units of weight and capacity.

e.g.   To change grams into kg, divide by 1000.
        To change litres into ml, multiply by 1000.

Time

The units for time are unlikely to be changed in the near future although since they are not based on ten they are not easy to use on a calculator. Perhaps, eventually, things will be changed so that there could be 10 new hours in a day, 10 new minutes in an hour, and even 10 days in a new week. But we cannot change the length of a year because that is the length of time that the earth takes to go round the sun, and that is approximately $365\frac{1}{4}$ days.

Here is the present table for time:

60 seconds = 1 minute		52 weeks = 1 year	
60 minutes = 1 hour		365 days = 1 year	
24 hours = 1 day		366 days = 1 leap year	
7 days = 1 week		12 months = 1 year	

Recording the time of day can either be by the 12-hour clock, when morning times are denoted by a.m. and afternoon times by p.m., or by the 24-hour clock. To avoid confusion, timetables are often printed with times using the 24-hour clock.

Examples

	12-hour clock	24-hour clock
1 o'clock early morning	1.00 am	1.00 or 01.00
5 past 1 early morning	1.05 am	1.05 or 01.05
Noon	12.00 pm	12.00
Quarter-to-1 early afternoon	12.45 pm	12.45
1 o'clock early afternoon	1.00 pm	13.00
Half-past 8 in the evening	8.30 pm	20.30
One minute to midnight	11.59 pm	23.59
Midnight	12.00 am	0.00 or 00.00
One minute past midnight	12.01 am	0.01 or 00.01

(The day changes at the instant of midnight so when the time is shown as 12.00 am or 0.00 the date has changed.)

On a timetable the 24-hour times would be printed as 4-figure numbers. The full stop separating the hours and minutes could be left out.
e.g.   1.23 am would be printed as 0123,
       1.23 pm would be printed as 1323.

1323 would be pronounced as thirteen twenty-three or thirteen twenty-three hours.
But 1300 would be pronounced as thirteen hundred hours.

The calendar

There are 7 days in a week:-
Sunday, Monday, Tuesday, Wednesday, Thursday, Friday, Saturday.

There are 12 months in a year:-
January, February, March, April, May, June, July, August, September, October, November, December.

April, June, September and November have 30 days.
February has 28 days, and 29 days in leap years.
All the other months have 31 days.

Thirty days hath September,
April, June and dull November,
All the rest have 31,
Excepting February alone,
Which has 28 days clear,
And 29 in each leap year.

FEBRUARY 1996						
Sun	Mon	Tu	Wed	Th	Fri	Sat
				1	2	3
4	5	6	7	8	9	10
11	12	13	14	15	16	17
18	19	20	21	22	23	24
25	26	27	28	29		

There are 4 weeks (+ usually some extra days) in a month.

There are 52 weeks (+ 1 extra day) in a year.
There are 52 weeks (+ 2 extra days) in a leap year.

A year has 365 days.
Every 4th year is a leap year and has an extra day, 29th February.

Leap years are years whose dates are divisible by 4, e.g. 1988 and 2000.

(A number divides by 4 if its last 2 figures divide by 4.
e.g. to check if 1992 divides by 4, just check if 92 divides by 4. Does it ? If so, 1992 was a leap year, if not, 1992 was not a leap year.)

The exceptions to the leap year rule were the years 1700, 1800 and 1900 which were not leap years. However, 2000 will be a leap year.
(The reason for these exceptions is that the actual length of a year is nearly $365\frac{1}{4}$ days, but not precisely.)

Use of a calculator

You cannot use your calculator directly for mixed calculations involving hours and minutes, minutes and seconds, days and weeks, etc. since these are not based on a scale of ten. You will have to do the calculations for the different units separately. Here are some examples:-

1   A plumber does two jobs. The first one takes 1 hour 37 minutes and the second takes 2 hours 46 minutes. What is the total time taken ?

$$
\begin{array}{ll}
1\,\text{hr} & 37\,\text{min} \\
2\,\text{hr} & 46\,\text{min} \\
\hline
4\,\text{hr} & 23\,\text{min}
\end{array}
$$

Use your calculator to add 37 and 46. This makes 83.   83 min = 1 hr 23 min so write down 23 min and carry 1 hour forward, making 4 hours altogether.

2   Of a school day of 5 hours, 2 hours 25 minutes was spent on rehearsals for a display. How much time was left for lessons ?

$$
\begin{array}{ll}
5\,\text{hr} & 0\,\text{min} \\
2\,\text{hr} & 25\,\text{min} \\
\hline
2\,\text{hr} & 35\,\text{min}
\end{array}
$$

Use your calculator to take 25 from 60, since you cannot take 25 from 0. This gives 35 min. Then adjust for the 1 hour you changed into 60 minutes, so, depending on the way you normally do subtraction, you will have either 5 hr − 3 hr or 4 hr − 2 hr. This gives 2 hours.

3   12 hr 22 min ÷ 7

$$
\begin{array}{r}
1\,\text{hr} \ \ 46\,\text{min} \\
7\,\overline{)12\,\text{hr} \ \ 22\,\text{min}}
\end{array}
$$

Do the hours part first. 7 into 12 goes 1 remainder 5. Write down 1 hr. Change the remainder, 5 hr, into 5×60 min = 300 min, so altogether there are 322 min. $322 \div 7 = 46$, so the answer is 1 hr 46 min.

4   A train left London at 12.25 pm and arrived in Penzance at 6.04 pm. How long did the journey take ?

One way to do this is:
From 12.25 pm to 1 pm is 35 minutes,
from 1 pm to 6 pm is 5 hours,
from 6 pm to 6.04 pm is 4 minutes,
Total time, 5 hours 39 minutes.

British units

The metric system originated in France at the time of the French Revolution. Since it is based on 10 and powers of 10 it is a very useful system for scientific work.

The British system of units for weights and measures is much older. It is still partly in use although it is not so convenient for use with calculators, not being based on 10.

Length

We use inch, foot, yard, mile.

12 inches	= 1 foot
3 feet	= 1 yard
1760 yards	= 1 mile

The old symbol for inches was ", and for feet was ', so 7' 6" means 7 feet 6 inches.

Other units which used to be used are rod, pole, perch (each $5\frac{1}{2}$ yards), chain (22 yards) and furlong (220 yards).

The approximate comparisons with the metric system which are useful are:

1 inch ... $2\frac{1}{2}$ cm
1 foot ... 30 cm
1 yard ... 0.9 m
1 mile ... 1.6 km
5 miles ... 8 km

1 cm ... 0.4 inches
1 m ... 40 inches = 4 ins longer than 1 yard
1 km ... $\frac{5}{8}$ mile
8 km ... 5 miles

Weight

We use ounces, pounds, stones, hundredweights and tons.

16 ounces	= 1 pound
14 pounds	= 1 stone
112 pounds	= 1 hundredweight
8 stones	= 1 hundredweight
2240 pounds	= 1 ton
20 hundredweights	= 1 ton

The symbol for ounces is oz, for pounds is lb (from Latin, libra for pound), for stones st, for hundredweight cwt (from the Roman C for a hundred). Another unit which used to be used is a quarter ($\frac{1}{4}$ of a hundredweight $= 28$ pounds).

The approximate comparisons with the metric system which are useful are:

1 lb ... 450 g (nearly $\frac{1}{2}$ kg)

1 ton ... 1 tonne

1 kg ... 2.2 lb (just over 2 lb)

1 tonne ... 1 ton

Capacity

We use pint, gallon.

8 pints $= 1$ gallon

Other units which used to be used are a gill ($\frac{1}{4}$ pint), although this unit is sometimes used for $\frac{1}{2}$ pint, e.g. when asking for a gill of beer; also fluid ounces. There are 20 fluid ounces in 1 pint.

The approximate comparisons with the metric system which are useful are

1 pint ... just over $\frac{1}{2}$ litre

1 gallon ... $4\frac{1}{2}$ litres

1 litre ... $1\frac{3}{4}$ pints

1 litre ... 0.22 gallon

It is useful to know that

1 pint of water weighs $1\frac{1}{4}$ lb

1 gallon of water weighs 10 lb

More exact comparisons with the metric system

You may need more accurate figures, and these are given at the front of the book on page xiii. You can also find them in many diaries and reference books. There is no need to learn them.

Use of a calculator

As with calculations with time, be careful if using your calculator when dealing with mixed units not based on 10, such as lb and oz, gallons and pints, feet and inches. You will have to deal with the different units separately.

Examples

5   One parcel weighs 14 lb 9 oz and another weighs 10 lb 12 oz. What is the total weight ?

14 lb 9 oz	First, do the ounces part. $9 + 12 = 21$.
10 lb 12 oz	Since $16 oz = 1 lb$, this is 1 lb 5 oz.
25 lb 5 oz	Write down 5 oz and carry forward 1 lb, making 25 lb altogether.

(It is usual to have only 2 units in our measurements, which is why stones are not used in this question, where there are already lbs and oz.)

6   6 gall 2 pints − 1 gall 7 pints.

6 gall 2 pints	First do the pints. You cannot take 7 from 2 so change 1 gall into
1 gall 7 pints	8 pints and take 7 from 10, answer 3.
4 gall 3 pints	Then either do 6 gall − 2 gall or 5 gall − 1 gall, depending on the way
	you usually do subtraction, leaving 4 gall.

7   The space between two gateposts is 3 ft 5 in. This space is to be blocked with 6 strands of wire. What is the total length of wire needed ?

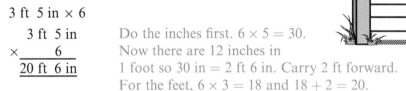

3 ft 5 in × 6

3 ft 5 in	Do the inches first. $6 \times 5 = 30$.
× 6	Now there are 12 inches in
20 ft 6 in	1 foot so 30 in = 2 ft 6 in. Carry 2 ft forward.
	For the feet, $6 \times 3 = 18$ and $18 + 2 = 20$.

8   A sackful of apples weighing 23 lb 7 oz is to be divided among 5 people. How much should they each get ?

5)23 lb 7 oz	5's into 23 goes 4 so they will each get 4 lb.
4 lb 11 oz	There is a remainder of 3 lb.
	This is $3 \times 16 oz = 48 oz$. Add this to the 7 oz making 55 oz.
	5's into 55 goes 11, so they will also get 11 oz.

Temperature

The temperature scale used nowadays is the Celsius scale (which used to be called the Centigrade scale).

In this scale:
0° is the temperature at which water freezes,
100° is the temperature at which water boils.

In Britain, we still often use the Fahrenheit scale.

In this scale:
32° is the temperature at which water freezes,
212° is the temperature at which water boils.

To change from Fahrenheit to Celsius, use the formula

$$C = \tfrac{5}{9}(F - 32)$$

To change from Celsius to Fahrenheit, use the formula

$$F = 1.8\,C + 32$$

where F is the temperature in deg F,
        C is the temperature in deg C.

Exercise 3.3

1. How many

1	mm in 5 cm	**11**	pints in 2 gallons
2	g in 3 kg	**12**	degrees in $1\frac{1}{2}$ right angles
3	pence in £10	**13**	mm in 2 m
4	cm in $\frac{1}{2}$ m	**14**	minutes in $2\frac{1}{2}$ hours
5	days in a year	**15**	inches in 1 yard
6	m in 4 km	**16**	weeks in a year
7	yards in $\frac{1}{2}$ mile	**17**	pounds in $\frac{1}{4}$ ton
8	mg in 6 g	**18**	seconds in $\frac{1}{2}$ minute
9	oz in 4 lb	**19**	feet in 1 mile
10	days in January	**20**	ml in 1 litre ?

2. Give the readings shown on these instruments.

    1 Weight in kg.

    10   ↑   11

    2 Temperature in °F.

2.   Give the readings shown on these instruments.

3 Weighing scale in kg and g.   4 Measuring glass.

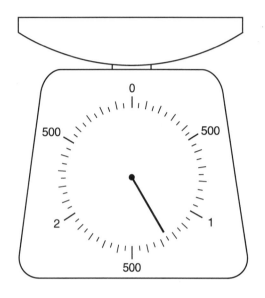

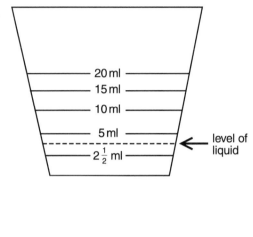

3.   1   Write 0.75 kg in g.   6   Write 1520 g in kg.
     2   Write 126 mm in cm.   7   Write 0.7 ℓ in cl.
     3   Write 2.6 m in cm.   8   Write 7.8 cm in mm.
     4   Write 400 ml in ℓ.   9   Write 1.2 m in cm.
     5   Write 160 cm in m.   10   Write 3040 kg in tonnes.

4.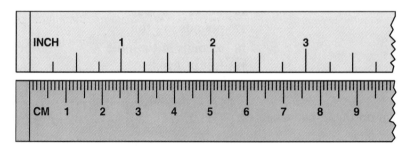

The two rulers show measurements in inches and in centimetres. The top ruler has inches and is divided into quarter inches. The other ruler has centimetres and is divided into millimetres.

1   What measurement in centimetres is equivalent to $2\frac{3}{4}$ inches ?
2   What measurement in inches is equivalent to 3.8 cm ?

5.   Give approximate metric equivalents for these measures.

   1   6 inches   **4**   2 tons
   2   4 lb   **5**   10 miles
   3   10 gallons

6.   Give approximate British equivalents for these measures.

   1   3 m   **4**   12 km
   2   5 kg   **5**   6 tonnes
   3   4 litres

7.   For these statements 4 alternatives are given in brackets. Which one makes the most sensible statement ?

   1   Jim's 20-year old brother is   (1.2)   (1.8)   (2.4)   (6)   metres tall.
   2   Mary's baby sister weighs   (35 g)   ($3\frac{1}{2}$ kg)   (35 kg)   (350 lb). Her other young sister weighs   (35 g)   ($3\frac{1}{2}$ kg)   (35 kg)   (350 lb).
   3   Tessa measured one of the other angles of a right-angled triangle and it was (72°)   (99°)   (100°)   (108°).
   4   Sam's car does 40 miles to the gallon. On his holiday he expects to drive about 500 miles, and he estimates that he will need about   (£3)   (£20)   (£30)   (£300)   for petrol, which costs £2.50 per gallon.
   5   The height of the oak tree in the field is   (1.5)   (20)   (50)   (75)   metres.

8.   John is 6 feet 6 inches tall and his son Keith is 5 feet 8 inches tall. How many inches is John taller than Keith ?

9.   Mary weighed 10 stones 8 lbs on New Year's Day and she decided to lose some weight. Now she weighs 9 stones 10 lbs. How many pounds has she lost ?

10.   A farmer has 108 gallons of milk to sell. How many pint bottles can he fill with this milk ?

11.   Fence posts are 3 yards apart. If there are 4 strands of barbed wire nailed to each post, how much wire is need to stretch between the first and the twentieth posts ?

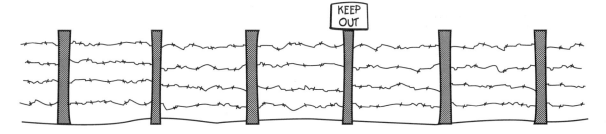

12.   Paul runs a race of 1500 metres. (1500 m = 1640 yards.) How many yards short of a mile is this ?

13.   Alan started school on his 5th birthday in 1993. In which year will he have his 16th birthday ?

14. Change these times to the 24-hour clock.

    4.05 am   2.00 pm   3.15 pm   6.05 pm   11.55 pm

    Change these times to the 12-hour clock.

    01.10   5.18   10.30   17.05   21.50

15. A train left a station at 9.30 am and
    arrived at its destination at 2.13 pm.
    How long did the journey take ?

16. Mike set off on a training ride at 11.50 am and cycled for $4\frac{1}{4}$ hours. At what time did he stop ?

17. How many days are/were there in February in these years ?

    1 1992   **2** 1946   **3** 1808   **4** 2012   **5** 1994

18. Name these months.

    1 It begins with the letter J and has only 30 days.
    2 It follows two months which have 31 days.
    3 It ends with the letter y and has less than 31 days.

19. On a timetable, a plane was due to leave an
    airport at 20.55 and arrive at its destination
    at 02.05 the next day. How long should the
    journey take ? It actually arrived 45 minutes
    early. At what time did it arrive ?

20. The distance all round the equator is approximately 24 900 miles. Taking 1 mile as
    equivalent to 1.61 km, find this distance in kilometres, to the nearest 100 km.

Exercise 3.4 Applications

Do not use your calculator, except for checking, in questions 1 to 11.

1. Work out the answers to these questions

1	60×30	**5**	10×0.1	**8**	$270 \div 0.9$
2	0.7×0.1	**6**	$4.2 \div 0.7$	**9**	$0.36 \div 0.6$
3	40×0.9	**7**	$0.56 \div 0.08$	**10**	$10 \div 0.1$
4	0.6×8				

2. Divide 1720 by 0.8

3. What is the square root of 0.16 ?

4. Simplify $0.1 \times 0.2 \times 0.3$.

5. 0.0035×8000

6. Express $\frac{5}{8}$ as an exact decimal.

7. Subtract 0.006 from 0.06.

8. Find the exact value of $4.2752 \div 0.4$.

9. Find the exact value of $\dfrac{1.4 \times 0.05}{0.07}$.

10. What fraction, in its simplest form, is equivalent to 0.075 ?

11. If $A = 5.14$, $B = 3.709$ and $C = 13.3$, find

    1 $A + B + C$ **2** $A \div 100$ **3** $10(C - A)$

12. Express 9876.524 correct to
    1 the nearest whole number,
    2 2 decimal places,
    3 3 significant figures.

13. Write these numbers in order of size, smallest first.

    0.35,   0.3,   0.299.

14. By using approximate values, estimate answers for these calculations. Then find the
    correct answers, using your calculator, correct to 3 significant figures.

    1 324×1058 **4** $(4235 \times 15) - (498 \times 18)$

    2 $24\,300 \div 325$ **5** $\dfrac{115 \times 32}{60}$

    3 $\dfrac{27 + 19}{15}$ **6** 29^3

15. Use your calculator to find the numbers represented by $\square$ in these statements.

    1 $122 + \square = 975$ **6** $125 \times (\square + 89) = 52875$

    2 $\square \times 17 = 442$ **7** $\dfrac{187 + 99}{\square} = 13$

    3 $\square - 169 = 2978$ **8** $(47 \times 63) + \square = 3852$

    4 $\square \div 36 = 1944$ **9** $\dfrac{127 + \square}{3} = 49$

    5 $893 - \square = 578$ **10** $(80 \times \square) - 1939 = 2221$

16. 329 marbles are shared equally among 32 children. How many did they each get, and how many were left over ?

17. The first prize of £180 in a competition was shared equally among 32 winners. How much did they each get, in £'s and pence, and how much was left over ?

18. Jane has a recipe which gives the quantities in grams. Her old scales, however, only give the weight in lbs and ounces. If the recipe uses 350 g of flour, how much should she weigh, to the nearest ounce ? (1 g = 0.035 oz)

19. 1 stone is 14 lbs. Marie weighs 8 stones 8 lbs. What is her weight in kg, to the nearest kg, taking 1 lb as equivalent to 454 g ?

Use trial and improvement methods to solve the problems in questions 20 to 22.

20. The sum of the squares of 3 consecutive odd numbers is 1883. Find the numbers.

21. Two positive integers have a sum of 70 and a product of 1216. Find the numbers.

22. A cubical tin has to be designed to hold 1.5 litres of liquid. The length of an edge of the cube, in cm, is found from $\sqrt[3]{1500}$. Find this length, to the nearest mm, without using the cube root key on your calculator.

23. Write down the number and the unit which together make the most sensible statement.
     1   To knit a pair of gloves you will need (2, 10, 60)   (g, kg) of wool.
     2   A good runner can run a mile in about (4, 20, 60)   (seconds, minutes, hours).
     3   If 200 new pencils were placed end-to-end to make a long straight line, the line would stretch for about (2, 10, 30)   (cm, m, km).

24. Equal pieces of ribbon 28 cm long are cut from a strip 5 m long. How many pieces are there, and how many cm are left over ?

25. Which size of packet of this tea is the better value for money ?

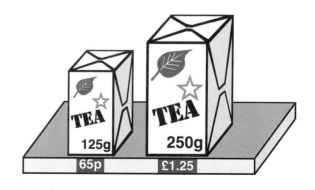

26. How many packets of sweets, each containing 110 g, can be made up from $5\frac{1}{2}$ kg of sweets ?

27. If a car travels 12 km on a litre of petrol, how much will petrol cost for a journey of 270 km, if the price is 60p per litre ?

28. Mrs Sharples wants to buy 2 curtains size 108 by 66, and 4 curtains size 54 by 46. (The measurements are in inches.)

    1 Show how she can find a quick estimate of the cost, and give the estimated total.

    2 Use your calculator, or another method, to find the exact cost.

Very good value! Price per pair			
54 × 46	£29.99	54 × 66	£49.99
72 × 46	£42.99	72 × 66	£59.99
90 × 46	£49.99	90 × 66	£74.99
108 × 46	£59.99	108 × 66	£89.99
54 × 90	£68.99	90 × 90	£99.99
72 × 90	£86.99	108 × 90	£124.99

29. A school's lessons begin at 9.20 am and end at 3.20 pm with an hour's break at lunchtime and 20 minutes break mid-morning. If there are 7 lessons of equal length, how long is a lesson ?

30. Here is part of a bus timetable:

Ashmead School	1554	1602	1608	1616	1622	1629
Brook Lane	1604	1612	1618	1626	1632	1639
Carlton Village	1619	1627	—	1641	—	1654
Denham Station	—	—	1640	—	1654	—

    1 Helen finishes school at 4.00 pm but it takes her 3 minutes to reach the bus stop. What is the time of the next bus she can catch to get to her home in Carlton Village ? How long does the journey take ?

    2 Ismail usually catches a train from Denham station at 4.45 pm. On which bus must he travel from school ? One day he stays late at school and catches the 1622 bus. The next train leaves at 5.30 pm. How long will Ismail have to wait at the station, for that train ?

31. The diagram shows a thermometer marked in
    degrees Celsius and degrees Fahrenheit.

    1   What temperature does the thermometer
        show in °F, and in °C ?
    2   What would be the temperature in °F
        if it was 35°C ?
    3   In cold weather, elderly people are advised
        to heat their living rooms to 68°F.
        What is this temperature in °C ?

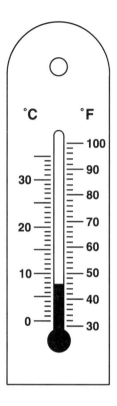

Practice test 3

1. Work out the answers to these questions without using your calculator.

1	$1.7 + 2.8 + 3.5$	**5**	1.05×1000	**8**	$1.8 \div 0.2$
2	$20.2 - 18.6$	**6**	$3.2 \div 100$	**9**	0.03×0.06
3	19.4×5	**7**	0.7×0.4	**10**	$0.235 \div 0.05$
4	$38.7 \div 9$				

2. By turning these fractions into decimals, or otherwise, write them in order of size,
    smallest first.

    $\frac{7}{10}, \quad \frac{3}{4}, \quad \frac{5}{6}, \quad \frac{5}{8}, \quad \frac{7}{9}.$

3. By using approximate values, estimate answers for these questions.

1	501×398	**4**	$336 \div 28$
2	$1305 \div 29$	**5**	$\sqrt{77.44}$
3	61^2		

4. Use your calculator to find exact answers to question 3.

5. Use your calculator to find answers to the following, correct to 1 decimal place.

    1 $2 \times 3.14 \times 17$

    2 $\dfrac{219}{0.7 \times 11}$

    3 $(81.7 + 1.52) \div 6.28$

    4 $\dfrac{3.14 \times 78.2}{22.4 - 15.5}$

    5 $7.36^2 - 2.64^2$

6. Find the whole number answer and the remainder when 529 is divided by 17.

7. Find the square root of 19, correct to 2 decimal places, by using a trial and improvement method, and without using the square root key on your calculator.

8.   **1**   Write 2380 g in kg.
    2   Write 20 cm in m.
    3   Write 5 litres in ml.
    4   Write 12 cm in mm.
    5   Write 2.6 m in cm.

    6   Write 3.1 kg in g.
    7   Write 28 mm in cm.
    8   Write 512 cm in m.
    9   Write 3200 cl in litres.
   10   Write 0.25 kg in g.

9. 500 sheets of paper weigh 3 kg. What is the weight, in g, of 1 sheet ? The pile of sheets is 7 cm thick. What is the thickness, in mm, of 1 sheet ?

10. Write down the time shown on this clock when it is in the afternoon,
    1   in the 12-hour system,
    2   in the 24-hour system.

11. Tessa works in a local shop from 1.30 pm to 5 pm on four afternoons each week. She is paid £2.70 per hour. How much is her weekly wage ?

12. An old knitting pattern for a child's jumper requires 8 oz of wool. How many 50 g balls of wool should Mrs Walsh buy to have enough to knit the jumper ?
(1 oz = 28 g.)

Quadrilaterals, polygons and solid figures

The topics in this chapter include:

- classifying and defining types of quadrilaterals,
- knowing and using angle and symmetry properties of quadrilaterals and other polygons, identifying the symmetries of various shapes,
- recognising and using common 2-D representation of 3-D objects, using accurate measurement and drawing in constructing 3-D models.

Quadrilaterals

A **quadrilateral** is a figure with 4 sides.

The sum of the angles of a quadrilateral is 360°.

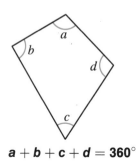

$$a + b + c + d = 360°$$

Names of some special quadrilaterals

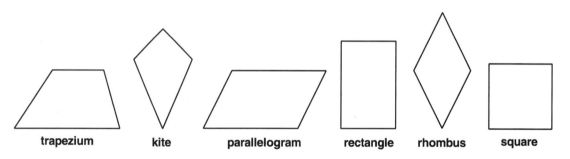

| trapezium | kite | parallelogram | rectangle | rhombus | square |

Special sorts of quadrilaterals

Here is a summary of the special quadrilaterals with their definitions and properties.

Trapezium

One pair of parallel sides.

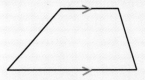

If the other 2 sides are equal it is an isosceles trapezium.

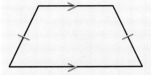

Kite

Two adjacent sides are equal and the other two adjacent sides are equal.

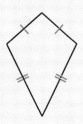

Parallelogram

Opposite sides are parallel.

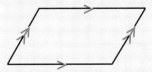

Opposite sides are equal.
Opposite angles are equal.

Rectangle

It is a parallelogram with one angle a right angle.

Opposite sides are parallel and equal.
All angles are right angles.

Rhombus

It is a parallelogram with one pair of adjacent sides equal.

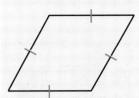

Opposite sides are parallel.
All sides are equal.
Opposite angles are equal.

Square

It is a rectangle and a rhombus.

Opposite sides are parallel.
All sides are equal.
All angles are right angles.

Diagonals

A diagonal of a quadrilateral is a line which joins opposite points.

Here is a summary of the properties of diagonals.

Isosceles trapezium

Diagonals are equal (but do not bisect each other).

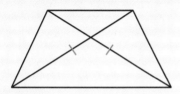

Kite

One diagonal is a line of symmetry.
It bisects the other diagonal at right angles.

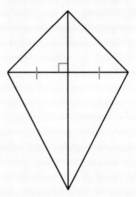

Parallelogram

Diagonals bisect each other.

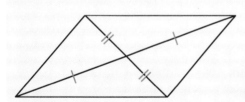

Rectangle

Diagonals bisect each other.
Diagonals are equal.

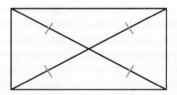

Rhombus

Diagonals bisect each other at right angles.
They also bisect the angles of the rhombus.

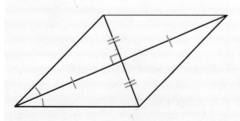

Square

Diagonals bisect each other at right angles.
Diagonals are equal.
Diagonals make angles of 45° with the sides of the square.

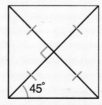

Symmetry

An isosceles trapezium has one axis of symmetry.
A kite has one axis of symmetry. (It is a diagonal of the kite.)
A parallelogram has no axes of symmetry.
A rectangle has 2 axes of symmetry.
A rhombus has 2 axes of symmetry. (They are the diagonals of the rhombus.)
A square has 4 axes of symmetry. (Two of them are the diagonals of the square.)

The parallelogram, rectangle, rhombus and square have a point of symmetry at the point where the diagonals cross each other. They have rotational symmetry of order 2, except for the square, which has rotational symmetry of order 4.

Example

ABCD is a square and CDEF is a rhombus.
Explain why $AD = DE$.
Find the sizes of the angles a, b, c, d.

$AD = DC$ sides of a square are equal
$CD = DE$ all sides of a rhombus are equal
So $AD = DE$

$a = 90°$ angle of a square
$b = 56°$ opposite angles of a rhombus are equal

In $\triangle ADE$,
$\angle ADE = a + b = 146°$
$\triangle ADE$ is isosceles so $c = e$
$c = 17°$ angle sum of triangle $= 180°$
                  $180° - 146° = 34°$
                  $34° \div 2 = 17°$

$\angle DEF = 180° - 56° = 124°$ interior angles
$d = 124° - 17°$
   $= 107°$

Exercise 4.1

1.   Three angles of a quadrilateral are 50°, 75° and 123°. Find the size of the fourth angle.

2.   Two angles of a quadrilateral are 72° and 118° and the other two angles are equal. What size are they ?

3. Draw sketch diagrams of these figures and mark on your drawings any lines or points of symmetry.

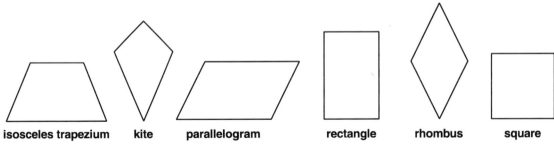

isosceles trapezium   kite   parallelogram   rectangle   rhombus   square

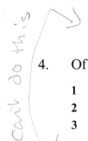
can't do this

4. Of the figures parallelogram, rhombus, rectangle and square,

    1   which have diagonals which bisect each other,
    2   which have diagonals which bisect the angles of the figure,
    3   which have diagonals which are equal ?

5. What is the order of rotational symmetry of

    1   a parallelogram,
    2   a rectangle,
    3   a rhombus,
    4   a square ?

6. Find the sizes of the marked angles.

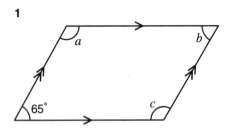

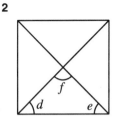

(this is a square)

7. Two angles of a trapezium are 106° and 93°. Find the size of each of the other two angles.

8. *ABCD* is a kite with *AB* = *BC* and *AD* = *DC* = diagonal *AC*. ∠*ABC* = 80°. Find the size of ∠*BAD*.

9. What sort of triangles are these ?

    1 △ABC, where $ABCD$ is a rectangle.

    2 △PQR, where $PQRS$ is a square.

    3 △XYZ, where $WXYZ$ is a rhombus.

10. $ABCD$ is a trapezium with AD parallel to BC and diagonals cutting at X.

    1 If $BX = XC$, which angles are equal to $\angle XBC$?

    2 Explain why $AX = XD$.

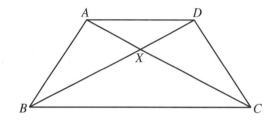

11. If △ABC is reflected in the line BC, with A reflected into a point D, what sort of quadrilateral is $ABDC$, with the following conditions:

    1 if AB is not equal to AC, and $\angle A$ is an obtuse angle,

    2 if $AB = AC$, and $\angle A$ is an obtuse angle,

    3 if $AB = AC$, and $\angle A$ is a right angle ?

12. Draw an accurate, full-size drawing of this figure. Join AD and measure it to the nearest mm. What sort of figure is $ABCD$?

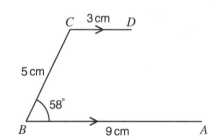

13. Draw a triangle ABC with $BC = 6$ cm, $\angle B = 70°$, $\angle C = 55°$.
Find, using compasses, a point D to complete the quadrilateral $ABCD$ such that $AD = CD = 8$ cm.
Measure the length of AC and the size of the angle ADC.
If the quadrilateral has a line of symmetry show it on your diagram by a dotted line.

14. Draw accurately a parallelogram $ABCD$ with $AB = 9$ cm, $BC = 6$ cm and $\angle ABC = 42°$.
Draw its diagonals and measure the acute angle between them.

15. Construct the quadrilateral $ABCD$ in which $AB = 4$ cm, $BC = 6$ cm, $CD = 5$ cm, $\angle B = 60°$ and $\angle C = 90°$. Measure $\angle A$, and the length of AD.

Polygons

A **polygon** is a figure with straight sides.

Number of sides	Name
3	triangle
4	quadrilateral
5	pentagon
6	hexagon
7	heptagon
8	octagon

pentagon

hexagon

octagon

Regular Polygons

A regular polygon has all sides equal and all angles equal.

Number of sides	Name
3	equilateral triangle
4	square
5	regular pentagon
6	regular hexagon
7	regular heptagon
8	regular octagon

Regular polygons

pentagon

hexagon

heptagon

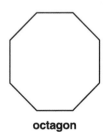

octagon

Exterior angles of a convex polygon are the angles formed when each side is extended in order.

The sum of the exterior angles is 360°.

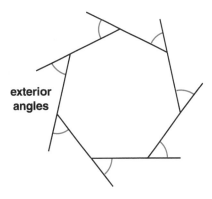

exterior
angles

Sum of the angles in a polygon

Split the polygon into triangles as shown. The sum of the angles in each triangle is 180°. The number of triangles is 2 less than the number of sides of the polygon.

Pentagon

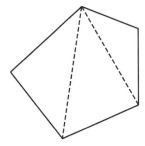

Hexagon

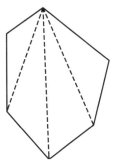

Heptagon

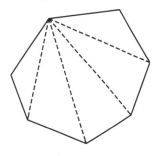

3 triangles
Sum of angles in a pentagon
= 3 × 180°
= 540°

4 triangles
Sum of angles in a hexagon
= 4 × 180°
= 720°

5 triangles
Sum of angles in a heptagon
= 5 × 180°
= 900°

Size of each angle in a regular polygon

To find the size of an exterior angle in a **regular** polygon, divide 360° by 'number of sides'.

At each vertex,
    interior angle + exterior angle = 180°,
so interior angle = 180° − exterior angle.

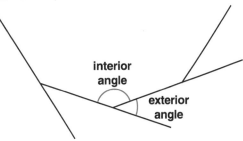

interior
angle

exterior
angle

Angles of regular polygons

Number of sides	Name	Each interior angle	Each exterior angle
3	equilateral triangle	60°	120°
4	square	90°	90°
5	regular pentagon	108°	72°
6	regular hexagon	120°	60°
7	regular heptagon	$128\frac{4}{7}°$	$51\frac{3}{7}°$
8	regular octagon	135°	45°
n	n-sided regular polygon	$\left(180 - \dfrac{360}{n}\right)°$	$\left(\dfrac{360}{n}\right)°$

Symmetry of regular polygons

e.g.

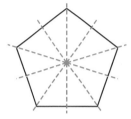

A regular pentagon has 5 axes of symmetry.

It has rotational symmetry of order 5.

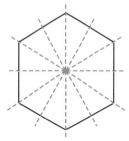

A regular hexagon has 6 axes of symmetry.

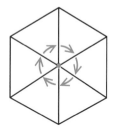

It has rotational symmetry of order 6.

Diagonals of a polygon

A diagonal is a line which joins two non-adjacent points.

e.g.

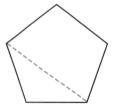

A diagonal of a pentagon.

A pentagon with all diagonals drawn.

Examples

1   Find the angles of a regular octagon.

Either:

Sum of the exterior angles $= 360°$
Each exterior angle $= 360° \div 8 = 45°$
Each interior angle $= 180° - 45° = 135°$

or:

An octagon can be split into 6 triangles as shown.
Sum of angles in an octagon $= 6 \times 180°$
$\qquad\qquad\qquad\qquad\qquad = 1080°$
Each interior angle in a regular octagon
$\qquad\qquad\qquad\qquad = 1080° \div 8$
$\qquad\qquad\qquad\qquad = 135°$

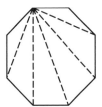

2   A regular polygon has interior angles of 160°. How many sides has it ?

Each exterior angle $= 180° - 160° = 20°$
Sum of exterior angles $= 360°$
Number of exterior angles $= 360 \div 20 = 18$
The polygon has 18 sides.

Exercise 4.2

1.   Sketch these figures and mark any axes of symmetry or centres of rotational symmetry:
      equilateral triangle, square, regular pentagon, regular hexagon, regular heptagon, regular
      octagon.
      Copy and complete this table.

Name of figure	Number of axes of symmetry	Order of rotational symmetry
equilateral triangle		
square		
. . .		

      Is there a pattern in your answers ?

2.   A regular polygon has 10 sides. What is the size of
      1   an exterior angle,   **2**   an interior angle ?

3.   A regular polygon has 20 sides. What is the size of an interior angle ?

4. A regular polygon has exterior angles of 30°. How many sides has it ?

5. A regular polygon has interior angles of 135°.
    1   What is the size of an exterior angle ?
    2   How many sides has it ?

6. A regular polygon has interior angles of 170°. How many sides has it ?

7. What is the sum of the angles of a pentagon ? Four of the angles of a pentagon are 75°, 110°, 124° and 146°. Find the size of the fifth angle.

8. What is the sum of the angles of a hexagon ? Five of the angles of a hexagon are 108°, 106°, 115°, 120° and 124°. Find the sixth angle.

9. What is the sum of the angles of an octagon ? Five of the angles of an octagon are each 130°, two other angles are 140° and 155°. Find the size of the remaining angle.

10. Five of the exterior angles of a hexagon are 45°, 55°, 60°, 65° and 85°. Find the sixth exterior angle.

11. *ABCD* is part of a regular pentagon. *PCBQ* is part of a regular octagon. State or find the sizes of $\angle BCD$ and $\angle BCP$ and hence find the size of angle *a*.

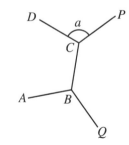

12. Sketch this regular hexagon and join points as necessary.

    What sort of quadrilaterals are
    1   *ABCD*,   2   *ABDE* ?

    What sort of triangles are
    3   $\triangle ABC$,   4 $\triangle ABD$,   5 $\triangle ACE$?

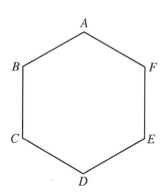

Solid figures

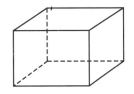

Cuboid, or rectangular block

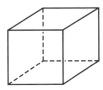

Cube

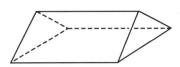

Triangular prism

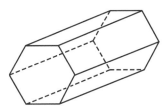

Hexagonal prism

Triangular pyramid, or tetrahedron

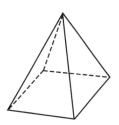

Pyramid with square base

Cylinder

Cone

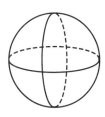

Sphere

Practice in drawing cubes and cuboids

1   **Cube**
    Draw a square.   Draw 4 parallel lines of equal length.   Draw a square joining the 4 ends.

   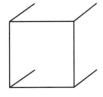

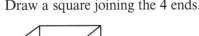

    Make some lines dotted lines.   or   Leave out the dotted lines.

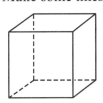

2   Use a similar method to draw a cuboid.

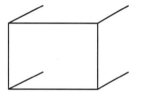   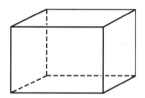

3   Using isometric paper.

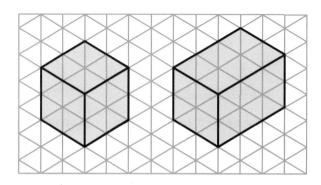

To draw a triangular prism

Draw a triangle and translate it to form a second triangle.

Join the corresponding points of the triangles, making the rectangular faces.

Make some lines into dotted lines.

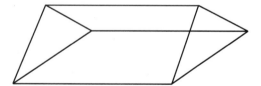   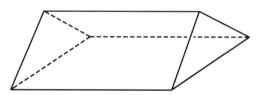

To draw a triangular pyramid

Draw a triangle and put a dot somewhere inside it.

Draw dotted lines from the dot to the vertices of the triangle.

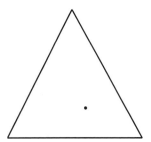
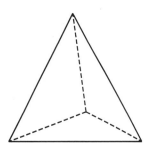

To draw a pyramid with a square base

Draw a parallelogram *ABCD* as shown. Find where the diagonals cross and put a dot vertically above this point.

Join the dot to *A*, *B* and *C*, using solid lines, and to *D* with a dotted line. Make *AD* and *DC* into dotted lines.

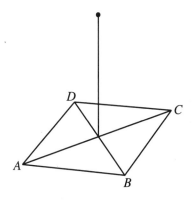
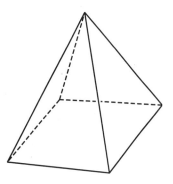

Drawing a cylinder

Begin with a rectangle.
Make curved lines at the top and the bottom.
Rub out the straight lines there, and make part of the bottom curve dotted.

Drawing a cone

Begin with an isosceles triangle.
Make curved lines at the bottom.
Rub out the bottom straight line and make some of the curve dotted.

Nets of solid figures

These are patterns which when cut out and folded will make the solid figures.

Net of a cube

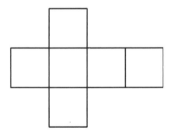

Here are nets for some other figures you can make. Decide which lengths on the nets should be equal.

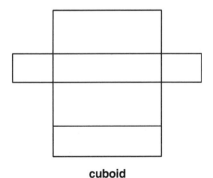

cuboid

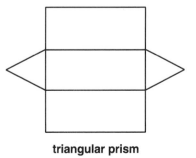

triangular prism

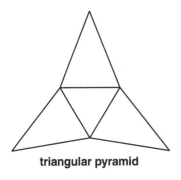

triangular pyramid

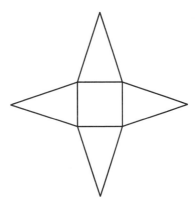

pyramid with square base

There are other arrangements possible, to make the same solid figures.

Making models from thin cardboard, using their nets

1   Draw the pattern of the net of the solid figure, on paper. Then place it over thin cardboard, with something underneath to protect the desk or table, and prick through the main points using the point of your compasses. Remove the pattern and join up the marks on the cardboard. (Keep the pattern for future use.)

2   Draw a tab on every alternate edge, i.e. starting at any edge, put tabs on edges 1, 3, 5, 7, . . . in order. Tabs can be drawn freehand. They should be large enough to stick easily.

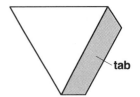

3   Score every line.
     This means making a nick in the line so that it folds neatly. Put your ruler along the line and drag your compass point along it. (When you fold the cardboard, always fold **away** from the side you scored on. Do not bend the cardboard backwards **and** forwards.)

4   Cut out the net and fold it along the scored lines.

5   Glue it together, doing one tab at a time and waiting until it has stuck before doing the next one, except at the last face where more than one tab may have to be glued at the same time. You may need to poke your compass point through a corner hole to help to make the last tab stick down properly.

To make a cube
Making the sides of the squares 4 cm long, copy the net of the cube shown on page 90 onto paper. (Graph paper or squared paper is useful.)
Carry out the instructions above for making the model.

To make a cuboid
Decide on the measurements your finished cuboid
will have, and design and draw the net. Here is the net
for a cuboid which will be 8 cm by 3 cm by 2 cm.
Carry out the instructions for making the model.

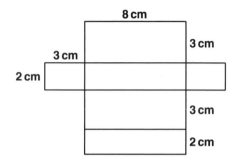

Exercise 4.3

1. Name the solid figures with these shapes.

    1   **2**   **3**   **4**

    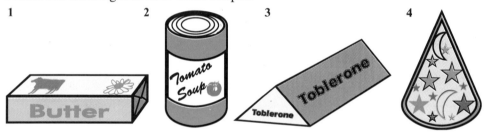

2. Give an example of a common object, not shown above, which has the shape of

    1 a cuboid,   **4** a sphere,
    2 a cylindrical disc,   **5** a prism.
    3 a cube,

3. These solid figures have planes of symmetry. How many do they have ?

    1   **2**

    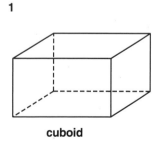

    cuboid

    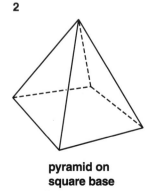

    **pyramid on
    square base**

4. Look at the drawings of the solid figures
    which have no curved faces, or look at
    actual objects if you have them available.
    Count the number of faces, vertices (corners)
    and edges on each.
    For example, this prism with pentagonal ends
    has 7 faces, 10 vertices and 15 edges.
    Copy and complete this table and add other
    solid figures to the list.
    F = number of faces, V = number of vertices,
    E = number of edges.

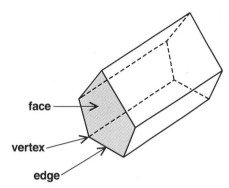

Solid figure	F	V	E
cuboid			
triangular prism			
prism with pentagonal ends	7	10	15
tetrahedron			
pyramid on square base			

Can you discover the relationship between $F + V$ and E ?

5. The net of a cube can be arranged in several different ways. Which of these drawings of
    arrangements of six equal squares, if cut out and folded, would make a cube ?

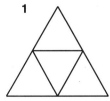
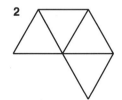
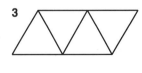

6. This is a triangular pyramid with all edges 4 cm long.
    Since all the faces are equilateral triangles it can also be called
    a **regular tetrahedron**.

Which of these arrangements of 4 triangles can be used as nets of the pyramid ?

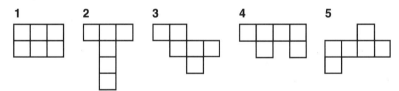

Draw a net of the pyramid accurately. (Isometric paper is useful.)
Make a model of the pyramid using cardboard.

Exercise 4.4 Applications

1. *ABCD* is a parallelogram.

    1 What is the size of ∠*A* ?
    2 Find the size of ∠*AYX*.
    3 What sort of triangle is △*AYX* ?

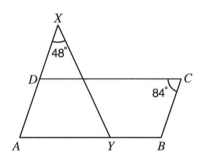

2. In these rectangles, find the sizes of *a* and *b*.

    1 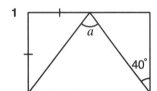   **2**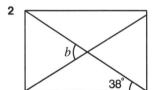

3. *ABCD* is a square.
    △*CDE* is an equilateral triangle.

    1 Explain why *AD* = *DE*.
    2 What sort of triangle is △*ADE* ?
    3 Find the sizes of angles *g*, *h*, *j* and *k*.

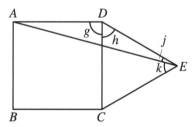

4. The diagonals *AC* and *BD* of a parallelogram *ABCD* are 8 cm and 10 cm long respectively, and intersect at an angle of 56°. Construct the parallelogram. Estimate and then measure the lengths of *AB* and *AD* and the size of ∠*DAB*.

5. For each part of this question, sketch a quadrilateral *ABCD* and mark on it the information given, then say whether it is necessarily a trapezium, parallelogram, rectangle, rhombus or square.

    1 *AB//CD*, *AB* = *CD*.
    2 ∠*B* = ∠*C* = 90°.
    3 *AB//CD*, *AD//BC*, *AC* = *BD*.
    4 *AC* and *BD* are axes of symmetry.

6. If △ABC is rotated about M, the mid-point of BC, through 180°, so that B is rotated onto C, C onto B, and A onto a point D, what sort of quadrilateral is ABDC, with the following conditions:

   1 if AB is not equal to AC, and ∠A is an obtuse angle,
   2 if AB is not equal to AC, and ∠A is a right angle,
   3 if AB = AC, and ∠A is an obtuse angle,
   4 if AB = AC, and ∠A is a right angle ?

7. In this regular 12-sided polygon with centre O, find the sizes of angles a, b, c.

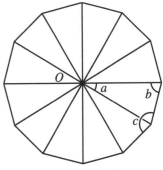

8. Three regular polygons fit exactly together at a point P.

   1 If they all have the same number of sides, what are the sizes of the angles at P? What sort of polygons are they?
   2 If one polygon is a square and the other two have an equal number of sides, what are the sizes of the angles of P? What sort of polygons are they?

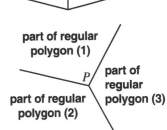

9. Sketch the regular pentagon ABCDE and join points as necessary to answer the following.

   1 What is the size of ∠A?
   2 What sort of triangle is △BCD?
   3 What is the size of ∠CBD?
   4 What is the size of ∠ABD?
   5 What sort of figure is ABDE?
   6 If CE cuts BD at K, what sort of figures is ABKE?

10. ABCDE is a non-regular pentagon. The dotted line is a line of symmetry. ∠B = 90°, ∠C = 110°. Find the size of angle BAE.

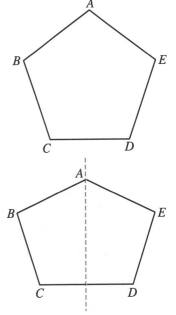

11.   Nine of the ten angles of a decagon are each 150°. What are the sizes of their exterior angles ? Find the size of the tenth exterior angle and hence find the size of the tenth interior angle.

12.   **To construct a regular pentagon *ABCDE***

Method 1

Draw $AB = 6$ cm, make angles of 108° for $\angle BAE$ and $\angle ABC$.
Mark off 6 cm on these lines for points E and C.
To find D, with compasses centre C, draw an arc of radius 6 cm, with centre E draw an arc of radius 6 cm, to meet the first arc at D.
Join CD and ED.

Check the accuracy of your drawing by measuring angles C, D and E, which should all be 108°.

Measure the distance from A to D. (You can also measure the other 4 diagonal lengths of the pentagon, which should all be equal.)

Method 2

Starting at a point O, draw 5 lines OA, OB, OC, OD and OE, each 5 cm long, with an angle of 72° between each one and the next.
Join AB, BC, CD, DE, EA and measure these lines (which should be equal in length).

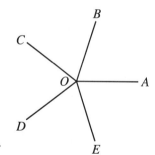

Similar methods can be used to construct other regular polygons.

13.   **To construct a regular hexagon *ABCDEF* of side 6 cm**

With compasses mark a centre O and draw a circle, radius 6 cm.
Take 1 point on the circumference to be A.
With compasses, radius 6 cm, centre A, mark off an arc to cut the circumference at B.
Repeat with centre B to get point C.
Continue this method to get points D, E and F.
As a check, $FA = 6$ cm.
Join the sides AB, BC, CD, DE, EF and FA.

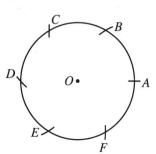

14. **Tessellations**

These are congruent shapes arranged in a pattern to cover an area.
At every point where shapes join, for them to fit exactly, the sum of the angles is 360°.

Examples

triangles covering a surface   **hexagons**   **rhombuses**

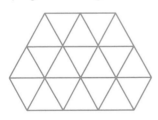 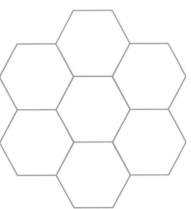 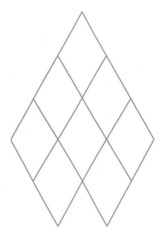

If we take triangles or other shapes out of 2 sides of a square

and add them to the other 2 sides

the shapes will still fit together, and make a more interesting pattern.

This second pattern is made by taking out equal curved shapes from 2 sides of the square.

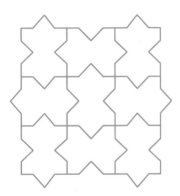

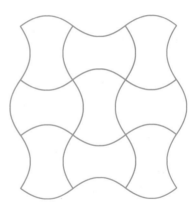

Tessellations can also be made using some combinations of regular polygons.
The sum of the angles at each point must be 360°, for the pieces to fit together.

Examples

equilateral triangles and regular hexagons

squares, hexagons and dodecagons

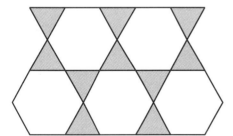

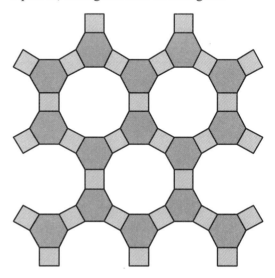

Draw a regular hexagon with side 4 cm on thick card. Cut it out. By drawing round the
outside, make several more hexagons. Also make some equilateral triangles and some
squares of side 4 cm.

Draw sketches of these tessellated areas:

1   Use equilateral triangles and regular hexagons, so that every point is the join of
     1 hexagon and 4 triangles.
2   Use equilateral triangles, regular hexagons and squares. How many of each meet at
     every point ?
3   Use equilateral triangles and squares.

Draw a regular octagon. Cut it out, and make several more of the same size.
Make several squares with sides the same length as those of the octagon.
Arrange the octagons and squares to make a tessellated area and show your design on a
sketch.

The possibilities are endless. Notice any tessellations you see, for example, on tiled floors.
Make up your own designs.

15. **Using a computer**

If you have a computer which will **draw**, you can investigate quadrilaterals and polygons.

If you have had no previous experience, begin by finding out how to draw rectangles and squares. Then by altering the angles you can produce parallelograms or rhombuses, and by altering lengths you can make trapeziums and kites. You can investigate the diagonals of such figures. For instance, by making a sequence of small changes to the angles of a parallelogram until it becomes a rectangle, you can notice how the diagonals which are unequal in length finally become equal. Similarly you can watch what happens to the diagonals when you turn a parallelogram into a rhombus. You can also draw polygons, especially regular polygons, on the screen, and use these to make patterns such as tessellations. You can also include curves such as circles, or arcs of circles, into your designs. You can reflect shapes in a line, or lines, or rotate them about a point. You can move shapes around the screen by translation, or enlarge or reduce them.

16. The circular cylinder has an axis of symmetry. Sketch 3 other solid figures which have an axis of symmetry.

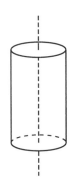

17. On a proper die, the numbers on opposite faces add up to 7. A cardboard cube was to be made into a die by labelling the squares on the net with the numbers 1, 2, 3, 4, 5, 6.

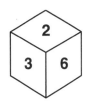

On these nets, some of the squares have been labelled. Sketch these diagrams and label the other squares correctly.

1

1	2

3

2

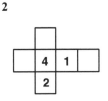

3

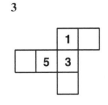

18. If small triangular pyramids are sliced off the corners of a cube, how many faces, vertices and edges has the remaining solid figure ?

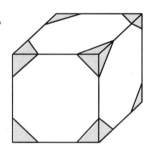

19. **To make a pyramid with a square base**

Begin by drawing a semicircle, centre *O*, of radius 10 cm, and from it make 4 triangles, as shown.

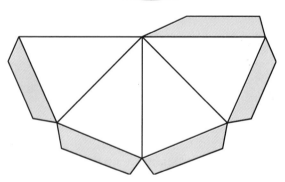

Add tabs. Score all lines and cut out the figure. Make an open pyramid by glueing along the long tab.
Make a square base of side 7.7 cm and glue it to the other tabs.

20. **The Regular Solid Figures**

These are solid figures made with regular polygons. There are just five of them. You could make them and display them.

The smallest, the regular tetrahedron, is made with equilateral triangles, with 3 triangles meeting at each point. See page 93, question 6.
(The word **tetrahedron** means that it has four faces.)

If equilateral triangles are arranged with 4 triangles meeting at a point, an octahedron is formed, and if there are 5 triangles meeting at a point, an icosahedron is formed.
You can make these solid figures from their nets. (You may find it useful to copy the patterns on isometric paper.)

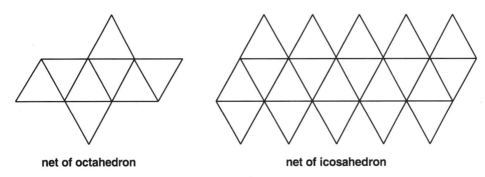

net of octahedron   **net of icosahedron**

These are the only regular solid figures which can be made with equilateral triangles.

The only regular solid figure made with squares is the cube.

The 5th regular solid figure is made from 12 regular pentagons, meeting 3 at a point. It is called a dodecahedron.
It can be made from its net, but as pentagons are not easy to draw, you may prefer to make it from separate pentagons.
Draw a regular pentagon carefully as a pattern and transfer it to cardboard 12 times by pricking through the main points. Put a tab, drawn freehand, on each edge, and score along the edges. (You will only use half of these tabs, cutting the rest off when you know which ones are not needed.)
Glue two pentagons together, using one tab and cutting one off, and when the glue is dry glue two edges of a 3rd pentagon to these two, to make 3 pentagons meeting at a point. Add all the other pentagons in turn.

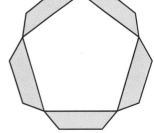

Practice test 4

1.   Four rods are placed together to make the outline of a plane shape.

   1   If the rods are, in order, 4 cm, 6 cm, 4 cm and 6 cm, what two possible shapes can be made ?

   2   If the rods are, in order, 4 cm, 4 cm, 6 cm and 6 cm, what shape can be made ?

   3   If all the rods are 8 cm long, what two possible shapes can be made ?

   [Turn over]

2.   In the parallelogram *ABCD*, $\angle B = 76°$.
     E is a point on *BC* such that *BA = BE*,
     and $\angle EDC = 27°$.
     Find the sizes of the marked angles.

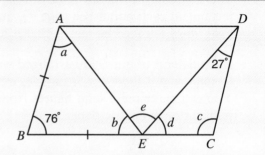

3.   Construct a square *ABCD* with side *AB* = 5 cm. Join its diagonals and let them meet
     at *X*. Measure *AC* and *BD*, and also measure the sizes of the angles at *X*.

4.   *ABCDEF* is a regular hexagon. *O* is the centre of rotational
     symmetry, and *AD*, *BE*, *CF* are axes of symmetry.

     1   State or find the size of an interior angle of the hexagon.
     2   Find the sizes of the angles *a*, *b*, *c*.
     3   What sort of triangle is △*OAB* ?
     4   What sort of quadrilateral is *ABCO* ?

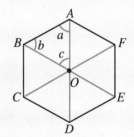

5.   The diagram shows part of a regular
     polygon with 9 sides.

     1   What is the size of an exterior angle
         of the polygon ?
     2   What is the size of an interior angle
         of the polygon ?
     3   Find the size of angle *a*.

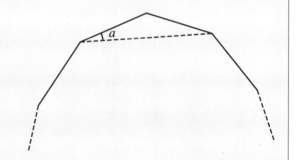

6.   A solid figure consists of a triangular pyramid fitted exactly
     on top of a triangular prism.
     State how many faces, vertices and edges the solid figure has.

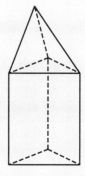

7.   This net can be folded to make a
     triangular prism.
     Which letter(s) will point *A* join ?

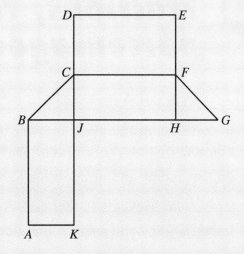

8.   This diagram is part of the
     net for a pyramid with a
     square base.
     Sketch the drawing and
     complete the net.

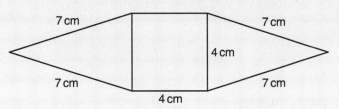

PUZZLES

7.   How many triangles are there in this figure ?

8.   S H A R O N
     + S A R A H
     ─────────────
     S A N D R A
     ─────────────

     Each figure is represented by a different letter.
     Find which figure each letter represents.
     There are three different solutions, so begin with the
     one where A = 9.

5 Fractions, ratios and percentages

The topics in this chapter include:

● understanding and using equivalent fractions, calculating fractions of quantities, relating fractions to ratios and percentages,

● understanding and using ratios,

● calculating using direct and inverse proportion,

● understanding and using compound measures,

● understanding and using percentages, calculating percentages of quantities.

Fractions

Fractions are numbers such as $\frac{1}{4}, \frac{1}{3}, \frac{2}{5}, \frac{5}{9}$.

The number on top is called the **numerator** and the number underneath is called the **denominator**.

The shaded part represents $\frac{1}{4}$ (one-quarter) of the circle.
(The whole circle is divided into 4 equal parts and 1 part is shaded.)
The unshaded part represents $\frac{3}{4}$ (three-quarters) of the circle.

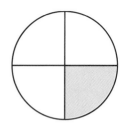

The shaded part represents $\frac{2}{5}$ (two-fifths) of the rectangle.
(The whole rectangle is divided into 5 equal parts and 2 parts are shaded.)
The unshaded part represents $\frac{3}{5}$ of the rectangle.

Equivalent fractions

This diagram shows that $\frac{2}{5}$ is equivalent to $\frac{4}{10}$.

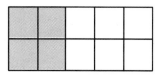

This diagram shows that $\frac{2}{5} + \frac{1}{10} = \frac{4}{10} + \frac{1}{10} = \frac{5}{10} = \frac{1}{2}$.

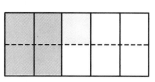

Improper fractions are numbers with a greater numerator than denominator, such as $\frac{6}{5}$ and $\frac{5}{2}$.

Mixed numbers are numbers with a whole number part and a fraction part, such as $1\frac{1}{5}$ and $2\frac{1}{2}$.

This diagram shows that $\frac{6}{5} = 1\frac{1}{5}$.

This diagram shows that $\frac{5}{2} = 2\frac{1}{2}$.

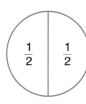

Examples

1   Reduce $\frac{60}{75}$ to its lowest terms.

    60 and 75 both divide by 5 so reduce the fraction by dividing the numerator and the denominator both by 5. This process can be called **cancelling**.

    $\frac{\overset{12}{\cancel{60}}}{\underset{15}{\cancel{75}}}$ This gives the fraction $\frac{12}{15}$ but this is still not in its lowest terms because 12 and 15 both divide by 3. So divide the numerator and the denominator both by 3.

    $\frac{\overset{4}{\cancel{\overset{12}{\cancel{60}}}}}{\underset{5}{\cancel{\underset{15}{\cancel{75}}}}} = \frac{4}{5}$ This is the fraction in its lowest terms.

2   Change $\frac{5}{6}$ into a fraction with denominator 24.

    6 becomes 24 when multiplied by 4, so multiply the numerator and the denominator by 4.

    $\frac{5}{6} = \frac{5 \times 4}{6 \times 4} = \frac{20}{24}$

3   Change $3\frac{7}{8}$ into an improper fraction.

Multiply the whole number 3 by 8 to change it into eighths. This is 24 eighths and another 7 eighths makes 31 eighths.

$3\frac{7}{8} = \frac{24}{8} + \frac{7}{8} = \frac{31}{8}$

4   Change $\frac{45}{7}$ to a mixed number.

Divide 7 into 45. It goes 6 times so there are 6 whole ones. $6 \times 7 = 42$ and the remainder is 3 so there is also $\frac{3}{7}$.

$\frac{45}{7} = \frac{42 + 3}{7} = 6\frac{3}{7}$

5   Express 24 pence as a fraction of £3.

$\frac{24p}{£3} = \frac{24p}{300p} = \frac{\overset{2}{\cancel{24}}}{\underset{25}{\cancel{300}}} = \frac{2}{25}$ Both quantities must be in the same units before cancelling.

6   Find $\frac{2}{3}$ of £2.40.

$\frac{1}{3}$ of £2.40 = 80 pence

So $\frac{2}{3}$ of £2.40 = £1.60

7   Which is greater, $\frac{5}{6}$ or $\frac{7}{8}$?

$\frac{5}{6} = \frac{20}{24}$, $\frac{7}{8} = \frac{21}{24}$,   so $\frac{7}{8}$ is greater.

Exercise 5.1

1.   What fraction of the shape is shaded ?

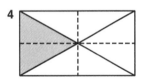

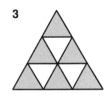

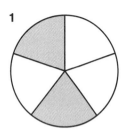

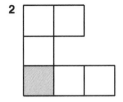

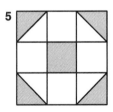

1.   Copy these figures and shade the fraction stated.

   6 $\frac{3}{8}$ 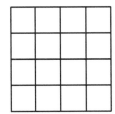   **7** $\frac{5}{12}$ 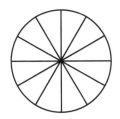   **8** $\frac{1}{2}$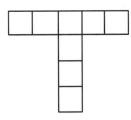

   9 $\frac{2}{3}$ 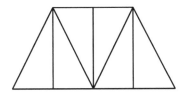   **10** $\frac{1}{4}$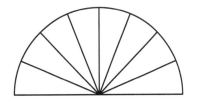

2.   **1** Find one-half of each of these numbers
          88   18   8   14   60   24   42   52   90   96
      2 Find one-third of each of these numbers
          18   99   60   24   45   27   3   21   39   75
      3 Find one-quarter of each of these numbers
          8   28   80   100   52   44   4   24   160   36
      4 Find one-fifth of each of these numbers
          60   20   45   10   100   15   35   75   55   200
      5 Find two-thirds of each of these numbers
          6   15   24   9   30   60   33   90   75   18

3.   Reduce these fractions to their lowest terms.

   1 $\frac{6}{9}$ **2** $\frac{10}{12}$ **3** $\frac{5}{30}$ **4** $\frac{30}{100}$ **5** $\frac{24}{80}$

   6 $\frac{18}{45}$ **7** $\frac{35}{36}$ **8** $\frac{21}{56}$ **9** $\frac{24}{54}$ **10** $\frac{15}{20}$

4.   **1** Change $\frac{7}{9}$ into a fraction with denominator 18.

      2 Change $\frac{3}{5}$ into a fraction with denominator 20.

      3 Change $\frac{5}{6}$ into a fraction with denominator 18.

      4 Change $\frac{7}{8}$ into a fraction with denominator 24.

      5 Change $\frac{3}{10}$ into a fraction with denominator 20.

5.   Change these mixed numbers to improper fractions.

   1   $1\frac{3}{4}$ 5 $2\frac{7}{8}$ 8 $7\frac{1}{2}$
   2   $2\frac{1}{3}$ 6 $4\frac{2}{5}$ 9 $3\frac{1}{3}$
   3   $3\frac{7}{10}$ 7 $1\frac{1}{8}$ 10 $2\frac{3}{10}$
   4   $1\frac{5}{6}$

6.   Change these improper fractions to mixed numbers.

   1   $\frac{23}{5}$ 2 $\frac{17}{6}$ 3 $\frac{31}{10}$ 4 $\frac{21}{8}$ 5 $\frac{11}{4}$
   6   $\frac{20}{3}$ 7 $\frac{13}{5}$ 8 $\frac{17}{4}$ 9 $\frac{25}{3}$ 10 $\frac{13}{4}$

7.   1   Express 8 hours as a fraction of 1 day.
     2   Express $20°$ as a fraction of 1 right angle.
     3   Express 6 inches as a fraction of 1 yard.
     4   Express 45 seconds as a fraction of 1 minute.
     5   Express 60p as a fraction of £1.
     6   Express £1.60 as a fraction of £2.40.
     7   Express 10 oz as a fraction of $2\frac{1}{2}$ lb.
     8   Express 50p as a fraction of £4.50.
     9   Express 12 minutes as a fraction of 1 hour.
    10   Express $120°$ as a fraction of 1 complete turn.

8.   1   Find $\frac{3}{4}$ of £3.60.   6   Find $\frac{1}{6}$ of 1 right angle.
     2   Find $\frac{2}{3}$ of 1 foot.   7   Find $\frac{3}{8}$ of 2 gallons.
     3   Find $\frac{3}{10}$ of £2.   8   Find $\frac{1}{9}$ of 1 yard.
     4   Find $\frac{3}{5}$ of 1 hour 40 minutes. 9   Find $\frac{1}{4}$ of 2 stones 8 lb.
     5   Find $\frac{5}{8}$ of 1 lb 8 oz.   10   Find $\frac{7}{10}$ of 4 feet 2 inches.

9.   Which is greater ?

   1   $\frac{5}{6}$ or $\frac{7}{9}$ 2 $\frac{1}{3}$ or $\frac{3}{10}$ 3 $\frac{2}{3}$ or $\frac{3}{5}$ 4 $\frac{3}{4}$ or $\frac{5}{6}$ 5 $\frac{7}{10}$ or $\frac{3}{4}$

10. 2 pints of milk are poured into an urn containing 10 pints of coffee. What fraction of the mixture is milk ?

11. In a club, two-fifths of the members are Junior members. The remaining 90 members are Senior members. How many members are there altogether ?

Ratio and Proportion

A ratio is a way of comparing the sizes of two quantities.
e.g. A quantity divided in the ratio 2 : 3 (read as 2 to 3)
means that the 1st share is $\frac{2}{3}$ of the 2nd share,

and the 2nd share is $\frac{3}{2}$ times the 1st share.

Ratios have no units, they are just numbers.

Here is a reminder of methods for using ratios.

Examples

1   Express 25 cm : $1\frac{1}{2}$ m as a ratio in its simplest form.

$\dfrac{25\,\text{cm}}{1\frac{1}{2}\,\text{m}} = \dfrac{25\,\text{cm}}{150\,\text{cm}} = \dfrac{25}{150} = \dfrac{1}{6}$. Ratio is 1 : 6.   Both quantities must be in the same units before simplifying.

2   Divide £24 in the ratio 3 : 5.

3 : 5 gives 8 parts. 1 part is $\dfrac{£24}{8} = £3$.

Shares are 3 × £3 and 5 × £3, i.e. £9 and £15.

3   Increase 12 kg in the ratio 5 : 3.

New weight is $\dfrac{5}{3}$ of 12 kg $= \dfrac{5}{3} \times 12\,\text{kg} = 20\,\text{kg}$.

4   Decrease £120 in the ratio 9 : 10.

New amount is $\dfrac{9}{10}$ of £120 $= £\dfrac{9}{10} \times 120 = £108$.

Exercise 5.2

1.   Express as ratios in their simplest forms

1	24 : 64	**6**	13.2 cm : 16.5 cm
2	1.5 : 3.5	**7**	75p : £1.80
3	18 cm : 12 cm	**8**	3 hours 20 minutes : 5 hours 20 minutes
4	£9 : £27	**9**	750 g : 3.6 kg
5	16 kg : 8 kg	**10**	600 ml : 2 litres

2. **1** Divide £2.25 in the ratio 2 : 3
    2 Divide £1.54 in the ratio 4 : 7
    3 Divide 60p in the ratio 7 : 3
    4 Divide £1.75 in the ratio 6 : 1
    5 Divide £4 in the ratio 7 : 3

3. **1** Increase £270 in the ratio 5 : 3
    2 Increase £37.50 in the ratio 9 : 5
    3 Decrease £280 in the ratio 4 : 7
    4 Decrease £12 in the ratio 5 : 8
    5 Increase £25 in the ratio 11 : 10

4. A line AB of length 9 cm is divided at P so that $AP : PB = 3 : 7$. Find the length of AP.

5. Children aged 12 years, 9 years and 4 years share £5 in proportion to their ages. How much does the youngest child get ?

6. The angles of a triangle are in the ratio 4 : 5 : 6. Find their sizes.

7. A concrete mixture is made by mixing cement, sand and gravel by volume in the ratio 1 : 2 : 4. How much sand and gravel must be added to $0.5 \, \text{m}^3$ of cement ?

Unitary method and proportion

Quantities which increase in the same ratio are in **direct proportion**.

Example

1 If 21 notebooks cost £7.56, what do 28 similar notebooks cost?

1st method, unitary method

21 notebooks cost £7.56
 1 notebook costs £0.36   (dividing by 21)
28 notebooks cost £10.08   (multiplying by 28)

2nd method, proportion

The prices are in direct proportion to the quantities.
Ratio of quantities, new : old $= 28 : 21 = 4 : 3$
Ratio of prices $= 4 : 3$

New price $= \dfrac{4}{3}$ of £7.56 $= £\dfrac{4}{3} \times 7.56 = £10.08$.

Quantities which vary so that one increases in the same ratio as the other decreases are in **inverse proportion**.

Example

2   If there is enough food in an emergency pack to last 12 men for 10 days, how long would the food last if there were 15 men?

1st method, unitary method

The food lasts 12 men for 10 days.

The food lasts 1 man for 120 days.   (multiplying by 12 because it would last twelve times as long)

The food lasts 15 men for 8 days.   (dividing by 15)

2nd method, proportion

As the number of men increases, the time the food will last decreases.

Ratio of number of men, new : old $= 15 : 12 = 5 : 4$

Ratio of times, new : old $= 4 : 5$

New time the food lasts for $= \dfrac{4}{5}$ of 10 days $= 8$ days.

Compound measures

The word **rate** is used in many real-life situations.

Examples

A woman is paid for doing a job at the rate of £6.75 per hour.
Grass seed is sown to make a lawn at the rate of 2 oz per square yard.
Income tax is paid at the standard rate of 25 p in the £ (or whatever the current rate is).
A car uses petrol at the rate of 40 miles to the gallon.
Wallpaper paste powder is added to water at the rate of 1 packet to 6 pints of water.

Density

The density of a material $=$ the mass per unit volume.
It is measured in units such as g/cm^3.

(In Physics it is important to use the exact word 'mass', but in Mathematics we often use the more everyday word 'weight' to mean mass.)

$$\text{Density} = \frac{\text{mass}}{\text{volume}}$$

The formula rearranged gives:

$$\text{Volume} = \frac{\text{mass}}{\text{density}}$$

$$\text{Mass} = \text{density} \times \text{volume}$$

Example

3   If copper has density of $8.9\,\text{g/cm}^3$, what will be the mass of a copper block with volume $45\,\text{cm}^3$?

$$\text{Mass} = 8.9 \times 45 \ \text{g}$$

$$= 400.5\,\text{g}$$

$$= 401\,\text{g, to 3 sig. fig.}$$

Speed

The rate at which distance is travelled is called **speed** and it is found from the formula

$$\text{Speed} = \frac{\text{distance}}{\text{time}}$$

It is measured in units such as miles per hour, kilometres per hour, metres per second. The abbreviation for metres per second is m/s or ms^{-1}.

The formula can be rearranged to give:

$$\text{Time} = \frac{\text{distance}}{\text{speed}}$$

$$\text{Distance} = \text{speed} \times \text{time}$$

The units have to correspond, e.g. metres, seconds, metres per second or km, hours, km per hour.

If the speed is variable, these formulae will give or use the **average speed**.

Velocity is a word used instead of speed when the direction of motion is included, so that if the direction from point A to point B is being regarded as positive, a speed in the opposite direction will have a negative velocity.

Examples

4   If a train travels 64 km in 40 minutes, what is its average speed?

$$\text{Speed} = \frac{\text{distance}}{\text{time}} = \frac{64}{\frac{2}{3}} \text{ km/h} = 64 \times \frac{3}{2} \text{ km/h} = 96 \text{ km/h}.$$

Note that to get the speed in km/h, the time 40 minutes had to be written as $\frac{40}{60}$ or $\frac{2}{3}$ hours.

5   A car travels 45 km at an average speed of 30 km/h and then travels 175 km at 70 km/h. What is the average speed for the whole journey?

(Do **not** just average the two speeds 30 and 70, getting 50, since this is wrong.)

$$\text{Average speed} = \frac{\text{total distance}}{\text{total time}}$$

The total distance is 220 km.
The time for the first part of the journey is $1\frac{1}{2}$ hours.
The time for the second part of the journey is $2\frac{1}{2}$ hours.
The total time is 4 hours.

$$\text{Average speed} = \frac{220}{4} \text{ km/h} = 55 \text{ km/h}.$$

Exercise 5.3

1.   28 bars of chocolate cost £6.16. What would be the cost of 35 similar bars?

2.   If 20 boxes weigh 36 lb, what is the weight of 45 similar boxes?

3.   If a car travels for 100 miles on fuel costing £4.80, what would the fuel cost be, at the same rate, for a journey of 250 miles?

4.   If a store of emergency food would last 20 men for 36 days, how long would the same food last if there were 45 men?

5.   10 men can build a wall in 9 days. How long would 6 men take, working at the same rate?

6.   A carpet to cover a floor of area 20 square yards costs £250.
     How much would it cost for a similar carpet to cover
     a floor of area 24 square yards?

7.   If 3000 Portuguese escudos are equivalent to £12, what is the value in £'s of 10 000 escudos ?

8.   If 25 cm on a plan represents a length of 20 m, what is the length represented by a line 35 cm long ?

9.   A party of 4 volunteers can pack a batch of emergency parcels in 7 hours. How long would it take if there were 10 more volunteers helping, and they all worked at the same rate ?

10. Tanya saves £12 in 8 weeks. How long would it take her to save £45, if she saved at the same rate ?

11. A train journey will take 50 minutes if the train has an average speed of 36 mph. On one day, because of track repairs, the journey took 75 minutes. What was the average speed then ?

12. The weekly wages paid by a firm to 8 workers total £760. What will be the weekly wages if they employ 2 extra women and pay them all at the same rate ?

13. If grass seed is to be sown at the rate of 2 oz per square yard, how many lbs will be needed to make a rectangular lawn, 10 yards long by 8 yards wide ? (16 oz = 1 lb.)

14. 1 What is the density of a piece of wood which has a mass of 15 kg and a volume of 25 000 cm^3 ?
     2 What is the mass of a block of gold of volume 200 cm^3, if the gold has a density of 19.3 g/cm^3 ?
     3 What is the volume of a block of ice weighing 23.25 kg, if the ice has a density of 0.93 g/cm^3 ?

15. If petrol has a density of 0.8 g/cm^3 and the petrol in a can weighs 3.6 kg, how much petrol, in litres, does the can contain ?

16. 1 A car travels 210 km in 3 hours. What is its average speed ?
     2 A train is travelling at 60 km/h. How far will it travel in $1\frac{1}{2}$ hours ?
     3 A plane is travelling at 900 km/h. How long will it take to travel 300 km ?

17. A helicopter passes a point *A* at 3.58 pm and reaches a point *B* 25 km distant at 4.03 pm. What was its average speed ?

18. A main road through a village has a speed limit of 40 miles per hour. A motorist covers the $1\frac{1}{2}$ mile section in 2 minutes. Did he break the speed limit?

19. A train travels for 2 hours at 100 km/h and then for 1 hour at 85 km/h. Find its average speed for the whole journey.

20. A motorist has to make a journey of 175 miles. She estimates that for 143 miles on the motorway she can maintain an average speed of 65 mph, but the last 32 miles is in a built-up area where her average speed will be 20 mph. How long will the total journey take?

Percentages

'Per cent' means 'per hundred', so 17% means $\dfrac{17}{100}$ or 0.17.

Here is a reminder of methods for percentage calculations.

Examples

1   Express $87\frac{1}{2}\%$ as a fraction.

$$87\tfrac{1}{2}\% = \frac{87\frac{1}{2}}{100} = \frac{175}{200} = \tfrac{7}{8}$$

2   Express $63\frac{1}{4}\%$ as a decimal.

$$63\tfrac{1}{4}\% = \frac{63\frac{1}{4}}{100} = \frac{63.25}{100} = 0.6325$$

To change a fraction or decimal to a percentage, multiply by 100 and write the % sign.

3   $\dfrac{5}{6} = \dfrac{5}{6} \times 100\% = \dfrac{250}{3}\% = 83\tfrac{1}{3}\%$

$0.575 = 0.575 \times 100\% = 57.5\%$

4   Find 24% of 60 cm, and find $16\frac{2}{3}\%$ of 9 litres.

24% of 60 cm $= 0.24 \times 60$ cm $= 14.4$ cm

$16\frac{2}{3}\%$ of $9\,\ell = \dfrac{16\frac{2}{3}}{100} \times 9\,\ell = \dfrac{50}{300} \times 9\,\ell = 1.5\,\ell$

5   What percentage is 34 g of 2 kg?

(First find what fraction 34 g is of 2 kg, then change this fraction to a percentage.)

$\dfrac{34\text{ g}}{2\text{ kg}} = \dfrac{34\text{ g}}{2000\text{ g}} = \dfrac{34}{2000} \times 100\% = 1.7\%$

6   Increase £50 by 15%.

The new amount will be $(100 + 15)\%$, i.e. 115% of £50.

115% of £50 $= £1.15 \times 50 = £57.50$

(Alternatively, you could find 15% of £50, i.e. £7.50, and then add this to the original £50, making £57.50.)

7   Decrease £900 by 12%.

The new amount will be $(100 - 12)\%$, i.e. 88% of £900.

88% of £900 $= £0.88 \times 900 = £792$

(Alternatively, you could find 12% of £900, i.e. £108, and then subtract this from the original £900, leaving £792.)

Profit and Loss

Examples

8   A dealer buys an article for £75 and sells it for £90. What is his percentage profit?

Percentage profit is always based on the cost price, unless otherwise stated.
Here the profit is £15 on a cost price of £75.

% profit $= \dfrac{15}{75} \times 100\% = 20\%$

9   A dealer buys an article, adds 30% to the cost price for his profit, and marks the selling price at £6.50. What did the article cost him?

The selling price is $(100 + 30)\%$, i.e. 130% of the cost price.

The cost price is $£\dfrac{100}{130} \times 6.50 = £\dfrac{6.50}{1.30} = £5.00$

The article cost £5.

VAT. Value Added Tax

This tax is added to the cost of many things you buy. In most shops the price marked includes the tax so you do not have to calculate it.

Occasionally, however, the prices are given without VAT and it has to be added to the bill. The present rate of this tax is $17\frac{1}{2}\%$ so the final price is $117\frac{1}{2}\%$ of the original price. To find the final price, multiply the original price by 1.175.

Examples

10 A builder says he will charge £80 for doing a small job. To this, VAT at $17\frac{1}{2}\%$ is added. What is the total cost?

The total cost is £80 × 1.175 = £94.

If a price includes VAT, to find the original price divide by 1.175.

11 A video recorder costs £350. How much of this cost is tax?

The original price was $£\dfrac{350}{1.175} = £297.87$

The VAT is £350 − £297.87 = £52.13

The rate of tax might be changed. If it has, work out these examples using the up-to-date rate.

Interest

If you invest money, this money earns money which is called Interest. e.g. If you invested money in a Building Society which was paying interest at 8% (per year), then for every £100 invested you would get £8 every year your money was invested.

With **Simple Interest**, the interest is paid out each year, not added to the investment.

Example

12   If £800 is invested at $6\frac{1}{2}$% per annum, what is the interest paid each year ?
(per annum means 'for a year'. It is sometimes abbreviated to p.a.)

Every £100 invested gains £6.50 interest per year, so £800 invested gains
£6.50 × 8 interest per year = £52.

If the interest earned on money invested is added to the investment, then that money earns interest in future years. This is called **Compound Interest**, and it is explained further on page 428.

Loans

If you borrow money then you probably have to pay interest on the loan. Usually you agree to make repayments at so much per month or per week and these amounts include the interest, so that you pay back more than you borrowed. The sooner you repay a loan the less the interest will be. The bank, finance company or other lender must tell you the true rate of interest. In advertisements look for the letters APR (Annual Percentage Rate), for instance APR 24.6% means that you will pay at that rate of interest over the period of the loan. It might be possible to find another source from which you could borrow money at a cheaper rate of interest.

Exercise 5.4

1.   Express these percentages as fractions in their simplest forms.

    1   36%   **2**   45%   **3** $17\frac{1}{2}$%   **4** $3\frac{1}{3}$%   **5** $66\frac{2}{3}$%

2.   Express as decimals.

    1   47%   **2**   95%   **3** $22\frac{1}{2}$%   **4** $6\frac{1}{4}$%   **5**   99.9%

3.   Change these fractions or decimals to percentages.

    1 $\frac{3}{4}$ **2** $\frac{5}{8}$ **3**   0.15   **4** $\frac{1}{3}$ **5**   0.875

4.   Find

    1   48% of 3 m   **4** $62\frac{1}{2}$ % of 2.4 cm

    2   30% of 2 kg   **5**   115% of £4

    3 $16\frac{2}{3}$ % of $\frac{1}{2}$ hour

5. Find what percentage the 1st quantity is of the 2nd.

   1   £3.60, £5.00   **4**   750 g, 2 kg

   2   16 cm, 2 m   **5**   50p, 75p

   3   36 minutes, 1 hour

6. **1**   Increase £6 by 4%   **4**   Decrease £75 by 20%

   2   Increase £2.50 by 16%   **5**   Increase £300 by 12%

   3   Decrease £120 by 10%

7. **1**   Find the percentage profit if an article costing £2.50 to make is sold for £3.

   2   Find the percentage loss if an article costing £3 is sold for £2.50.

   3   A restaurant bill for £15 became £16.80 after a service charge was added. What was the percentage rate of the service charge?

   4   Find the percentage profit if a car is bought for £800 and sold for £980.

   5   Find the percentage loss if furniture which costs £600 is sold for £480.

8. **1**   By selling a car for £980 a dealer made 40% profit on what he had paid for it. How much had he paid for it?

   2   To clear goods during a sale a shopkeeper reduced the price by 10% and sold them for £3.60. What was the original price?

   3   This bottle of shampoo contains 330 ml of liquid. What quantity should an ordinary bottle hold?

   4   After an 8% pay-rise Miss Scott earned £9720 per year. What was she earning before the rise?

9.   Mr Parmar buys some DIY materials marked £24. VAT at $17\frac{1}{2}$% is added to this price. What is the total cost, including the tax?

10.   Mr Kent employed a firm to do some repairs and the bill, including VAT at $17\frac{1}{2}$%, came to £423. How much of this was the price for the work, and how much was the tax?

11.   How much interest must be paid each year on the following loans?

   1   Loan £1500, interest 12% p.a.

   2   Loan £600, interest 10% p.a.

   3   Loan £240, interest $7\frac{1}{2}$ % p.a.

12. Mrs Evans wants to borrow some money to finance a special project. Four firms are willing to lend her the money.

    1 Which firm charges the cheapest rate of interest ?

    2 Which firm charges the dearest rate of interest ?

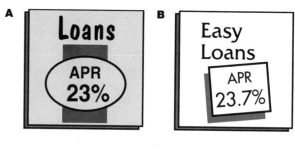

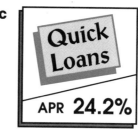

13. A grocer bought 10 cases of tinned fruit at £7.50 per case, each case containing 24 tins. He sold 200 tins at 42p each but the remainder were damaged and unfit for sale. Find his percentage profit.

14. A firm buys petrol and diesel oil in the ratio 5 : 7, spending £2700 altogether per week. If the price of petrol is increased by 5% and the diesel oil by 3%, find the percentage increase in the total cost, correct to 1 decimal place.

Exercise 5.5 Applications

1. There were two candidates, Mr A and Mr B, in an election. Mr A got $\frac{7}{12}$ of the votes.
What fraction did Mr B get ? Who won the election ?
If 2400 people altogether voted, how many extra votes did the winner get more than the loser ?

2. A farmer had 240 animals on his farm. $\frac{5}{8}$ of them were sheep, $\frac{1}{10}$ of them were pigs, he had 2 horses, 4 dogs and the rest were cows. How many cows had he ? What fraction of the total were cows ?

3. I think of a number. Two-thirds of this number is 18. What is the number ?

4. Maureen was trying to save £7. For 6 weeks she saved 70p a week. What fraction of the £7 had she still to save ?

5. A tank containing liquid is two-thirds full. When 60 more gallons of liquid are put in the tank is full. How many gallons does the tank hold altogether ?

6. A man gave some money to his four children in the ratio 2 : 4 : 5 : 9. If the difference between the largest and the smallest share was £175, how much did he give altogether ?

7. £900 is raised and is divided among 3 charities, A, B and C in the proportion 4 : 5 : 6. Find the amount each charity receives.

8. The costs of manufacture of an article are divided among labour, materials and overheads in the ratio 8 : 4 : 3. If the materials for 1000 articles cost £650, what is the total cost of these articles ?

9. Three men invest £2000, £3500 and £4500 respectively into a business and agree to share the profits in the ratio of their investments. The profits in the first year were £8000. How much did they each receive ?

10. A shade of paint is made up of 3 parts blue and 4 parts purple. How many litres of blue are needed to make up 10.5 litres of this paint ?

11. Mrs Robins and Mrs Webb both do a similar part-time job. Mrs Robins works for 9 hours and earns £30.60. Mrs Webb earns £40.80. How many hours does she work ?

12. A car journey takes 42 minutes when the average speed is 56 miles/hour. How long would it take if the average speed was 48 miles/hour?

13. The weekly wages paid by a firm to 5 workmen total £825. What will the weekly wages be if they employ two extra men, and pay them all at the same rate?

14.   A pond can be emptied in 12 hours using 4 pumps.
If the owner wants it emptied in 8 hours, how
many extra pumps, which work at the same rate,
will be needed?

15.   A recipe for 12 small cakes uses 75 g butter, 75 g castor sugar, 100 g flour and 2 eggs.
 1   How much flour is needed to make 30 of these cakes?
 2   How many eggs are needed to make 30 of these cakes?

16.   Mrs Khan earns £3.40 per hour for a basic week of 40 hours. Overtime is paid at
time-and-a-half. If she works 42 hours one week, what will she earn? If one week she
earns £176.80, how many hours altogether did she work?

17.   The insurance for the contents of a house is charged at £6.50 per £1000 of value. How
much will the insurance cost for contents valued at £18 500?

18.   1250 cm^3 of a liquid weighs 1 kg.
What is the density of the liquid, in g/cm^3?

19.   Two motorists, Mr Bowen and Mrs Crane, set off at 9 am to travel to a town 120 km
away. Mr Bowen arrives there at 11.30 am and Mrs Crane arrives there at noon.
 1   What is the ratio of their times taken?
 2   What is the ratio of their average speeds?

20.   On a holiday journey the car mileage indicator readings and times were as follows:

Time	9.05 am	11.45 am	12.15 pm	2.00 pm
Mileage indicator reading	16335	16463	16463	16526

(I had stopped to visit a place of interest from 11.45 am to 12.15 pm.)

 1   What was the average speed for the part of the journey up to 11.45 am?
 2   What was the average speed for the part of the journey from 12.15 pm?
 3   I estimate that my car used 5 gallons of petrol on the journey. What is the
approximate fuel consumption in miles per gallon?

21. Mrs Modi wants to buy some toothpaste. Which size, 50 ml, 125 ml or 175 ml, is the best value for money ?

22. **1** Write down the percentages equivalent to these fractions.

$\frac{1}{2}$, $\frac{1}{4}$, $\frac{1}{5}$ $\frac{1}{10}$, $\frac{1}{20}$, $\frac{1}{100}$

2 Write down the fractions equivalent to these percentages.

30%, $33\frac{1}{3}$%,   40%, $66\frac{2}{3}$%,   75%

3 Copy this table and complete it, also including the fractions $\frac{1}{5}$, $\frac{2}{5}$, $\frac{3}{5}$, $\frac{4}{5}$, $\frac{1}{10}$, $\frac{1}{20}$, $\frac{1}{25}$, $\frac{1}{50}$, $\frac{1}{100}$.

Equivalent fractions, ratios, decimals and percentages

Fraction	Ratio	Decimal	Percentage
$\frac{1}{2}$	1 : 2	0.5	50%
$\frac{1}{4}$			
$\frac{3}{4}$			
$\frac{1}{3}$	1 : 3	0.333...	$33\frac{1}{3}$ %
$\frac{2}{3}$			

23. Debbie knits a jumper from 12 balls of wool costing 60p per ball. In addition the pattern costs 30p. She sells the jumper for £12. What is the percentage profit on her outlay ?

24. A car insurance premium is £250 but there is a deduction of 60% of this for 'no claims discount'. How much is deducted, and how much remains to be paid ?

25. The price of a camera is increased by 30%. Later, in a sale, the price is reduced by 20% of its new value. This final price is £78. What was the original price ?

26.   If £1000 is invested at 9% per annum, find the interest paid at the end of the first year. If the interest is added to the money invested, find the interest which will be paid at the end of the second year.
      What is the total interest paid for the 2 years ?

27.   One firm will lend £800 at 10% per annum Simple Interest while another will lend it at 9% per annum Simple Interest. If the money is needed for 2 years, how much cheaper would it be to borrow from the second firm ?

Practice test 5

1.   **1**   Reduce $\frac{60}{72}$ to its lowest terms.

     2   Change $\frac{3}{7}$ into a fraction with denominator 35.

     3   Change the mixed number $4\frac{4}{5}$ into an improper fraction.

     4   Change $\frac{18}{5}$ into a mixed number.

     5   Express 60 cm as a fraction of 2 metres.

     6   Find $\frac{5}{8}$ of £2.24.

2.   There are 144 eggs in a crate. One-eighth of them are cracked. How many are whole ?

3.   To make gunmetal, copper, tin and zinc are used in the ratio 43 : 5 : 2. What quantities of tin and zinc are used with 21.5 kg of copper ?

4.   Two girls share some apples in the ratio 4 : 3. The girl with the larger share took 56 apples. How many did the other girl take ?

5.   In an hour 10 people can pick 40 kg of fruit. How much can be picked in an hour if there are 25 people ?

6.   A farmer has enough food for his 30 cows for 12 days. If he buys 6 more cows, how long will the food last then ?

7.   What is 48 minutes as a percentage of $1\frac{1}{4}$ hours ?

8. When Ron visits his mother, the journey takes $2\frac{1}{2}$ hours if he goes at an average speed of 30 miles per hour. If he reduces his average speed to 25 miles per hour in wet weather, how much longer will his journey take ?

9. This tin of paint will cover an area of $45\,\text{m}^2$.
What is the rate in square metres per litre ?

10. A computer game is for sale at £45. In a sale, the price is reduced by 5%. What is the new price ?

PUZZLES

9. If it takes a clock 6 seconds to strike 6, how long does it take to strike 12 ?

10. How many times in 12 hours do the hands of a clock point in the same direction ?

11. Jill has lost her timetable. She remembers that tomorrow's lessons end with Games, but she cannot remember the order of the first 5 lessons. She asks her friends, who decide to tease her.
Alison says, 'Science is 3rd, History is 1st'.
Brenda says, 'English is 2nd, Maths is 4th'
Claire says, 'History is 5th, Science is 4th'.
Denise says 'French is 5th, English is 2nd'.
Emma says 'French is 3rd, Maths is 4th'
Naturally, Jill is very confused by all this. Then her friends admit that they have each made one true statement and one untrue one.
When is Maths ?

Miscellaneous Section A

Exercise A1   Aural Practice

If possible find someone to read these questions to you.
You should do all of them within 10 minutes.
Do not use your calculator.
Write down the answers only.

1. If £10 was equally divided among 4 children, how much would they each receive ?

2. If 32 cm was cut from 1 metre of ribbon, how much was left ?

3. If 1 litre of petrol costs 54p, how much will 10 litres cost ?

4. A water tank holding 48 litres of water lost one-quarter of it through a leak. How much was left ?

5. 6 men can build a wall in 9 days. How long would 3 men take, working at the same rate ?

6. What is left when 0.05 is subtracted from 1 ?

7. Write down the prime numbers between 50 and 60.

8. There are two parcels with total weight 18 kg. One is 4 kg heavier than the other. What does the heavier one weigh ?

9. What is the order of rotational symmetry of a square ?

10. If 1 kg of a mixture cost 34p, what will 100 kg cost ?

11. Two angles of a triangle are 20° and 50°. What size is the third angle ?

12. A girl was 3 years old in 1992. When will she be 16 years old ?

13. What is 8% of £10 ?

14. A train which was due at 2.53 pm arrived 30 minutes late. At what time did it arrive ?

15. What fraction of 1 metre is 75 cm ?

Exercise A2   Revision

1.   Write correct to 2 significant figures

   1   639
   2   263
   3   0.0847
   4   5256
   5   0.517

2.   **1**   The marks on a harbour wall show the
         water level at −2 (feet). Where will it be
         when the water has risen 5 feet ?
     2   At its highest point the water level was at
         10 (feet), and several hours later it was at
         −6 (feet). What was the fall in the tide ?

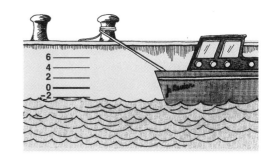

3.   Find the size of angle *a*.

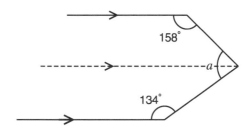

4.   Write down any number less than 10, add 3 to it and square the result. Then add 1 and
     multiply by 10. Subtract 100 and divide by the number you started with. Add 5 and then
     divide by 5. Subtract 9 and halve the result. Subtract the number you started with. What
     is your answer ?

5.   Name the solid figures with the shape of

   1   a cricket ball,
   2   a tin of soup,
   3   a clown's hat,
   4   a match box,
   5   a child's building block.

6.   Construct a quadrilateral *ABCD* as follows:
     Draw a line *AC*, 10 cm long.
     Draw the perpendicular bisector of *AC*, cutting *AC* at *M*.
     Find points *B* and *D* on the bisector, such that $BM = MD = 3$ cm.
     Join *AB, BC, CD, DA*.
     Measure *AB*, to the nearest mm.
     Measure $\angle ABC$.
     What sort of quadrilateral is *ABCD* ?

7. The profits on a business were £4800. The three partners divided this amount amongst themselves in the ratio 3 : 5 : 7. How much did each receive ?

8. Write in order of size, smallest first, $\frac{3}{8}$, 0.4, $\frac{3}{10}$, $\frac{1}{3}$, 38%.

9. Here is one quarter of a symmetrical pattern. Copy it and complete the other three quarters to match, so that the dotted lines are axes of symmetry.

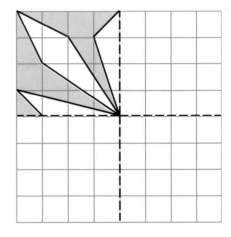

10. *ABCDEFGH* is a regular octagon, whose point of symmetry is *O*.

    1   What is the size of ∠*AOB* ?
    2   What is the size of ∠*ABC* ?
    3   If *AC*, *CE*, *EG* and *GA* are joined, what sort of quadrilateral is formed ?

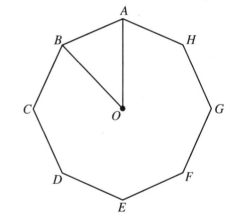

11. The air service between London and Kereva, together with connecting train services to Veefield, are given in a time-table as follows:

London dep.	23.00	10.20	11.20	15.25	16.55
Kereva airport arr.	00.30	11.40	12.50	16.45	18.10
Kereva station dep.	04.30	13.31	15.17	17.55	20.01
Veefield arr.	06.13	14.43	16.25	19.03	21.09

    1   What is the time of departure from London of the fastest service to Kereva ?
    2   What is the time taken for the slowest journey from London to Veefield ?
    3   The single fare from London to Kereva is £190, and the distance is 760 km. How much is the cost per km ?
    4   From Kereva to Veefield is 84 km. What is the average speed of the 13.31 train ?

12. Find the total cost of the ingredients used in making a cake from 150 g of butter, 150 g of sugar, 3 eggs and 200 g of flour, when flour costs 45p for a 1.5 kg bag, butter 65p for 250 g, sugar 60p for a kg bag and eggs £1 per dozen.

Exercise A3   Revision

1. The number of insects in a colony doubles each week. If there were 100 insects initially, how many would there be after 5 weeks ?

2. These flags have been rotated with ● as centre of rotation. In each case 1 is rotated into 2. Estimate, then measure, the angle of rotation. If it is anticlockwise give it as positive, e.g. +30°, if it is clockwise give it as negative, e.g. −30°.

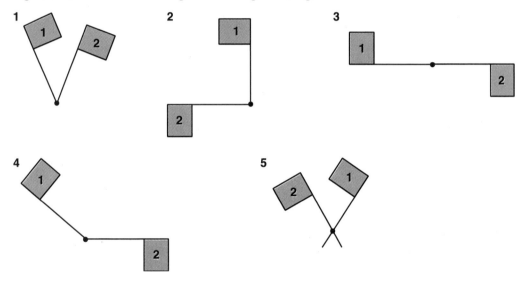

3. **1** Find 36% of $2\frac{1}{2}$ hours.

   2 What percentage is 40 cm of 5 m ?

4. From this list of numbers:

   15   21   24   27   31   34   44   47   51   57

   1 Find the largest prime number.
   2 Find two numbers whose product is 765.
   3 Find two numbers whose sum is 104.
   4 Find two numbers which as numerator and denominator of a fraction reduce to $\frac{2}{3}$.
   5 Find two numbers which as numerator and denominator of a fraction simplify to 1.8.

5. If 20 fence-posts cost £48, what would be the cost of 25 posts ?

6. These diagrams represent the nets of solid figures. Give the names of the solid figures.

1 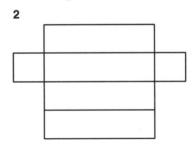   **2** 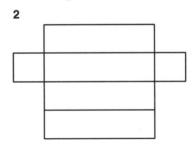   **3**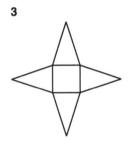

7. Write these numbers correct to 2 decimal places.

   1   5.628   **4**   0.0976
   2   3.2296   **5**   0.0628
   3   37.283

8. In the diagram, AD bisects $\angle BAC$.
   Find the size of $\angle C$.

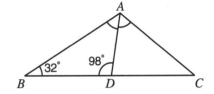

9. Find the values of the following, without using your calculator.

   1 $0.07 + 0.05$
   2 0.07×0.05
   3 $0.07 \div 0.05$

10. Three years ago the cost of an article was £24, made up of charges for labour, materials and other expenses in the ratio 9 : 4 : 3. Since then labour costs have increased by one-third, the price of materials has increased by one-fifth and the cost of other expenses has increased by one-tenth. What is the cost of the article now ?

11. Identify whether the quadrilateral $ABCD$ is necessarily a parallelogram, trapezium, rectangle, square or rhombus, if it has the following properties.

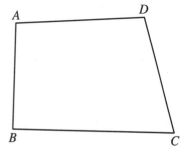

   1 $AD // BC$.
   2 $AB = DC$ and $AD = BC$.
   3 $\angle A = \angle C$ and $\angle B = \angle D$.
   4   Angles A, B, C, D are right angles.
   5 $AB = BC = CD = DA$.

12. If Denise travels to work by train it is quicker, but costs her three times as much as if she had travelled by bus. She decides that she could save £500 a year by going by bus. What would be the cost of travel by bus, for the year ?

To the student : 2

Activities

As part of your Mathematics course, you should choose and make use of knowledge, skills and understanding of Mathematics in practical tasks, in real-life problems and to investigate within Mathematics itself.

You may be tested on this section by doing practical work during your course, or you may be tested by taking an extra examination paper which includes suitable practical tasks.

Some suggestions are given here for activities. If you are being tested by coursework, you should discuss with your teacher the sort of activities which will be acceptable. As well as the activities suggested here, you may gain ideas from other sources. There may be cross-curricular activities, school or locally-based projects, national or international current affairs which may suggest suitable investigations. You can also get ideas from other textbooks, library books, worksheets, etc.

If you are being tested in an extra examination paper you should use some of the activities here for practice in doing the investigational type of questions.

The organisation of an activity

First of all, decide what is to be the **aim** of the activity or investigation, and write this down. Decide how much time you have available for it, and then make a detailed plan of what you are actually going to do.
Decide where you are going to find any further information you need. Sources can include library books, newspapers, magazines, or asking other people.
Carry out the activity. Work methodically and check information and results. Write a logical account of your work. Give reasons for any choices made. Examine and comment on any results and justify any solutions.
You may choose to present your work in a booklet, on a poster or by another form of display, including drawings or photographs.
After doing an activity you may be able to extend your investigations and make further discoveries. (See the examples on page 231.)

Exercise A4   Activities

1.   **Magic squares**

Here is a 4 by 4 magic square, used by the German artist
Albrecht Durer in an engraving 'Melancholia' to show the
date, 1514.

What are the totals of each row, each column and the two
main diagonals ?

16	3	2	13
5	10	11	8
9	6	7	12
4	15	14	1

Make a 3 by 3 magic square using the numbers 1 to 9.

If a 5 by 5 magic square uses numbers 1 to 25, what is the number to which all rows and
columns should add up ?
Try to find a general formula for the totals of rows and columns for an n by n magic
square using numbers 1 to n^2.

One way of constructing a magic square with an odd number of rows or columns is:
(1)   Put 1 in the middle of the top row.
(2)   Put each following number above and to the right of the preceding number. If this is
      above the top row go to the bottom row and if it is to the right of the right-hand
      column go to the left-hand column.

The 1st 5 numbers are shown.

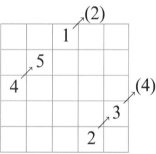

(3)   If a number cannot be placed because its square has already been filled (as 6 cannot
      be placed because 1 is there), put the number below the last number written. (Thus
      put 6 below 5 and continue as before.)

Copy and complete this magic square according
to this method.
Check that the rows, columns and main diagonals
all add up to the same number.

Make a 7 by 7 magic square using the same method.

Here is an 8 by 8 magic square.
Check that the rows, columns and main diagonals
all add up to the same number.

7	53	41	27	2	52	48	30
12	58	38	24	13	63	35	17
51	1	29	47	54	8	28	42
64	14	18	36	57	11	23	37
25	43	55	5	32	46	50	4
22	40	60	10	19	33	61	15
45	31	3	49	44	26	6	56
34	20	16	62	39	21	9	59

What happens if you replace each number by
its square ?

Look for other patterns in the square.
For instance, copy the square just writing in
the odd numbers and leaving the other squares
blank, or just writing in the numbers 1 to 32
and leaving the other squares blank.

2. ## The four 4's problem

Using the figure 4, four times, and any mathematical symbols, can you express all the
numbers from 1 to 100 ?

e.g. $1 = \dfrac{4 \times 4}{4 \times 4}$

$2 = \sqrt{4} + \sqrt{4 \times 4} - 4$

You may like to use the symbol !   This is called 'factorial'.

Factorial $1 = 1! = 1$
factorial $2 = 2! = 2 \times 1 = 2$
factorial $3 = 3! = 3 \times 2 \times 1 = 6$
factorial $4 = 4! = 4 \times 3 \times 2 \times 1 = 24$
and so on.

You may like to use .4 and .$\dot{4}$. You cannot write the 0's but the numbers have their usual
meanings if the decimal points are clear.

.$\dot{4}$ is $\dfrac{4}{9}$. What are the values of $\dfrac{4}{.4}$, $\dfrac{4}{.\dot{4}}$, $\sqrt{\dfrac{4}{.4}}$ and $\dfrac{4}{\sqrt{.4}}$?

Another useful symbol is %. What is $\dfrac{4}{4\%}$?

If you succeed is getting expressions for all the numbers from 1 to 100, well done! You
may like to do the same using the figure 9 four times.

3. **A holiday abroad**

Plan a holiday abroad for your family, or for you and your friends. Decide on the type of holiday you want and how much you want to spend on it. Include details of travel, destination, plans and costs.

4. **Banking**

Many people have a bank account nowadays. Many firms pay wages directly into employees' bank accounts as this is safer and quicker than paying by cash.
Find out from the main banks in your district full details of how to open an account and how to manage it.

5. **A guess-the-number trick**

Ask a friend to:
(1) Write down a 4-digit number, e.g. 7291,
(2) then multiply it by 100,
(3) and subtract the original number;
(4) then add up the figures of the answer.
    $(7 + 2 + 1 + 8 + 0 + 9 = \ldots)$

$$
\begin{array}{r}
7\,2\,9\,1\,0\,0 \\
-\qquad 7\,2\,9\,1 \\
\hline
7\,2\,1\,8\,0\,9 \\
\hline
\end{array}
$$

Now say you can guess the total, if you are allowed 3 guesses.
What numbers must you use for your 3 guesses ?

6. **Regular polygons**

   1   Investigate the number of diagonals for polygons with 3, 4, 5, ... sides. Find a formula for the number of diagonals of an *n*-sided polygon.

   2   When all the diagonals are drawn, how many regions are there inside the polygon ?

   3   Paper knots. Use strips of paper of uniform width. Practise with narrow strips first. Tie an ordinary knot to get a pentagon. Go round an extra turn to get a heptagon. Tie a reef knot in two strips of paper for a hexagon. By bending the paper in a different way you get an octagon.

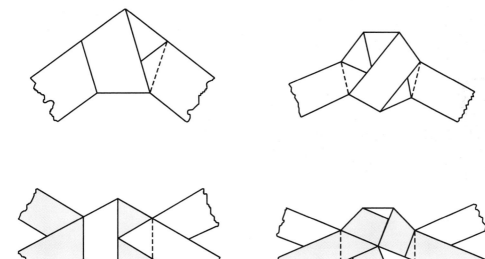

   4   Draw a regular pentagon and join its diagonals. Find in the figure an acute-angled isosceles triangle, an obtuse-angled isosceles triangle, an isosceles trapezium, a rhombus, a kite, a pentagon. Find non-regular polygons with different numbers of sides. How many triangles are there altogether in the figure ?

        Do a similar investigation for a regular hexagon and a regular octagon.

PUZZLES

12.   If 1 m^3 of earth weighs 1600 kg, how much would there be in a hole 50 cm by 50 cm by 50 cm ?

13.   Lorraine said 'Two days ago I was 13, next year I shall be 16'. What is the date today and when is her birthday ?

6 Collecting and displaying statistics

The topics in this chapter include:

- specifying an issue for which data are needed, designing and using observation sheets to collect data, collating and analysing results; constructing and interpreting information through two-way tables; inserting and interrogating data in a computer database, drawing conclusions,

- constructing and interpreting pie charts,

- collecting, ordering and grouping continuous data and creating frequency tables, and constructing and interpreting frequency diagrams,

- drawing a frequency polygon, making comparisons between two frequency distributions.

Statistics

Statistics involves numerical data.

Firstly, the data must be collected. Sometimes you carry out an investigation or experiment and collect data for yourself. Sometimes you can use data which someone else has collected. This includes data in government publications, newspapers, scientific textbooks, etc.

Secondly, the data is displayed in the form of a list, a table or a diagram.

Thirdly, it is studied, in order to make conclusions from it, often involving decisions for the future.

Tally tables

Example

1 The vehicles passing along a road were as follows: lorry, bus, car, lorry, lorry, lorry, car, lorry, bus, bus, lorry, car, car, van, car, car, bus, car, car, lorry, car, lorry, car, car, lorry, car, van, lorry, lorry, car, van, car, bus, van, lorry, car, bus, car.

The items are entered in a tally chart as they occur.

Vehicle	Tally	Total
Car	ⲜⲜ ⲜⲜ ⲜⲜ Ⅰ	16
Van	ⅠⅠⅠⅠ	4
Bus	ⲜⲜ Ⅰ	6
Lorry	ⲜⲜ ⲜⲜ ⅠⅠ	12
		38

Notice that the numbers are grouped in fives, the fifth number going diagonally through the first four. ⲜⲜ
The groups of 5 are kept in neat columns.
Grouping in 5's makes the totals easier to count.

Presenting data in a table

Example

2   **Method of transport to and from school**

Copy the table and fill in the figures to show this information.

Of the 50 boys, 10 walk to school, 5 cycle, 3 come on their motorbikes, 8 come by car and 4 come by train. The rest come by bus. All go home by the same method except that 2 who walk to school go home by car and 3 who come by car go home by bus.

	Morning			Afternoon		
	Boys	Girls	Total	Boys	Girls	Total
Walk						
Cycle						
Motorbike						
Car						
Bus						
Train						
Total						

Of the girls, 12 walk to school, 8 cycle, 1 comes on her motorbike, 3 come by car and 16 come by bus. No-one comes by train. 4 of the girls who come by bus walk home and 2 others go home by car instead of by bus.

What fraction of the pupils come to school by public transport (bus or train) ?
What fraction of the pupils go home by public transport ?

Diagrams

Here are shown some types of diagrams which can be used to display data.

Pictogram

Example

3

Eating habits of 100 students at lunch-time		
Canteen meal	20	🚶🚶🚶🚶
Canteen snack	36	🚶🚶🚶🚶🚶🚶🚶ı
Bring sandwiches	24	🚶🚶🚶🚶🚶
Eat out	8	🚶ı
Go home	12	🚶🚶ı

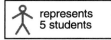
represents
5 students

Unless you are spending time on a special project, do not draw elaborate symbols. Use simple ones that are quick and easy to draw.

Bar chart

Example

4

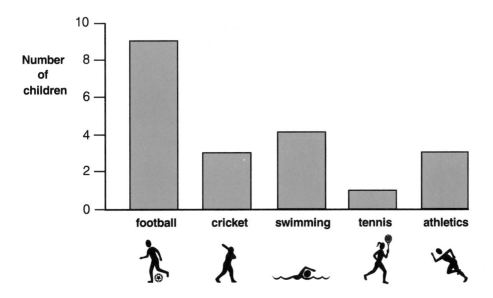

(The rectangles should all have the same width.)

Bar charts could be horizontal instead of vertical.

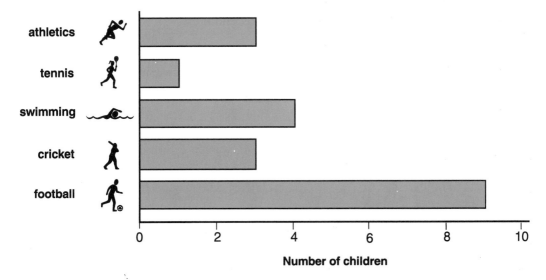

Statistical diagrams and graphs should have headings to describe them.
Scales should be clearly marked. Axes should be labelled.

Line graph (Time-series graph)

Example

5   These figures show the numbers attending a youth club over the past ten weeks.

20, 35, 28, 25, 33, 41, 37, 46, 48, 42.

We can plot these figures on a graph, putting time on the horizontal axis and attendance on the vertical axis.

Youth club attendance

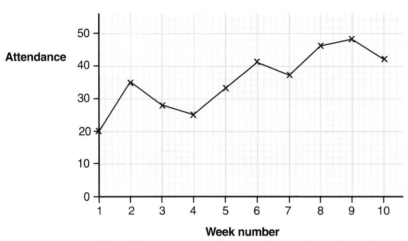

The points are joined from one to the next by straight lines, because this shows increases and decreases more easily, but in this graph the lines have no other meaning. We cannot use the graph to find the attendance at in-between times, because that would be meaningless. The graph does show an upward trend in attendance and we might use this to make a very cautious prediction for future attendances.

From the graph find

1   in which week the attendance was greatest,

2   between which two weeks there was the greatest increase in attendance.

Pie chart

Example

6   A family with a weekly income of £225 spend it as follows:

	£
Rent	50
Fuel	35
Food	75
Clothing	25
Household goods	15
Other expenses	25
	225

Spending by a family

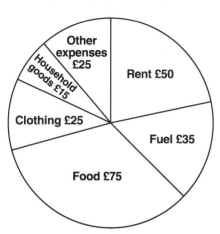

(Working for the pie chart.)
Since £225 is represented by 360°,

£1 is represented by $\dfrac{360^{\circ}}{225} = 1.6^{\circ}$

Rent	$50 \times 1.6^{\circ} = 80^{\circ}$
Fuel	$35 \times 1.6^{\circ} = 56^{\circ}$
Food	$75 \times 1.6^{\circ} = 120^{\circ}$
Clothing	$25 \times 1.6^{\circ} = 40^{\circ}$
Household goods	$15 \times 1.6^{\circ} = 24^{\circ}$
Other expenses	$25 \times 1.6^{\circ} = 40^{\circ}$

Total $= 360°$

this is a useful check

(It is not necessary to mark the sizes of angles on the diagram but show your working clearly as above. The diagram shows the statistical figures and is clearer without the angle markings.)

Which diagram to draw

A **pictogram** shows information in a similar way to a bar chart, but by making attractive drawings it makes it look more interesting than a bar chart, so people are more likely to look at it.

A **bar chart** shows clearly the different frequencies. It is easy to compare them. You can see at a glance which of two similar bars is longer.

A **pie chart** shows more easily the fraction of the total which each item takes. A sector using more than half of the circle represents more than half of the total, a sector with a small angle represents a small part of the total, and so on. It is not so easy to compare sectors with each other if they are nearly the same size.

Exercise 6.1

1. The numbers of matches in 60 boxes were counted. Tally the information and show the totals in a separate column.

48	49	47	45	48	49	48	49	49	49	49	48	48	44	48
47	49	45	49	50	48	49	47	48	49	46	50	48	46	46
47	48	47	49	45	47	45	46	47	47	48	45	50	49	46
47	49	48	46	49	46	49	47	46	49	49	49	45	49	49

2.   A firm made a table showing sales of a product.

	Standard model	De-luxe model	Total
Red			
Green			
Blue			
Total			

Copy the table and fill in the details.
In the standard model there were 60 sold altogether of which $\frac{1}{2}$ were red and $\frac{1}{5}$ were green.
For sales in the de-luxe range, 5 more red ones were sold than of the standard model and 4 fewer blue ones than of the standard model. Altogether 31 green items were sold.
What fraction of the total items sold were blue ones ?

3.   24 teenagers going on an Activity Day each have to choose from these five activities: abseiling, orienteering, canoeing, archery, mystery event. They have to give their choice of activity (1) for the morning session, (2) for the afternoon session, (3) as a reserve, in case they cannot do one of their choices for (1) or (2).

Design a sheet which the organiser could use to record the choices from each person and the totals for each category.

4.   A camping holiday cost £36. This pie chart shows how the money was used.

Measure the angles with your protractor to the nearest 5° in each case.
Find how much was spent on each of the four items.

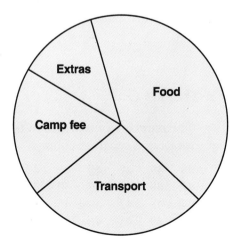

5. An arable farm of 90 hectares grows four main crops.

Barley	56 hectares
Potatoes	11 hectares
Carrots	9 hectares
Green vegetables	14 hectares

    (1 hectare $= 10\,000\,\text{m}^2$)

    Represent the data on a pie chart.

6. In a shopping survey, 4 different brands of butter, which we will call brands A, B, C and D, were on sale. The first 60 customers' choices were as follows:

    ```
    C  C  A  D  D  D  C  C  D  C  B  A
    C  A  D  D  C  C  A  D  C  A  A  C
    C  A  B  C  C  A  A  A  A  C  D  C
    C  C  A  A  A  A  A  C  C  C  A  C
    B  B  D  C  D  C  C  C  B  D  B  D
    ```

    Summarise this information. Draw a pie chart to illustrate the results.

7. Each £1 collected in Council Tax was used by a Council as follows:

Education	53p
Social services	17p
Police	12p
Highways and transport	8p
Fire Service	3p
Other expenses	2p

    The rest was kept in reserve. How much per £1 was this ?
    Represent this information on a pie chart.

Frequency Distributions

Discrete data

(i.e. the variables are numbers, not measurements)

Example

1   The numbers of children in 50 families (with at least 1 child) are as follows:

    ```
    4  5  2  2  3  4  4  3  5  4  7  3  3  4  2  2  2  2  2  6  3  2  3  3  1
    2  3  2  2  6  5  5  3  2  4  4  2  4  1  2  2  2  1  3  3  2  2  4  5  3
    ```

Frequency distribution table

Number of children	Number of families f
1	3
2	18
3	12
4	9
5	5
6	2
7	1
	50

The most suitable diagram to represent the data is a bar-line graph, but a histogram is sometimes used.

Bar-line graph

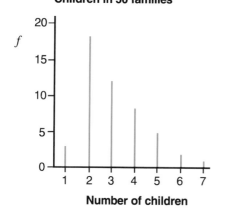

Histogram

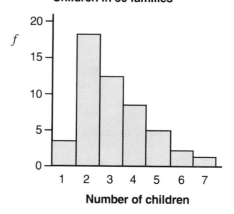

Grouped data

If the range of data is wide we can put it into convenient groups, called classes.

Example

2   The distribution of examination marks of 120 students.

Mark	0–9	10–19	20–29	30–39	40–49	50–59	60–69
f (number of students)	5	14	22	29	27	19	4

The data can be represented by a histogram.

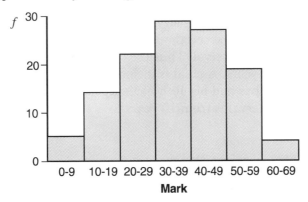

In a histogram, the **area** of each block represents the frequency.
In the histograms here the class intervals are of equal width, so the heights of the columns are in proportion to their frequencies, and can be labelled to represent the frequencies.

Continuous data

(i.e. the variables are measurements, such as lengths, weights, times, which go up continuously, not in jumps.)

Example

3   The lengths of leaves from a bush, using a sample of 60 leaves.

Length in cm	5.0–5.4	5.5–5.9	6.0–6.4	6.5–6.9	7.0–7.4	7.5–7.9
f	2	12	20	15	8	3

Measurements in the 1st class interval will include lengths from 4.95 to 5.45 cm, in the 2nd class interval from 5.45 to 5.95 cm, and so on.

In the histogram, since the measurements are continuous, we can label the edges of the intervals.

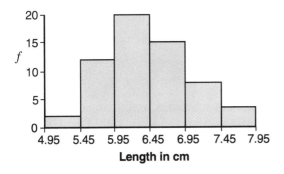

Age distributions

Ages are usually given in completed years so in a table such as this a child who has not quite reached the age of 10 years will be included in the 5–9 class interval. Thus the class interval is from 5 years to 10 years. A child is included in the 10–14 class interval if he has had his 10th birthday but not his 15th, and the class interval is from 10 years to 15 years.

Age in years	f
5–9	2
10–14	3
15–19	5

Compare this with a table for weight. Weights are usually measured to the nearest kg so a weight of 9.7 kg will go in the 10–14 class interval. But the 5–9 class interval can also include weights over 4.5 kg. So the class intervals are 4.5–9.5 kg, 9.5–14.5 kg, 14.5–19.5 kg.

Weight in kg	f
5–9	2
10–14	3
15–19	5

Histograms

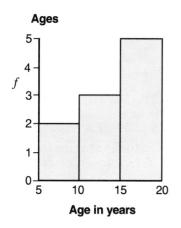

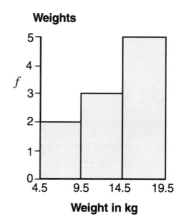

Frequency Polygons

A frequency polygon is an alternative diagram which is sometimes used instead of a histogram. One use is for when two or more frequency distributions with the same total frequencies have to be compared. It is possible to draw their frequency polygons on the same graph, whereas this is not possible with histograms.

The simplest way to see how to draw a frequency polygon is to draw one on the same diagram as a histogram. It is constructed by joining the mid-points of the top lines of the histogram.

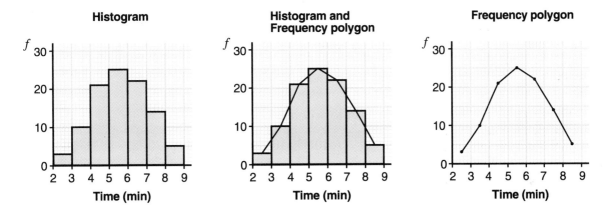

You can see that the word 'polygon' was chosen because it consists of a series of straight lines.

Some people say that the polygon should be closed, by meeting the horizontal axis on both sides.
You cannot do this if you are drawing the frequency polygon on the same diagram as a histogram, as you will not have left an empty class interval.
If you are drawing a separate frequency polygon, you can add an extra class interval on each side. These have frequency 0. Join the polygon to the mid-point of each.

Frequency polygon with extra intervals added.

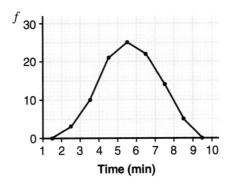

Exercise 6.2

In questions 1, 2, 3, draw a histogram of the distribution.

1. The heights of 80 students.

Height in cm	150–154	155–159	160–164	165–169	170–174	175–179	180–184	185–189
Number of students	3	4	9	16	18	17	7	6

2. Times taken by 100 children to travel to school.

Time in minutes	0–5	5–10	10–15	15–20	20–25	25–30
Number of children	3	15	27	34	19	2

3. Lengths of 30 leaves, each measured to the nearest 0.5 cm.

Length in cm	6.0	6.5	7.0	7.5	8.0	8.5
Number of leaves	1	5	7	11	4	2

4. The weights of a group of children are given in this frequency distribution.

    Show the frequencies of each class of weights, in a table.

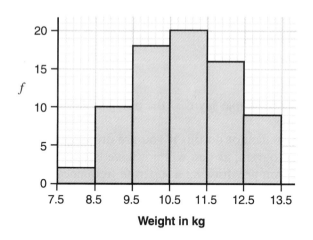

5. 30 students were asked in a survey to say how many hours they spent watching television in the previous week. Their answers, in hours to the nearest hour, were as follows:

    12 20 13 15 22 3 6 24 20 15 9 12 5 6 8
    30 7 12 14 25 2 6 12 20 20 18 3 18 8 9

    Tally these data in classes 1–5, 6–10, 11–15, etc.
    (The class 1–5 includes actual times from 0.5 to 5.5 hours,
    the class 6–10 includes times from 5.5 to 10.5 hours, and so on.)
    Draw a histogram of the distribution.

Questions 6 to 8

For the questions 1 to 3, either add a frequency polygon to the histogram you have already drawn, or draw a separate frequency polygon of the data.

9. Draw a frequency polygon of the data shown in the histogram of question 4. Label the horizontal axis from 6.5 to 14.5 and make the polygon a closed one.

10. The distributions of examination marks in two examinations are shown in this table. Draw frequency polygons for these distributions on the same graph and comment on them.

Mark	0–9	10–19	20–29	30–39	40–49	50–59	60–69	70–79	80–89	90–99
1st exam	3	8	7	11	14	18	21	10	6	2
2nd exam			1	3	6	8	15	38	22	7

Exercise 6.3   Applications

1. The scores in 42 matches on a particular Saturday were as follows:

0–2	0–2	2–2	0–3	1–4	1–0	1–0	2–1	4–1	5–1	5–0
3–2	2–1	1–4	2–0	3–0	1–1	2–1	0–1	1–2	2–1	2–0
1–1	1–2	0–0	2–2	1–2	0–3	2–0	1–0	0–0	1–0	1–2
1–0	2–2	3–0	2–0	3–1	1–2	1–2	2–2	1–3		

Copy and fill in this table showing the **number of teams** in each category.

Number of teams		Goals by home team						
		0	1	2	3	4	5	Total
Goals by away team	0							
	1							
	2							
	3							
	4							
	Total							

What was the total number of goals scored by the home teams ?
What was the total number of goals scored by the away teams ?

Draw two bar-line graphs or histograms, one showing the distribution of goals by the home teams and the other showing the distribution of goals by the away teams. Comment on these graphs.

2. Design a table which could be used by a doctor to record the number of patients visiting the surgery on any one day. The table could include separate categories for men, women and children, and also the numbers for the morning surgery and the evening surgery, and all totals.

3. The pie chart represents the numbers of sheep, cattle and pigs in Britain in a certain year.

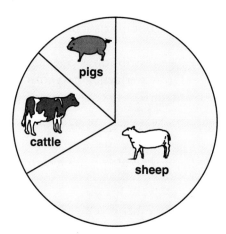

   1　Approximately what fraction of the total numbers were sheep ?

   2　By measuring the angles with your protractor, find how many cattle and how many pigs there were, both to the nearest million, if there were 40 million sheep.

4. In an electricity company, the cost of electricity at £7.20 per 100 units is made up as follows:

Cost of electricity from generators	£4.40
Cost of transporting electricity	£1.72
Fossil fuel levy	£0.72
Company profit	£0.36

This information is to be represented in a pie chart.
What size of angle in the pie chart will represent 1p ?
Calculate the sizes of angles to be used in the 4 sectors of the pie chart, and list them.
Draw the pie chart, labelling the sectors.

5. Each £1 collected by a children's charity is used in the following ways:

To child care	79p
Fundraising	11p
Information and education	7p
Administration	3p

Represent this information on a pie chart.

6. In a particular year, the destinations of British holidaymakers travelling to other European countries were as follows:
Spain 30%, France 14%, Italy 8%, Greece 7%, Eire 5%, Other countries 36%.
Represent the data on a pie chart.

In questions 7 to 10, draw histograms to represent the data, and comment on the shape of the histogram.

7. Heights of 60 men.

167·5

Height in cm	168–170	171–173	174–176	177–179	180–182	183–185	186–188	189–191
Number of men	2	4	8	13	14	9	7	3

8. Ages of children in a club.

Age (in completed years)	11	12	13	14	15
Number of children	8	10	6	4	2

9. The weights of 120 men are as follows:

59·5   64·5   69·5   74·5   79·5   84·5   9

Weight in kg	60–	65–	70–	75–	80–	85–90
Number of men	4	18	36	50	10	2

(The 1st class includes weights between 60 and 65 kg.)

10. The ages of 100 cars in a survey are as follows:

7·5   9·5   11·5   13·5

Age in years	0–2 1·5	2–4 3·5	4–6 5·5	6–8	8–10	10–12	12–14
Number of cars	16	23	24	17	12	7	1

(The 1st class includes cars up to just under 2 years old, the 2nd class includes cars from 2 years to just under 4 years old, and so on.)

Questions 11 to 14

For questions 11 to 14, draw frequency polygons of the data of questions 7 to 10 above.

15. The table shows the age distribution of the population of the UK in 1901 and 1981. Draw frequency polygons on the same graph to represent the data, and comment on them. (Figures in 100 000's.)

Age (years)	Population	
	1901	1981
0–9·5	85	70
10–19·5	78	90
20–29·5	70	78
30–39·5	53	76
40–49·5	40	62
50–59·5	28	64
60–69·5	18	56
70–79·5	8	40
80–89·5	2	15

(A few people in the last group are over 89 years old.)

16.   The lengths of 50 rods were measured to the nearest cm.
      Here are the results, in cm:

      87 80 69 90 80 84 73 78 79 71 74 85 62 79 72
      81 65 76 82 70 74 75 82 66 71 78 72 73 86 76
      81 73 70 67 78 84 75 70 77 82 83 76 77 88 75
      75 83 78 79 68

      Tally the data using classes 60 – 64, 65 – 69, etc. and show the frequencies.
      Draw a histogram of the distribution.

17.   **A statistical investigation**
      Choose a topic that interests you, or has some practical purpose, and carry out an
      investigation.
      First of all, decide what is the **aim** of the investigation. It is no use spending time
      collecting data without knowing whether it will be of any use.
      You need not collect the data for yourself. You may use data that someone has already
      collected, or you may use data from books, magazines, etc. or from a computer database.

      Nowadays there are many types of computer programs which you can use to present and
      analyse your data. After you have entered your data, many programs produce a variety
      of diagrams to illustrate the data, and will work out averages and dispersion. This is very
      useful, especially if you have a large amount of data.

      Here are some brief notes which may give you ideas for choosing what to do.

      1   Investigations into heights of people, shoe sizes, heights of teenagers compared with
          parents' heights, etc.

      2   Financial matters, e.g. children's spending money, family budgets, money spent on
          leisure, transport, etc.

      3   Television, e.g. amount of time devoted to different kinds of programmes, comparing
          different channels. Time taken by advertising, kinds of advertising.
          Time people spend watching TV or videos. Favourite types of programme.
          Percentage of people who have satellite or cable television.

      4   Sports, e.g. football results, goals scored, differences between home and away
          matches, comparisons with other years. Similar analysis of other sports.
          Popularity of various sports by people taking part, by spectators or by watching them
          on television.

      5   Leisure interests, e.g. costs of a hobby, time needed for it.

      6   Holidays, e.g. destinations, type, cost, length of time, method of travel.

      7   Traffic, e.g. surveys, number of people in each car. Ages of cars. Traffic flow at
          different times. Distances travelled. Use of public transport or taxis. Travel costs.

8 School or college issues, e.g. any plans to alter existing arrangements for uniform, meals, homework. Survey of attendance and punctuality. Distances from homes to school. Examination results.

9 Local issues, e.g. whether people want a new by-pass built and their views for and against. Council spending. Ages of local population.

10 Employment, e.g. types of work and numbers of jobs available locally. Pay and prospects.

11 National issues, e.g. whether people support Government proposals on some matter and their views for or against.

12 Health issues, e.g. healthy eating, types of exercise.

13 International problems such as third world famine. Ecological issues.

14 Work linked with other school or college subjects such as experiments in Biology and other Sciences, links with Geography fieldwork, plans in technology.

Practice test 6

1. In a certain firm there were 4 workshops, A, B, C, D, with men and women workers in each.
   Design a table to show the categories of (1) men, (2) women, (3) total workers, in each workshop, and the totals in the firm.
   Fill in the table using this information. There were 175 workers in workshop A of whom 40% were men and the rest were women. There were 200 men and 50 women in workshop B. There were 45 women in workshop C and twice as many men, and in workshop D there were 80 workers of whom 15% were men.
   How many workers were there altogether ?

2. A family's income of £240 in a particular week was spent as follows:

Food	£72
Rent	£42
Car expenses	£36
Clothes	£18
Fuel	£24
Miscellaneous	£48

   Represent the data on a pie chart.

   [Turn over]

3. The heights of 40 plants, given to the nearest cm, are as follows:

Height in cm	3	4	5	6	7	8
Number of plants	1	7	10	12	8	2

Draw a histogram of this distribution.

4. The marks of 30 children in an examination were as follows:

62 73 52 59 66 82 73 51 37 42 86 63 32 77 49
57 85 65 79 93 46 68 60 83 79 56 84 74 98 61

Tally these marks in classes 30–39, 40–49, etc.
Draw a histogram of the distribution.
On the same diagram, draw a frequency polygon of the distribution.

5. The number of words per sentence in the first 50 sentences of two books are recorded below.
Draw frequency polygons on the same graph to represent the data.
Compare the two sets of data and comment on them.

(1) 'The Children of the New Forest'
(2) 'The Adventures of Tom Sawyer'

Number of words	Number of sentences	
	(1)	(2)
1–10	2	27
11–20	9	11
21–30	14	9
31–40	7	0
41–50	4	3
51–60	8	0
61–70	3	0
71–80	2	0
81–90	1	0

PUZZLES

14. What is the area of a square of side 21 cm ?
Draw a square of side 21 cm on cardboard
and divide it into 4 pieces as shown. Cut
the pieces out and rearrange them to form
a rectangle.
What are the measurements of the rectangle ?
What is the area of the rectangle ?
Where has the extra 1 cm^2 come from ?

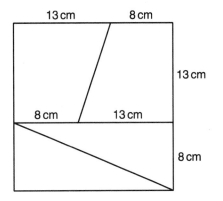

15. A shop sells one brand of chocolate bars which are priced at, small, 16p; medium, 23p
and large 39p; and a second brand where the prices are, small, 17p; medium, 24p and
large 40p. A customer buys some of these bars of chocolate and they cost him exactly
£1. What does he buy ?

16. In this sentence, each letter of the alphabet has been substituted by another letter
chosen at random (the same one each time that letter occurs). Can you decode the
sentence, and say whether it is a true statement ?

XWN DJKSUN RV XWN WQORXNVKDN RL S UCIWX-SVIZNF
XUCSVIZN CD NJKSZ XR WXN DKP RL XWN DJKSUND RV
XWN XER SFMSTNVX DCFND.

17. Write the numbers from 100 to 200 as the sum of consecutive integers.
e.g. $100 = 18 + 19 + 20 + 21 + 22$
$101 = 50 + 51$
$102 = 33 + 34 + 35$
$104 = 2 + 3 + 4 + \cdots + 13 + 14$
It is possible to do this for every number except one of them. Which number is this ?

18. Whilst Mr Mercer's car was being repaired, he travelled to and from work either by
train or by bus. When he went to work on the train, he came home on the bus. If he
came home on the train, he had taken the bus to work. During this time he travelled
on the train 9 times and travelled on the bus 10 times going to work and 15 times
coming home from work. For how many days was his car off the road ?

7 Introduction to algebra

The topics in this chapter include:

- expressing simple functions symbolically,
- understanding and using simple formulae,
- using the rules of indices for positive integer values,
- solving linear equations,
- solving polynomial equations by trial and improvement methods,
- using symbolic notation to express the rules of sequences.

Expressions and formulae

Examples

If there are 8 parcels each weighing w kg, the total weight is $8w$ kg.

If a roll of ribbon b metres long is to be cut into 10 equal pieces, the length of each piece is $\dfrac{b}{10}$ metres.

The total cost of 5 kg of potatoes at p pence per kg and 3 kg of carrots at q pence per kg is $(5p + 3q)$ pence.

The formula for the perimeter of a rectangle, P cm, when the length is l cm and the breadth is b cm, is $P = 2(l + b)$.

The formula for the time taken, t seconds, to run 200 m at a speed of x m/s is $t = \dfrac{200}{x}$.

Simplifying expressions

Addition and subtraction

$a + a = 2a$

$5b - 4b = b$

$3c - 3c = 0$

$3d + 4e + d - e = 4d + 3e$

Multiplication and division

$a \times a = a^2$

$2 \times b \times c = 2bc$

$d \times d \times d = d^3$

$e \div f = \dfrac{e}{f}$

$g \div g = 1$

Indices

The rules are

$$a^m \times a^n = a^{m+n}$$

$$(a^m)^n = a^{mn}$$

$$a^m \div a^n = a^{m-n}$$

Examples

$$x^5 \times x^3 = x^8$$

$$x^7 \div x^5 = x^2$$

$$\left(x^3\right)^4 = x^{12}$$

Further expressions

$a^2 + a^2 = 2a^2$

$3b^2 \times 2b^3 = 6b^5$

$4c^3 \div 3c = \dfrac{4c^3}{3c} = \tfrac{4}{3}c^2$

$\sqrt{9d^2} = 3d$

Removing brackets

$3(a + 4b) = 3a + 12b$

$c(2c - 3d) = 2c^2 - 3cd$

$2e(3e + 5f - 1) = 6e^2 + 10ef - 2e$

$3(g + 4h) + 2(3g - h)$

$\qquad = 3g + 12h + 6g - 2h = 9g + 10h$

Negative numbers

Examples

$(-5a) + 4a = -a$

$(-5a) + 7a = 2a$

$5a - 8a = -3a$

$(-5a) - a = -6a$

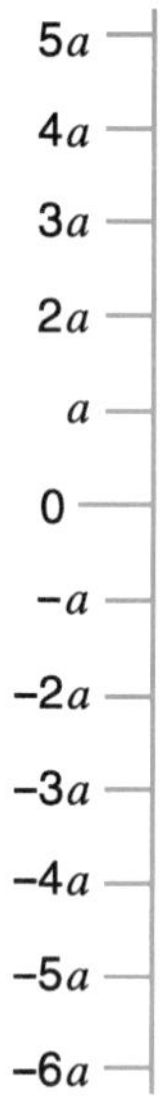

$5a$ —

$4a$ —

$3a$ —

$2a$ —

a —

0 —

$-a$ —

$-2a$ —

$-3a$ —

$-4a$ —

$-5a$ —

$-6a$ —

Replace two signs by one, and then work as shown above.

The rules are

$$x + (+y) = x + y$$
$$x - (+y) = x - y$$
$$x + (-y) = x - y$$
$$x - (-y) = x + y$$

Examples

$(-5a) + (+a) = (-5a) + a = -4a$

$(-5a) - (+3a) = (-5a) - 3a = -8a$

$(-5a) + (-2a) = (-5a) - 2a = -7a$

$(-5a) - (-8a) = (-5a) + 8a = 3a$

Multiplication and division

The rules are

$$(+x) \times (+y) = xy$$
$$(+x) \times (-y) = -xy$$
$$(-x) \times (-y) = xy$$

$$(+x) \div (+y) = \frac{x}{y}$$

$$(+x) \div (-y) = -\frac{x}{y}$$

$$(-x) \div (+y) = -\frac{x}{y}$$

$$(-x) \div (-y) = \frac{x}{y}$$

Examples

$$4a \times (-6) = -24a \qquad\qquad 12a \div (-3) = -4a$$

$$(-4b) \times 6b = -24b^2 \qquad\qquad (-12b) \div 3b = -4$$

$$(-4c) \times (-6d) = 24cd \qquad\qquad (-12c^2) \div (-3c) = 4c$$

Rules for removing brackets

$$a + (b + c) = a + b + c$$

$$a + (b - c) = a + b - c$$

$$a - (b + c) = a - b - c$$

$$a - (b - c) = a - b + c$$

Note that the minus sign immediately in front of the bracket changes any signs inside the bracket when the bracket is removed.

Examples

$$5(x + 2y) + 2(x - 8y) = 5x + 10y + 2x - 16y = 7x - 6y$$

$$4(x + y) - (3x + 5y) = 4x + 4y - 3x - 5y = x - y$$

$$3(2x + y) - 2(3x - y) = 6x + 3y - 6x + 2y = 5y$$

Substitution

1   If $a = 2$, $b = 5$ and $c = 0$ then

$$3a + b^2 = (3 \times 2) + 5^2 = 6 + 25 = 31$$

$$4abc = 4 \times 2 \times 5 \times 0 = 0$$

$$a^3 + 2b^2 = 2^3 + (2 \times 5^2) = 8 + 50 = 58$$

Note that $2b^2$ means $2 \times b^2 = 2 \times 5^2 = 2 \times 25 = 50$. It is not the same as $(2b)^2$ which means $2b \times 2b$ and equals 100.

2   If $x = 3$ and $y = -5$,

$$5x + 10y = 5 \times 3 + 10 \times (-5) = 15 - 50 = -35$$

$$x^2 + y^2 = 3^2 + (-5)^2 = 9 + 25 = 34$$

3 A formula used to calculate distance is $s = ut + \frac{1}{2}ft^2$.
Find the value of s when $u = 5$, $t = 3$ and $f = -10$.

$$s = ut + \tfrac{1}{2}ft^2$$
$$= 5 \times 3 + \tfrac{1}{2} \times (-10) \times 3^2$$
$$= 15 - 45$$
$$= -30$$

Exercise 7.1

1. **1** What is the cost, in pence, of 5 kg of butter at a pence per kg ?

2 How many minutes are there in $2b$ hours ?

3 What is the total cost, in pence, of 3 lb of apples at e pence per lb and 2 lb of pears at f pence per lb ?

4 What is the change, in pence, from £1, after buying g packets of sweets at h pence each ?

2. **1** If pencils cost k pence each, and k pencils cost £C, find a formula for C in terms of k.

2 If a dozen eggs cost m pence and 4 eggs cost e pence, find a formula for e in terms of m.

3 If m minutes is equivalent to $3n$ seconds, find a formula for m in terms of n.

3. Simplify these expressions

1	$3c + 2c - 4c$	**10**	$f^8 \div f^4$	**18**	$3n^2 \div 2n^2$
2	$6d - 4d - 2d$	**11**	$9a \times 5a$	**19**	$ab + ba$
3	$5e + f + 3e - f$	**12**	$8b \times 2c$	**20**	$c^3 + c^3$
4	$2g - 3h + g - h$	**13**	$4e \times 5e^2$	**21**	$4d^2 + 4d^2$
5	$a \times a$	**14**	$15f^3 \div 5f^2$	**22**	$ef + 3ef - 2ef$
6	$b \times b \times b$	**15**	$(3g)^2$	**23**	$6ab \times 6ac \div 6bc$
7	$c \div c$	**16**	$\sqrt{(25h^2)}$	**24**	$(3g^2h^3)^2$
8	$d^3 \div d$	**17**	$8m \div 2n$	**25**	$\sqrt{(16j^2k^4)}$
9	$e^3 \times e^2$				

4. Simplify

1	$a^3 \times a^4$	**5**	$(e^4)^2$	**8**	$3h^4 \times 2h^3$
2	$(b^3)^2$	**6**	$f \times f^2 \times f^3$	**9**	$j^5 \div j^4$
3	$c^5 \div c^3$	**7**	$g^4 \div g^4$	**10**	$3k^6 \div k^2$
4	$d^5 \times d^4$				

5. Remove the brackets in these expressions

   1 $2(3a - 5)$ **4** $5e(e^2 - e + 2)$

   2 $3(6b + 5c)$ **5** $3(f^2 - 18f + 4)$

   3 $4d(d + 1)$

6. Simplify

   1 $5a + (-2a)$ **6** $(-3f) - (-f)$

   2 $b - (+2b)$ **7** $g + (-g)$

   3 $(-4c) - (-9c)$ **8** $(+2h) - (-5h)$

   4 $(-2d) + (-d)$ **9** $5x + (-6x) - (+2x)$

   5 $7e + (+2e)$ **10** $(-7x) + (+9x) - (-3x)$

7. Simplify

   1 $8x \times 2y$ **5** $(-6x) \div 6x$ **8** $(-5) \div (-5x)$

   2 $(-4x) \times 7y$ **6** $3 \times (-2xy)$ **9** $(-2x)^2$

   3 $(+2x) \div (-3x)$ **7** $(-6) \times 4x^2$ **10** $0 \times (-3xy)$

   4 $(-3x) \times (-9x)$

8. Simplify

   1 $2(a + 2b) + (a - b)$ **6** $5(p - 2q - r) + 3(p - q + 2r)$

   2 $4(c - d) - 3(c + 2d)$ **7** $3(s + 8) - 4(2s - 5)$

   3 $3(2e + f) + 2(e - 2f)$ **8** $x(x - 4) + 3(x - 2)$

   4 $(g - h) - 4(g + 2h)$ **9** $x(2x + 3) - 4(3x - 1)$

   5 $2j + 3k - (j - 3k)$ **10** $x(x^2 + 1) - x^2(x + 1)$

9. If $a = 5$, $b = 3$ and $c = 1$, find the values of

   1 $4a + b$ **4** $\dfrac{a + c}{b - c}$

   2 $a^2 + b^2$

   3 $2a^2$ **5** $(3a - 5c)^2$

10. If $p = 4$, $q = -2$, $r = 3$, find the values of

   1 $p + q$ **7** $4r - 3q$

   2 $4p + 3q$ **8** $4r^2 - 3q^2$

   3 $r - q$ **9** $\dfrac{p + r}{7q}$

   4 $8pqr$

   5 $p^2 + 4r^2$ **10** $q(2p + r)$

   6 $\dfrac{p}{.q}$

11. The formula for the sum, s, of the cubes of the numbers from 1 to n is $s = \frac{1}{4}n^2(n+1)^2$. Use this formula to find the value of $1^3 + 2^3 + 3^3 + \ldots + 10^3$.

12. The formula to convert Fahrenheit temperatures to Celsius temperatures is
$C = \frac{5}{9}(F - 32).$

Find the value of C
1   when $F = 95$.
2   when $F = -22$.

Solving equations

You can add equal numbers to both sides.

You can subtract equal numbers from both sides.

You can multiply both sides by the same number.

You can divide both sides by the same number, (not 0).

Examples

1   $x + 10 = 17$
Subtract 10 from both sides.
$x = 7$

2   $x - 8 = 5$
Add 8 to both sides.
$x = 13$

3   $5x = 16$
Divide both sides by 5.
$x = 3\frac{1}{5}$

4   $\dfrac{x}{4} = 5$
Multiply both sides by 4.
$x = 20$

5 $13x - 20 = 6x + 8$

Subtract $6x$ from both sides.

   $7x - 20 = 8$

Add 20 to both sides.

       $7x = 28$

Divide both sides by 7.

        $x = 4$

To check the equation, substitute $x = 4$ into both sides of the equation separately.
The two sides should be equal.
Left-hand side (LHS) $= 13x - 20 = (13 \times 4) - 20 = 52 - 20 = 32$.
RHS $= 6x + 8 = (6 \times 4) + 8 = 24 + 8 = 32$.
The two sides are both 32, so the equation checks.

If you are not required to do a check as part of the answer, do it at the side of your
work, as rough working, or even mentally.

6 $3(x + 11) = 24 - 4(x + 3)$
         $3x + 33 = 24 - 4x - 12$
             $7x = -21$
              $x = -3$

To check the equation, substitute $x = -3$ into both sides of the equation separately.
LHS $= 3(x + 11) = 3(-3 + 11) = 3 \times 8 = 24$
RHS $= 24 - 4(x + 3) = 24 - 4(-3 + 3) = 24 - 4 \times 0 = 24$
The two sides are both 24, so the equation checks.

7 $\dfrac{2x + 3}{5} = 4$

Multiply both sides by 5.
$2x + 3 = 20$
Subtract 3 from both sides.
   $2x = 17$
Divide both sides by 2.
    $x = 8\frac{1}{2}$

As a check, LHS $= \dfrac{2x + 3}{5} = \dfrac{\left(2 \times 8\frac{1}{2}\right) + 3}{5} = \dfrac{17 + 3}{5} = \dfrac{20}{5} = 4$. RHS $= 4$.

The two sides are both 4, so the equation checks.

Exercise 7.2

1. Solve these equations

   1 $a - 7 = 14$
   2 $b + 17 = 36$
   3 $7c = 56$
   4 $\dfrac{d}{7} = 20$
   5 $11e - 6 = 71$

   6 $2f + 3 = 17$
   7 $g + 3g = 24$
   8 $3h = 90 - h$
   9 $j - 5 = 0$
   10 $15 - k = 12$

2. Solve these equations

   1 $3a + 1 = 13 - a$
   2 $16 - 4b = 0$
   3 $12c - 5 = 15 + 8c$
   4 $2d + 7 = 31 - 4d$
   5 $3(e + 2) - e = 26$

   6 $4(2f - 6) + 3(f + 5) = 35$
   7 $\frac{1}{4}(g - 2) = 6$
   8 $\dfrac{h + 7}{4} = 5$
   9 $\frac{1}{5}j - 6 = 8$
   10 $8k - 5 = 2k + 43$

3. Solve the equations

   1 $3(2x - 5) - 4(x + 7) = 13$
   2 $5(x + 3) + (x - 5) = 9$
   3 $2(5 + x) - 3(6 - x) = 42$

   4 $5(x - 1) + 3(x - 4) = -11$
   5 $22 - 5x - (x + 10) = 0$

4. Carol's father was 24 years old when Carol was born. Now he is four times as old as Carol. How old is Carol now ?
   (Let Carol be x years old, write down an equation and solve it.)

5. **1** Write down an equation involving x and solve it to find the value of x.

   2 Write down an equation involving y and solve it to find the value of y.

   3 Write down an equation involving z and solve it to find the value of z.

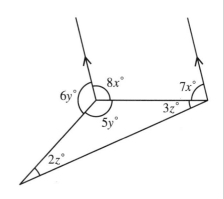

Solving equations by trial and improvement methods

An equation such as $5x - 8 = 22$ is called a **linear** equation.

Equations can include powers of x, such as x^2, x^3 or higher powers.

An equation such as $x^2 - 5x + 3 = 0$, with highest power x^2, is called a **quadratic** equation. A quadratic equation can have 2, 1 or 0 solutions.

An equation such as $x^3 - 5x^2 + 3x + 7 = 0$, with highest power x^3, is called a **cubic** equation. A cubic equation can have 3, 2 or 1 solutions.

Example

1   Solve the equation $x^3 - 3x = 52$, given that the solution is a positive number.

Write this as $x^3 - 3x - 52 = 0$.
Make a table of values.

x	0	1	2	3	4	5	6
x^3 $-3x$ -52	0 0 -52	1 -3 -52	8 -6 -52	27 -9 -52	64 -12 -52	125 -15 -52	216 -18 -52
$x^3 - 3x - 52$	-52	-54	-50	-34	0	58	146

The solution is $x = 4$.

From looking at the table it seems unlikely that there will be another solution with x positive.

Equations whose solutions are not whole numbers

Examples

2   Solve the equation $2x^2 = 5x + 10$, correct to 1 decimal place, finding the positive solution.

Rewrite the equation as $2x^2 - 5x - 10 = 0$.
Make a table of values.

x	0	1	2	3	4	5
x^2	0	1	4	9	16	25
$2x^2$ $-5x$ -10	0 0 -10	2 -5 -10	8 -10 -10	18 -15 -10	32 -20 -10	50 -25 -10
$2x^2 - 5x - 10$	-10	-13	-12	-7	2	15

When $x = 3$, $2x^2 - 5x - 10 = -7$ (negative)
When $x = 4$, $2x^2 - 5x - 10 = 2$ (positive)
So the value of $2x^2 - 5x - 10$ will be 0 somewhere between $x = 3$ and $x = 4$ (and probably nearer to 4 than to 3).

We now use trial and improvement methods to find the solution correct to 1 decimal place.
Find the value of the function when $x = 3.7$, using your calculator. (We chose 3.7 because we think the solution is greater than 3.5.)
We can set the working down in the table of values, but it is probably just as easy to work it out in one stage.
Press 2 $\boxed{\times}$ 3.7 $\boxed{x^2}$ $\boxed{-}$ 5 $\boxed{\times}$ 3.7 $\boxed{-}$ 10 $\boxed{=}$ and you will get -1.12, which is negative.
Now we know that the solution is between $x = 3.7$ and $x = 4$.

Try $x = 3.8$ next.
Using your calculator, you will get -0.12, still negative.
Now we know that the solution is between $x = 3.8$ and $x = 4$, and seems quite near to $x = 3.8$.

Trying $x = 3.9$ gives the value 0.92, which is positive.
So now we know that the solution is between $x = 3.8$ and $x = 3.9$.
Since we want the answer correct to 1 decimal place, we want to know whether it is nearer to 3.8 or to 3.9. So we find the value of the function for x halfway between 3.8 and 3.9, i.e. for $x = 3.85$.
The value is found to be 0.395, which is positive.

So the solution is between $x = 3.8$ and $x = 3.85$, and correct to 1 decimal place it is $x = 3.8$.

If you wanted the solution correct to 2 decimal places you would have to continue using this method, trying (say) 3.82 next. To 2 decimal places the solution is $x = 3.81$.

3   Solve the equation $x^3 + 3x - 20 = 0$, correct to 1 decimal place, given that the solution is a positive number.

Make a table of values.

x	0	1	2	3	4	5
x^3	0	1	8	27	64	125
$3x$	0	3	6	9	12	15
-20	-20	-20	-20	-20	-20	-20
$x^3 + 3x - 20$	-20	-16	-6	16	56	120

The table shows that there will be a value 0 somewhere between $x = 2$ and $x = 3$, and probably nearer to 2 than to 3.

Find the value of the function when $x = 2.3$.

Press 2.3 $\boxed{y^x}$ 3 $\boxed{+}$ 3 $\boxed{\times}$ 2.3 $\boxed{-}$ 20 $\boxed{=}$ and you will get -0.933, which is negative. Try $x = 2.4$ and you will get 1.024, which is positive. So the solution is between $x = 2.3$ and $x = 2.4$.

Since we want the answer correct to 1 decimal place, we find the value of the function when $x = 2.35$. This is 0.028, which is positive.

So the solution lies between $x = 2.3$ and $x = 2.35$, and correct to 1 decimal place it is $x = 2.3$.

Exercise 7.3

1. Solve these quadratic equations by trial, finding solutions which are positive whole numbers.

   1 $x^2 - x = 30$
   2 $x^2 + 4x = 21$
   3 $x^2 - 7x + 6 = 0$ (2 solutions)

   4 $x^2 = 8x - 15$ (2 solutions)
   5 $3x^2 + 8 = 14x$

2. Solve these cubic equations by trial, finding solutions which are positive whole numbers.

   1 $x^3 - x^2 - x = 95$
   2 $x^3 = 10x - 3$
   3 $x^3 = x^2 + 5x - 6$

   4 $x^3 - x^2 = 14x + 30$
   5 $(x + 1)(x + 2)(x - 2) = 60$

3. Solve these equations by trial and improvement, finding solutions which are positive numbers, correct to 1 decimal place.

   1 $x^2 - 2x = 18$
   2 $2x^2 + x = 5$
   3 $x^2 - 4x - 3 = 0$
   4 $x^3 - x^2 = 56$
   5 $x^3 + x = 59$

   6 $x^3 - x - 2 = 0$
   7 $x^3 = 2x + 100$
   8 $2x^2 = x + 85$
   9 $x^3 + 6x = 29$
   10 $x^2 - 10 = 8x$

4. Ann is 4 years older than Bobby. The sum of the squares of their ages is 400. Find their ages.

5.   If a stone is thrown vertically upwards with a velocity of u m/s, its height, s metres, above the ground after t seconds is given by the formula $s = ut - 5t^2$.
      How long does it take, to the nearest 0.1 s, for a stone thrown upwards with a velocity of 20 m/s to reach a height of 17.5 m above the ground ?

Sequences

By looking at the pattern of the numbers in a sequence we can find an expression for the nth term.

To find the expression for the nth term if the terms of the sequence increase by a constant number.

e.g. 3, 8, 13, 18, ... goes up by 5 each time.
The nth term will include a term $5n$.
In fact, it is $5n - 2$.

If the sequence decreases by a constant number:

e.g. 28, 25, 22, 19, ... goes down by 3 each time.
The nth term will include a term $-3n$.
In fact, it is $31 - 3n$.

For other sequences, look for patterns including squares, 1, 4, 9, 16; cubes, 1, 8, 27; powers, e.g. powers of 2; 2, 4, 8, 16, $(2, 2^2, 2^3, 2^4)$; and so on.

You can use the expression for the nth term to find any term of the sequence.

Example

The nth term of a sequence is $\dfrac{n}{2n + 1}$

The 1st term is $\dfrac{1}{(2 \times 1) + 1} = \frac{1}{3}$

The 2nd term is $\dfrac{2}{(2 \times 2) + 1} = \frac{2}{5}$

The 3rd term is $\dfrac{3}{(2 \times 3) + 1} = \frac{3}{7}$

The 10th term is $\dfrac{10}{(2 \times 10) + 1} = \frac{10}{21}$

and so on, for any term.

You can use a computer program to generate many such terms quickly, and perhaps make some discoveries about the patterns.

Exercise 7.4

1. Write down the next 2 terms in these sequences, and find an expression for the *n*th term.

   1 3, 7, 11, 15, ...
   2 16, 15, 14, 13, ...
   3 10, 13, 16, 19, ...
   4 95, 90, 85, 80, ...
   5 $1, \frac{1}{2}, \frac{1}{3}, \frac{1}{4}, \ldots$

   6 2, 9, 28, 65, 126, ...
   7 15, 5, −5, −15, ...
   8 0, 2, 6, 12, 20, ...
   9 $\frac{1}{3}, \frac{2}{4}, \frac{3}{5}, \frac{4}{6}, \ldots$
   10 11, 14, 19, 26, ...

2. These expressions are the *n*th terms of sequences. By putting $n = 1, 2, 3$ and 4 in turn, write down the 1st 4 terms of each sequence.

   1 $3n - 1$
   2 $100 - 10n$
   3 $n^2 + 1$
   4 10^n
   5 $n(n + 2)$

   6 3^n
   7 $\dfrac{n}{n + 1}$
   8 $n^3 - 1$

Exercise 7.5 Applications

1. If £*p* is shared equally among *q* children, how much, in pence, do they each receive ?

2. If a clock gains *s* seconds per hour, and it is set to the right time, how many minutes fast will it be *t* days later ?

3. For this video recorder, find a formula
   for the amount, £*A*, paid after *n* months,
   where *n* is less than or equal to 12.
   What is the total amount paid for the recorder ?

Deposit £60
£25 per month
for 12 months

4. Simplify   **1** $a + a$ **2** $a - a$ **3** $a \times a$ **4** $a \div a$ **5** $\sqrt{a^2}$

5. Simplify   **1** $5a^7 \times 4a^6$ **2** $27b^5 \div 9b$ **3** $\dfrac{(c^4)^2 \times c^5}{c^{12}}$

6. Simplify

    1 $4(x-4)-3(x-5)$ **4** $8(1+x)+12(1-x)$

    2 $x-2(x+y)+3(x-y)$ **5** $4(3x-1)-3(x+2)$

    3 $2(1+3x)-3(5-x)$

7. If $p=1$, $q=2$, $r=3$ and $s=0$, find the values of

    1 $5p+2q-r+s$ **5** $\dfrac{p^2+q^2+r^2+s^2}{2pq}$ **8** $\frac{1}{2}(2pq+3qr-4rs)$

    2 $r-(p+q)$ **9** $\sqrt{6pqr}$

    3 $\dfrac{2p+5q+2s}{4r}$ **6** $(2r-q)(2q-p)$ **10** $(q+3r)^2-p^2$

    4 $2r^2+q^3+2ps$ **7** $\dfrac{q}{r}-\dfrac{p}{q}+\dfrac{s}{p}$

8. If $a=1$ and $b=-1$, find the values of

    1 $5(a+b)$ **4** a^3-b^3

    2 $6b-4a$ **5** $2a^2+3b^2$

    3 $(a-b)^3$

9. A formula to find velocity is $v=u+at$. Find the value of v when $u=7.5$, $a=-3$ and $t=2.5$.

10. A formula to find kinetic energy is $E=\frac{1}{2}mv^2$. Find E when $m=8$ and $v=-3$.

11. Solve the equations

    1 $3x-7=2$ **6** $3-x=6+2x$

    2 $2x+17=3$ **7** $6(x+1)-10=-4$

    3 $\dfrac{x}{2}-6=-10$ **8** $3-3x=13-2x$

                                  9 $3(x-3)=x+6$

    4 $15x-4=3x-12$ **10** $5x-x=1$

    5 $3(1-2x)=12$

12. Solve the equations

    1 $4(x+3)-2(x-9)=24$ **4** $3(x+2)+2(x-4)=x-3(x+3)$

    2 $4(x-4)-2(x+7)=0$ **5** $x(2x+5)-(x-2)=2x(x+5)$

    3 $2(3x-4)+(x+8)=2(x-4)$

13. 20 paperback books are bought, some costing £1.80 each and the others costing £3.20 each. The total cost was £54.20. How many of the cheaper kind were there? (Let there be x at £1.80 and $(20-x)$ at £3.20.)

14. (In each part of this question write down an equation involving x, and solve it.)

1 The three angles of a triangle are $(x + 25)°$, $(x + 35)°$ and $2x°$. Find x. What is the size of the largest angle ?

2
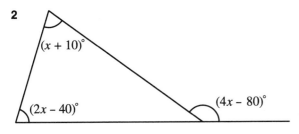

3
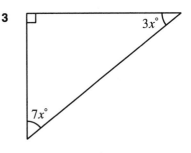

Find x. What sort of triangle is it ?

Find x.

15. Write down two equations, one involving x, the other involving y, and solve them.
Hence find the numerical values of the lengths of the sides of this parallelogram.

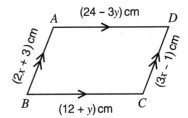

Use trial and improvement methods in questions 16, 17, 18.

16. A polygon with n sides has $\dfrac{n(n-3)}{2}$ diagonals. How many sides has a polygon with 65 diagonals ?

17. The perimeter of a rectangular field is 220 m. Find an expression for the breadth in terms of the length x m.
If the area of the field is 2800 m^2, find its length.

18. There are 12 containers of cuboid shape with length and width x m and height 5 m, and one cubical container of edge x m. Find the value of x, to 1 decimal place, if the total capacity of the containers is 360 m^3.

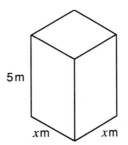
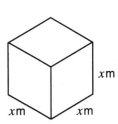

19. Write down the next 3 terms in these sequences, and find an expression for the nth term.

1 11, 19, 27, 35, ...
2 2, 4, 8, 16, ...
3 21, 17, 13, 9, ...

20.   These matchstick patterns form sequences. For each one, draw the next pattern, write
      down the next 3 terms of the sequence, and find an expression for the *n*th term.

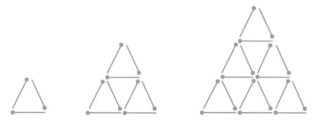

   1   Number of small triangles, 1, 4, 9, ...
   2   Number of matches used, 3, 9, 18, ...

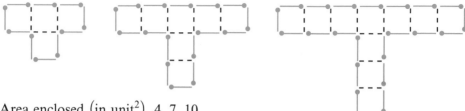

   3   Area enclosed $\left(\text{in unit}^2\right)$, 4, 7, 10, ...
   4   Number of matches used, 10, 16, 22, ...

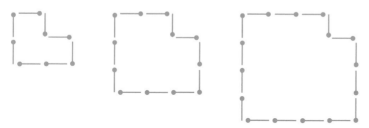

   5   Number of matches used, 8, 12, 16, ...
   6   Area enclosed, 3, 8, 15, ...

Practice test 7

1.   If *k* lb of apples are bought for *x* pence per lb and sold for *y* pence per lb, what is the
      profit in £'s ?

2.   The time taken to cook a chicken is given as 20 minutes per lb plus 20 minutes extra.
      Find a formula for the time, *T* hours, needed for a chicken weighing *c* lb.

3.　Simplify　**1** $3a^3 + 4a^3$　　**2** $3a^3 \times 4a^3$　　**3** $3a^3 \div 4a^3$

4.　Simplify　$2(2x + y) + 3(2x - y)$

5.　A formula used to find gradients of lines is $m = \dfrac{a - b}{1 + ab}$.

Find the values of m when
1　$a = 4, b = 1,$
2　$a = -2, b = -1.$

6.　Solve the equations

1　$3 + 5x = 11 + x$
2　$7 + 2x = 13 - 3x$
3　$5x + 10 = 0$

4　$\dfrac{4x}{5} = 8$
5　$5(3x + 1) - 3(2x + 1) = 50$

7.　I think of a number, multiply it by 5 and add 28. The result is 5 less than eight times the original number.
Write down an equation, letting x be the original number, and solve it. What number did I start with ?

8.　Use angle properties to write down an equation involving x and hence find the value of x in the following figures.

1

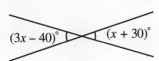

$(3x - 40)°$　　　$(x + 30)°$

2

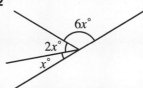

$6x°$
$2x°$
$x°$

9.　Solve these equations by trial, finding solutions which are positive numbers.

1　$(x + 3)(x - 2) = 84,$

2　$x^3 + 6x = 29,$ correct to 1 decimal place.

10.　Write down the next 3 terms in these sequences, and find an expression for the nth term.

1　$8, 5, 2, -1, \ldots$　　　　　　　　　**2**　$\frac{1}{4}, \frac{2}{5}, \frac{3}{6}, \frac{4}{7}, \ldots$

Lengths, areas and volumes

The topics in this chapter include:

- using Pythagoras' theorem,
- length, area and volume calculations,
- distinguishing between formulae by considering dimensions.

A theorem is a mathematical statement which can be proved to be true.

Pythagoras' theorem

Pythagoras' theorem states that:

In a right-angled triangle, the area of the square on the hypotenuse is equal to the sum of the areas of the squares on the other two sides.

$$a^2 = b^2 + c^2$$

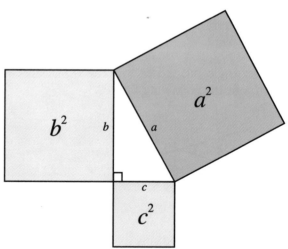

Here, because it is simpler, we have labelled the sides, using small letters, instead of labelling the vertices of the triangle.

a^2 means the area of the square with side a, and in this diagram, side a is the hypotenuse (the side opposite to the right angle).
b^2 means the area of the square with side b.
c^2 means the area of the square with side c.

Although the theorem is about areas of squares on the sides of the triangles, we use it mainly for calculating lengths of sides of right-angled triangles.

Examples

1   To find a.

$a^2 = b^2 + c^2$

$\quad = 8^2 + 5^2 \quad (a \text{ in cm})$

$\quad = 64 + 25 = 89$

$a = \sqrt{89}$ cm

$\quad = 9.4$ cm, to the nearest mm.

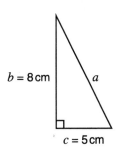

You can find the square root using your calculator. Since you know that $9^2 = 81$ and $10^2 = 100$, you know that $\sqrt{89}$ is a number between 9 and 10, so you can make a rough check of your answer.

(If you do not have to set down your working, you can do the whole calculation in one step on your calculator.

Press 8 $\boxed{x^2}$ $\boxed{+}$ 5 $\boxed{x^2}$ $\boxed{=}$ $\boxed{\sqrt{}}$ and you will get 9.43 ...)

We can use the result of Pythagoras' theorem to find the length of one of the other sides.

2   Find b.

Notice that c is the hypotenuse.

$c^2 = a^2 + b^2$

$30^2 = 10^2 + b^2 \quad (b \text{ in cm})$

$900 = 100 + b^2$

$b^2 = 800$

$b = \sqrt{800}$ cm

$\quad = 28.3$ cm, to the nearest mm.

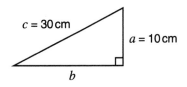

Triangle *ABC*

A triangle can have the vertices labelled by capital letters, as usual.
In this triangle, BC is the hypotenuse.

$$BC^2 = AB^2 + AC^2$$

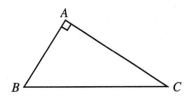

Example

3   If, in this triangle, $AB = 2.6$ cm and $BC = 3.5$ cm, calculate AC.

Notice that the hypotenuse is BC.

$$BC^2 = AB^2 + AC^2$$

$$3.5^2 = 2.6^2 + AC^2 \quad (AC \text{ in cm})$$

$$12.25 = 6.76 + AC^2$$

$$AC^2 = 5.49$$

$$AC = \sqrt{5.49} \text{ cm}$$

$$= 2.3 \text{ cm, to the nearest mm.}$$

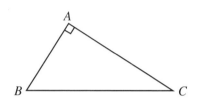

If we want to use small letters for sides, we use
a for the side opposite $\angle A$ (the side BC),
b for the side opposite $\angle B$ (the side AC), and
c for the side opposite $\angle C$ (the side AB).

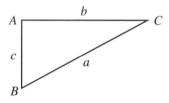

There are certain groups of numbers which give exact answers, and it is useful to learn the ones which involve small numbers.

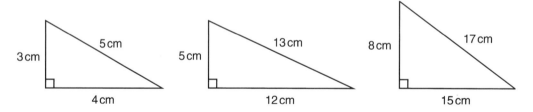

There are many others, including multiples of these numbers such as 6, 8, 10;   10, 24, 26; 30, 40, 50;   ...

Exercise 8.1

Give answers which are not exact correct to the nearest mm.

1.   Find the hypotenuse, a, in these triangles.
      1    $b = 5$ cm, $c = 10$ cm
      2    $b = 6$ cm, $c = 8$ cm
      3    $b = 1$ cm, $c = 2$ cm
      4    $b = 7$ cm, $c = 4$ cm
      5    $b = \sqrt{7}$ cm, $c = 3$ cm

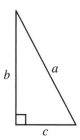

2.   Find the third side in these triangles.

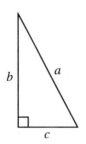

1 $b = 8$ cm, $a = 17$ cm
2 $b = 6$ cm, $a = 9$ cm
3 $c = 24$ cm, $a = 25$ cm
4 $c = 5$ cm, $a = 6$ cm
5 $c = 7$ cm, $a = 11$ cm

3.   Find the lengths of sides x and y.

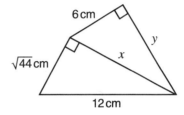

4.   Find the lengths of

1 BD,
2 BC,
3 AC.

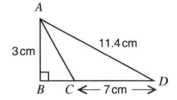

5. AB is a chord 24 cm long, in a circle centre O. C is the mid-point of AB and $\angle OCA = 90°$. The radius of the circle is 13 cm.
Find the length of OC.

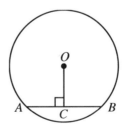

Perimeters

The perimeter of a plane figure is the total length of the edges.

The perimeter of a rectangle $= 2 \times$ (length $+$ breadth)
$$= 2(l + b)$$

Areas

Area of a rectangle = length × breadth = lb

Area of a square = (length)^2 = l^2

Area of a triangle = $\frac{1}{2}$ × base × perpendicular height = $\frac{1}{2}bh$

Area of a parallelogram = base × perpendicular height = bh

Area of a trapezium = $\frac{1}{2}$ × sum of the parallel sides × the perpendicular distance between them

$$= \frac{1}{2}(a+b)h$$

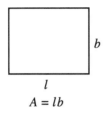

$A = lb$

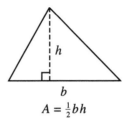

$A = \frac{1}{2}bh$

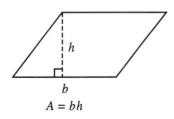

$A = bh$

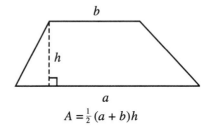

$A = \frac{1}{2}(a+b)h$

Examples

1   **Rectangle**

    Perimeter = $2(l+b)$

             = $2 × (10+8)$ cm

             = $2 × 18$ cm = 36 cm

      Area = lb

           = $10 × 8$ cm^2

           = 80 cm^2

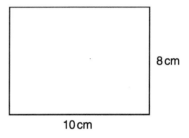

2 Triangle

Area $= \frac{1}{2}bh$

$\quad = \frac{1}{2} \times 10 \times 6$ cm^2

$\quad = 30$ cm^2

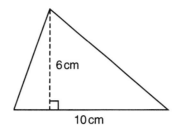

6 cm

10 cm

3 Parallelogram

Area $= bh$

$\quad = 9 \times 5$ cm^2

$\quad = 45$ cm^2

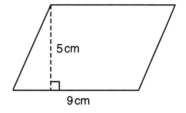

5 cm

9 cm

4 Trapezium

Area $= \frac{1}{2}(a+b)h$

$\quad = \frac{1}{2} \times (11+7) \times 8$ cm^2

$\quad = \frac{1}{2} \times 18 \times 8$ cm$^2 = 72$ cm^2

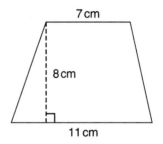

7 cm

8 cm

11 cm

Exercise 8.2

1. Find the areas of these figures.

1

11 cm

Square

2

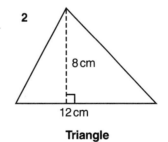

8 cm

12 cm

Triangle

3

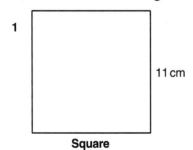

7 cm

11 cm

Parallelogram

4

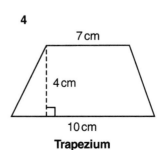

7 cm

4 cm

10 cm

Trapezium

2. Find the area of this trapezium.

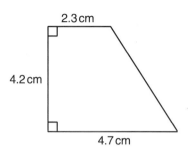

3. The area of a rectangle is 54.4 cm². Its breadth is 6.4 cm.
Find
1 the length of the rectangle,
2 the perimeter.

4. Find the total area of the quadrilateral *ABCD*.

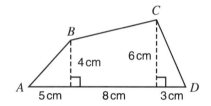

5. 1 Find the area of this parallelogram.
   2 Find the value of *x*.

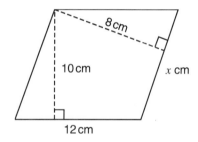

6. If the perimeter of a square is 36 cm, what is its area ?

7. Find the area and perimeter of a rectangular lawn 7 m long and 4 m wide.

8. A rectangle $9\frac{1}{2}$ cm by 6 cm is cut out of the corner of a square piece of paper of side 12 cm. What area is left ? What is the perimeter of the piece that is left ?

9. *ABCD* is a square of side 8 cm. Find the areas of the four triangles, and hence find the area of the quadrilateral *PQRS*.

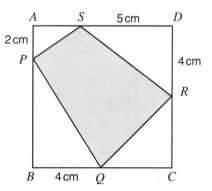

Surface areas

The surface area of a solid figure is the sum of the areas of all the faces.
A **cuboid** has 6 rectangular faces.

Volumes

> Volume of a cuboid = length × breadth × height = lbh
>
> Volume of a cube = (length)^3 = l^3
>
> Volume of a prism = area of cross-section × height

(The formula for the volume of a prism applies to any solid of uniform cross-section.
The height is sometimes expressed as 'length'.)

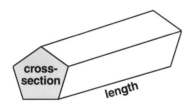

Examples

1   **Cuboid**

Volume = lbh

$= 10 \times 8 \times 5 \,\text{cm}^3$

$= 400 \,\text{cm}^3$

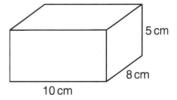

Total area of surfaces $= 2 \times [(10 \times 8) + (10 \times 5) + (8 \times 5)] \,\text{cm}^2$

$= 2 \times (80 + 50 + 40) \,\text{cm}^2 = 340 \,\text{cm}^2$

Total length of its edges $= 4 \times (10 + 8 + 5) \,\text{cm} = 92 \,\text{cm}$

2   Prism

Find the volume of this prism.

Area of triangle $= \frac{1}{2}bh$

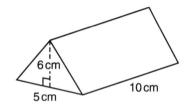

$$= \frac{1}{2} \times 5 \times 6 \text{ cm}^2$$

$$= 15 \text{ cm}^2$$

Volume of prism = area of triangle × length

$$= 15 \times 10 \text{ cm}^3$$

$$= 150 \text{ cm}^3$$

Exercise 8.3

1.   Find the volumes of these figures.

   1   A rectangular box 12 cm by 10 cm by 5 cm.
   2   A cube of edge 5 cm.
   3   A rectangular room 5 m by 4 m with height $2\frac{1}{2}$ m.
   4   A matchbox 7.5 cm by 4 cm by 1.5 cm.
   5   A case 50 cm by 30 cm by 18 cm.

2.   This swimming pool is 1.8 m deep.
      Find the volume of water which
      it will hold.

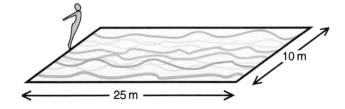

3.   The end of this prism is a right-angled triangle.
      1   Find the area of the triangle.
      2   Find the volume of the prism.

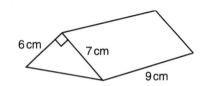

4.   This sketch shows the side of a shed.
      1   Find its area.
      2   Find the volume of the shed, if it is
              4 m long.

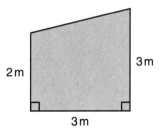

5.   What is the surface area of a solid cube whose volume is $27 \, \text{cm}^3$?

6.   If a large rectangular room has length $9 \, \text{m}$, breadth $8 \, \text{m}$ and its volume is $360 \, \text{m}^3$, what is its height ?

Circles and cylinders

The perimeter of a circle is called the circumference.

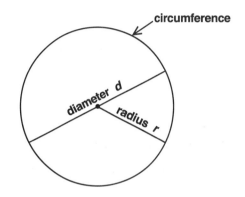

Circumference $= \pi \times$ diameter $= 2 \times \pi \times$ radius

$$C = \pi d$$

$$C = 2\pi r$$

Area of a circle $= \pi \times (\text{radius})^2$

$$A = \pi r^2$$

A **cylinder** has two circular ends and a curved surface.

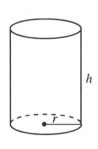

The area of the curved surface of a cylinder $= 2 \times \pi \times$ radius $\times$ height

$$S = 2\pi r h$$

Volume of a cylinder $= \pi \times (\text{radius})^2 \times$ height

$$V = \pi r^2 h.$$

π (pi) is the Greek letter which represents the special number 3.14159... used in circle formulae. This number cannot be written exactly. For practical purposes it is usually sufficient to use 3.14 or 3.142 but if there is a $\boxed{\pi}$ key on your calculator it is quicker to use that. Do not leave more than 3 or 4 significant figures in the final answer.

e.g. For 6π press $6 \boxed{\times} \boxed{\pi} \boxed{=}$ getting 18.849 ...

To 3 significant figures this is 18.8

For $\dfrac{\pi}{2}$ press $\boxed{\pi} \boxed{\div} 2 \boxed{=}$ getting 1.5707 ...

To 3 significant figures this is 1.57.

Examples

1   Find the circumference of a circle with radius 25 cm.

$C = 2\pi r$

$\quad = 2 \times \pi \times 25 \text{ cm}$

$\quad = 157.07\ldots \text{ cm}$

$\quad = 157 \text{ cm, to 3 sig. fig.}$

2   Find the area of a circle with radius 4 cm.

$A = \pi r^2$

$\quad = \pi \times 4^2 \text{ cm}^2$

$\quad = 50.26\ldots \text{ cm}^2$

$\quad = 50.3 \text{ cm}^2, \text{ to 3 sig. fig.}$

3   Find the curved surface area of a cylinder, radius 4 cm, height 10 cm.

Curved surface area $= 2\pi rh$

$\qquad\qquad\qquad = 2 \times \pi \times 4 \times 10 \text{ cm}^2$

$\qquad\qquad\qquad = 251.32\ldots \text{ cm}^2$

$\qquad\qquad\qquad = 251 \text{ cm}^2, \text{ to 3 sig. fig.}$

4   Find the volume of a cylinder, radius 2.5 cm, height 6.5 cm.

Volume $= \pi r^2 h$

$\qquad = \pi \times 2.5^2 \times 6.5 \text{ cm}^3$

$\qquad = 127.62\ldots \text{ cm}^3$

$\qquad = 128 \text{ cm}^3, \text{ to 3 sig. fig.}$

Exercise 8.4

Take π as 3.142 or use the π key on your calculator, and give approximate answers correct to 3 significant figures.

1.   Find the lengths of the circumferences and the areas of these circles.
    1   Radius 14 cm.   **3**   Diameter 2 m.
    2   Radius 6 cm.   **4**   Radius 4.5 cm.

2. **1** Find the volume of a cylinder with radius 3 cm, height 7 cm.
    2 Find the area of the curved surface of a cylinder with radius 15 cm, height 40 cm.
    3 Find the volume of a cylinder with diameter 5.6 cm, height 10 cm.
    4 Find the area of the curved surface of a circular metal pipe with length 1 m and diameter 10 cm.

3. The circle is inscribed in a square of side 6 cm.
    Find the total shaded area.

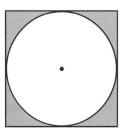

4. Find the outside curved surface area of a cylindrical storage tank with diameter 5.8 m and height 3.2 m.

5. The perpendicular height, h, of a cone is 16 cm.
    The slant height, l, of the cone is 16.4 cm.
    Find the radius, r, of the base, and hence find
    the area of the base of the cone.

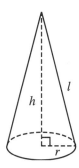

6. 6 cylindrical tins with radius 5 cm and height 10 cm are packed in a rectangular box with measurements 30 cm by 20 cm by 10 cm. The space around the tins is filled with sawdust for packing. What is the volume of the space to be filled with sawdust ?

7. A square has a side of 1.7 cm and a circle has radius 1 cm. Which has the greater   **1** perimeter,   **2** area,   and by how much ?

Area units

$$100 \, mm^2 = 1 \, cm^2$$

$$10\,000 \, cm^2 = 1 \, m^2$$

$$1\,000\,000 \, m^2 = 1 \, km^2$$

Volume units

$$1000 \, mm^3 = 1 \, cm^3$$

$$1\,000\,000 \, cm^3 = 1 \, m^3$$

Units in formulae

To find a length, e.g. a perimeter, you use **length** units such as cm, m or km.
Any formula to find a length only involves units of length, and **has** to involve units of length.
Such formulae are said to be of dimension 1.

Examples are
$P = 2(l + b)$
$C = 2\pi r$

To find an area you use area units such as cm^2, m^2, km^2.
Any formula to find an area involves units of length × units of length.
Area formulae are of dimension 2.

Examples are
$A = lb$
$A = \pi r^2$
$S = 2lb + 2lh + 2bh$

To find a volume you use volume units such as cm^3, m^3.
Any formula to find a volume involves units of length × units of length × units of length,
or units of area × units of length.
Volume formulae are of dimension 3.

Examples are
$V = lbh$
$V =$ area of base × height
$V = \frac{4}{3}\pi r^3$

Formulae which involve combinations of these units such as $2\pi r + \pi r^2$, $lbh + 5r$, are not giving
either lengths, areas or volumes.
$2\pi r$ is a length formula because it involves r, in length units. It is of dimension 1.
πr^2 is an area formula because it involves r^2, in area units. It is of dimension 2.
$2\pi r + \pi r^2$ does not represent length or area.

lbh is a volume formula because it involves l, b, h, all lengths. It is of dimension 3.
$5r$ is a length formula because it involves r, in length units. It is of dimension 1.
$lbh + 5r$ does not represent volume or length.

A formula which involves area units ÷ length units will give a length.
e.g. Height of triangle $= \dfrac{2 \times \text{area}}{\text{base}}$

A formula which involves $\sqrt{\text{area units}}$ will give a length.

e.g. Radius of circle $= \sqrt{\dfrac{A}{\pi}}$

A formula which involves volume units $\div$ area units will give a length.

e.g. Height $= \dfrac{\text{volume of cylinder}}{\text{area of base}}$

A formula which involves $\sqrt[3]{\text{volume units}}$ will give a length.

e.g. Radius of sphere $= \sqrt[3]{\dfrac{3V}{4\pi}}$

A formula which involves volume units $\div$ length units will give an area.

e.g. Area of cross-section $= \dfrac{\text{volume}}{\text{height}}$

Exercise 8.5

1.   For these formulae, decide if X represents a length, area or volume.
     a, l, b, h, r are all lengths. A is an area and V is a volume.

   1 $X = 4\pi r^3$ **6** $X = \frac{1}{3}\pi r^2 h$ **11** $X = \dfrac{A}{h}$

        7 $X = Ah$

   2 $X = \dfrac{A}{\pi h}$ **8** $X = \pi ab$ **12** $X = \dfrac{V}{A}$

   3 $X = 2\pi r^2$ **9** $X = \dfrac{V}{\pi r h}$ **13** $X = \dfrac{l^3}{a}$

   4 $X = b + h$ **14** $X = \sqrt{2A}$

   5 $X = lb + \frac{1}{2}\pi r^2$ **10** $X = \dfrac{l^2 b}{A}$ **15** $X = \sqrt[3]{8V}$

2.   From this list of expressions, where p, q, r are lengths,

   $p^2 + 4pqr,$

   $\dfrac{pq}{r} + \sqrt{\pi r^2}\,,$

   $\pi p^3 + 2q^2 r\,,$

   $\dfrac{3pr}{q^3}\,,$

   $\dfrac{3pqr}{\sqrt{p^2 + q^2}}\,,$

   write down the expression which represents
   1 a length,   **2** an area,   **3** a volume.

3.   In this list of formulae, each one has an error.
      Explain how you can tell, by considering dimensions, why each one is wrong.
      r, b, h are lengths, A is an area.
      Write down the correct formulae.

      1   The volume of a cylinder. $V = \pi r^3 h$
      2   The height of a triangle. $h = 2Ab$
      3   The radius of a circle. $r = \dfrac{A}{\pi}$
      4   The volume of a prism. $V = Ah^2$
      5   The curved surface area of a cylinder. $S = 2\pi h$

Exercise 8.6   Applications

Take π as 3.142 or use the π key on your calculator, and give approximate answers correct to 3 significant figures.

1.   The longer side of a rectangular field is 52 m and a footpath crossing the field along a diagonal is 65 m long. Find the length of the shorter side of the field.

2.   A patrol boat goes 7 km South, then 8 km East, then 8 km South. Find how far it is, in a direct line, from its starting point.

3.   A gardener is making a rectangular concrete base for a greenhouse 7 feet wide and 24 feet long. Having measured out the edges he checks that it is truly rectangular by measuring both diagonals. How long should these diagonals be ?

4.   A ladder is 5.4 m long. The foot of the ladder is placed on horizontal ground 2.2 m from a vertical wall, and the ladder is leaning against the wall.
      How high up the wall will the ladder reach, to the nearest 0.1 m ?

5. O is the centre of a circle. The tangent
      PT is 24 cm long. The radius is 10 cm
      and $\angle OTP = 90°$.
      Find the length of OP and hence
      find the length of AP.

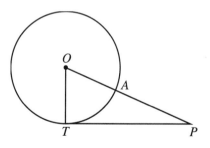

6. **The converse of Pythagoras' theorem**

If, in a triangle, $a^2 = b^2 + c^2$, then the angle
opposite side a is a right angle.

Which of these triangles are right-angled ?
1   The sides have lengths 3.5 cm, 12 cm, 12.5 cm.
2   The sides have lengths 4 cm, 5 cm, 6 cm.
3   The sides have lengths 2.4 cm, 7.0 cm, 7.4 cm.
4   The sides have lengths 1.1 cm, 6 cm, 6.1 cm.
5   The sides have lengths 9.1 cm, 9.1 cm, 12.8 cm.

7. A room 8 m by $7\frac{1}{2}$ m contains a carpet 6 m by $5\frac{1}{2}$ m.
    1   What is the area of the uncarpeted floor ?
    2   What is the cost of buying floor-covering for the uncarpeted floor at a cost of £8 per m^2 ?

8. A floor 12 m long and 7.5 m wide is to be covered by tiles 30 cm square. How many tiles
    will be needed ?
    If the tiles are sold in boxes of 24 how many boxes must be bought ?

9. There is a path 1 m wide all round a
    rectangular lawn of size 10 m by 8 m.
    Find the area of the path.

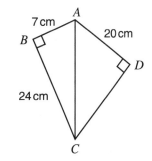

10. Find the area and the perimeter
    of this triangle.

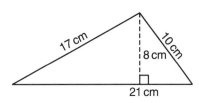

11. 1   Find the length of AC.
    2   Find the length of DC.
    3   Find the perimeter of $ABCD$.
    4   Find the area of $ABCD$.

12. Construct a triangle ABC with $AB = 9$ cm, $BC = 7.5$ cm and $AC = 6.5$ cm.
    Construct and measure an additional line needed to calculate the area of $\triangle ABC$, and
    find this area.

13. A child's sandpit is rectangular in shape, 2 m long and $1\frac{1}{2}$ m wide. What weight of sand is needed to fill it to a depth of 50 cm ? (Assume 1 m³ of sand weighs 1500 kg.)

14. The diagram shows the side of a swimming pool which slopes steadily from a depth of 1 m to 3 m. It is 25 m long.

    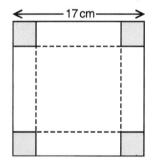

    1 Find the area of the side.
    2 The pool is 10 m wide. Find its volume.

15. The internal dimensions of the base of a rectangular tank are 2 m by 1 m and it can contain water to a depth of 80 cm. How long will it take to fill the tank by means of an inlet pipe delivering water at the rate of 50 litres per minute ?

16. Ice 10 cm thick covered a pond whose surface area is 300 m². Find the weight of the ice, if 1 m³ of ice weighs 920 kg.

17. A new road 4 km long and 25 m wide is to be constructed.

    1 How many square metres of land will be required ?
    2 If the soil has to be removed to a depth of 30 cm, how many cubic metres of soil will have to be removed ?

18. A square sheet of cardboard has sides of length 17 cm. Out of each corner a square of side 4 cm is cut, and the flaps remaining are turned up to form an open box of depth 4 cm. Find the volume of the box.

19. A circular pond of radius 2.6 m is surrounded by a circular path of width 40 cm.
    Find the area of the path
    1 in cm²,
    2 in m².

20. **1** If a circle has a circumference of 100 m, what is its radius ?

    2 If a circle has an area of 100 m², what is its radius ?

21. A cylinder, diameter 60 cm, contains water to a depth of 70 cm. This water is then poured into an empty rectangular tank 1.1 m long and 0.9 m wide. What will be the depth of water in this tank ?

22. For these formulae, decide if X represents a length, area, volume or none of these. a, b, c, h, r, s are lengths, A is an area and V is a volume.

    1 $X = \frac{1}{2}(a + b + c)$

    2 $X = \sqrt{s(s-a)(s-b)(s-c)}$

    3 $X = \dfrac{a^2 + b^2 + c^2}{abc}$

    4 $X = a^2 h$

    5 $X = \sqrt{\dfrac{V}{\pi h}}$

    6 $X = A + \pi b h$

    7 $X = \dfrac{V}{ab}$

    8 $X = \pi ab + h^3$

    9 $X = 2\pi r + 2r$

    10 $X = \dfrac{5(a+b)^2}{3a}$

Practice test 8

1. Find the lengths of
   1 AB,
   2 BC,
   3 AC.

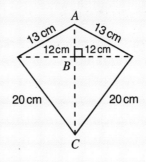

2. $ABCD$ is a square.
   Find the areas of
   1 $\triangle ABE$,
   2 $\triangle CEF$,
   3 $\triangle ADF$,
   4 $\triangle AEF$.

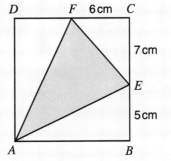

[Turn over]

3.   Find
      1   the area of $\triangle ABC$,
      2   the length of AC,
      3   the length of BX.

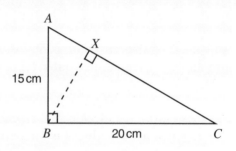

4.   Find the volume of this prism.

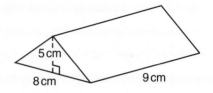

5.   A room is 4 m wide, 3 m long and $2\frac{1}{2}$ m high. What is the total area of the four walls ?

6.   A rectangular tank is 4 m long, $2\frac{1}{2}$ m wide and 3 m deep. How many cubic metres of water does it contain when it is half-full ?

7.   There is a circular running-track with diameter 35 m. How far has Peter run when he has made 10 complete circuits ?

8.   Some cylindrical tins have radius $3\frac{1}{2}$ cm and height 10 cm. Find the volume of a tin.
      The tins are packed in a rectangular box of length 28 cm, width 21 cm and height 10 cm. How many tins will fit in the box ?

9.   Look at the list of expressions below, where b, r, h are lengths.

      $b + 2\pi r$

      $\frac{1}{2} b^2 + \pi r^2 h$

      $b^2 + \pi r h$

      $b^3 + \pi b r$

      $\frac{1}{3} b^3 + \pi r^2 h$

      Write down the expression which represents

      1   a length,   **2**   an area,   **3**   a volume.

PUZZLE

19.   **A Cross-figure**

Across

1   Number of miles I can travel in
    24 minutes at 60 mph.
3   Number of diagonals of a parallelogram.
4   Number of mm in 1 cm.
5   Three angles of a quadrilateral are 16°,
    27° and 150°. What is the 4th angle ?
7   $\sqrt{\text{LXIV}}$
8   75% of (11 across) −40% of (4 across)
9   $(1\frac{3}{4} − 1\frac{1}{3}) \times 7.2$
10 The base of a triangle, in cm, if its
    height is 8 cm and its area is 20 cm².
11 *A* is south-west of *C*, *B* is on a bearing
    of 273° from *C*. What is the size of
    angle *ACB*, in degrees ?
12 Christine bought 2 tins of meat at 47p
    each. How much change, in pence, did she get from £1 ?
13 Number of days in a leap year + number of degrees in the angles of a triangle −
    number of sides of a triangle.
15 $3^2 + 4^2 + 5^2$
16 If the numbers 4 to 12 are placed in a magic square so that each row, column
    and diagonal add up to 24, what is the number in the centre square ?
17 An article cost £1.80 less a discount of 15%. What was the discount, in pence ?

Copy this diagram and fill in the answers on your copy.

Down

1   If 5 pumps all working together can empty the water out of a tank in 36 minutes,
    how long would it take if there were 9 pumps working ?
2   A circular running-track has diameter 70 yards. How many times must an athlete
    run round it to run $\frac{1}{2}$ mile, to the nearest whole number ?
3   In a cuboid, number of faces + number of edges + number of vertices.
4   If 'THE LOVELY FIRE' is coded as 'pug cksgcz bang', decode 'puanpz-basg'
    and 'babpz-pungg' and write down their product.
5   The next number in the sequence 8, 16, 32, 64.
6   The number of metres in 8 km − the number of cm in 8 metres + the number of
    articles in 8 score.
8   One number in this sequence is incorrect. What should it be ?
    1, 8, 27, 64, 125, 216, 333, 512, 729, 1000.
14 A lawn is 12 m long and 8 m wide. There is a path 1 m wide all the way round.
    How many metres of fencing would be needed to go all round the outer edge of
    the path ?
15 125 equal cubes are placed on the table to form a solid cube. The top and the
    four side faces of this large cube are then painted red. How many of the original
    cubes have just one face painted red ?
17 Write down any number less than 6. Double it and to the result add 2. Then
    square the total, subtract 4 and then divide by 4. Divide then by the number you
    started with, and finally subtract the number you started with. What is your answer ?

Coordinates and graphs

The topics in this chapter include:

- understanding and using coordinates,
- drawing graphs of simple functions,
- using coordinates in 3-D.

Graphs

Coordinates

A point on a graph can be specified by giving its coordinates, i.e. its x-value and its y-value.

Example

Point A has x-value 1 and y-value 2.
This can be written as the point (1, 2).
A is (1, 2),
B is (−2, 1),
C is (0, −3).
Copy this diagram and plot the
point D (3, −2).
Join AB, BC, CD and DA.
What sort of figure is $ABCD$?

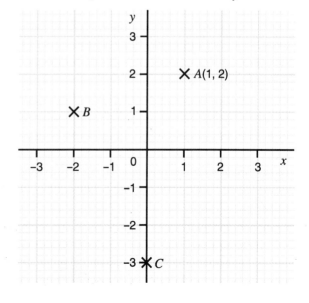

Exercise 9.1

1. Copy and complete the figure *PQRSTU* so that *PS* is a line of symmetry. State the coordinates of *T* and *U*.

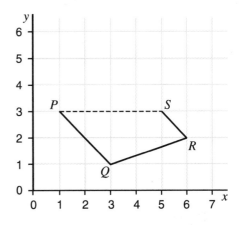

2. Draw the *x* and *y* axes from 0 to 6. Find a triangle whose sides lie on the three lines $x = 6$, $y = 4$ and $y = x$.

3. Draw the *x*-axis from 0 to 6 and the *y*-axis from 0 to 4 using a scale of 1 cm to 1 unit.

   1 Plot the points *A* (6, 0), *B* (6, 4) and *C* (0, 4). *O* is the origin.
     Join *AB* and *BC*.
     What is the area of the rectangle *OABC*?

   2 Plot the points *D* (6, 2) and *E* (2, 4). Join *OD* and *OE*. What are the areas of $\triangle OAD$ and $\triangle OCE$?

   3 What is the area of the quadrilateral *ODBE*?

4. Draw axes for *x* and *y* from −8 to 8 using equal scales on both axes.

   1 Plot points *A* (0, 1), *B* (6, 4), *C* (8, 8), *D* (2, 5). Join *AB*, *BC*, *CD*, *DA*.
     What sort of quadrilateral is *ABCD*?
     Mark the point of symmetry, *E*, and state its coordinates.

   2 Plot points *F* (−8, 5), *G* (−6, 2), *H* (−3, 4). Join *FG* and *GH*.
     Find a point *J* such that *FGHJ* is a square. Complete the square.
     What are the coordinates of *J*?
     Draw the axes of symmetry of the square on your diagram. How many axes of symmetry are there?

   3 Plot points *K* (−7, −6), *L* (−4, −8), *M* (−1, −6), *N* (−4, −4).
     Join *KL*, *LM*, *MN*, *NK*.
     What sort of quadrilateral is *KLMN*?
     What are the equations of its axes of symmetry?

5.   Draw the *x*-axis from 0 to 8 and the *y*-axis from 0 to 10 using equal scales on both axes.

   1   Plot the points J (0, 2), K (2, 4), L (3, 6), M (8, 10). Three of these points lie on a
         straight line. Draw this line.
         Write down the coordinates of 4 more points which lie on the line.
         What is the connection between the *x* and *y* values for all points on the line ?

   2   Complete this pattern.
         (0, 6), (1, 5), (2, 4), (3, _), (4, _), (5, _), (6, _).
         Plot these points and join them with a line.
         What are the coordinates of the point where this line crosses the line drawn in **1** ?

Functions

If a set of values, *x*, is connected to another set of values, *y*, and for each value of *x* there is
only one value of *y*, then *y* is said to be a function of *x*.

A function can be represented by ordered pairs of numbers.
e.g. (1, 1), (2, 4), (3, 9), (4, 16).
The 1st number of each pair is the value of *x*, the 2nd number is the value of *y*.

A function can be represented by a mapping diagram.
e.g.

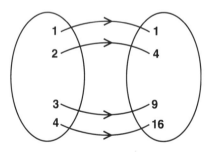

A function can be represented by a table.

e.g.

x	1	2	3	4
y	1	4	9	16

A function can be represented by an equation. The equation for this function is $y = x^2$.
The notation $x \mapsto x^2$ can also be used. This is read as 'the function such that *x* is mapped onto
x^2'.

Graphs of functions

If the values of x are continuous, the function can be represented by its graph.

This is the graph of $y = x^2$.

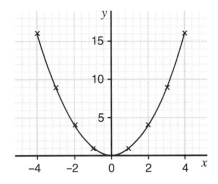

Examples

1   For this question, use graph paper with x from -1 to 3 and y from -3 to 9 using scales of 1 cm to 1 unit on both axes.

(1)   This is a table connecting values of x and y, for the function $y = x$ or $x \mapsto x$.

x	-1	0	1	2	3
y	-1	0	1	2	3

To represent this table on graph paper, plot the points $(-1, -1)$, $(0, 0)$, $(1, 1)$, $(2, 2)$, $(3, 3)$. These points lie on a straight line. Draw it.

$y = x$ is the equation of the line.

(2)   Here is another table, for the function $y = 2x$ or $x \mapsto 2x$.

x	-1	0	1	2	3
y	-2	0	2	4	6

To represent this, plot the points $(-1, -2)$, $(0, 0)$, $(1, 2)$, $(2, 4)$, $(3, 6)$ on the same graph as before, and draw the straight line through these points.
The equation of this line is $y = 2x$.

It is a steeper line than the first one.

(3)   Make similar tables for $y = 3x$, and $y = \frac{1}{2}x$, and plot these lines on your graph.

2 For this question use graph paper with x from -1 to 3 and y from -4 to 5, using equal scales on both axes.
Plot the points given in this table, and draw the line.

x	-1	0	1	2	3
y	1	2	3	4	5

The equation of this line is $y = x + 2$.
Draw the line $y = x$ on the same graph.
These lines are parallel. $y = x + 2$ cuts the y-axis at $(0, 2)$, but $y = x$ passes through the origin $(0, 0)$.
Make a table of values for the line $y = x - 3$, and draw this line on the same graph.

3 Draw the graph of $y = 5 - 2x$.

Find the values of y when $x = -1$, 0 and 3.
When $x = 0$, $y = 5 - (2 \times 0) = 5$
When $x = 3$, $y = 5 - (2 \times 3) = 5 - 6 = -1$.
When $x = -1$, $y = 5 - (2 \times (-1)) = 5 + 2 = 7$

Here are these results in a table.

x	-1	0	3
y	7	5	-1

Draw axes with x from -1 to 3 and y from -1 to 7.
Plot the points $(-1, 7)$, $(0, 5)$, $(3, -1)$ and draw the line.
It slopes downwards.

(It is unnecessary to plot many points when you know the graph is a straight line. Two points are sufficient but a third point is also useful as a check on accuracy.)

Exercise 9.2

1. Make a table of values for these functions, for values of $x = -2, -1, 0, 1, 2, 3$.

   1 $y = x + 3$ **3** $y = 7 - x$
   2 $y = 2x - 1$ **4** $y = 4 - 2x$

   Draw axes for x from -2 to 3 and for y from -6 to 10, using a scale of 2 cm to 1 unit on the x-axis and 1 cm to 1 unit on the y-axis.
   Plot the points given in the tables and draw the lines, labelling each one.

2.   Make a table of values for these functions, for $x = 0, 1, 2, 3, 4$.

1 $y = 2x - 4$ **3** $y = 9 - 3x$
2 $y = \frac{1}{2}x + 3$

Draw axes for x from 0 to 4 and for y from -4 to 10, using a scale of 2 cm to 1 unit on the x-axis and 1 cm to 1 unit on the y-axis.
Plot the points given in the tables and draw the lines, labelling each one.

3.   **To draw the graph of $y = x^2$**
This is not a straight line and several points must be plotted.
Copy and complete this table showing the connection between x and y.

x	-4	-3	-2	-1	0	1	2	3	4
y	16	9				1			

Draw the x-axis from -4 to 4 and the y-axis from 0 to 16.
Plot these 9 points and join them with a smooth curve.
This shape is called a parabola.

4.   Make a table of values for the function $y = \dfrac{60}{x}$ for $x = 2, 3, 4, 5, 6, 8, 10$.

Draw the x-axis from 0 to 10 and the y-axis from 0 to 30, taking a scale of 1 cm to 1 unit on the x-axis and 2 cm to 5 units on the y-axis.
Plot the points given in the table and join them with a smooth curve.

Coordinates in 3-dimensions

Coordinates are used to indicate position.
By introducing another axis (the z-axis) we can represent positions in 3-dimensions.
If the x and y axes are in a horizontal plane (such as on a level table), the z-axis goes vertically upwards.
The origin is the point $(0, 0, 0)$. The axes are all at right angles to each other.

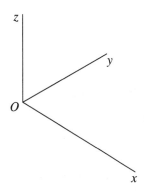

To find the point $(4, 3, 2)$, first find the point $(4, 3)$ as usual, using the axes Ox, Oy.
Then move upwards (i.e. in the direction of the z-axis) for 2 units.

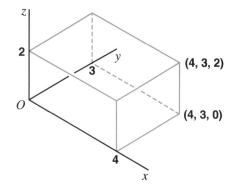

Example

A cuboid has one vertex at the origin and three of its edges on the x, y and z axes.
One vertex is at the point $(3, 1, 2)$.
What are the coordinates of the other vertices ?

These are shown on the diagram.
Notice that all the points on the base of the cuboid have z-coordinate 0, the others have z-coordinate 2.
Notice which vertices have x-coordinate 0, and which have x-coordinate 3.
Notice which vertices have y-coordinate 0, and which have y-coordinate 1.

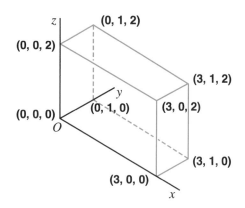

Exercise 9.3

1. *ABCDEFGH* is a cuboid.
    A is the point $(2, 1, 0)$.
    B is the point $(8, 1, 0)$.
    D is the point $(2, 4, 0)$.
    E is the point $(2, 1, 6)$.
    Find the coordinates of the points C, F, G and H.

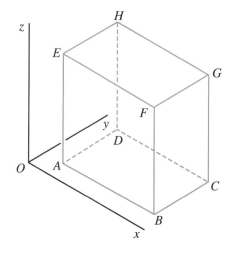

2. *ABCDEFGH* is a cuboid.
    A is the point $(1, 4, 5)$.
    G is the point $(12, 7, 9)$.
    If *AB*, *AD* and *AE* are parallel to the *x*, *y* and *z*
    axes respectively, find the coordinates of
    B, *C*, *D*, *E*, *F* and *H*.

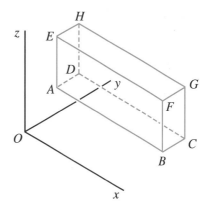

3. *ABCDEFGH* is a cuboid.
    A is the point $(-1, -4, -2)$.
    AB has length 10 units and is parallel to
    the *x*-axis.
    BC has length 9 units and is parallel to
    the *y*-axis.
    AE has length 6 units and is parallel to the
    z-axis.
    Find the coordinates of the points
    B, *C*, *D*, *E*, *F*, *G* and *H*.

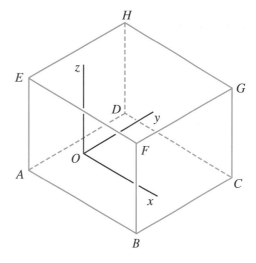

Exercise 9.4 Applications

1. Draw the *x*-axis from 0 to 10 and the *y*-axis from 0 to 8 using equal scales on both axes.
    1 Plot points $A(6, 3)$ and $B(10, 5)$.
       Draw the line *OAB* (where *O* is the origin). What is the equation of this line ?
    2 Plot the point $C(9, 7)$ and join *BC*.
       Find the point *D* such that *ABCD* is a rectangle. Join *AD* and *DC*.
       What are the coordinates of *D* ?
    3 What is the equation of the line *BD* ?

2. Draw the x-axis from −6 to 10 and the y-axis from −4 to 11 using equal scales on both axes. Draw triangles labelled A to F by plotting and joining the 3 points given in each case.

Triangle A   (2, 6), (2, 9), (3, 10)
Triangle B   (5, 3), (6, 6), (7, 6)
Triangle C   (9, 0), (6, −2), (6, −3)
Triangle D   (−5, 7), (−3, 10), (−2, 10)
Triangle E   (−5, 4), (−2, 4), (−1, 5)
Triangle F   (−4, −2), (−4, −3), (−1, −1)

Which pairs of triangles are congruent (exactly the same shape and size) ?

3. On a graph, draw the x-axis from −3 to 5 and the y-axis from −1 to 6, using equal scales on both axes.
Plot the points A (3, 2), B (5, 6) and C (0, 4). Join AB and BC.
Plot point D such that AD is parallel and equal in length to BC.
What are the coordinates of D ?
Join AD and DC. What kind of quadrilateral is ABCD ?

4. On a graph draw the x-axis from −3 to 4 and the y-axis from −3 to 4, using scales of 1 cm to 1 unit on both axes.
Plot points A (4, 0), B (1, 4), C (−3, 1) and D (0, −3). Join AB, BC, CD, DA.
What kind of quadrilateral is ABCD ?
Plot the point E (−1, 0) and join BE. Find the area of △ABE.

5. Draw the x-axis from −3 to 5 using 2 cm to 1 unit, and draw the y-axis from −4 to 12 using 1 cm to 1 unit.
Plot the points and draw the lines represented by these patterns.

1

x	−3	−1	1	3	5
y	−4	0	4	8	12

2

x	−3	−1	1	3	5
y	12	10	8	6	4

3 Make a similar pattern for the equation $y = x - 1$ and draw this line on the graph.

4 Make a similar pattern for the equation $y = 12 - 3x$ for $x = 0, 1, 2, 3, 4, 5$ and draw this line on the graph.

5 Find the coordinates of the point where the lines $y = x - 1$ and $y = 12 - 3x$ intersect.

6 Draw the line $x = -2$ on the graph. Find the coordinates of the point where this line intersects the line drawn in part **2**.

6. Make a table of values for $x = -5, -1, 3, 7$ for the function $y = \dfrac{3(x+1)}{4}$.

    Draw the x-axis from -5 to 7 and the y-axis from -3 to 6. Plot the points from the table and draw the graph.

7. Make a table of values for $x = -4, -3, -2, -1, 0, 1, 2, 3, 4$ for the function $y = \frac{1}{2}x^2$. Draw the x-axis from -4 to 4 and the y-axis from 0 to 8. Plot the points from the table and draw the graph, joining the points with a smooth curve.

8. Make a table of values for $x = 1, 1.5, 2, 3, 4, 5, 6, 7.5, 9$ for the function $y = \dfrac{9}{x}$.

    Draw both axes from 0 to 9. Plot the points from the table and draw the graph for values of x between 1 and 9, joining the points with a smooth curve.

9. *ABCDEFGH* is a cuboid.
    A is the point $(2, 3, 4)$.
    AB has length 7 units and is parallel to the x-axis.
    AD has length 1 unit and is parallel to the y-axis.
    AE has length 3 units and is parallel to the z-axis.
    Find the coordinates of the points B, C, D, E, F, G and H.

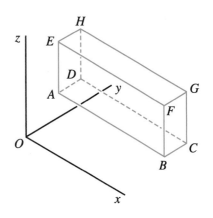

10. *ABCDEFGH* is a cuboid.
    A is the point $(2, 3, 5)$.
    B is the point $(6, 3, 5)$.
    D is the point $(2, 6, 5)$.
    E is the point $(2, 3, 17)$.
    Find the coordinates of the points C, F, G and H.

    State the lengths of AB and BC and use Pythagoras' theorem to find the length of AC.
    State the length of CG.
    What is the size of $\angle ACG$?
    Find the length of AG.

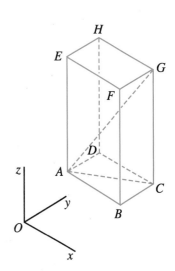

Practice test 9

1. Draw the x-axis from 0 to 4 and the y-axis from 0 to 3. Plot the points A, B, C, D
    where A is $(3, 0)$, B is $(4, 1)$, C is $(1, 3)$ and D is $(0, 2)$.
    What sort of quadrilateral is $ABCD$?

2. On a graph, draw the x-axis from -7 to 3 and the y-axis from 0 to 6, using a scale of
    1 cm to 1 unit on both axes.
    Plot the points A, B, and C where A is $(-7, 1)$, B is $(3, 1)$ and C $(1, 6)$.
    Join AB, BC, CA.
    Find the area of $\triangle ABC$.

3. Make a table of values for these functions, for $x = -4, -2, 0, 2, 4, 6$.

    1 $y = 10 - 2x$ **2** $y = 3x - 2$

    Draw the x-axis from -4 to 6 and the y-axis from -14 to 18, taking a scale of 2 cm to
    1 unit on the x-axis and 1 cm to 1 unit on the y-axis.
    Plot the points given in the table and draw the lines, labelling each one.

4. Copy and complete this table for the function $y = x^2 - 2$.

x	-4	-3	-2	-1	0	1	2	3	4
y	14	7			-2				

    Draw the x-axis from -4 to 4 and the y-axis from -2 to 14, taking a scale of 2 cm to
    1 unit on the x-axis and 1 cm to 1 unit on the y-axis.
    Plot the points from the table and draw the graph of the function, joining the points
    with a smooth curve.

5. $ABCDEFGH$ is a cuboid.
    G is the point $(7, 9, 4)$.
    HG has length 15 units and is parallel to
    the x-axis.
    FG has length 13 units and is parallel to
    the y-axis.
    CG has length 7 units and is parallel to the
    z-axis.
    Find the coordinates of the points A, B, C,
    D, E, F and H.

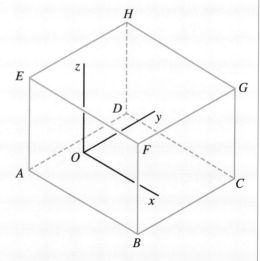

PUZZLES

20. Here is the final table in the local league. Every team has played every other team once. What was the score in the match between the Allsorts and the Dribblers ?

	played	won	drawn	lost	goals for	goals against	points
Allsorts	3	3	0	0	4	0	6
Buskers	3	1	1	1	4	4	3
Cobblers	3	0	2	1	3	4	2
Dribblers	3	0	1	2	0	3	1

21. How many squares are there in this figure, and how many contain the dot ?

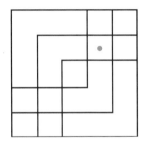

22. Start from *, going horizontally or vertically (not diagonally), and spell out the names of 7 plane figures.

T	A	N	T	R	I	X	A
N	G	O	R	T	A	E	G
E	G	O	A	E	N	H	O
P	R	L	P	L	G	M	N
M	A	E	E	Z	I	U	Q
A	L	L	A	R	E	A	U
R	A	*P	L	S	T	D	R
E	R	A	U	Q	A	L	I

23. Seasonal greetings. On graph paper, label the *x*-axis from 0 to 12 and the *y*-axis from 0 to 8, using the same scale on both axes. Mark these points. Join each point to the next one with a straight line, except where there is a cross after the point.

(5, 6)   (4, 6)   (4, 8)   (5, 8)×   (8, 6)   (8, 8)   (8.8, 8)   (9, 7.8)
(9, 7.2)   (8.8, 7)   (8, 7)   (9, 6)×   (1, 2)   (3, 4)×   (1, 6)   (1, 8)
(2, 7)   (3, 8)   (3, 6)×   (11, 7)   (12, 8)×   (6, 6)   (6, 8)   (6.8, 8)
(7, 7.8)   (7, 7.2)   (6.8, 7)   (6, 7)   (7, 6)×   (10, 8)   (11, 7)   (11, 6)×
(4, 7)   (4.8, 7)×   (3, 2)   (1, 4)×
Complete the diagram.

10 *Probability*

The topics in this chapter include:

- understanding that different outcomes may result from repeating an experiment,

- understanding and using relative frequency as an estimate of probability,

- knowing that if each of n events is equally likely, the probability of one occurring is $\frac{1}{n}$,

- recognising situations where estimates of probability can be based on equally likely outcomes, and others where estimates must be based on statistical evidence,

- appreciating that relative frequency and equally likely considerations may not be appropriate and subjective estimates of probability may have to be made.

Probability

Probability or chance is the likelihood of an event happening.
It is measured on a numerical scale from 0 to 1 and can be given as a fraction, a decimal or a percentage.

A probability of 0 means that there is no chance of the event happening.
A probability of 1 means that it is certain that the event will happen.
A probability of $\frac{1}{2}$ means that there is a 50–50 chance of the event happening. In the long run, $\frac{1}{2}$ of the trials will give successful results.
A probability of $\frac{2}{3}$ means that in the long run $\frac{2}{3}$ of the trials will give successful results.
The nearer the value of the probability is to 1, the more chance there is of a successful outcome.
The nearer the value of the probability is to 0, the less chance there is of a successful outcome.

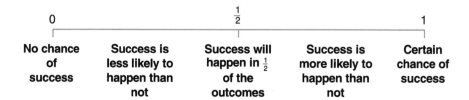

When we know the probability of an event happening we can use its value to predict the likelihood of a future result. That is why Probability is linked to Statistics. Government departments, business firms, industrialists, scientists, medical researchers and many other people and organisations use the figures from past events to predict what is likely to happen in the future, and thus they can plan ahead. For example, insurance companies use their knowledge of past claims to predict future ones, and they can then decide what premiums they must charge. If you want to gamble on a sporting event it is useful to estimate the probability of winning. You might then realise that you are unlikely to win in the long run and decide not to waste your money on the bet.

You learn about probability by doing simple experiments with coins, dice, cards, etc. but probability is an important subject, and affects all our lives.

Relative frequency

If we have trials with different outcomes, some of which are successful, then

the relative frequency of a successful outcome $= \dfrac{\text{number of successful outcomes}}{\text{total number of trials}}$.

The relative frequency gives an estimate of the probability of a successful outcome.

e.g. There are a number of beads in a bag, some red and some blue, and to find the probability of picking a red bead out if picking a bead at random, a large number of trials are made. A bead is picked out, its colour noted, and the bead is replaced. This experiment is repeated 1000 times altogether, and the number of red beads noted was 596.

So, the probability of a red bead $= \dfrac{\text{number of trials giving a red bead}}{\text{total number of trials}}$

$$= \frac{596}{1000} = 0.60, \text{ to 2 dec. pl.}$$

We can only use this method for estimating probability if we do enough trials to show that the fraction is settling down to a steady value. Some events are completely unpredictable and in those cases the fraction would not settle down and we could not find a value for the probability.

Exercise 10.1 includes suggestions for experiments.
All the trials should be done randomly and fairly. Toss a coin properly. Give a die (dice) a good shake before rolling it out onto a flat surface. Shuffle a pack of cards properly and for most experiments you should take out the jokers first so that the pack contains the 52 cards of the 4 suits. If you have not got proper equipment it is often possible to think of a substitute. If you can combine other people's results with yours to give more trials, do so. Keep a record of your results to use again later.

If you compare your results with another person's, you will probably find that the outcomes are different, but for a large number of trials the final estimates for probability should be similar.

Using random numbers to simulate results

Instead of actually doing the experiments, you may prefer to use a graphics calculator or a computer to produce random numbers.

To simulate the throwing of a die, on the graphics calculator, press

$\boxed{\text{Int}}$ $\boxed{(}$ $\boxed{\text{Ran\#}}$ $\boxed{\times}$ 6 $\boxed{+}$ 1 $\boxed{)}$ $\boxed{\text{EXE}}$ $\boxed{\text{EXE}}$ $\boxed{\text{EXE}}$ ...

and you will get a sequence of random numbers between 1 and 6.

By changing 6 into 2 in the instructions, you will get a sequence of 1's or 2's which you can use as the results of tossing coins, with 1 for heads and 2 for tails.

You can produce similar results on a computer using a simple basic program.

However, you may have commercial computer programs available which will do these and other simulated experiments.

Exercise 10.1

1. Toss a coin 200 times. Record your results in order, in a grid of 10 columns by 20 rows. Put H for head and T for tail.
    The grid starts like this:

H	H	T	H	T	T	H			

    Before you begin, estimate how many heads you are likely to get.

    Make a table similar to this one and fill it in.

number of tosses (n)	number of heads (h)	fraction $\frac{h}{n}$	$\frac{h}{n}$ to 2 decimal places
1			
2			
3			
4			
5			
10			
20			
50			
100			
150			
200			

Is $\dfrac{h}{n}$ settling down to a steady value ? If so, this gives the estimated probability of a toss of a coin showing a head.

The value from 200 tosses gives the most reliable estimate, as it involves most trials. From your results, what is the estimated probability of a toss showing a head ?

2. Instead of tossing coins again, use the results of question 1 in pairs, as if you had tossed two coins together, so that the possible results are HH, HT, TH, TT. If you had 200 single results you will have 100 results for pairs. Count the number of heads in each pair and put your results on a tally chart. Before you begin estimate how many of each you will get.

Heads	Tally marks	Frequency (f)
0		
1		
2		
		100

What is the most likely result ?
What are your estimates for the probabilities of 0 heads, 1 head, 2 heads ?

3. Throw a die 400 times. Record the number which lands face upwards, in a grid of 20 columns by 20 rows.
If the total number of throws is n and the number of sixes is s,
find the fraction $\dfrac{s}{n}$, to 2 decimal places.
This gives the estimated probability of a throw showing a six.

Work out the probabilities of getting the other numbers, 1 to 5.
Is the die a fair one ?

4. Put 10 similar drawing-pins into a cup and holding it approximately 20 cm above a table, gently tip the drawing-pins out so they land on the table. They come to rest point upwards, like this $\underline{\perp}$, or on their side, like this $\swarrow$. Count and record how many land point upwards. Repeat the experiment 50 times.

If the total number of drawing-pins tipped out is n, and the number which rest point upwards is s, find the fraction $\dfrac{s}{n}$, to 2 decimal places, after 5, 10, 20, 30, 40 and 50 repetitions.

If the results are settling down to a certain value this gives the value of the probability that a drawing-pin in this type of experiment will land point upwards. (There is no theoretical way of checking this result.)
The height through which the drawing-pins fall may affect the result. You could investigate this by repeating the experiment from different heights. Different makes of drawing-pins may also give different results.

5. Shuffle a pack of cards and pick out 3 cards.
    Record as P if they contain at least one picture-card
    (i.e. Jack, Queen or King). Record as N if there is
    no picture card.
    Replace the cards, shuffle and repeat 100 times
    altogether.
    Before you begin, estimate how many times P will occur.

    Find the fraction $\dfrac{\text{number of times P occurs}}{\text{total number of trials}}$ as a

    decimal to 2 decimal places.
    From your results, what value would you give for the
    probability that of three cards drawn at random,
    at least one card is a picture-card ?

6. Collect 200 single-figure random numbers by taking the last figure of a list of phone
    numbers out of a random page of a directory. (If a firm has consecutive numbers listed,
    only use the first one.) Record these numbers in a grid, as in question 1.
    Before you begin, estimate how many of each number 0 to 9 you expect to get.

    Count up your results and show them in a table.

    Now add up the frequencies of the odd numbers.

    Find the fraction $\dfrac{\text{number of odd numbers}}{\text{total number of numbers}}$ as a

    decimal to 2 decimal places.
    From your results, what value would you give for
    the probability that a number picked at random
    from the numbers 0 to 9 is odd ?

Number	Frequency
0	
1	
2	
3	
4	
5	
6	
7	
8	
9	

Subjective estimates

Probability may be worked out using the formula

$$\text{Probability} = \frac{\text{number of successful outcomes}}{\text{number of equally likely outcomes}}$$

If it is not possible to use that formula the probability can be estimated by finding the relative
frequency.

$$\text{Probability} = \frac{\text{number of successful trials}}{\text{total number of trials}}$$

provided that the number of trials is large, and the fraction settles down to a steady value.

But there are many times in life when we have to estimate the probability or chance of something happening, and we cannot use calculation.

e.g. What is the probability that this year there will be a White Christmas ?

(This means that there will be snow on Christmas Day.)

Now if you live in Northern Canada, you might estimate the probability as 1 (certain to happen), and if you live in the Sahara Desert you might estimate the probability as 0 (certain not to happen).

If you live in Southern England, and there has never been snow on Christmas Day for many years, you may think that there is a very slight chance, and estimate the probability as 0.1, or 0.05.

If you live in the Scottish Highlands, and most years there has been snow, you might estimate the probability as 0.8, 0.9 or 0.95. For other parts of Britain you might make estimates at some other point on the probability scale. If you think there is an even chance, the probability will be 0.5. If it is more likely to snow than not, the probability will be over 0.5. And so on ...

Some people may have a bet on an outcome such as this. For other people, the result is more serious. Shepherds have to make sure the sheep are safe. Transport authorities have to keep their vehicles running, and people planning journeys may have to change their plans.

Exercise 10.2

1.   Here are some statements. Some of them may not apply to you, or they may be certainties. Choose 5 statements from the rest and put them in order of likelihood. Then decide which probabilities are less than 0.5 and which are greater than 0.5. Finally, give estimated probabilities for them.

(a) Tomorrow will be wet.
(b) You will give some useful help at home this evening.
(c) You will be late for school/college one day next week.
(d) You will go to the cinema next weekend.
(e) During the next fortnight, you will get some new clothes.
(f) During the next month, you will win a prize in a competition.
(g) For your next holiday you will go to the USA.
(h) When you take GCSE Maths you will achieve a satisfactory result.
(i) Next year, you will continue your education (at school or college).
(j) When you take your driving test, you will pass at the first attempt.
(k) Make up your own statement.

2.   Imagine a young couple, Mr and Mrs Kaye, who are going to spend 10 days holiday in
     Greece.
     Give estimated probabilities for these statements.

   1   The plane's departure will be delayed.
   2   There will be fine, sunny weather every day during the
          holiday.
   3   The hotel accommodation will be satisfactory.
   4   The couple will spend more money than they expected to.
   5   They will make new friends.
   6   Mrs Kaye will buy some new clothes.
   7   Mr Kaye will go water-skiing.
   8   One of them will need medical treatment during the
          holiday.
   9   They will buy some duty-free goods on the plane
          coming home.
  10   They will go again to the same place next year.

Equally likely outcomes

If a trial has n equally likely outcomes, then the probability of each outcome ocurring is $\dfrac{1}{n}$.

If a trial has n equally likely outcomes, and of these s outcomes are successful ones, then:

$$\text{Probability (or chance) of a successful outcome} = \frac{\text{number of successful outcomes}}{\text{total possible outcomes}} = \frac{s}{n}$$

Examples

1   Find the probability of a tossed coin showing heads.

   There are 2 outcomes, heads or tails, and these are equally likely.

   Probability of heads $= \dfrac{1}{n} = \tfrac{1}{2}$.

2   Find the probability of a fair die showing a five when thrown.

   There are 6 outcomes, the numbers 1, 2, 3, 4, 5, 6, and these
   are equally likely.

   Probability of a five $= \dfrac{1}{n} = \tfrac{1}{6}$.

3   Find the probability of a number picked at random from the numbers 1 to 10 being exactly divisible by 4.

There are ten equally likely outcomes of which two (4 and 8) are successful.

Probability of picking a number exactly divisible by $4 = \dfrac{s}{n} = \dfrac{2}{10} = \tfrac{1}{5}$

4   If a letter is chosen at random from the 11 letters of the word **PROBABILITY**, what is the probability that it is A, B, either A or B ?

There are 11 equally likely outcomes, including one A and two B's.

Probability of letter A $= \dfrac{1}{n} = \tfrac{1}{11}$,

probability of letter B $= \dfrac{s}{n} = \tfrac{2}{11}$,

probability of either A or B $= \dfrac{s}{n} = \tfrac{3}{11}$.

Exercise 10.3

1.   A fair die is thrown once. What is the probability of getting
      1   a three,
      2   a square number ?

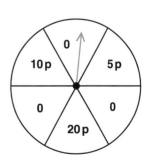

2.   20 discs, numbered from 1 to 20, are placed in a bag and one is drawn out at random. What is the probability of getting a disc with
      1   a number greater than 15,
      2   a number which includes the digit 1,
      3   a number which is divisible by 3 ?

3.   In a fairground game a pointer is spun and you win the amount shown in the sector where it comes to rest. Assuming that the pointer is equally likely to come to rest in any sector, what is the probability that
      1   you win some money,
      2   you win 20p ?

4.   In a tombola game, $\frac{7}{8}$ of the counters are blank. The rest have a number on them and they win a prize. If you take a counter out of the drum at random what is the probability that you win a prize ?

5.   If you choose a card at random from a pack of 52 playing-cards, what is the probability that it is
     1   an ace,
     2   a diamond,
     3   a red card with an even number ?

6   A letter is chosen at random from the 11 letters of the word MATHEMATICS. What is the probability that it is
     1   the letter M,
     2   a vowel,
     3   a letter from the second half of the alphabet ?

7.   In a pack of playing-cards, the 2 of diamonds and the 2 of hearts have been removed. If you choose a card at random from the remaining cards, what is the probability that it is
     1   a diamond,
     2   a two,
     3   the 2 of diamonds ?

8.   A box contains 2 red, 3 yellow and 5 green sweets. One is taken out at random, and eaten. A second sweet is then taken out.
     1   If the 1st sweet was green, what is the probability that the 2nd sweet is also green ?
     2   If the 1st sweet was not red, what is the probability that the 2nd sweet is red ?

9.   In a survey of 36 boys, the numbers playing football, cricket and rugby are given in the diagram.
     If a boy is picked at random from this group what is the probability that he plays
     1   football,
     2   cricket and football but not rugby,
     3   only rugby ?
     4   If a boy who plays cricket is chosen at random, what is the probability that he also plays football ?

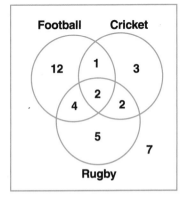

10. Two cards are drawn from a pack of 52 cards. What is the probability that the second card is from the same suit as the first
     1   if the 1st card is replaced before the 2nd card is drawn,
     2   if the 1st card is not replaced before the 2nd card is drawn ?

Use of sample spaces

Example

Five discs numbered 1 to 5 are placed in a bag and one is drawn out at random and not replaced. A second disc is then drawn out at random.
(1) What is the probability that the second disc has a number higher by at least 2 than the first disc ?
(2) What is the probability that the total of the two numbers is 6 ?

Set down the possible equally likely results in a diagram called a sample space.

		1st disc				
		1	2	3	4	5
2nd	1		.	.	.	.
disc	2	.		.	.	.
	3	.	*a*	.	.	.
	4	.	▸	.		.
	5	.	.	.	.	

A dot represents one of the equally likely outcomes, e.g. dot (*a*) represents the outcome that the first disc is 2 and the second disc is 4. There are 20 dots so there are 20 equally likely outcomes. (It might be more useful to write the actual outcomes e.g. (2, 4), or the total score, instead of just dots.)

We will mark in some way all the outcomes where the second disc has a number higher by at least 2 than the first disc, and in a different way where the total of the two numbers is 6. (Normally these would go on the original diagram but here to make it clearer we have two new diagrams.)

(1)

		1st disc				
		1	2	3	4	5
2nd	1		.	.	.	.
disc	2	.		.	.	.
	3	⊡	.		.	.
	4	⊡	⊡	.		.
	5	⊡	⊡	⊡	.	

(2)

		1st disc				
		1	2	3	4	5
2nd	1		.	.	.	⊙
disc	2	.		.	⊙	.
	3	.	.		.	.
	4	.	⊙	.		.
	5	⊙	.	.	.	

⊡ represents a successful outcome.
There are 6 successful outcomes.

⊙ represents a successful outcome.
There are 4 successful outcomes.

(1) The probability that the 2nd disc has a number higher by at least 2 than the first disc
$$= \frac{s}{n} = \frac{6}{20} = 0.3$$

(2) The probability that the total of the two numbers is $6 = \frac{s}{n} = \frac{4}{20} = 0.2$

Exercise 10.4

1. In a bag there are 5 cards numbered 1, 3, 5, 7, 9.
    In a second bag there are 4 cards numbered 2, 4, 6, 8.
    One card is drawn at random from each bag.
    Copy and complete the sample space diagram showing the sum of the numbers on the two cards.

    What is the probability that
    1   the sum is an odd number,
    2   the sum is an even number,
    3   the sum is 13,
    4   the sum is less than 10,
    5   the sum is exactly divisible by 5 ?

		1st card				
		1	3	5	7	9
	2	3	5			
2nd	4	5				
card	6					
	8					

2. A regular triangular pyramid (tetrahedron) has its four faces numbered 1, 2, 3, 4 and it is used as a die by counting as the score the number on the bottom face. Make a sample space diagram showing the outcomes when this die is thrown twice.

    Find the probability that
    1   in each of the two throws the score is 4,
    2   in the two throws the sum of the scores is 4,
    3   in the two throws the product of the scores is 4.

    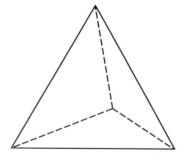

3. Two dice are thrown together. Make a sample space diagram of the equally likely results.

    What is the probability
    1   that the sum of the two numbers is greater than 10,
    2   that the sum of the two numbers is 7,
    3   of a double (the two dice showing the same number),
    4   of both dice showing numbers less than 3 ?

4. There are six cards numbered 1 to 6. One card is selected at random and not replaced, and then a second card is selected. Make a sample space diagram of the equally likely results.
    What is the probability
    1   that the sum of the two numbers is greater than 10,
    2   that the sum of the two numbers is 7,
    3   that the product of the two numbers is odd ?

Exercise 10.5   Applications

1.   Use a set of dominoes going up to double six.
     (If you have no dominoes, label cards 0–0,
     0–1, up to 0–6; then 1–1, 1–2, up to 1–6;
     then 2–2, etc., ending 6–6. There are 28 cards
     altogether.)
     Pick out a domino at random and record the
     total score. Replace and repeat 200 times.
     The scores range from 0 to 12. Make a tally
     chart of the results.
     What is the estimated probability of getting a
     score of 6 if a domino is picked at random ?

2.   In an experiment with a biased die, the following results were obtained for the number
     facing uppermost when the die was thrown 400 times.

Number	1	2	3	4	5	6
Number of times	39	72	57	111	25	96

Using these results, find the probability of throwing
   1 number 6,
   2 an odd number,
   3 a number greater than 3.

3.   The students in a school club belong to two forms 11X and 11Y.

	11X	11Y
Girls	12	16
Boys	8	14

If from this club one member is chosen at random,
what is the probability that it is
   1 a boy,
   2 a member of 11Y,
   3 a girl from 11X ?
   4 If a girl has to be chosen at random what is the
       probability that she is from 11X ?

4.   These five tiles are placed in a bag.
     One tile is drawn out and replaced and
     then a second tile is drawn out.
     Make a sample space diagram of the
     equally likely results.

     Find the probability of getting
       1 A first and then B,
       2 A and B in either order.
       3 Repeat the questions if the second tile
           is drawn out without the first tile
           being replaced.

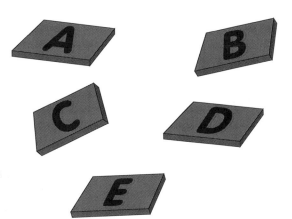

5.   Find the theoretical results for the experiments you carried out in Exercise 10.1, questions 1, 2, 3 and 6, and compare them with your experimental results.

6.   A   B   C   D

A collection of blue or white table-tennis balls are placed in 4 bags, as shown.
Sheila wants to pick a blue table-tennis ball from a bag, without looking.

1   Find the probability of selecting a blue ball from each of the 4 bags.
2   Which bag should Sheila choose to pick from, to have least chance of picking a blue ball ?
3   Which bag should Sheila choose to pick from, to have most chance of picking a blue ball ?
4   Of the other two bags, which one would give Sheila a greater chance than the other one, of picking a blue ball ?

The table-tennis balls from two of the bags are put together in a box. A ball is picked out at random from the box.
Which two bags were used if the probability of picking out a blue ball is

5    $\frac{1}{2}$,   6 $\frac{8}{17}$?

7   Which two bags should be used together to make the probability of drawing out a blue ball from the box as small as possible, and what is this probability ?
8   Which two bags should be used together to make the probability of drawing out a blue ball from the box as large as possible, and what is this probability ?

Practice test 10

1.   Write down a list of all possible results if a coin is tossed 3 times in succession, e.g. HHH, HTH, HHT, . . .

What is the probability of getting
1   3 heads,
2   2 or more tails,
3   exactly 2 heads and 1 tail ?

2. 100 discs, numbered from 1 to 100, are placed
    in a bag and one is drawn out at random.
    What is the probability of getting a disc with
    1   a number greater than 70,
    2   a number which includes the digit 1,
    3   a number whose digits add up to 9 ?

3. This table shows the numbers of boys and girls in 200 families.

		Number of boys				
		0	1	2	3	4
Number of girls	0	45	6	7	8	3
	1	7	15	25	12	1
	2	5	23	13	1	0
	3	10	9	2	0	0
	4	2	3	0	2	1

e.g. There are 45 families with no children, and 6 families with 1 boy but no girls.

Find the probability that in a family chosen from these at random, there are
1   two boys and one girl,
2   an equal number of boys and girls (at least one of each),
3   more than two boys.

4. A bag contains 6 cards numbered 1 to 6. Two cards are selected at random. Show the
    outcomes in a sample space diagram.
    Find the probability that
    1   there is a difference of 2 between the numbers on the two cards,
    2   the two cards have a sum of 6,
    3   the two cards have a difference of 2 and a sum of 6.

Miscellaneous Section B

Exercise B1 Aural Practice

If possible find someone to read these questions to you.
You should do all of them within 10 minutes.
Do not use your calculator.
Write down the answers only.

1. Pat's mother is 30, and is five times as old as Pat. How old will Pat be next year ?

2. How many pieces of ribbon of length 30 cm can be cut from a piece 6 metres long ?

3. What is the total cost of 9 articles at 99p each ?

4. Give an approximate answer to 31×49.

5. Two angles of an isosceles triangle are each 65°. What is the size of the other angle of the triangle ?

6. Which is larger, $\frac{2}{3}$ or $\frac{3}{5}$?

7. How many lines of symmetry does a rectangle have ?

8. 25% of 60 kg of potatoes were bad, and $\frac{1}{3}$ of the remainder were too small for sale. What weight were fit for sale ?

9. If the scale of a plan is 1 : 20, what length is represented by 5 cm on the plan ?

10. Write 42 in prime factors.

11. What is the total surface area of a cube of edge 3 cm ?

12. What is 0.05 as a fraction in its simplest form ?

13. What is the size of an interior angle of a regular hexagon ?

14. If the sum of two numbers is 20 and one is 4 more than the other, what is the larger number ?

15. A rectangular piece of paper measuring 50 cm by 30 cm is cut into squares with side 5 cm. How many squares can be made ?

Exercise B2   Revision

1. A shop allows a discount of 10% on all purchases during a sale. What was the original price of an article which was sold for £35.10 ?

2. The bar chart shows sales of 5 products *A*, *B*, *C*, *D* and *E*, by a manufacturing company in two years, this year and last year.

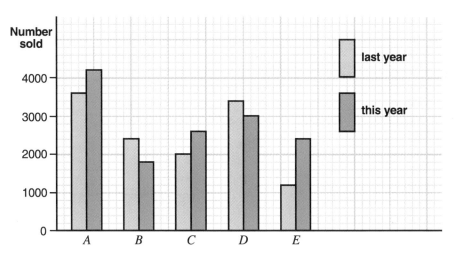

1 How many items of product *A* were sold last year ?

2 Of which products were fewer sold this year than last year ?

3 Of which product were approximately 2000 sold last year ?

4 Find the total sales of all 5 products this year, to the nearest 1000.

3. *ABCD* is a square and *CDE* is an equilateral triangle. Find the sizes of

   1 $\angle ADE$,
   2 $\angle AED$,
   3 $\angle AEC$.

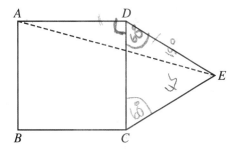

4. Write down the next two numbers in each sequence.

   1 1, 9, 25, 49, ...
   2 1, 3, 6, 10, 15, ...
   3 2, 4, 8, 16, ...

   4 100, 93, 86, 79, 72, ...
   5 1, $\frac{1}{2}$, $\frac{1}{3}$, $\frac{1}{4}$, $\frac{1}{5}$, ...

5. The internal dimensions of the base of a rectangular tank are 2 m by 1 m and it can contain water to a depth of 80 cm. How long will it take to fill the tank by means of an inlet pipe delivering water at the rate of 50 litres per minute ?

6. One of the numbers   5,   6,   7,   8,   9,   10,   11,   12   is drawn at random. What is the probability that it is a factor of 60 ?

7. Solve the equations

    1 $7x + 1 = x - 14$ **4** $3(x - 4) - 2(2x - 3) + 16 = 0$

    2 $4(x - 5) - (x + 1) = 3$ **5** $3(x^2 + x - 2) - 2(x^2 + 3x - 5) = x^2 - 2$

    3 $5 - 8x = 9 - 3x$

8. **1**   If the point P with coordinates $(-3, 5)$ is reflected in the line $y = 1$, what are the coordinates of the image point ?

    2   If $P\,(-3, 5)$ is reflected in the line $x = -1$, what are the coordinates of the image point ?

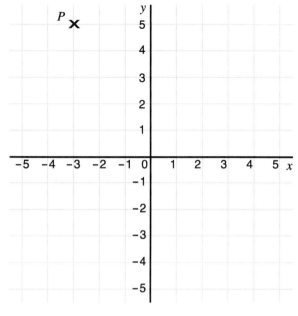

9. This pie chart represents the expenses of a catering firm. The total expenses were £54 000. If the angles at the centre of each sector were Wages, 150°; Food, 120°; Fuel, 40°; Extras, 50°; find the cost of each item.
In the following year the cost of food rose by 6%, fuel increased by 10% and wages increased by 8%. The cost of the extras decreased by 10%. Find the new total cost.

10. If an object is thrown straight upwards with a speed of 50 m/s, its height above the ground after t seconds is approximately $(50t - 5t^2)$ metres. Find, by trial, the two times at which the height above the ground is 45 m.

11. A firm prints photographs on paper of size 10 cm square. If they decide to make larger prints, size 11.2 cm square,
    1   what is the new area ?
    2   The firm have advertised their prints as being 25% larger. Is this correct ?

12. A spherical wire cage for holding a plant pot is formed by fastening together 3 circular hoops of diameter 30 cm and one smaller hoop of diameter 20 cm. Find the total length of wire needed, giving the answer to the nearest 0.1 m.

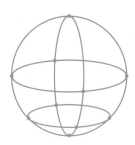

Exercise B3   Revision

1. A floor 12 m long and 7.5 m wide is to be covered by tiles 30 cm square. How many tiles will be needed ?

2. The table shows the dinners ordered for the 1st year forms at a school, for a week in September.

	1P	1Q	1R	1S	Total
Mon	35	28	22	25	110
Tues	34	28	18	26	
Wed	33		21	26	104
Thur	33	21			
Fri		26	22		106
Total for week	166		105	131	

Copy the table and fill in the missing figures, including the total number of dinners ordered for the week by all the 1st year forms.

1 On which day were the fewest dinners ordered ?
2 If the dinners cost 90p each, what was the total cost of the dinners ordered for the week by form 1Q ?

3. The following numbers were written on pieces of paper, put into a hat, and drawn out at random.

10,   13,   16,   17,   21,   25,   30,   36,   39,   49,   110,   121.

What is the probability of drawing out
1 a number greater than 100,
2 a number less than 20,
3 a prime number,
4 a number which is not a square number ?
5 If an odd number is drawn out and not replaced, what is the probability of drawing out a second odd number ?

4.   The end of this solid prism is a right-angled triangle.

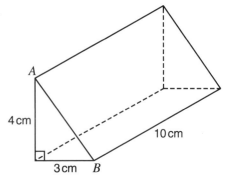

   1   Find the length of *AB*.
   2   Find the total surface area of the prism.
   3   Find the volume of the prism.

5.   Find the total cost of 4 kg of sugar at 67p per kg, $\frac{1}{4}$ kg of cheese at £3.68 per kg, $\frac{1}{2}$ kg of apples at 74p per kg and 2 dozen eggs at 72p for 6. How much change would there be from a £20 note ?

6.   Construct a triangle *ABC* with *BC* = 7 cm, $\angle B = 95°$ and $\angle C = 40°$. Bisect $\angle A$, letting the bisector cut *BC* at *D*. Measure the length of *BD*, to the nearest mm.

7.   Simplify

   1 $x^3 \times x^4 \div x^6$ **2** $\left(x^3\right)^2$ **3** $x^6 \div x^3$

8.   A train starts at 2.30 pm and reaches the next stop at 3.45 pm. If its average speed is 52 km/h, what is the distance it has travelled ?

9.   A householder paid £360 in council tax last year. This compound bar chart shows how this money is used by the County.

   1   How much goes into the Reserve Fund ?
   2   What percentage of the tax is spent on Education ?
   3   Show the data on a pie chart.

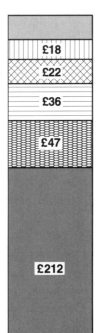

10. **1** If $s = ut + \frac{1}{2} ft^2$, what is the value of s when $u = 9$, $f = 10$, $t = 4$?

2 If $I = \dfrac{PRT}{100}$, what is the value of I when $P = 750$, $R = 8$, $T = 4$?

3 If $g = \dfrac{v - u}{t}$, find t when $v = 90$, $u = 20$ and $g = 10$.

4 If $S = 90(2n - 4)$, find n when $S = 720$.

5 If $a = \dfrac{b(100 + c)}{100 - c}$, find b when $a = 9$ and $c = 20$.

11. **1** What is the probability of getting a six when a fair die is thrown ? In 120 throws, what is the approximate number of sixes you would expect to get ?

2 What is the probability of getting an ace if a card is dealt to you from a full pack of 52 cards ? If a card was dealt in this way 120 times, what is the approximate number of times you would expect to get an ace ?

3 If the probability that the bus to take you to school is late on any one morning is reckoned to be $\frac{1}{10}$, how many times approximately would you expect to be late out of 120 mornings ?

12. The angles of a quadrilateral, in order, are $(x + 5)°$, $(x - 25)°$, $(2x - 95)°$ and $(175 - x)°$. Write down an equation and solve it to find the value of x. What are the numerical values of the sizes of the angles ? What sort of quadrilateral is it ?

Exercise B4   Activities

1. ### Motoring

How much does it cost to run a car (or, if you prefer, a motor bike) ? Before buying a car (or a motor bike) you should estimate how much it will cost you.
Make a list of all the necessary expenses and find the total annual cost, and hence the weekly cost.

2.   **History of numbers and calculation**

Counting can be traced back to very ancient times, and yet it is only a few years ago that modern calculators and computers were invented. You could make a topic booklet about this, including early methods of writing numbers in different parts of the world, and methods of calculation such as the abacus, Napier's bones and logarithms, and ending with a section on the development of the computer.

3.   **Probability of winning in competitions**

There are many competitions in newspapers, magazines and leaflets available in shops. Other competitions such as raffles are organised to raise money for Charities.

Examples:

1   If there are 8 items which you have to put in order of merit, find how many different entries are possible. Often the winning entry depends on the judge's opinion, so assume that all entries are equally likely to win. What is the probability that your entry is the correct one ?

2   If there are 8 questions each with possible answers, A, B, C, D, how many possible combinations of answers are there ? If you choose answers at random, what is the probability that your entry is the correct one ?

3   Premium Bonds are a form of gambling where you do not lose your original investment, but instead of earning interest on it the interest is paid out in prizes to the winners. You can get a leaflet from the Post Office which gives details about how the scheme works, and from this you can work out your chances of winning a prize.

4   You may like to try to work out the probability of winning on various 'fairground' games, fruit machines, or other forms of gambling such as the football pools, poker or roulette. But note that the promoter arranges things so that he makes a profit in the long run.

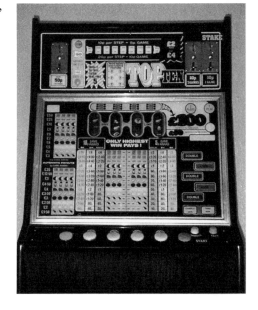

4. **The Sieve of Eratosthenes and prime numbers**

Write down the numbers from 1 to 200 in columns of 10.

```
1    2    3    4    5    6    7    8    9    10
11   12   13   14   15   16   17   18   19   20
21   22    ·    ·    ·
```

Draw a circle round 2 and then cross out all other
numbers which divide by 2. The 1st number not circled
or crossed out is 3. Draw a circle round 3 and then
cross out all other numbers which divide by 3. The next
number not crossed out or circled is 5. Draw a circle
round 5 and then cross out all other numbers which
divide by 5. The next number not crossed out is 7.
Draw a circle round 7 and then cross out all other
numbers which divide by 7.

Continue similarly with the numbers 11 and 13.

Now draw a circle round all the remaining numbers which are not crossed out.

The circled numbers are the prime numbers.

Why was it sufficient to stop at 13 ? If we had made a list up to 300 what other number
would need to be crossed out ?

This method can be used to find the prime numbers up to any large number.

1 is a special number, so mark it in a different way. It is not counted as a prime number
although it has no factors other than itself.

This method is known as 'The Sieve of Eratosthenes'. See if you can find out anything
about Eratosthenes who lived a long time ago.

Carry out further investigations with prime numbers.

First, get a list of more prime numbers, up to 500 or 1000.

Does the number of prime numbers in a range of 100 numbers decrease as the numbers
get larger ? E.g. Are there fewer prime numbers between 400 and 500 than between 300
and 400 ?

Prime numbers with a difference of 2 are called **prime pairs**. Examples are 29, 31; 41, 43.
Make a list of these for numbers less than 200. It is thought that the number of prime
pairs is infinite.

However, there is sometimes a sequence of consecutive numbers which are not prime, for
example, between the prime numbers 113 and 127 there are 13 numbers which are not
prime. Can you find a longer run of numbers which are not prime ?

With modern computers, searches can be made for larger prime numbers. The largest one
found (in 1992) was $2^{756839} - 1$. By now, a larger one may have been discovered. But it
can be proved that the number of prime numbers is infinite, so there is no such thing as
the largest prime number, only the largest one **known**.

5.   **Pentominoes and hexominoes**

Pentominoes are arrangements of 5 equal squares which join together with edges of
adjacent squares fitting exactly together, such as

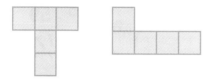

Pieces which would be identical if turned round or turned over are counted as the same.
Thus 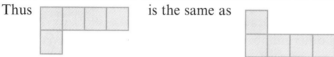 is the same as

There are 12 different pieces. Find them. Some of them will form the net of an 'open'
cube. Which ones ? The 12 pieces can be fitted together to form various rectangles.
Make some cardboard pieces and investigate.

Hexominoes consist of 6 squares joined together. Investigate these shapes and see how
many you can find. Some of them will form the net of a cube. Which ones ? Which
pieces can be used to make tessellations ?

6.   **Pythagoras' theorem**

State the theorem.
One way to prove the theorem is to use
similar triangles *ABC*, *DBA* and *DAC*.
See if you can discover this proof.
Can you find other ways of proving the theorem ?

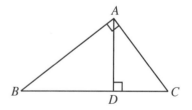

Dissections

1   Find the centre *X* of the square *BCRS*.
Draw lines through *X* parallel to *AC* and to *CT*.
This divides the square into 4 sections which you
can cut out. Also cut out square *ABPQ*.
Rearrange these 5 pieces to make the square *ACTU*.

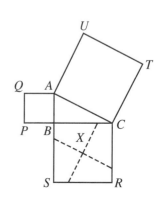

2   **Tangrams**. Use thin cardboard to make this.

Start with two equal squares and cut into 7 pieces as shown.

Rearrange these 7 pieces to make one large square.

This is an ancient puzzle. The pieces make many more shapes, using all 7 pieces each time. The pieces can be turned over.

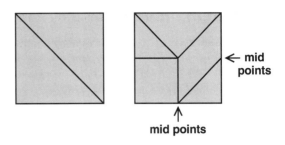

Make a parallelogram, an isosceles trapezium, a rectangle, an isosceles right-angled triangle and a trapezium with 2 adjacent right angles. Here are some other designs to make, and you can invent others.

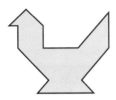

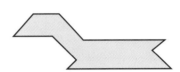

Problem

If you had a long piece of rope, divided by knots into 12 equal parts, how could you use it to make a right angle on the ground, e.g. to mark out a rectangular playing-area ?

Sets of numbers

The ones you probably know are 3 : 4 : 5, 5 : 12 : 13 and 8 : 15 : 17.
Investigate these and similar patterns to find others.

hypotenuse	1 other side	sum	difference	3rd side
5	4	9	1	3
13	12	25	1	5
...	...	...	1	7
5	3	8	2	4
17	15	32	2	8
...	...	72	2	12

Pythagoras

Consult library books and try to find out something about him. When did he live ? Where ? Like you, he tried to investigate patterns in numbers.

7. **Making models of a cylinder and a cone**

Cylinder

Use thin cardboard.

The circular ends are made from 2 circles, radius 3 cm.
The curved surface is made from a rectangle.
Length = 3.14 × diameter of cylinder
       = 3.14 × 6 cm = 18.8 cm
Breadth = height of cylinder = 8 cm

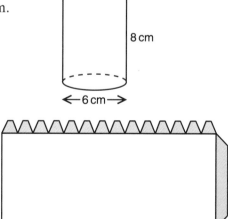

To stick the pieces together, tabs should be added
to the rectangle, as shown.
Score along the top and bottom edges with tabs,
but it is better not to score the edge with the
long tab.
Bend the rectangle carefully, and stick the long tab
behind the opposite edge.
Stick the circles onto the ends.

Cone

The base is made from a circle, radius 3 cm.
The curved surface is made from a sector of a circle
with radius 8 cm.
To find angle a, use the formula

$$a = \frac{\text{radius}}{\text{slant height}} \times 360°$$

In this case, $a = \frac{3}{8} \times 360° = 135°$

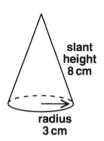

Tabs should be added to this piece,
as shown.
Score along the curved edge with tabs,
but it is better not to score the edge with
the long tab.
Bend the cone carefully, especially at its
point, and stick the long tab behind the
opposite edge.
Stick the circle onto the base.

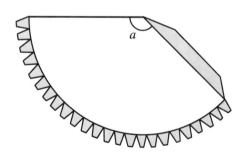

8. **Following new lines of enquiry**

When you are doing a mathematical activity, you may be able to extend your investigation and make further discoveries.
Here are some examples of how **you** could think of extending an investigation.

1   After investigating diagonals of polygons and finding a formula for the number of diagonals of a polygon with n sides, you could decide to investigate diagonals of solid figures such as the 5 regular solid figures (tetrahedron, cube, octahedron, dodecahedron and icosahedron). You could find a formula for the number of diagonals in terms of the numbers of vertices and edges.

2   After investigating the possible units digits of square numbers, decide to investigate the tens digits of the same numbers. Depending on what the units digit is, what can you discover about the tens digit ?

3   Having found a formula for the nth triangular number, decide to find a formula for the sum of the first n triangular numbers. Investigate any links between the numbers, the sums and Pascal's triangle. (In the song 'On the 12th day of Christmas', how many gifts were there altogether ?)

4   Having learnt Pythagoras' theorem, decide to see if a similar result is true for areas of semicircles or equilateral triangles drawn on the sides of a right-angled triangle.

You could, of course, carry out the above activities if you have not already done so, even though they are not your own ideas. Maybe you can extend them still further.

9. **Cardioids and other designs from circles**

Draw a circle and divide the circumference into 72 equal parts. (If you choose a radius just larger than that of your protractor you can mark off points every $5°$ along the protractor edge.)
Number the points from 1 to 72 in order.
Join 1 to 2, 2 to 4, 3 to 6, 4 to 8, and so on, with straight lines. After joining 36 to 72 imagine the numbering continues past 72, or continue numbering, so that the point numbered 2 is also number 74. Continue joining 37 to 74, 38 to 76, etc. Number 72 will join to 144, which is the same point, so just make a dot there.

You can investigate similar ideas by joining 1 to 3, 2 to 6, 3 to 9 etc., then 1 to 4, and so on. You can also number points in a positive direction and a negative direction and join 1 to −2, 2 to −4, etc.

The curves in the first group are called epicycloids.
The one joining k to $2k$ is a cardioid, and the one joining k to $3k$ is a nephroid.
The second group, joining k to $−2k$, k to $−3k$, etc. are called hypocycloids. For these, do not draw the circle, only mark the points, and manage without numbering them.
Draw another concentric circle with a radius 3 cm larger. When you join 2 points extend the line in both directions until it meets the outer circle.

10. **Using a computer**

If you have the use of a computer and a selection of computer programs then there are many investigations or activities which you can do.

The choice of activities will depend on the programs available, but here are a few general suggestions. If you have not got suitable software, it is often possible to do some investigations using simple programs which you can write yourself.

1   Statistical investigations, using spreadsheets to produce graphs and diagrams, and to calculate averages and measures of dispersion. Inserting and interrogating data in a database and drawing conclusions from it.

2   Probability investigations, using computer-generated random numbers to simulate throws of dice, tosses of coins, selections of discs, etc.

3   To investigate prime numbers and prime factors of numbers.

4   To investigate sequences, number chains, etc.

5   To draw graphs of algebraic functions. To draw graphs of growth, e.g. Compound Interest, or decay.

6   To solve equations by trial and improvement methods.

7   To do calculations using mathematical formulae, e.g. finding areas and volumes, or finding lengths and angles using trig. formulae.

8   Using LOGO or similar methods to generate and transform 2-D shapes. Devising instructions for the computer to produce certain shapes and paths.

The computer is a very powerful tool. Do make use of it.

PUZZLES

24.   What is the next prime number after 113 ?

25.   Five children were playing a game of cards.
      A set of cards numbered 1 to 10 are dealt so that they get two each. Paul has two cards which total 11, Mike has two cards which total 7, Laura has two cards which total 17, Kate has two cards which total 4 and Jane has two cards which total 16.
      In this game the winner is the person who has the card numbered 10. Who wins the game ?

To the student : 3

Improving your work

Check your handwriting and if necessary, improve it. It must be legible even when you are working quickly. Badly written work means that you confuse 6 with 0 or b, 2 with z, 5 with s, and so on. Show minus signs clearly. Do not alter figures, e.g. a 2 into a 3, by overwriting. Cross the 2 out and write the 3 nearby. Do not change $+$ into $-$ except by crossing it out and re-writing clearly. $+$ which might mean either $+$ or $-$ cannot be marked as correct because you have not made it clear which it is. Altered figures which are not clear cannot be marked as correct. So always make clear alterations.

Try to work at a reasonable speed. If you tend to work slowly, try to speed up, because in an examination you must give yourself a reasonable chance of completing the paper to gain good marks. When you are doing a question, concentrate completely on it so that you immediately think about the method, start it quickly, and continue working it out without a pause until you finish it. Work out any simple arithmetic in your head so that you do not break your concentration, and waste time, by pressing calculator keys. (You could do a check later, using the calculator, if you want to.)

Make sure that you use brackets correctly. $180 - 30 + 40$ is not the same as $180 - (30 + 40)$. The first expression equals 190, the second one equals 110. Be careful when you work out algebraic expressions or equations, especially those involving brackets.

Sketch diagrams, or rough plans of what you are going to do, are very useful even if they are not required as part of the answer.

When you have found an answer, consider if it is reasonable, especially if you have pressed calculator keys to get it. Look at the relative sizes of lengths or angles on the diagram, which should give a general idea even if the diagram is not drawn to an exact scale. A man earning £12 000 per year would not pay £30 000 per year in tax! It would also be rather unlikely for him to pay only £30 in tax. A circle with radius 10 cm cannot have a chord of length 24 cm. (Why ?) If the answer to a simple algebraic equation is an awkward number such as $x = -3\frac{10}{71}$, this **could** be correct, but it is more likely that you have made a mistake. When you have found an answer, give it correct to a suitable degree of accuracy. e.g. to 3 significant figures, and do not forget the units, e.g. £, cm, m^2, kg, where necessary.

11 Conversion graphs and other graphs

The topics in this chapter include:

- constructing and interpreting conversion graphs,

- interpreting graphs which describe real-life situations, including travel graphs,

- using networks to solve problems, constructing and interpreting information through network diagrams.

Conversion Graphs

Example

1   Draw a graph to convert kilometres into miles, given that 1 km = 0.62 miles.

Draw the 'kilometres' axis horizontally, label from 0 to 100.
Draw the 'miles' axis vertically, label from 0 to 70.

You know that 0 km = 0 miles, so plot a point at (0, 0).
Also 100 km = 100 × 0.62 miles = 62 miles, so plot a point at (100, 62).
A third point would be useful as a check.
50 km = 50 × 0.62 miles = 31 miles, so you can plot a point at (50, 31).
Join the points with a straight line.

You can use this graph to convert km into miles or miles into km.

1   Convert 23 km into miles.
2   Convert 50 miles into km.

Frankfurt
23 km

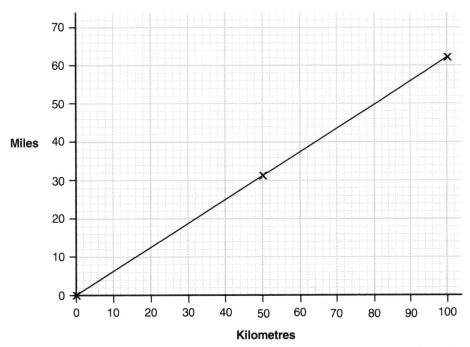

For **1**, draw a dotted line up from the horizontal axis where the reading is 23 km, to the graph. Then draw a dotted line sideways from this point on the graph to the vertical axis, where its value can be read. (It is 14 miles.)

For **2**, start with a dotted line sideways from the vertical axis where the reading is 50 miles, to the graph. Then draw a dotted line downwards from this point on the graph to the horizontal axis, where its value can be read. (It is 81 km.)

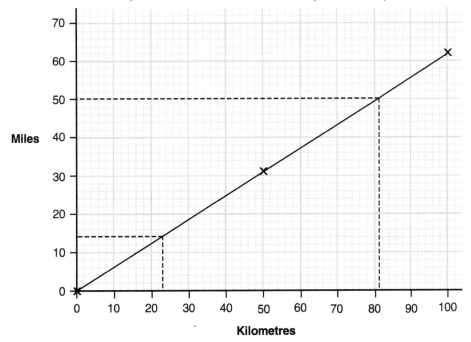

Other graphs

Example

2   A Gas Company makes a standing charge of £10 a quarter plus a cost of 1.5p for every
     kilowatt hour (kWh) of gas used.
     What would be the total bill if 8000 kWh were used ?
     What would be the total bill if 4000 kWh were used ?
     If no gas was used, there would still be the £10 standing charge to pay.

     Draw an accurate graph, with the number of kWh on the horizontal axis, from 0 to 8000,
     using a scale of 2 cm to represent 1000 kWh, and with cost in £'s on the vertical axis,
     from 0 to 130, using a scale of 2 cm to £20.

     Plot the 3 points corresponding to 0 kWh,
     4000 kWh and 8000 kWh used, and join
     them with a straight line.

     Use your graph to find the amount of the
     bill when 2800 kWh were used. Also find
     the number of kWh used if a gas bill was
     for £88.

     (This sketch graph shows how your
     accurate graph will look, and how it
     can be used.)

     8000 kWh cost £130,
     4000 kWh cost £70,
     2800 kWh cost £52,
     £88 is the cost of 5200 kWh.

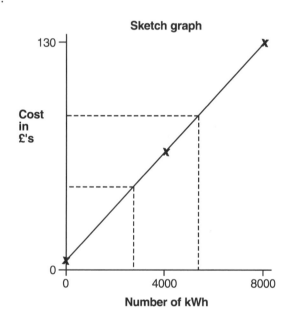

Sketch graph

Exercise 11.1

1.   Draw a graph to convert U.S. dollars into £'s at a time when the rate of exchange was
     1 dollar = £0.69. Draw the 'dollars' axis horizontally, label from 0 to 100. Draw the £'s
     axis vertically, label from 0 to 70. Plot the point representing 100 dollars on the graph
     and join it to the origin (0, 0) with a straight line.

     Use your graph to convert
     1   75 dollars into £'s,
     2   £22 into dollars.

     (If you know the up-to-date rate of exchange you may prefer to use that.)

2. Draw a graph to convert gallons into litres.
    Draw the 'gallons' axis horizontally, label from 0 to 10.
    Draw the 'litres' axis vertically, label from 0 to 50.
    10 gallons is equivalent to 45.5 litres.
    Plot this point on the graph and join it to the origin (0, 0) with a straight line.

    Use your graph to convert 6.5 gallons into litres, and to convert 10 litres into gallons.

3. When a local firm is called out to service machinery, it charges £40 for coming out plus
    an amount for time spent on the job, at the rate of £30 per hour.

    Draw a graph of the costs for jobs taking up to 5 hours.

    Use the graph to find
    1   the cost for a job taking $2\frac{1}{4}$ hours,
    2   the time spent, if the bill was for £175.

4. A tank contains water, and when it is drained by means of a tap the water level falls by
    2.5 cm each second. At the start, the depth of the water is 50 cm.
    Show on a graph the relationship between the depth of water and the time after opening
    the tap.

    Use the graph to find
    1   the depth of water in the tank after 12 seconds,
    2   the time taken for the tank to empty.

5. These times are taken from a table of 'lighting-up times for vehicles', on the Sunday of
    each week.

Week number	1	2	3	4	5	6	7	8
Time of day	16.32	16.40	16.50	17.02	17.14	17.26	17.39	17.52

Plot these values on a graph. Draw the 'week number' axis horizontally with 2 cm to each
unit. Draw the 'time of day' axis vertically, from 16.00 hours to 18.00 hours taking 1 cm
to 10 minutes. Join the plotted points with a smooth curve.

Travel graphs

Distance-time graphs

On a distance-time graph, the horizontal axis is the time axis and the vertical axis is the distance axis.

The graph is a straight line when the speed is steady. If the speed is not steady, the graph will not be a straight line.

When the speed is steady, its value is given by the gradient (slope) of the line. The greater the speed, the greater the gradient of the line.

If the gradient is negative, the object is travelling in the opposite direction to that in which the distance is measured.

Velocity is a word used instead of speed when the direction of motion is included.

Speed between A and B = gradient of line AB

$$= \frac{\text{increase in distance}}{\text{increase in time}}$$

$$= \frac{BC}{AC}$$

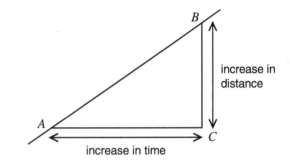

Example

1   This graph represents a boy's journey from a town P.

He leaves at 12 noon and walks for 30 minutes at a steady speed. This is represented by the line AB. The gradient of the line gives the speed. At what speed does he walk ?

The line BC represents the next stage, where he cycles.
For how long does he cycle ?
What distance does he cycle ?
At what speed does he cycle ?

The line CD represents a rest of 30 minutes.
How far is he away from P ?

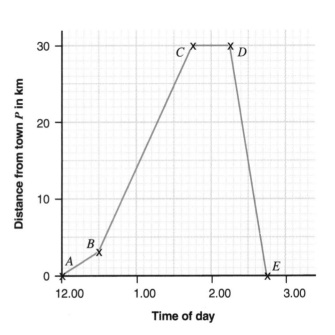

The line *DE* represents his journey home by bus.
What time does the bus journey begin ?
How long is the bus journey ?
What is the speed of the bus ?
(The gradient of the line *DE* gives the velocity which is negative because the direction of motion is in the opposite direction to that at first.)

Speed-time graphs

Example

2   Draw a graph to represent the journey of a car which starts from rest and increases its speed at a constant rate for 10 seconds, reaching a speed of 30 m/s. It maintains this speed for 30 seconds and then decreases its speed constantly at the rate of 2 m/s per second until it comes to rest.

Put time on the horizontal axis, from 0 to 55 s.
Put speed on the vertical axis, from 0 to 30 m/s.
For the first part of the journey, join the point (0, 0) to the point (10, 30) with a straight line.
Then draw a straight line with the speed 30 for the next 30 seconds.
Finally, the slowing down period from 30 m/s to 0 at the rate of 2 m/s per second will take 15 seconds. Draw the line to represent this.

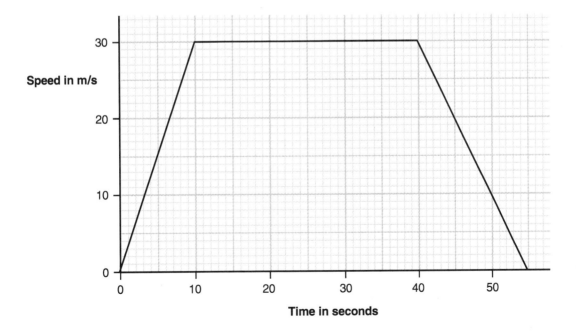

Use your graph to find the speed of the car at time 6 seconds, and at time 42 seconds.

Exercise 11.2

1. The graph represents the journey
   of a cyclist.
   What is the cyclist's speed ?

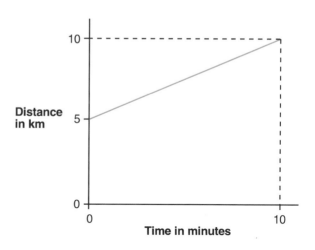

2. The diagram represents the journeys of 4 trains, 3 of them travelling from town *A*
   to town *B*, 100 km away, and one going in the opposite direction.

   1 Which two trains
         travel at the same
         speed ? What speed
         is it ?

   2 Which train has the
         slowest speed ?
         What speed is it ?

   3 Train (2) should have
         been travelling at a
         speed of 40 km/h.
         How many minutes
         late was it on reaching
         town *A* ?

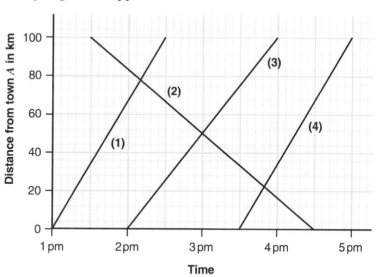

3. Paula leaves home to go to school. She walks at a steady speed of 5 km/h to her friend's
   home, which is $2\frac{1}{2}$ km away. There she waits for 20 minutes until her friend is ready to
   leave. The two girls are then taken by car to the school, which is 5 km away. The car
   travels at a steady speed of 30 km/h.
   Draw a graph to represent Paula's journey.

4. The graph represents the journeys of two motorists, one in a car and one in a van.

    1   At what time did the car reach *B* ?
    2   What was the speed of the van ?
    3   At what time, and how far from *A*, did the car pass the van ?
    4   How far apart were the car and the van at 2 pm ?
    5   What was the average speed of the car over the whole journey from A to B ?

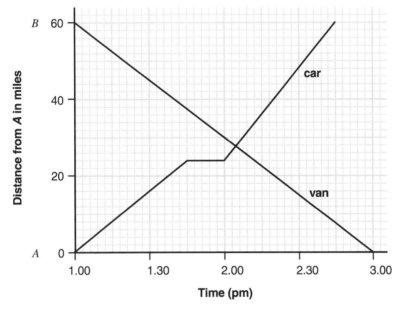

5. John cycled from home to a friend's house. He stayed for a while and then cycled home, stopping on the way to buy some sweets at a shop.
    The graph shows his journeys.

    1   How long did it take John to cycle to his friend's house ?
    2   How long did he stay at his friend's house ?
    3   How far from his friend's house was the shop ?
    4   How long did he spend in the shop ?
    5   After leaving the shop, what was John's speed on the homeward journey ?

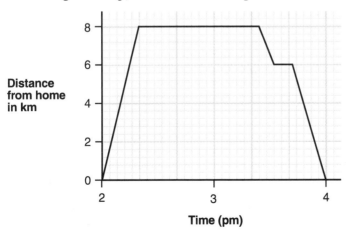

6.   A train starts from rest at a station *A* and increases speed at a steady rate for 2 minutes until it reaches a speed of 100 km/h. It maintains this steady speed for 12 minutes, and then slows down at a steady rate of 20 km/h per minute until it comes to a stop at station *B*.

Represent this information graphically on a speed-time graph.
Draw the time axis from 0 to 20 minutes and the speed axis from 0 to 100 km/h.

1   How far does the train travel at its highest speed ?

2   What is its speed after $\frac{1}{2}$ minute, and at what time is it next travelling at this speed ?

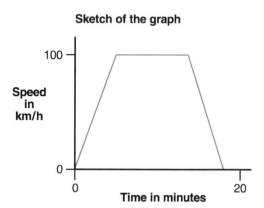

Sketch of the graph

7.   The table shows the speed of a train at various times as it travels between two stations.

Time from start, in seconds	0	15	30	45	60	75	90	105	120
Speed, in m/s	0	9	14	18	21	21	18	11	0

Draw a speed-time graph, joining the points with a smooth curve.
Draw the time axis from 0 to 120 seconds and the speed axis from 0 to 25 m/s.

Find from the graph
1   the greatest speed,
2   the two times when the train was travelling at half its greatest speed.

Sketch graphs

These can show the general relationship between two variables, without showing exact details. Often, one of the variables is time, and that usually goes on the horizontal axis.

Examples

Distance-time graphs

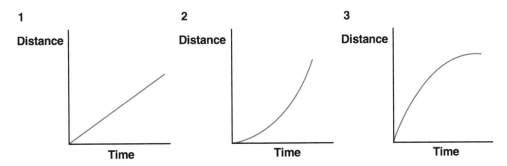

1   shows an object moving with a steady speed.
2   shows an object moving with an increasing speed (i.e. it is accelerating).
3   shows an object moving with a decreasing speed (i.e. it is slowing down).

Profits of a firm

4   shows that there is a steady increase in profits.
5   shows that there is a steady decrease in profits.
6   shows that for the first few months of the year, profits increased, but the rate of increase slowed down and profits reached a maximum, and then slowly fell. (If these profits were plotted every month, then the graph would not be a curve, because the readings are not continuous. It would be a line-graph (time-series graph), with points joined by a series of straight lines. However, in a sketch graph which shows the general relationship, it is reasonable to draw a curve.)

Other graphs

7

A wave graph

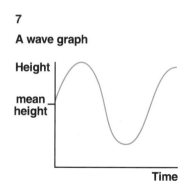

8

A cooling graph

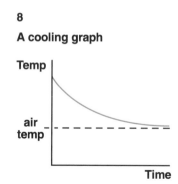

7   E.g. the height of the tide in a harbour.

8   The hot liquid cools quickly at first, then more slowly as it gets nearer to air temperature.

Filling containers

9   **10**   **11**

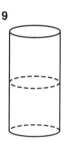  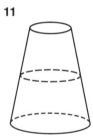

If liquid is poured into these containers at a steady rate of volume per second, then the rate at which the height of liquid increases depends on the shape of the container.

9   **10**   **11**

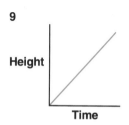 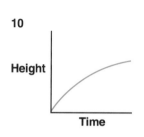 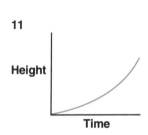

In **9**, the height will increase steadily.

In **10**, the height will increase quickly when there is a small area of cross-section, and increase more slowly as the area of cross-section increases.

In **11**, the height will increase slowly at first and increase more quickly as the area of the cross-section decreases.

A good way to decide what the graph looks like is to make a possible table of values, even though you are not going to plot them exactly.

Examples

12   A man's wages stay constant over several years.

Make a table of values. Suppose he earns £9000 per year.

Year	1	2	3	4	5
Wage (£)	9000	9000	9000	9000	9000

The graph looks like this.

13   The distance travelled by a car going at a constant speed, at different times.

Make a table of values. Suppose the speed is 30 mph.

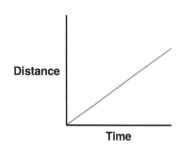

Time (hours)	0	1	2	3	4
Distance (miles)	0	30	60	90	120

The graph looks like this.

14   The level of water in a rectangular tank at different times when it is being drained and running out at a constant rate.

Make a table of values. Suppose the level is falling 10 cm/minute and it is 60 cm deep at the beginning.

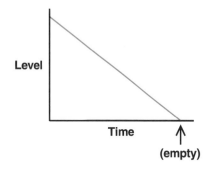

Time (min)	0	1	2	3	4	5	6
Level (cm)	60	50	40	30	20	10	0

The graph looks like this.

15   The connection between the area and radius of a circle.

$A = \pi r^2$ but take π as 3 to get a rough idea, in the table of values.

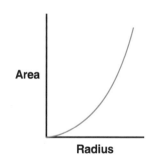

r	0	1	2	3	4
A	0	3	12	27	48

The graph looks like this.

16   The connection between the length and breadth of a
rectangle with a fixed area.

Make a table of values. Suppose the area is $12\,\text{cm}^2$.

Then length × breadth = 12, so length = $\dfrac{12}{\text{breadth}}$.

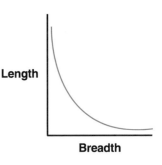

Length

Breadth	1	2	3	4	6	8	10	12
Length	12	6	4	3	2	1.5	1.2	1

Breadth

This is an inverse relationship so the graph looks like this.

Exercise 11.3

1.   These sketch graphs show the costs of running a business over several months.
Identify which sketch graph matches each of these statements.
1   The costs are rising steadily.
2   The costs are falling after having reached a peak.
3   The costs are rising at an increasing rate.
4   The costs have been rising but now seem to have levelled out.

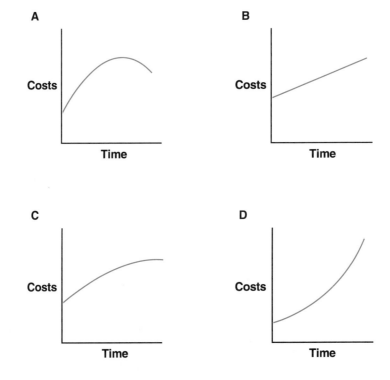

2. Draw sketch graphs to show the relationships between time and speed under these conditions.

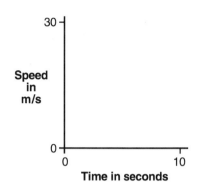

  1 The speed is kept constant, at 15 m/s.
  2 The speed increases at a steady rate, from rest to 30 m/s over 10 seconds.
  3 The speed decreases at a steady rate, from 30 m/s to 10 m/s in 10 seconds.

3. The graph shows the temperature recorded in the room of a house between 6 am and 6 pm.
Describe the changes in temperature and suggest likely reasons for them.

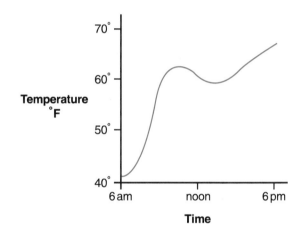

4. Draw sketch graphs to show the general relationships between these variables.
It may help you to make a table of values first, in some cases.
If the relationship is represented by a straight line, draw it using a ruler, not freehand.

  1 The connection between the number of trees bought and their cost, if they cost £8 each.
     (Number on the horizontal axis, cost in £'s on the vertical axis.)

  2 The connection between the time taken and the speed, to go a distance of 60 miles at various average speeds.
     (Time in hours on the horizontal axis, speed in mph on the vertical axis.)

  3 The distance-time graph of a runner in a race, who starts off quickly and gradually reduces speed until he is running very slowly, until the last quarter of the race where he makes a final burst of speed.
     (Time on the horizontal axis, distance on the vertical axis.)

5. Which of these graphs shows the true relationship between the perimeter of a square and the length of an edge ?

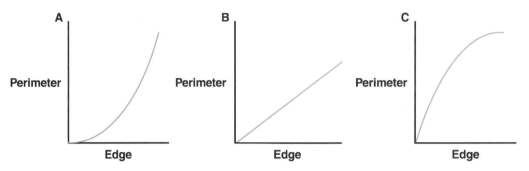

Networks

A network consists of a set of lines connecting a set of points.

Example

1 A messenger has to deliver magazines to 7 houses, *A, B, C, D, E, F* and *G*.
   He sets out and finishes at the shop. The network of possible routes is shown here.
   What is his shortest route ?

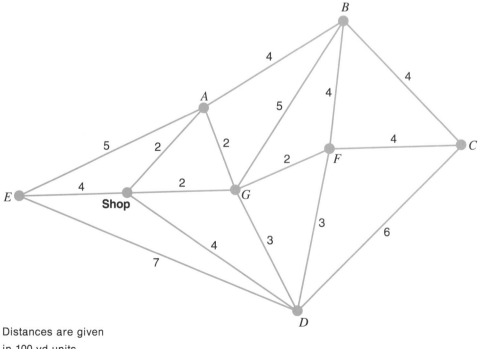

Distances are given
in 100 yd units,
i.e. 4 means 400 yd

There does not seem to be any better way to do this than by trying several routes. If he went round the outside paths in the order A, B, C, D, E, then the distances (in units) are

$$A \smile B \smile C \smile D \smile E$$
$$4 \quad 4 \quad 6 \quad 7$$

The longest distance here is from D to E so perhaps it might be shorter to start by going to one of these places first and finishing from the other.

$$\text{shop} \smile E \smile A \smile B \smile C \smile D \smile \text{shop}$$
$$4 \quad 5 \quad 4 \quad 4 \quad 6 \quad 4$$

Now F and G have to be fitted in.

To go to F between C and D just takes an extra 1 unit. This seems the best diversion for F.

To visit G after D and then return to the shop takes an extra 1 unit. This seems the best diversion for G.

So the route is

$$\text{shop} \smile E \smile A \smile B \smile C \smile F \smile D \smile G \smile \text{shop}$$
$$4 \quad 5 \quad 4 \quad 4 \quad 4 \quad 3 \quad 3 \quad 2 \quad = 29$$

We could do the same route in reverse order.

The total distance in 2900 yd.

Is this the shortest route ? We think it is.

This route is shown on the plan.

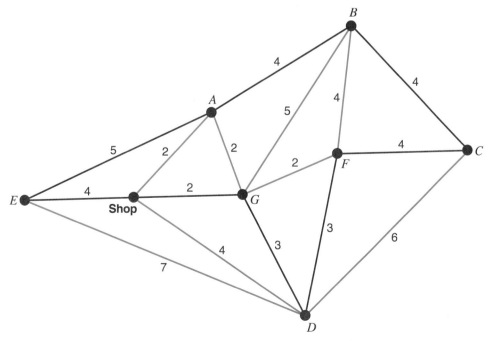

Using a network map, the London Undergound

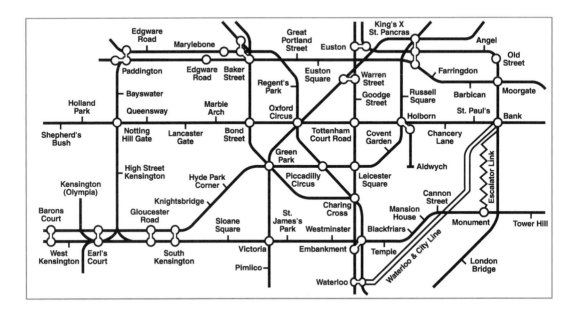

Try to find a proper map, because it will be in colour and you can give a more complete answer. You will probably have one if you live near London. If you have not, you often find them published in diaries or Guide books of London.

Example

2　　How would you get from Holland Park to South Kensington ?

First, find these two places. Holland Park is on the West of the above map, on the line running through the middle of the map. South Kensington is roughly South-East of it.

From Holland Park you would go 1 stop to Notting Hill Gate. This station is marked by a circle because it is a station where you can change to other lines. Change lines and go 3 stops to South Kensington. This makes 4 stops altogether with 1 change.
If you have a proper map, you would also know that you start on the Central Line, and then change to the Circle Line.

Exercise 11.4

1. Use the same network as in example **1** on page 248.
    On one particular week the person at *E* is on holiday so the messenger does not have to deliver there. In addition, there are roadworks which mean that he cannot go along the road between *G* and the shop. Which is the shortest route now ?

2. This map shows the network of local bus services. All the routes start from and return to the bus station.

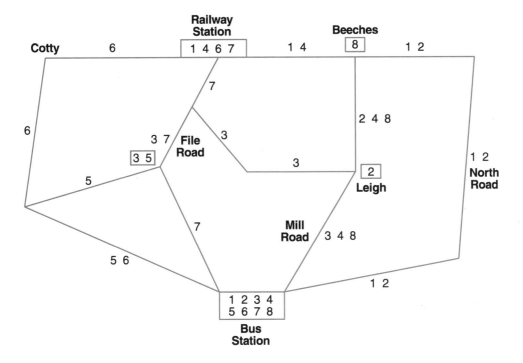

    Which number of bus must I get
    1   from Mill Road to Beeches,
    2   from Leigh to the Railway station,
    3   from the bus station to Cotty,
    4   from North Road to Leigh,
    5   from File Road to Mill Road ?

3.   Here is a map of the district around Wishby.

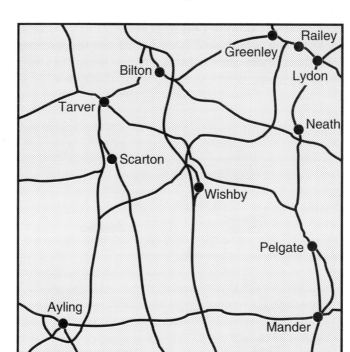

A salesman has to visit the 11 towns shown on the map, by car. He lives in Bilton so he will start and finish his journey there. Plan a suitable route for him to follow.

When you have decided on the best route, put tracing paper over the map and mark the 11 towns and the route joining them on your tracing paper.

Exercise 11.5 Applications

1.   Draw a graph to convert metres/second into km/h for speeds up to 50 m/s. Label the horizontal axis from 0 to 50 (m/s) and the vertical axis from 0 to 180 (km/h). Use the information that 0 m/s = 0 km/h and 50 m/s = 180 km/h to draw the straight-line graph. What speed is equivalent to   **1**   13 m/s,   **2**   100 km/h ?

2.   Draw a graph to convert temperature from °F to °C.
      Draw the °F axis horizontally, labelling it from 0 to 240, and draw the °C axis vertically, labelling it from 0 to 120.
      When the temperature is 32°F, it is 0°C. (Freezing point.)
      When the temperature is 212°F, it is 100°C. (Boiling point.)
      Plot these two points on the graph, and join them with a straight line.
      Use your graph to convert 70°F into °C, and to convert 80°C into °F.
      A person's 'normal' temperature is 98.4°F. What is the approximate value in °C ?

3. The cost, £C, of making n articles in a certain factory is given by the formula
C = 160 + 20n.
Draw a graph showing the cost for making up to 30 articles.
From the graph find how many articles can be made for £500.

4. Three workmen charge for doing a job as follows:
Mr A charges £240 for the 1st 40 hours and £10 an hour for any hours over 40.
Mr B charges a flat-rate of £12 per hour.
Mr C charges £300 for the job regardless of how long it will take.

Copy and fill in this table showing the charges by the three men for jobs up to 50 hours.

Number of hours	1	10	20	30	40	50
Mr A	£240					
Mr B	£12					
Mr C	£300					

Draw a graph with time on the horizontal axis, from 0 to 50 hours, and cost on the vertical axis from £0 to £600.
Plot the points in the table for Mr B, and join them with a straight line.
Draw the straight line representing the costs for Mr C.
For Mr A the graph consists of two straight lines, one to the point (40, 240) and one past that point. Draw this graph.
Label the graphs for Mr A, Mr B and Mr C.

From your graphs find
1 which man charges least for a job taking 15 hours,
2 which man charges least for a job taking 25 hours,
3 which man charges least for a job taking 48 hours.

5. The temperature of water in a jug is shown in this table.

Time in minutes	0	2	4	6	8	10	12
Temperature in °C	100	60	40	30	25	23	21

Plot the points on a graph with time on the horizontal axis, from 0 to 12 minutes, and temperature on the vertical axis, from 0° to 100°.
Join the points with a smooth curve.
Use the graph to estimate the temperature of the water after 7 minutes.

6. Karen walks from school to a bus stop and then catches a bus which takes her to the village. She then walks the remaining distance home. The journey is shown by the graph.

    1 How long does Karen wait at the bus stop ?
    2 At what speed does the bus travel ?
    3 How far does Karen walk after getting off the bus ?

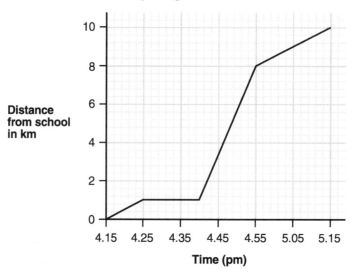

7. A train leaves town A for town B at 1 pm and maintains a steady speed of 60 km/h. At 2 pm another train leaves B for A maintaining a steady speed of 60 km/h. The distance between A and B is 180 km. Draw the distance-time graphs for these two trains using the same axes. Draw the time axis with times from 1 pm to 5 pm and the distance axis with distances from A from 0 to 180 km with A at 0 and B at 180.
    When do the trains pass one another and how far are they from A at this time ?

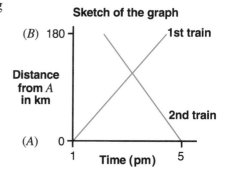

8. The table gives the distances travelled by a car at various times.

Time after start, in seconds	0	1	2	3	4	5	6	7	8
Distance from start, in metres	0	0.6	2.5	5.5	9.8	15.3	20.7	22.6	23.2

Draw a distance-time graph, joining the points with a smooth curve.

Use the graph to estimate
1 the distance from the starting point after 3.5 s,
2 the time taken to travel a distance of 20 m.

9. A rocket is fired vertically into the air from ground level, and its height h metres after t seconds is given in the table.

t	0	5	10	15	20	25	30
h	0	625	1000	1125	1000	625	0

Draw a distance-time graph, joining the points with a smooth curve.

1   What is the greatest height achieved by the rocket ?
2   At what times is the rocket at half of its greatest height ?
3   For how many seconds is the rocket 900 m or more above the ground ?

10. The speed of a racing-car during the first minute after starting from rest is given in this table.

Time in seconds	0	10	20	30	40	50	60
Speed in m/s	0	28	46	51	47	43	46

Draw the speed-time graph, joining the points with a smooth curve.
Use the graph to estimate the speed 15 seconds after the start.

11. The graph shows a man's weight at different ages.
Describe the changes in weight and suggest possible reasons for them.

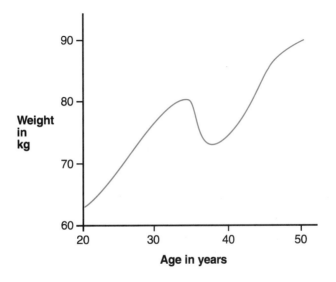

12. The graph shows how the depth
     of water in a harbour varies
     throughout the day.

     1   At what times were high tide ?
     2   At what times were low tide ?
     3   Estimate the time of the next high
             tide.

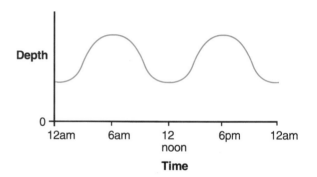

13. Draw sketch graphs to show the daily attendances at a show at a theatre over 6 weeks,
     for the following descriptions.

     1   We started off with half-full attendance, but the attendances rose steadily and we
             have had a full house for the last two weeks.
     2   We started off with a full house for the first three weeks but then the numbers started
             falling and we are now running to a nearly empty theatre.
     3   We started off with half-full attendances. The numbers rose quite rapidly and we had
             a full house after two weeks. This state lasted for two weeks but now the numbers are
             falling slowly. We are still quite full, though.

14. Draw sketch graphs showing the relationship between time and height of water when
     these containers are being filled with water which is being poured in at a steady rate of
     volume per second.

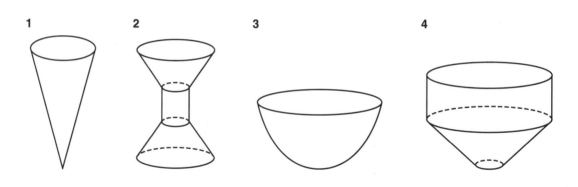

15. These sketch graphs show these relationships. Identify which is which.
    1   The diameter, x cm, of a circle, and the circumference, y cm.
    2   The length, x cm, and the breadth, y cm, of a rectangle of constant area 48 cm^2.
    3   The distance travelled by a young child over several seconds when running to meet his mother who is waiting for him 100 m away.
    4   The amount £y in a savings account after x years when the rate of interest is 10%.

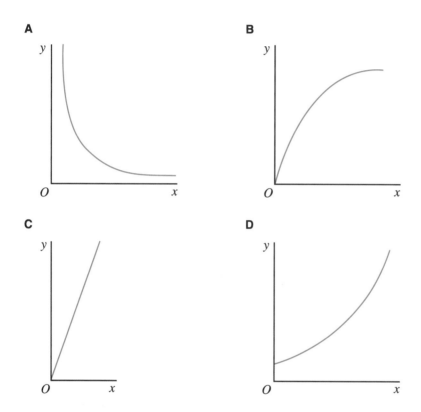

16. The most famous problem connected with a network is 'The Bridges of Königsberg'.

There were 7 bridges over the various parts of the river. The townspeople suspected that the 7 bridges could not be crossed in one continuous walk without recrossing the route somewhere. In 1735, Euler, one of the world's great mathematicians, was asked to give a proof of this, which he did. Now, if there was an 8th bridge, just out of view on the left side of the picture, would it be possible to cross the 8 bridges in one continuous walk ?

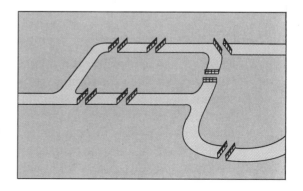

17. Use the map of the London Underground on page 250, or a coloured map, to answer these questions.

How would you get by the most direct way
  1 from Bond Street to Blackfriars,
  2 from Oxford Circus to Westminster,
  3 from Victoria to Euston,
  4 from Tottenham Court Road to Knightsbridge,
  5 from Farringdon to Bank,
  6 from Green Park to Baker Street,
  7 from Euston Square to Russell Square,
  8 from Sloane Square to Marble Arch,
  9 from Bayswater to Pimlico,
  10 from Tower Hill to Piccadilly Circus ?

18. This is a map of Queensbury village.

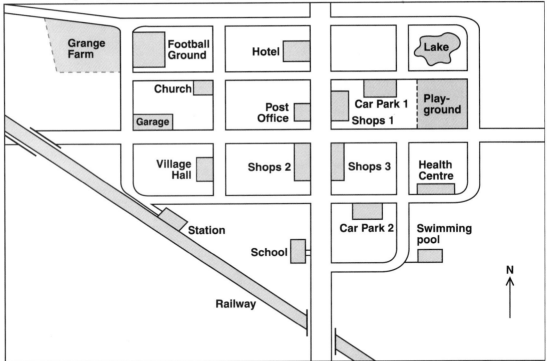

  1 The postman comes into the village by van to deliver parcels. On one morning he has parcels to deliver to the Church, garage, Grange Farm, Health Centre, hotel, railway station, shops (2), shops (3), swimming pool, school and Village Hall. He enters the town from the West and leaves the same way, but just before leaving he calls at the Post Office to collect any parcels to be taken to town. Plan a suitable route for the postman to take. The village roads are not too busy so he can approach places from either direction and walk across the roads when necessary.
  Put tracing paper over the map to mark your route on.

2   The local policeman does a patrol of the village on his motorcycle. He wants to go along every part of every road in the village. He comes into the village from the East, and leaves by the road going South. Plan a suitable route for him to take, keeping to a minimum the places where he travels along the same stretch of road more than once. Put tracing paper over the map to mark your route on.

19.   It is possible to draw the networks (a) and (b) without taking your pencil off the paper and without going along any line more than once. However, this cannot be done for (c). Copy the diagrams for (a) and (b) and show how you can draw the networks, labelling the starting and ending points and marking the route by drawing over it freehand with a coloured pen.

(a)   **(b)**   **(c)**

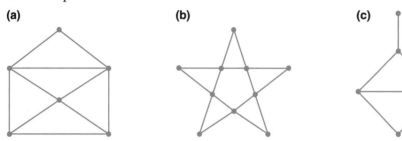

Find out whether these networks can be drawn similarly, and for those which can, copy them and show your solution.

1   **2**   **3**   **4**

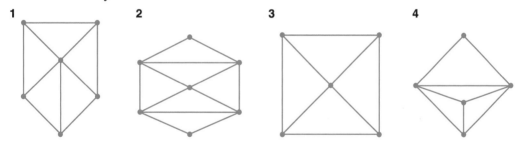

Practice test 11

1.   Draw a graph to convert between British and Spanish currency at a time when the rate of exchange was £1 = 190 pesetas.
  On the horizontal axis, for £'s, label from 0 to 10 with 1 unit to 1 cm. On the vertical axis, for pesetas, label from 0 to 2000 with 200 units to 1 cm.
  Plot the point representing £10 in pesetas and join this to the origin with a straight line.

  From your graph find
  1   the amount you would get if you changed £3 into pesetas,
  2   the value in British money of a present which cost you 1500 pesetas.

  (If you know the up-to-date rate of exchange you may prefer to use that.)

2.   The graph shows the journeys of 2 girls, Pam and Ruth.
      Pam cycles from town *A* to village *B*, stopping for a rest on the way. Ruth cycles from
      village *B* to town *A*.

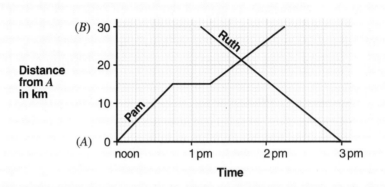

1   For how long did Pam rest ?
2   What was Pam's average speed on the part of her journey after her rest ?
3   When did the two girls pass each other and how far from *B* were they at this time ?
4   How far apart were the girls at 2.00 pm ?
5   How far did Ruth travel between 2.00 pm and 3.00 pm ?
6   What was Ruth's average speed ?

3.   Two cars start at 9 am, one from place *A* and the other from place *B*, which is
      60 miles from *A*. They move towards each other, the first car travelling at 30 mph
      and the other one at 40 mph.
      Show these journeys on a graph.
      At what time do the cars meet, and how far are they from *A* when they meet ?

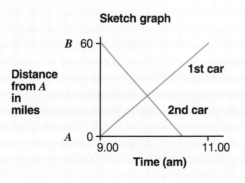

Sketch graph

4. The following values of the speed of an object at different times are obtained by experiment. Plot the values on a graph with time on the horizontal axis and speed on the vertical axis, and show that the plotted points lie approximately on a straight line. Draw this line and use it to estimate the speed at time 3.5 seconds.

Time in seconds	1	2	3	4	5	6
Speed in m/s	2.0	2.7	3.6	4.4	5.3	5.9

5. These sketch graphs show the amount of water in a storage tank, during a day when it was being filled.

Identify which sketch matches each of these statements.
1   The tank has been filling all day at a steady rate.
2   The tank has been filling all day, and at an increasing rate as the day progressed.
3   This morning the tank was gradually filled until it was full and since then it has been kept topped up.
4   The tank was filled gradually this morning until it was full. Since then some water has been taken out and not yet replaced.

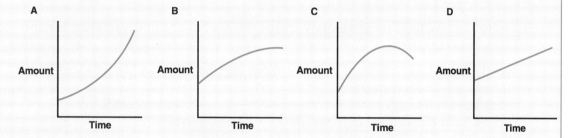

6. Find out whether these networks can be drawn without taking your pencil off the paper and without going along any line more than once. For those that can be drawn in this way, copy them and show your solution, labelling the starting and ending points and marking the route by drawing over it freehand with a coloured pen.

1   2   3   4

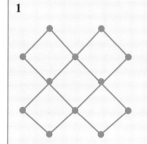

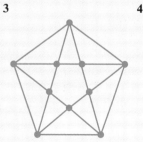
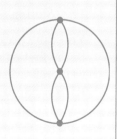

12 *Simultaneous equations*

The topics in this chapter include:

- using algebraic methods to solve simultaneous equations.

Simultaneous equations

Examples

1   Solve the equations $5x + 2y = 53$
$$3x - 2y = 19$$

The first equation has an unlimited number of solutions such as $x = 0$, $y = 26\frac{1}{2}$ or $x = 10$, $y = 1\frac{1}{2}$, and the second equation also has an unlimited number of solutions, e.g. $x = 7$, $y = 1$ or $x = \frac{1}{3}$, $y = -9$.

To solve the equations **simultaneously** means that we have to find a solution which satisfies both equations.

If we add the left hand sides of both equations together, they will be balanced by the right hand sides added together.
The left hand sides added together are $5x + 2y + 3x - 2y$ which equals $8x$.
The right hand sides added together are $53 + 19$ which equals 72.
So $8x = 72$
$\qquad x = 9$
To find y, substitute the value $x = 9$ into either of the original equations.
$$\begin{aligned} 5x + 2y &= 53 \\ 5 \times 9 + 2y &= 53 \\ 45 + 2y &= 53 \\ 2y &= 8 \\ y &= 4 \end{aligned}$$
The solution of the simultaneous equations is $x = 9$, $y = 4$.

You can check the solution in both equations.
In the first equation, when $x = 9$ and $y = 4$,
LHS $= 5 \times 9 + 2 \times 4 = 45 + 8 = 53$.
RHS $= 53$, so the solution is correct.
In the second equation, when $x = 9$ and $y = 4$,
LHS $= 3 \times 9 - 2 \times 4 = 27 - 8 = 19$.
RHS $= 19$, so the solution is correct.

Notice that:
If the equations are written down underneath each other with the x's in one column and the y's in another, it is easy to add them up.

$$5x + 2y = 53$$
$$\underline{3x - 2y = 19}$$

Adding, $8x\qquad = 72$

By adding the equations together the terms involving y disappeared. Then we were able to find the value of x.

The terms involving y disappeared because they had the same numerical **coefficient**, both 2. Also one term was $+2y$ and the other $-2y$.
Often the coefficients are not the same so we have to make them the same before we add the equations.

(In the next example, to make it simpler to describe what we are doing, we label the equations (1) and (2).)

2   Solve the equations $3x + 2y = 5$ (1)
$5x - 6y = 27$ (2)

The coefficients of y are 2 and -6.
We can make $2y$ into $6y$ by multiplying by 3. We must multiply every term of (1) by 3.

Multiply (1) by 3, and write down (2) again.
$9x + 6y = 15$ (1a)
$5x - 6y = 27$ (2)

Add (1a) and (2).
$14x = 42$
$x = 3$

Substitute $x = 3$ in (1).
$3 \times 3 + 2y = 5$
$9 + 2y = 5$
$2y = -4$
$y = -2$
The solution is $x = 3$, $y = -2$.

To check the solution:
For (1), LHS $= 3x + 2y = 3 \times 3 + 2 \times (-2) = 9 - 4 = 5$, and RHS $= 5$
For (2), LHS $= 5x - 6y = 5 \times 3 - 6 \times (-2) = 15 + 12 = 27$ and RHS $= 27$.
The solution is correct.

3   Solve the equations $3x - 5y = 15$ (1)
$$2x + 3y = 29 \quad (2)$$

Make both coefficients of y into 15.
Multiply (1) by 3 and (2) by 5.

$9x - 15y = 45$ (1a)
$10x + 15y = 145$ (2a)

Add (1a) and (2a).
$19x = 190$
$x = 10$

Substitute $x = 10$ in (2).
$2 \times 10 + 3y = 29$
$20 + 3y = 29$
$3y = 9$
$y = 3$
The solution is $x = 10$, $y = 3$.

You can check for yourself that this solution is correct.

Exercise 12.1

Solve these simultaneous equations.

1. $x + y = 8$
$x - y = 4$

6. $5x + 4y = 39$
$6x - y = 70$

2. $5x + y = 14$
$7x - y = 22$

7. $4x + 3y = 12$
$3x - 2y = 9$

3. $5x - 3y = 0$
$2x + 3y = 10\frac{1}{2}$

8. $2x + 3y = -7$
$3x - 4y = -2$

4. $2x + 3y = -2$
$3x - y = 8$

9. $7x - 5y = -11$
$3x + 2y = -13$

5. $2x - 3y = -18$
$4x + y = 6$

10. $2x - 3y = 5\frac{1}{2}$
$3x + 2y = -1\frac{1}{2}$

11. $5x + 8y = 7x - 3y = 71$

12. $3x + 5y = 5x - 3y = 19 - 2y$

Using subtraction

Examples

1 Solve the equations $3x + 2y = 10$ (1)
$$7x + 2y = 26 \quad (2)$$

Although the coefficients of the terms in y are the same, they are both $+2$. To eliminate the terms in y, we must subtract.

Subtract (1) from (2).
$$4x = 16$$
$$x = 4$$

If, instead, you subtract (2) from (1) you get
$$-4x = -16$$
$$4x = 16$$
$$x = 4, \text{ as before.}$$

Substitute $x = 4$ in (1).
$$3 \times 4 + 2y = 10$$
$$12 + 2y = 10$$
$$2y = -2$$
$$y = -1$$
The solution is $x = 4$, $y = -1$.

To check the solution:
In (1), LHS $= 3x + 2y = 3 \times 4 + 2 \times (-1) = 12 - 2 = 10$, and RHS $= 10$.
In (2), LHS $= 7x + 2y = 7 \times 4 + 2 \times (-1) = 28 - 2 = 26$, and RHS $= 26$.
The solution is correct.

2 Solve the equations $5x - 3y = 29$ (1)
$$4x - 2y = 24 \quad (2)$$

Make both terms in y into $-6y$.
Multiply (1) by 2 and multiply (2) by 3.
$$10x - 6y = 58 \quad (1a)$$
$$12x - 6y = 72 \quad (2a)$$

Subtract (1a) from (2a).
$$2x = 14$$
$$x = 7$$

Notice that when subtracting, $(-6y)$ take away $(-6y)$
$$= (-6y) - (-6y)$$
$$= (-6y) + 6y$$
$$= 0$$

Substitute $x = 7$ into (2).

$$28 - 2y = 24$$
$$28 = 24 + 2y$$
$$4 = 2y$$
$$y = 2$$

The solution is $x = 7$, $y = 2$.

You can check for yourself that this solution is correct.

Sometimes it may be easier to eliminate x rather than y.

3   Solve the equations $3x + 5y = \quad 9$ (1)
$\qquad\qquad\qquad\qquad\quad x + 6y = -10$ (2)

Multiply (2) by 3. Write down (1) again, if you want to.
$3x + 18y = -30$ (2a)
$3x + \quad 5y = \quad 9$ (1)
Subtract (1) from (2a).

$$13y = -39$$
$$y = -3$$

Substitute $y = -3$ in (2).
$x + 6 \times (-3) = -10$
$x - 18 \qquad\quad = -10$
$\qquad\quad x = 8$

The solution is $x = 8$, $y = -3$.

To check the solution:
For (1), LHS $= 3x + 5y = 3 \times 8 + 5 \times (-3) = 24 - 15 = 9$, and RHS $= 9$.
For (2), LHS $= x + 6y = 8 + 6 \times (-3) = 8 - 18 = -10$, and RHS $= -10$.
The solution is correct.

Be very careful if subtracting numbers or terms with negative signs.
e.g. in a case like $3x - 6y = \quad 6$ (1)
$\qquad\qquad\qquad\quad 3x - 5y = 11$ (2)
When subtracting (2) from (1), $(-6y) - (-5y) = (-6y) + 5y = -y$.
When subtracting (1) from (2), $(-5y) - (-6y) = (-5y) + 6y = y$.

Exercise 12.2

Solve these simultaneous equations.

1. $2x + y = 13$
$\qquad x + y = \quad 8$

2. $x + 7y = 33$
$\qquad x + 2y = \quad 8$

3. $2x - 6y = 18$
$\qquad 2x - 5y = 15\frac{1}{2}$

4. $2x - \quad y = \quad 9$
$\qquad 3x - 2y = 11$

5. $2x + 3y = 0$
    $x + 6y = 9$

8. $3x + 2y = 2$
    $7x + 3y = 3$

6. $3x - y = 6$
    $x - 5y = 2$

9. $2x - 3y = 5$
    $3x - 2y = 25$

7. $x + 5y = -3$
    $2x + 3y = 1$

10. $5x + 3y = -7$
     $7x + 5y = -13$

11. $3x + 8y = 5x + 2y = 51$

12. $4x + 5y = 5x + 4y = 3x + y - 10$

Solving by substitution

This method is useful when we have a term containing x (i.e. not $2x$, $3x$, etc.) or y.

Example

1   Solve the equations $x - 8y = 3$ (1)
                            $3x - 10y = 2$ (2)

(1) can be written as $x = 3 + 8y$ (1a)
Substitute this expression for x in (2).
$3(3 + 8y) - 10y = 2$
Remove the bracket and solve in the usual way.
$9 + 24y - 10y = 2$
$\qquad 9 + 14y = 2$
$\qquad\qquad 14y = -7$
$\qquad\qquad\quad y = -\frac{1}{2}$

Use (1a) again, substituting $y = -\frac{1}{2}$.

$x = 3 + 8 \times \left(-\frac{1}{2}\right)$
$\quad = 3 - 4$
$\quad = -1$

The solution is $x = -1$, $y = -\frac{1}{2}$.

To check the solution $x = -1$, $y = -\frac{1}{2}$:
For (1), LHS $= x - 8y = (-1) - 8 \times \left(-\frac{1}{2}\right) = (-1) + 4 = 3$, and RHS $= 3$.
For (2), LHS $= 3x - 10y = 3 \times (-1) - 10 \times \left(-\frac{1}{2}\right) = (-3) + 5 = 2$, and RHS $= 2$.
The solution is correct.

2   Solve the equations $2x - 3y = 5$ (1)
$$3x + y = 2 \quad (2)$$

(2) can be written as $y = 2 - 3x$ (2a)
Substitute this expression for y in (1).
$$2x - 3(2 - 3x) = 5$$
$$2x - 6 + 9x = 5$$
$$11x - 6 = 5$$
$$11x = 11$$
$$x = 1$$
Use (2a) again, substituting $x = 1$.
$$y = 2 - 3 \times 1$$
$$= 2 - 3$$
$$= -1$$

The solution is $x = 1$, $y = -1$.

You can check for yourself that this solution is correct.

Using simultaneous equations to solve problems

Example

3   3 lamps and 4 metres of wire cost £38,
and 5 lamps and 14 metres of wire cost £67.
What is the cost of a lamp, and how much
does a metre of wire cost ?

Let a lamp cost £x and a metre of wire cost £y.
Then $3x + 4y = 38$ (1)   (working in £'s)
$$5x + 14y = 67 \quad (2)$$
Multiply (1) by 5 and (2) by 3.
$$15x + 20y = 190 \quad (1a)$$
$$15x + 42y = 201 \quad (2a)$$
Subtract (1a) from (2a).
$$22y = 11$$
$$y = \tfrac{1}{2} \quad \text{(Thus wire costs £}\tfrac{1}{2}\text{ per metre.)}$$
Substitute $y = \tfrac{1}{2}$ in (1).
$$3x + 4 \times \tfrac{1}{2} = 38$$
$$3x + 2 = 38$$
$$3x = 36$$
$$x = 12 \quad \text{(Thus a lamp costs £12.)}$$

A lamp costs £12 and a metre of wire costs 50p.

You can check the solution using the details of the question.

Exercise 12.3

Solve these equations by the method of substitution.

1. $x - 4y = -1$
    $3x + 2y = 11$

2. $4x - 3y = 22$
    $2x + y = 6$

3. $x - y = 2$
    $3x - 4y = 5\frac{1}{2}$

4. $x - 2y = -7$
    $7x + y = -4$

5. $x + 2y = 18$
    $3x + 5y = 47$

6. $5x + 3y = -25$
    $7x + y = -19$

Solve these equations using any suitable method.

7. $4x + 3y = 34$
    $x - 3y = 1$

8. $3x - 4y = 5$
    $2x + y = -4$

9. $3x + 4y = 10$
    $2x + 3y = 8$

10. $x + 5y = 7$
    $3x - y = -11$

11. $3x + 8y = 7$
    $5x - 6y = 2$

12. $7x - 3y = 26$
    $9x - 5y = 30$

13. $2x + 3y = -10$
    $4x - y = 15$

14. $2x - 3y = -1$
    $4x - y = -2$

15. $3x + 4y = 6$
    $4x - y = -11$

16. $3x + 4y = 0$
    $2x + 5y = -7$

17. $3x - 2y = 1$
    $5x - 6y = 3$

18. $x + 3y = 3x - 5y = 7$

19. $5x - 2y = 7x + 2y = x - 5$

20. $10x + y = 7x - y + 18 = 77$

21. Write down two equations connecting x and y, simplify them, and solve them simultaneously. Hence find the numerical values of the lengths of the sides of this parallelogram.

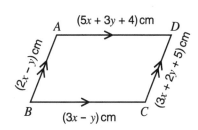

22. At a snack-bar, 5 cups of tea and 3 cups of coffee cost £2.30, and 3 cups of tea and 2 cups of coffee cost £1.45. What is the price of a cup of tea, and of a cup of coffee? (Let a cup of tea cost x pence and a cup of coffee cost y pence. Write down two equations and solve them simultaneously.)

Exercise 12.4 Applications

1. Patrick buys a bunch of 10 roses and 5 carnations for his wife, and they cost £3.50. At the same stall, Margaret buys a bunch of 8 roses and 10 carnations for her mother, and they cost £4.
Find the cost of 1 rose, and 1 carnation.
(Let 1 rose cost r pence and 1 carnation cost c pence.)

2. Write down two equations connecting x and y, simplify them, and solve them simultaneously. Hence find the numerical values of the three angles.

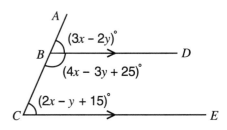

3. If this triangle is equilateral, write down an equation connecting x and y and simplify it. Write down a second equation connecting x and y and simplify it. Solve the equations simultaneously to find x and y. What is the numerical value of the perimeter of the triangle ?

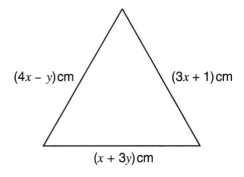

4. The law of a machine is given by $E = aR + C$. When $R = 10$, $E = 5.5$ and when $R = 40$, $E = 7$.   Find the values of a and C.

5. An employer pays some of his workers £50 per day, and others £40 a day. Altogether he has 30 workers and the daily wages amount to £1440. How many workers get the £40 wage ?
(Let x workers get £50 per day and y workers get £40 per day.)

6. Two rolls of carpet are together worth £1200. The first roll costs £20 per metre. The second, which is 12 m longer than the first, costs £16 per metre. How many metres were there in each roll ?

7.   If $y = ax + b$, and x and y satisfy this table of values, what are the values of a and b ?

x	1	2	3
y	−1	2	5

8. $7x + 5y = 47$
$5x + 7y = 49$.
Find the values of   1 $x + y$,   2 $x - y$.
Hence find the values of x and y.

Practice test 12

1.   The sum of two numbers is 168 and their difference is 18. What are they ?
(Let the numbers be x and y.)

2.   Solve the simultaneous equations.

1    $2x - 9y = 19$
$5x + 9y = 16$

4    $3x + 5y = 8$
$5x + 3y = 16$

2    $8x - 2y = 48$
$6x - y = 38$

5    $x = 15 - y$
$3x + 2y = 34$

3    $5x - 2y = -11$
$6x + 7y = 15$

3.   Entrance fees to a show for 3 adults and 2 children total £6.80; for 2 adults and
5 children it costs £8.20. How much is the cost for an adult, and for a child ?

PUZZLE

26.   How many triangles are there in this figure ?

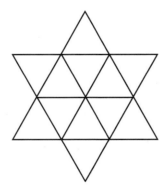

13 Statistical investigations and averages

> **The topics in this chapter include:**
>
> - specifying a simple hypothesis, designing and using a questionnaire, collecting and analysing results,
> - designing and using a questionnaire with multiple responses,
> - using and recording grouped data, producing a frequency table, calculating the mean, comparing the mean, median, mode and range of a frequency distribution for given sets of data and interpreting the results.

A statistical investigation

To carry out a statistical investigation, first of all decide what is the **aim** of the investigation. Then you can decide where to obtain the data you need, whether you will collect it for yourself or whether you will find it elsewhere.
If you are collecting data for yourself, you will probably need to make a tally table on which to record it.

When you have carried out the investigation, you should then display your information in an interesting way, so that other people can read about it. Make neat lists or tables, and include statistical diagrams.

Questionnaires

To conduct a survey amongst a group of people one way is to ask them to answer a questionnaire. You can either give them the questionnaire to fill in themselves or you can ask the questions and write down their answers.
Decide exactly what information you want and how you are planning to use the answers.
Keep the questionnaire as short as possible, and keep the questions short, clear and precise.
Avoid questions which people may not be willing to answer because they are embarrassing or offensive.

The best questions can be answered by categories, such as the ones below, where you can put a tick in one of the boxes.

Age

Under 20	
20–under 40	
40–under 60	
60 or over	

No	
Yes	
Don't know	

Strongly agree	
Agree	
Don't know/no opinion	
Disagree	
Strongly disagree	

'How long do you spend watching TV ?' This is a very vague question, and will produce equally vague answers, so you will find it difficult to analyse the data.

'How long did you spend watching TV yesterday ? Tick one of the following:'

Not at all	
Up to 1 hour	
Between 1 and 3 hours	
Between 3 and 5 hours	
Over 5 hours	

This is much more precise, and you have only to count the ticks in each category to have some useful data about viewing habits.

It is a good idea to try out your questionnaire on a few people first to see if it is clear enough and likely to give you the data you need, or whether it needs improving. This is called a **pilot survey**.

If you are asking members of the public for their views, you have not the resources, time or authority to make a proper sample. You will probably have to question people in the street or shopping area, and your sample will have to consist of people in that area at that time. (But a survey on where people shop could be biased if you select your sample from outside the largest supermarket in the area.) Try to make your sample representative by including people of different ages, and equal numbers of men and women. Be very polite when you approach people, and thank them afterwards for their help. Remember that some people will be in too much of a hurry to stop to talk to you. Before you do such a survey, discuss your plans with your teacher and with your parents.

Analysing a questionnaire

A hypothesis

A theory that you are putting to a test is called a **hypothesis**.
For example, you may wish to test people's opinion on a particular matter and your hypothesis would be that most people had a certain preference.
To test your hypothesis, you could question a sample of people and analyse the results.

Now, if you asked 100 people and 90 of them agreed with the preference, then you could consider that you have proved your hypothesis.

If only 30 agreed with it, then you would decide that you had not proved your hypothesis. The difficulty is knowing whether to say you have proved your hypothesis if only about 55 people out of 100 agreed with it. With a slightly different sample of people you could have got different results, so if the result is near 50–50 you cannot be sure that your hypothesis is proved. A statistician would have further tests to use in deciding when to accept a hypothesis, but as a rough rule, for a sample of 100, only accept the hypothesis when you get at least 60 people agreeing with it.

Multiple responses

In a more detailed questionnaire, people may be asked to put items in order of merit, order of preference, or some other order.
You have to decide how to analyse such results.

Example

Here 10 people, identified by the letters A to J, have put 5 drinks in order of preference.

$1 = $ 1st choice, $2 = $ 2nd choice, etc.

	A	B	C	D	E	F	G	H	I	J
Poppo	2	3	3	3	4	3	4	5	3	3
Quencho	4	2	4	1	2	1	5	1	2	2
Ribbo	3	5	5	5	5	5	2	3	5	4
Squasho	5	4	2	2	1	4	1	4	4	1
Tisso	1	1	1	4	3	2	3	2	1	5

How would you analyse these results ?

This is a complicated process and you might use one of several methods.

1st idea

You can see how many 1's there are for each product.

Drink	Number of 1st choices
Poppo	0
Quencho	3
Ribbo	0
Squasho	3
Tisso	4
	10

Tisso has 4 1's and this is the most popular.

However, only 4 out of 10 people voted for Tisso so you may think that this is not sufficient to say it is the best. You might have been more sure if more than half the people had voted for it.

So you might go on to another method.

2nd idea

Count the 1st and 2nd choices.

Drink	Number of 1st choices	Number of 2nd choices	Total 1st and 2nd choices
Poppo	0	1	1
Quencho	3	4	7
Ribbo	0	1	1
Squasho	3	2	5
Tisso	4	2	6
	10	10	20

It now looks as if Quencho is the most popular, using this way of analysing the results.

3rd idea

You may think that all the choices should be taken into consideration.

You can add up all the 'scores' for each drink from the 1st table of choices.
e.g. For Poppo, $2 + 3 + 3 + 3 + 4 + 3 + 4 + 5 + 3 + 3 = 33$
This gives a table like this:

Drink	Total of scores
Poppo	33
Quencho	24
Ribbo	42
Squasho	28
Tisso	23
	150 ←

Since each column adds up to 15, this should add up to 10×15, and is a useful check.

Since 1 is best and 5 is worst, it is the drink with the lowest total (not the highest) which is best, so using this method it seems that Tisso is the most popular, although Quencho is a close second.
If you had asked people to give 5 marks for the best, 4 for the next best, and so on, or you had done this yourself when tabulating the results, then it would be the item with the highest total which would be considered the most popular.
You can change all the results in the table to marks in this way, and check this.
This method of scoring would be useful if, for instance, there were 10 products and you only asked for the 1st five to be put in order. After scores of 5, 4, 3, 2 and 1, the rest would be given marks of 0.

These methods have been suggested as possible ways in which you can come to a conclusion.
Choose whichever way you want.
Perhaps you will invent your own rules to decide which item is best.

Exercise 13.1

1.   Here are some questions which might be used in surveys.
     In each case, re-write the question, or the answer categories, so that the answers will be more useful for the survey.

   1   How much water do you think your
           household uses ?

More than average	
About average	
Less than average	

   (A survey about water meters.)

   2   How often do you drink our product ?

Daily	
Weekly	
Monthly	
Other (please specify)	

   (A health-food drink.)

   3   Which figure best describes your annual household income ?

Less than £25 000	
£25 001–£30 000	
£30 001–£40 000	
£40 001–£50 000	
More than £50 000	

   (A holiday survey given to a group of friends.)

   4   How many times do you eat out at restaurants ?

Seldom/never	
Once a month	
2–4 times a month	
More than 4 times a month	

   (Market research survey.)

2.   Imagine that you are the cook at an adventure holiday centre for teenagers.
     Design a questionnaire which you could give to a group of teenagers at the end of their stay, to see whether the meals you are providing are satisfactory, or whether any improvements should be made.
     (Include about 4 to 8 questions.)

3. Certain community leaders thought that there ought to be a swimming pool and other community amenities in the local area. They sent questionnaires to 500 households. One question was: Do you think a local swimming pool is needed ?

Highly desirable	
Desirable	
Not needed	

Replies were received from 170 households and of these
72 ticked 'Highly desirable',
20 ticked 'Desirable',
63 ticked 'Not needed',
15 did not answer that question.

On the basis of these replies, do you think that the community leaders should approach the Council saying that there is a good local demand for a swimming pool ?

Questions 4 to 8
Here are some (fictitious) results in which people A, B, C, ... have put some products P, Q, R, ... in order of preference.
1 = 1st choice, 2 = 2nd choice, etc.

If these were the results of surveys that you had carried out, analyse them and write down your conclusions, including saying which product you would decide is the most popular.

(Choose for yourself the methods you will use. There are no definite correct answers although some answers may be more acceptable than others.)

4.

Product	Person				
	A	B	C	D	E
P	4	3	2	3	1
Q	3	1	1	4	4
R	2	4	4	1	3
S	1	2	3	2	2

5.

Product	Person				
	A	B	C	D	E
P	1	1	3	3	2
Q	3	2	1	2	1
R	2	3	2	1	3

Read the general instructions on the previous page.

6.

Product	Person					
	A	B	C	D	E	F
P	1	3	1	2	4	2
Q	2	1	2	4	3	4
R	4	2	4	1	2	1
S	3	4	3	3	1	3

7.

Product	Person				
	A	B	C	D	E
P	3	2		1	1
Q			1		2
R				2	3
S	2	3	2		
T	1	1	3	3	

(People only asked for 1st 3 preferences.)

8.

Product	Person							
	A	B	C	D	E	F	G	H
P		1		4	2		1	1
Q	2	4		1	3	1		2
R	1		1	2		4	3	3
S		3	2		4		2	
T	4	2	3			3		
U	3		4	3	1	2	4	4

(People only asked for 1st 4 preferences.)

Averages

When statistical data has been collected, we often need to find an average measurement. There are several kinds of average. Here we will use the mean, the median and the mode.

1   **The mean** $= \dfrac{\text{the total of the items}}{\text{the number of items}}$.

The formula is written as

$$\bar{x} = \frac{\Sigma x}{n},$$

where $\bar{x}$ (read as x bar) is the symbol for the mean;

Σ, the Greek capital letter sigma, means 'the sum of', so Σx means the sum of the x-values;

n is the number of items.

2   **The median.** When the items are arranged in order of size, the median is the value of the middle item, or the value halfway between the middle two if there is an even number of items.

3   **The mode** is the value which occurs most often. (Sometimes a set of values will not have a mode, as there may not be any value which occurs more often than any of the others.)

Example

1   **Numbers of members of a club attending the meetings**

Week number	1	2	3	4	5	6	7	8	9	10	Total
Attendance	20	19	24	22	20	23	20	28	24	20	220

Find the mean, median and mode attendances.

The mean attendance

$$\bar{x} = \frac{\Sigma x}{n} = \frac{220}{10} = 22$$

The median

(Arrange the items in order of size.)

19   20   20   20   20   ↑   22   23   24   24   28

middle

The median is halfway between 20 and 22, i.e. 21.
(Half the values are less than 21 and half are greater than 21.)

The mode

The value which occurs most often is 20 (as there were 4 weeks when 20 members were present), so the mode is 20.

Summary:- Mean = 22, median = 21, mode = 20.

All these averages can be used in different circumstances, although the most usual one is the mean, as this is the one which involves all the values. If one of the values is very high or low compared to the others, this will affect the mean and in this case the median might be a better average to use. The mode is the simplest average to find, but generally it is not as useful as the other two.

Example

2   In a class test, the marks were

5   10   25   25   25   30   30   30   30   35

The mean mark is 24.5, the median mark is 27.5 and the mode mark is 30.

Comment about the averages.

The fairest average to quote here is the median. Half the students have less than 27.5 and half have more.
The mean has been distorted by the two low values, and only two students have marks less than the mean.
The mode is not a representative average, as only 1 student has a better mark.

If the word 'average' is used without specifying which one in an arithmetical question, it refers to the mean.

In your answers, remember to give the unit of measurement, e.g. cm, kg. Check that your answer seems to be reasonable. Do not give too many decimal places. If the data is accurate to the nearest whole number then it is reasonable to give the averages to 1 decimal place.

Using a statistical calculator to find the mean

e.g. To find the mean of 23, 24, 28, 29, 31.

Set the calculator to work in statistical mode, then press

23 $\boxed{\text{DATA}}$ 24 $\boxed{\text{DATA}}$ 28 $\boxed{\text{DATA}}$ 29 $\boxed{\text{DATA}}$ 31 $\boxed{\text{DATA}}$

When you have entered all the data, pressing
$\boxed{n}$ will tell you the number of items entered, 5,
$\boxed{\Sigma x}$ will tell you the sum of the items entered, 135,
$\boxed{\bar{x}}$ will tell you the mean of the items entered, 27.

Dispersion

The average (mean, median or mode) gives us a general idea of the data, but two sets of numbers can have the same mean but be very different in other ways. The other main statistic we find is a measure of dispersion (or spread).

There are several measures of dispersion, of which we will use two:
1   the range,
2   the interquartile range (used in Chapter 24).

The range is the simplest measure of dispersion to find.

Range = highest value – lowest value

The range only uses the extreme values so it is not always very representative.

In example **1** on page 279, the range = 28 – 19 = 9 members.
In example **2** on page 280, the range = 35 – 5 = 30 marks.

Exercise 13.2

1. Find the mean, median and range of these sets of numbers.

    1   4   5   5   7   7   8   9   10   12   15   17
    2   12   20   31   35   39   48   55   71   85
    3   2   14   5   12   7
    4   25   53   37   17   62   93   41   27   33   19
    5   1.5   1.7   1.8   1.9   2.0   2.0   2.1   2.2

2. Find the median, mode and range of these sets of numbers.

    1   4   5   5   7   7   7   8   9   9   10   12   12   12   12   13
    2   26   27   29   25   31   33   27   32   28   27   33
    3   3   5   1   6   2   5   4   8   1   5   2   5   7   2   1   5   4   3   6   9   4   1   6   7

3. Find the mean of

    1   59.2,   90.0,   75.8,   32.6.
    2   £985,   £863,   £904,   £967,   £868.
    3   1 hr 20 min,   2 hr 30 min,   1 hr 45 min,   3 hr 10 min,   2 hr 8 min,   1 hr 13 min.
    4 $1\frac{1}{4}$, $3\frac{1}{4}$, $4\frac{1}{2}$.
    5   2.5 kg,   3.4 kg,   2.7 kg,   1.9 kg,   4.0 kg.

4. **1**   The weights in kg of 10 children are
            54,   52,   62,   49,   61,   56,   51,   64,   54,   67.
            Find the mean and the median weights.

    2   The ages of 5 boys are
            12 y 1 m,   12 y 5 m,   13 y 7 m,   11 y 2 m,   11 y 7 m.
            Find the mean age.

    3   The weights of 10 helpings of potatoes
            (to the nearest 10 g) are
            150 g,   170 g,   190 g,   160 g,   180 g,
            140 g,   170 g,   170 g,   150 g,   160 g.
            Find the mean weight.

5.   The 1971 census recorded 7.45 million people living in Greater London in 2.65 million households. Find the mean number of people per household.
The figures for the North-west region of England were 6.74 million people and 2.27 million households. Were there more people per household in London or in the North-west region ?

Frequency Distributions

Discrete data

(i.e. the variables are numbers, not measurements)

Formula for the mean

$$\bar{x} = \frac{\Sigma fx}{\Sigma f}$$

where Σf is the total of the frequencies,
        Σfx is the total of the fx values.

Example

1   The numbers of children in 50 families (with at least 1 child) are as follows:

Number of children	Number of families f
1	3
2	18
3	12
4	9
5	5
6	2
7	1
	50

Mode. There are most families with 2 children (18), so the mode is 2 children per family.

Median. If the numbers were arranged in order of size
1 1 1 2 2 2 . . . 5 6 6 7
the middle value would be halfway between the 25th and 26th numbers, and these are both 3, so the median is 3 children per family.
(This is easier to find by making a cumulative frequency table as explained in Chapter 24.)

Mean. Write down a frequency table. x is the number of children, f is the frequency. Add a column for fx. Find the sums of the columns f and fx.

x	f	fx
1	3	3
2	18	36
3	12	36
4	9	36
5	5	25
6	2	12
7	1	7
	50	155

(1×3)
(2×18)

$$\bar{x} = \frac{\Sigma fx}{\Sigma f} = \frac{155}{50} = 3.1$$

The mean is 3.1 children per family.

The range = highest value − lowest value = $7 - 1 = 6$ children.

Grouped data

If the range of data is wide we can put it into convenient groups, called classes.

Example

2   The distribution of examination marks of 120 students.

Mark	0–9	10–19	20–29	30–39	40–49	50–59	60–69
f (number of students)	5	14	22	29	27	19	4

The modal class is the class which includes most students, here it is the class 30–39 marks.

The median mark is best found using a cumulative frequency graph (see Chapter 24).

To find the mean mark we assume that each student has the mark corresponding to the centre of the class interval in which it lies, e.g. the centre of the marks 0–9 is 4.5, of 10–19 is 14.5, and so on. Of the 14 students who got between 10 and 19 marks, some probably got less than 14.5 marks and some more, so 14.5 is the best estimate we can make.

Use the formula $\bar{x} = \dfrac{\Sigma fx}{\Sigma f}$, taking x as the value at the centre of the interval.

If you are using your calculator to find the numbers in the fx column, add them into the memory as you go along, then to get the total you only have to press the 'recall memory' key.

If you do not need to show the separate totals you may be able to add them up directly. But it is advisable to do a check in case you have missed out some. Does the answer **look** right ? Anything above 69 is bound to be wrong. Looking at the distribution we would make a rough estimate that the average mark is between 30 and 39 marks.

Mark	f	x centre of interval	fx
0–9	5	4.5	22.5
10–19	14	14.5	203.0
20–29	22	24.5	539.0
30–39	29	34.5	1000.5
40–49	27	44.5	1201.5
50–59	19	54.5	1035.5
60–69	4	64.5	258.0
	120		4260.0

$$\bar{x} = \frac{\Sigma fx}{\Sigma f}$$

$$= \frac{4260}{120}$$

$$= 35.5 \text{ marks.}$$

Using a statistical calculator

Set the calculator to work in statistical mode then press

4.5 $\boxed{\text{x}}$ 5 $\boxed{\text{DATA}}$ 14.5 $\boxed{\text{x}}$ 14 $\boxed{\text{DATA}}$ and so on.

When you have entered all the data,
$\boxed{n}$ will tell you the number of items, Σf, and gives 120,
$\boxed{\Sigma x}$ will tell you the sum of the items, Σfx, and gives 4260,
$\boxed{\bar{x}}$ will tell you the mean, and gives 35.5.

Continuous data

(i.e. the variables are measurements, such as lengths, weights, times, which go up continuously, not in jumps.)

Example

3   The lengths of leaves from a bush, using a sample of 60 leaves.

Length in cm	5.0–5.4	5.5–5.9	6.0–6.4	6.5–6.9	7.0–7.4	7.5–7.9
f	2	12	20	15	8	3

Measurements in the 1st class interval will include lengths from 4.95 to 5.45 cm, in the 2nd class interval from 5.45 to 5.95 cm, and so on.
The centre of the 1st class interval is 5.2 cm, of the 2nd one is 5.7 cm, and so on.

The modal class is the class interval from 6.0 to 6.4 cm. (This actually includes measurements from 5.95 to 6.45 cm.)

To find the mean length of leaf, copy and complete this table.

x centre of interval	f	fx
5.2	2	10.4
5.7	12	
6.2		
6.7		
7.2		
7.7		
	60	

$$\bar{x} = \frac{\Sigma\,fx}{\Sigma f}$$
$$= \frac{\ldots}{60}\ \text{cm}$$
$$= \ldots\ \text{cm}$$

Give your answer to 1 decimal place.
(The correct answer is 6.4 cm.)

Exercise 13.3

For the frequency distributions in questions 1 to 4, find
1   the mean,
2   the median,
3   the mode, of the distribution.

1.   Number of people per household in a sample of 50 households.

Size of household, x	1	2	3	4	5	6
Number of households, f	10	18	9	7	4	2

2.   Number of goals scored by 30 teams in a league.

Goals	0	1	2	3	4	5
f (number of teams)	8	9	5	4	2	2

3.   Apexa plays a computer game in which she can score from 0 to 10 in each game.
The scores she achieved in several games are shown here.

Score	0	1	2	3	4	5
Frequency	2	3	0	4	3	8

Score	6	7	8	9	10
Frequency	5	9	3	1	2

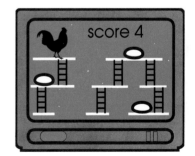

4.   Number of heads when 8 coins were tossed together 60 times.

Number of heads	0	1	2	3	4	5	6	7	8
f		1	2	7	15	17	11	5	2	0

5.　Number of pupils per class in 30 classes in a school.

Number in class	29	30	31	32	33
f	6	10	5	5	4

Find the mean number of children per class.

6.　A machine is set to cut metal into 40 cm lengths. 60 bars cut by the machine had lengths as follows:

Length in cm	39.7	39.8	39.9	40.0	40.1	40.2	40.3
Number of bars	1	6	15	17	14	5	2

Find the mean length of the bars.

7.　The marks of 40 children in a test were as follows:

Mark	0–2	3–5	6–8	9–11	12–14	15–17	18–20
Number of children	4	3	5	7	10	6	5

1　What is the modal class of this distribution ?
2　Find the mean mark, using the centres of intervals for the marks. These are 1, 4, 7, 10, 13, 16 and 19 respectively.

8.　The times a doctor takes to deal with each of 100 patients at her surgery are given in the table (each to the nearest minute).

Time in minutes	1	2	3	4	5	6	7	8	9	10
Number of patients	5	19	21	20	15	11	4	3	1	1

Find the mean time taken per patient.

9.　The heights of 40 women are as follows:

Height in cm	150–154	155–159	160–164	165–169	170–174
Number of women	5	10	12	9	4

(The 1st class interval includes heights from 149.5 to 154.5 cm, the centre of interval is 152 cm. The 2nd class interval includes heights from 154.5 to 159.5 cm, the centre of interval is 157 cm; and so on.)

1　What is the modal class of the distribution ?
2　Find the mean height of the women.

10.　The lengths of 50 rods are as follows:

Length in cm	5–9	10–14	15–19	20–24	25–29
Number of rods	1	14	20	11	4

1　What is the modal class of the distribution ?
2　What is the centre of interval of the modal class ?
3　Find the mean length of the rods.

11. The ages of 200 cars in a survey are as follows:

Age in years	0–2	2–4	4–6	6–8	8–10	10–12	12–14
Number of cars	42	41	32	29	23	21	12

(The 1st class includes cars up to just under 2 years old, the centre of interval is 1 year. The 2nd class includes cars from 2 years to just under 4 years old, the centre of interval is 3 years; and so on.)

1   What is the modal class ?
2   Find the mean age of the cars in the survey.

Exercise 13.4 Applications

1. Imagine that you are the manager of a seaside caravan park.
Design a questionnaire which you could ask your customers to fill in, to give you some idea of whether the amenities on the site are satisfactory, and whether certain extra ones would be welcomed.

2. The owners of a local radio station wish to obtain information on any improvements that could be made to increase the listening figures. They decide to send out a questionnaire, asking the following questions:

1   What is your name ?
2   Do you enjoy listening to our station ?
3   What type of programme do you enjoy most ?
4   Do you listen in the mornings ?
5   Do you like quizzes and competitions ?
6   What kind of work do you do ?
7   How much do you earn ?

Are the questions suitable ? Where necessary, replace them by more useful ones, including categories of answers.

3. You are trying to test whether people prefer a certain brand of a product rather than any other brand.
You ask a sample of people whether they prefer this brand.

'Do you like this brand in preference to other brands ?'

	Number of replies
Strongly prefer	52
Prefer	81
Don't know	21
Prefer some other brand	67

On the basis of these results, assuming that the sample was correctly chosen, would you say that this brand is preferred ?

Questions 4 to 7

Here are the results of some (fictitious) surveys in which people were given a list of activities they could take part in, and they were asked to give their 1st 3 choices for what they wanted to do. Here are the results.

If these were surveys that you had carried out, analyse the results and write down your conclusions, including saying which one of the activities you would choose as being the one most people wanted to do.

4.

Activity	Number putting it		
	1st	2nd	3rd
P	11	7	10
Q	11	8	8
R	6	11	12
S	9	10	8
T	8	9	7

5.

Activity	Number putting it		
	1st	2nd	3rd
P	8	7	6
Q	7	7	14
R	9	9	7
S	8	9	5

6.

Activity	Number putting it		
	1st	2nd	3rd
P	2	5	7
Q	6	8	8
R	8	7	4
S	4	3	3
T	5	2	3
U	5	5	5

7.

Activity	Number putting it		
	1st	2nd	3rd
P	7	8	5
Q	7	3	10
R	6	9	5

8. In a year-group of 60 pupils, the number of subjects each pupil passed in an examination was as follows:

    5 8 8 7 8 7 6 4 8 7 8 7 7 8 5 6 6 3 6 6
    8 7 9 5 7 8 7 7 8 6 7 9 4 7 8 9 6 5 9 8
    3 8 7 4 5 8 4 5 6 9 9 9 9 7 8 8 5 6 7 6

    Tally the results to form a frequency distribution. Draw a histogram or a bar-line graph of the distribution. Find the mean, median and mode of the number of subjects passed.

9. The number of seeds germinating in 40 pots when 6 seeds were planted in each pot was as follows:

Number of seeds	0	1	2	3	4	5	6
Number of pots	0	1	3	12	10	11	3

    Draw a bar-line graph of the distribution.
    Find the mean, median and mode of the distribution.
    If you pick a pot at random from this batch what is the probability that it will have 4 or more germinating seeds ?

10. The lengths of 60 leaves on a plant.

Length in cm	7–9	10–12	13–15	16–18	19–21
Number of leaves	4	16	24	13	3

    1 What are the boundaries of the length measurements in the 1st class interval ? What is the centre of this interval ?
    2 Find the mean length of the leaves.
    3 Draw a histogram of the distribution.

11. The histogram shows the times taken by a group of boys to run a race.

    1 How many boys were there altogether ?
    2 What percentage of boys took less than 7 minutes ?
    3 What is the modal class of the distribution ?
    4 What is the centre of interval of the modal class ?
    5 Find the mean time taken by the boys.

    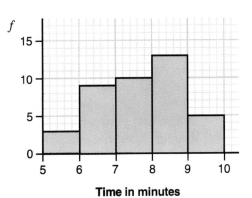

12. The marks of 25 children in an examination were as follows:

68 78 64 67 73 94 69 86 62 67 82 79 61
87 71 81 79 82 77 73 81 84 74 76 66

Tally these data in classes 60–64, 65–69, 70–74, etc.
Find the mean of the grouped distribution.

13. **Statistical investigations**

You should continue to do your own statistical investigations. Suggestions were given in question 17, page 152, and you should refer to these for further ideas.
In particular, carry out an investigation where you can compare two related fequency distributions by finding the means and, if suitable, the medians, the modes and the ranges.

Here are some suggestions:

The heights and shoe sizes of boys, and of girls, in your class.

The weekly amounts spent on snacks, sweets, drinks, etc. by students of your age, and by younger children.

The numbers of goals scored in football matches by home teams, compared with those scored by away teams.

The numbers of passengers in cars, compared at different times of day, or on weekdays and at weekends.

The ages of cars (estimates based on the registration letter) in a town and in a rural area.

The number of customers entering a shop at 1-minute intervals, compared at different times of day.

The times taken to do a manual task using the hand you write with and using the other hand.

Here also are suggestions for multi-response surveys you can do with your friends:
Find about 8 or 10 cartoons from magazines or newspapers. Cut them out and stick them on cards and label them P, Q, R, . . .
Then ask your friends, one by one, to put them in order of preference, or just to choose their 1st 3 preferences. When all your friends have given you their answers, analyse the results and say which is the best cartoon.
You can do similar surveys using pictures of fashions, cars, TV personalities, pop groups, etc.
You can just produce a list, without pictures, if you are asking about people's favourite TV series, favourite sport, favourite food, etc.

Decide on a survey about something which interests you. Plan it and carry it out.
Analyse the results and state your conclusions.

Practice test 13

1. Imagine that you are running a pre-school playgroup.
    Design a questionnaire which you could ask the parents of the children to fill in, to give you their views on how well the playgroup meets their needs and those of their children.
    (Include about 4 to 8 questions.)

2. Here are the results of a (fictitious) survey in which people were given a list of activities they could take part in, and they were asked to give their 1st 3 choices for what they wanted to do. Here are the results.
    Analyse the results of the survey and write down your conclusions, including saying which one of the activities you would choose as being the one most people wanted to do.

Activity	Number putting it		
	1st	2nd	3rd
P	10	9	9
Q	10	10	10
R	12	8	10
S	9	13	9
T	9	10	12

3. A manufacturer notes the number of faults in 100 machines.

Number of faults	0	1	2	3	4	5	6 or more
Number of machines	14	31	25	16	9	5	0

    Find the mean number of faults per machine.

4. The weekly wages of 30 women are shown in the table.

Wage (to nearest £20)	60	80	100	120
Number of women	3	7	15	5

    Find the mean wage.

5. The times taken by 50 workers to travel to work are as follows:

Time (minutes)	0–10	10–20	20–30	30–40	40–50	50–60
Number of workers	18	13	11	4	3	1

    1 What is the modal class of the distribution ?
    2 What is the centre of interval of the modal class ?
    3 Find the mean time taken.

14 Enlargement and similar figures

> **The topics in this chapter include:**
>
> - enlarging a shape by a whole number or a fractional scale factor,
> - understanding and using similarity,
> - understanding the notion of scale in maps and drawings.

Enlargements

A figure and its enlargement have the same shape.

The **scale factor** of the enlargement is the number of times the original has been enlarged.

e.g. If the scale factor is 2, all lines on the enlargement are twice as long as corresponding lines on the original.

If the scale factor is 3, all lines on the enlargement are three times as long as corresponding lines on the original.

Examples

1   Enlargement with scale factor 2

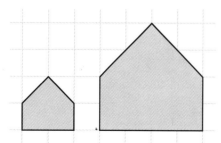

2   Enlargement with scale factor 3

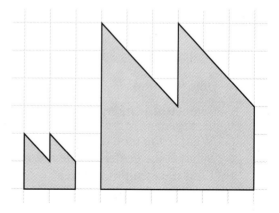

Length of line on enlargement $=$ scale factor $\times$ length of line on original

Scale factor $= \dfrac{\text{length of line on the enlargement}}{\text{length of line on the original}}$

The scale factor need not be a whole number.
e.g. If the scale factor is $1\frac{1}{2}$, all lines on the enlargement are $1\frac{1}{2}$ times as long as the corresponding lines on the original.
Since $1\frac{1}{2} = \frac{3}{2}$, this is equivalent to the ratio $3:2$.
The length on the enlargement : length on original $= 3:2$.

Enlargement with scale factor $1\frac{1}{2}$.

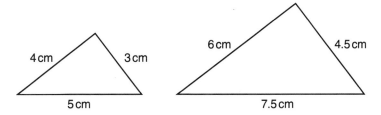

Example

Trapezium $PQRS$ is an enlargement of trapezium $ABCD$.
Find the scale factor of the enlargement, and the lengths of QR, RS and SP.

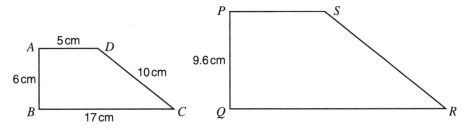

Scale factor $= \dfrac{\text{length of } PQ}{\text{length of } AB} = \dfrac{9.6 \text{ cm}}{6 \text{ cm}} = 1.6 \quad \left(\text{or } 1\frac{3}{5}\right)$

Length of $QR =$ scale factor $\times$ length of BC

$\qquad = 1.6 \times 17 \text{ cm}$

$\qquad = 27.2 \text{ cm}$

Length of $RS = 1.6 \times 10 \text{ cm}$

$\qquad = 16 \text{ cm}$

Length of $SP = 1.6 \times 5 \text{ cm}$

$\qquad = 8 \text{ cm}$

Reduction

If you 'enlarge' a shape by a scale factor less than 1, then you are actually making a reduction of the figure.

e.g. Enlargement by a scale factor $\frac{3}{4}$.

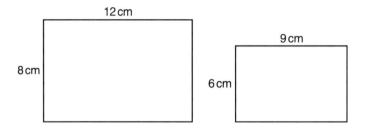

Centre of enlargement

If there is a centre of enlargement O and a scale factor k, then each point A is mapped to a position A_1 on the line OA such that distance $OA_1 = k \times$ distance OA.

Examples

When the scale factor is 2

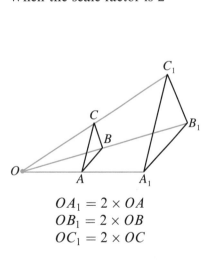

$$OA_1 = 2 \times OA$$
$$OB_1 = 2 \times OB$$
$$OC_1 = 2 \times OC$$

When the scale factor is 3

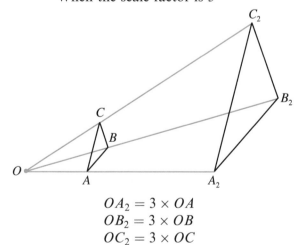

$$OA_2 = 3 \times OA$$
$$OB_2 = 3 \times OB$$
$$OC_2 = 3 \times OC$$

Since lines are altered in the same ratio the mapped figure has the same shape as the original figure with lengths in the ratio $k : 1$.

In the 1st diagram:
$A_1B_1 = 2AB, \quad B_1C_1 = 2BC, \quad A_1C_1 = 2AC.$

In the 2nd diagram:
$A_2B_2 = 3AB, \quad B_2C_2 = 3BC, \quad A_2C_2 = 3AC.$

Exercise 14.1

1. Copy these figures and for each one draw an enlargement with scale factor 2.

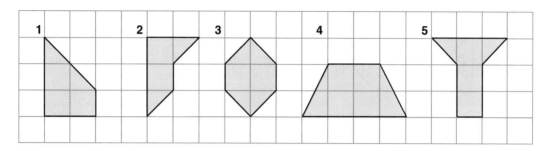

2. **1** What is the scale factor of the enlargement which transforms figure *A* into figure *B* ?

    2 What is the scale factor of the reduction which transforms figure *B* into figure *A* ?

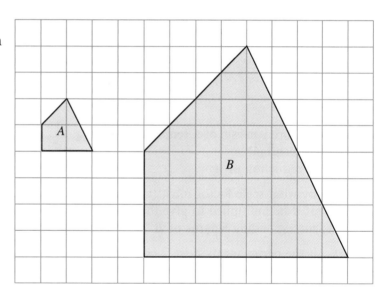

3. Copy these diagrams onto squared paper.
    Using *O* as the centre of enlargement and a scale factor 2, transform the line *AB* into a line *A'B'*.

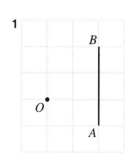
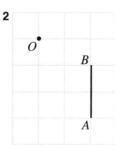
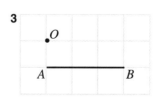
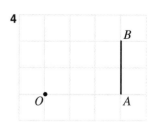

4. Copy these diagrams onto squared paper.
    Using O as the centre of enlargement and a scale factor of 3, transform triangle T into a
    triangle T'.

1

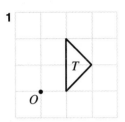

2

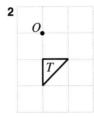

3

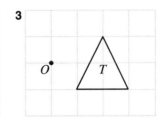

5. Copy this drawing of a box, on
    squared paper, and then draw an
    enlarged box using a scale factor of $1\frac{1}{2}$.

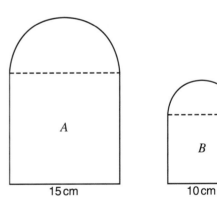

6. Each figure consists of a semicircle
    above a rectangle.
    B is a reduction of A.

    1 By what scale factor must the lengths
           of A be multiplied to give the
           corresponding lengths of B?

    2 If the perimeter of A is 72 cm, what is
           the perimeter of B?

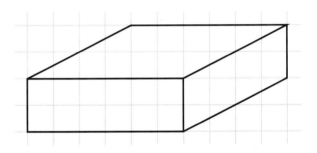

7. A triangle is transformed by enlargement with scale factor 3 into a similar triangle.

    1 One side of the new triangle has length 4.5 cm. What is the length of the
           corresponding side of the original triangle?
    2 One angle of the new triangle has size 66°. What is the size of the corresponding
           angle of the original triangle?

8. A photograph with length 15 cm is enlarged and the corresponding length on the
    enlargement is 36 cm.
    1 What is the scale factor of the enlargement?
    2 The breadth of the original photograph is 10 cm.
           What is the breadth of the enlargement?

Similar figures

Similar figures have the same shape.

All corresponding angles are equal.

All corresponding lengths are in proportion, i.e. they are in the same ratio as all other corresponding lengths.

Examples

1   The lengths of these rectangles are in the
ratio $4 : 10 = 2 : 5$
The breadths of these rectangles are
in the ratio $3 : 7.5 = 6 : 15 = 2 : 5$
(All angles are 90°.)
The rectangles are similar.

2   Two similar cylinders have heights of 6 cm and 10 cm.
If the smaller one has a radius of 4.2 cm, what is
the radius of the larger one ?

Ratio of heights $= 6 : 10 = 3 : 5$
Because the cylinders are similar, the radii are in
the same ratio as the heights.
The larger radius is $\frac{5}{3}$ of the smaller radius
$= \frac{5}{3} \times 4.2$ cm $= 7$ cm.

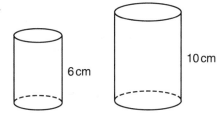

Exercise 14.2

1.   **1**   In what ratio, in its simplest form, are
the lengths of these rectangles ?
2   In what ratio, in its simplest form,
are the breadths of these rectangles ?
3   Are these rectangles similar ?
4   What is the ratio of the lengths of
their diagonals ?

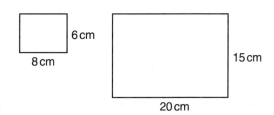

2. These pairs of figures are similar. State the ratios of corresponding lengths. Calculate the lengths of the unknown, marked sides.

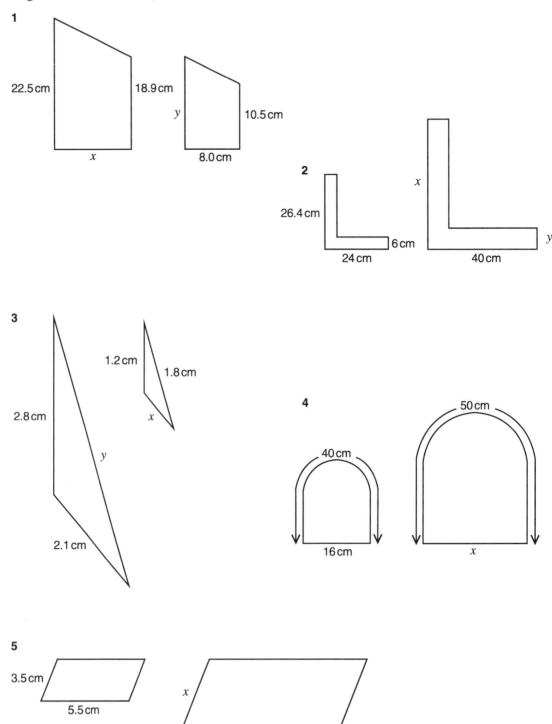

3. These pairs of solid figures are similar. State the ratios of corresponding lengths. Calculate the unknown, marked lengths.

1

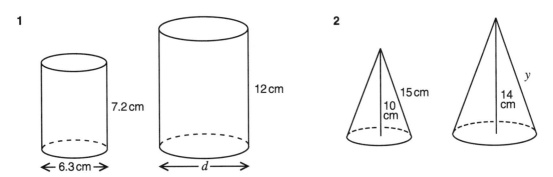

12 cm

7.2 cm

← 6.3 cm →

← d →

2

15 cm

10 cm

14 cm

y

3

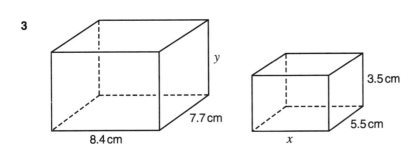

y

7.7 cm

8.4 cm

3.5 cm

5.5 cm

x

4

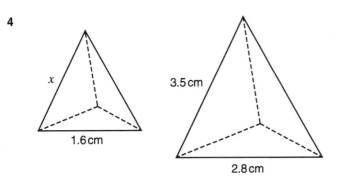

x

1.6 cm

3.5 cm

2.8 cm

5

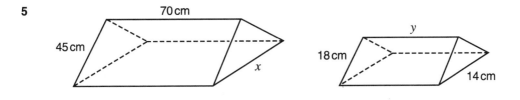

70 cm

45 cm

x

18 cm

y

14 cm

4.   These concentric circles have radii 3 cm and 4 cm.
      Without substituting any numerical value for π, find
      the ratio of the lengths of their circumferences.

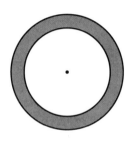

5.   These pyramids have square bases with edges 4 cm and
      6 cm. Their heights are 6 cm and 9 cm.

      1   What is the ratio, in its simplest form, of the edges
             of their bases ?
      2   What is the ratio, in its simplest form, of their heights ?
      3   Are the pyramids similar ?

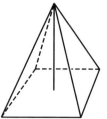

Similar triangles

Similar triangles have the same shape.
(If they have the same size also, they are called congruent triangles.)

(1)   (2)   (3)

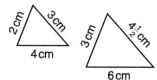

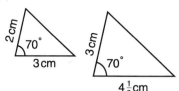

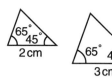

We recognise that the triangles are similar because:

In (1), the three sides of the first triangle are proportional to the three sides of the second
         triangle.

In (2), two sides of the first triangle are proportional to two of the sides of the second triangle,
         and the angles included between the two sides are equal.

In (3), the three angles of the first triangle are equal to the three angles of the second triangle,
         (i.e. the triangles are equiangular).
         (The 3rd angle in each triangle is $180° - (65° + 45°) = 70°$.)

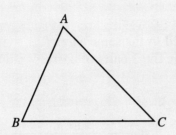

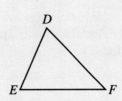

If two triangles ABC, DEF are similar, then we know

1   $\angle A = \angle D$, $\angle B = \angle E$, $\angle C = \angle F$.

2   $\dfrac{AB}{DE} = \dfrac{AC}{DF} = \dfrac{BC}{EF}$,   i.e. corresponding sides are proportional.

Examples

1   Triangles ABD, ACE are similar because

$\qquad \angle A = \angle A$ (same angle)

$\qquad \angle ABD = \angle C$ (corresponding angles)

$\qquad \angle ADB = \angle E$ (corresponding angles)

So $\dfrac{AB}{AC} = \dfrac{AD}{AE} = \dfrac{BD}{CE}$

So $\dfrac{3}{5} = \dfrac{4}{AE}$, $3AE = 20$ cm

$\qquad\qquad\qquad AE = 6\frac{2}{3}$ cm

$\qquad\qquad\qquad DE = 2\frac{2}{3}$ cm

$\dfrac{BD}{7.5} = \dfrac{3}{5}$, $BD = \dfrac{3 \times 7.5}{5}$ cm $= 4.5$ cm.

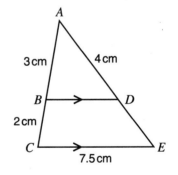

2   Triangles ABC, DEC are similar because

$\dfrac{AC}{DC} = \dfrac{BC}{EC}\ \left(= \frac{2}{3}\right)$ and $\angle ACB = \angle DCE$.

So $\angle A = \angle D$ and $\angle B = \angle E$.

$\dfrac{AB}{DE} = \dfrac{AC}{DC} = \dfrac{2}{3}$,   i.e. AB is $\frac{2}{3}$ of DE.

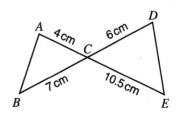

Exercise 14.3

1. In these questions, equal angles are marked in the same way.
   Say why the triangles are similar and name the 3 pairs of corresponding sides, and any other equal angles.

1

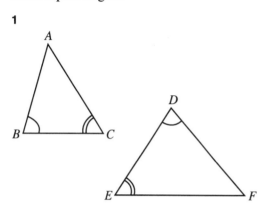

2

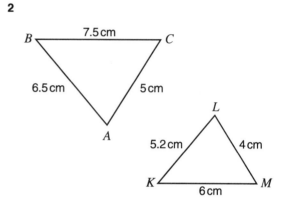

3

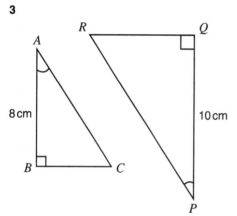

4

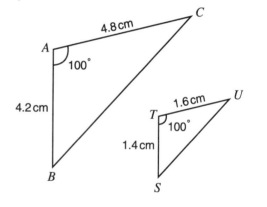

2. ' **1** Explain why these triangles are similar.

   2 What is the ratio $BC : EF$?

   3 Which angle is equal to $\angle C$?

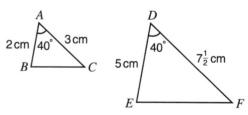

3. **1** Explain why these triangles are similar.

   2 Name an angle equal to $\angle B$.

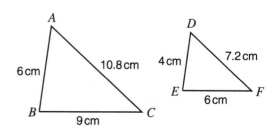

4. 1 What are the values of $\dfrac{AD}{AC}$ and $\dfrac{AE}{AB}$?

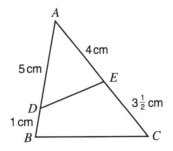

    2 Are triangles ADE, ACB similar ?

    3 What angle is equal to $\angle ADE$?

    4 What is the ratio $DE : CB$?

5. 1 Explain why triangles ABC, ADE are similar.
    2 What is the ratio $AD : AB$?
    3 What is the ratio $ED : CB$?
    4 If $DE = 2.7$ cm, what is the length of BC ?

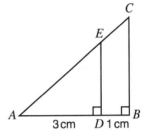

6. ACD and BCE are straight lines.
    Show that these triangles are similar
    and name the equal angles.
    What does this prove about the
    lines AB and ED ?

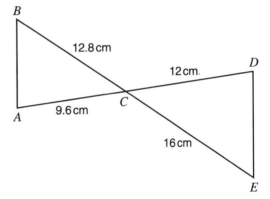

Scale drawing

Scales can be given in various ways, such as
    1 cm represents $\frac{1}{2}$ m,
or, 2 cm represents 1 m,
or, Scale 1 : 50,
or, $\frac{1}{50}$ scale.

In any scale drawing, the scale should be stated.

The scale of a map

Some possible scales are 1 : 1250, 1 : 2500, 1 : 10 000, 1 : 25 000, etc.

The scale of a map can be called the Representative Fraction, or R.F.

R.F. $= \frac{1}{100\,000}$ or R.F. $= 1 : 100\,000$ means that 1 unit represents 100 000 units, so 1 cm
represents 100 000 cm, which is 1 km.

Example

1   On a map, 3 cm represents 15 km. What is the scale of the map, in ratio form ?

3 cm represents 15 km
1 cm represents 5 km
1 cm represents 500 000 cm
The scale of the map is 1 : 500 000

Angles of elevation and depression

Angles of elevation and depression are both measured from the horizontal direction.

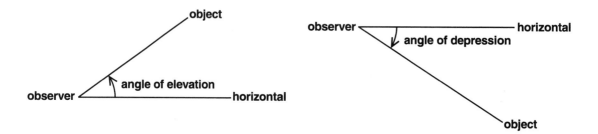

Example

2   A coastguard on a vertical cliff 80 m high sees a dinghy out to sea at an angle of
depression of 18°.
Draw an accurate scale drawing and use it to find how far the dinghy is from the foot of
the cliff.

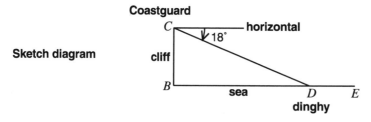

A suitable scale to use would be 1 cm to represent 20 m.
Begin by drawing a horizontal line BE for the sea and make an accurate right angle at B.
Draw the cliff BC, making this line 4 cm long.
The angle of depression is 18° so the angle in the triangle at the top of the cliff is 72°.
Measure an angle of 72° giving the direction of the line CD.
Draw this line and extend it to meet BE at D. Measure BD.
BD is 12.3 cm, so the actual distance is 12.3 × 20 m.
The dinghy is 246 m from the foot of the cliff.
(It would be sensible to give this distance as approximately 250 m.)

Exercise 14.4

1. The scale of a map is 5 cm to 1 km. What is the distance between two places which are 17.5 cm apart on the map ?

2. The scale of a map is 1 : 25 000. What is the actual distance in km between two places which are 8 cm apart on the map ?

3. A hall is 20 m long and 13.5 m wide. What measurements should be used on a plan to a scale of 1 : 250 ?

4. On a map the distance between two villages is 7.2 cm. The villages are actually 18 km apart. What is the scale of the map, in ratio form ?

5. On a scale drawing, a rectangular enclosure which is 228 m long and 66 m wide is drawn with a length of 11.4 cm.
    What is the scale of the drawing ?
    What is the width of the building on the drawing ?

6. On this plan of the park, the scale is 1 : 5000.
    How far is it from the main gate to the swings ?
    (Measure to the crosses.)
    How far is it from the swings to the aviary ?
    A jogger goes all round the park, running on a path at the edge of the park. How far does she run ?

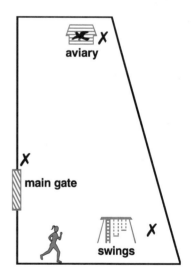

7. Draw an accurate scale drawing of a rectangular field, 75 m long and 45 m wide, using a scale of 1 : 1000.
    By measurement on your drawing, find the actual distance from a corner of the field to the opposite corner.

8. A boy stands 60 m from the base of a tower and on the same level as the base.
    He finds that the angle of elevation of the top of the tower is 14°. Draw an accurate scale drawing using a scale of $\frac{1}{500}$. Use it to find the height of the tower, to the nearest metre. (Ignore the height of the boy.)

Exercise 14.5 Applications

1.   On graph paper draw the *x*-axis from −4 to 8 and the *y*-axis from 0 to 8.
     Plot these points and join them in order, to make a letter *Z*, $(-4, 6)$, $(-1, 6)$, $(-4, 3)$,
     $(-1, 3)$.
     Enlarge this letter *Z*, starting with the top left-hand point at $(1, 8)$ and using a scale
     factor of $2\frac{1}{3}$.

2.   △*DEF* is an enlargement of △*ABC*.

     1 What is the scale factor of
            the enlargement ?

     2 What is the length of *DF* ?

     3 What is the length of *BC* ?

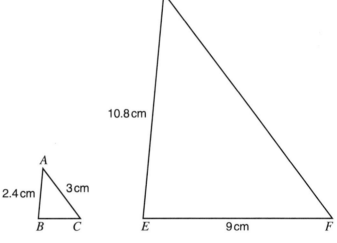

3.   Copy this diagram onto squared
     paper. Triangle *ABC* has been
     enlarged into triangle *A'B'C'*.
     What is the scale factor of the
     enlargement ?
     By joining *A'A*, *B'B*, *C'C* and
     continuing these lines, find on
     your diagram the position of the
     centre *O* of the enlargement.

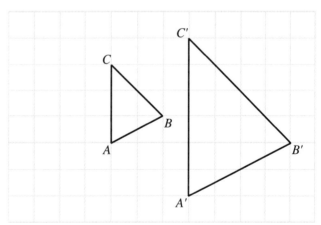

4.   **1** What is the ratio of the heights of these cylinders ?
     2 What is the ratio of the radii of these cylinders ?
     3 Are these cylinders similar ?

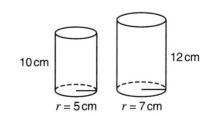

5. Two similar cones have heights in the ratio 3 : 7. If the base radius of the larger one is 14 cm, what is the base radius of the smaller one ?

6. The cylinders are similar.
    1   What is the scale factor of the enlargement to turn the small cylinder into the large one ?
    2   The radius of the small cylinder is 2.4 cm. What is the radius of the large one ?

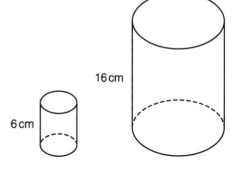

7. Two model boats are similar in shape. Their lengths are in the ratio 2 : 5. The smaller one is 10 cm wide. How wide is the larger one ?

8. A model of a hall of rectangular shape is made using a scale of 2 cm to 1 m. The height of the model is 16 cm and its floor measurements are 25 cm by 32 cm. Find the height and floor measurements of the hall and hence calculate its volume.

9. 1   Name two similar triangles.
    2   Find the ratio $AX : XC$.

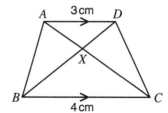

10. 1   Name 3 similar triangles.
    2   In what ratio are $BC : DE : GF$?
    3   Which point is the mid-point of AG ?

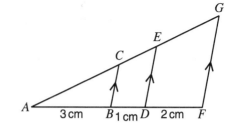

11. A stick 2 m long is placed vertically so that its top is in line with the top of a cliff, from a point A on the ground 3 m from the stick and 120 m from the cliff. How high is the cliff ?

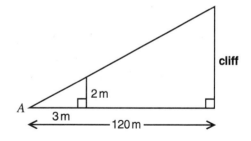

12. The length of the shadow of a vertical post 2.4 m high is 3.3 m. At the same time and place the length of the shadow of a vertical flagpole is 17.6 m. Find the height of the flagpole.

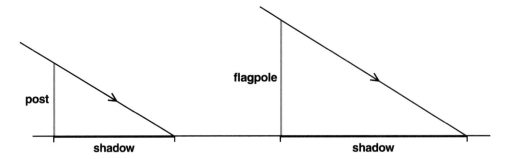

(The sun is so far away that its rays form parallel lines.)

13. In △*ABC*, *AB* = 16 cm, *BC* = 12 cm. *D* is the mid-point of *AC* and *DE* is perpendicular to *AC*.

    1 Find the length of *AC*.
    2 Show that triangles *ADE*, *ABC* are similar.
    3 Find the length of *DE*.

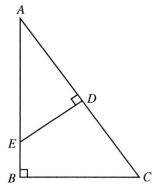

14. The diagram shows a regular pentagon with all diagonals drawn.

    1 Name a triangle similar to △ *ABE*, with *AB* as one of its sides.
    2 Name two triangles, of different sizes, similar to △ *ASR*, each with *AB* as one of its sides.

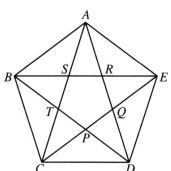

15. This diagram shows a sketch of one end of a building. Draw an accurate scale drawing, using a scale of 1 : 100. By measurement, find how high the highest point is from ground level.

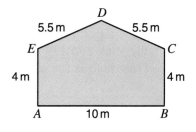

16. This plan of the ground floor of a house is drawn to a scale of 1 cm represents 1 m.

What are the measurements of
1 the lounge,   2 the dining-room,   3 the kitchen ?

4 What is the area of the lounge ? A carpet for this room costs £18 per m². What is the cost of the carpet ?

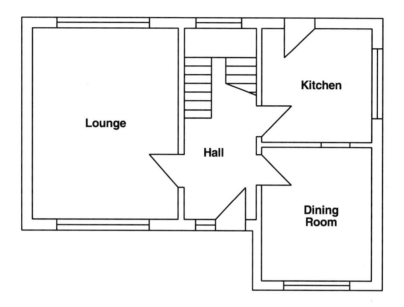

17. Draw an accurate scale drawing of this garden which is 25 m long and 15 m wide, using a scale of 1 cm to represent 2 m.

The lawn is 17 m long and 11 m wide and the path round three sides of it is 1 m wide.

In the centre of the lawn, draw in a circular pond of diameter 5 m.

Find the area of the vegetable plot.

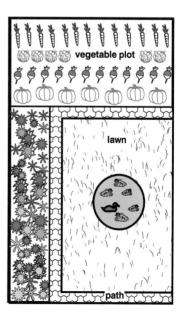

18. From a point A on top of a cliff 60 m high two boats B and C have angles of depression of 24° and 39°, and both boats are due East of A. Draw an accurate scale drawing, and find how far apart the boats are.

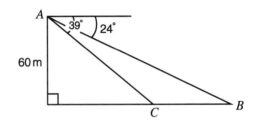

Practice test 14

1. This rectangle is enlarged with a scale factor $2\frac{2}{3}$.
   What are the measurements of the enlarged rectangle ?

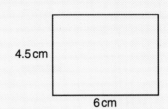

2. These cylinders are similar.
   What is the ratio of corresponding lengths ?
   What is the height of the 2nd cylinder ?

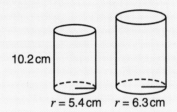

3. **1** Explain why these triangles are similar.
   2 Name an angle equal to $\angle B$.

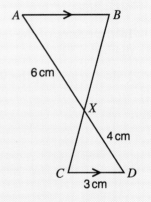

4. AXD and BXC are straight lines.

   1 Explain why triangles AXB, DXC are similar.
   2 What is the ratio $AX : XD$ in its simplest form ?
   3 Find the length of AB.

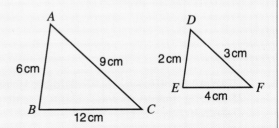

5. A map has a scale of 2 cm to represent 1 km. What is the scale in ratio form ?
   If two villages are 8.4 cm apart on the map, what is the actual distance between them ?

6. Two rectangular boxes are similar in shape. The smaller one has length 20 cm, width 16 cm and height 10 cm.
   1 The larger one has height 15 cm. What are its other measurements ?
   2 Find the volumes of these boxes and hence find the ratio of the volumes, in its simplest form.

7. The angle of elevation of a balloon due West of an observer *A* and 300 m high is 32°. Draw an accurate scale drawing using a scale of 1 : 5000, and use it to find how far the observer is from a point on level ground vertically below the balloon.

PUZZLES

27. Fill in the missing numbers in this division problem, which has no remainder.

```
          * *
   5 * ) 2 * * *
         * 5 *
         * * *
         4 0 0
```

28. Alan, Bob and Charles are allowed to pick apples in an orchard. Alan picks 7 sackfuls containing 16 kg each, Bob picks 7 sackfuls containing 14 kg each, Charles has smaller sacks and he picks 10 sackfuls holding 9 kg each. They had agreed beforehand that they would share the fruit equally. How can they do this without opening any of the sacks ?

29. How many squares of side 24 cm can be cut from a piece of paper 65 cm square ?

30. Write in figures; eleven thousand, eleven hundred and eleven.

31. By crossing out just SIX LETTERS in the following, leave the name of a topic in this book.

P S R I O X B L A E B T I T L E I R T S Y

15 Inequalities and flow diagrams

The topics in this chapter include:

- solving inequalities,
- constructing and interpreting flow diagrams.

Inequalities

$<$ is the symbol for 'is less than', so $3 < 4$ means '3 is less than 4'.
$>$ is the symbol for 'is greater than'.
$\leqslant$ is the symbol for 'is less than or equal to'.
$\geqslant$ is the symbol for 'is greater than or equal to', so $x \geqslant 3$ means 'x is greater than or equal to 3'.

Examples

1 If x is an integer (whole number), what are the possible values of x if $-1 \leqslant x < 5$?

x is greater than or equal to -1.
x is less than 5.
The possible values of x are $-1, 0, 1, 2, 3, 4$.

Inequalities on the number line

2 $x > 1$

$x \leqslant 2$

$-2 < x < 4$

$x \leqslant -1$ or $x \geqslant 6$

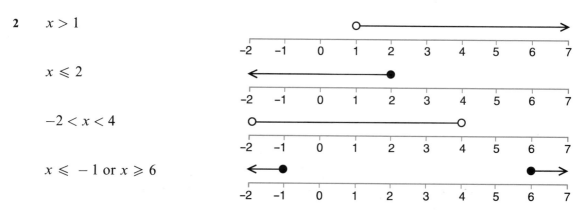

We have used the symbol ● if the end point is included and the symbol ○ if the end point is not included.

Solving inequalities

To solve simple inequalities, use the same methods as for solving simple equations.

> You can add equal numbers to both sides,
> you can subtract equal numbers from both sides,
> you can multiply both sides by the same **positive** number,
> you can divide both sides by the same **positive** number,
>
> and the inequality remains true.

If you multiply or divide both sides by a **negative** number, the inequality sign must be reversed at the same time.

Examples

3   Find the values of x which satisfy the inequality $13x - 20 > 6x + 8$.

$13x - 20 > 6x + 8$ Subtract $6x$ from both sides.

$7x - 20 > 8$ Add 20 to both sides.

$7x > 28$ Divide both sides by 7.

$x > 4$

4   Find the values of x which satisfy the inequality $8 - 3x \geqslant 14$.

$8 - 3x \geqslant 14$ Subtract 8 from both sides.

$-3x \geqslant 6$ Divide both sides by -3, reversing the inequality sign.

$x \leqslant -2$

Other inequalities

Examples

5   Solve the inequality $x^2 < 9$.

First, think of the **equation** $x^2 = 9$.
Take the square root of both sides.
$x = \sqrt{9} = 3$.
There is also a negative solution, $x = -\sqrt{9} = -3$.
The equation has two solutions, $x = -3$ or $x = 3$.

Now, if x has any value between -3 and 3, then x^2 is less than 9.
If x has any value less than -3 or greater than 3, x^2 is greater than 9.

So the solution to $x^2 < 9$ is 'x lies between -3 and 3'. This is written as $-3 < x < 3$.
It is shown here on a number line.

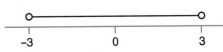

6   Solve the inequality $x^2 \geqslant 25$.

This means $x^2 = 25$ or $x^2 > 25$.
$x^2 = 25$ when $x = -5$ or $x = 5$.
If x has any value less than -5 or greater than 5 then $x^2 > 25$.

So the solution to $x^2 \geqslant 25$ is $x \leqslant -5$ or $x \geqslant 5$.

This cannot be written any simpler as it is
represented by two distinct regions on the
number line.

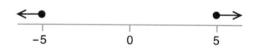

7   Solve the inequality $3x^2 \geqslant 75$.

Divide both sides by 3.
$x^2 \geqslant 25$
The solution is $x \leqslant -5$ or $x \geqslant 5$.

Exercise 15.1

1.   Describe these statements in words.

    1 $x > 7$ **4** $1 < x < 4$

    2 $x \leqslant 8$ **5** $x \geqslant -5$

    3 $x < 1$

2.   Write these statements in symbols.

    1 x is less than 6.

    2 x is greater than or equal to -2.

    3 x is greater than 0.

    4 x is less than 10 but greater than -3

    5 x is less than or equal to 5.

3.   Write a statement linking a, b, c using the symbol $<$, e.g. if $a = 3$, $b = -2$, $c = 5$ you can
write $b < a < c$.

    1 $a = -2, b = 4, c = -1$ **4** $a = -3, b = 1\frac{1}{2}, c = 1\frac{3}{4}$

    2 $a = 3, b = 0, c = -4$ **5** $a = 4, b = -4\frac{1}{2}, c = -3\frac{1}{2}$

    3 $a = -1, b = 5, c = -6$

4.   If x is an integer, what are the possible values of x if

    1 $3 < x < 7$ **4** $-8 < x < -4$

    2 $4 \leqslant x < 6$ **5** $0 \leqslant x \leqslant 5$

    3 $-2 \leqslant x \leqslant 2$

5. Show these inequalities on a number line. Draw a separate number line for each part, labelling each line from -4 to 4.

1   $x > -3$ 5 $-2 < x < -1$
2   $x < -1$ 6 $-3 \leqslant x \leqslant 4$
3   $x \geqslant 0$ 7 $x < -3$ or $x > 2$
4   $x \leqslant 3$ 8 $x \leqslant 1$ or $x \geqslant 2$

6. If x is an integer such that $-4 \leqslant x \leqslant 4$, write down the possible values for x, for the inequalities of question 5.

7. Find the values of x which satisfy these inequalities.

1   $6(x - 7) < 6$ 6 $5(x + 1) \leqslant x + 8$
2   $x - 1 > 2x + 5$ 7 $3(x - 4) < 5(x - 7)$
3   $5 - x \geqslant 6 - 3x$ 8 $\dfrac{x - 2}{3} \geqslant -1$
4   $\dfrac{x}{2} - 8 \leqslant -10$ 9 $12x - 5 > 15 - 8x$
5   $12 - 2x < 0$ 10 $3(2x - 1) + 2(x + 1) \leqslant 39$

8. Find the values of x which satisfy these inequalities.

1   $x^2 > 36$ 4 $x^2 < 1$
2   $x^2 > 2.25$ 5 $x^2 \geqslant \frac{1}{16}$
3   $x^2 \leqslant 100$

9. Find the values of x which satisfy these inequalities.

1   $2x^2 \leqslant 98$ 2 $x^2 + 4 \geqslant 85$ 3 $\frac{1}{2}x^2 < 72$

10. If x is a positive whole number such that $1 \leqslant x \leqslant 10$, state the values of x satisfied by these inequalities.

1   $x^2 \geqslant 45$ 3 $5x^2 > x^2 + 320$
2   $2x^2 + 1 \leqslant 20$ 4 $35 < x^2 < 65$

11. The values of x satisfy the inequality $4x + 3 \leqslant 40 \leqslant 6x - 4$.

   1 Find the largest possible value of x.
   2 Find the smallest possible value of x.
   3 If x is an integer, write down all the possible values of x.

12. Mrs Taylor wants to buy some oranges and lemons to make marmalade. If she decides to buy x oranges and y lemons, write down 4 inequalities to represent these statements.
    She decides to buy at least 2 oranges and 3 lemons, and not more than 9 fruits altogether.
    Oranges cost 20p each, and lemons 24p each, and Mrs Taylor has only £2 to spend.

    If she buys 3 oranges, what is the greatest number of lemons she can buy?

Flow diagrams

Instead of giving instructions in a simple list, they can be arranged in a **flow diagram**. You start by reading the box at the top, or sometimes at the left side, and follow the direction of the arrows, reading the boxes in turn, and carrying out the instructions or answering the questions in them.

You can put all the instructions in rectangular boxes, but if you use the other shapes shown it makes the flow diagrams clearer.

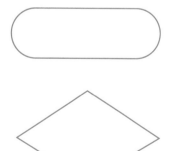

A rounded box is used at the beginning and end.

A diamond box is used for a question. The path you take from it will depend on the answer. In the next example the two paths are for the answers 'Yes' and 'No'. The path 'Yes' returns to a previous part of the diagram. This is called a **loop**.

Example

Here is a flow diagram which gives a sequence of numbers.

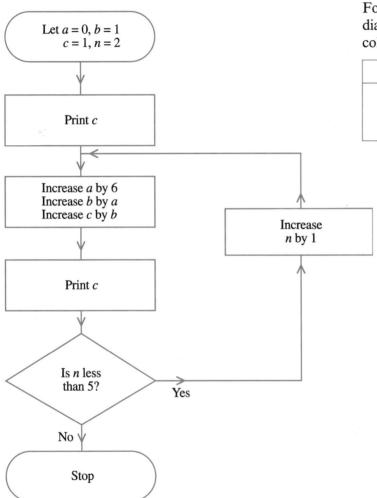

For working through the flow diagram, write down a, b, c, n in columns, which begin like this:

a	b	c	n
0	1	1	2
6	7	8	3
.	.	.	.

Write the numbers given by the instruction 'Print c' in a row, separated by commas.

What sequence of numbers is formed ?

Exercise 15.2

1. Here is a flow diagram.

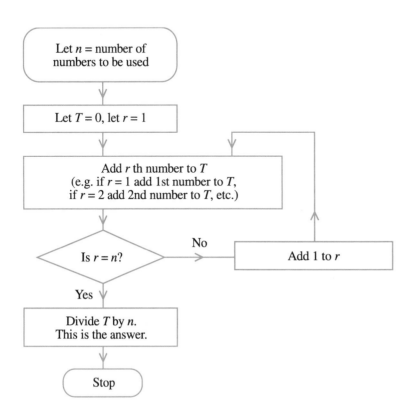

Use the set of numbers 6, 8, 12, 15, 17 in this flow diagram.
What is the answer ?
What does the answer represent ?

2. Construct a simple flow diagram which will print the sequence of numbers $3, 6, 9, \ldots$ up to 30.

3. Construct a simple flow diagram which will print the terms of the sequence of powers of 2, (2, 4, 8, ...) ending with the first term $> 10\,000$.

4.   Here is a flow diagram which gives a sequence of numbers.

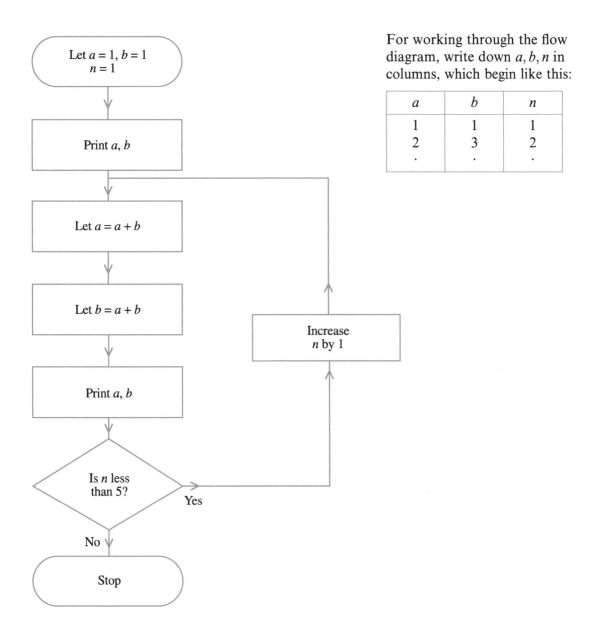

For working through the flow diagram, write down a, b, n in columns, which begin like this:

a	b	n
1	1	1
2	3	2
.	.	.

Write the numbers given by the instruction 'Print a, b' in a row, separated by commas. What sequence of numbers is formed ?

5. **Here is a flow diagram which gives a number chain.**

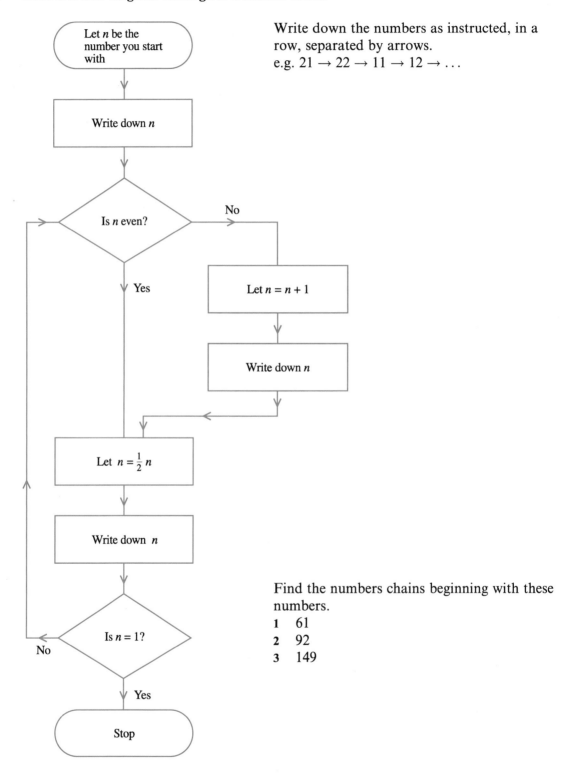

Write down the numbers as instructed, in a row, separated by arrows.

e.g. $21 \rightarrow 22 \rightarrow 11 \rightarrow 12 \rightarrow \ldots$

Find the numbers chains beginning with these numbers.

1   61

2   92

3   149

6. Here is a flow diagram which tells you which coins to use to pay a sum of money less than 50p.

Use the flow chart to find out how to pay out
1 40p, **2** 37p, **3** 4p.
Write down in order a list of the coins you should pay.

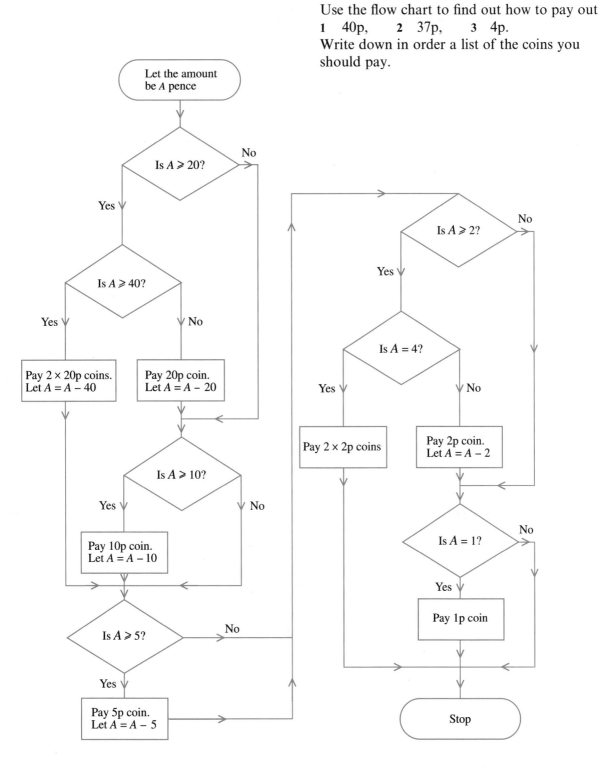

Exercise 15.3 Applications

1. Find the range of values of x for which

    1 $3 - 2(4 - x) \geqslant 3x$ **2** $x - 3 < 7 < 5x + 2$

2. Find the smallest integer n such that $n + 9 \leqslant 3n - 4$.

3. Find all pairs of positive integers (x, y) such that $3x + 2y \leqslant 11$.

4. Find the prime number which satisfies both these inequalities.

    $13x - 20 \geqslant 10(x + 25), \quad 23(x - 40) \geqslant 8(3x - 125) - 20.$

5. A coach firm has to carry 300 people on an outing. It has 5 coaches which can carry up
    to 50 passengers each and 7 minibuses which can carry up to 20 passengers each. There
    are 10 drivers available.
    If x coaches and y minibuses are used, write down 4 inequalities satisfied by x and y.
    By trial, find how many coaches and how many minibuses should be used, so as to use
    the least number of drivers.

6. This flow diagram will convert °C into °F.

    Use the flow diagram to convert 30°C into °F.
    Design a similar flow diagram to convert temperatures in °F to temperatures in °C, and
    use it to convert 77°F into °C.

7. Construct a simple flow diagram which will print the first 10 terms of the sequence of
    triangular numbers, 1, 3, 6, ...

8.   **To check whether a number (less than 275) is a prime number**

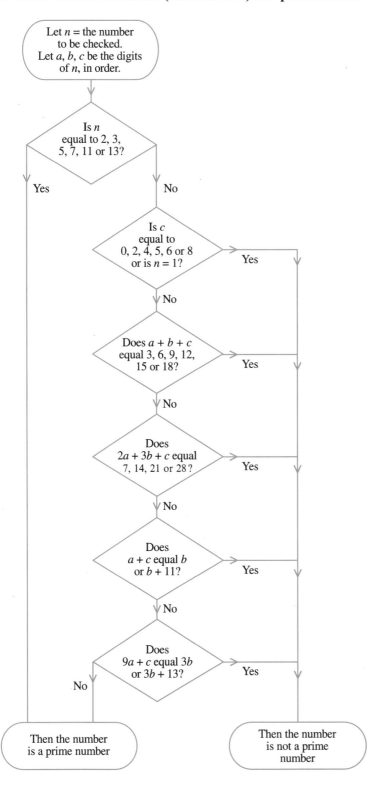

e.g. when $n = 231$, $a = 2$, $b = 3$, $c = 1$; when $n = 97$, $a = 0$, $b = 9$, $c = 7$.

Use the flow diagram to find whether or not these numbers are prime numbers.

1   119
2   151
3   165
4   221
5   257

For each answer, indicate the path taken by writing, e.g., no, no, yes.

9. Here are 2 flow diagrams for finding the size of each interior angle of a regular polygon.

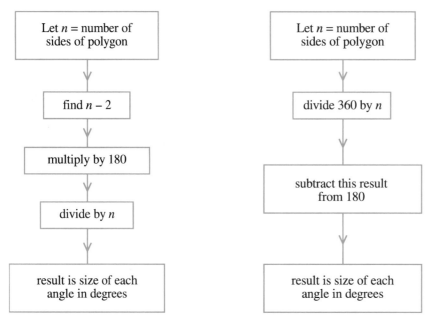

Use each flow diagram to find the size of an interior angle in
1   a hexagon,   2   a regular 20-sided polygon.
Which flow diagram do you prefer to use ?

10. Use the flow diagram on the opposite page to identify the countries which have these flags

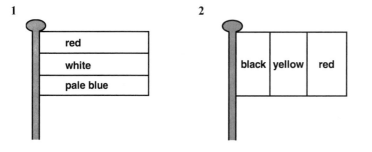

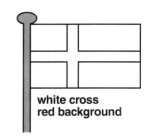

4   It is possible that Austria may join the EC. The flag is

    Explain how you could alter the flow diagram to
    include Austria.

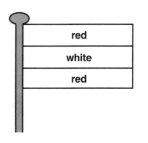

This flow diagram identifies the flags of the EC countries

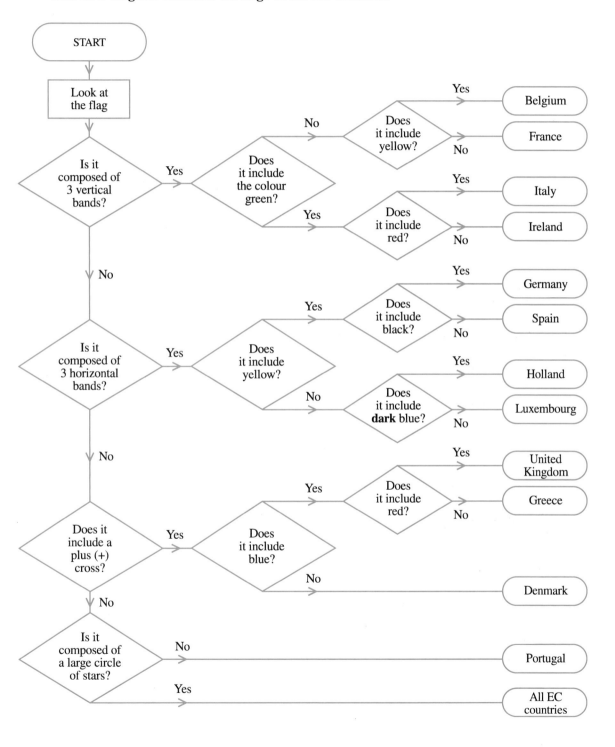

11.   Here is a flow diagram which gives a solution to the equation $x^2 + x - 1 = 0$.

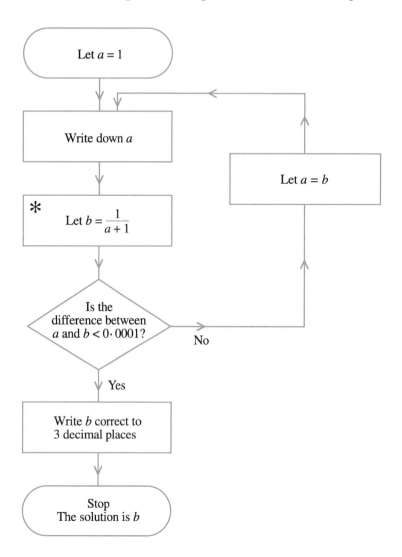

$*$On your calculator, start by entering a.

Press $\boxed{+}$ $\boxed{1}$ $\boxed{=}$ $\boxed{1/x}$ and leave this on the calculator for the next time.

On a graphics calculator, press a $\boxed{\text{EXE}}$

then press $\boxed{(}$ $\boxed{\text{ANS}}$ $\boxed{+}$ 1 $\boxed{)}$ $\boxed{1/x}$ $\boxed{\text{EXE}}$, then press $\boxed{\text{EXE}}$ each time.

1   Write down the 1st 5 decimal places of successive values of a in a column, and state the answer, b, correct to 3 decimal places.

2   By changing the instruction, let $b = \dfrac{1}{a+1}$, into let $b = \dfrac{1}{a+3}$, find a solution of the equation $x^2 + 3x - 1 = 0$, correct to 3 decimal places.

Practice test 15

1. Solve the inequalities.

   1 $8x + 3 \geqslant 12 - 4x$ **3** $x^2 - 11 \leqslant 14$

   2 $12 - x < 19 - 2x$ **4** $3x^2 > 108$

2. Mrs Jones makes toy animals, dogs and elephants, to sell. She can make not more than 10 of these animals in a week. There is more demand for elephants so she always makes at least 6 elephants, although she also makes at least 2 dogs.

   If in one week she makes x dogs and y elephants, write down inequalities satisfied by x and y.

   List the possible combinations of animals she could make, e.g. 2 dogs and 6 elephants. If she makes £3 profit on each dog and £2 profit on each elephant, consider the possible combinations and decide what she should make to get most profit. How much profit will this be ?

3. Here is a flow diagram which gives a sequence of numbers.

   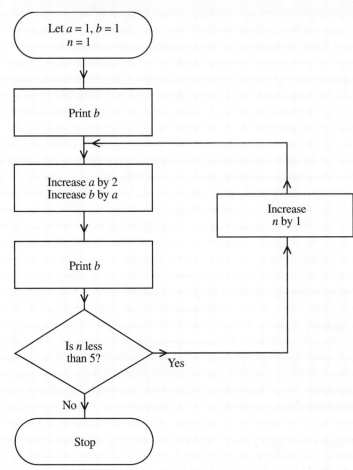

   For working through the flow diagram, write down a, b, n in columns, which begin like this:

a	b	n
1	1	1
3	4	2
.	. .	.

   Write the numbers given by the instruction 'Print b' in a row, separated by commas.

   What sequence of numbers is formed ?

Miscellaneous Section C

Exercise C1   Aural Practice

If possible find someone to read these questions to you.
You should do all of them within 10 minutes.
Do not use your calculator.
Write down the answers only.

1.   What is 6 less than one-quarter of 48 ?

2.   How many centimetres is 8 cm short of 1 metre ?

3.   If 20 equal packages weigh 70 kg, what is the weight of 1 package ?

4.   One angle of a triangle is 80° and the other two angles are equal. What size are they ?

5.   A rectangular lawn is 9 metres long and 6 metres wide. What is its perimeter ?

6.   What is the cube root of 125 ?

7.   When $17\frac{1}{2}\%$ tax is added to £100, what is the new price ?

8.   A water tank is 5 m long, 4 m wide and 2 m deep. How many cubic metres of water does it hold ?

9.   What is the next prime number after 31 ?

10.   How many faces has a triangular prism ?

11.   If 43 students out of 50 passed an exam, what percentage failed ?

12.   What is the median of the numbers 3, 4, 6, 7, 7 ?

13.   The base of a triangle is 10 cm and the height is 9 cm. What is its area ?

14.   How many kilometres are equivalent to 5 miles ?

15.   I think of a positive number, square it and subtract 15. The result is 34. What was the number I thought of ?

Exercise C2 Revision

1. Find the range of values of x if

    1 $2(5x + 4) > 3(2x - 1)$
    2 $12 + x > 5 - x > 1$

2. The rainfall records for a town in England for one year were as given in this bar diagram.

    1   Which was the wettest month and how much rain fell then ?
    2   Which was the driest month and how much rain fell then ?
    3   In which month was the rainfall double that of the preceding month ?

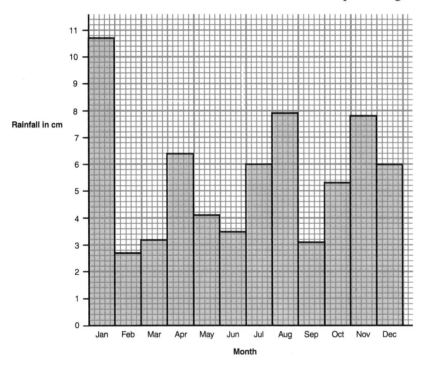

3. A closed cylinder has a radius of 14 cm. Find the area of one end.
    If its volume is 10 000 cm³, find its height, to the nearest mm.

4. Find the size of angle d.

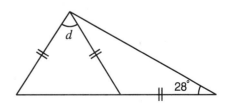

5. **1** Find the value of the number x if the ratio of $x : 3$ is the same as the ratio $4 : 5$.

2 Find the value of the positive number x if the ratio of $4 : x$ is the same as the ratio $x : 25$.

6. A certain estate of 660 hectares consists of ploughed land, pasture land and woodland. This is represented in the pie chart shown.

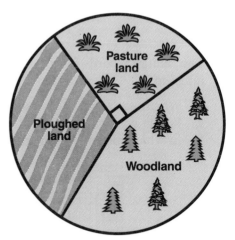

1 The angle in the pasture land sector is 90°. How many hectares are pasture land ?

2 There are 220 hectares of ploughed land. The angle in this sector has not been drawn accurately. What should it be ?

3 What fraction of the estate is woodland ?

7. Copy this drawing of a prism on your own squared paper, then using the squares to help you, draw an enlargement of your prism with scale factor 2.

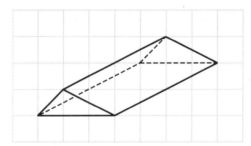

8. Raffle tickets are numbered from 1 to 50. What is the probability that the winning ticket is a multiple of 7 or includes a figure 7 ?

9. A man went abroad taking £200 which he changed into francs at the rate of 12.5 francs to the £. He stayed 7 days in a hotel for 180 francs per day, and his other expenses averaged 60 francs per day. In addition he spent 340 francs on presents. After 7 days how many francs had he left ? On his return he changed his remaining money back into £'s but the rate this time was 12 francs to the £. How much did he get ?

10. The perimeter of this triangle is 28 cm. The side BC is 5 cm longer than the side AB. Write down two equations, simplify them, and solve them simultaneously.
Hence find the numerical values of the lengths of the sides of the triangle.

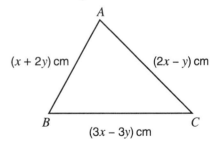

11. The graph represents the journey of a boy who cycles from a town A to a town B, and after a rest there, cycles back to A.

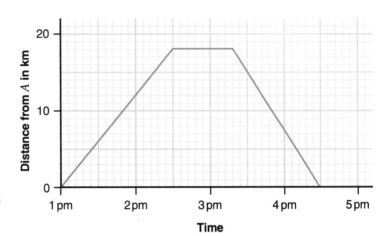

1 For how long did the boy stay in town B ?
2 What was his speed on the outward journey ?
3 What was his speed on the return journey ?

12. The time spent on homework by 30 students in a certain week was as follows:

(Times in hours, to the nearest hour.)

| 8 | 3 | 3 | 6 | 9 | 5 | 20 | 7 | 12 | 14 | 25 | 2 | 6 | 12 | 20 |
| 20 | 18 | 18 | 12 | 9 | 20 | 15 | 24 | 5 | 3 | 22 | 15 | 13 | 16 | 20 |

Make a frequency distribution table of the data using class intervals 1–5, 6–10, 11–15, 16–20, 21–25.
Draw a histogram of the distribution.
What is the modal class ?
Find the mean of the grouped distribution, to the nearest 0.1 hour.

Exercise C3 Revision

1. On a small photograph, a building is 4 cm high and its width is 10 cm.
On an enlargement, if the building is 10 cm high, what is its width ?

2. State how many axes of symmetry these figures have.

1 Isosceles triangle
2 Equilateral triangle
3 Parallelogram
4 Circle
5 Regular hexagon

State the order of rotational symmetry of these figures.

6 Square
7 Rectangle
8 Equilateral triangle
9 Regular pentagon
10 Outline of a 50 pence coin

3. Find the positive value of $\sqrt{b^2 - 4ac}$ when $a = 3$, $b = -5$ and $c = -8$.

4. A baby was weighed at the Health Clinic every month and the weights recorded for the first year were as follows:

Age in months	1	2	3	4	5	6	7	8	9	10	11	12
Weight in kg	4.5	5.0	6.0	6.5	7.0	7.5	8.0	8.5	9.0	9.2	9.4	9.5

Show this information on a graph, joining the points with a series of straight lines.
In which month was there the greatest gain in weight ?

5. **1** Express 96 in its prime factors.
   2 A number expressed in its prime factors is $2^6 \times 3^4 \times 5^2$. What is the square root of this number ?
   3 Which numbers between 40 and 50 are prime ?

6. Five people measured the length of a field and the lengths were 53 m, 55 m, 56 m, 52 m, 55 m.
   What is the average of the measurements ?

7. Which point does **not** lie on the line $3y = 7 - x$?

   $A(-5, 4)$, $B(-2, 1\frac{2}{3})$, $C(0, 2\frac{1}{3})$, $D(1, 2)$, $E(4, 1)$.

8. In a certain school, students must learn either French or Spanish, or both languages.
   The numbers studying each subject are shown in the diagram.

   1 If a student of the school is chosen at random, what is the probability that this student studies both French and Spanish ?
   2 If a student is chosen at random from those who study Spanish, what is the probability that this student also studies French ?

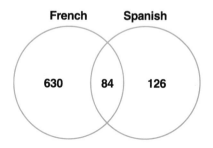

9. The distributions of examination marks in two examinations are shown in this table. Draw frequency polygons for these distributions on the same graph and comment on them.

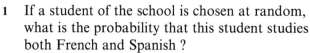
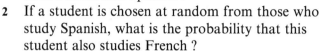

Mark	20–29	30–39	40–49	50–59	60–69	70–79	80–89	90–99
1st exam	4	14	38	30	11	3		
2nd exam		5	18	25	31	15	4	2

10. Which statement best describes this graph, showing profits
    of a firm over several months.

    A   The profits of the firm show a steady increase.
    B   The firm's profits are increasing at an increasing rate.
    C   Although the profits are increasing, the rate of
        increase is slowing down.
    D   The firm is making a steady profit.
    E   After an initial decrease the profits then increased.

    Draw similar sketch graphs to describe the other four statements, and label them.

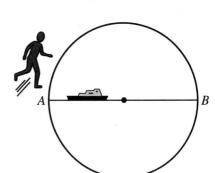

11. A boy is playing near a circular pool of
    diameter 20 m. He sends his toy boat
    across the centre of the pool from *A* to *B*
    at a speed of 2.5 m/s, and at the same time
    as the boat leaves *A* he starts to run round
    the edge of the pool from *A* to *B* at a speed
    of 4 m/s. Which gets to *B* first, the boy or
    his boat ?

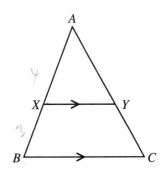

12. Imagine that you decide to do a statistical investigation about pocket money of young
    children. For example, you might like to find out how much pocket money they get, what
    it is spent on, and whether any is regularly saved in a savings account.
    Write a brief questionnaire (about 4 to 8 questions) which you could use to give you
    suitable information.

Exercise C4   Revision

1. If $AX = 4$ cm and $XB = 3$ cm, what are the ratios of

    1   $AX : AB$
    2   $XY : BC$?

2. Find the values of x which satisfy these inequalities.

    1   $3x^2 + 5 \leqslant 113$
    2   $5x^2 - 6 \geqslant x^2 + 94$

3. In a road survey, the cars passing a certain point in 1 minute intervals were counted, for
    30 minutes. Here are the results.

9	11	3	15	11	1	13	12	1	10	15	0	9	11	0
10	5	5	4	5	11	7	13	7	9	12	5	9	10	6

    1 Show the results in a tally chart in classes 0–3, 4–7, 8–11, 12–15.
    2 Find the mean number of cars per minute, using the original data. (The total number
        of cars is 239.)
    3 Find the mean number of cars per minute, using the grouped data.

4. The diagram shows the cross-section of a
    railway cutting, in the form of a trapezium.
    What is the area of this cross-section ?
    If the cutting is 200 m long, what volume of
    earth will have to be removed in constructing
    the cutting ?

    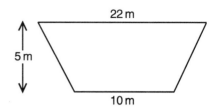

5. Solve the simultaneous equations

    1 $4x - 3y = 11$ **2** $3x + 2y = 5$
        $2x + y = 13$ $7x + 3y = 15$

6. Draw a graph to convert between British and French currency at a time when the rate of
    exchange was £1 = 8.5 francs.
    On the horizontal axis, for £'s, label from 0 to 10 with 1 unit to 1 cm. On the vertical
    axis, for francs, label from 0 to 90 with 10 units to 1 cm.

    From your graph, find
    1 the amount you would get if you changed £3 into francs,
    2 the value in British money of a present which cost you 50 francs.

7. *ABCD* is a rhombus with $\angle ABC = 60°$.

    What sort of triangles are
    1 $\triangle ABC$,
    2 $\triangle ABD$,
    3 $\triangle ABX$?

    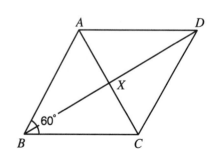

8. The histogram shows the distances from
    home to school of a group of children.
    What is the probability that a child chosen
    at random from this group lives within
    1 mile of the school ?

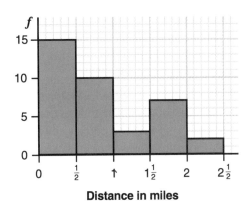

Distance in miles

9. *ABCD* is a rectangle.

    Find
    1   the length of *DE*,
    2   the area of △*ADE*,
    3   the length of *AB*.

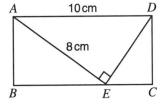

10. Solve these equations by trial, finding solutions which are positive whole numbers.

    1 $x^2 + x = 56$
    2 $x^2 - 2x = 120$
    3 $(x + 3)(x - 2) = 104$.

11. It is estimated that 5 men can lay a pipeline in 16 days. To do the work in 10 days, how
    many extra men should be used (assuming that all men work at the same rate) ?

12. Here are the results of a (fictitious) survey in which people were given a list of activities
    they could take part in, and they were asked to give their 1st 3 choices for what they
    wanted to do. Here are the results.

    Analyse the results and write down your conclusions, including saying which one of the
    activities you would choose as being the one most people wanted to do.

| Activity | Number putting it | | |
	1st	2nd	3rd
P	4	2	0
Q	3	5	1
R	5	1	1
S	0	2	3
T	0	2	7

Exercise C5   Activities

1. **A scale model**

   Design a study-bedroom suitable for a teenager and make a scale model of the room, showing the door, windows and heating source. Make scale models of the furniture and include those. Show where the lighting is and where the power points are. Paint your model to show the colour scheme.

   A more ambitious project would be to make a model of a house, a famous building or a village.

2. **Planning for a wedding**

   This is a most important occasion in a couple's life and deserves proper planning. You can imagine it is your own wedding in a few years' time or the wedding of imaginary friends.

   Decide what type of wedding. Church, other place of worship, Registry Office ? It can be a very simple wedding with just two witnesses or a very grand one. Plan all the details of the wedding, and make a list of costs involved, with a separate note of who pays for each. Traditionally the bride's father paid for most things but that is not always the case nowadays. There are many small details to include, for instance, transport to the wedding, legal costs, wedding ring or rings.

   Plan the timetable for the day, so that the ceremony begins on time, and the couple leave for their honeymoon on time, especially if they have a train or plane to catch.

   Illustrate your booklet with pictures, e.g. of the bride's dress.

3. **To find the probability that 2 dominoes will match each other**

Get a set of dominoes which go from
0–0 (double blank) to 6–6 (double six).

Put the set of dominoes in a bag and draw two out at random. Count it as a success (s) if the dominoes match and a failure (f) if they do not.

e.g. 2–4 and 3–5 have no number in common and do not match, (f),
         2–4 and 4–4 have 4 in common and match, (s),
         2–4 and 1–2 have 2 in common and match, (s),
         0–0 and 0–6 have 0 in common and match, (s).

Before you begin, estimate how many times out of 100 trials the 2 dominoes will match.

Repeat the experiment 100 times, recording your results.

How close was your estimate ?

From your results, the experimental probability that 2 dominoes will match each other is $\dfrac{S}{100}$, where S is the total number which match.

If you have a set of dominoes going up to double nine, you can repeat the experiment with these.

(The theoretical result for the set up to double six is 0.39, and for the set up to double nine it is 0.30. Do your experimental results match these ?)

4. **Using a counter-example in disproving statements**

Prove that these statements are not always true, by finding an example where the statement is not true.

1   $2x^2$ is always greater than x.

2   If $x^2 > 16$ then $x > 4$.

3   If two triangles have equal areas then they have equal perimeters.

4   If the probability of event A happening is $\frac{1}{3}$ and the probability of event B happening is $\frac{1}{2}$ then the probability of either A or B happening is $\frac{1}{3} + \frac{1}{2} = \frac{5}{6}$.

5   $\triangle ABC$, $\triangle DEF$ have $AB = DE = 8$ cm, $BC = DF = 6$ cm and $\angle A = \angle D = 20°$. Therefore the triangles are congruent (exactly alike).

5. **Shapes in everyday life**

Make a display about these, with
drawings, pictures, postcards,
photographs and models.

Ideas:
symmetry in nature, and in man-made
objects,

triangles: pylons, etc.

circles: wheels, drainpipes,

tins and boxes of different solid shapes,

shapes in nature: spirals in snails, jellyfish,
pattern on a sunflower centre, cone of a
volcano,

shapes in building: unusual
modern designs, bridges, the Pyramids,
radio telescopes (paraboloid), cooling towers
(hyperboloid), spheres of an early warning system.

6. **Investigating π**

Measure the circumference C and diameter D of circles of different sizes from a penny
to a large wheel and find the value of π from $\dfrac{C}{D}$.

Set your results down in a table. One item has been given here, as an example.

Object	C	D	$\dfrac{C}{D}$ as a fraction	$\dfrac{C}{D}$ as a decimal
tin of soup	23.6 cm	7.5 cm	$\dfrac{23.6}{7.5}$	3.15

Study your results and comment on them. If the results in the last column are nearly the
same, you could find the average of all these results.

Show that the area of a circle is πr^2 by cutting a circle into small sectors and rearranging
them into the shape of an approximate parallelogram with length πr and height r.

Write π to as many decimal places as are shown on your calculator. See if you can find a list giving more decimal places. People have invented phrases to help them to remember the first few decimal places of π. One of these is 'Sir, I have a number.' The number of letters in each word gives π as 3.1416. Can you invent a phrase of your own, or even a rhyme ?

There are various infinite series which give π, such as

$$\pi = 4 - \frac{4}{3} + \frac{4}{5} - \frac{4}{7} + \frac{4}{9} - \frac{4}{11} + \frac{4}{13} - \frac{4}{15} + \cdots$$

Use your calculator to work out several terms of this.

Archimedes, who lived about 200 BC, found a value for π by considering a pattern for the perimeters of regular polygons with 6, 12, 24, 48 and 96 sides inscribed in a circle, and then polygons outside and touching a circle. (The circumference is greater than the perimeter of polygons inside, and less than the perimeter of polygons outside the circle.) He gave π as a number between $3\frac{1}{7}$ and $3\frac{10}{71}$. Write these numbers as decimals to see how close he was.

Make a list of all the formula you know which involve π.

Find π using probability and by tossing sticks. If you toss sticks over a set of parallel lines then the sticks may either land touching or across a line, or land completely between the lines. The probability that a stick will touch a line is $\dfrac{2s}{\pi d}$, where the sticks are s cm long and the lines are d cm apart.

Use the floorboards of the room if they form parallel lines, otherwise draw lines on the floor. Find 10 thin sticks with length about $\frac{3}{4}$ of the distance between the lines. Toss the sticks randomly 50 times, and find the total number n, out of 500, which land touching or across a line. Then $\dfrac{n}{500}$ is an estimate of the probability. Put $\dfrac{n}{500} = \dfrac{2s}{\pi d}$ and rearrange this equation to find an experimental value for π.

Find π using probability and random numbers. If you choose 2 numbers at random they can either have a common factor, e.g. 40 and 75 have a common factor 5, or they can be prime to each other, i.e. have no factor in common, e.g. 40 and 63 have no common factor although they both have factors.

The probability that 2 numbers are prime to each other is $\dfrac{6}{\pi^2}$.

Get 500 pairs of random numbers from random number tables, a computer, or using the numbers from a phone directory. Numbers less than 100 will do. Find how many pairs are prime to each other. If there are n pairs, then $\dfrac{n}{500}$ is an estimate of the probability.

Put $\dfrac{n}{500} = \dfrac{6}{\pi^2}$, and rearrange this equation to find an experimental value for π.

7.   **The number of throws of a die needed to get a six**

In many children's dice games, you need to get a six to begin, and sometimes it seems a long time before you get one. What is the average number of throws needed ?

Before you begin the experiment, estimate
(1) what is the most likely number (mode number) of throws until you get a six,
(2) what is the average number (mean number) of throws until you get a six.

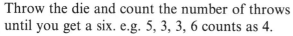

Throw the die and count the number of throws until you get a six. e.g. 5, 3, 3, 6 counts as 4.
Repeat about 200 times. (You can use the results of a previous experiment if you have kept them. You can also use simulated numbers from a computer or calculator.)
Put the results in a tally chart.
Draw a bar-line graph of the results and describe its shape.
Find the mode number and the mean number of throws.
How close were your estimates ?

PUZZLES

32.   A friend offered £100 to provide prizes for a Charity Tombola on condition that exactly 100 prizes were bought. The committee running the Tombola wanted to buy prizes costing £10, £2 and 50 pence, with more than one at each price. How could they fulfil the conditions of the gift ?

33.   Mark, the racing driver, did his first practice lap at 40 miles per hour. What speed would he have to average on his second lap if he wanted to produce an average for the two laps of 80 miles per hour ?

34.   Arrange (a) three 1's, (b) three 2's, (c) three 4's, without using any mathematical signs, so that you represent the highest possible number in each case.

35 .   A group of six children have to send a team of four of them to take part in a quiz. But they all have their own views on whether they will take part or not.
Laura won't be in the team unless Michelle is also in it.
Michelle won't be in the team if Oliver is.
Naomi won't be in the team if both Laura and Michelle are in it.
Oliver won't be in the team if Patrick is.
Patrick will be in the team with any of the others.
Robert won't be in the team if Laura is, unless Oliver is in it too.
Which 4 took part in the quiz ?

To the student : 4

Making plans for revision

As the time of the examination draws nearer you should look back over your progress and see if you are satisfied with it, and make a plan of action for the future. If you have been working steadily from the beginning of the course, you may not need to make any extra effort. If you enjoy the challenge of Maths you are probably working well and learning everything as you go along. But if you find some of the work difficult and are feeling discouraged, perhaps a little extra effort at this stage, and perhaps a change in the way you approach your work, will help to improve your standard, and you will feel more confident.

In addition to lessons and set homework you should spend some time each week on individual study. Make a plan for this depending on how much time you have available and what you need to learn or practise. In addition to Maths, you will have work to do in all your other subjects, so take these into consideration. If you have to do a 'Project' in any subject, then start it in good time or you will find yourself at the last minute spending all your time on it, and your other work is neglected.

You must plan how you are going to revise the work. You could work through this book again in order, spending so much time on each chapter. Choose a suitable selection of questions to do, either straightforward ones if you need practice in these, or the more challenging questions if you are more confident with the topic. Alternatively, you could use the revision exercises in the miscellaneous sections A to E of the book. You might prefer to revise all the arithmetic, then the algebra, then the geometry, and so on. The important thing is that **you** should decide for yourself what **you** need to do, and then plan how you are going to do it.

Sort out your difficulties as you go along. Try to think things out for yourself as far as possible, rather than having to be shown how to do everything. But if you need extra help, then **ask** someone to help you, either your teacher, someone in your class or a higher class, a parent or a friend.

Keep a list of what you are doing. At first there will be a lot to do and not much done, but you will find it encouraging when after a few weeks you can see that you are making real progress.

16 Scatter diagrams

The topics in this chapter include:

- creating scatter diagrams,
- having an understanding of correlaton,
- drawing a line of best fit on a scatter diagram.

Scatter diagrams

Scatter diagrams can be drawn to look at the relationship between 2 sets of data.

Simple scatter diagrams for data with few values.

Example

1   The number of goals scored by the home team and the number of goals scored by the away team in football matches.
Here are the results for one particular Saturday.

4–0	1–0	1–0	1–1	1–3	0–1	2–0	1–2	1–1	2–2
0–2	3–2	1–2	2–1	3–1	0–0	0–0	1–1	2–4	0–1
2–1	3–1	1–1	2–2	3–3	3–0	2–3	1–1	1–1	0–2
2–2	1–0	1–0	1–1	2–1	1–1	0–2	4–2	3–1	3–2
3–0	2–4

Show these results on a simple scatter diagram.

Draw and label the axes like this.

If the first score is 4–0, put a cross in the space which represents 4 goals by the home team and 0 by the away team.

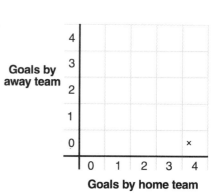

Here is the graph showing the results.

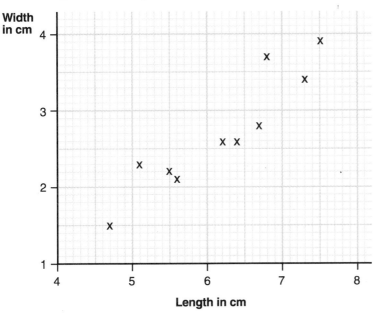

This example uses a few whole numbers only, on each axis, and these were represented in blocks. When the numbers have a bigger range, or if the data involves measurements, we label the axes in a different way.

Example

2   The length and width of 10 leaves from a bush.

| Length (in cm) | 6.4 | 7.5 | 6.7 | 7.3 | 6.8 | 5.6 | 5.1 | 4.7 | 5.5 | 6.2 |
| Width (in cm) | 2.6 | 3.9 | 2.8 | 3.4 | 3.7 | 2.1 | 2.3 | 1.5 | 2.2 | 2.6 |

Scatter diagram of the lengths and widths of 10 leaves

This diagram shows that there is some relationship between the length and width of a leaf from the bush. Longer leaves tend to be wider, although the relationship is not exact. This relationship is called **correlation**.

Note that the labelling on the axes need not start at 0.

The 1st set of data is usually plotted on the horizontal axis. You do not need to use the same scale on both axes.

Correlation

Here are some pictures of scatter diagrams, with axes not labelled.

This shows that there is good (positive) correlation between the variables.

Here there is an exact relationship. This can be described as perfect correlation.

There is some correlation but it is not very close.

This is a relationship where as one variable increases, the other decreases.
This is said to be inverse or negative correlation.

Perfect inverse correlation.

There does not seem to be any relationship. There is no correlation, or there is zero correlation.

With a suitable computer program, a scatter diagram can be plotted on a computer screen. This is very useful if you have a large amount of data, because it is much quicker than drawing your own graph and plotting the points on it. You can see if there seems to be evidence of correlation.

Statisticians use a formula to work out a numerical value for correlation. They would not make any assumptions about whether two variables have correlation unless they had at least 30 pairs of data. However, we have used less items here, so that the questions do not take too long.

When there is evidence of correlation between two sets of data, you have to decide if they are really connected, or whether they are both linked to a third item.
For example, someone found a strong positive correlation between size of feet and maths ability, but the real reason for the connection was that the boys with the bigger feet were older boys, and they had learnt more maths. Both these items, size of feet, and maths knowledge, would show some correlation with age of boys, but there is no other connection.

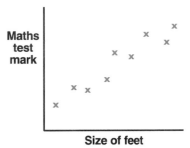

Exercise 16.1

1. The marks out of 10 for some children in two tests are given below.
    Draw axes like these and put crosses in
    the squares to represent the marks.
    Comment about the relationship shown by
    the graph.

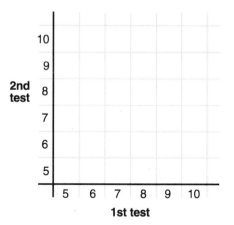

    The marks are given for each child in turn. 6, 7 means 6 in the first test and 7 in the
    second test.

6, 7	5, 6	10, 10	7, 8	9, 9	9, 9	7, 6
9, 10	8, 9	5, 7	6, 9	5, 7	8, 8	8, 8
9, 10	9, 9	7, 7	8, 7	7, 9	8, 8	7, 8
6, 8	9, 9	8, 7	9, 9	6, 7	8, 7	6, 5
8, 6	8, 8	6, 8	7, 9	9, 8	6, 6	10, 10
10, 9	8, 9	9, 9	7, 8	9, 9	10, 10	9, 10
8, 9	9, 8	9, 8				

2. The football results on a particular Saturday are given below. Draw axes with blocks
    labelled from 0 to 5 and put crosses in the squares to represent the goals scored by the
    home team and by the away team.

1–0	1–1	1–0	0–2	1–5	4–2	2–0	1–1	0–1	0–1	1–1
2–0	4–1	0–0	0–0	0–1	2–0	0–1	1–1	2–1	2–0	1–2
3–1	2–3	1–0	0–2	1–0	1–3	1–1	2–0	4–0	0–0	4–1
0–0	1–0	3–0	0–4	3–2	5–1	1–3	3–3	1–0		

    Comment on the results.

For question 3 onwards the axes should be labelled as in example 2 on page 343.
Keep the graphs you draw to use again in Exercise 16.2.

Questions 3 to 7
Sets of two related variables x and y are given in the tables. Plot the values on scatter
diagrams, with x on the horizontal axis, from 10 to 70, and y on the vertical axis, from 0
to 50.
Say whether the correlation is positive or negative.

3.

x	10	20	30	40	50	60	70
y	2	3	12	25	33	36	47

4.

x	10	15	20	25	30	40	50	55	60	70
y	44	40	39	32	31	25	17	15	9	7

5.

x	15	20	25	30	40	50	60	70
y	8	17	20	19	24	39.	41	46

6.

x	15	20	25	30	35	40	50	55	60	70
y	45	31	35	25	22	12	15	8	5	6

7.

x	10	15	20	25	30	40	50	55	60	65	70
y	6	7	18	17	25	26	42	39	43	49	48

8.   8 plots were treated with different amounts of fertilizer and the crop yield recorded.

Amount of fertilizer (units/m^2)	1	2	3	4	5	6	7	8
Yield (in kg)	36	41	58	60	70	76	75	92

Plot a scatter diagram of these results and comment on the relationship between the
amount of fertilizer and the yield.

9.   The marks of 10 students in a Maths exam were as follows:

Paper 1	32	38	42	45	48	51	57	62	70	72
Paper 2	45	44	49	51	50	55	60	60	68	70

Plot the points on a scatter diagram and comment on the relationship between the marks in the two papers.

A line of best fit

A line of best fit is a straight line which shows the possible relationship between the two sets of data. It is drawn so that points on one side of it are balanced by points on the other side.

We may not all agree on what is the 'best' line.

To draw a line of best fit

You just draw the best line you can, deciding by putting your ruler (or your set-square may be better) on the graph and trying it in various positions, until you have a slope which matches the general slope of the points, and an average position where the points are balanced with some on both sides of the line.

Diagrams showing lines of best fit

(Scales are not shown.)

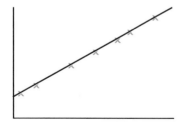  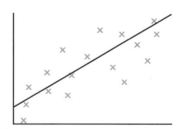

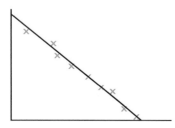 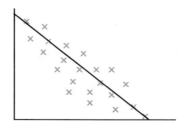

Line of best fit drawn on the scatter diagram of the lengths and widths of 10 leaves. (Example 2, page 343.)

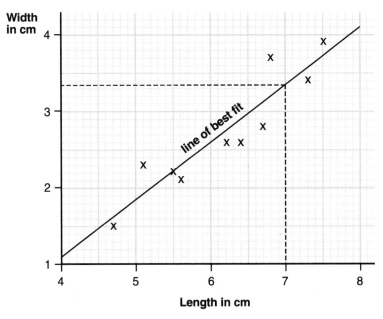

This line can be used to estimate the likely width of a leaf with a certain length, but the result will only be a 'best estimate', not a fixed measure.
For a leaf of length 7 cm the estimate for the width is 3.3 cm.

If you use a computer program, it will also draw a line of best fit, and estimate *y*-values to correspond with given *x*-values.

Exercise 16.2

1. An experiment is carried out with readings of values of *x* and *y*. Here are the results.

x	12	18	28	37	52	64	71	76
y	43	53	52	60	70	75	77	84

    Plot these values on a scatter diagram and draw the line of best fit.
    Find an approximate value for *y* when *x* = 60.

2. *x* and *y* are two related variables. Plot the values on a scatter diagram. Comment on the relationship between the variables.
    Draw a line of best fit, and use it to find an approximate value for *y* when *x* = 80.

x	53	57	66	70	72	85	90	97
y	42	37	35	37	30	28	25	24

Questions 3 to 7
Use the scatter diagrams drawn for questions 3 to 7 of Exercise 16.1, page 347.
For each one, draw a line of best fit.
Use your line to estimate a *y*-value which would correspond with an *x*-value of 45.

8.   Draw a line of best fit on the scatter diagram drawn for question 8 of Exercise 16.1.

9.   Draw a line of best fit on the scatter diagram drawn for question 9 of Exercise 16.1.
      Another student scored 55 marks on Paper 1 but was absent for Paper 2. Use your
      diagram to estimate what he might have scored on Paper 2.

Exercise 16.3 Applications

1.   In each of the following cases say whether you think that the correlation would be
      positive, negative or zero.
      Give reasons and sketch the kind of scatter diagram you would expect.

      1   The daily rainfall, and the number
            of umbrellas sold.
      2   The number of empty chairs, and
            the number of occupied chairs in a
            classroom in each lesson during
            the week.
      3   The heights of children, and their
            house numbers.
      4   The distances that children live from
            school, and the cost of their fares to school.
      5   The daily air temperature, and the
            amount of fuel used for heating by
            households in a certain town.

2.   A manufacturing company gives these figures for each quarter in a two-year period.

Quarter	1	2	3	4	1	2	3	4
Output units	10	20	40	25	30	40	50	45
Total cost (in £1000's)	41	48	67	53	61	70	79	73

Draw a scatter diagram for the data, with output units on the horizontal axis and total
cost on the vertical axis. Draw a line of best fit. What is the estimate for the total cost
likely to be incurred at an output level of 35 units ?

3.   The heights and weights of 8 young men are given in this table.

Height (in cm)	168	170	173	178	181	182	183	185
Weight (in kg)	68	70	70	74	75	76	78	79

Plot the points on a scatter diagram and draw a line of best fit.
Estimate the likely weight of a young man if he is 1.75 m tall.

4.   The exam marks for 10 students for Maths and Physics are as follows:

Maths mark	63	89	53	45	47	74	69	79	64	37
Physics mark	44	65	38	32	35	53	50	59	51	26

Plot these marks on a scatter diagram and draw a line of best fit.
Another student scored 56 in Maths but was absent for the Physics exam. Use your
diagram to give an estimated mark for Physics.

5.   A test was carried out on seven fields by treating them with different amounts of nitrogen
fertilizer and measuring the percentage of protein in the grass.
Here are the results.

Units of fertilizer applied	0	1	2	3	4	5	6
Percentage of protein	14.0	15.2	17.0	19.4	21.4	22.6	23.2

Plot a scatter diagram of these results and draw a line of best fit.

6.   Eight paintings were entered for a competition and were examined by two judges, who
marked them out of 100.
The marks are shown in the table.

Painting	1	2	3	4	5	6	7	8
1st Judge	45	55	65	40	25	45	35	65
2nd Judge	50	65	80	50	35	60	40	75

Plot a scatter diagram of the data and draw a line of best fit.
Another painting arrived unavoidably late, and was given a mark of 50 by the 1st judge,
but it was not possible for the 2nd judge to examine it. Use the line of best fit to estimate
the mark it might have gained from the 2nd judge.

7.   Carry out an investigation using data with which you expect to find some kind of paired relationship.
     Collect the data and represent it on a scatter diagram.
     Comment on the relationship, but do not be too disappointed if your scatter diagrams do not show good correlation. Statistical data rarely matches perfectly as the figures are often affected by other factors as well as those you are measuring.

     Here are some suggestions for possible investigations.

     Heights and weights of children of the same age.
     Heights of mothers and their 16 year old daughters.
     Ages of young children and their bedtimes.
     Heights and arm-spans.
     Exam marks in similar subjects such as Maths and Science, French and German, or in different subjects such as Art and Science.
     Times spent learning a piece of work, and marks gained in a test on it.
     Times taken to do a piece of work using (1) normal hand and (2) other hand.
     Shoe sizes and collar (or hat) sizes.
     Amounts of pocket money and amounts saved.

Practice test 16

1.   Draw 5 sketch diagrams, with 10 crosses shown on each, to show examples of pairs of variables which have
     1   good positive correlation,
     2   positive correlation which is fairly good,
     3   good negative correlation,
     4   perfect negative correlation,
     5   no correlation.
     (Do not label axes or show scales.)
     In diagrams **1** to **4**, add a line of best fit to your sketch.

2.   The heights of 10 boys and their fathers are given in this table.

Height of father (in cm)	167	168	169	171	172	172	174	175	176	182
Height of son (in cm)	164	166	166	168	169	170	170	171	173	177

     Plot the points on a scatter diagram and draw a line of best fit. Use your diagram to estimate the height of a boy of this age if his father is 1.7 m tall.

3. The marks gained by 10 students in each of two papers of a Maths examination were as follows:

Student	A	B	C	D	E	F	G	H	J	K
Marks for Paper 1	30	39	44	60	28	64	70	56	32	46
Marks for Paper 2	48	55	56	75	35	78	86	70	46	56

Draw a scatter diagram for the data, putting the marks for Paper 1 on the horizontal axis. Draw a line of best fit.
Another student got 52 marks on Paper 1 but was absent for Paper 2. Use the line of best fit to estimate a mark for this student for Paper 2.

PUZZLES

36. Barry was given a box containing 125 small bars of chocolate. On the wrapper of each bar there was a token, and Barry could exchange 5 tokens at the local shop for a similar bar of chocolate. How many extra bars of chocolate did he get ?

37. In the 'Tower of Hanoi' puzzle, there are 8 discs of different sizes on 1 peg, with two empty pegs.

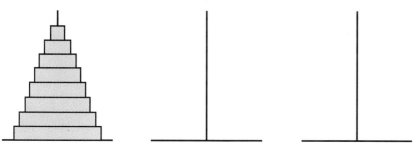

The game is to transfer all the discs to one of the empty pegs.
Only one disc can be moved at a time. A disc can only be placed on an empty peg or onto a larger disc, never onto a smaller one.
Make your own version of this game using circles of cardboard, and see how many moves are needed. You may prefer to discover the pattern of moves by starting with less than 8 discs. Notice the moves of the smallest disc.
The legend has it that there is such a peg with 64 discs on it. At the rate of 1 move per second, how long will it take to move all 64 discs ?

17 Using decimals

The topics in this chapter include:

- multiplying and dividing mentally single digit multiples of any power of 10,

- solving problems and using multiplication and division with numbers of any size, using a calculator efficiently,

- estimating and approximating to check the results of calculations,

- understanding the meaning of reciprocals and exploring relationships,

- recognising that measurement is approximate and when expressed to a given unit is in possible error of half a unit,

- expressing and using numbers in standard index form.

Multiplying and dividing mentally

Multiplying

Examples

1
$$300 \times 60 = 3 \times 100 \times 6 \times 10$$
$$= 18 \times 1000$$
$$= 18\,000$$

(In your head)

or

$$300 \times 60 = 300 \times 6 \times 10$$
$$= 1800 \times 10$$
$$= 18\,000$$

(In your head)

2 80×0.2 $80 \times 2 = 160$

Restore 1 decimal place   (In your head)

$80 \times 0.2 = 16.0$

$ = 16$

or

$80 \times 0.2 = 0.2 \times 80$

$ = 0.2 \times 10 \times 8$ (In your head)

$ = 2 \times 8$

$ = 16$

3 0.04×0.9 $4 \times 9 = 36$ (In your head)

Restore 3 decimal places

$0.04 \times 0.9 = 0.036$

Notice that when you multiply by a decimal which is a number less than 1, the answer will be smaller than the number you are multiplying.
e.g. 80×0.2 will be smaller than 80.
    0.04×0.9 will be smaller than 0.04 and also smaller than 0.9.

Dividing

Examples

4 $6300 \div 90 = 6300 \div 10 \div 9$

$ = 630 \div 9$ (In your head)

$ = 70$

5 $40 \div 0.8 = 400 \div 8$

(making 0.8 into 8)   (In your head)

$ = 50$

6 $3 \div 0.05 = 300 \div 5$

(making 0.05 into 5)   (In your head)

$ = 60$

7 $0.06 \div 0.3 = 0.6 \div 3$

        (making 0.3 into 3)   (In your head)

        $= 0.2$

Notice that when you divide by a decimal which is a number less than 1, the answer will be greater than the number you are dividing.

e.g. $40 \div 0.8$ will be greater than 40.
      $3 \div 0.05$ will be greater than 3.
      $0.06 \div 0.3$ will be greater than 0.06.

Using your calculator

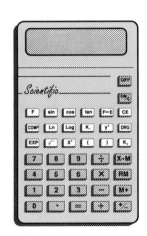

Read the notes of page 52 again, to remind you.
Here are some further examples.

8   Find the value of $\dfrac{27.6 + 1.2}{19.3 - 14.2}$

Using brackets, press

$\boxed{(}\ 27.6\ \boxed{+}\ 1.2\ \boxed{)}\ \boxed{\div}\ \boxed{(}\ 19.3\ \boxed{-}\ 14.2\ \boxed{)}\ \boxed{=}$

Using the memory instead, make sure it is cleared before you begin, then press

$19.3\ \boxed{-}\ 14.2\ \boxed{=}\ \boxed{M+}\ 27.6\ \boxed{+}\ 1.2\ \boxed{=}\ \boxed{\div}\ \boxed{RM}\ \boxed{=}$

With either method, you should get $5.64705\ldots$, which is 5.65, to 3 sig. fig.

9   Find the vaue of $\sqrt{11.3^2 - 1.5^2}$

Press $11.3\ \boxed{x^2}\ \boxed{-}\ 1.5\ \boxed{x^2}\ \boxed{=}\ \boxed{\sqrt{}}$

The answer is 11.2.

10   Find the value of $x^3 - 5x^2 + 13$, when $x = 9.6$.

Press $9.6\ \boxed{x^y}\ 3\ \boxed{-}\ 5\ \boxed{\times}\ 9.6\ \boxed{x^2}\ \boxed{+}\ 13\ \boxed{=}$

or $9.6\ \boxed{\times}\ \boxed{x^2}\ \boxed{-}\ 5\ \boxed{\times}\ 9.6\ \boxed{x^2}\ \boxed{+}\ 13\ \boxed{=}$

You should get 437, to 3 sig. fig.

11 $\sqrt[4]{\dfrac{1287}{36.2 \times 23.8}}$

Press 1287 $\boxed{\div}$ 36.2 $\boxed{\div}$ 23.8 $\boxed{=}$ $\boxed{\sqrt{}}$ $\boxed{\sqrt{}}$

You should get 1.11, to 3 sig. fig.

12 Make a rough check of your calculations to see if the calculator answer seems to be about the right size.

For example **8**, $27.6 + 1.2$ is approximately $28 + 1 = 29$.
$19.3 - 14.2$ is approximately $19 - 14 = 5$.
$29 \div 5$ is approximately $30 \div 5 = 6$.
The answer 5.65 seems to be about the right size.

For example **9**, $11.3^2 - 1.5^2$ is approximately $11^2 - 2^2 = 121 - 4 = 117$.
$\sqrt{117}$ is approximately $\sqrt{121} = 11$.
The answer 11.2 seems to be about the right size.

For example **10**, 9.6 is approximately 10.
$10^3 - 5 \times 10^2 + 13 = 1000 - 500 + 13 = 513$.
The answer 437 seems to be about the right size.

For example **11**, $\dfrac{1287}{36.2 \times 23.8}$ is approximately $\dfrac{12\cancel{0}\cancel{0}}{4\cancel{0} \times 2\cancel{0}} = 1.5$

Now $1^4 = 1$ and $2^4 = 16$ so $\sqrt[4]{1.5}$ is just over 1.
The answer 1.11 seems to be about the right size.

Reciprocals

If x is a number (not 0) then $\dfrac{1}{x}$ is called the reciprocal of x.

A number multiplied by its reciprocal equals 1.

e.g. The reciprocal of 5 is $\frac{1}{5}$ since $5 \times \frac{1}{5} = 1$.

The reciprocal of $\frac{1}{3}$ is 3 since $\frac{1}{3} \times 3 = 1$.

The reciprocal of $\frac{4}{5}$ is $\frac{5}{4}$ since $\frac{4}{5} \times \frac{5}{4} = 1$.

The reciprocal of 0.7 is $\frac{10}{7}$ since 0.7 is $\frac{7}{10}$ and $\frac{7}{10} \times \frac{10}{7} = 1$.

In general, the reciprocal of $\dfrac{a}{b}$ is $\dfrac{b}{a}$.

There will be a reciprocal key on your calculator. It will be labelled $\dfrac{1}{x}$.

Press 8 $\boxed{\frac{1}{x}}$ and you will get 0.125 since $\frac{1}{8} = 0.125$

Press 1.1 $\boxed{\frac{1}{x}}$ and you will get 0.909090 ... since $\frac{1}{1.1} = \frac{10}{11} = 0.909090\ldots$

Recurring decimals

If you want to show that a decimal is a recurring one, then you write dots over the first and last number of the recurring pattern.

$0.\dot{7}$ means $0.77777\ldots$

$0.1\dot{6}$ means $0.166666\ldots$

$0.\dot{4}\dot{1}$ means $0.414141\ldots$

$0.\dot{2}9\dot{3}$ means $0.293293293\ldots$

$0.31\dot{2}8\dot{5}$ means $0.31285285285\ldots$

Exercise 17.1

1. Work out the answers to these questions in your head, just writing down the answers.

1	100×0.01	**5**	80×0.05	**8**	$0.4 \div 0.8$
2	500×0.7	**6**	$4 \div 0.04$	**9**	$540 \div 0.9$
3	20×0.8	**7**	$60 \div 0.2$	**10**	$0.64 \div 8$
4	0.7×0.9				

2. These numbers are approximations of the numbers used in question 3. Find the answers, if possible without using your calculator. Keep the answers to use in question 3.

1	$3 + 2 + 8$	**6**	4×300
2	0.1×2	**7**	$1 \div 2$
3	$7 \div 0.2$	**8**	$400 + 800 - 600$
4	$13 - 3$	**9**	$2 + 2 + 2$
5	$(20 \times 20) + (10 \times 10)$	**10**	$1000 \div 5$

3.   Work out the following, using your calculator. Compare each answer with the corresponding answer from question 2. If they are very different, check your work again.

   1 $3.17 + 2.4 + 7.73$ **6** 3.63×280
   2 0.09×2.1 **7** $1.32 \div 2.4$
   3 $6.8 \div 0.17$ **8** $379 + 821 - 560$
   4 $13.3 - 2.84$ **9** $2.35 + 2.4 + 1.85$
   5 $19^2 + 11^2$ **10** $1008 \div 4.8$

4.   Find approximate anwers to the following, then use your calculator to work out the exact answers.

   1 1.4×2.32 **4** 6.3^2
   2 $203.7 - 114.9$ **5** $319.2 + 97.5$
   3 $8.74 \div 3.8$

5.   Use your calculator to work out the following, giving the answers correct to 3 significant figures.

   1 $\dfrac{98.4 + 103.2}{22.9}$ **4** $\sqrt{2.7^3 + 28}$

   2 $\dfrac{21.7}{82.6 - 41.8}$ **5** $\dfrac{84.1 - 62.3}{22.5 + 17.9}$

   3 $1.6^2 - (1.4 \times 1.8)$

6.   A formula used in engineering is $M = \dfrac{WR(\pi - 2)}{2\pi}$.
     Find the value of M when $R = 2.35$ and $W = 4.8$.

7.   A formula to find the Simple Interest, £I, earned if £P is invested at $R\%$ per year for T years is $I = 0.01\ PRT$.
     Find the total Simple Interest if £880 is invested at 4.75% per year for $7\frac{1}{2}$ years.

8.   Write down the reciprocal of 22

   1 as a recurring decimal,
   2 correct to 3 significant figures,
   3 correct to 3 decimal places.

9.   Find the reciprocals of the numbers from 2 to 12, as decimals. If they are not exact, write them as recurring decimals and also correct to 3 decimal places.

   1 Which of the numbers have reciprocals which are exact decimals ?
   2 Which of the numbers have reciprocals which have 1 recurring figure ?
   3 Which of the numbers have reciprocals which have 2 recurring figures ?

Accuracy of measurements

There is a difference between counting, which is usually in whole numbers, but in any case goes up in jumps, and measurement, which goes up continuously.

We can never measure **exactly**, but by using appropriate instruments we can get measurements as accurately as they are needed for a particular purpose.

When measuring a line in Geometry, it is usual to give the length to the nearest mm. In measuring the width of a desk, it is probably sufficient to measure to the nearest cm. In measuring larger distances the measurement would be taken to the nearest 10 cm, the nearest metre, the nearest 10 m or 100 m, or the nearest km.

With weighing, 1 gram is such a small weight that it would only be used for scientific or medical purposes or when an expensive substance was being bought. In cookery it is sufficient to weigh to the nearest 25 g. Heavier items can be weighed to the nearest kg, and very heavy objects are weighed in tonnes.

For capacity, medicines are often given using a 5 ml spoonful, and in the kitchen liquids are measured in a litre jug, with markings for every 50 ml. Larger quantities can be measured to the nearest 10 ℓ, 100 ℓ, etc.

Time can be measured to the nearest hour, to the nearest minute or to the nearest second. Athletes will want to measure their times in tenths or hundredths of a second.

Range of measurement

If a measurement is 7 m, to the nearest metre, the actual measurement can be anything between 6.5 m and 7.5 m, i.e. it can be up to 0.5 m less or 0.5 m more.

If a weight is 8.3 kg, to the nearest 0.1 kg, the actual weight can be anything between 8.25 kg and 8.35 kg, i.e. it can be up to 0.05 kg less or 0.05 kg more.

Similar rules apply to measurements correct to 2 decimal places, 3 decimal places, to the nearest 10 units, etc.

If a length is given as 7 m, then you must assume that it has been measured to the nearest metre. If the length has been measured to the nearest 0.1 m, then it is better to write it as 7.0 m. In this case the length lies between 6.95 m and 7.05 m. If the length has been measured to the nearest cm (0.01 m) then it is better to write it as 7.00 m. The actual length lies between 6.995 m and 7.005 m. It could be up to 0.005 m (5 mm) less or 0.005 m more.

Exercise 17.2

1. Give the limits between which these measurements must lie.

   1 A weight of 60 kg, weighed to the nearest 10 kg.
   2 A weight of 56 kg, weighed to the nearest kg.
   3 A capacity of 250 ml, measured to the nearest 10 ml.
   4 A length of 4.6 m, measured to the nearest 0.1 m.
   5 An amount of £700, given to the nearest £100.

2. Name a sensible metric unit for measuring or weighing

   1 the height of a tall tree,
   2 the amount of sugar in a bowl,
   3 the amount of water in a pond,
   4 the perimeter of a field,
   5 the height of a child.

3. Write these measurements as stated.

   1 8.732 m, to the nearest 0.1 m,
   2 279.3 g, to the nearest 10 g,
   3 4160 ℓ, to the nearest 100 ℓ,
   4 5.51 m, to the nearest metre,
   5 156.92 cm, to the nearest mm,
   6 4.087 ℓ, to the nearest 0.1 ℓ,
   7 4.96 m, to the nearest 0.1 m,
   8 5.438 kg, to the nearest 10 g,
   9 2504 ℓ, to the nearest 10 ℓ,
   10 47.03 s, to the nearest 0.1 s.

4. Give limits between which these measurements must lie.
   1 A line 5.0 cm long, measured to the nearest mm.
   2 A weight of 200 g, weighed to the nearest 10 g.
   3 A time of 3 minutes, measured to the nearest minute.
   4 A capacity of 60 ml, measured to the nearest ml.
   5 An amount of £30, given to the nearest £1.

5. 1 Rob says that he is 1.62 m tall.
     How accurately do you think he has measured his height ?
     Using your answer, what are the limits between which his true height lies ?

   2 Rob says that his weight is 38 kg.
     To what accuracy do you think he has weighed himself ?
     Using your answer, what are the limits between which his true weight lies ?

Powers of 10

You have used powers of 10 with positive indices.
e.g. $10^5 = 10 \times 10 \times 10 \times 10 \times 10 = 100\,000$

We can also use powers of 10 with negative indices.
e.g. $10^{-2} = \dfrac{1}{10^2} = \dfrac{1}{100} = 0.01$

There are two general rules.

$$10^0 = 1$$
$$10^{-n} = \dfrac{1}{10^n}$$

Here is a table showing these indices.

$10^6 \quad = 1\,000\,000$
$10^5 \quad = \quad 100\,000$
$10^4 \quad = \quad\quad 10\,000$
$10^3 \quad = \quad\quad\quad 1\,000$
$10^2 \quad = \quad\quad\quad\quad 100$
$10^1 \quad = \quad\quad\quad\quad\quad 10$
$10^0 \quad = \quad\quad\quad\quad\quad\quad 1$
$10^{-1} = \quad\quad\quad\quad 0.1 \quad\quad$ or $\quad \frac{1}{10}$
$10^{-2} = \quad\quad\quad\quad 0.01 \quad\quad$ or $\quad \frac{1}{100}$
$10^{-3} = \quad\quad\quad\quad 0.001 \quad\quad$ or $\quad \frac{1}{1000}$
$10^{-4} = \quad\quad\quad\quad 0.0001 \quad$ or $\quad \frac{1}{10000}$

These powers of 10 are useful in expressing very large or very small numbers.

Standard Index Form

A number is written in standard index form when it is written as $a \times 10^n$, where a is a number between 1 and 10 (not including 10) and n is an integer (positive or negative whole number, or 0).

Standard index form is often referred to as **standard form**. It can also be called **scientific notation**.

Examples

$6579 = 6.579 \times 1000 = 6.579 \times 10^3$
$71\,800\,000 = 7.18 \times 10\,000\,000 = 7.18 \times 10^7$
$20 = 2 \times 10 = 2 \times 10^1$
$220.56 = 2.2056 \times 100 = 2.2056 \times 10^2$

$0.6423 = 6.423 \times \frac{1}{10} = 6.423 \times 10^{-1}$
$0.00912 = 9.12 \times \frac{1}{1000} = 9.12 \times 10^{-3}$
$0.00001 = 1 \times \frac{1}{100000} = 1 \times 10^{-5}$

Your calculator will turn numbers into standard form. (Calculators do not all work in the same way so you may have to investigate to see how yours will do this.)

To turn 840 000 into standard form.
Press 840 000 $\boxed{=}$ $\boxed{F \leftrightarrow E}$ and it will show 8.4   05 which means 8.4×10^5.
Press $\boxed{F \leftrightarrow E}$ again and it will return to showing 840 000.

To enter a number which is already given in standard form, use the $\boxed{EXP}$ key.
To enter 8.4×10^5 press 8.4 $\boxed{EXP}$ 5 $\boxed{=}$ and it will work it out to 840 000.
You can get back to 8.4   05 by pressing $\boxed{F \leftrightarrow E}$.
You can also find the value of 8.4×10^5 by pressing 8.4 $\boxed{\times}$ 10 $\boxed{y^x}$ 5 $\boxed{=}$.

Press 0.0047 $\boxed{=}$ $\boxed{F \leftrightarrow E}$ and the calculator will show 4.7   −03 which means 4.7×10^{-3}.

To enter 4.7×10^{-3} press 4.7 $\boxed{EXP}$ 3 $\boxed{^+/_-}$ $\boxed{=}$ and it will work it out to 0.0047.
You can get back to 4.7   −03 by pressing $\boxed{F \leftrightarrow E}$.
You can also find the value of 4.7×10^{-3} by pressing 4.7 $\boxed{\times}$ 10 $\boxed{y^x}$ 3 $\boxed{^+/_-}$ $\boxed{=}$.

If a number is too big or too small for the calculator to display it normally it cannot change it out of standard form.

For numbers already between 1 and 10, there is usually no need to express them in standard form, but if this is needed then the power of 10 is 10^0, (since $10^0 = 1$).
e.g. $8.3 = 8.3 \times 10^0$. A calculator would show 8.3   00

Examples

Use your calculator to find the values of:
$(2.46 \times 10^7) \times (1.23 \times 10^2)$, $(3.92 \times 10^{-5}) \div (9.8 \times 10^{-3})$, $(2.46 \times 10^7)^2$, $\sqrt{4.9 \times 10^{-7}}$.

For $(2.46 \times 10^7) \times (1.23 \times 10^2)$ press
2.46 $\boxed{EXP}$ 7 $\boxed{\times}$ 1.23 $\boxed{EXP}$ 2 $\boxed{=}$ and the calculator will show 3 025 800 000
If you press $\boxed{F \leftrightarrow E}$ this will change to 3.0258   09, which means 3.0258×10^9.

For $(3.92 \times 10^{-5}) \div (9.8 \times 10^{-3})$ press
3.92 $\boxed{EXP}$ 5 $\boxed{^+/_-}$ $\boxed{\div}$ 9.8 $\boxed{EXP}$ 3 $\boxed{^+/_-}$ $\boxed{=}$ and the calculator will show 0.004
If you press $\boxed{F \leftrightarrow E}$ this will change to 4.   −03 which means 4×10^{-3}.

For $(2.46 \times 10^7)^2$ press 2.46 $\boxed{EXP}$ 7 $\boxed{x^2}$ and the calculator will show 6.0516   14
This means 6.0516×10^{14}, which is 605 160 000 000 000.
This number is too big to be shown on the calculator as an ordinary number.

For $\sqrt{4.9 \times 10^{-7}}$ press 4.9 $\boxed{EXP}$ 7 $\boxed{^+/_-}$ $\boxed{\sqrt{}}$ and the calculator will show 0.0007
If you press $\boxed{F \leftrightarrow E}$ this will change to 7.   −04 which means 7×10^{-4}.

Exercise 17.3

1. Express these numbers in standard index form. Try to do them first without using your calculator, then do them again with your calculator to check the answers.

1	506	**6**	0.027	**11**	93 070
2	2187	**7**	0.00051	**12**	0.00000013
3	15.07	**8**	0.000006	**13**	11.57
4	2300	**9**	0.345	**14**	0.1157
5	7 000 000	**10**	0.0208	**15**	0.0099

2. These numbers are given in standard form. Write them as ordinary numbers. Try to do them first without using your calculator, then do them again with your calculator to check the answers.

1	1.05×10^2	**9**	2.93×10^2
2	9.6×10^4	**10**	1.1×10^6
3	4.12×10^{-1}	**11**	4.3×10^{-2}
4	5.2×10^3	**12**	8×10^5
5	2.89×10^{-2}	**13**	2.03×10^{-4}
6	7.5×10^5	**14**	9.9×10^3
7	4×10^{-3}	**15**	1.072×10^{-1}
8	6.11×10^{-1}		

3. Use your calculator to work out these calculations. Express the answers in standard form.

1	$5.7 \times 10^3 \times (8.2 \times 10^4)$	**7**	$(3.4 \times 10^{-1}) \times (2.9 \times 10^{-2})$
2	$4.2 \times 10^5 \div (5.6 \times 10^3)$	**8**	$(4.06 \times 10^{-2}) \div (7 \times 10^{-4})$
3	$(4.7 \times 10^3)^2$	**9**	$(5.9 \times 10^{-3})^2$
4	$\sqrt{4.84 \times 10^6}$	**10**	$(1.3 \times 10^{-1}) \div (5.2 \times 10^5)$
5	$(5.4 \times 10^4) \div (1.8 \times 10^6)$	**11**	$\dfrac{8 \times 10^{-3}}{5 \times 10^3}$
6	$(1.1 \times 10^5) \times (2.4 \times 10^{-2})$	**12**	$\sqrt{6.4 \times 10^{-3}}$

4. Find the value of n if

1	$0.0064 = 6.4 \times 10^n$	**2**	$3280 = 3.28 \times 10^n$

5. The mass of the Earth is 5.974×10^{21} tonnes.
    The Moon's mass is 0.0123 of the Earth's mass.
    Find the Moon's mass, giving your answer
    in standard form, correct to 3 significant figures.

Exercise 17.4   Applications

1. Work out the answers to these questions in your head, just writing down the answers.

    1 100×0.3 **2** $3000 \div 40$ **8** $48 \div 0.3$
    2 4000×70 **6** $72 \div 0.06$ **9** $370 \div 10$
    3 20×0.9 **7** $200 \div 0.2$ **10** $1.3 \div 0.1$
    4 500×0.6

2. These questions are approximations of the numbers used in question 3. Find the answers, if possible without using your calculator. Keep the answers to use in question 3.

    1 $\dfrac{200 \times 0.1}{10}$ **6** $(6 \times 7) - (3 \times 4)$

    2 $(35 - 30) \times 60$ **7** $\dfrac{30 + 60}{20}$

    3 $2 + \left(\frac{1}{4} \times 8\right)$ **8** $\frac{30}{4} + \frac{8}{2}$
    4 $20 \div (3 + 2)$ **9** $(20 \times 3) - (10 \times 3)$
    5 $(5 \times 3) - 5$ **10** $\frac{3}{4}$ of $28 + \frac{1}{4}$ of 32

3. Work out the following, using your calculator. Compare each answer with the corresponding answer from question 2. If they are very different, check your work again.

    1 $\dfrac{216 \times 0.084}{9.6}$ **7** $\dfrac{33.6 + 61.8}{21.2}$

    2 $(35 - 29.7) \times 61.3$
    3 $1.93 + (0.25 \times 7.64)$ **8** $\dfrac{28.7}{3.5} + \dfrac{8}{1.6}$
    4 $23.75 \div (2.8 + 2.2)$ **9** $(19 \times 3.14) - (9 \times 3.14)$
    5 $(4.7 \times 3.1) - 5.07$ **10** $\frac{3}{4}$ of $29.6 + \frac{1}{4}$ of 31.2
    6 $6.5^2 - 3.5^2$

4. Use your calculator to find the numbers represented by $\square$ in these statements.

    1   $\square + 22.5 = 103.1$ 6 $1760 - \square = 990$
    2   $\square \times 13 = 22.1$ 7 $12.6 \times \square = 10.08$
    3   $\square - 5.3 = 12.7$ 8 $136.8 \div \square = 15.2$
    4   $\square \div 2.4 = 1.5$ 9 $2 \times (\square + 5.3) = 17.8$
    5   $1967 + \square = 1988$ 10 $(5.1 \times 7.3) - \square = 27.23$

5. In each of these calculations a mistake has been made. Find the correct answers. Can you also discover what mistake was made in each case ?

    1   $1.32 + 2.5 + 3.79 = 7.09$ 4 $5.32 \times 6.15 = 34.6332$
    2   $10 - 0.918 = 0.82$ 5 $1234 \div 0.032 = 3856.25$
    3   $(13.1 + 17.9) \times 1.2 = 34.58$

6. Using your calculator, find the value of $\sqrt[4]{\dfrac{360}{0.0738 \times 92.1^3}}$, giving the answer correct to 3 significant figures.

7. If $v^3 = \dfrac{64P}{wA}$, find the value of v, correct to 3 significant figures, when $P = 1450$, $w = 62.3$ and $A = 0.0105$.

8. A formula for the area of a triangle is $A = \sqrt{s(s-a)(s-b)(s-c)}$.

    If $a = 2.5$, $b = 3.2$ and $c = 4.1$,
    1   find the value of s, where $s = \frac{1}{2}(a+b+c)$,
    2   find the value of A.

9. A rectangular tank has internal measurements 2.5 m by 2.4 m by 1.25 m. How many litres of liquid will it hold ? ($1 \, m^3 = 1\,000$ litres.)

10. A sample of petrol weighs 722 g/litre. How many litres of this petrol weigh 5 kg ?

11. A formula to find distances is $s = ut + \frac{1}{2} ft^2$. Find the value of s when $u = 25.2$, $t = 7.9$ and $f = -3.6$.

12. Find the reciprocals of the numbers from 30 to 40, writing them to 4 decimal places if they are not exact decimals.
    Say which of the numbers have reciprocals which

    1   are exact decimals,
    2   are decimals with 1 recurring figure,
    3   are decimals with 2 recurring figures,
    4   are decimals with 3 recurring figures.

13. Name a sensible metric unit for measuring or weighing

    1   the weight of a loaded lorry,
    2   the capacity of a car's fuel tank,
    3   the weight of a letter, to be sent by air-mail,
    4   the distance between two towns,
    5   the width of a piece of paper.

14. Tara says that it takes her 20 minutes to cycle to school.
How accurately do you think she has stated this time ?
Using your answer, what are the limits between which the true time lies ?

15. The sides of a rectangle, each measured to the nearest cm, are 6 cm and 4 cm.
Find
    1   the largest possible length of the rectangle,
    2   the largest possible breadth,
    3   the largest possible length of the perimeter,
    4   the largest possible area of the rectangle,
    5   the smallest possible length of the rectangle,
    6   the smallest possible breadth,
    7   the smallest possible length of the perimeter,
    8   the smallest possible area.

16. Express in standard index form.

    1   15 000   **2**   364   **3**   0.000 952   **4**   0.5276   **5**   23.2

17. Find the values of

    1 1.86×10^3 **4** $(8.64 \times 10^4) \div (4.32 \times 10^{-1})$
    2 7.65×10^{-3} **5** $\sqrt{8.1 \times 10^{-5}}$
    3 $(9.34 \times 10^{-2}) \times (1.35 \times 10^5)$

18. The Earth is approximately 93 million miles from the Sun. Taking 1 mile as equivalent to 1.6 km, find this distance in km, to 2 significant figures, expressing your answer in standard form.

19. The weight of a litre of hydrogen is 0.0899 g. Find the weight of 1 cm^3 of hydrogen, expressing your answer in standard form.

20. The Amazon river discharges 2×10^{11} cm^3 of water per second into the Atlantic Ocean, when it is in flood. How many tonnes of water is this per day (24 hours) ? Give the answer in standard form correct to 2 significant figures. (1 cm^3 of water weighs 1 g.)

Practice test 17

1. Work out the answers to these questions in your head, just writing down the answers.

   1   600×50 5 8×0.05 8 $630 \div 90$
   2   70×0.2 6 $4500 \div 50$ 9 $8.8 \div 0.8$
   3   0.8×0.6 7 $33 \div 0.3$ 10 $0.3 \div 0.5$
   4   40×0.9

2. By using approximate values, estimate answers for these questions. Then find the correct answers, using your calculator, giving them correct to 3 significant figures.

   1   3.99×5.01 4 $29.12 \div 2.9$
   2   $17.82 \div 5.82$ 5 395×0.103
   3   3.9^2

3. A formula used for electrical circuits is $W = \dfrac{RE^2}{(R+r)^2}$.
   Find the value of W if $R = 1.76$, $r = 1.38$ and $E = 2.92$.

4. Write down the reciprocal of 66,
   1   as a recurring decimal,
   2   correct to 3 significant figures,
   3   correct to 3 decimal places.

5. Give the limits between which these measurements must lie.

   1   A line 6.5 cm long, measured to the nearest mm.
   2   A weight of 8.75 kg, weighed to the nearest 0.01 kg.
   3   A capacity of 4.2 ℓ, measured to the nearest 0.1 ℓ.
   4   A time of 2 hours 10 minutes, measured to the nearest 10 minutes.
   5   A time of 8 hours 5 minutes, measured to the nearest minute.

6. Express in standard index form.

   1   2100   4   0.637
   2   544   5   10.71
   3   0.0018

7. Find the values of

   1   1.265×10^2 4 6.78×10^5
   2   2.38×10^{-2} 5 5.999×10^3
   3   7.021×10^{-1}

8. Work out $(9 \times 10^{-2}) \div (1.2 \times 10^3)$, and express your answer in standard index form.

PUZZLES

38. How far would someone have to travel to get to 'the opposite end of the Earth' assuming that the Earth is a sphere of diameter 12 750 km ?
    If instead of travelling over the surface, the person went by plane which travelled at a height of 10 km over the earth, how much further would the journey be ?

39. This map shows the roads where Jenny lives. How many different routes are there for her to cycle from home to school, (never going Northwards, of course) ?

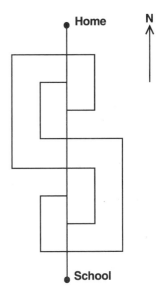

40. The rail journey from Ashfield to Beechgrove takes exactly 4 hours and trains leave each way on the hour and on the half-hour. If you were on a train going from Ashfield to Beechgrove, how many trains going from Beechgrove to Ashfield would you pass during the journey ?

41. In a 2-digit number the units digit is 2 more than the 10's digit.
    On reversing the digits a number is formed whose square exceeds the square of the original number by 2376.
    Find the original number.

42. Copy the diagram and starting in the top left-hand square, draw a continuous line passing through each square once only, so that the sum of the numbers in each group of four squares is 24.

6	6	3	15	5	3
6	9	3	10	6	3
3	3	3	8	8	5
5	10	4	2	3	10
3	6	11	2	3	9
5	8	4	7	10	9

18 Loci, vectors and bearings

> **The topics in this chapter include:**
>
> - finding the locus of a point,
> - understanding and using vector notation,
> - understanding and using bearings.

Locus

The locus of a point is the path traced by the point as it moves so as to satisfy certain conditions.

Examples

1 A flower-bed is to be made round the edge of a rectangular lawn, and every part of the flower-bed is not more than 1 m from the lawn. What is the locus of the outer edge of the flower-bed ?

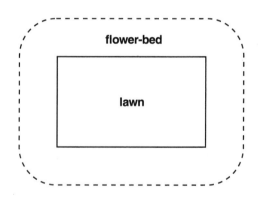

The locus is shown in the diagram. There are 4 straight lines 1 m from the edge of the lawn and 4 quarter-circles radius 1 m with centres at the corners of the lawn.

2 What is the locus of the path of a girl running across a field keeping as far from the hedge as from the fence ? (This path can be said to be 'equidistant from the hedge and the fence'.)

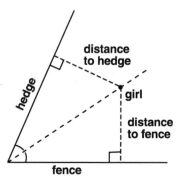

The locus is shown in the diagram. It is the line which bisects the angle between the hedge and the fence.

The distance measured from any point on the locus to the hedge (or fence) would be the shortest distance, and that is the length of the perpendicular line from the point to the hedge (or fence).

Special results

1. The locus of a point at a fixed
    distance r units from a given point A
    is a circle, centre A, radius r.

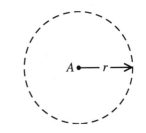

2. The locus of a point at a fixed
    distance r units from a given line
    AB is a pair of lines, each parallel
    to AB, and distance r from AB.

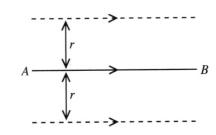

3. The locus of a point equidistant
    from two given points A and B is
    the perpendicular bisector of AB.

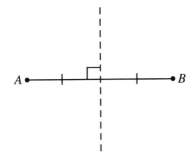

4. The locus of a point, within the shaded
    region, equidistant from two given lines
    OA and OB, is the line which bisects $\angle AOB$.

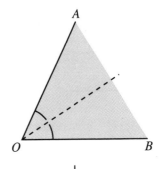

    The locus of a point equidistant
    from two given lines AOC, BOD is
    the pair of lines which bisect the
    angles at O.

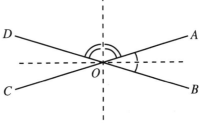

Constructions

To draw accurately a line a fixed distance from a given line

e.g. to draw a line 5 cm from AB.

Draw lines at right angles to AB at A and B
(or at any two points on AB).

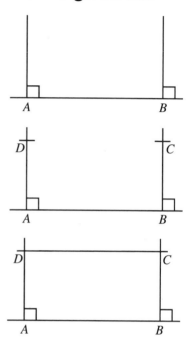

Measure off 5 cm along these lines so that
$AD = 5$ cm and $BC = 5$ cm.

Join CD.
Then every point on CD is 5 cm from the
nearest point on AB.

Here is a reminder of two constructions using ruler and compasses. (You can also do these
constructions without compasses by using a ruler and a protractor.)

To find the perpendicular bisector of a line *AB*

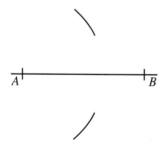

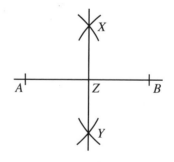

With centre A and a radius more than
half of AB, draw two arcs.

With centre B and the same radius,
draw two arcs to cut the first two arcs
at X and Y.

Join XY, cutting AB at Z.

Then Z is the mid-point of AB, and XZY
is the perpendicular bisector of AB.

To bisect an angle *ACB*

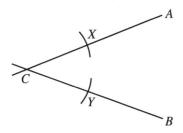

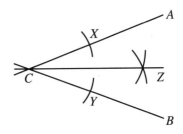

With centre *C*, draws arcs to cut *CA* and *CB* at *X* and *Y*.

With centres *X* and *Y* in turn, and a suitable radius, draw arcs to cut at *Z*.

Join *CZ*, which is the bisector of angle *ACB*.

Example

3   Draw a triangle *ABC* with *AB* = 9 cm, *AC* = 7 cm and ∠*BAC* = 66°.
Find
  1 the locus of points inside the triangle which are 4.5 cm from *C*,
  2 the locus of points inside the triangle which are equidistant from *AB* and *AC*.
Mark the point *P* inside the triangle which is 4.5 cm from *C* and is as far from *AB*
as it is from *AC*.
How far is *P* from *B*?

First, draw the triangle accurately.

For **1**, the locus of the points 4.5 cm from a point *C* is a circle, centre *C*, radius 4.5 cm.
In this question you only need the part of the circle which is inside the triangle.
Draw this locus and label it (**1**).

For **2**, the locus of points inside the triangle which are equidistant from
AB and *AC* is the bisector of ∠*A*.
You can construct the bisector
using your protractor. Since
∠*A* = 66°, the bisector makes
angles of 33° with *AB* and *AC*.
Alternatively, you can use the
method for bisecting an angle
using ruler and compasses.
Draw this locus and label it (**2**).

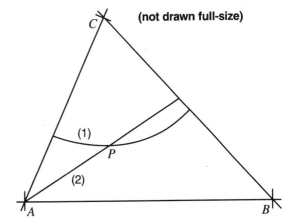

(not drawn full-size)

P is the point where the loci intersect.
Measure the distance *PB*.
(It should be 6.4 cm.)

Exercise 18.1

In questions 1 to 4 draw sketches showing the loci and describe each locus.

1.   There are 2 rocks 100 m apart. A boat passes between the rocks keeping an equal distance from each. Show the locus of the boat.

2.   Show the locus of the top of a child's head as the child sits on a slide and slides down.

3.   Show the locus of a hand of a child who is swinging on a swing and holding onto the ropes.

4.   A disc of radius 5 cm is fixed to a board. A disc of radius 3 cm is placed touching the first disc, and is moved to circle round it, always keeping in contact with it. Show the locus of the centre of the moving disc.

5.   Draw a triangle *ABC* with *AB* = 8 cm, *BC* = 9 cm and *CA* = 7 cm. Draw the locus of points inside the triangle which are (1) 5 cm from *B*, (2) 6 cm from *C*.
     Mark a point *P* inside the triangle which is 5 cm from *B* and 6 cm from *C*.
     Measure *PA*.

6.   Draw a triangle *ABC* with *AB* = 7 cm, *BC* = 9.5 cm and ∠*B* = 90°. Draw the locus of points inside the triangle which are (1) 2 cm from *AB*, (2) 3 cm from *BC*.
     Find a point *P* inside the triangle which is 2 cm from *AB* and 3 cm from *BC*.
     Measure *PB*.

7.   There are radio stations at 3 places, *A*, *B*, *C*. Broadcasts from *A* can be heard within a distance of 30 km, those from *B* within a distance of 40 km, and those from *C* within a distance of 45 km.
     Draw an accurate scale drawing and mark the loci of the boundaries of the three broadcast receiving areas. Shade in the region where all three stations can be heard.

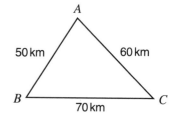

8.   The diagram shows an open space bounded by 2 walls of a building. It is planned to erect a safety barrier which will be 20 m from the walls. Copy the diagram and using a scale of 1 cm to represent 5 m show the locus of the barrier.
     At the corner where the 2 walls meet, a spotlight is fixed which lights up the area for a distance of 35 m. Show the locus of the boundary of the region lit by the spotlight.
     Shade the region which is the far side of the barrier from the walls but is lit by the spotlight.

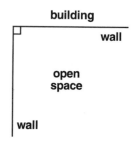

9. Treasure is hidden in the triangular field ABC
    (1) equidistant from AB and BC, (2) 10 m from AC.
    Draw a scale drawing of the field and draw
    loci for conditions (1) and (2). Mark with T
    the position of the treasure.
    How far is it from corner A ?

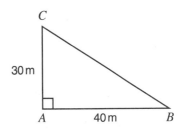

Vectors

A vector quantity has a size and a direction.

Examples:
Velocity. A plane overhead is travelling towards London at a speed of 600 mph.
Displacement. A boy is 400 m from home, and due South of it.
Force. Kick the ball as hard as you can in the direction of the goal.

The line AB can represent the vector of a displacement from A to B.

If A is $(1, 2)$ and B is $(5, 3)$ then the displacement is
4 units in the x-direction and 1 unit in the y-direction.

This vector can be represented by the matrix $\begin{pmatrix} 4 \\ 1 \end{pmatrix}$.

Any other line parallel to AB with the same length
also represents the vector $\begin{pmatrix} 4 \\ 1 \end{pmatrix}$.

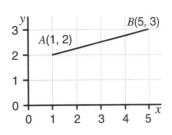

Notation

In printed books vectors are denoted by small letters in heavy type, e.g. **a**.
In writing, the letters are underlined instead, e.g. a̲.

If the vector is represented by a line AB this is written as $\overline{AB}$, $\overrightarrow{AB}$ or **AB**.

Numbers, which have size but no direction, are called scalars.
0 is the zero vector. It has no direction.

Equal vectors have the same size and the same direction.

$-\mathbf{a}$ is a vector with the same length as **a** but in the opposite
direction.

The lines on diagrams can be marked with arrows to
show the directions of the vectors. In this diagram,

a is $\begin{pmatrix} 3 \\ 2 \end{pmatrix}$ and $-\mathbf{a}$ is $\begin{pmatrix} -3 \\ -2 \end{pmatrix}$.

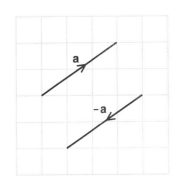

Translation

We can represent a translation by a vector.

Example

A (1, 1) is translated into A' (8, 2),
B (2, 5) is translated into B' (9, 6),
C (5, 3) is translated into C' (12, 4).

The translation is 7 units in the
x-direction and 1 unit in the
y-direction, and it can be

represented by the vector $\begin{pmatrix} 7 \\ 1 \end{pmatrix}$.

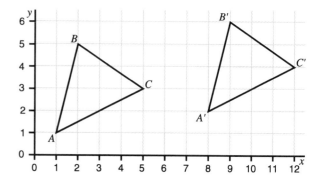

Every point on the line AB is translated into a point on the line $A'B'$.
Every point on BC is translated into a point on $B'C'$.
Every point on AC is translated into a point on $A'C'$.
Every point on $\triangle ABC$ is translated into a point on $\triangle A'B'C'$.

Exercise 18.2

In the diagrams, the lines are drawn on a unit grid.

1. **1** What vector would translate $\triangle A$ into $\triangle B$?
    2 What vector would translate $\triangle B$ into $\triangle C$?
    3 What vector would translate $\triangle C$ into $\triangle A$?

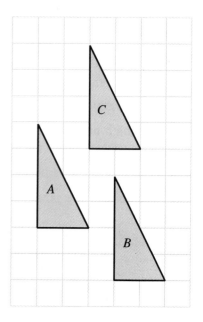

2. **1** Write down the vectors **a, b, c, d, e, f** and **g** as column vectors.
    2 Which two vectors are equal ?
    3 Which vector is equal to **a** in size but not in direction?
    4 Which vector is equal to 2**b** ?

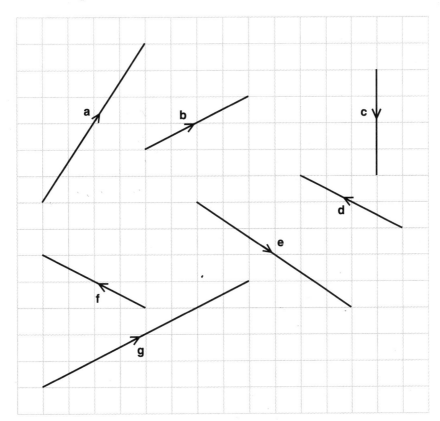

3. Write $\overrightarrow{AB}$ and $\overrightarrow{BC}$ in column form. D is a

    point such that $\overrightarrow{CD} = \begin{pmatrix} -2 \\ 1 \end{pmatrix}$, and E is a point such

    that $\overrightarrow{AE} = \begin{pmatrix} 0 \\ -1 \end{pmatrix}$.

    Show A, B, C, D, E on a diagram
    and find the length of $\overrightarrow{DE}$.

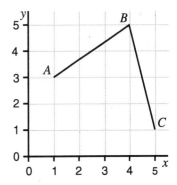

4. Use squared paper for this question.

    O is the origin and $\overrightarrow{OA} = \begin{pmatrix} 2 \\ 2 \end{pmatrix}$, $\overrightarrow{OB} = \begin{pmatrix} 6 \\ 5 \end{pmatrix}$, $\overrightarrow{OC} = \begin{pmatrix} 2 \\ 0 \end{pmatrix}$, $\overrightarrow{OD} = \begin{pmatrix} -2 \\ -3 \end{pmatrix}$.

    Find $\overrightarrow{AB}$, $\overrightarrow{BC}$, $\overrightarrow{AD}$, $\overrightarrow{DC}$. Show that $ABCD$ is a parallelogram.

5. From the diagrams, write down the vectors $\overrightarrow{AB}$ and $\overrightarrow{BC}$ in column form.
    Also write down the vector which would translate point A into point C.

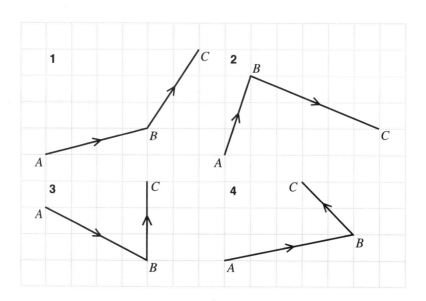

Compass directions

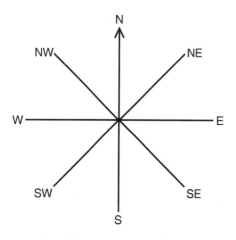

8-points compass directions

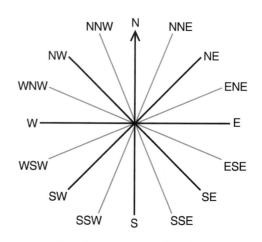

16-points compass directions

3-figure bearings

Bearings (directions) are measured from North, in a clockwise direction. They are given in degrees, as 3-figure numbers.

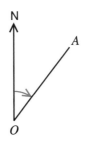

Examples

1   Show the directions given by the bearings 040°, 310°.

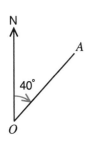

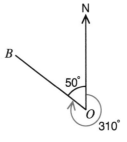

Direction OA has a bearing of 040°.   Direction OB has a bearing of 310°.

Opposite directions

To face the opposite direction, you turn through 180°. So to find the bearing of a reverse direction, add 180°. If this comes to 360° or more, subtract 180° instead.

2   Find the bearings of the directions AO and BO from example 1.

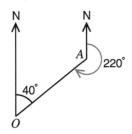

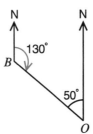

The bearing of A from O is 040°   The bearing of B from O is 310°
The bearing of O from A is 040° + 180°   The bearing of O from B is 310° − 180°
$$= 220°$$ $$= 130°$$

Exercise 18.3

1. Find the bearings given by the directions *OA, OB, OC, OD* and *OF*.

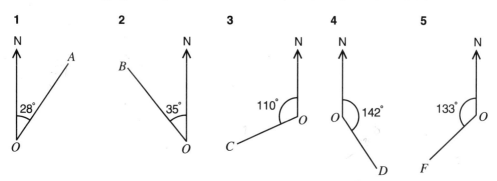

2. Draw sketches to show the directions given by the bearings

    1 200°   **2** 020°   **3** 290°   **4** 135°   **5** 002°

3. Find the bearings of the directions *AO, BO, CO, DO* and *FO* in question 1.

4. In a sailing race the boats go round a triangular course
    ABC, with *AB* = 7 km, *BC* = 5 km and *CA* = 6 km.
    The direction of *AB* is due North.
    Show this information on a scale drawing, with *C* to
    the East of the line *AB*.
    On what bearing do the boats head from *B* to *C* ?

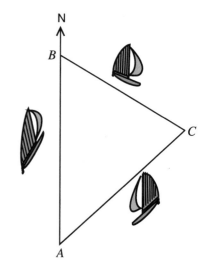

5. Find the bearings of these places from a point *O*.

    1 *A* is south-west of *O*,   **4** *D* is north-east of *O*,
    2 *B* is east of *O*,   **5** *F* is west of *O*.
    3 *C* is north-west of *O*,

6. **1** The bearing of *P* from *Q* is 080°. What is the bearing of *Q* from *P* ?
    2 The bearing of *P* from *Q* is 125°. What is the bearing of *Q* from *P* ?
    3 The bearing of *P* from *Q* is 260°. What is the bearing of *Q* from *P* ?
    4 The bearing of *P* from *Q* is 015°. What is the bearing of *Q* from *P* ?
    5 The bearing of *P* from *Q* is 301°. What is the bearing of *Q* from *P* ?

7. By measuring with your protractor, find the bearings given by the directions *OA*, *OB*, *OC*, *OD*, *OF* in these scale drawings.

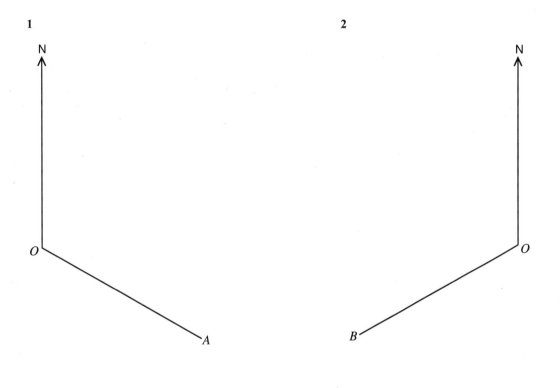

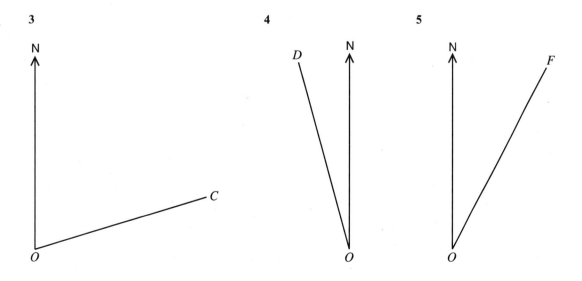

8.   **1**   Find the bearings of B and C from A.

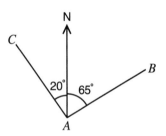

2   Find the bearings of B and C from A.

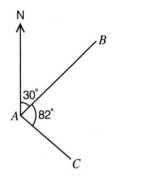

3   The bearing of B from A is 068° and the bearing of C
from B is 130°.
Find the size of $\angle ABC$.

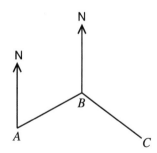

4   The bearing of B from A is 070° and $\angle ABC$ is 109°.
Find the bearing of B from C.

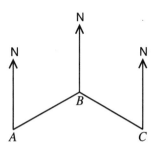

5   Find the bearing of C from A, and of C from B.

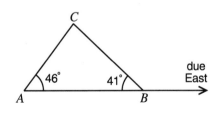

9.

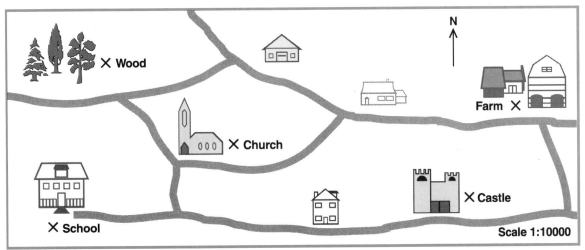

Use tracing paper to mark the positions shown by the crosses for the school, church, castle, wood and farm, and also mark the North direction.

Find the distances and bearings of

1   the church from the school,
2   the farm from the wood,
3   the wood from the castle,
4   the farm from the church,
5   the castle from the farm.

Exercise 18.4   Applications

1.   Draw a triangle ABC with $AB = 8$ cm, $BC = 10$ cm and $\angle B = 90°$. Draw the locus of points inside the triangle which are (1) 1 cm from BC, (2) equidistant from A and C, (3) 9 cm from A.
Using these loci, mark P, a point 1 cm from BC and equidistant from A and C, and shade the region of points inside the triangle which are more than 1 cm from BC and more than 9 cm from A.

2.   ## To construct the circumscribed circle of a triangle

Draw an acute-angled triangle ABC.
Draw the perpendicular bisectors of AC and BC to meet at O.
With centre O, radius OA, draw the circle.
(This circle is also called the circumcircle of the triangle.)

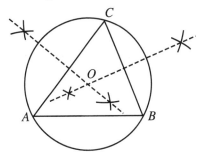

3. A camper pitches his tent equidistant from
    the farm, the shop and the cafe. Show on
    an accurate scale drawing where this is.
    How far is he from any of the three places ?

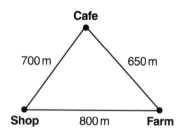

4. **To construct the inscribed circle of a triangle**

Draw an acute-angled triangle ABC.
Draw the bisectors of angles A and B to
meet at I.
Draw a line from I, perpendicular to AB,
meeting AB at X.
With centre I, radius IX, draw the circle.
(This circle is also called the in-circle of
the triangle.)

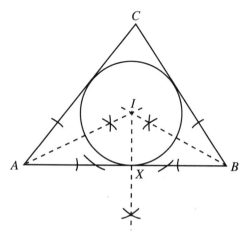

5. A camper pitches his tent equidistant from
    the beach, the river and the road. Show on
    an accurate scale drawing where this is.
    How far from the beach is it ?

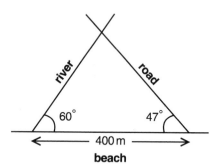

6. A ladder 6 m long is standing on horizontal
    ground, leaning against a vertical wall. As its
    foot slides along the ground, find the locus of
    the rung at the middle of the ladder.

    (Draw a scale drawing, starting with $AC = 1$ m.
    Use compasses to find point B, draw the ladder
    and then find M.
    Repeat when $AC = 2$ m, 3 m, etc.)

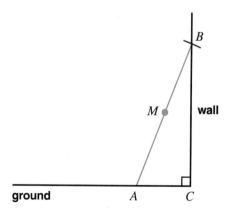

7.

The triangle is rotated clockwise about B until C lies on the table. Then it is rotated clockwise about the new position of C until A lies on the table. On an accurate drawing show the loci of C, B and A. Mark each locus clearly.

8. As the minute hand of a clock rotates, an insect starts to move at a constant speed along the hand starting at the centre of the clock when the hand is pointing to 12 and moving towards the tip of the hand, reaching it when the hand again points to 12.
Draw a circle of radius 6 cm to represent the clock face and draw 12 equally-spaced radii to represent the hand as it points to each number in turn. Mark the position the insect has reached on each one. Join these points with a curve to represent the path of the insect.

Use squared paper for questions 9 to 11.

9. A is the point with coordinates (3, 1). If $\overrightarrow{AB} = \begin{pmatrix} -2 \\ 4 \end{pmatrix}$ and $\overrightarrow{AC} = \begin{pmatrix} 2 \\ 3 \end{pmatrix}$, find the coordinates of B and C.
D is a point such that $\overrightarrow{CD} = \frac{1}{2}\overrightarrow{AB}$ and E is a point such that $\overrightarrow{DE} = \overrightarrow{BD}$. Find $\overrightarrow{CE}$. What can be deduced about the points A, C and E ?

10. O is the origin, A is the point (2, 3), B is (−1, −2), C is (4, 0) and D is the mid-point of BC. Find the vectors representing the lines

   1 $\overrightarrow{AB}$ 2 $\overrightarrow{AC}$ 3 $\overrightarrow{AD}$

11. Use squared paper for this question.

If O is the origin and $\overrightarrow{OA} = \begin{pmatrix} 3 \\ 1 \end{pmatrix}$, $\overrightarrow{OB} = \begin{pmatrix} 0 \\ -1 \end{pmatrix}$, $\overrightarrow{OC} = \begin{pmatrix} -2 \\ -5 \end{pmatrix}$, and $\triangle ABC$ is

translated using the vector $\begin{pmatrix} -3 \\ 5 \end{pmatrix}$, state the coordinates of the points A', B', C' of the

new triangle.

12. Draw the x and y axes labelled from 0 to 60, taking a scale of 2 cm to 10 units on both axes.

Plot the point A (18, 5).

Draw the lines representing these vectors:

$\overrightarrow{AB} = \begin{pmatrix} 12 \\ 53 \end{pmatrix}$, $\overrightarrow{BC} = \begin{pmatrix} 12 \\ -53 \end{pmatrix}$, $\overrightarrow{CD} = \begin{pmatrix} -34 \\ 42 \end{pmatrix}$, $\overrightarrow{DE} = \begin{pmatrix} 49 \\ -23 \end{pmatrix}$,

$\overrightarrow{EF} = \begin{pmatrix} -54 \\ 0 \end{pmatrix}$, $\overrightarrow{FG} = \begin{pmatrix} 49 \\ 23 \end{pmatrix}$,

Draw $\overrightarrow{GA}$ and state the vector $\overrightarrow{GA}$.

Describe the figure you have drawn.

13. (On tracing paper mark the positions shown for A, B, C, and also mark the North direction.)

A boat is just off the cape at A and it wants to reach the harbour at B. On what bearing must the boat sail ?

The distance AB is actually 6.6 km. What is the scale of the map ?

After reaching B, the boat then sails to a bay at C. What is the actual distance from B to C ?

From C, on what bearing must the boat sail to return round the cape at A ?

14. (On tracing paper mark the positions shown for *B* and *D*, and also mark the North direction.)

The map shows the positions of 4 towns *A*, *B*, *C*, *D*.

This table shows the distances by road between the towns, in km.

A			
60	B		
69	75	C	
48	90	46	D

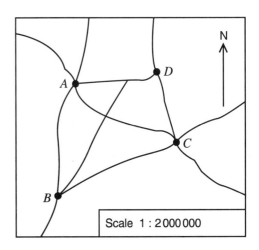

Scale 1 : 2 000 000

1   A helicopter must fly directly from *B* to *D*. On what bearing must it fly ?
2   How much further is it for a motorist to travel from *B* to *D* than for the helicopter ?
3   How much further is it for a motorist to travel from *A* to *C* via *D*, than travelling directly from *A* to *C* ?

15. An explorer walks 1000 m on a bearing of 070° and he then walks 2000 m on a bearing of 160°. Draw an accurate scale drawing of his route.
By measurement, find the bearing he must follow to return directly to his starting point, and find how far he has to go.

16. A fishing boat is 20 km due North of its harbour. It sails on a bearing of 110° at an average speed of 12 km/h.

After 2 hours there is a gale warning on the radio. Show on a scale drawing the position of the boat at that time.

In what direction should the boat be headed to get straight back to the harbour, and how far has it to go ?
If it increases its speed to 16 km/h, how long will it take ?

17. There are 2 coastguard stations, *A* and *B*, 50 km apart, with
     B being due East of *A*.
     A ship is shown on radar on a bearing of 068° from *A*, and
     on a bearing of 316° from *B*.
     Draw an accurate scale drawing showing *A*, *B* and the ship.
     (Use a scale of 1 cm to represent 5 km.)
     How far is the ship from *A*, and from *B* ?

     • ship

     A —————————————— *B*

18. **Alternative notation for bearings**

     You may still find instances where the old method of stating bearings is used, so here are
     some examples of how the method works.

     Bearings are measured from North or South, whichever is the nearer direction, and they
     are measured towards the East or towards the West.
     N 20° E means measure 20° from the North, turning towards the East.

     Examples

     N 20°E   N 30°W   S 40°W   S 5°E

     Using this notation, find the bearings given by *OA*, *OB*, *OC*, *OD*, *OF*.

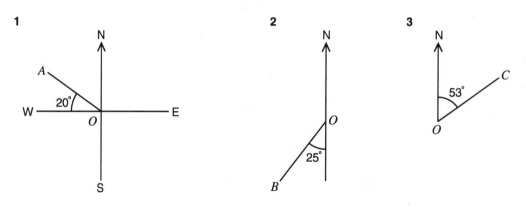

4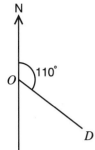

5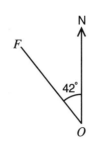

Draw sketches to show the directions given by the bearings

6 N 40° E   **7** S 15° W   **8** N 80° W   **9** N 4° E   **10** S 10° E

Practice test 18

1   *P* is a point which moves inside the rhombus *ABCD*
     so that its distance from *AB* is less than its distance
     from *AD* and its distance from *A* is greater than its
     distance from *C*. Sketch the rhombus and shade the
     region in which *P* must lie.

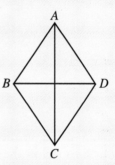

2.   The diagram shows a rectangular field.
     Treasure is hidden in the field (1) 60 m from *A*,
     (2) equidistant from *B* and *D*.
     Draw a scale drawing of the field and draw
     loci for conditions (1) and (2). Mark with *T* the
     position of the treasure.
     How far is the treasure from corner *B*?

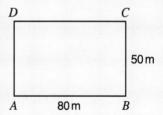

3.   On squared paper plot the points *A* (3, 2), *B* (5, 6), *C* (0, 4) and *D* (−2, 0).
     Find $\overrightarrow{AD}$ and $\overrightarrow{BC}$.

     What kind of quadrilateral is *ABCD*?

     What vector would translate the line $\overrightarrow{DA}$ into the line $\overrightarrow{CB}$?

     [Turn over]

4. From the diagrams, write down the vectors $\overrightarrow{AB}$ and $\overrightarrow{AD}$ as column vectors. Also write down the vector which would translate point B into point D.

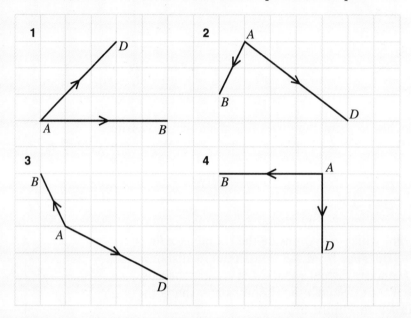

The lines are drawn on a unit grid.

5. A ship sailing in the direction 158° alters course to sail in the opposite direction. What is its new course ?

6. There are four towns A, B, C, D. B is 100 km North of A, C is 90 km on a bearing of 140° from A, D is 120 km on a bearing 260° from A. Draw an accurate scale drawing and find the distances between the towns B and C, C and D, B and D.

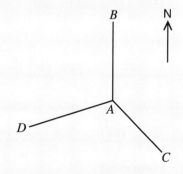

PUZZLES

43.   When Katie and Roger were married, they hadn't much money, and on their first wedding anniversary Roger was unable to buy his wife a decent present. So he gave her 1p, and said that it was all he could afford, but he would try to double the amount each year from then on. Sure enough, the next year he gave her 2p, and the following year 4p. Katie was quite pleased to get £5.12 this year, and says she is looking forward to their Silver Wedding anniversary when they will have been happily married for 25 years. Roger, however, doesn't seem quite so enthusiastic about this. Why ?

44.   Is it correct to say 'Half of 13 **is** $7\frac{1}{2}$' or 'Half of 13 **are** $7\frac{1}{2}$' ?

45.   Find 8 small counters.
      Put one counter on any point A to H, and move it along one of the lines to the point at the other end of the line and leave it there.
      Repeat this with 6 more counters in turn, always putting a counter on an **empty** point and moving it along one of the lines to the point at the other end, which should also have been empty.
      When you have done this, put the 8th counter on the remaining empty point.

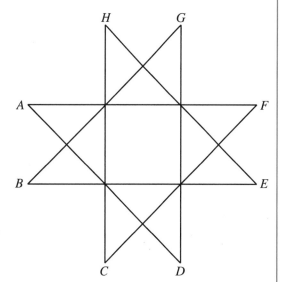

46.   A group of people on a coach outing went into a cafe for a snack. The party leader ordered a cup of tea and a sandwich for everyone, and the total bill came to £18.49. How many people were on the coach ?

47.   In a dress shop there were six dresses in the window, marked for sale at £15, £22, £30, £26, £16 and £31. Five of the dresses were sold to two customers, the second customer spending twice as much as the first one. Which dress was unsold ?

48.   If it takes 5 men 5 days to plough 5 fields, how long does it take 1 man to plough 1 field, working at the same rate ?

19 *Using straight-line graphs*

> **The topics in this chapter include:**
>
> - drawing and interpreting the graphs of linear functions,
> - interpreting and using m and c in $y = mx + c$,
> - using graphical methods to solve simultaneous equations,
> - using graphs to locate regions given by linear inequalities.

Graphs of linear functions

Linear functions are functions which can be written in the form $y = mx + c$, where m and c are numbers. Their graphs are straight lines.

e.g. $3y = 2x - 5$ can be written as $y = \frac{2}{3} x - \frac{5}{3}$.

Here, $m = \frac{2}{3}$ and $c = -\frac{5}{3}$.

Graphs of straight lines were drawn in Chapter 9.
In example 1, page 197, the graphs
of $y = x$ and $y = 2x$ were drawn.
The lines both pass through the origin,
but $y = 2x$ is a steeper line than
$y = x$.

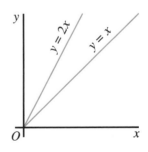

The slope of a line is called its gradient.

To find the gradient of a line drawn on a graph

Choose 2 points A and B on the line, a reasonable distance apart.

$$\text{Gradient of } AB = \frac{\text{increase in } y}{\text{increase in } x}$$

$$= \frac{y\text{-coordinate of } B - y\text{-coordinate of } A}{x\text{-coordinate of } B - x\text{-coordinate of } A}$$

If A is (1, 2.2) and B is (8.6, 7.9),

$$\text{gradient of } AB = \frac{7.9 - 2.2}{8.6 - 1} = \frac{5.7}{7.6} = 0.75$$

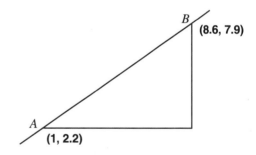

If the line slopes the other way the gradient will be negative.

e.g. $\text{gradient of AC} = \dfrac{-5.4 - 2.2}{5 - 1} = \dfrac{-7.6}{4}$

$$= -1.9$$

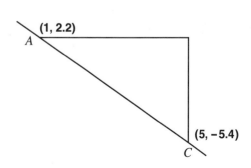

The lines $y = x$, $\quad y = 2x$, $\quad y = -\frac{1}{2}x$, $\quad y = -3x$

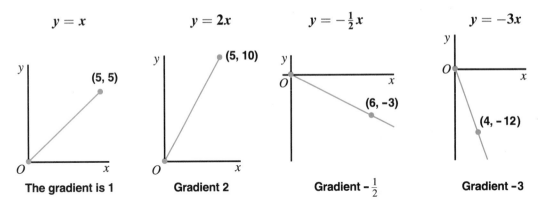

You will notice that the line $y = mx$ has gradient m.

In example **2**, page 198, the graphs of $y = x$ and $y = x + 2$ were drawn.

The lines are parallel, and both have gradient 1. However $y = x$ passes through the origin, but $y = x + 2$ cuts the y-axis at $(0, 2)$.

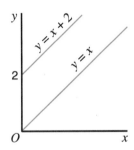

The lines $y = 2x$, $y = 2x + 4$, $y = 2x - 3$ all have gradient 2, so they are parallel.

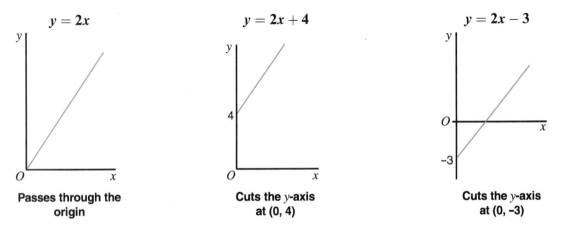

You will notice that the line $y = mx$ passes through the origin, but the line $y = mx + c$ passes through the point $(0, c)$.

c is said to be the **intercept** on the y-axis.

In general, the graph with equation $y = mx + c$, where m and c are numbers, is a straight line with gradient m, and it cuts the y-axis at the point $(0, c)$.

Examples

1   A line crosses the y-axis at $(0, -2)$ and has gradient $3\frac{1}{2}$. What is its equation ?

The general equation of a straight line is $y = mx + c$.
Here, $m = 3\frac{1}{2}$ and $c = -2$.
The equation of the line is $y = 3\frac{1}{2}x - 2$.
This can be written as $2y = 7x - 4$.

2   A line cuts the y-axis at A $(0, 5)$ and passes through the point B $(4, 2)$. Find its equation.

Its equation is $y = mx + c$.

The gradient of the line $= \dfrac{\text{increase in } y}{\text{increase in } x}$

$$= \frac{2 - 5}{4 - 0} = -\frac{3}{4}.$$

So $m = -\frac{3}{4}$.

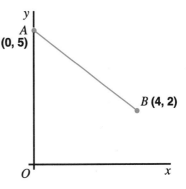

The line cuts the y-axis at $(0, 5)$ so $c = 5$.

The equation is $y = -\frac{3}{4}x + 5$.

This can be written as $4y = 20 - 3x$.
You can use the coordinates of B to check this equation.

Lines of best fit

If variables satisfy a straight line law, then results obtained experimentally may have slight errors so that plotted values may not exactly lie on a line. In that case, a line may be drawn to fit as nearly as possible to the plotted points, and this is called the line of best fit. Further readings may be made from that line.

Example

3   The following values of the speed y m/s of an object at times t seconds are obtained by experiment. Plot the values of y against t and show that they lie approximately on a straight line. Use the line to estimate the value of y when $t = 3.5$.

t	1	2	3	4	5	6
y	2.05	2.75	3.6	4.45	5.3	5.9

Draw an accurate graph and draw a line of best fit.
Find the gradient of the line. It is approximately 0.8.

The graph meets the y-axis at approximately 1.2, so
the equation of the line is $y = 0.8t + 1.2$.

Using the line on the graph, or using its equation,
when $t = 3.5$, $y = 4.0$.

Sketch graph

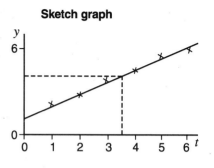

Exercise 19.1

1. Draw the x-axis from -2 to 6 and the y-axis from -15 to 20, using suitable scales.
   For the functions given, find the values of y when $x = -2, 0, 3, 6$, and draw the graphs.
   For each function, state the gradient of the graph.

   1 $y = 2x + 8$ **3** $y = 3x - 9$
   2 $y = 9 - x$ **4** $y = 4 - 3x$

2. Find the gradients of the lines (1), (2), (3), (4), (5).

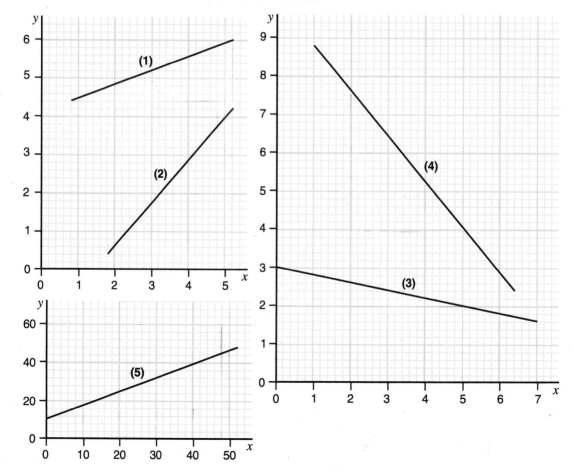

3. Find the equations of these lines:

    1 With gradient -1 and passing through the point $(0, 7)$.
    2 With gradient 2 and passing through the point $(0, -5)$.
    3 With gradient $\frac{1}{3}$ and passing through the point $(0, 1)$.

4. Draw the x-axis from -6 to 8 and the y-axis from -8 to 8.
    Plot the points $A\,(5, 3)$ and $B\,(2, 6)$. Join AB and find the gradient of this line.
    Plot the points $C\,(-4, -2)$ and $D\,(-2, 4)$. Join CD and find the gradient of this line.
    Plot the point $E\,(2, -6)$. Through E draw a line with gradient 3.
    Plot the point $F\,(-6, 2)$. Through F draw a line with gradient -1.

5. State the gradients of these lines, and also give the coordinates of the points where the lines cut the y-axis.

    1 $y = 4x - 1$ **4** $y = 2 - 5x$
    2 $y = 3 - x$ **5** $3y = x + 3$
    3 $y = \frac{1}{2}x + 7$

6. On graph paper, label the x-axis from -2 to 6 and the y-axis from -8 to 12.
    Draw these graphs and label them. Show as much of each graph as fits on the graph paper.

    1 $y = 2x + 2$ **4** $y = 3x - 6$
    2 $y = 8 - 4x$ **5** $5y = 50 - 2x$
    3 $y = -x - 4$

7. These sketch graphs represent the functions $y = 2$, $y = 2x$, $y = x + 2$, $y = 2x + 2$, $y = 2 - x$, $y = 2 - 2x$. Identify each graph.

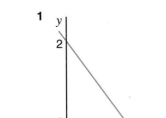

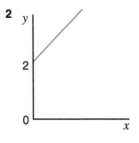

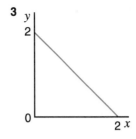

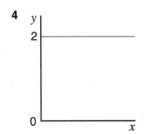

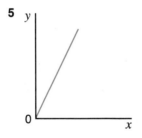

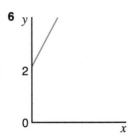

8. An experiment is carried out and readings of x and y are made.
    Here are the results:

x	6	8	10	12	14	20
y	13.5	17.5	19.5	22	26.5	36

Plot these values on a graph and draw the line of best fit.
Find the equation of the line.
Use the equation or the graph to find an approximate value for y when $x = 17.5$.

Simultaneous equations

Example

Use a graphical method to solve the simultaneous equations $x - 3y = -9$ and $8x + 6y = 3$.

$x - 3y = -9$ can be rearranged as $3y = x + 9$, and then as $y = \frac{1}{3}x + 3$.

$8x + 6y = 3$ can be rearranged as $6y = -8x + 3$, and then as $y = -\frac{4}{3}x + \frac{1}{2}$.

Find the y-values when $x = -3, 0, 3$.

For $y = \frac{1}{3}x + 3$

x	-3	0	3
y	2	3	4

For $y = -\frac{4}{3}x + \frac{1}{2}$

x	-3	0	3
y	$4\frac{1}{2}$	$\frac{1}{2}$	$-3\frac{1}{2}$

Draw the x-axis from -3 to 3 and the y-axis from -4 to 5.
Plot the points for each line and draw the lines on the graph.
Label each one with its equation.

The equations are satisfied simultaneously
at the point which lies on both lines.
Draw dotted lines from this point to both
axes, to read off the coordinates. The point
is $(-1\frac{1}{2}, 2\frac{1}{2})$.
The solution of the equations is
$x = -1\frac{1}{2}, y = 2\frac{1}{2}$.

Sketch graph

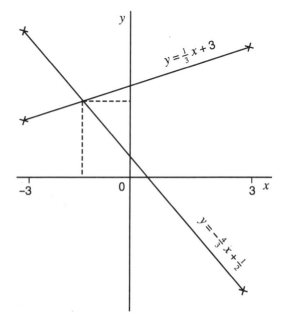

Using a computer or graphics calculator

If you have the use of a computer then you probably
have a graph-plotting program which you can use to
plot graphs of various functions. You could also use
a graphics calculator, although the graphs are shown
much smaller than on a computer screen.
One use of plotting the graphs on the computer screen
or calculator is so that you can see the general shape
of the graph. If you need to find solutions of equations
from the points of intersection of 2 graphs, you can see
where these values are, approximately.

By zooming into an area around a value, or by re-scaling the axes to draw that area to a larger
scale, you can get a more accurate value. The trace facility will help you to find approximate
values of x and y at a point of intersection. This is equivalent to using trial and improvement
methods algebraically. It is also useful to use a computer or calculator to check graphs you
have drawn, and the solutions of equations you have found.

Exercise 19.2

Use a graphical method to solve the simultaneous equations in questions 1 to 6.

1. $2y = 12 - x$ Draw the x-axis from 0 to 16 and the y-axis from -2 to 6.
    $3y = x - 2$

2. $3y = 4x - 14$ Draw the x-axis from 0 to 12 and the y-axis from -6 to 10.
    $4y = 3x$

3. $3x + y + 1 = 0$ Draw the x-axis from -4 to 4 and the y-axis from -20 to 20.
    $2y = 20 + 5x$

4. $3y = 2x + 8$ Draw the x-axis from -1 to 6 and the y-axis from 0 to 8.
    $6y = 30 - 5x$

5. $2y = 3 - x$ Draw the x-axis from -4 to 4 and the y-axis from -5 to 5.
    $2y = 4x - 7$

6. $2y = x - 3$ Draw the x and y axes from -3 to 5.
    $4y = 7 - 3x$

7. Draw x and y axes from 0 to 8.
    1 To draw the graph of $2x + 3y = 6$.

    If $x = 0$, what is the value of y ? Mark the point corresponding to these values on the graph.
    If $y = 0$, what is the value of x ? Mark the point corresponding to these values on the graph.
    Join these two points.

    In a similar way, draw the graphs of

    2 $5x + 4y = 20$,
    3 $8x + 5y = 40$,
    4 $6x + 7y = 42$.

    From your graphs find the solution of the simultaneous equations $6x + 7y = 42$, $8x + 5y = 40$.

8. A bag contains £2.80 in ten-pence and five-pence coins. If there were x ten-pence and y five-pence coins, write down an equation connecting x and y, and simplify it.
    If there were half as many ten-pence coins and twice as many five-pence coins, the total amount would be £3.20. Write down another equation connecting x and y, and simplify it.
    Draw axes with x from 0 to 70 and y from 0 to 60.
    Draw the lines represented by the equations and hence solve the equations simultaneously. How many of each kind of coin were there originally ?

Linear inequalities

A line divides the plane into two regions.

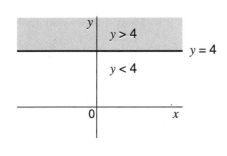

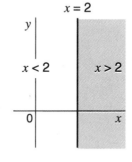

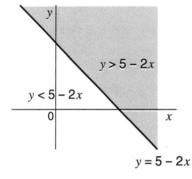

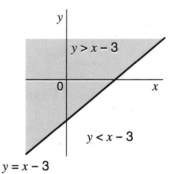

Example

On a graph, draw the lines $x = 3$, $y = 4$,
$5y = 30 - 6x$.
Identify the regions where
1    $x \leqslant 3$, $y \leqslant 4$ and $5y \geqslant 30 - 6x$,

2    $0 \leqslant x \leqslant 3$, $0 \leqslant y \leqslant 4$ and $5y \leqslant 30 - 6x$.

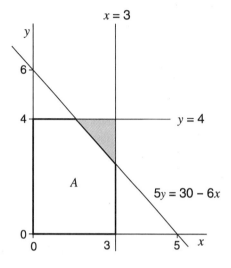

In the diagram, the shaded region is where
$x \leqslant 3$, $y \leqslant 4$ and $5y \geqslant 30 - 6x$.

The pentagon A is where $0 \leqslant x \leqslant 3$,
$0 \leqslant y \leqslant 4$ and $5y \leqslant 30 - 6x$.

If the region does **not** include the boundary line then this line can be drawn as a dotted line.

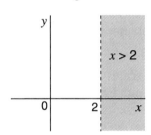

A region can be identified by shading it, but sometimes it is better to shade the unwanted parts and leave the required region unshaded.

The region where $x \geqslant 0$, $y \geqslant 0$, $x + y \leqslant 5$, is the region left unshaded.

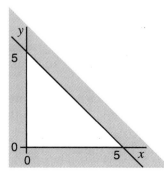

Exercise 19.3

1. Draw x and y axes from 0 to 10. Draw the lines $x = 2$, $y = 3$ and $y = 10 - x$.
    Identify the region where $x \geqslant 2$, $y \geqslant 3$ and $y \leqslant 10 - x$.

2. Draw x and y axes from 0 to 6, and draw the lines $y = 2$, $y = 2x$ and $x + y = 6$.
    Identify the region where $y \geqslant 2$, $y \leqslant 2x$ and $x + y \leqslant 6$.

3. Draw x and y axes from 0 to 8, and draw dotted lines for $y = x$, $2y = 8 + x$ and
    $2y = 8 - x$.
    Identify the regions A, B, C, where
    for A, $x \geqslant 0$, $y > x$ and $2y < 8 - x$;
    for B, $y \geqslant 0$, $y < x$ and $2y < 8 - x$;
    for C, $y > x$, $2y > 8 - x$ and $2y < 8 + x$.

4. Sketch on a graph the line $y = x$. Identify on your graph the region where $x \geqslant 0$, $y \geqslant x$
    and $y \leqslant 10$.

5. Draw the graph of $y = 10 - 3x$.
    If x and y are positive integers, mark on the graph the points whose coordinates satisfy
    the inequality $3x + y \leqslant 10$. How many such points are there ?

6. Draw axes for x and y from -3 to 9 using equal scales on both axes.
    Draw the lines AB, $2y = x + 8$; CD, $2y = x - 2$ and EF, $2y = 6 - x$.
    What are the coordinates of the points where EF meets AB, and CD ?
    Identify the region on the graph where $y \geqslant 0$, $2y \leqslant x - 2$ and $2y \leqslant 6 - x$.
    What shape is this region ?

7. On graph paper, label x and y axes from 0 to 10.
    Draw the lines $y = x - 1$, $y = 9 - x$, $3y = 12 - 2x$ and $x = 1$.
    Identify the region where $y \geqslant x - 1$, $y \leqslant 9 - x$, $3y \geqslant 12 - 2x$ and $x \geqslant 1$.

8. A trainee is tested on two pieces of work. In order to pass the test he must spend at least
    1 minute on the first piece of work but complete it within 5 minutes, and take between
    2 and 7 minutes on the second piece of work. In addition he must not take longer than
    9 minutes to complete both pieces.
    If the time in minutes taken for the 1st piece is represented by x and the time in minutes
    taken for the 2nd piece is represented by y, write down the inequalities which must be
    satisfied by x and y.
    Draw x and y axes from 0 to 9 and draw the lines representing the boundaries of these
    inequalities. Identify the region representing the times which are satisfactory.

Exercise 19.4 Applications

1. If A is $(3, 0)$, B is $(4, 1)$, C is $(1, 3)$ and D is $(0, 2)$, find the gradients of the lines AB, BC, AD and DC.
    Show that $ABCD$ is a parallelogram.

2. Find the gradient of the line AB.
    Find the equation of the line AB in the form $ax + by = c$, where a, b and c are integers.

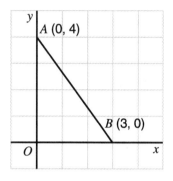

3. The line $y + 4x = 8$ meets the x-axis at A. Find the coordinates of A. Find the equation of the line with gradient 4 passing through A.

4. A straight line with gradient 4 passes through $(-1, -2)$ and $(3, a)$. Find the value of a.

5. Draw the x-axis from 0 to 5 and the y-axis from 0 to 3. Draw the straight line which passes through $(1, 2)$ and $(5, 3)$. Find the gradient of the line and the coordinates of the point where the line meets the y-axis.

6. An experiment is carried out with readings of values of x and y. Here are the results.

x	8	17	30	42	54	66	78
y	46	71	94	118	142	176	190

    Plot these values on a graph and draw the line of best fit.
    Find the equation of the line.
    Find an approximate value for y when $x = 60$.

7. Draw axes with x from -4 to 4 and y from -12 to 24. Draw the graph of $y = 3x + 2$, by finding values of y when $x = -4$, 0 and 4 and plotting the three points.
    Also draw the graph of $y = 16 - 2x$ in a similar way.
    Using your graphs, solve the simultaneous equations $y = 3x + 2$ and $y = 16 - 2x$.
    Solve these equations by another method, to check your solution.

8. The diagram shows two lines with
    equations $y = 2x - 3$ and $x + 2y = 7$.

    1   State the coordinates of P and R.
    2   Find the distance between Q and S.
    3   Which equations are solved by finding
           the coordinates of T ?
    4   Solve these equations by another
           method and hence find the coordinates
           of T.

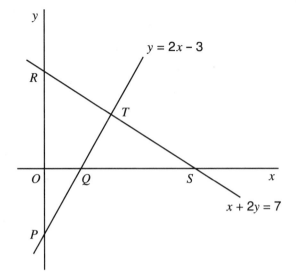

9. For prizes for a children's party Mrs Davies decides to buy packets of sweets at 16p each
    and bars of chocolate at 32p each.
    If she buys x packets of sweets and y bars of chocolate, what is the total cost ?
    She needs 25 prizes altogether. Write down an equation using this fact.
    On graph paper draw x and y axes from 0 to 40. Draw the graph of the equation.
    Mrs Davies decides to spend £6.40 on the prizes. Write down another equation using this
    fact and draw its line on your graph.
    How many packets of sweets and bars of chocolate does she buy ?

10. On graph paper, label the x and y axes from 0 to 16, using a scale of 1 cm to 1 unit on
    both axes.
    Draw the lines $y = x$, $y = 6 - 2x$, $y = 24 - 3x$ and $2y = 3x + 12$, showing as much of
    the lines as fit on the graph.

    Identify the region
    $y \geqslant x$
    $y \geqslant 6 - 2x$
    $y \leqslant 24 - 3x$
    $2y \leqslant 3x + 12$.

11. The diagram shows 3 lines whose equations
    are $x = 3$, $y = 2$ and $x + 2y = 11$.
    Write down the inequalities satisfied by all
    points inside $\triangle ABC$.

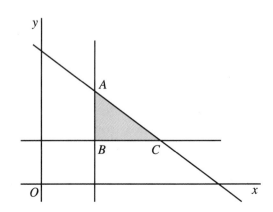

12.

A builder has a plot of land available on which he can build houses.

He can either build luxury houses or standard houses.

He decides to build at least 15 luxury and at least 5 standard houses, and he cannot build more than 40 houses altogether.

If he builds x luxury houses and y standard houses, write down 3 inequalities satisfied by x and y.

Draw the x-axis from 0 to 40 and the y-axis from 0 to 50, taking a scale of 2 cm to 5 units on both axes.

Draw the boundary lines of the inequalities on the graph.

The luxury houses require 240 m^2 of land each, and the standard houses require 120 m^2 each. The total area of the plot is 7200 m^2. Write down a 4th inequality, simplify it and draw its boundary line on the graph.

Identify the region in which all 4 inequalities are satisfied.

Practice test 19

1. Find the gradients of the lines
    AB, CD, EF, GH.

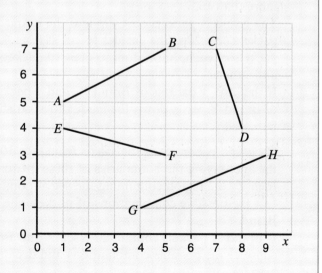

[Turn over]

2. Draw the x-axis from −2 to 6 and the y-axis from −10 to 20.
    If $y = 3x − 2$, find the values of y when $x = −2, 0$ and 5.
    For the graph of $y = 3x − 2$ plot 3 points and join them with a straight line.
    What is the gradient of this line ?
    Where does the line cut the y-axis ?

3. The diameter and circumference of different-sized circular objects were measured, with
    the following results:

Diameter, d, in cm	2.6	5.4	8.2	13.2	15.8
Circumference, c, in cm	7.8	17.5	26.2	41.0	49.5

    Plot the values of c (vertical axis) against d (horizontal axis), and show that the points
    lie approximately on a straight line.
    Draw a line of best fit for these points. This line should pass through the origin. Find
    the gradient of this line.
    What is the equation connecting c and d ?

4. Use a graphical method to solve these simultaneous equations:
    $y = 8 − 2x$
    $2y = 3x − 14$
    Draw the x-axis from 0 to 8 and the y-axis from −8 to 8.

5. Mrs Parmer wants to buy some biscuits for a
    children's party. She does not want to spend
    more than £3.
    The brand X packets cost 40p and the brand Y
    packets cost 20p. She decides to get at least 4
    packets of each, but not more than 10 packets
    altogether.
    If she buys x packets of Brand X, and y packets
    of Brand Y, write down the inequalities satisfied
    by x and y.

    On graph paper, draw the x-axis from 0 to 10 and the y-axis from 0 to 15, and draw
    the lines giving the boundaries of these inequalities.
    Identify the region containing the set of points (x, y) satisfying all these inequalities.
    List the possible combinations of packets she could buy, e.g. 4 of Brand X and 4 of
    Brand Y.
    If Brand X packets contain 20 biscuits and Brand Y packets contain 25 biscuits,
    consider the possible combinations and decide which combination will give most
    biscuits.

6. Draw the x-axis from -2 to 2 and the y-axis from -2 to 10.
    Draw the lines $y = -2$, $y = -x$ and $y = 3x + 4$.
    Identify the region A where $y \geqslant -x$, $y \leqslant 3x + 4$ and $x \leqslant 0$, and the region B where
    $x \geqslant 0$, $y \leqslant -x$ and $y \geqslant -2$.
    Describe in a similar way the region bounded by 4 lines containing the point $(-1, -1)$.

PUZZLES

49. What is the next symbol in this sequence ?

50. There are two discs; one is red on both sides, the other is red on one side and green on
     the other, but they are otherwise identical. Without looking, one is picked at random
     and placed flat on the table. If the top of this disc is red, what is the probability that
     the hidden side is also red ? Is it $\frac{1}{4}$, $\frac{1}{3}$, $\frac{1}{2}$, $\frac{2}{3}$ or $\frac{3}{4}$?

51. An explorer wants to estimate the width of a river, flowing East–West. He stands due
     South of a tree growing on the opposite bank, and then walks due West, counting his
     paces, until the tree is in the North-East direction. If by that time he has taken 120
     paces, and his usual pace-length is 90 cm, what estimate can he make of the width of
     the river ?

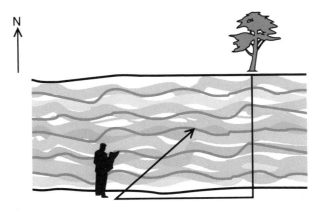

52. Yesterday a trader bought a number of vases for £63. Today he bought 28 similar
     vases at the same price, and he paid the same number of £'s for them as the number of
     vases he bought yesterday. How many vases has he altogether ?

20 Fractions

> **The topics in this chapter include:**
>
> ● calculating with fractions,
>
> ● using fractions in Algebra,
>
> ● using index notation to represent roots.

Fractions were introduced in Chapter 5. Look at that chapter again to remind yourself about the methods shown there.

Calculating with fractions

Examples

1   **Addition**

$\frac{5}{6} + \frac{3}{4}$

Change $\frac{5}{6}$ and $\frac{3}{4}$ into fractions with denominator 12, because 12 is the smallest number into which the denominators 6 and 4 both divide.

$\frac{5}{6} = \frac{10}{12}$ and $\frac{3}{4} = \frac{9}{12}$

$\frac{5}{6} + \frac{3}{4} = \frac{10}{12} + \frac{9}{12} = \frac{19}{12} = 1\frac{7}{12}$

$\left(\text{The stage } \frac{10}{12} + \frac{9}{12} \text{ can be written as } \frac{10+9}{12} \right)$

2   **Subtraction**

$\frac{5}{6} - \frac{7}{12} = \frac{10-7}{12} = \frac{3}{12} = \frac{1}{4}$

$1 - \frac{4}{9} = \frac{9-4}{9} = \frac{5}{9}$

3   In addition and subtraction questions with **mixed numbers** do the whole number part and the fraction part separately.

$3\frac{5}{6} + 2\frac{3}{4} = 5\frac{10+9}{12} = 5\frac{19}{12} = 5 + 1 + \frac{7}{12} = 6\frac{7}{12}$

$3\frac{5}{6} - 1\frac{7}{12} = 2\frac{10-7}{12} = 2\frac{3}{12} = 2\frac{1}{4}$

$3\frac{5}{8} - 1\frac{3}{4} = 2\frac{5-6}{8} = 1\frac{8+5-6}{8} = 1\frac{7}{8}$ Since we cannot take 6 from 5, one of the whole numbers was changed into 8 eighths.

In **multiplication and division** questions, mixed numbers must be changed to improper fractions.

4    $5\frac{5}{6} \times 2\frac{7}{10} = \frac{\overset{7}{\cancel{35}}}{\underset{2}{\cancel{6}}} \times \frac{\overset{9}{\cancel{27}}}{\underset{2}{\cancel{10}}} = \frac{63}{4} = 15\frac{3}{4}$

5    $2\frac{5}{6} \div 1\frac{1}{4} = \frac{17}{6} \div \frac{5}{4}$

Instead of dividing by $\frac{5}{4}$, multiply by $\frac{4}{5}$.

$= \frac{17}{\underset{3}{\cancel{6}}} \times \frac{\overset{2}{\cancel{4}}}{5} = \frac{34}{15} = 2\frac{4}{15}$

Using a calculator
You may have a calculator which will calculate with fractions, and if so, you can learn how to use it. You must find out how to enter fractions or mixed numbers, and how to read the displayed answers. Do not rely on your calculator entirely. You still need to know the methods for working out fractions.

Exercise 20.1

1.   Reduce these fractions to their lowest terms.

   1 $\frac{24}{88}$ 2 $\frac{60}{84}$ 3 $\frac{33}{132}$ 4 $\frac{26}{39}$ 5 $\frac{75}{200}$ 6 $\frac{11}{110}$

2.   Change these mixed numbers to improper fractions.

   1 $4\frac{5}{6}$ 2 $7\frac{7}{10}$ 3 $9\frac{1}{11}$ 4 $5\frac{7}{8}$ 5 $3\frac{1}{7}$ 6 $8\frac{2}{5}$

3.   Change these improper fractions to mixed numbers.

   1 $\frac{37}{10}$ 2 $\frac{25}{8}$ 3 $\frac{55}{9}$ 4 $\frac{40}{11}$ 5 $\frac{100}{3}$ 6 $\frac{105}{12}$

Find the values of the following.

4.   1 $\frac{1}{2} + \frac{1}{3} + \frac{1}{4}$ 5 $2\frac{5}{12} + 2\frac{1}{3}$ 8 $\frac{1}{2} + 2\frac{5}{6}$

     2 $\frac{5}{8} + \frac{1}{6}$ 6 $4\frac{3}{8} + 3\frac{1}{3}$ 9 $2\frac{3}{4} + 1\frac{4}{5}$

     3 $2\frac{7}{10} + 1\frac{3}{5}$ 7 $5\frac{5}{9} + \frac{1}{6}$ 10 $4\frac{1}{8} + 1\frac{7}{12}$

     4 $3\frac{3}{8} + 1\frac{4}{5}$

Find the values of the following.

5. **1** $\frac{5}{8} - \frac{1}{6}$ **5** $1\frac{7}{20} - \frac{4}{5}$ **8** $\frac{1}{2} + \frac{1}{3} - \frac{1}{6}$

   2 $2\frac{11}{12} - \frac{7}{8}$ **6** $5\frac{5}{14} - 3\frac{6}{7}$ **9** $2\frac{1}{2} + \frac{7}{10} - \frac{2}{5}$

   3 $2\frac{5}{6} - 1\frac{1}{4}$ **7** $2\frac{2}{3} - 2\frac{5}{9}$ **10** $1\frac{3}{4} - \frac{4}{5} + 2\frac{7}{8}$

   4 $7\frac{5}{12} - 5\frac{8}{9}$

6. **1** $\frac{3}{8} \times \frac{2}{3}$ **5** $2\frac{1}{6} \times \frac{9}{13}$ **8** $3\frac{3}{8} \times 1\frac{1}{9}$

   2 $\frac{5}{6} \times \frac{7}{8}$ **6** $\frac{5}{6} \times \frac{9}{10}$ **9** $4\frac{1}{2} \times 1\frac{5}{6}$

   3 $\frac{2}{3} \times 1\frac{1}{8}$ **7** $1\frac{1}{7} \times 10$ **10** $5\frac{5}{9} \times 6\frac{3}{4} \times 1\frac{1}{15}$

   4 $1\frac{3}{4} \times 2\frac{2}{5}$

7. **1** $\frac{5}{6} \div \frac{7}{8}$ **5** $\frac{7}{12} \div \frac{14}{15}$ **8** $4\frac{4}{9} \div 5\frac{5}{6}$

   2 $\frac{3}{10} \div 1\frac{1}{6}$ **6** $2\frac{4}{5} \div 7$ **9** $2\frac{1}{12} \div 5\frac{5}{8}$

   3 $4\frac{1}{8} \div 2\frac{3}{4}$ **7** $3\frac{3}{4} \div 2\frac{2}{5}$ **10** $11\frac{1}{4} \div 2\frac{3}{16}$

   4 $7 \div 1\frac{3}{4}$

8. **1** $6\frac{3}{4} - 1\frac{2}{3}$ **5** $1\frac{5}{8} \times 1\frac{3}{5}$ **8** $3\frac{1}{3} \times \frac{3}{10}$

   2 $5\frac{1}{12} \div 7\frac{5}{8}$ **6** $4\frac{2}{3} - 4\frac{1}{6}$ **9** $3\frac{1}{6} + 1\frac{3}{4}$

   3 $2\frac{2}{3} \times 2\frac{3}{4}$ **7** $2\frac{3}{5} \div 1\frac{3}{10}$ **10** $3\frac{1}{7} \times \frac{4}{11}$

   4 $1\frac{3}{4} + 2\frac{5}{12} + 3\frac{5}{6}$

9. **1** $\left(\frac{15}{28} \times \frac{7}{30}\right) + \frac{7}{8}$ **5** $\left(3\frac{1}{7} \times 8\frac{3}{4}\right) - 2\frac{1}{3}$ **8** $12\frac{1}{5} - \left(2\frac{2}{9} \times 4\frac{1}{2}\right)$

   2 $\left(2\frac{2}{3} - 1\frac{3}{4}\right) \times 4$ **6** $\left(\frac{2}{3} - \frac{1}{6}\right)^2$ **9** $2\frac{1}{4} - \left(1\frac{1}{2} \times \frac{2}{5}\right)$

   3 $\left(2\frac{1}{2} \div \frac{1}{4}\right) - 6\frac{1}{2}$ **7** $1\frac{5}{12} \div \left(3\frac{1}{5} + 1\frac{1}{3}\right)$ **10** $2\frac{1}{10} - 1\frac{3}{5} + 6\frac{1}{2}$

   4 $8\frac{3}{4} \times 1\frac{3}{5} \div 4\frac{2}{3}$

10. Eleanor had a box of chocolates. She put aside $\frac{1}{4}$ of them for her sister and $\frac{1}{3}$ of them for her brother. What fraction had she left ?

11. Mr Taylor's weekly wage is £240. He reckons that $\frac{1}{4}$ of his wages go in tax and insurance. Of the remainder, $\frac{1}{5}$ pays the rent and $\frac{1}{10}$ is put aside to pay the household fuel bills. How much has he left to spend ?

12. Mr Brown decided to dig his garden. On the first fine day he dug $\frac{2}{5}$ of it. On the next day he dug $\frac{1}{6}$ of it, then he stopped because it was raining. What fraction remained to be dug ?

Algebraic fractions

Example

1 Simplify $\dfrac{3x^2}{9x}$

$$\frac{3x^2}{9x} = \frac{\cancel{3} \times \cancel{x} \times x}{\underset{3}{\cancel{9}} \times \cancel{x}}$$
Cancel by 3 and by x.

$$= \frac{x}{3}$$

Addition and subtraction

Examples

2 $\dfrac{a}{6} + \dfrac{2a}{3}$

The lowest number into which 6 and 3 both divide is 6,
so change $\dfrac{2a}{3}$ into $\dfrac{4a}{6}$.

$$= \frac{a + 4a}{6} = \frac{5a}{6}$$

3 $\dfrac{2b}{5} - \dfrac{b}{4}$

The lowest number into which 5 and 4 both divide is 20,
so change $\dfrac{2b}{5}$ into $\dfrac{8b}{20}$ and $\dfrac{b}{4}$ into $\dfrac{5b}{20}$.

$$= \frac{8b - 5b}{20} = \frac{3b}{20}$$

Multiplication and division

Examples

4 $\dfrac{3a}{5c} \times \dfrac{10c^2}{a}$

$$= \frac{3 \times \cancel{a}}{\cancel{5} \times \cancel{c}} \times \frac{\overset{2}{\cancel{10}} \times \cancel{c} \times c}{\cancel{a}}$$
Cancel by 5, a and c.

$$= \frac{6c}{1} = 6c$$

5 $\dfrac{3x^2}{y^2} \div \dfrac{x}{y}$

Instead of dividing by $\dfrac{x}{y}$, multiply by $\dfrac{y}{x}$.

$$= \frac{3 \times x \times \cancel{x}}{y \times \cancel{y}} \times \frac{\cancel{y}}{\cancel{x}}$$
Cancel by x and y.

$$= \frac{3x}{y}$$

Equations involving fractions

Examples

6    $\dfrac{3x}{4} = 10$ Multiply both sides by 4.

    $3x = 40$ Divide both sides by 3.

    $x = 13\frac{1}{3}$

As a check, LHS $= \frac{3}{4} \times 13\frac{1}{3} = \frac{3}{4} \times \frac{40}{3} = 10$. The two sides are both 10, so the equation checks.

7    $\dfrac{x}{4} + \dfrac{x}{6} = 15$ Multiply both sides by 12, because 12 is the lowest number into which 4 and 6 both divide.

    $3x + 2x = 180$ $\dfrac{x}{4}$ multiplied by 12 is $3x$, $\dfrac{x}{6}$ multiplied by 12 is $2x$.

        $5x = 180$

         $x = 36$

As a check, LHS $= \dfrac{x}{4} + \dfrac{x}{6} = \dfrac{36}{4} + \dfrac{36}{6} = 9 + 6 = 15$. The two sides are both 15, so the equation checks.

8    $\dfrac{2x-1}{6} = \dfrac{4x+3}{8}$ Multiply both sides by 24.

    $4(2x-1) = 3(4x+3)$ Remove the brackets.

        $8x - 4 = 12x + 9$

          $-13 = 4x$

           $x = -3\frac{1}{4}$

As a check, LHS $= \dfrac{2x-1}{6} = \dfrac{-6\frac{1}{2}-1}{6} = \dfrac{-7\frac{1}{2}}{6} = -1\frac{1}{4}$

RHS $= \dfrac{4x+3}{8} = \dfrac{-13+3}{4} = \dfrac{-10}{8} = -1\frac{1}{4}$

The two sides are both $-1\frac{1}{4}$, so the equation checks.

Substitution in expressions or formulae

Examples

9   If $x = \frac{1}{2}$ and $y = \frac{4}{5}$,

$$\frac{x}{3y-1} = \frac{\frac{1}{2}}{3 \times \frac{4}{5} - 1} = \frac{\frac{1}{2}}{\frac{7}{5}} = \frac{1}{2} \div \frac{7}{5} = \frac{1}{2} \times \frac{5}{7} = \frac{5}{14}$$

$$2x^2 + 5y^2 = 2 \times \left(\tfrac{1}{2}\right)^2 \; + \; 5 \times \left(\tfrac{4}{5}\right)^2 = \overset{1}{\cancel{2}} \times \frac{1}{\underset{2}{\cancel{4}}} \; + \; \overset{1}{\cancel{5}} \times \frac{16}{\underset{5}{\cancel{25}}}$$

$$= \tfrac{1}{2} + \tfrac{16}{5} = \tfrac{5+32}{10} = \tfrac{37}{10} = 3\tfrac{7}{10}$$

10   A formula used to calculate distance is $s = ut + \frac{1}{2}ft^2$. Find the value of s when $u = 5\frac{1}{3}$, $t = \frac{3}{5}$ and $f = -10$.

$$s = ut + \tfrac{1}{2}ft^2$$

$$= 5\tfrac{1}{3} \times \tfrac{3}{5} \; + \; \tfrac{1}{2} \times (-10) \times \left(\tfrac{3}{5}\right)^2$$

$$= \frac{16}{\underset{1}{\cancel{3}}} \times \frac{\overset{1}{\cancel{3}}}{5} \; - \; \frac{1}{\underset{1}{\cancel{2}}} \times \overset{1}{\cancel{10}} \times \frac{9}{\underset{5}{\cancel{25}}}$$

$$= \tfrac{16}{5} - \tfrac{9}{5} = \tfrac{7}{5} = 1\tfrac{2}{5}$$

Fractional indices

$\sqrt{49}$ can be written in index form as $49^{\frac{1}{2}}$, so $49^{\frac{1}{2}} = 7$.

$36^{\frac{1}{2}} = \sqrt{36} = 6$, $81^{\frac{1}{2}} = \sqrt{81} = 9$.

$\sqrt[3]{125}$ can be written in index form as $125^{\frac{1}{3}}$, so $125^{\frac{1}{3}} = 5$.

$8^{\frac{1}{3}} = \sqrt[3]{8} = 2$, $1000^{\frac{1}{3}} = \sqrt[3]{1000} = 10$.

The general rules are

$$a^{\frac{1}{2}} = \sqrt{a}$$

$$a^{\frac{1}{3}} = \sqrt[3]{a}$$

$$a^{\frac{1}{4}} = \sqrt[4]{a}$$

$$a^{\frac{1}{n}} = \sqrt[n]{a}$$

Exercise 20.2

1. Simplify

   1 $\dfrac{12a^2}{3a}$ **2** $\dfrac{6c^2}{54c}$ **3** $\dfrac{25e^3}{15e}$

2. Simplify

   1 $\dfrac{3a}{8} + \dfrac{a}{6}$ **4** $\dfrac{d}{14} + \dfrac{3d}{7}$

   2 $\dfrac{10b}{3} - \dfrac{2b}{9}$ **5** $\dfrac{3e}{2} - \dfrac{4e}{3}$

   3 $\dfrac{4c}{15} + \dfrac{5c}{6}$

3. Simplify

   1 $\dfrac{8a}{15b} \times \dfrac{5b}{4}$ **4** $\dfrac{2g^2}{5} \div \dfrac{4g}{15}$

   2 $\dfrac{3}{8b} \div \dfrac{15}{16b^2}$ **5** $\dfrac{6pq}{5} \times \dfrac{25q}{18p}$

   3 $\dfrac{3c}{10e} \times \dfrac{2e^2}{9}$

4. Solve the equations

   1 $\dfrac{2x}{3} = 20$ **5** $\dfrac{4}{5}x - \dfrac{1}{10}x = 21$ **8** $\dfrac{2x}{9} - \dfrac{x}{6} = -\frac{1}{3}$

   2 $\dfrac{3x-4}{7} = 8$ **6** $\dfrac{5x}{6} = -15$ **9** $\dfrac{2(x+1)}{3} = 1$

   3 $\dfrac{5x+1}{6} = 11$ **7** $\dfrac{5x-7}{3} = -1$ **10** $\dfrac{x+1}{8} = \dfrac{2x-3}{4}$

   4 $\dfrac{x}{2} + \dfrac{2x}{3} = 14$

5. If $p = \frac{1}{2}$, $q = \frac{2}{3}$, $r = 1\frac{1}{4}$, find the values of

   1 $p + q$ **7** $4r - 3q$

   2 $4p - 3q$ **8** $4r^2 - 3q^2$

   3 $r - q$ **9** $\dfrac{p+r}{7q}$

   4 $8pqr$

   5 $p^2 + 4r^2$ **10** $q(2p + r)$

   6 $\dfrac{p}{q}$

6. If $a = \frac{1}{3}$ and $b = \frac{1}{2}$, find the values of

    1 $4a + b$
    2 $a^2 + b^2$
    3 $2a^2$

7. Find the values of

    1 $25^{\frac{1}{2}}$ **4** $64^{\frac{1}{3}}$

    2 $100^{\frac{1}{2}}$ **5** $81^{\frac{1}{4}}$

    3 $27^{\frac{1}{3}}$

8. A formula for horse-power is $H = \dfrac{PV}{550}$.

    Find H when $P = 30$ and $V = 44$.

9. The formula for the volume of a pyramid with a square base is $V = \frac{1}{3}x^2 h$.
    Find V when $x = 2\frac{2}{3}$ and $h = 3\frac{3}{8}$.

Exercise 20.3   Applications

1. How many half-pint glasses of fruit juice can be filled from a container which holds 2 gallons ?

2. An engine turns at 1200 revolutions per minute. Find, as a fraction of a second, how long it takes to turn through one revolution ?

3. Eric spends half his pocket money on the day he gets it, and one-third on the following day. This leaves him with 50p. How much pocket money does he get ?

4.

    Pauline's ruler measures in inches and twelfths. From A to B is $3\frac{5}{12}$ inches and from B to C is $2\frac{1}{12}$ inches. What is the distance from A to C ?

5. Mrs Jenkins has a roll of ribbon which is 10 feet long. She cuts 5 pieces off it, each of length $1\frac{1}{4}$ feet. What length remains on the roll ?

6. A cinema is $\frac{1}{3}$ full. After another 60 people come in it is $\frac{1}{2}$ full. How many people does the cinema hold ?

7. How many litres are there in a 5-gallon drum, taking 1 litre as $1\frac{3}{4}$ pints ?

8. A man walks $3\frac{3}{8}$ miles in $\frac{3}{4}$ hour. At what speed does he walk, in mph ? At the same speed, how far will he walk in 50 minutes ?

9. Copy and complete the 1st 9 rows of this pattern.

$$1 \qquad\qquad = \frac{1 \times 2}{2} = 1$$

$$1 + 2 \qquad\quad = \frac{2 \times 3}{2} = 3$$

$$1 + 2 + 3 \quad\; = \frac{3 \times 4}{2} = 6$$

$$1 + 2 + 3 + 4 = \qquad =$$

. . .

Now using the method of this pattern, work out the sum of the numbers from 1 to 40.

10. On a canal holiday, the family planned to make
a round trip of 72 miles in 4 days.
On the first 3 days the distances they covered
were $12\frac{3}{4}$ miles, $20\frac{1}{2}$ miles, $23\frac{3}{4}$ miles.
How far would they have to travel on the 4th day ?
What fraction of the total distance is this ?

11. Two rods, AB of length $4\frac{1}{2}$ inches and CD of length $5\frac{5}{8}$ inches, overlap by $\frac{3}{4}$ inch. What is
the total length AD ?

A   B

                                            C   D

12. The outside measurements of a picture frame are $14\frac{7}{8}$ inches and
$10\frac{3}{4}$ inches. The wood is $\frac{5}{8}$ inch wide.
What are the inside measurements ?

13. Simplify   **1** $\dfrac{3xy \times 4xy}{xy}$ **2** $\dfrac{1}{3xy} + \dfrac{1}{4xy}$ **3** $\dfrac{1}{3xy} \div \dfrac{1}{4xy}$

14. Solve the equations

    1 $\dfrac{x}{2} - 6 = -10$

    2 $\frac{1}{2}(x - 3) = x + 6$

    3 $\dfrac{x}{2} - \dfrac{x}{4} = 1$

15. I think of a number. Two-thirds of this number is 15 more than one-quarter of the number. What is the number ? (Let the number be x.)

16. If $a = \frac{1}{2}$, $b = \frac{1}{3}$ and $c = \frac{1}{5}$, find the values of

    1 $5c - (a + b)$ **2** $2a^2 + 3b^2$ **3** $a(b - c)$

17. Three regular polygons with a sides, b sides and c sides respectively meet at a point P.
What is the size of the exterior angle of a polygon with a sides ?
What is the size of the exterior angle of a polygon with b sides ?
What is the size of the **interior** angle of a polygon with c sides ?

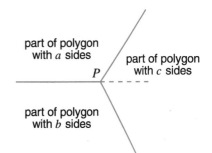

part of polygon with a sides

part of polygon with c sides

P

part of polygon with b sides

Find an equation connecting a, b and c, and simplify it to show that

$$\dfrac{1}{a} + \dfrac{1}{b} + \dfrac{1}{c} = \dfrac{1}{2}.$$

If $b = 12$ and $c = 6$, use this equation to find a.
If one polygon has 12 sides and another has 6 sides, what sort of polygon is the third one ?

18. Find the value of $\dfrac{a + b}{a - b}$ when $a = 2\frac{1}{2}$ and $b = 1\frac{1}{3}$.

19. If $x = 4y$, find the value of $\dfrac{x^2 - 4y^2}{x^2 + 4y^2}$.

20. If $a = 121$ and $b = 27$, find the values of

    1 $a^{\frac{1}{2}} - b^{\frac{1}{3}}$ **2** $(11a)^{\frac{1}{3}} + (3b)^{\frac{1}{4}}$.

21. If $y = x^{\frac{1}{5}}$, find the value of y when $x = 32$.

22. A formula used in optics is $f = \dfrac{uv}{u+v}$. Find the value of f when $u = \frac{1}{2}$ and $v = 2\frac{1}{2}$.

23. A rule used in piloting an aircraft is $C = \dfrac{H}{500}(50 - T)$. Find C when $H = 12\,500$ and $T = 42$.

Practice test 20

1. A plank of wood is $10\frac{1}{2}$ feet long. 3 pieces each $1\frac{3}{4}$ feet long are cut off. What length remains?

2. Mrs Carr wins some money in a competition. She gives $\frac{1}{3}$ of it to her husband and $\frac{2}{5}$ of the remainder to her daughter. She keeps the remaining money, £300, for herself. How much did she win?

3. $3\frac{1}{4}$ metres of material is needed for a loose cover for an armchair and $\frac{3}{4}$ metre for a small chair. Find the cost of the material for covering a suite of 2 armchairs and 6 small chairs with material costing £5.50 per metre.

4. Simplify

    1 $\dfrac{3a}{2} - \dfrac{a}{5}$ **2** $\dfrac{3b^2}{4c} \times \dfrac{2c^2}{9b}$

5. Solve the equation $\dfrac{3x+2}{3} - \dfrac{3x}{4} = \dfrac{7}{12}$.

6. Find the value of $(x+y)^2 - (x^2 + y^2)$ when $x = 5$ and $y = 3\frac{1}{2}$.

7. If $c = 29$ and $d = 7$, find the values of

    1 $(c+d)^{\frac{1}{2}}$ **2** $(2c+d-1)^{\frac{1}{3}}$

8. If $s = \dfrac{a}{1-r}$, find s when $a = 9$ and $r = \frac{1}{4}$.

9. A formula for calculating electrical resistance is $\dfrac{1}{R} = \dfrac{1}{a} + \dfrac{1}{b}$. Find the value of R when $a = 30$ and $b = 20$.

PUZZLES

53. Copy and complete this magic square. All rows, columns and the main diagonals should add up to 111, and when complete all numbers from 1 to 36 are used.

1		24			31
35	8			26	
34		15	21		4
3		16		10	33
	11	14	20		
	7		18	25	36

54. Make 12 pieces like this (with 3 squares) out of cardboard.

Colour them red (*R*), yellow (*Y*), blue (*B*) as follows.

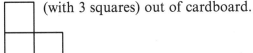

R		Y		Y		B		R		Y
B	**Y**	**B**	**R**	**R**	**B**	**R**	**Y**	**Y**	**Y**	**Y**	**B**

3 of these   2 of these   3 of these   2 of these   1 of this   1 of this

Rearrange the pieces to form a rectangle. How many different-sized rectangles can you make ?
Now rearrange the pieces to form a rectangle such that only two of the three colours appear on the perimeter.

55. Mrs Richards left her umbrella on the bus so she went into the local gift shop to buy a new one at £6.75. She paid with a £20 note, but since it was early in the morning, Mr Jenkins who owned the gift shop had no change so he took the £20 note next door to Mrs Evans at the confectioner's, and got £20 in change. Then he gave Mrs Richards her £13.25 change and she went on her way.
Later on, Mrs Evans came in, very worried, because she had just discovered that the £20 note was a forgery. Mr Jenkins had to give her a cheque for £20, and give the forged note to the police. Later on he told his wife the sad tale—that he had lost a good umbrella, £13.25 in change and a cheque for £20, total value £40.
Was he correct ?

Miscellaneous Section D

Exercise D1   Aural Practice

If possible find someone to read these questions to you.
You should do all of them within 10 minutes.
Do not use your calculator.
Write down the answers only.

1.   The sides of a triangle have lengths 5 cm, 6 cm and 9 cm. What is its perimeter ?

2.   What is the next number in the sequence 1, 4, 9, 16, ... ?

3.   What is 0.6×70 ?

4.   A boy jogs $2\frac{1}{2}$ km every evening. How far does he go in a week ?

5.   What is the gradient of the line with equation $2y = 7 - x$?

6.   The product of two girls' ages is 65. How old is the older girl ?

7.   What is the mean of the numbers 2, 3, 6, 7, 7 ?

8.   What is one-quarter of one-half ?

9.   What is the total cost of 200 badges at 6p each ?

10.   How long will it take to go 15 km at an average speed of 10 km/h ?

11.   Two children share £3.50 in the ratio 5 : 2. What is the smaller share ?

12.   What is the name of a quadrilateral which has all sides equal, but no right angles ?

13.   What must be added to $\frac{1}{3}$ to make it up to $\frac{1}{2}$?

14.   Give an approximate value for the square root of 4×20.

15.   A woman buys a bicycle for £150 and sells it to gain 20%. What is the selling price ?

Exercise D2 Revision

1. The angles of a quadrilateral are in the ratio $2 : 3 : 5 : 8$. Find their sizes.

2. The diagram represents an octagon formed by
    cutting equal isosceles triangles from the corners
    of a square of side 12 cm.
    Find, in terms of x, the total area of the four corners.
    If the area of the octagon is $\frac{7}{8}$ of the area of the
    original square, find the value of x.
    Find the perimeter of the octagon, correct to the nearest mm.

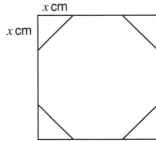

3. A group of 6 children held a money-raising event and raised £90, which they decided to
    split between 2 charities, X and Y.
    They each wrote down the amounts they wanted to send to each, (in £'s).

Child	Adam	Ben	Claire	Donna	Edward	Farida
To charity X	70	85	20			
To charity Y	20	5		55		

    Edward wanted to send equal amounts to each charity. Farida wanted to send twice as
    much to charity X as to charity Y.
    Copy and complete the table.
    Plot the data on a scatter diagram with charity X on the horizontal axis and charity Y on
    the vertical axis.
    The children found the mean of the amounts they wished to send to X, and this was the
    money they sent, with the rest going to Y. Draw a line on your graph and represent these
    amounts by a point on the line. How much did each charity receive ?

4. *A* and *B* are two harbours 15 km apart on a straight
    coastline running West–East. A ship, *C*, out at sea
    is seen from *A* on a bearing of 056° and from *B* on a
    bearing of 288°.
    Use scale drawing to find the distance of the ship
    from *B*, to the nearest 0.1 km.

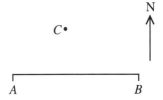

5. Solve these quadratic equations by trial, finding solutions which are positive integers.
    1 $2x^2 - 5x - 88 = 0$
    2 $(2x + 1)(x - 4) + 10 = 0$

6. Find the values of

1 $1\frac{3}{4} + 4\frac{5}{6}$ **3** $2\frac{2}{3} \times 2\frac{1}{4} \times \frac{5}{6}$ **5** $(3\frac{1}{4} + 1\frac{1}{3}) \times 1\frac{1}{5}$

2 $3\frac{1}{10} - 2\frac{3}{5}$ **4** $2\frac{1}{12} \div 1\frac{1}{4}$

7. What numbers are these ?

1 It is less than 100, it is a prime number, it is one less than a multiple of 7 and its digits add up to 5.

2 It is less than 100, it is 2 more than a square number and it is a multiple of 11. When divided by 9 there is a remainder of 3.

3 It is a factor of 180, it is 4 less than a square number, and when it is divided by 7 there is a remainder of 3.

8. **1** Find the largest integer n where $\dfrac{n}{12} < \dfrac{5}{7}$.

2 List the positive integers n such that n is less than 25% of $(2n + 11)$.

9. **1** Multiply 3.8×10^4 by 5×10^{-2}, giving the answer in standard index form.

2 Divide 3.8×10^4 by 5×10^{-2}, giving the answer in standard index form.

10. Draw axes as shown and show the journey of a boy on his bicycle and his father in the car.
The boy starts from A at 1 pm and cycles at a steady speed of 10 km/h for 2 hours. He then rests for $\frac{1}{2}$ hour and then continues cycling to B, which is 40 km from A, and he arrives at 6 pm.

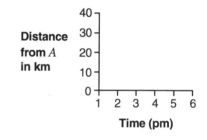

His father starts from A at 4 pm and arrives at B at 5.20 pm, travelling at a steady speed.

1 On the second part of the journey the boy travelled at a steady speed. What was his speed ?

2 What was his father's speed ?

3 When and where did the father overtake his son ?

11. A firm employs skilled workers and trainee workers. The skilled workers are paid £40 per day and the trainees are paid £20 per day.
If there are altogether 30 workers, of whom x are skilled and y are trainees, write down an equation involving x and y.
If the daily wage bill is £800, write down a second equation and simplify it.
Solve the equations simultaneously to find how many trainees there are.

12. This table gives the lengths of time of 80 phone calls.

Time (in minutes)	0–2	2–4	4–6	6–8	8–10	10–12
Number of calls	18	22	16	14	8	2

Draw a histogram of this distribution.
Find the mean time per call.

Exercise D3   Revision

1. The weights of 8 eggs were, in grams,

    47,   53,   53,   57,   48,   57,   55,   46.

    Find the mean and the range of the weights.

2. $C = \dfrac{1000P}{V}$, where P is power in kilowatts, V is voltage in volts, C is current in amps.

    If the local voltage is 240 volts, what is the current for a 2 kW fire, to the nearest amp ?

3. The graph shows how the temperature varied with time during a day in a certain tropical country.

    1   What was the minimum temperature and at what time of day did it occur ?

    2   What was the hottest time of day and what was the maximum temperature ?

    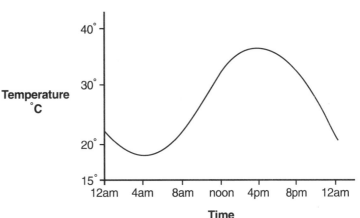

4. The points A and B have coordinates $(1, -1)$ and $(4, -5)$.
    Find
    1   the length of the line AB,
    2   the gradient of the line AB.

5. This shows the reading when Bert had filled his car with some petrol.

    1   How many litres had he bought ?

    2   He paid for the petrol with a £20 note. How much change did he get ?

    3   What is the price per gallon, to the nearest penny, if 1 gallon = 4.546 litres ?

    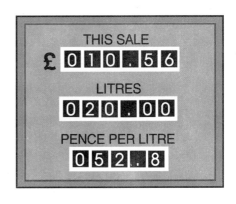

6. Use the map of the London Underground on page 250, or a coloured map, to say how you would travel on these journeys, using the Underground. Name the stations where you have to change from one line to another. The nearest stations to each place are given in brackets.

1   From Buckingham Palace (Victoria or St James's Park or Green Park) to the Tower of London (Tower Hill).
2   From St Paul's Cathedral (St Paul's) to Westminster Abbey (Westminster).
3   From Victoria Station (Victoria) to King's Cross Station (Kings Cross St Pancras).
4   From the Museum of London (Barbican, St Paul's or Moorgate) to Madame Tussauds (Baker Street).
5   From Trafalgar Square (Charing Cross) to Harrods (Knightsbridge).

7. 1   If 1 franc is worth p pence, how many pence will f francs be worth ?
    2   If x kg of potatoes are bought for y pence, what is the price per kg ?
    3   The sum of two numbers is 12. One of them is x. What is the other ? What is their product ?
    4   Elaine is 3 years younger than Eric. If Eric is x years old, how old will Elaine be next year ?
    5   A man earned £x per month and his wife earned £y per week. What were their total earnings in a year ?

8. With centre of enlargement A, P is mapped into B and Q is mapped into C.
    1   What is the scale factor of the enlargement ?
    2   What is the ratio of lengths $BC : PQ$?

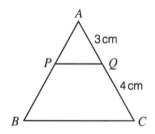

9. A group of people were asked how they prefer to spend their leisure time, choosing from reading (R), playing sports (S), watching television (T), other activities (U). The results were as follows:

```
R   T   T   S   T   R   T   R   T   S   R   T   R   S   T
U   T   R   U   R   T   S   U   U   S   S   T   U   T   T
T   T   T   T   R   R   T   R   S   U   S   T   R   U   S
T   R   T   U   R   T   R   R   U   T   R   T   U   S   U
```

Tally these results and show them on a pie chart.

10. A triangular field has sides 900 m, 700 m, 600 m. Treasure is hidden in the field (1) 200 m from the longest side, (2) equidistant from the two other sides.
Draw a scale drawing using a scale of 1 cm to represent 100 m, showing the loci for (1) and (2). Mark the position of the treasure. Find its distance from the nearest corner of the field, to the nearest 10 m.

11. Draw the x-axis from -1 to 3 and the y-axis from -8 to 13.
Draw the graphs of $y = 3x - 5$ and $y = 9 - 4x$.
Use your graphs to solve the simultaneous equations $y = 3x - 5$, $y = 9 - 4x$.

12. In a certain quarter the quarterly charge for a telephone was £19.54, and each unit used cost 4.20 pence. To the total amount, VAT was added at $17\frac{1}{2}\%$. What was the phone bill in that quarter if 600 units had been used ?

Exercise D4   Revision

1. How many

1	cm in 1 metre,	**6**	pence in £1,
2	m in 1 km,	**7**	mm in 1 metre,
3	seconds in 1 minute,	**8**	minutes in 1 hour,
4	g in 1 kg,	**9**	mm^2 in $1\,cm^2$,
5	cm^3 in 1 litre,	**10**	cm^3 in $1\,m^3$?

2. A die is thrown twice. What is the probability that both scores are greater than 4 ?

3. If $a = 9.5$, $b = 11.2$ and $c = 7.3$, find the values of
   1   s, where $s = \frac{1}{2}(a + b + c)$,

   2   $\sqrt{\dfrac{s(s-a)}{bc}}$, where s has the value found in **1**.

4.   Find the size of angle *b*.

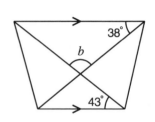

5.   Copy this sketch graph and identify these
     regions on it.
     A $y < x$, $x < 3$, $y > 3 - x$

     B $y > -1$, $x > 3$, $y < 3 - x$

     C $y > 0$, $y < x$, $y < 3 - x$

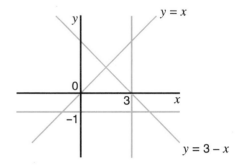

6.   These windows are similar in shape,
     consisting of a semicircle above a rectangle.
     What is the ratio of their perimeters ?

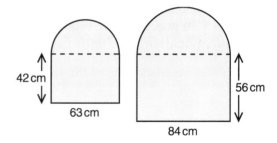

7.   5 oranges and 2 lemons cost £1.05.   9 oranges and 1 lemon cost £1.37. Find the cost of
     1 orange, and of 1 lemon.

8.   Copy and complete this table showing the size of an interior angle of a regular polygon.

Number of sides	3	4	5	6	8	9	10
Size of each interior angle (in degrees)	60						144

     On graph paper, label the horizontal axis for 'number of sides' from 3 to 10, and label
     the vertical axis for 'size of angle in degrees' from 0 to 180.
     Plot the values in the table on the graph.
     Join the points with a smooth curve. (Note that intermediate points on the curve have no
     meaning, except where the number of sides is 7.)
     Estimate the size of an interior angle of a regular polygon with 7 sides.

9. Use graph paper or squared paper for this question.

If O is the origin and $\overrightarrow{OA} = \begin{pmatrix} 1 \\ 3 \end{pmatrix}$, $\overrightarrow{OB} = \begin{pmatrix} 9 \\ 15 \end{pmatrix}$, $\overrightarrow{OC} = \begin{pmatrix} 5 \\ 7 \end{pmatrix}$,

find $\overrightarrow{OD}$, where D is the mid-point of BC.

Find $\overrightarrow{AD}$. What is the length of AD ?

10. Use the flow diagram given in question 8 page 323 to find out whether or not these numbers are prime numbers.

    1   67   4   143
    2   68   5   169
    3   137

11. The circle centre O, radius 5 cm, has a regular hexagon inscribed in it.

    1   Find the circumference of the circle.
    2   What is the size of $\angle AOB$?
    3   What kind of triangle is $\triangle AOB$?
    4   What is the length of the chord AB ?

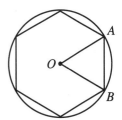

12. The Council Tax payable by 6 householders is as follows:

Value of the property (£1000's)	30	50	65	80	120	150
Tax (to nearest £10)	430	510	580	650	800	940

Draw a scatter diagram of the data, with the value of the property on the horizontal axis and tax on the vertical axis.
Draw a line of best fit.
Use the line of best fit to determine how much tax a householder with a house worth £100 000 should pay.
In fact, the prices are calculated in bands, not as gradual increases, and that householder will pay the same as the one with a house worth £120 000. How much extra is this above your previous answer ?

Exercise D5 Activities

1. **My house**

   Imagine that it is a few years into the future and you are about to buy a house.
   Design the house and draw a plan of each floor.
   Then draw the plan of each room, showing where the doorways and windows are, and
   where each item of furniture will go.
   Find the approximate cost of each item of furniture (by looking in shops, catalogues or
   advertisements).
   For each room make a list of the furniture and fittings you will need and find the total
   cost. Find the total cost for all the rooms in the house.
   If you intend to have a garden you could include a plan for this, and add on the costs of
   garden tools and garden furniture.
   Find the up-to-date price of a similar house by looking at advertisements, and find the
   total cost of everything.
   Cut pictures from magazines and catalogues to illustrate your booklet, and make an
   attractive cover for it.
   This is your dream house so you need not be too practical about being able to afford it,
   if you wish to design a really luxurious one, on the other hand you may prefer to be
   practical and plan for an inexpensive one. You may prefer to choose a flat, or a
   bungalow, instead of a house.

2. **Compound Interest**

   If an amount of money is invested and the interest is added
   to the investment, then the interest gets bigger each year.
   Suppose you begin with £1000 and the interest is
   8% each year.
   Then the interest in the first year is 8% of £1000, which
   is £80.
   The amount at the end of the first year is £1080.

   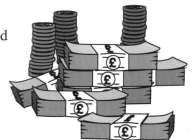

Now in the second year the interest is 8% of £1080, which is £86.40.

The amount at the end of the second year is £1166.40.

You can continue working out the amounts in this way.

However, to find the amount at the end of any year, you are finding 100% + 8% = 108% of the amount at the beginning of the year. So you can multiply by 1.08 each time.

On your calculator press

1.08 $\boxed{\times}$ 1000 $\boxed{=}$ $\boxed{=}$ $\boxed{=}$ ...   and you will get the amounts at the end of 1 year,

2 years, 3 years, ...

(On some calculators you may have to press $\boxed{\times}$ twice, or reverse the order of 1.08 and 1000.)

Show your results on a graph, joining the points with a smooth curve.

These are the **amounts** at compound interest. If you subtract the original amount, £1000, the money remaining is the **compound interest**.

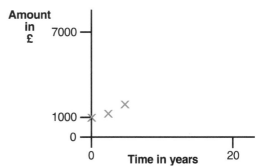

Investigate how money grows at different rates of interest. Illustrate this by drawing graphs. How long would it take to 'double your money' at different rates of interest ? A magazine article quoted this as 'the rule of 72'. If the rate is R% per annum then the number of years needed to double the money is found by dividing 72 by R. You can check to see how reliable this rule is.

If money is invested at 12% per annum and interest is added twice a year instead of annually, then 6% is added every 6 months. If interest is paid monthly, this is 1% added at the end of every month. Does it make any difference how often the interest is added, in the long run ?

You could link this investigation with (1) what happens to a population which increases at a constant rate, and (2) what happens when the value of an object depreciates at a constant rate.

3.   **History of measurement**

It is interesting to find out about the measures which were used long ago in Britain. Land is still measured in acres. An acre is the area of land that could be ploughed in a day, in the days when oxen were used for ploughing.

If you have an interest in another country, maybe you could find out about how its system developed.

In France at the time of the Revolution, the old measures were abolished and the Metric System adopted. This is now used worldwide for scientific work and is being introduced gradually into Britain.

You could make a topic booklet about measurements. You could include weights as well. You could also find out about the measurement of time, and about coinage, or these could be topics in themselves.

4. **Which lorry ?**

Moveall Haulage Company want to buy a new lorry. They have looked at many suitable lorries and finally have to decide between the Truckmaster and the Freightliner. They have to consider the cost of the lorry, which is made up of a chassis plus a body, the payload (the weight that the lorry can carry) and the fuel consumption under different driving conditions.

The manufacturers of the lorries provide the following information.

	Truckmaster		Freightliner	
Chassis price	£42508		£44349	
Body price	£7437		£8894	
Payload	14.28 tons		15.16 tons	
	miles per gallon (mpg)	average speed (mph)	miles per gallon (mpg)	average speed (mph)
Motorway	9.68	56.0	8.74	54.1
Hills	7.65	28.7	7.84	29.8
Main roads	12.76	42.5	13.12	41.6

Using the information given, find
1   the total cost of the Truckmaster,
2   the total cost of the Freightliner.
3   Which is the more expensive lorry, and by how much ?
4   Which lorry has the greater payload, and by how much ?

The Company estimate that the lorry will travel 30 000 miles on motorways, 4000 miles along hilly routes and 16 000 miles along main roads, each year.
They work out the amount of fuel to be used, using the formula

$$\text{Number of gallons of diesel} = \frac{\text{number of miles}}{\text{miles per gallon}}.$$

5   Using the estimated distances, find out how many gallons of diesel each lorry will use on the three types of road, in a year. Copy and complete this table, giving each answer to the nearest gallon and the totals to the nearest 10 gallons. (The first answer has been filled in.)

	Number of gallons	
	Truckmaster	Freightliner
Motorway	3099	
Hills		
Main roads		
Total		

Which lorry would use the least amount of diesel in a year, and how much less is this than the other one would use ?

The Company have just won an additional contract to move 4800 tons of gravel for a local quarry.

What is the least number of trips needed to transport the gravel

6   using the Truckmaster,

7   using the Freightliner ?

If these delivery journeys involve a total distance of 90 miles each time, what is the total mileage involved

8   for the Truckmaster,

9   for the Freightliner ?

Estimate the total time needed for all the gravel delivery journeys, if the route is a hilly one,

10 using a Truckmaster,

11 using a Freightliner ?

12 Write a short report for the Company, suggesting which lorry should be bought, and giving reasons.

5.   Cubes

Work out the cubes from 1^3 to 10^3.

Copy and complete this pattern.

natural numbers	sum	cubes of natural numbers	sum
1	1	1^3	1
$1+2$	3	1^3+2^3	9
$1+2+3$	6	$1^3+2^3+3^3$	36
...		...	
$1+2+\cdots+10$	55	$1^3+2^3+\cdots+10^3$	

What do you notice about the connection between the 2nd and 4th columns ?

Double the numbers in column (2) and divide each by the largest number of the same row in column (1). What do you notice ? Can you use this to find a formula for

(1) $1+2+3+\cdots+n,$

(2) $1^3+2^3+3^3+\cdots+n^3$?

It is not so easy to find a formula for $1^2+2^2+3^2+\cdots+n^2$, but using a similar method, finding $1^2, 1^2+2^2, 1^2+2^2+3^2,\ldots$, and multiplying the sums by 6, you may discover the formula.

6.   Moebius bands

These are long strips of paper glued together at the ends to form a loop. Some of the strips have a twist, or several twists, put in them before they are glued. Make one each with 0 twists, 1 twist, 2 twists, etc. For each loop, investigate whether it is one-sided or two-sided, and how many edges it has. Continue your investigations by seeing what happens when you cut each strip lengthwise down a centre line. It is interesting to try to predict the result in advance. Investigate sides and edges again, and the lengths of the new strips in comparison with the original. Finally, make new strips which you can cut lengthways by a cut which is $\frac{1}{3}$ of the width across. Investigate the results.

Moebius was a mathematician who lived in the 19th century. Can you find out anything about him ?

7. **Geometrical models**

Instructions for making models of solid figures, including the 5 regular solid figures, were given in Chapter 4.
There are other models you could make.

There are 13 semi-regular solids, made with combinations of regular polygons. You could try to make these.
With 6 squares and 8 equilateral triangles, with the same length of edge, putting 2 of each alternately at each point, you get a cuboctahedron. With 18 squares and 8 triangles, with 3 squares and 1 triangle meeting at a point, you can make a rhombicuboctahedron. With 6 squares and 32 triangles, with 4 triangles and a square meeting at a point, you can make a snub cube. Other solids use different combinations of equilateral triangles, squares and regular pentagons, hexagons, octagons and decagons. Can you discover them all ?

There are 4 other regular solids called the Kepler-Poinsot Polyhedra, which are interesting models.
To make the great stellated dodecahedron, first make a regular icosahedron as a base. Then make 20 triangular pyramids to stick on the 20 faces of the icosahedron. The long slant edges of these pyramids must be 1.62 times the length of the base edges, which are the same length as the edges of the icosahedron.

If you are interested in making mathematical models you can find details of many others from library books.

8. **The arrangement of red cards in a pack of cards**

If a pack of cards has been shuffled properly, then when you turn up the top card it is equally likely to be a red card (heart or diamond) or a black one (club or spade). In this experiment you should investigate how many cards are turned over before a red card appears.
Shuffle the pack of cards and turn over the cards one-by-one, counting until a red card appears. If it is the first card it counts as 1. If it is only the second card it counts as 2, and so on. Record the result. Then continue turning the cards over, beginning the count again at 1, and carrying on until another red card appears. Repeat until you have 10 results.

Before you go any further, make two guesses:
1   What is the mode number of the results ?
2   What is the mean of the results ?

To continue the experiment, shuffle all the cards again properly and begin again using the full pack.
Carry on in this way. After every 10 results shuffle the cards and begin again with a full pack. Repeat until you have got 100, or more, results.
Make a frequency table of the results and show them in a bar-line graph. Comment on the shape of the graph.
Find the mode. Does it agree with your guess ?
Find the mean. Does it agree with your guess ?

To the student : 5

Learning formulae

There are certain formulae which you will need to know by heart. The best way to learn a formula is to know where it comes from.

There is a formula checklist on page 520. Copy the list, completing each formula, then check your answers from the relevant chapters of the book. Learn those you do not know.

Learning formulae in isolation is not very useful. You need to link this with learning methods, so that you can use the formulae correctly.

Practice exams

You may have a practice exam at school. This will give you some idea of your present standard. It will show you that you can do well if you have learnt the work. It will give you practice in working to time and working under pressure.

After the exam, you will be told your marks or grade and given back your paper. Perhaps your teacher will go through all the questions with the class or you may have to correct them yourself. Ask about anything you do not understand.

If you get a low mark, do not be too discouraged if you know that you can do better next time. But decide what you are going to do to improve your standard.

In an exam it is the marks which count. Could you have got more marks if you had spent less time on some questions and more on others ? Should you have revised some topics more thoroughly ?

Did you throw away any marks by:
not reading a question carefully enough,
not showing the necessary working with the answer,
writing so badly that the marker could not read it,
writing so badly that **you** could not read it and copied it wrongly on the next line,
not checking an answer that was obviously wrong,
not giving an answer to the accuracy asked for, e.g. to the nearest cm ?

Since this was a practice exam, having made some of these mistakes, you can see that by avoiding them in future you can gain more marks.

Make a list of topics you still need to revise, and plan how you will use the remaining time before the proper examination.

Your teacher may give your further practice papers to do at home. If not, you may like to give yourself some. You can use the practice test questions or the revision exercises in this book. Try to do them as in a proper exam, spending the correct time on them and working in a quiet room without referring to books or notes.

21 Mutually exclusive or independent events

> **The topics in this chapter include:**
>
> - appreciating that the total sum of the probabilities of mutually exclusive events is 1 and that the probability of something happening is 1 minus the probability of it not happening,
>
> - understanding and applying the addition of probabilities for mutually exclusive events,
>
> - identifying all the outcomes when dealing with two combined events which are independent,
>
> - calculating the probability of a combined event given the probabilities of two independent events, and illustrating the combined probabilities of several events using tabulation or tree-diagrams,
>
> - understanding that when dealing with two independent events, the probability of both happening is less than the probability of either of them happening.

Mutually exclusive events

When there are two or more outcomes of an event and at each time only one of the outcomes can happen (because if one outcome happens, this prevents any of the other outcomes happening), then the outcomes are called mutually exclusive events.

The sum of the probabilities of all possible mutually exclusive events is 1, because it is certain that one of them will occur.

If the probability of an event happening is p, then the probability of the event not happening is $1 - p$.

The OR rule

If there are two mutually exclusive events A or B, then the probability of A or B occurring = the probability of A occurring + the probability of B occurring.
i.e.

$$P(A \text{ or } B) = P(A) + P(B)$$

If there are 3 events, A or B or C, then

$$P(A \text{ or } B \text{ or } C) = P(A) + P(B) + P(C)$$

The rule is similar if there are more than 3 events.

Examples

1   In the last year in a certain school, pupils must study one of the subjects music, or art, or Latin.

25% of the pupils study music and 60% of the pupils study art.

If a pupil from that year is chosen at random, what is the probability that the pupil studies music, art, music or art, Latin ?

$P(\text{music}) = \frac{25}{100} = \frac{1}{4}, \quad P(\text{art}) = \frac{60}{100} = \frac{3}{5}$

$P(\text{music or art}) = \frac{25}{100} + \frac{60}{100} = \frac{85}{100} = \frac{17}{20}$

$P(\text{Latin}) + P(\text{music or art}) = 1$

so $P(\text{Latin}) = 1 - \frac{17}{20} = \frac{3}{20}$

2   In a pack of 52 cards one card is drawn at random. What is the probability that it is **1** a heart,   **2** an ace,   **3** an ace or a heart ?

1 $P(\text{heart}) = \dfrac{13}{52} = \frac{1}{4}$

2 $P(\text{ace}) = \dfrac{4}{52} = \frac{1}{13}$

3 It would be wrong to use the OR rule because the two events, ace and heart, can occur together with the ace of hearts. They are not mutually exclusive events. Instead, find the number of successful outcomes. There are 13 hearts, including the ace, and the other 3 aces, making 16 successful outcomes altogether.

$P(\text{ace or heart}) = \dfrac{s}{n} = \dfrac{16}{52} = \frac{4}{13}$

Exercise 21.1

1.   A biscuit jar contains 7 shortbread biscuits, 8 cream biscuits, 10 chocolate biscuits and 15 wafer biscuits.

    If a biscuit is picked out at random, what is the probability that

    1 it is either a cream biscuit or a chocolate biscuit,

    2 it is not a wafer biscuit ?

2.   6 men, 4 women, 3 girls and 7 boys enter for a contest.
      If they each have an equal chance of winning, what is the probability that the winner is
      1   a man,
      2   a child,
      3   a female ?

3.   In a raffle, Mrs Andrews buys 10 tickets
      and Mr Andrews buys 5 tickets. There are
      200 tickets sold altogether.
      What is the probability that the 1st prize is
      won by either Mr or Mrs Andrews ?

4.   A bag contains a number of sweets, some red and some green. The probability of taking
      out a red sweet, at random, is $\frac{7}{12}$.
      1   What is the probability of taking out a green sweet ?
      2   If 35 of the sweets are green sweets, how many red sweets are there ?

5.   A box contains cartons of orange juice,
      grapefruit juice and pineapple juice.
      If a drink is taken out at random the probability
      that it is orange or pineapple is $\frac{5}{8}$.

      1   What is the probability that it is grapefruit ?
      2   The probability that it is orange is $\frac{3}{8}$. What is
            the probability that it is pineapple ?

6.   A number of corks are placed in a bag. Most corks are marked with a number 1, 2, 3, 4
      or 5. If a cork is picked out at random the probabilities of the different scores are:
      P(1) = 0.05
      P(2) = 0.3
      P(3) = 0.25
      P(4) = 0.2
      P(5) = 0.15

      What is the probability of getting
      1   a cork marked 4 or 5,
      2   a cork marked with an odd number,
      3   a cork which is not marked with a number ?

7. Jan estimates that the probability of the bus being early is 0.1, of it being on time is 0.7, and otherwise it will be late.

1 What is the probability that the bus will be late ?

2 If the bus is early, Jan will miss it, and thus be late for school. If the bus is late, Jan will also be late for school.
    What is the probability that Jan will be late for school ?

Independent events

Two events, where the outcome of the second event does not depend on the outcome of the first event, are called independent events.

The AND rule

If there are two independent events A and B, then the probability of both A and B occurring = the probability of A occurring × the probability of B occurring.

$$P(A \text{ and } B) = P(A) \times P(B)$$

If there are 3 independent events, A, B and C, then

$$P(A \text{ and } B \text{ and } C) = P(A) \times P(B) \times P(C)$$

The rule is similar if there are more than 3 events.

(Compare this with the OR rule for mutually exclusive events on page 434.)

Examples

1 If two dice are thrown, find the probability of getting two sixes.

The 1st event is tossing the 1st die. $P(\text{six}) = \frac{1}{6}$

The 2nd event is tossing the 2nd die. $P(\text{six}) = \frac{1}{6}$

$P(\text{two sixes}) = P(\text{six}) \times P(\text{six}) = \frac{1}{6} \times \frac{1}{6} = \frac{1}{36}$

(This result can also be found using a sample space diagram.)

2   A playing card is drawn from a pack of 52 cards and after replacing it and shuffling the pack, a second card is drawn.
What is the probability that both cards drawn are aces ?
What is the probability that the 1st card is a heart and the 2nd card is not a heart ?

These events are independent because the 1st card is replaced before the 2nd card is drawn.

P(1st card an ace) $= \frac{1}{13}$

P(2nd card an ace) $= \frac{1}{13}$

P(both cards are aces) $=$ P(1st an ace and 2nd an ace) $= \frac{1}{13} \times \frac{1}{13} = \frac{1}{169}$

P(1st card a heart) $= \frac{1}{4}$

P(2nd card not a heart) $= \frac{3}{4}$

P(1st card a heart and 2nd not a heart) $= \frac{1}{4} \times \frac{3}{4} = \frac{3}{16}$

3   A seed manufacturer guarantees that 90% of a particular type of flower seed will germinate.
If 5 seeds of this type are sown, what is the probability that they will all germinate ?
What is the probability that none of them will germinate ?

P(one seed germinates) $= 90\% = 0.9$

P(all seeds germinate) $=$ P(1st, 2nd, 3rd, 4th and 5th seeds germinate)
$= 0.9 \times 0.9 \times 0.9 \times 0.9 \times 0.9$
$= 0.59049$
$= 0.59$, to 2 dec pl.

P(one seed does not germinate) $= 0.1$

P(no seeds germinate) $=$ P(1st, 2nd, 3rd, 4th and 5th do not germinate)
$= 0.1 \times 0.1 \times 0.1 \times 0.1 \times 0.1$
$= 0.00001$

(These answers assume that the results are independent and that the conditions are satisfactory. If the seeds were not planted in the right soil, not kept at a suitable temperature or not watered properly, it is much more probable that none of the seeds would germinate.)

4   The probabilities of 3 independent events taking place are $\frac{1}{3}$, $\frac{3}{4}$ and $\frac{2}{5}$, respectively.
What is the probability that at least one of these events takes place ?

The simplest way to find this is to first find the probability that none of the events takes place.

The probabilities that the events do not happen are $\frac{2}{3}$, $\frac{1}{4}$ and $\frac{3}{5}$.

P(no event takes place) $= \frac{2}{3} \times \frac{1}{4} \times \frac{3}{5} = \frac{1}{10}$

P(at least one event takes place) $= 1 - \frac{1}{10} = \frac{9}{10}$

Two events are less likely to happen than one of the events

When finding the probability of two or more independent events, the probabilities of the separate events are **multiplied**.
Since these probabilities are numbers less than 1, the result is smaller than any of the separate probabilities.
(This is assuming that neither probability is 0 or 1.)

Repeated trials

A coin or die has no memory so the probabilities are not affected by any previous tosses. Suppose a fairly-tossed coin has come down heads 5 times in succession. The 6th toss is not affected by the previous results and the probability of it being a head is still $\frac{1}{2}$.

But the probability of getting 6 heads in succession is

$$\text{P(head)} \times \text{P(head)} \times \text{P(head)} \times \text{P(head)} \times \text{P(head)} \times \text{P(head)} = \tfrac{1}{2} \times \tfrac{1}{2} \times \tfrac{1}{2} \times \tfrac{1}{2} \times \tfrac{1}{2} \times \tfrac{1}{2}$$
$$= \tfrac{1}{64}$$

Exercise 21.2

1. In a computer game the probability of scoring a hit is $\frac{2}{5}$. What is the probability that the first two players both score hits ?

2. There are 7 beads in a bag, 4 red, 1 white, 2 blue. One is taken out at random and replaced, and then another one is taken out. What is the probability that
    1 the 1st one is red,
    2 the 2nd one is blue,
    3 the 1st one is red and the 2nd one is blue ?

3. Hank usually has lunch at Dan's cafe. The probability that sausage and mash is on the day's menu is $\frac{2}{3}$. The probability that there is apple pie on the menu is $\frac{3}{4}$, quite independently of whether there is sausage and mash or not. Hank's favourite meal is sausage and mash followed by apple pie.
    What is the probability that he can have this today ?

4. On this spinner, the probability of getting any number from 1 to 5 is equally likely.
    1 If Betty spins twice, what is the probability that she scores a 5 and then a 4 ?
    2 What is the probability that she scores the same number twice in succession ?

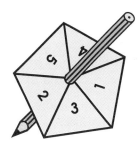

5. In Mrs Wright's job if extra work comes in during the afternoon she has to work late. The probability that she has to work late on any one evening is $\frac{1}{8}$. What is the probability that she will have to work late this Friday and also next Friday ?

6. Ronnie's bus ticket always has a different 4-figure number on it.
    1   What is the probability that the number on this morning's ticket has a unit figure of 7 ?
    2   What is the probability that he gets a ticket with a unit figure of 7 on the way to school and also on the way home from school ?

7. A card is drawn from a full pack of 52 cards and a second card is drawn from another full pack. What is the probability that
    1   both cards are hearts,
    2   both cards are red ones ?

8. A biased coin is tossed 4 times. At each toss the probability of heads is 0.6. What is the probability of getting heads, heads, tails, tails, in that order ?

9. Three table-tennis players, Nasir, Bilal and Sundip play in different matches.
    Their probabilities of winning are respectively $\frac{1}{2}$, $\frac{1}{4}$ and $\frac{1}{5}$.
    What is the probability that
    1   Nasir and Bilal win their matches, but Sundip loses his match,
    2   all three boys win their matches ?

Tree-diagrams

When there are two or more independent events we can show the combined results on a tree-diagram or in a table.

Examples

1   Emily goes to school by bus or car, or she walks. The probability of going by bus is $\frac{1}{2}$, of going by car is $\frac{1}{3}$, and of walking is $\frac{1}{6}$.

    When she comes home from school, she either walks, with probability $\frac{1}{2}$, or goes by bus, with probability $\frac{2}{5}$, or occasionally gets a lift home in a friend's car, with probability $\frac{1}{10}$. This is regardless of which way she travelled to school in the morning.

Here is a tree-diagram showing the combined outcomes.
W = walk, B = by bus, C = car.

Going	Coming	Outcome	Probability

Tree diagram:

Going branches: W ($\frac{1}{6}$), B ($\frac{1}{2}$), C ($\frac{1}{3}$)

Coming branches for each: W ($\frac{1}{2}$), B ($\frac{2}{5}$), C ($\frac{1}{10}$)

	Outcome	Probability
W – W	WW	$\frac{1}{6} \times \frac{1}{2} = \frac{1}{12}$
W – B	WB	$\frac{1}{6} \times \frac{2}{5} = \frac{1}{15}$
W – C	WC	$\frac{1}{6} \times \frac{1}{10} = \frac{1}{60}$
B – W	BW	$\frac{1}{2} \times \frac{1}{2} = \frac{1}{4}$
B – B	BB	$\frac{1}{2} \times \frac{2}{5} = \frac{1}{5}$
B – C	BC	$\frac{1}{2} \times \frac{1}{10} = \frac{1}{20}$
C – W	CW	$\frac{1}{3} \times \frac{1}{2} = \frac{1}{6}$
C – B	CB	$\frac{1}{3} \times \frac{2}{5} = \frac{2}{15}$
C – C	CC	$\frac{1}{3} \times \frac{1}{10} = \frac{1}{30}$

Write all the results as fractions with denominator 60 to check that the total probability is 1.

We can also show the outcomes and the probabilities in a table.

		Going		
		W $\left(\frac{1}{6}\right)$	B $\left(\frac{1}{2}\right)$	C $\left(\frac{1}{3}\right)$
Coming home	W $\left(\frac{1}{2}\right)$	WW $\frac{1}{6} \times \frac{1}{2}$	BW $\frac{1}{2} \times \frac{1}{2}$	CW $\frac{1}{3} \times \frac{1}{2}$
	B $\left(\frac{2}{5}\right)$	WB $\frac{1}{6} \times \frac{2}{5}$	BB $\frac{1}{2} \times \frac{2}{5}$	CB $\frac{1}{3} \times \frac{2}{5}$
	C $\left(\frac{1}{10}\right)$	WC $\frac{1}{6} \times \frac{1}{10}$	BC $\frac{1}{2} \times \frac{1}{10}$	CC $\frac{1}{3} \times \frac{1}{10}$

What is the probability of Emily walking either to or from school, or both ways ?
Look at all the results in the diagram or table which include W. These are mutually exclusive events and must be added.

P(walks at least one way) = P(WW) + P(WB) + P(WC) + P(BW) + P(CW)

$$= \tfrac{1}{12} + \tfrac{1}{15} + \tfrac{1}{60} + \tfrac{1}{4} + \tfrac{1}{6}$$

$$= \frac{5 + 4 + 1 + 15 + 10}{60}$$

$$= \tfrac{35}{60} = \tfrac{7}{12}$$

What is the probability of Emily using transport both ways ?

This can be found in a similar way.
However, either Emily walks at least one way **or** she uses transport both ways.
So you can find this answer by subtraction.

P(using transport both ways) = 1 − P(walks at least one way)

$$= 1 - \tfrac{7}{12} = \tfrac{5}{12}$$

2   The outcomes when 3 coins are tossed

1st coin	2nd coin	3rd coin	Outcome	Probability
		$\frac{1}{2}$ H	HHH	$\frac{1}{2} \times \frac{1}{2} \times \frac{1}{2} = \frac{1}{8}$
	$\frac{1}{2}$ H			
		$\frac{1}{2}$ T	HHT	$\frac{1}{8}$
H	$\frac{1}{2}$ T	$\frac{1}{2}$ H	HTH	$\frac{1}{8}$
$\frac{1}{2}$				
		$\frac{1}{2}$ T	HTT	$\frac{1}{8}$
		$\frac{1}{2}$ H	THH	$\frac{1}{8}$
$\frac{1}{2}$	$\frac{1}{2}$ H			
T		$\frac{1}{2}$ T	THT	$\frac{1}{8}$
	$\frac{1}{2}$ T	$\frac{1}{2}$ H	TTH	$\frac{1}{8}$
		$\frac{1}{2}$ T	TTT	$\frac{1}{8}$

Since there are 3 events, we cannot show the outcomes in a table, but we can show them in a list.

HHH
HHT
HTH
HTT
THH
THT
TTH
TTT

$P(3 \text{ heads}) = \frac{1}{8}$

$P(2 \text{ heads and 1 tail}) = \frac{1}{8} + \frac{1}{8} + \frac{1}{8} = \frac{3}{8}$

$P(1 \text{ head and 2 tails}) = \frac{3}{8}$

$P(3 \text{ tails}) = \frac{1}{8}$

(The probability of 2 heads and 1 tail involves the 3 possible orders, either HHT, HTH or THH, each with probability $\frac{1}{8}$. These are mutually exclusive events and their probabilities are added.)

Exercise 21.3

1.   A bag contains 8 blue marbles and 2 red ones. A marble is taken out at random, replaced, and then another marble is taken out.
Copy and complete the tree-diagram.

What is the probability of getting
1   2 red marbles,
2   1 marble of each colour,
3   2 blue marbles ?

1st marble   **2nd marble**   **Outcome**   **Probability**

R
R
B

R
B
B

2.   A coin and a die are tossed together. What is the probability of getting
1   a head on the coin and a one on the die,
2   a head on the coin or a one on the die (or both) ?

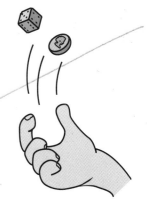

3.   In a large batch of seed, 80% of the plants which can be grown from it will have red flowers and the rest will have pink flowers.
Using a tree-diagram or otherwise, find the probability that two plants grown from this batch of seed will have flowers of the same colour.

4.   A die is thrown 3 times. Draw a tree-diagram showing 'six' or 'not six' and find the probabilities that there will be
   1   no sixes,
   2   1 six only,
   3   2 sixes,
   4   3 sixes.

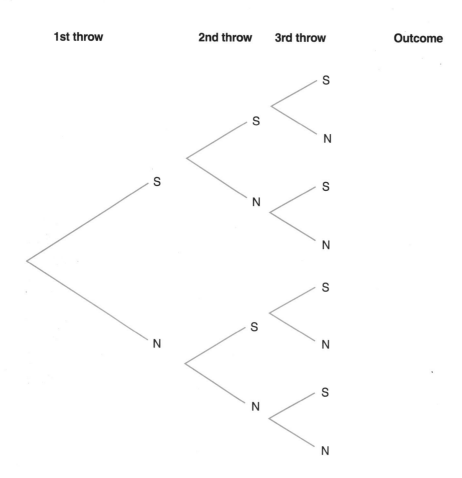

| **1st throw** | **2nd throw** | **3rd throw** | **Outcome** | **Probability** |

5.   Tom has 3 goes on an amusement machine. At each go, the probability of him winning a prize is $\frac{1}{4}$.
   What is the probability of him winning
   1   no prizes,
   2   1 prize,
   3   2 prizes,
   4   3 prizes ?

Exercise 21.4 Applications

1. There are a number of red, white and blue beads in a bag. The probability of picking a
    red bead is $\frac{1}{3}$ and the probability of picking a blue bead is $\frac{1}{5}$.
    1 What is the probability of picking a bead which is red or blue ?'
    2 What is the probability of picking a white bead ?

2. Seeds are planted with 5 in each pot. The probabilities of 0, 1, 2, 3, 4 or 5 seeds in a
    pot germinating are as follows:

Number of seeds germinating	0	1	2	3	4	5
Probability	0.002	0.008	0.02	0.14	0.39	0.44

What is the probability of having a pot in which
1 less than 2 seeds germinate,
2 at least 1 seed germinates,
3 4 or 5 seeds germinate ?

3. At a certain set of traffic lights,
    the probability of the lights showing red = 0.3,
    the probability of the lights showing red and amber = 0.04,
    the probability of the lights showing green = 0.6,
    the probability of the lights showing amber = x.

    1 What is the value of x ?
    2 A motorist passes through the junction every day.
        Unless the lights are showing green he has to stop.
        What is the probability that he has to stop ?
    3 A pedestrian crosses the road at the junction every day. He can
        cross safely when the lights are showing red. Unless the lights are
        showing red, he has to wait.
        What is the probability that he has to wait ?

4. In a batch of components the probabilities of the number of faults per component are as
    follows:

    P(0 faults) = 0.8,

    P(1 fault) = 0.12,

    P(2 faults) = 0.06.

    The other components have more than 2 faults.

    What is the probability that a component picked at random has
    1 1 or 2 faults,
    2 more than 2 faults,
    3 at least 1 fault ?

5. A tin contains 2 red, 1 orange and 4 yellow counters, and another tin contains 1 green, 2 blue and 3 violet counters.
    If two counters are taken at random, one from each tin, what is the probability that they are
    1   red and violet,
    2   orange and green ?

6. The probability that Gavin wins the 100 m race is $\frac{2}{5}$. The probability that Frank wins the 400 m race is $\frac{4}{15}$.
    What is the probability that
    1   both of them win their races,
    2   neither of them wins his race ?

7. Two cards are drawn, one from each of two packs.
    What is the probability that they are
    1   a club from the 1st pack and a diamond from the 2nd pack,
    2   a red ace from the 1st pack and a black ace from the 2nd pack,
    3   an even numbered card from the 1st pack and a picture card, Jack, Queen or King, from the 2nd pack ?

8. When Fiona goes to buy a certain gift, the chances of finding it in three different shops are, independently, $\frac{1}{3}$, $\frac{1}{4}$ and $\frac{1}{5}$ respectively. What is the chance of Fiona being able to buy the gift ?

9. Two dice are thrown together. Draw up a sample space showing the total scores.
    1   List in a table the probability of scoring each total from 2 to 12.
    2   What is the most likely total score ?
    3   What is the chance of getting this score three times in successive throws ?

10. If 5% of a large batch of light bulbs manufactured by a certain firm are defective, and a sample of 4 bulbs is chosen from the batch at random, what is the probability that
    1   there will be no defective bulbs in the sample,
    2   there will be at least one defective bulb ?

11. Susan travels to school by bus, and the probability that the bus will be late on any

   morning is $\frac{1}{5}$.

   Copy and complete the tree-diagram and find the probability that
   1   the bus is late on both Monday and Tuesday,
   2   the bus is late on just one of the two mornings.

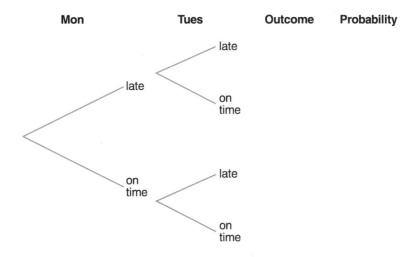

12. There is a bag containing a large number of marbles, of which 25% are red and the rest
   are white.
   Using a tree-diagram, find the probability that if two marbles are taken at random from
   the bag,
   1   both will be red,
   2   both will be white,
   3   there will be one of each colour.

13. The probability of a marksman hitting a target is 0.7.
   1   What is the probability of him missing the target ?

   Show the results of 3 shots (hit or miss) on a tree-diagram,
   and, assuming that the results are independent, find the
   probability that, out of 3 shots,
   2   the marksman hits the target each time,
   3   the marksman hits the target twice,
   4   the marksman hits the target at least twice.

14. A circuit includes three valves. The probabilities, which are independent, of the valves
   being defective are 0.1, 0.2 and 0.25, respectively.
   Find the probability that
   1   all three valves work properly,
   2   two valves work properly and one does not.

15. Some parachute jumpers are landing on the target shown.

1	2	3	4	3	2	1
2	5	6	7	6	5	2
3	6	8	9	8	6	3
4	7	9	10	9	7	4
3	6	8	9	8	6	3
2	5	6	7	6	5	2
1	2	3	4	3	2	1

There is an equal probability of them landing on any of the small squares.
They never fail to land somewhere within the target.
Points, ranging from 1 to 10, are scored for landing on different squares. These points are shown in the diagram.

What is the probability of a parachutist scoring
1   10 points,
2   8 or 9 points,
3   5 or more points,
4   3 or less points ?

Two parachutists jump in turn.
What is the probability that
5   they both score 10,
6   the total of their two scores is 19 or 20,
7   the total of their two scores is 4 ?

Practice test 21

1.   Raffle tickets are sold from books of three different colours, blue, green and pink. The probability that the winning ticket is blue is $\frac{1}{3}$ and the probability that the winning ticket is green is $\frac{2}{5}$. What is the probability that the winning ticket is pink ?

2.   When 6 coins are tossed, the probabilities of different numbers of heads and tails are as follows:

P(6 heads) $= \frac{1}{64}$

P(5 heads, 1 tail) $= \frac{6}{64}$

P(4 heads, 2 tails) $= \frac{15}{64}$

P(3 heads, 3 tails) $= \frac{20}{64}$

P(2 heads, 4 tails) $= \frac{15}{64}$

P(1 head, 5 tails) $= \frac{6}{64}$

P(6 tails) $= \frac{1}{64}$

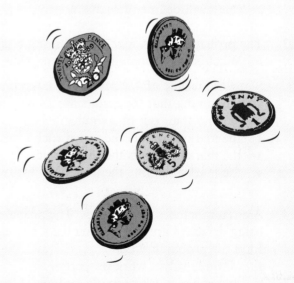

If you toss 6 coins once, what is the probability of getting
1   at least 4 heads,
2   at least 3 heads,
3   at least 1 tail ?

3. It is estimated that the probability that Rajesh will win in the 100 m race is $\frac{1}{4}$, and that he will win in the javelin event is $\frac{1}{3}$. What is the probability that he wins both events ?

4. A pack of 52 cards is split into two piles with the Kings, Queens and Jacks in the first pile and the rest of the cards in the second pile.
    1   If a card is drawn at random from the 1st pile what is the probability that it is the Queen of hearts ?
    2   If a card is drawn at random from the 2nd pile what is the probability that it is an ace ?
    3   If you take one card from each pile what is the probability that you get the Queen of hearts and an ace ?

5. Box A contains 2 green discs and 1 red disc. Box B contains 3 green discs and 2 red discs. Two discs are drawn out at random, one from each box. Copy and complete the tree-diagram to show the probabilities of each colour.
    What is the probability of getting
    1   2 green discs,
    2   1 disc of each colour,
    3   2 red discs ?

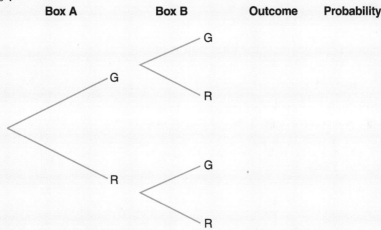

Box A   **Box B**   **Outcome**   **Probability**

6. On the way to work Mrs Cole passes through three sets of traffic lights.
    The probability that the first set is green when she gets to them is $\frac{2}{3}$, the probability that the second set is green is $\frac{3}{4}$ and the probability that the third set is green is $\frac{1}{2}$. Show the probabilities (for green or not green) on a tree-diagram.

    What is the probability that
    1   she finds all three sets of lights green as she gets to them,
    2   she has to stop at at least two of the three sets of lights ?

22 Algebraic expressions and formulae

The topics in this chapter include:

- multiplying out two brackets,
- finding common factors,
- understanding the relationship between powers and roots,
- transforming and using formulae,
- understanding direct and inverse proportions.

Expanding brackets

The diagram shows the geometrical illustration of $(x+6)^2$.

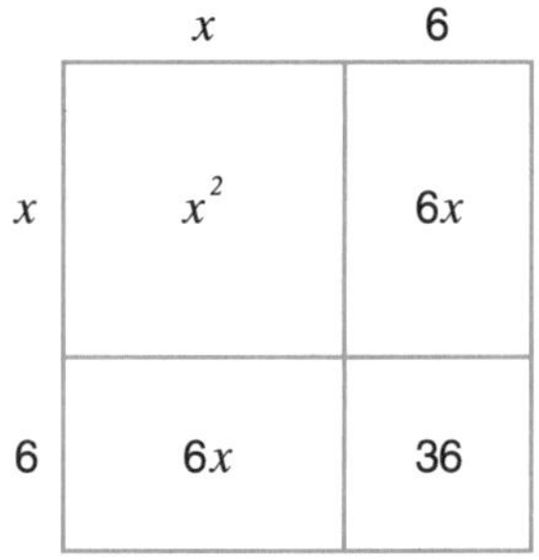

Total area $= (x+6) \times (x+6) = (x+6)^2$

4 separate areas $= x^2 + 6x + 6x + 36$
$$= x^2 + 12x + 36$$

So $(x+6)^2 = x^2 + 12x + 36$.

	x	6
x	x^2	$6x$
6	$6x$	36

Examples

1 $(x+8)(x-10) = x(x-10) + 8(x-10)$

$$= x^2 - 10x + 8x - 80$$

$$= x^2 - 2x - 80$$

You can work this out more quickly in this way.

$(x+8)(x-10)$ Multiply x by x. Answer x^2. Write this down.
Multiply $+8$ by -10. Answer -80. Write this down, leaving a space between x^2 and -80 for two more terms.

$(x+8)(x-10)$ Multiply x by -10. Answer $-10x$.
Multiply $+8$ by x. Answer $+8x$.

The answer so far is $x^2 - 10x + 8x - 80$
$$= x^2 - 2x - 80$$

2 $(2x - 1)(x - 3) = 2x^2 - 6x - x + 3$

$$= 2x^2 - 7x + 3$$

3 $(x - 3y)(3x + y) = 3x^2 + xy - 9xy - 3y^2$

$$= 3x^2 - 8xy - 3y^2$$

4 $(3x + 2)^2 = (3x + 2)(3x + 2)$

$$= 9x^2 + 6x + 6x + 4$$

$$= 9x^2 + 12x + 4$$

Exercise 22.1

1.   Draw diagrams to show the following geometrically.

   1 $(x + 4)(x + 6) = x^2 + 10x + 24$
   2 $x(x + y) = x^2 + xy$
   3 $(x + 1)(x + 2) = x^2 + 3x + 2$
   4 $(x + 5)^2 = x^2 + 10x + 25$
   5 $3(x + 4) = 3x + 12$

2.   Expand the following

   1 $(x + 6)(x + 1)$ **11** $(3x + 4y)(x - 6y)$
   2 $(x - 7)(x - 3)$ **12** $(2x + 5y)(x - y)$
   3 $(x + 5)(x - 3)$ **13** $(3x + y)^2$
   4 $(x + 4)^2$ **14** $(2x - 3y)(2x + 7y)$
   5 $(x + 1)(2x + 5)$ **15** $(4x - 3y)(x + y)$
   6 $(3x - 5)(2x + 1)$ **16** $(3x + 2)^2$
   7 $(2x - 3)(x - 1)$ **17** $(4x - 3)(4x + 3)$
   8 $(2x + y)(2x - y)$ **18** $(2x - y)^2$
   9 $(15 - x)(4 + x)$ **19** $(x + 4y)(x - 4y)$
   10 $(x - y)^2$ **20** $(3x + 2y)(3x - y)$

3.   Remove the brackets and simplify the expression $(2x + 1)^2 - (x + 5)(x - 3)$.

Common factors

Examples

1 Factorise $6xy + 9xz$.

This is the opposite process to removing brackets.
The two terms have a common factor 3 and a common factor x.
Dividing $6xy$ by $3x$ gives $2y$.
Dividing $9xz$ by $3x$ gives $3z$.
So $6xy + 9xz = 3x(2y + 3z)$
This is the expression expressed in its factors.
It has factors 3, x and $(2y + 3z)$.

You can check that you have the correct factors by multiplying out the bracket.

2 Factorise $x^2 - x$.

The common factor is x.
$x^2 - x = x(x - 1)$

3 Factorise $6x^3 - 8x^2$.

$6x^3 - 8x^2 = 2x^2(3x - 4)$

4 $6x^3 + 4x^2 + 2x = 2x(3x^2 + 2x + 1)$
All terms divide by 2 and by x, so $2x$ is a common factor.

5 Use factors to find the value of $(2.1 \times 6.9) + (2.1 \times 3.1)$.

2.1 is a common factor.
$(2.1 \times 6.9) + (2.1 \times 3.1) = 2.1 \times (6.9 + 3.1)$
$$= 2.1 \times 10 = 21$$

Exercise 22.2

1. Factorise

1	$10x - 15y$	**11**	$a^2 + a^3$
2	$3xy - 12yz$	**12**	$a^2 + 2ab - ac$
3	$4\pi a - 4\pi b$	**13**	$49 + 7x^3$
4	$20abc + 10a - 5b + 25c$	**14**	$2\pi r^2 + 2\pi rh$
5	$14x^2y + 21xy^2$	**15**	$x^2y - xy^2$
6	$3a + 6b + 12c$	**16**	$6c^2 - 4d^2$
7	$4x^2 + 3x$	**17**	$5e^2 - 10ef + 15eg$
8	$a^3 + a^2b$	**18**	$4a^2x + 8ax^2$
9	$y^2 - 6y$	**19**	$21x^3 - 14x^2$
10	$2x^3 + xy^2$	**20**	$t^2 + 3t^2 + t$

2. Factorise, and hence find the values of the following without using your calculator.

 1 $(24.3 \times 12.1) - (24.3 \times 11.1)$
 2 $(8.67 \times 16.9) + (1.33 \times 16.9)$
 3 $97^2 + (3 \times 97)$
 4 $(2 \times 3.142 \times 12.1) - (2 \times 3.142 \times 7.1)$
 5 $68^2 - (24 \times 68) + (56 \times 68)$

3. Factorise the expression $\pi r l + \pi r^2 + 2\pi r h$ and find its value, without using your calculator, when $l = 17$, $r = 5$ and $h = 9$, taking π as 3.14.

4. If n is a positive odd integer, write down in terms of n the next four consecutive odd integers. Find an expression for the sum of these 5 numbers.
Factorise the expression, and show that it is divisible by 5 but not divisible by 10.

Powers and roots

If $x^2 = a$ (where a is a positive number).
Take the square root of both sides.

$$x = \sqrt{a}$$

There is also a negative solution, $x = -\sqrt{a}$
The complete solution can be written $x = \pm \sqrt{a}$
This means x equals plus $\sqrt{a}$ or minus $\sqrt{a}$

Examples

1   If $x^2 = 36$

$\qquad x = \sqrt{36} = 6$ or $x = -\sqrt{36} = -6$

$\qquad x = \pm 6$

2   If $x^2 = 12$

$\qquad x = \sqrt{12}$ or $-\sqrt{12}$

$\qquad x = \pm 3.46$, correct to 2 dec pl.

If $x^3 = b$

Take the cube root of both sides.

$x = \sqrt[3]{b}$

3   If $x^3 = 125$

$\qquad x = \sqrt[3]{125} = 5$

(There is no negative solution.)

4   If $x^3 = 60$

$\qquad x = \sqrt[3]{60}$

$\qquad x = 3.91$, correct to 2 dec pl.

If $\sqrt{x} = c$

Square both sides.

$x = c^2$

If $\sqrt[3]{x} = d$

Cube both sides.

$x = d^3$

5   If $\sqrt{x} = 8$

     $x = 64$

6   If $\sqrt[3]{x} = 10$

     $x = 1000$

Transformation of formulae

Examples

7   If $ax + b = c$, find x in terms of a, b, c.

$ax + b = c$ Subtract b from both sides.
$ax = c - b$ Divide both sides by a.

$x = \dfrac{c - b}{a}$

8   If $y = \dfrac{x^2}{2}$, find x in terms of y, if x is a positive number.

$y = \dfrac{x^2}{2}$ Multiply both sides by 2.

$2y = x^2$

$x^2 = 2y$ Take the square root of both sides.

$x = \sqrt{2y}$

9   If $I = \dfrac{PRT}{100}$, find R in terms of the other letters.

$I = \dfrac{PRT}{100}$ Multiply both sides by 100.

$100I = PRT$ Divide both sides by PT.

$R = \dfrac{100I}{PT}$

10 If $a\sqrt{x} - b = c$, find x in terms of the other letters.

$a\sqrt{x} - b = c$ Add b to both sides.

$\quad a\sqrt{x} = c + b$ Divide both sides by a.

$\quad\quad \sqrt{x} = \dfrac{c + b}{a}$ Square both sides.

$\quad\quad\quad x = \dfrac{(c + b)^2}{a^2}$ $\left(\text{Note that } x \text{ does not equal } \dfrac{c^2 + b^2}{a^2}\right)$

11 If $F = \frac{9}{5}C + 32$, find C in terms of F.

$F = \frac{9}{5}C + 32$ Take 32 from both sides.

$\quad F - 32 = \frac{9}{5}C$ Multiply both sides by 5.

$5(F - 32) = 9C$ Divide both sides by 9.

$\frac{5}{9}(F - 32) = C$

i.e. $C = \frac{5}{9}(F - 32)$

Using formulae

Examples

12 If $S = 4\pi r^2$ and $S = 80$, what is the value of r (which is a positive number) ?

Either transform the formula.   **Or** use the formula directly.

$r^2 = \dfrac{S}{4\pi}$ $S = 4\pi r^2$

$r = \sqrt{\dfrac{S}{4\pi}}$ $80 = 4\pi r^2$

                                              $20 = \pi r^2$

When $S = 80$, $r = \sqrt{\dfrac{80}{4\pi}} = 2.523\ldots$ $r^2 = \dfrac{20}{\pi}$

                    $= 2.52$, to 3 sig. fig. $r = \sqrt{\dfrac{20}{\pi}} = 2.523\ldots$

Using your calculator, $= 2.52$, to 3 sig. fig.

press 80 $\boxed{\div}$ 4 $\boxed{\div}$ $\boxed{\pi}$ $\boxed{=}$ $\boxed{\sqrt{}}$

13   If $T = 2\sqrt{l}$ and $T = 6$, what is the value of l ?

Either transform the formula.   **Or** use the formula directly.

$T = 2\sqrt{l}$ $T = 2\sqrt{l}$

$T^2 = 4l$ $6 = 2\sqrt{l}$

$l = \dfrac{T^2}{4}$ $3 = \sqrt{l}$

When $T = 6$, $l = \dfrac{6^2}{4} = \dfrac{36}{4} = 9$ $l = 9$

Exercise 22.3

1.   Solve the equations. If the solutions are not exact, give them correct to 2 decimal places.

  1 $x^2 = 144$ **6** $x^2 = 3.61$
  2 $x^3 = 343$ **7** $\sqrt[3]{x} = 1.3$
  3 $x^2 = 0.06$ **8** $x^3 = 1.04$
  4 $\sqrt{x} = 7$ **9** $\sqrt{x} = 0.9$
  5 $\sqrt[3]{x} = 6$ **10** $x^2 = 10$

2.   **1**   If $ax - b = c$, find x in terms of a, b, c.
     2   If $E = 3v^2$, find v in terms of E, if v is a positive number.
     3   If $v = u + at$, find t in terms of u, v, a.
     4   If $s = 5t^2$, find t in terms of s, if t is a positive number.
     5   If $area = length \times breadth$, find $length$ in terms of $area$ and $breadth$.
     6   If $A = P + RP$, find R in terms of A and P.
     7   If $t = 180n - 360$, find n in terms of t.
     8   If $speed = \dfrac{distance}{time}$, find $distance$ in terms of $speed$ and $time$.
     9   If $3y = 2x - 4$, find x in terms of y.
     10   If $P = \dfrac{V^2}{R}$, find V in terms of P and R, if V is a positive number.

3.   If $S = 2\pi rh$ and $V = \pi r^2 h$,
     1   express h in terms of S, r and π,
     2   express h in terms of V, r and π,
     3   write down an equation not involving h,
     4   hence express V in terms of S and r.

4.   If $3a = \sqrt{x+2}$,
     1   find x in terms of a,
     2   find the value of x when $a = 2$.
     3   Repeat the question if $3a = \sqrt{x} + 2$.

5.   If $T = 2\pi\sqrt{\dfrac{l}{g}}$,
     1   find l in terms of T, g and π,
     2   find the value of l when $T = 2$ and $g = 10$.

Variation

In Chapter 5, questions involving proportion were worked out using arithmetical methods.
Quantities which are in proportion can be linked by equations.

Direct Variation

If y is directly proportional to x, i.e. y varies directly as x,
then $y = kx$, where k is a positive constant number.

The word 'directly' need not be included as it is assumed that the variation is direct variation if
the word 'inverse' is not included.

The square law

If y varies as the square of x, then $y = kx^2$.

The cube law

If y varies as the cube of x, then $y = kx^3$.

If we know some corresponding values of x and y, we can find the value of k.

Example

1   If y varies as the cube of x, and $y = 40$ when $x = 2$, find the equation connecting x and y,
    and find the value of y when $x = 3$.

$$y = kx^3$$

When $x = 2$, $y = 40$ so $40 = k \times 2^3$
$$40 = 8k$$
$$k = 5$$

The equation is $y = 5x^3$.
When $x = 3$, $y = 5 \times 3^3 = 135$.

Inverse Variation

If y is inversely proportional to x, i.e. y varies inversely as x, then $y = \dfrac{k}{x}$.

The inverse square law

If y varies inversely as the square of x, then $y = \dfrac{k}{x^2}$.

Example

2   If y varies inversely as the square of x, and $y = 5$ when $x = 3$, find the equation connecting x and y, and find the value of y when $x = 6$.

$$y = \frac{k}{x^2}$$

When $x = 3$, $y = 5$ so $5 = \dfrac{k}{3^2}$

$$5 = \frac{k}{9}$$

$$k = 45$$

The equation is $y = \dfrac{45}{x^2}$.

When $x = 6$, $y = \dfrac{45}{6^2} = 1\tfrac{1}{4}$.

Exercise 22.4

1.   If y varies directly as x and $y = \tfrac{1}{2}$ when $x = 5$, find y when $x = 20$.

2.   If y varies as the square of x and $y = 4$ when $x = 4$, find the equation connecting y with x and find the value of y when $x = 5$.

3.   If y varies inversely as x and $y = 15$ when $x = 3$, find the value of y when $x = 5$.

4.   If y varies inversely as the square of x and $y = 18$ when $x = 2$, find the value of y when $x = 3$.

5.   If y varies as the cube of x and $y = 1000$ when $x = 5$, find the equation connecting y with x. What is the value of y when $x = 10$?

6. If y is inversely proportional to x and $y = \frac{1}{2}$ when $x = 3$, what is the value of y when $x = 6$?

7. A variable A is proportional to r^2. If $A = 20$ when $r = 2$, find the value of A when $r = 5$.

8. If w is directly proportional to d and $w = 24$ when $d = 6$, find the value of w when $d = 7$.

9. If y varies inversely as the square root of x, and $y = 12$ when $x = 56.25$, find the equation connecting y with x, and find the value of y when $x = 64$.

10. The weights of a set of similar articles are proportional to the cubes of their heights. One article is 15 cm high and weighs 10.8 kg. Find the height of the article which weighs 400 g.

11. The areas of two similar windows are proportional to the squares of corresponding heights. If the smaller one has height 1.2 m and area 3.6 m^2, what is the area of the larger one, which has height 1.6 m ?

Exercise 22.5 Applications

1. Expand the following.

1	$(x + 5)(x + 1)$	**6**	$(3x + 4)(2x - 3)$
2	$(x - 6)(x - 2)$	**7**	$(2x - 5)^2$
3	$(x + 4)(x - 4)$	**8**	$(x + y)(x - y)$
4	$(x + 3)^2$	**9**	$(x - 5y)(x + 3y)$
5	$(3x + 2)(x + 7)$	**10**	$(2x - 3y)(2x + 5y)$

2. The diagram represents a square $ABCD$ of side $(x + 4)$ cm.

1 What is the area of $ABCD$?
2 What is the total area of the 4 triangles ?
3 Find the area of the square $PQRS$ by subtraction. Simplify your answer and verify that the answer is the same as that found by using Pythagoras' theorem.

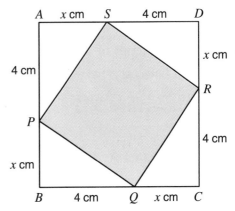

3. Write down an equation connecting the
   lengths of the sides of this right-angled triangle.
   Simplify the equation and solve it, to find x.
   What is the numerical value of the area of
   the triangle ?

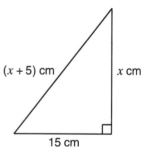

$(x+5)$ cm x cm

15 cm

4. Start with any number between 1 and 10, double it, from the result subtract 20, then
   multiply by 3 and add 6.
   Next divide by 6, subtract 1 and square the result.
   Subtract 100, divide by the number you started with, and then add 20. Subtract the
   number you started with. What is your answer ?

   Repeat the question beginning with the number n, checking that your previous answer is
   correct.

5. Factorise the following:

1	$14x - 21y$	**5**	$15x^2 - 25x$	**8**	$9 + 3x^3$
2	$3xy + 9yz$	**6**	$t^2 + t$	**9**	$2x^2 + 2xy$
3	$2\pi a - 2\pi b$	**7**	$a^2 + ab - 2ac$	**10**	$4b - 2$
4	$6a - 3b + 9c$				

6. Use factors to find the value of

   1 $(3.5 \times 1.3) + (3.5 \times 8.7)$
   2 $(96 \times 2.04) + (4 \times 2.04)$
   3 $(12.9 \times 3.1) - (2.9 \times 3.1)$
   4 $(15.3 \times 5.6) - (15.3 \times 4.6)$
   5 $3.7^2 + (3.7 \times 6.3)$

7. Factorise $n^2 + n$ and explain why the value of this expression is always even, if n is any
   positive integer.

8. Find x in terms of the other letters.

   1 $a(x + b) = c$
   2 $a^2 = b^2 + x^2$, where $a > b$ and x is positive.
   3 $5 = \dfrac{2x}{x - a}$
   4 $b = 2\sqrt{x} + 5$

9. If $V = \frac{1}{6}x^2 h$,   **1** find the value of h when $V = 50$ and $x = 4$,   **2** find x in terms of V
   and h, where x is positive.

10. If $\dfrac{a}{b} = \dfrac{b}{c}$, where a, b and c are positive, find   **1** c in terms of a and b,

    2 b in terms of a and c.

11.

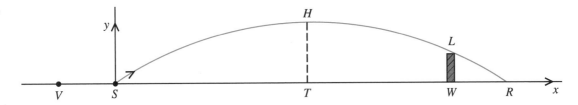

The path of the jet of water from the sprinkler at S describes a parabola with equation $y = 0.6x - 0.01x^2$, where x metres is the horizontal distance travelled and y metres is the height of the water.

1   Show that the water reaches a distance of 60 m along the ground (i.e. $SR = 60$ m), by substituting $x = 60$ in the equation and finding y.

2   The water reaches its greatest height when it has travelled horizontally for half its greatest distance. By substituting $x = 30$ in the equation, find the greatest height (TH).

3   The water just clears the wall WL, which is 2.5 m high. Substitute $y = 2.5$ in the equation, and show that this can be rearranged as $x^2 - 60x + 250 = 0$.
It is known that the wall is over 50 m distant from the sprinkler. Find this distance to the nearest metre, using trial and improvement methods.

4   The sprinkler is moved away from the wall to a point V, so that the water just reaches the foot of the wall at W. What is the distance that the sprinkler should be moved ?

12. The weight of liquid contained in a cylindrical tin of fixed radius varies as the height of the tin. When the height was 20 cm the liquid weighed 8 kg. Find the weight of similar liquid in a tin of the same radius with height 15 cm.

13. The time taken to travel a given distance varies inversely as the average speed. When the average speed is 25 miles/hour the time taken is 3 hours. What is the time taken when the average speed is 30 miles/hour ?

14. The electrical resistance, R ohms, of two connected wires of lengths a cm and b cm varies directly as $\dfrac{ab}{a + b}$. When the length of each wire is 50 cm the resistance is 4 ohms.
Find the resistance when the two wires are 25 cm and 75 cm long.

15. The load which can just be carried by a metal girder of a certain type varies inversely as its length. A load of 10 tonnes can just be carried by a girder 2 m long. What load can just be carried by a girder of the same type which is 1.6 m long ?

Practice test 22

1.　Expand the brackets.

　1　$(x+4)(x+2)$　　　　　　　　　**4**　$(x+10y)(x-10y)$
　2　$(x+7)^2$　　　　　　　　　　　**5**　$(5x+8)(x-6)$
　3　$(3x-2)(2x-3)$

　Give geometrical illustrations for parts **1** and **2**.

2.　If a square of side $(x+2)$ cm has the same area as a rectangle with length $(x+8)$ cm and breadth $(x-2)$ cm, write down an equation, simplify it, and solve it to find the value of x.
　What are the measurements of the square and the rectangle ?

3.　Factorise the following:

　1　$5x+15y$　　　　　　　　　　　**4**　$6x^3+12$
　2　$3x^2-6x$　　　　　　　　　　　**5**　x^3+xy
　3　$4ab-12bc$

4.　**1**　If $a=180n+360$, find n in terms of a.
　2　If $s=a+ar$, find r in terms of s and a.
　3　If $b=2\sqrt{x}$, find x in terms of b.
　4　If $C=\frac{5}{9}(F-32)$, find F in terms of C.

　5　If $s=\frac{n}{2}(a+l)$, find n in terms of s, a and l.

5.　If $A=P\left(1+\dfrac{R}{100}\right)$

　1　find R in terms of A and P,
　2　find the value of R when $A=172$ and $P=160$.

6.　If y is inversely proportional to the square of x and $x=3$ when $y=4$, find the equation connecting y with x, and find the value of y when $x=4$.

7.　The weight W kg of a bar varies directly as ld^2, where l cm is its length and d cm its diameter. If $W=4.9$ when $d=3.5$ and $l=50$, find the equation for W in terms of l and d. Hence find the weight of a bar of this type of length 42 cm and diameter 5 cm.

PUZZLES

56. How many mathematical words can you find reading horizontally, vertically or diagonally, in both directions ?

P	Y	R	O	T	C	E	V	R	H
E	E	S	H	A	R	E	A	P	Y
Q	M	R	T	N	A	F	A	Y	P
U	N	E	C	G	O	R	N	R	O
A	O	T	A	E	G	A	G	A	T
T	G	E	M	N	N	C	L	M	E
I	Y	M	E	T	I	T	E	I	N
O	L	A	X	I	S	I	A	D	U
N	O	I	T	A	R	O	C	G	S
E	P	D	O	H	E	N	O	C	E

57. A ship in the harbour has a ladder with 12 rungs, each 30 cm apart, hanging over the side. At low tide 4 rungs are covered by the sea. If the tide rises at 40 cm per hour, how many rungs will be covered 3 hours later ?

58. There are three married couples having dinner together.
George is older than Michelle's husband.
Frank's wife is older than Nadia.
Lynnette's husband is older than George.
Michelle is not Edward's wife.
The oldest man is married to the youngest woman.
The oldest woman paid the the bill. Who was this ?

59. Mary is the eldest of five children and she is responsible for bringing her brothers, Tony and James, and her sisters, Patricia and Wendy, home from school. This journey includes crossing a river by a small rowing-boat, which only holds two of them at a time, and only Mary and Tony can row this. Usually they all get across quite quickly, but one particular afternoon the children were quarrelsome and Mary did not want to leave the two boys together, or the two girls together, unless she was with them to keep them in order. She usually sent Wendy across the river first, with Tony, but on this afternoon Wendy refused to go with Tony and insisted she would only go in the boat with Mary. Then James said it was his turn to go across before Wendy did.
How did Mary get them all across the river peacefully ?

60. The ages of my father, my son and myself total 85 years. My father is just twice my age, and the units figure in his age is equal to the age of my son. How old am I ?

23 Trigonometry

The topics in this chapter include:

- using sine, cosine and tangent ratios in right-angled triangles.

There are three main relationships in a right-angled triangle.

Sine, cosine and tangent ratios

$$\sin A = \frac{\text{opp}}{\text{hyp}}$$

$$\cos A = \frac{\text{adj}}{\text{hyp}}$$

$$\tan A = \frac{\text{opp}}{\text{adj}}$$

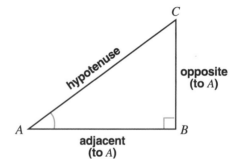

To find a side

Examples

1   To find AB.

$$\cos A = \frac{\text{adj}}{\text{hyp}}$$

$$\cos 32° = \frac{x}{8}$$

$$x = 8 \times \cos 32°$$

$$= 6.784$$

$AB = 6.78$ cm, to 3 sig. fig.

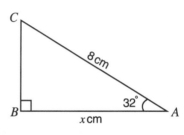

To use your calculator, make sure it is set to work in degrees, then press

8 $\boxed{\times}$ 32 $\boxed{\cos}$ $\boxed{=}$ and you will get 6.784...

(On some calculators you may have to press $\boxed{\cos}$ 32 instead of 32 $\boxed{\cos}$.)

For practical uses you would probably give the answer to the nearest mm. However, to check that you have done a correct calculation your answer may be wanted to 3 significant figures.

Make a rough check of the size of the answer. Here, it should be less than 8 cm, and 6.78 cm seems about right.

(Note that the formula $\cos A = \dfrac{\text{adj}}{\text{hyp}}$ can be rearranged as $\text{adj} = \text{hyp} \times \cos A$. This will give $x = 8 \times \cos 32°$ directly.)

2   To find AC.

Use the tangent ratio. Also use the angle opposite to AC, i.e. angle B, which is 54°.

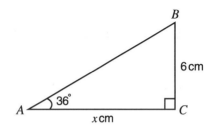

$\tan B = \dfrac{\text{opp}}{\text{adj}}$

$\tan 54° = \dfrac{x}{6}$

$\qquad x = 6 \times \tan 54°$

$\qquad\quad = 8.258$

$AC = 8.26$ cm, to 3 sig. fig.

On your calculator, make sure it is set to work in degrees then press 6 $\boxed{\times}$ 54 $\boxed{\tan}$ $\boxed{=}$

(Note that the formula $\tan B = \dfrac{\text{opp}}{\text{adj}}$ can be rearranged as $\text{opp} = \text{adj} \times \tan B$. This will give $x = 6 \times \tan 54°$ directly.)

If you prefer to use $\angle A$, the working goes like this:

$\tan A = \dfrac{\text{opp}}{\text{adj}}$

$\tan 36° = \dfrac{6}{x}$

$\qquad x = \dfrac{6}{\tan 36°}$

$\qquad\quad = 8.258$

$AC = 8.26$ cm, to 3 sig. fig.

3   To find AC.

$$\sin A = \frac{\text{opp}}{\text{hyp}}$$

$$\sin 40° = \frac{5}{x}$$

$$x = \frac{5}{\sin 40°}$$

$$= 7.779$$

$AC = 7.78$ cm, to 3 sig. fig.

On your calculator press $5 \boxed{\div} 40 \boxed{\sin} \boxed{=}$

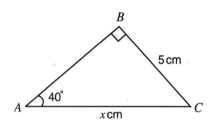

Exercise 23.1

Give all answers correct to 3 significant figures.

1.   Use the sine ratio to find the length of side AC in these triangles.

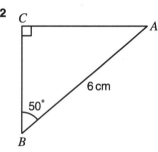
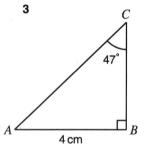

2.   Use the cosine ratio to find the length of side BC in these triangles.

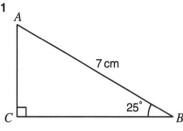
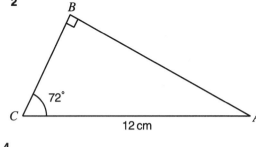

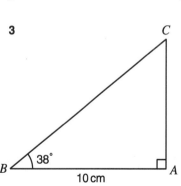
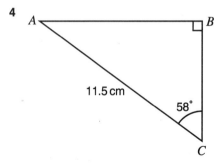

3. Use the tangent ratio to find the length of side *AC* in these triangles.

1

A

B 41° *C*

8 cm

2

B

20°

9 cm

A   *C*

3

A

5 cm

62°

C   *B*

4. Calculate the length of the side *AC* in these right-angled triangles.

1

C

B 23° *A*

6 cm

2

C   10 cm   *B*

50°

A

3

C

34°

A   *B*

4 cm

4

A

12 cm

25°

C   *B*

5

A

21°

B   *C*

8 cm

6

C

11 cm

52°

A

B

7

C

5 cm

20°

B   *A*

8

A

55°

3 cm

C

B

9

B

9 cm

30°

C   *A*

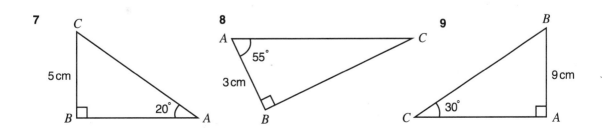

5. AC is a diameter of a circle, centre O, radius 3 cm.
    $\angle ABC = 90°$.
    Calculate the length of BC.

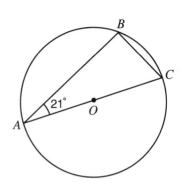

6. When a kite is flying, the string makes
    an angle of 22° with the horizontal,
    and the string is 200 m long.
    How high is the kite ?

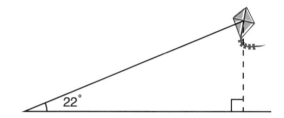

To find an angle, given two sides

If one of the sides is the hypotenuse, use the sine or cosine ratio. Otherwise use the tangent ratio.

Examples

1   To find $\angle A$.

$$\sin A = \frac{\text{opp}}{\text{hyp}}$$

$$= \frac{3}{8} \ (= 0.375)$$

$$\angle A = 22.0°$$

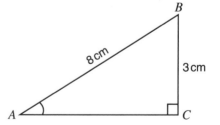

(Give the answer in degrees correct to 1 decimal place. On your calculator, make sure it
is set to work in degrees. Find the key for the inverse of the sine function. It might be
labelled $\sin^{-1}$, or arcsin. You will probably have to press the second function key and
then the sine key to get it.

Press 3 $\boxed{\div}$ 8 $\boxed{=}$ $\boxed{\text{inverse sine}}$)

You can now find $\angle B$ by subtraction.
$\angle B = 90° - 22.0° = 68.0°$

2   To find $\angle A$

$\tan A = \dfrac{\text{opp}}{\text{adj}}$

$\quad = \dfrac{5}{7} \; (= 0.7143)$

$\angle A = 35.5°$

On your calculator press $5\;\boxed{\div}\;7\;\boxed{=}\;\boxed{\text{inverse tan}}$

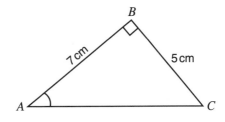

Isosceles triangles

An **isosceles triangle** can be split into two congruent right-angled triangles.

Example

3   To find BC.

$\sin \angle DAB = \dfrac{\text{opp}}{\text{hyp}}$

$\quad \sin 20° = \dfrac{x}{6}$

$\qquad\; x = 6 \times \sin 20°$

$\quad\; BC = 2x \text{ cm}$

$\qquad\;\; = 4.10 \text{ cm, to 3 sig. fig.}$

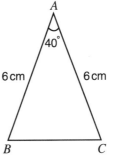
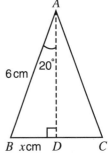

Exercise 23.2

In questions 1, 2, 3 and 5 give the angles in degrees, correct to 1 decimal place.

1.   Use the sine ratio to find the marked angle in these triangles.

1

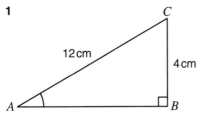

2

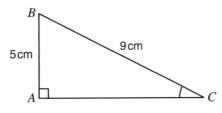

3

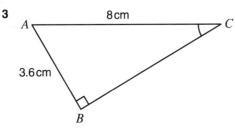

4

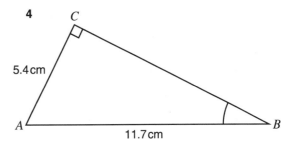

2.   Use the cosine ratio to find the marked angle in these triangles.

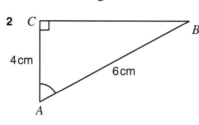

1

2

3

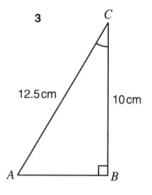

3.   Use the tangent ratio to find the marked angle in these triangles. By subtraction find the third angle of each triangle.

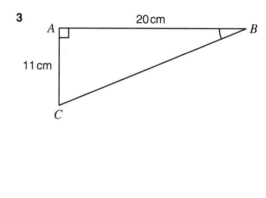

1

2

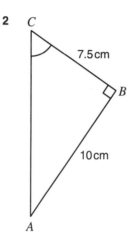

3

4.   **1** Write down, as fractions, the ratios for sin A, cos A, tan A, sin B, cos B, tan B.

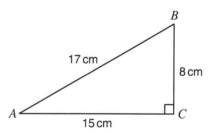

2 Calculate AB, and write down, as fractions, the ratios for sin A, cos A, tan A.

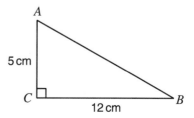

5. Calculate $\angle A$ in these right-angled triangles.

1

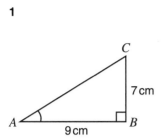

2

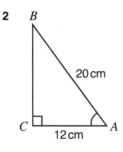

3

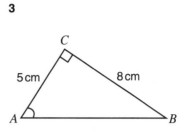

4

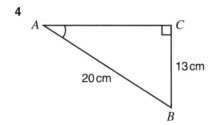

5

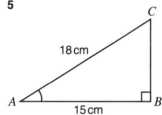

6. A ladder 6 m long is placed against a wall so that the foot of the ladder is 2.5 m from the wall. What angle does the ladder make with the ground?

7. Sketch this isosceles triangle and draw the axis of symmetry. Use the right-angled triangles formed to calculate the size of $\angle BAC$ to the nearest degree.

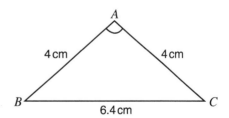

8. Triangle ABC is isosceles with $AB = AC$.
   $BC = 10$ cm.
   1 Find the height AD.
   2 Find the area of $\triangle ABC$.

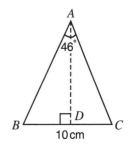

Using trig. ratios

Examples

1   A tower 30 m high stands at a point A. At a point B on the ground which is level with
the foot of the tower, the angle of elevation of the top of the tower is 28°.
Find the distance of B from A.

Let T be the top of the tower. $\angle TAB$ is a
right angle since TA is vertical and AB is
horizontal.
To find AB use $\angle BTA$, which is 62°.

$$\tan 62° = \frac{\text{opp}}{\text{adj}}$$

$$\tan 62° = \frac{x}{30}$$

$$x = 30 \times \tan 62°$$

$$= 56.42$$

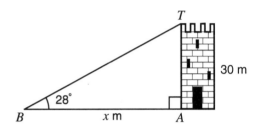

B is 56 m from the tower (to the nearest m).

2   There are three landmarks A, B and C. A is due North of B and C is due West of B.
From A the distance to B is 56 m and the distance to C is 113 m. Find the bearing of
C from A.

$\angle ABC$ is a right angle since A is North of B
and C is West of B.

$$\cos \angle CAB = \frac{\text{adj}}{\text{hyp}}$$

$$= \frac{56}{113} \ (= 0.4955\ldots)$$

$$\angle CAB = 60.29\ldots°$$

$$= 60°, \text{ to the nearest degree.}$$

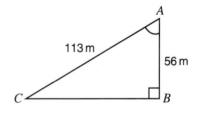

The bearing of C from A is $180° + 60° = 240°$.

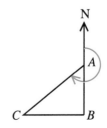

Exercise 23.3   Applications

1. The angle of elevation of the top of a church
    steeple from a point on the ground 120 m
    away is 32°.
    Find the height of the steeple.

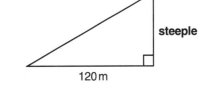

2. From a point at the top of a tower 30 m
    high, what is the angle of depression of
    a landmark on the ground 100 m away
    from the foot of the tower ?

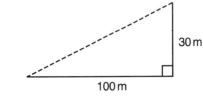

3. *ABCD* is a parallelogram.
    $BC = 10$ cm, $\angle ABC = 57°$ and
    $\angle BAC = 90°$.

    Calculate
    1   *AB*,
    2   *AC*,
    3   the area of $\triangle ABC$,
    4   the area of the parallelogram.

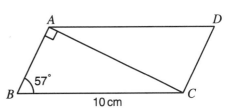

4. *P* and *Q* are places 900 m apart on a coastline running East–West.
    A ship *S* is at sea on a bearing of 341°
    from *P*, and on a bearing of 071° from *Q*.
    1   What size is $\angle QSP$?
    Find
    2   *SP*,
    3   *SQ*,
    4   the distance of *S* from the nearest point
    on the coast.

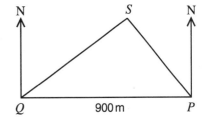

5. A surveyor who wishes to find the
    width of a river stands on one bank
    at point *X* directly opposite a tree *T*.
    He then walks 80 m along the river bank
    to a point *C*. The angle *XCT* is found
    to be 72°.
    Find the width of the river.

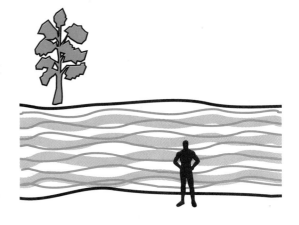

6. A plane flies due East from A to B.
   C is a town 80 km from A on a bearing
   of 038°.

   1 Find the distance of the plane from
     C when it is at D, the nearest point to C.
   2 Find the distance of the plane from C
     when it is at B, where $\angle ACB = 90°$.

   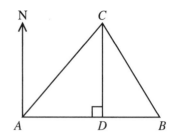

7. AB and CD are walls of two blocks
   of flats, which are 200 m apart. From
   E, the mid-point of AC, the angle of
   elevation of B is 12° and the angle of
   elevation of D is 24°.

   Find   1 AB,   2 CD.
   3 If a person is standing on the roof
      at B what is the angle of elevation
      of D ?

   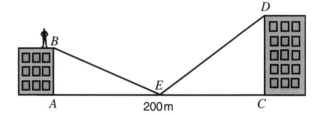

8. A man walks 10 km North-East and then 7 km South-East. How far is he from
   his starting-point, and on what bearing must he walk to go directly back to his
   starting-point ?

9. A and B are points on two mountain
   peaks. The distance between A and B
   on a map is 12 cm. The scale of the map
   is 1 : 50 000. Find the horizontal distance
   AC, in km.
   The heights of A and B are given as
   2900 m and 3650 m respectively.
   Find the angle of elevation of B from A.

   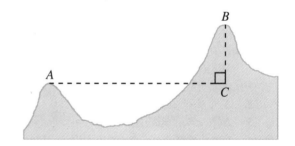

10. From the top of a tower which was 15 m tall, Jim saw
    his friend Ken at an angle of depression of 25°. Ken
    was standing on ground which was level with the foot
    of the tower. Calculate how far he was from the tower,
    to the nearest metre.
    Ken then walked on level ground in a straight line
    directly away from the tower, until he was twice as far
    from it as before. When Jim looked at him then, what
    was the new angle of depression ?

Practice test 23

1. Henry is 25 m due East from the foot of a tower, and on level ground. He measures the angle of elevation of the top of the tower as 38°. Calculate the height of the tower.

2. Find the height of △AOB, and hence find the area of △AOB.

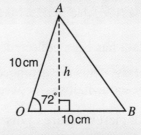

3.

A speedboat travels 8 km North and then 3 km East. On what bearing must it be steered to go directly back to the starting point ?

4. Triangle ABC is isosceles.
   1 Find the size of ∠ABC.
   2 Find the size of ∠BAC.

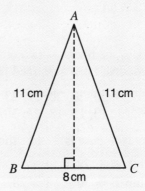

24 Cumulative frequency

The topics in this chapter include:

- constructing a cumulative frequency table,
- constructing a cumulative frequency curve, finding the median, upper quartile, lower quartile and interquartile range, and interpreting the results.

Averages and Dispersion

When statistical data has been collected, we often need to find an average measurement.

The median. When the items are arranged in order of size, the median is the value of the middle item, or the value halfway between the middle two if there is an even number of items.

The range is the simplest measure of dispersion to find.

Range = highest value − lowest value

The range only uses the extreme values so it is not always very representative.

The interquartile range is a measure of the middle half of the data, so it is more representative.

Quartiles are the quarter-way divisions in the data, found in a similar way to finding the median.

The interquartile range = upper quartile value − lower quartile value

Example

1   The numbers of members of two clubs attending meetings in different weeks are as shown. The numbers have been arranged in order of size.

Club A.   19, 20, 20, 20, 20, 22, 23, 24, 24, 28.
Club B.   8, 11, 13, 15, 18, 23, 30, 32, 34, 36.

The mean in each case is 22 but there is a much bigger dispersion in Club B.

Range in Club A = 28 − 19 = 9.
Range in Club B = 36 − 8 = 28.

In Club A.

19	20	20	20	20	22	23	24	24	28
	↓			↓			↓		
	lower quartile			median			upper quartile		
	(centre of lower half)						(centre of upper half)		

Interquartile range = 24 − 20 = 4.

Verify for yourself that the interquartile range in Club B = 19.

Cumulative Frequency

To find the median and the interquartile range of a grouped frequency distribution, it is useful to find the cumulative frequency and draw a cumulative frequency graph.

Examples

2   The frequency table shows the exam marks of 300 students. Make a cumulative frequency table and draw the cumulative frequency graph.
Find the median mark and the interquartile range of marks.

Frequency table

Mark	f
1–10	3
11–20	7
21–30	13
31–40	29
41–50	44
51–60	65
61–70	70
71–80	49
81–90	14
91–100	6
	300

Cumulative frequency table

Mark	Cum. freq.
0	0
10 or less	3
20 or less	10
30 or less	23
40 or less	52
50 or less	96
60 or less	161
70 or less	231
80 or less	280
90 or less	294
100 or less	300

← A useful beginning to the table

←i.e. 3 + 7
←i.e. 3 + 7 + 13
←i.e. 3 + 7 + 13 + 29

The points are plotted on a graph, with cumulative frequency on the vertical axis.

If the points are joined to each other by straight lines, this is called a **cumulative frequency polygon.**

If the points are joined by a smooth curve, this is called a **cumulative frequency curve** or **ogive.**

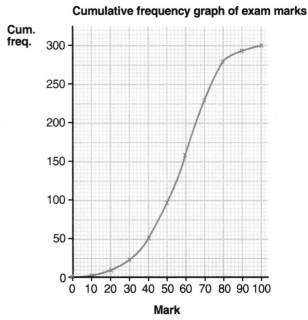

Cumulative frequency graph of exam marks

Median mark. The line to find the median mark is drawn at half the total frequency, that is at 150.

Quartiles. The line to find the lower quartile is drawn at one-quarter of the total frequency, that is at 75, and the line to find the upper quartile is drawn at three-quarters of the total frequency, that is at 225.

Sketch graphs

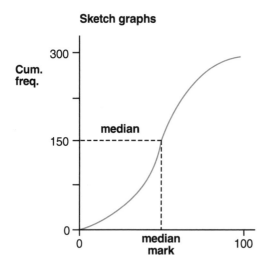

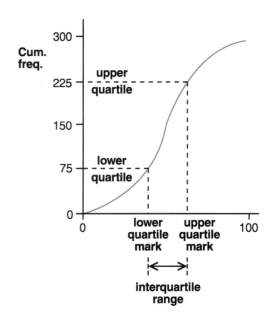

Reading from the actual graph:

The median mark is 59.
The lower quartile is 45, the upper quartile is 69.
The interquartile range = upper quartile − lower quartile = 69 − 45 = 24.

If the measurements are **continuous** then use the words 'less than x' instead of 'x or less' in the cumulative frequency table.

Example

3 The frequency table shows the lifetimes of a sample of 140 light bulbs. Make a cumulative frequency table and draw the cumulative frequency graph.
Find the median lifetime and the interquartile range of lifetimes.
Find how many bulbs last for more than 1500 hours.

Frequency table

Lifetime in hours (to the nearest 100 hours)	Frequency
800	3
900	9
1000	14
1100	23
1200	46
1300	26
1400	9
1500	6
1600	4
	140

Cumulative frequency table

Lifetime in hours	Cum. freq.
less than 750	0
less than 850	3
less than 950	12
less than 1050	26
less than 1150	49
less than 1250	95
less than 1350	121
less than 1450	130
less than 1550	136
less than 1650	140

(The 3 bulbs whose lifetimes are given as 800 hours to the nearest 100 hours have actual lifetimes between 750 and 850 hours. So there are no bulbs with lifetimes less than 750 hours and 3 bulbs with lifetimes less than 850 hours. Another 9 bulbs making 12 altogether have lifetimes less than 950 hours. All 140 bulbs have lifetimes less than 1650 hours.)

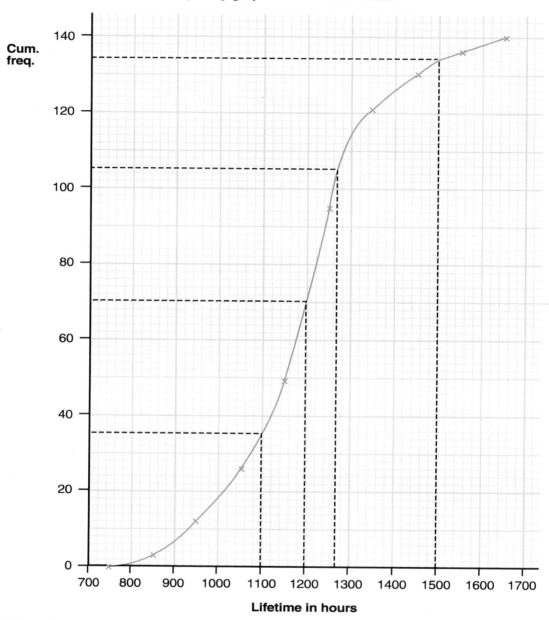

Cumulative frequency graph of lifetimes of bulbs

Using the graph, the median lifetime is found by drawing a line at 70.
The median lifetime is 1200 hours.

The quartile lifetimes are found by drawing lines at 35 and 105.
Lower quartile lifetime = 1100 hours.
Upper quartile lifetime = 1270 hours.
The interquartile range is (1270 − 1100) hours = 170 hours.

Drawing a line at 1500 hours shows that 134 bulbs last for less than 1500 hours, so 6 bulbs last longer.

Exercise 24.1

1. The distribution of examination marks of 80 students is as shown:

Marks	21–30	31–40	41–50	51–60	61–70	71–80	81–90	91–100
f	2	4	10	27	17	6	8	6

1 Use the frequency distribution to make a cumulative frequency table, which will begin like this:

Mark	Cum. freq.
20 or less	0
30 or less	2
40 or less	6
. . .	

2 Draw the cumulative frequency graph.

Find

3 the median mark,

4 the upper and lower quartile marks,

5 the interquartile range of marks.

2. The distribution of weights of 100 18 year-old boys is as follows:

Weight (kg)	30–40	40–50	50–60	60–70	70–80	80–90	90–100
f	3	10	27	33	20	6	1

1 Make a cumulative frequency table, which will begin like this:

Weight (kg)	Cum. freq.
less than 30	0
less than 40	3
less than 50	13

2 Draw the cumulative frequency graph.

Find

3 the median weight,

4 the upper and lower quartile weights,

5 the interquartile range of weights.

3.   The distribution of lengths of 60 leaves from a certain type of plant is as follows:
      (Lengths measured to the nearest mm.)

Length in mm	20–23	24–27	28–31	32–35	36–39	40–43
f	2	10	20	15	8	5

Make a cumulative frequency table, which will begin like this:

Length in mm	Cum. freq.
less than 19.5	0
less than 23.5	2
less than 27.5	12

Draw the cumulative frequency graph.
Find the median length, the upper and lower quartile lengths and the interquartile range
of lengths.

4.   The times 100 pupils take to travel to school are as follows:

Time (minutes)	0–10	10–20	20–30	30–40	40–50
Number of pupils	8	47	24	17	4

Make a cumulative frequency table for the data and draw the cumulative frequency
graph.
Find the median time taken, the upper and lower quartile times and the interquartile
range of times.

5.   A survey of distances travelled by a particular type of tyre gave these results:

Distance (in 1000 km)	f
10 to 20	6
20 to 30	20
30 to 40	40
40 to 50	54
50 to 60	45
60 to 70	15
	180

Make a cumulative frequency table for the data and draw the cumulative frequency
graph.
Find the median distance, the upper and lower quartile distances and the interquartile
range of distances.
What percentage of the tyres travelled over 55 000 km ?

Exercise 24.2   Applications

Questions 1 to 5.
Use the frequency distribution table given to make a cumulative frequency table of the data.
Draw the cumulative frequency graph.
Find the median value, the upper and lower quartile values and the interquartile range of values.

1.   The heights of 80 men.

Height in cm	168–170	171–173	174–176	177–179	180–182	183–185	186–188	189–191
Number of men	4	9	12	19	17	11	5	3

2.   The ages of 90 children in a Youth Club.

Age (in completed years)	11	12	13	14	15	16
Number of children	23	28	17	11	6	5

3.   The speeds of 200 vehicles passing along a road.

Speed (mph)	25–30	30–35	35–40	40–45	45–50	50–55	55–60
f	7	18	31	45	60	34	5

4.   The lengths of 72 pieces of cloth produced by a machine.

Length (m)	20–22	23–25	26–28	29–31	32–34	35–37
f	3	8	24	21	14	2

5.   The ages of 120 cars.

Age in years	0–2	2–4	4–6	6–8	8–10	10–12	12–14
f	19	28	30	19	13	9	2

6. 80 workers were tested on a particular piece of work and the times they took are recorded in the table.

Time in minutes	Number of workers
4.0–4.5	6
4.5–5.0	10
5.0–5.5	17
5.5–6.0	24
6.0–6.5	15
6.5–7.0	5
7.0–7.5	3

Make a cumulative frequency table for the data.
Draw the cumulative frequency graph.
Find the median time, the upper and lower quartile times and the interquartile range of times.
The management had planned that the maximum time needed for this piece of work was 6.3 minutes. What percentage of the workers took longer than this to complete the work?

7. The amounts spent by 120 customers in a shop were as follows:

Amount (£'s)	f
0 to under 5	10
5 to under 10	12
10 to under 20	27
20 to under 40	37
40 to under 60	22
60 to under 100	12

Make a cumulative frequency table for the data and draw the cumulative frequency graph. Find the median amount, the upper and lower quartile amounts and the interquartile range of amounts.

8. The percentages of the male and female populations in each age group for the UK in 1989 are given in the table:

Age (years)	males	females
0– 9	13.7	12.3
10–19	13.7	12.4
20–29	16.8	15.6
30–39	14.0	13.2
40–49	13.2	12.5
50–59	10.7	10.4
60–69	9.9	10.6
70–79	5.7	8.0
80–89	2.3	5.0

(A few people in the last group are 90 or over.)

Make cumulative frequency tables for men and for women.
Draw the cumulative frequency graphs using the same scales and axes for both. Label the graphs.
Find for men, and for women, the median age of the population, the upper and lower quartile ages and the interquartile range of ages.
Comment on the results.

Practice test 24

1. This cumulative frequency table shows the distribution of times of arrival of 50 children who were late for school on one particular day.

Minutes late	Cum. freq.
less than 5	22
less than 10	30
less than 15	43
less than 20	47
less than 25	49
less than 30	50

    Draw a cumulative frequency graph.

    Find the median number of minutes late, the upper and lower quartile values and the interquartile range of values.

2. Here are two distributions of examination marks, in each case for 60 students.
    Make cumulative frequency tables for Group A and Group B and draw the cumulative frequency graphs using the same scales and axes. Label the graphs.
    Find for each group the median mark, the upper and lower quartile marks and the interquartile range of marks.
    Comment on the results.

Mark	Group A f	Group B f
11–20	1	
21–30	4	1
31–40	5	2
41–50	13	4
51–60	15	5
61–70	12	9
71–80	6	13
81–90	3	15
91–100	1	11

25 Graphs of functions

> **The topics in this chapter include:**
>
> - drawing the graphs of simple functions,
> - knowing the form of graphs of simple functions.

Graphs of functions

Graphs of quadratic functions

Examples

1   Draw the graph of $y = x^2 - 5x + 2$, for values of x from -1 to 6.

Make a table of values, working out x^2 and $-5x$, and then $x^2 - 5x + 2$, for each value of x.

x	-1	0	1	2	3	4	5	6
x^2	1	0	1	4	9	16	25	36
$-5x$	5	0	-5	-10	-15	-20	-25	-30
2	2	2	2	2	2	2	2	2
y	8	2	-2	-4	-4	-2	2	8

Since the y-values are symmetrical about $x = 2\frac{1}{2}$, it is useful to find the value of y when $x = 2\frac{1}{2}$, as we can then plot the minimum point.

When $x = 2\frac{1}{2}$, $y = \left(2\frac{1}{2}\right)^2 - 5 \times 2\frac{1}{2} + 2 = -4\frac{1}{4}$.

On the graph we draw the x-axis from -1 to 6 and the y-axis from -5 to 8.
Plot the points and join them with a smooth curve.

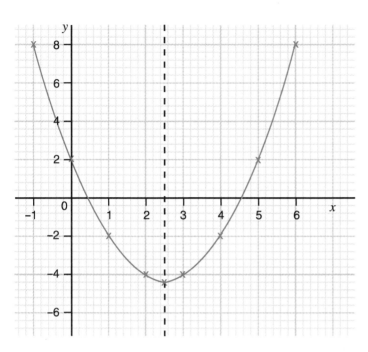

2   Draw the graph of $y = (x+2)(3-x)$ for values of x from -3 to 4.

Make a table of values, working out $x+2$, $3-x$ and then the product $(x+2)(3-x)$
for each value of x.

x	-3	-2	-1	0	1	2	3	4
$x+2$	-1	0	1	2	3	4	5	6
$3-x$	6	5	4	3	2	1	0	-1
y	-6	0	4	6	6	4	0	-6

An extra value which might be plotted is when $x = \frac{1}{2}$, $y = 2\frac{1}{2} \times 2\frac{1}{2} = 6\frac{1}{4}$.

Complete the question. Draw the x-axis from -3 to 4 and the y-axis from -6 to 7.
Plot the points and join them with a smooth curve.

Graphs of cubic functions

Example

3   Draw the graph of $y = x^3 - 3x - 5$ for values of x from -2 to 3.

Make a table of values.

x	-2	-1	0	1	2	3
x^3	-8	-1	0	1	8	27
$-3x$	6	3	0	-3	-6	-9
-5	-5	-5	-5	-5	-5	-5
y	-7	-3	-5	-7	-3	13

On the graph, draw the x-axis from -2 to 3 and the y-axis from -8 to 13. Plot the points and join them with a smooth curve.

Sketch graph

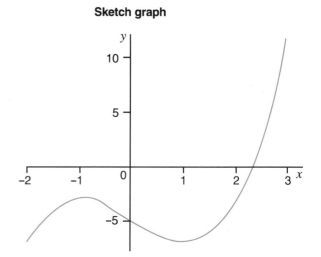

Sketch graphs of functions

A sketch graph should show the main shape of the graph and perhaps also the coordinates of a few important points on it, such as where it crosses the axes, and any maximum or minimum points.

It may be helpful to make a table of values to get an idea of the general shape of the graph, but do not plot unimportant points for just a few values of x near the origin. Consider what happens to the graph when x is a very big positive or negative number.

If you can use a computer graph plotting program, or a graphics calculator, you can investigate the shape of a graph quite quickly.

CHAPTER 25

Some basic functions

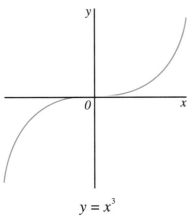

$y = x$

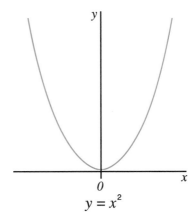

$y = x^2$

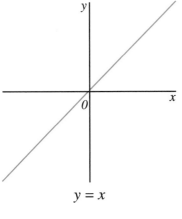

$y = x^3$

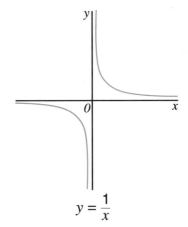

$y = \dfrac{1}{x}$

Linear functions

The general equation of a straight line is $y = mx + c$.
The gradient is m and the line cuts the y-axis at $(0, c)$.
c is called the **intercept** on the y-axis.

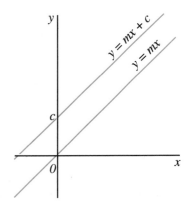

Quadratic functions

The general equation of a quadratic function is $y = ax^2 + bx + c$.
The shape of the graph is a parabola.

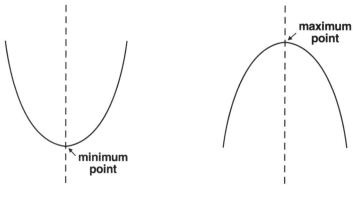

curve when a **is positive**   curve when a **is negative**

Exercise 25.1

1. The graph of $y = 4x^2$.
    Copy and complete this table of values.

x	-4	-3	-2	-1	0	1	2	3	4
x^2	16								
y	64								

    Draw axes with x from -4 to 4 and y from 0 to 70.
    Plot the points of the table on the graph, e.g. $(-4, 64)$, etc.
    Two extra points to plot are $(3.5, 49)$ and $(-3.5, 49)$.
    Join the points with a smooth curve.

2. Draw axes with x from -2 to 5 and y from -4 to 10.
    Copy and complete this table of values for the function $y = x^2 - 3x$.

x	-2	-1	0	1	$1\frac{1}{2}$	2	3	4	5
x^2	4				$2\frac{1}{4}$		9		
$-3x$	6				$-4\frac{1}{2}$		-9		
y	10				$-2\frac{1}{4}$		0		

    Draw the graph of $y = x^2 - 3x$.

3. Draw axes with x from -4 to 4, and y from -4 to 12.
   Copy and complete this table of values for the function $y = 12 - x^2$.

x	-4	-3	-2	-1	0	1	2	3	4
12	12							12	
$-x^2$	-16							-9	
y	-4							3	

Draw the graph of $y = 12 - x^2$.
What is the greatest value of y on the curve ?

4. Draw axes with x from -2 to 4 and y from -4 to 5. Copy and complete this table of values for the graph of $y = (x+1)(x-3)$.

x	-2	-1	0	1	2	3	4
$x+1$	-1				3		
$x-3$	-5				-1		
y	5				-3		

Draw the graph of $y = (x+1)(x-3)$.
What are the coordinates of the point on the graph where y has its lowest value ?

5. Draw axes with x from -3 to 4 and y from -6 to 8.
   Copy and complete this table of values for the function $y = x^2 - x - 5$.

x	-3	-2	-1	0	1	2	3	4
x^2	9				1			
$-x$	3				-1			
-5	-5	-5	-5	-5	-5	-5	-5	-5
y	7				-5			

Draw the graph of $y = x^2 - x - 5$.
Write down the equation of the line about which the curve is symmetrical.

6. Make a table of values for the function $y = x^2$, for x from -4 to 4 including $x = -\frac{1}{2}$ and $x = \frac{1}{2}$.
   Sketch the graph of $y = x^2$, not on graph paper.

7. Copy and complete this table of values for the function $y = x^3 - 4x$.

x	-4	-3	-2	-1	0	1	2	3	4
x^3	-64								
$-4x$	16								
y	-48								

Draw axes with x from -4 to 4, and y from -50 to 50.
Plot the points given by the table and also the points $(-3.5, -28.9)$, $(-0.5, 1.9)$, $(0.5, -1.9)$ and $(3.5, 28.9)$.
Draw the graph.
Comment on its shape.

8. Make a table of values for the function $y = x^3$, for x from -3 to 3, including $x = -\frac{1}{2}$ and $x = \frac{1}{2}$.
Sketch the graph of $y = x^3$.

9. **Graph of the positive part of $y = \dfrac{1}{x}$**

Draw the x and y axes from 0 to 10, using the same scale on both axes.
Copy and complete this table of values, using your calculator where necessary, and giving values correct to 1 decimal place.

x	0.1	0.2	0.3	0.4	0.5	0.6	0.8	1	2	3	4	5	6	8	10
y	10	5													

Plot the points on your graph. Two extra points to help you are $(0.15, 6.7)$ and $(0.125, 8)$.
Join the points with a smooth curve.

10. **The function $y = \sqrt{x}$**

x has to be positive or 0.
Make a table of values for x from 0 to 16, beginning like this:

x	0	1	2	3	4	5	...
y	0	1	1.41	1.73	2	2.24	...

Draw the graph, with x-axis from 0 to 16 and y-axis from 0 to 4.
(Where the square roots are not exact, use your calculator to find them to 1 or 2 decimal places, depending on your scale and how accurately you can plot them.)

Sketch graph

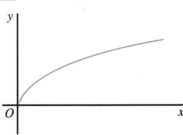

Exercise 25.2 Applications

1. Draw axes with x from -4 to 4, and y from -9 to 7.
    Copy and complete this table of values for the graph of $y = x^2 - 9$.

x	-4	-3	-2	-1	0	1	2	3	4
x^2	16							9	
-9	-9							-9	
y	7							0	

    Draw the graph of $y = x^2 - 9$
    What is the least value of y on the curve ?

2. Draw the graph of $y = x^2 - 7x + 10$ for values of x between 0 and 7. (Draw the x-axis from 0 to 7 and the y-axis from -4 to 10.)

3. Draw axes with x from -1 to 5 and y from -4 to 5.
    Make a table of values for the function $y = x^2 - 4x$ for values of x from -1 to 5.
    Draw the graph of $y = x^2 - 4x$.

4. Draw axes with x from -2 to 5 and y from -7 to 6. Make a table of values for the graph $y = (x + 1)(x - 4)$, for values of x from -2 to 5. Draw the graph.

5. Draw axes with x from -3 to 4 and y from -5 to 25. Make a table of values for the function $y = (2x + 1)(x - 2)$, for values of x from -3 to 4.
    Draw the graph of $y = (2x + 1)(x - 2)$.

6. Draw the graph of $y = x^3 - 3x^2$ for values of x from -1 to 4. (Draw the y-axis from -4 to 16.)

7. Identify these graphs from this list:
    $y = 4 - x^2$, $y = 4x^2$, $y = x^2 - 4x + 4$.

1
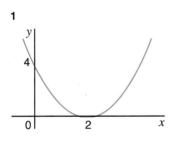

2
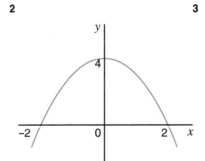

3
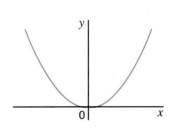

8.   The graph of $y = \dfrac{18}{x}$.

Copy and complete this table of values.

x	-4	-3	-2	-1	1	2	3	4
y	$-4\frac{1}{2}$	-6						

$x = 0$ has been omitted from the table because y does not exist when $x = 0$.
Draw axes with x from -4 to 4 and y from -30 to 30.
Plot the points on your graph. Find y when $x = 0.6$ and when $x = -0.6$ and add these two points.
The positive values of x give one part of the graph and the negative values give another part. Draw the graph.
This curve (which is in two parts) is called a rectangular hyperbola.

9.   A rectangular block has height 6 cm and a square base of side x cm. The total surface area is 160 cm^2.
Find an equation satisfied by x, and simplify it.
Draw the graphs of $y = x^2$ and $y = 80 - 12x$ for values of x from 0 to 8, labelling the y-axis from -20 to 80.
The value of x at the point of intersection of the graphs gives the length of a side of the base of the box.
Find this length, to the nearest mm.

10.   A paddock is rectangular in shape with width x metres and it is three times as long as it is wide. Find an equation connecting y with x, where y square metres is its area.
Draw axes for x from 0 to 50 and for y from 0 to 8000.
Make a table of values of x and y for $x = 0, 10, 20, 30, 40, 50$, and draw the curve representing the equation.
By drawing the line $y = 6000$ on the graph, and reading the value of x at the point where this line cuts the curve, find the measurements of the paddock when its area is $6000\,\text{m}^2$, giving them to the nearest metre.

11.   A storage tank is in the form of a cuboid with a square base of side x m and a height of $(5 - x)$ m. Its volume is y m^3.
Write down the equation connecting x and y.
Draw the graph of $y = x^2(5 - x)$ for values of x from -2 to 6. Label the y-axis from -40 to 20.
By drawing the line $y = 15$ on the graph and reading the values of x at the points where this line cuts the curve, find the possible measurements of the tank if its volume is 15 m^3.

Practice test 25

1. Draw axes with x from -3 to 5 and y from -7 to 9.
Copy and complete this table of values for the function $y = 8 + 2x - x^2$.

x	-3	-2	-1	0	1	2	3	4	5
8	8	8				8			
$2x$	-6					4			
$-x^2$	-9					-4			
y	-7					8			

Draw the graph of $y = 8 + 2x - x^2$.
What are the coordinates of the point on the graph where y has its greatest value ?

2. Draw the graph of $y = 2x^3$ for values of x from -3 to 3. Label the y-axis from -60 to 60.

3. Identify these sketch graphs from this list:
$$y = \frac{3}{x}, \quad y = \frac{x}{3}, \quad y = 3 - x, \quad y = 3x^2$$

1

2

3

4

4. Rectangular plots of land of area 600 m^2 are to be sold.
If the length of a plot is x m and the width is y m, express y in terms of x.
Draw axes for x and y from 0 to 60. Plot the corresponding values of x and y for $x = 10, 15, 20, 30, 40, 50, 60$. Join the points with a curve.

PUZZLE

61. Mine cost 52p, my neighbour's cost 26p and I got some for my friend who lives at the far end of the road, and they cost 78p. What was I buying in the hardware shop ?

Miscellaneous Section E

Exercise E1　Aural practice

If possible find someone to read these questions to you.
You should do all of them within 10 minutes.
Do not use your calculator.
Write down the answers only.

1.　What is $\frac{1}{2} + \frac{1}{4}$?

2.　If £1 is equal to 1.4 dollars, how many dollars will I get for £20 ?

3.　What is the smallest number into which 5, 6 and 10 all divide exactly ?

4.　How many edges has a cuboid ?

5.　If 5 similar books together weigh 4.5 kg, what will 3 of them weigh ?

6.　Where does the line with equation $y = 5 - 2x$ meet the y-axis ?

7.　The sides of a rectangle are 6 cm and 8 cm. What is the length of a diagonal ?

8.　When throwing a fair die, what is the probability of getting either a 1 or a 2 ?

9.　I think of a number, multiply it by 5 and add 12. The result is 57. What was the original number ?

10.　Three parcels weigh 7 kg, 6 kg and 11 kg. What is their average weight ?

11.　The area of a triangle is 36 cm^2 and the base is 9 cm. What is the height ?

12.　If a car costing £5000 is sold for £4000, what is the percentage loss ?

13.　Give an approximate value for the square root of $\left(7^2 + 7^2\right)$.

14.　What is the approximate weight in kilograms of 6.6 lb ?

15.　A rectangle 8 cm by 6 cm is cut out of a square piece of paper of side 10 cm. What area is left ?

Exercise E2   Revision

1. Find the size of angle *a*.

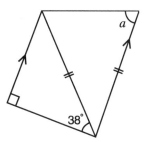

2. A parallelogram has base 8×10^{-2} m and height 6.5×10^{-2} m. Find its area in m², giving your answer in standard form.

3. The quantities, *w* grams, of a salt which can be dissolved in a given volume of water at different temperatures, *t* °C, are given in the table.

t (°C)	10	20	25	30	40	50	55	60
w (g)	41	44	45.5	47	50	53	54.5	56

Draw a graph to show this information using a scale of 2 cm to 10 units on both axes. Draw a line of best fit.

Use the graph to find
1 the amount of the salt which will dissolve in the given volume of water at a temperature of 34°C,
2 the temperature at which 52 g of the salt will dissolve in the given volume of water.

4. 1 If $v^2 = u^2 + 2as$, find *a* in terms of *u*, *v*, *s*.

   2 If $V = \frac{1}{3}\pi r^2 h$, find *h* in terms of *V*, *r* and π.

   3 If $S = 4\pi r^2$, and *r* is positive, find *r* in terms of *S* and π.

5. A hair shampoo is sold in two sizes costing 92p and £1.34. The cheaper bottle is marked as holding 110 ml and the other one holds 150 ml. Which bottle is the better value for money ?

6. This table shows the number of children in 100 families.

Children in family	0	1	2	3	4	5	6
Number of families	15	20	30	21	8	5	1

Draw a bar-line graph to illustrate the data.
Find the mean, median and mode number of children per family.

7. Which diagram represents the locus of points inside the triangle PQR which are

    1   equidistant from PQ and QR,
    2   equidistant from P and R ?

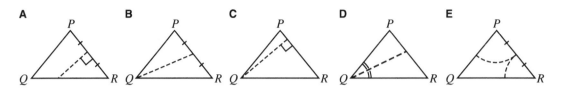

8. In the following lists, where values are given for $x = -2$, 0, 1 and 3, find the connection
    between y and x, in the form $y = mx + c$, where m and c are numbers.

1

x	y
-2	2
0	0
1	-1
3	-3

2

x	y
-2	-1
0	0
1	$\frac{1}{2}$
3	$1\frac{1}{2}$

3

x	y
-2	-3
0	-1
1	0
3	2

4

x	y
-2	5
0	3
1	2
3	0

5

x	y
-2	-3
0	1
1	3
3	7

On graph paper, draw axes for x from -2 to 3 and for y from -3 to 7.
For each list, plot the points on the graph and join them with a straight line.
Label each line with its equation.

9. Find the lengths of DE and DF.

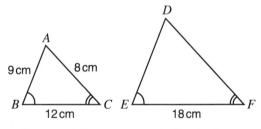

10. A box contains 12 discs. 3 are red, 4 are yellow and 5 are green. A disc is drawn out and
    replaced, then a second disc is drawn out.
    Show the results of the two drawings on a tree-diagram.
    What is the probability that
    1   both discs are red,
    2   both discs are the same colour ?

11. Calculate AC, and write down, as
    fractions in their simplest forms, the
    ratios for sin B, cos B, tan B.

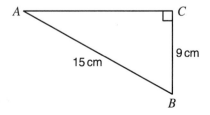

12. The percentages of the total male population in each age-group are given in the table. (Figures for UK, 1989.)

Age (years)	%
0–9	13.7
10–19	13.7
20–29	16.9
30–39	14.0
40–49	13.2
50–59	10.7
60–69	9.9
70–79	5.7
80–89	2.2

Make a cumulative frequency table of the data and draw a cumulative frequency graph.

Find the median age and the interquartile range of ages.

What percentage of the male population is over 65 years old ?

(A small number of the last group are 90 or over.)

Exercise E3 Revision

1. A plumber does three repair jobs as follows: the first from 9.35 am to 11.15 am, the second from 11.45 am to 12.50 pm and the third from 2.05 pm to 3.50 pm. Find the average time taken for a job.

2. Find the size of angle c.

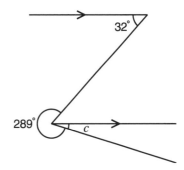

3. If $x = 3$ and $y = -5$, find the values of

   1 $\dfrac{2y + 2}{4x}$

   2 $2x^2 - y$

   3 $\sqrt{y^2 - x^2}$

4. A soil sample is found to have the following composition.

Air	25%
Water	25%
Mineral material	45%
Organic material	5%

   Draw a pie chart showing this information.

5.   Mary and Ann are hoping to be chosen for the position
     of shooter in the netball team. The probability that Mary
     will be chosen is 0.5 and the probability that Ann will be
     chosen is 0.3.

  1   What is the probability that Mary or Ann will be chosen ?
  2   What is the probability that someone else will be chosen ?

6.   A new road is being paid for by four towns A, B, C and D. Town A pays $\frac{1}{3}$ of the cost
     and B and C each pay $\frac{1}{4}$ of the cost. What fraction of the cost does D pay ? What does
     the road cost if D pays £40 000 ?

7.   There are 7 discs in a bag numbered from 1 to 7. A disc is drawn (and not replaced) and
     a second disc is drawn. Show the sample space of all possible pairs of results and find the
     probability that
  1   the sum of the numbers drawn is odd,
  2   the product of the numbers drawn is odd.

8. Here is a flow diagram which multiplies two numbers by halving and doubling.

    Use the flow diagram to multiply 278 by 92.
    Write down a, b, c in columns to keep a record of them.
    What is the answer ?

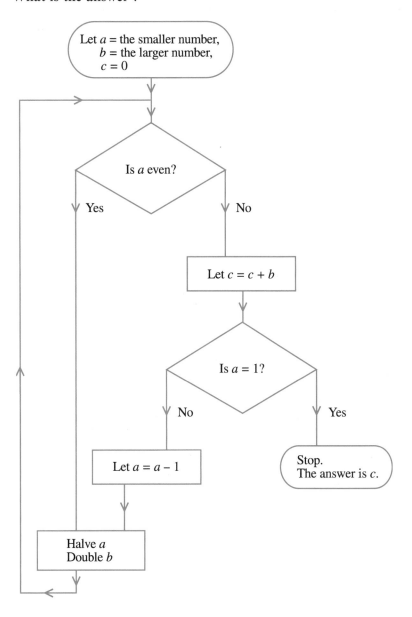

9. A road slopes at a steady angle of 17° to the
    horizontal. Calculate the increase of height
    of the road over a distance of 2 km.

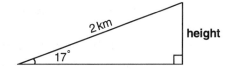

10. Use your calculator to find the answers to these questions.

   1 Which is larger, $\sqrt{225} + \sqrt{64}$ or $\sqrt{225 + 64}$, and by how much ?

   2 Which is larger, 2^{11} or 3^7, and by how much ?

   3 Find a prime factor of $69\,961$ between 30 and 50.

11. A rectangular block has height h cm and a square base of side x cm.

   1 If the total surface area is A cm^2, find an expression for A in terms of x and h.
   2 Find the value of A when $x = 5$ and $h = 3$.
   3 Find an expression for h in terms of A and x.
   4 Find the height when the total surface area is 440 cm^2 and the length of a side of the base is 10 cm.

12. The table shows the heights of 120 seedlings.

Height in cm	0–2	2–4	4–6	6–8	8–10	10–12
Number	14	34	22	30	18	2

   1 Draw a histogram of the distribution and describe its shape.
   2 Make a cumulative frequency table and draw a cumulative frequency graph.
   From the graph find the median height and the interquartile range of heights of the seedlings.

Exercise E4 Revision

1. Simplify, without using your calculator,

   1 5.32×100 **4** $55 \div 0.11$
   2 0.07×0.5
   3 $2.8 \div 70$ **5** $\dfrac{6.3 \times 0.8}{0.56}$

2. What is the gradient of the line joining the points $(-1, 2)$ and $(5, -1)$?

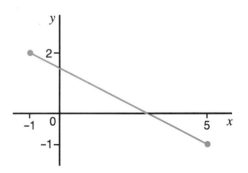

3. There are a lot of coloured beads in a bag, and some of them are green ones.
   When picking a bead at random the probability that it is green is 0.64.
   What is the probability of picking a bead that is not green ?

4. 1 What is the bearing of B from A ?
    2 What is the bearing of C from B ?
    3 What is the bearing of B from C ?

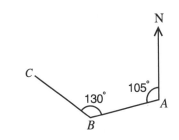

5. In the sunshine, a stick which is 1 m high
    has a shadow of length 0.8 m on the
    horizontal ground. At the same time and
    place a flagpole has a shadow which
    is 4.8 m long.
    How high is the flagpole ?

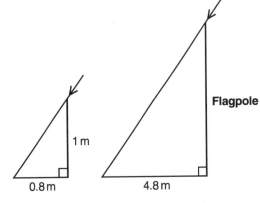

6. Draw the x-axis from -3 to 4 and the y-axis from -6 to 6. Draw the graphs of $y = 2 - x$
    and $2y = 3x - 2$.
    Use the graphs to solve the simultaneous equations $y = 2 - x$, $2y = 3x - 2$.

7. Identify these sketch graphs. The first quantity named is measured on the horizontal axis.

    1 The relationship between the radius and the volume of a cylinder with constant height.

    2 The relationship between speed and the time taken to travel a fixed distance.

    3 The relationship between money invested and Simple Interest gained per year, when
       the rate of interest is constant.

    4 The relationship between children present and children absent in a class of 30 pupils
       on different days.

    A   **B**   **C**   **D**

8. In this triangle PQR, the perimeter is 60 cm,
    and QR is 5 cm longer than PQ.
    Write down two equations involving x and y,
    simplify them and solve them.
    Find the numerical values of the sides
    of the triangle.

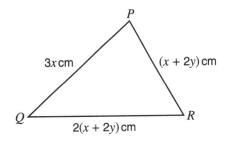

9.   From a point on horizontal ground 700 m away from the base of a very tall tower, the angle of elevation of the top of the tower is 15°. Find the height of the tower, to the nearest 10 m.

10. Three boys, Paul, Quentin and Robert enter for a job selection test, and their chances of passing it, independently, are $\frac{1}{2}, \frac{4}{5}$, and $\frac{2}{3}$ respectively.

     What is the probability that
     1   all 3 boys pass,
     2   none of the boys passes,
     3   2 of the boys pass and the other one does not ?

11. Write down the reciprocal of 54
     1   as a recurring decimal,
     2   correct to 3 decimal places,
     3   correct to 3 significant figures.

12. Make a table of values for the graph of $y = 2x - \dfrac{12}{x}$, for values of x from 1 to 6. Draw the x-axis from 0 to 6 and the y-axis from -10 to 10. Draw the graph for $1 \leqslant x \leqslant 6$. Write down the x-value of the point where the curve crosses the x-axis.

Exercise E5 Revision

1.   Find the values of

     1   $1\frac{1}{6} + \left(\frac{2}{3} \times 2\frac{1}{4}\right)$ 2 $\left(1\frac{1}{6} \div \frac{2}{3}\right) + 2\frac{1}{4}$ 3 $1\frac{1}{6} - \frac{2}{3} + 2\frac{1}{4}$

2.   Two sides of a regular pentagon are extended to meet at a point P. Find the size of $\angle P$.

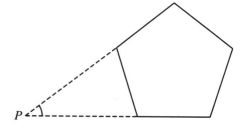

3.   Rearrange these formulae to give x in terms of the other letters.
     1   $y = mx + c$
     2   $y = 2\sqrt{x} - 3$
     3   $ax = b - cx$
     4   $y = x^2 + 4$, where x is positive.

4. An explorer setting out from his base camp C walks due West for 8 km and then due North for 5 km. Use trigonometry to find on what bearing he must now travel to go directly back to camp.

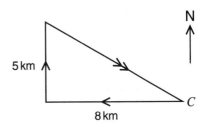

5. 1 Which is the largest number which divides into both 60 and 132 ?

2 When boxes are stacked in piles of 5 there are 2 left over. When they are stacked in piles of 8 there are still 2 left over. If the number of boxes is between 50 and 100, how many are there ?

6. The marks of 12 students in a test are 5, 5, 6, 6, 6, 7, 8, 8, 10, 10, 14, 17.

Find
1 the mode,
2 the median,
3 the mean,
4 the range, of the marks.

7. The table gives the distance, s m, travelled by a train, starting from rest, in t seconds. Draw a distance-time graph, joining the points with a curve.

t	10	15	20	30	40	60	80	100	120	140	160
s	15	35	65	135	230	480	785	1110	1440	1745	1990

8. $ABCDEFGH$ is a cuboid.
A is the point $(2, 2, 0)$.
B is the point $(18, 2, 0)$.
D is the point $(2, 14, 0)$.
E is the point $(2, 2, 15)$.
Find the coordinates of the points C, F, G and H.
Find the lengths of AC and AG.

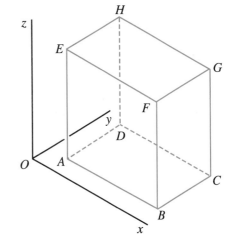

9. Use graph paper or squared paper for this question.

If O is the origin and $\overrightarrow{OA} = \begin{pmatrix} 3 \\ 2 \end{pmatrix}$, $\overrightarrow{OB} = \begin{pmatrix} 5 \\ 6 \end{pmatrix}$, $\overrightarrow{OC} = \begin{pmatrix} 4 \\ -4 \end{pmatrix}$, $\overrightarrow{OD} = \begin{pmatrix} 2 \\ -8 \end{pmatrix}$, find $\overrightarrow{AB}$, $\overrightarrow{BC}$, $\overrightarrow{AD}$, $\overrightarrow{DC}$.
What kind of quadrilateral is $ABCD$?

10. For a party, Eileen wants to buy some biscuits. She buys x packets of chocolate biscuits and y packets of cream biscuits.

Write down inequalities if she decides to buy at least 3 packets of each kind, but not more than 12 packets altogether.

Packets of chocolate biscuits cost 60p each and packets of cream biscuits cost 30p each. Eileen must not spend more than £4.80 altogether. Write down another inequality and simplify it.

11. A bag contains a number of fruit drops, some red, some yellow and some green.

The probability of taking a red sweet, at random, is $\frac{1}{3}$.

The probability of taking a yellow sweet, at random, is $\frac{1}{5}$.

What is the probability of taking
1   a red sweet or a yellow sweet,
2   a green sweet ?

3   If 28 of the sweets are green ones, how many sweets are there altogether ?

12. The data gives the marks of 10 students in Papers 1 and 2 of an examination. Show the data on a scatter diagram and draw a line of best fit.

Student	A	B	C	D	E	F	G	H	I	J
Mark on Paper 1	56	52	45	53	51	67	64	58	69	56
Mark on Paper 2	68	61	53	57	62	74	79	73	81	70

Another student gained 60 marks for Paper 1 but was absent through illness for Paper 2. Use your line of best fit to estimate the mark she might have gained on Paper 2.

Exercise E6   Revision

1. A man worked 48 hours in a week. For the first 40 hours he was paid £3.60 an hour. For the rest he was paid at the overtime rate of £5.40 an hour.

1   What were the man's wages that week ?
2   How many hours altogether had he worked in a week when he earned £198 ?

2. Expand the following:

1   $2x^2(3x^3 + x)$

2   $(x - 1)(x - 7)$

3   $(x + 3)(2x + 5)$

4   $(3x + y)(2x - 5y)$

5   $(2x + y)^2$

3. On a map a distance of 48 km is represented by a line of 2.4 cm. What is the scale of the map in ratio form ?

4. Alan plays a game where he can either win, draw or lose. The probability of him winning is $\frac{1}{3}$, the probability of him drawing is $\frac{1}{2}$. What is the probability of him losing ?
Show the results of two games on a tree-diagram and find the probability that he wins at least one of the two games.

5. In an auction, a dealer bought a table and a chair for £180. He then sold the table for twice as much as he had paid for it, and he sold the chair for half as much as he had paid for it, altogether making a profit of £60 over what he had paid.
Let £t be the price the dealer paid for the table and £c be the price he paid for the chair. Write down two equations and solve them simultaneously to find the prices paid for the table and the chair.

6. A boat owner runs pleasure cruises. His boat will carry 24 passengers, but of the passengers at least half of them, but not more than three-quarters of them, must be children.
The fares charged are £3 for an adult and £2 for a child. To cover expenses the fares on any trip must be at least £30.
If there are x children and y adults on a particular trip, write down 4 inequalities satisfied by x and y.

Draw a graph showing the region satisfying all these inequalities. (Label the x and y axes from 0 to 24.)

7. The distribution of the percentage yield of 112 top shares, quoted on a day in March, 1993, was as follows:

Percentage yield	0–1	1–2	2–3	3–4	4–5	5–6	6–7	7–8
f	2	3	14	23	44	18	5	3

1 Draw a histogram of the distribution and describe its shape.
2 Make a cumulative frequency table and draw a cumulative frequency graph. From the graph find the median percentage yield and the interquartile range of yields. Estimate how many of the shares had a yield of over 4.5%.

8. A man bought 600 eggs for £48 and planned to sell them at £1.20 per dozen. What percentage profit would he have made on his cost price ?
However, 60 of the eggs were broken and he could not sell them. What was his percentage profit after he had sold the rest ?

9. Here is a sequence of sets of numbers:

$(3, 4, 5)$,　　　$(5, 11, 13)$,　　　$(7, 24, 25)$,　　　$(9, 40, 41)$,　　　$(11, 60, 61)$,　　　$\ldots$

1 These numbers are connected with the sides of right-angled triangles. With which mathematician are they associated ?
2 One number in the sequence above is incorrect. Which one is incorrect, and what is the correct number ?
3 By finding the connection between the first number of a set and the **sum** of the other two, deduce the next set of numbers in the sequence.

10. Without using a calculator, find an approximate value of $\sqrt{3.92 \times 9.08}$.
    Now use your calculator to find its value correct to 3 significant figures.

11. The age distribution of the population of the Isle of Man in 1961 and 1971 is given in the
    table.
    Draw frequency polygons for both years on the same diagram. Assume the last
    age-group is 80–89 years.
    Comment about the data.

| Age (years) | Population (in 100's) | |
	1961	1971
0–9	60	77
10–19	64	70
20–29	43	68
30–39	54	54
40–49	62	63
50–59	76	73
60–69	66	85
70–79	41	53
80 and over	15	19

12. The graph shows the
    speed of a train which
    starts from A and
    increases speed steadily
    until it reaches 20 m/s.
    After keeping a steady
    speed for some time it
    then decreases its speed
    steadily until it stops
    at B.

    For how long altogether
    was its speed greater
    than 12 m/s ?

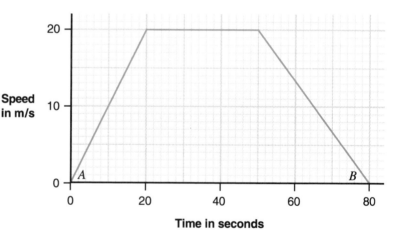

Exercise E7 Revision

1. Factorise

    1 $2x^2 + 8xy$ **2** $x^2 - 12x$ **3** $12x^2 + 4$

2. *ABCD* is a square, *BEC* is an isosceles triangle and
    $\angle CED = \angle AEB = 90°$. $\angle BEC = 42°$.
    Find the size of $\angle CDE$.

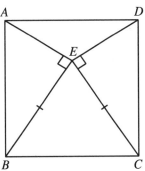

3. One number in each of these sequences is incorrect. Copy them, replacing the wrong
    number with the correct number.

    1 1, 3, 6, 9, 15, 21, 28.
    What is this sequence of numbers called ?
    Write down the next 3 numbers in the sequence.

    2 1, 1, 2, 3, 5, 8, 13, 22, 34.
    (Each number is connected to the previous two numbers.)
    Write down the next 3 numbers in the sequence.

    3 1, 6, 27, 64, 125, 216.
    Is 1000 a member of this sequence ?

    4 100, 93, 86, 79, 72, 66, 58, 51.
    Write down the next 3 numbers in the sequence.

4. Sketch the graphs of

    1 $y = x - 3$ **2** $y = x(x - 3)$

5. If $a = \frac{1}{2}$, $b = \frac{1}{4}$ and $c = 0$, find the values of

    1 $ab + 2bc$ **3** $3c(a + b)$

    2 $2b^2 + a^3$ **4** $\dfrac{2a + 3b + 4c}{2a - b}$

6. Find out whether these networks can be drawn without taking your pencil off the paper
    and without going along any line more than once.
    For those that can, copy them and show your solution, marking the route by drawing
    over it freehand with a coloured pen.

1

2
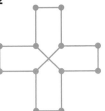

3
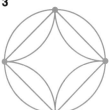

4
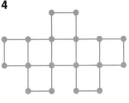

7. Here is a list of formulae. a and b are lengths.

$$W = \tfrac{1}{2}\sqrt{a^2 + b^2}$$

$$X = \tfrac{2}{3}\pi ab^2$$

$$Y = \pi(a^2 - b^2)$$

$$Z = 2\pi a + b^2$$

Which letter, W, X, Y or Z represents
1   a length,   2   an area,   3   a volume ?

8. Here are some (fictitious) results where people A, B, C, D, E, have put products P, Q, R, S, T, in order of preference.
1 = 1st choice, 2 = 2nd choice, etc.

Analyse the results and write down your conclusions, including saying which product you would decide is the most popular.

Product	Person				
	A	B	C	D	E
P	5	2	1	1	4
Q	4	4	4	2	3
R	3	5	2	3	2
S	1	3	5	5	5
T	2	1	3	4	1

9. Copy and complete the following table of values for the function $y = x^2 - 2x - 2$.

x	-2	-1	0	1	2	3	4
x^2	4		0				
$-2x$	4		0				
-2	-2		-2				
y	6		-2				

On graph paper, draw the graph of $y = x^2 - 2x - 2$ for values of x from -2 to 4.

10. On a stretch of straight coastline there is a coastguard station at A. Their rescue boats patrol a region within 10 km of the coast, and there is a lookout at the station who can see a distance of 15 km through a telescope. Using a scale 1 cm to 2 km, copy the diagram and mark in
(1) the boundary of the patrolled region, and
(2) the boundary of the region at sea that the lookout can see.
Shade the region of the sea which is not patrolled, but is visible to the lookout.

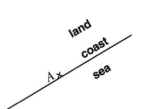

11. The equation $x^2 - 6x + 7 = 0$ has a solution for x between $x = 4$ and $x = 5$.
     Use your calculator and a trial method to find this solution correct to 1 decimal place.

12.

Share	Price in pence	
	Lowest	Highest
A	250	400
B	550	670
C	310	530
D	130	290
E	380	510
F	280	460
G	470	650
H	100	140
I	120	270
J	310	440

The price of shares changes according to the state of the Market.
Here are the lowest and highest prices for 10 selected shares in 1992. (Prices are to the nearest 10p.)

Draw a scatter diagram, with lowest price on the horizontal axis and highest price on the vertical axis.
Draw a line of best fit.

If the lowest price of another share was £2.20, estimate from the line of best fit what its highest price was likely to have been.

Exercise E8 Activities

1. **A budget for a year**

Imagine that you plan to move away from home into your own flat, in a few year's time. This is a big step to take and it deserves proper consideration.
You will have your wages from your work or your grant as a student. Plan how you are going to manage financially.

Firstly, there is necessary spending on the flat, e.g. rent, bills for water, electricity, gas and other fuel, insurance, TV licence, phone bills, etc. If you are over 18 and working you may have to pay a local tax.
Secondly, there is the necessary spending on yourself, e.g. food, travelling expenses (including car expenses if you have a car), clothes, etc.
Then there are all the extras such as things for the flat, holidays, presents, entertainment, sports or hobbies, etc.
If you have borrowed money or bought things on credit you will have regular repayments to make.

Make a complete list of expenditure (what you need to spend) with estimated costs for each item. Find the total amount.
Estimate the total income you will have. If you are working, deductions will be made from your wages for National Insurance contributions and Income Tax.
If the expenditure total exceeds the income total you will have to decide what you can do about it.

(If you prefer, instead of this you can work out a similar budget for a family.)

2. **Sevenths**

Work out the recurring sequences of decimals for $\frac{1}{7}, \frac{2}{7}, \frac{3}{7}, \frac{4}{7}, \frac{5}{7}, \frac{6}{7}$.
Investigate the patterns formed.
Also try adding the 1st and 4th figures, the 2nd and 5th, the 3rd and 6th.
Add the 1st 2 figures as a 2-figure number, with the 3rd and 4th, and 5th and 6th.
Add the 1st 3 figures as a 3-figure number with the last 3 figures as a 3-figure number.

Investigate the decimals for the thirteenths, $\frac{1}{13}, \frac{2}{13}$, etc.
You could also investigate the seventeenths, but the sequence is too long to get it all
displayed on your calculator. You can find it in stages, however.

3. **Number chains**

You can invent your own rules for number chains.

Here is one idea using 2-digit numbers and their squares.
e.g.
$77 \rightarrow 7^2 + 7^2 = 98 \rightarrow 9^2 + 8^2 = 145 \rightarrow 1^2 + 4^2 + 5^2 = 42 \rightarrow 4^2 + 2^2 = 20 \rightarrow 2^2 + 0^2 = 4$
Stop when you reach a 1-digit number.
The chain here is $77 \rightarrow 98 \rightarrow 145 \rightarrow 42 \rightarrow 20 \rightarrow 4$
Investigate for other 2-digit numbers. To which 1-digit number do most of them lead ?
Which are the exceptions, and which other 1-digit numbers are possible ?

You can do a similar investigation with 2-digit multiples of 3 and their cubes.

e.g. $36 \rightarrow 3^3 + 6^3 = 243 \rightarrow 2^3 + 4^3 + 3^3 = \ldots$
What happens ?

Here is a chain using 2 or 3 digit multiples of 7.
Multiply the hundreds digit by 2, the tens digit by 3, add them together and add on the
units digit.
e.g. $854 \rightarrow 8 \times 2 + 5 \times 3 + 4 = 35 \rightarrow 3 \times 3 + 5 = \ldots$
What happens ?

Another rule you can investigate using 2-digit numbers is:
If the number is odd, multiply it by 3 and add 1, if it is even, divide it by 2. Stop when
you get to 1.
e.g. $22 \rightarrow 11 \rightarrow 34 \rightarrow 17 \rightarrow 52 \rightarrow \ldots$

4.   **Packaging problems**

1   A square piece of cardboard has sides of length 30 cm.
    Out of each corner a square of side x cm, where $x < 15$,
    is cut, and the flaps remaining are turned up to form
    an open box.
    Find an expression for the volume of the box.
    By trial, find the value of x for which this volume
    is a maximum, and state this volume.

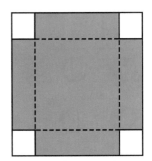

2   A modelling material is made in rods of length 15 cm
    and diameter 4 cm, and they are packed in sixes,
    in cardboard boxes with open ends. The cross-section
    is shown.
    Find the perimeter of this cross-section and hence
    the area of cardboard needed.
    (Ignore any overlap.)

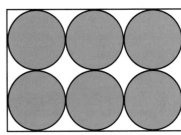

Two ways of using less cardboard are to be investigated.
(a) Making a new design of open box, with cross-section shown below.
(b) Making the modelling material with a square cross-section instead of a circular
cross-section but with the same cross-sectional area, and then enclosing the bars in a
rectangular box.

(a)

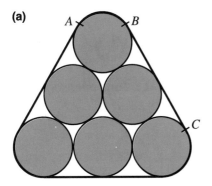

(b)

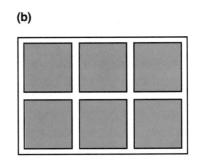

For each way, what is the new perimeter of the cross-section and hence what area of
cardboard is needed ?
(From A to B, the curved distance is $\frac{1}{3}$ of the circumference of a circular rod. From
B to C the distance is twice the diameter of a rod.)

Which method uses the least cardboard and what percentage of cardboard is saved,
compared with the original method ?

You can think of other packaging problems to solve.

5. **NIM**

This a very old mathematical game for 2 players.
It is played with a number of counters (or match sticks) which are placed in 3 groups.

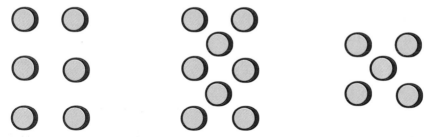

When it is your turn you can remove one or more counters, but they must all be taken from one group only.
You win the game if your opponent takes the last counter.

Play several games, beginning with a number of counters between 12 and 30. It need not be the same number in each game, and the 3 groups can contain unequal numbers of counters at the start of a game.

After playing several games, you may have noticed that if you leave one counter in each of 3 piles then you are bound to win.

You can also win if one pile is empty and there are 2 counters in each of the other two piles.

If you leave 3 counters in one pile, 2 in another and 1 in the third pile, show that whatever your opponent takes away, you can win.

In some cases, this is because you can reduce the position to 1, 1, 1 or 2, 2, 0 and then win, as above.

Find other positions which are such that whatever your opponent moves, you can reduce the counters to 3, 2, 1;   1, 1, 1;   2, 2, 0 or another winning position already discovered.

Make a list of all positions which guarantee you a win if you play carefully.

Now, suppose that 10, 9, 3 is such a position. We now write the numbers as sums of powers of 2, using each power once only. The powers of 2 are 1, 2, 4, 8, 16, ... (1 is 2^0.) Every number can be written in this way. $10 = 8 + 2$, $9 = 8 + 1$, $3 = 2 + 1$. We can show the three numbers with ticks in columns.

	16	8	4	2	1
10		✓		✓	
9		✓			✓
3				✓	✓
		2		2	2

(Total ticks in each column)

Make such a table for all the winning positions you have found. Then make tables for some combinations which are not winning positions.

Apart from the positions 1, 1, 1; and 1, 0, 0; what do you notice about all the winning positions, and what about the losing positions ?

If when it is your turn, there is a losing position, how can you work out what counters to remove to make it into a winning posiion ?

When you have worked out a winning strategy you can challenge all your friends to try to beat you. You can only lose when it is your first turn and the groups already form a winning combination.

6.   **Weighing scale problems**

1   You are given 27 coins and told that 26 of them are of equal weight but 1 is slightly lighter. You are also given balance-type weighing scales so that you can weigh some coins on one side against some on the other side. However, you are only allowed to make 3 weighings. How can you find the lighter coin ?

2   You are given 12 coins and told the 11 of them are of equal weight but 1 is different, either lighter or heavier. Using 3 weighings with coins on either side of the scales, find which coin is the wrong one, and whether it is heavy or light.

7. **The ninth stellation of the icosahedron**

Here are instructions for making this solid figure.
It is made from 12 star points.

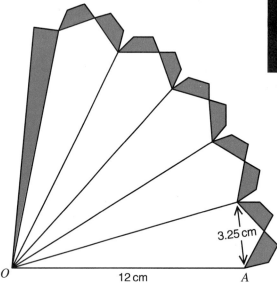

3.25 cm

O　　　　　　12 cm　　　　　　*A*

To make a star point:
Draw the pattern on paper.
With centre *O*, draw a faint arc, radius 12 cm.
Starting at *A*, with radius 3.25 cm, mark off 5 more points on the arc.
Using *A* and the other points as centres in turn, with radius 2.05 cm, find the 5 outer points.
Draw all the lines, and add tabs as shown.
If you alter the measurements, keep them in the same proportion.

Transfer the pattern to cardboard. You need 12 pieces altogether. Cut them out.
Score along all the lines on the right side, and bend them away from the side they were scored on.
Glue the long tab to the opposite face to make a star point.
Then glue 2 pieces together along 2 small tabs of each, one of each on either side of a long edge.
Glue a third piece in a similar way to each of the first two pieces.
Continue glueing on other pieces until you have a complete, closed model. For the last star point, you may find it easier to make an incomplete point with 4 faces and tabs on both long edges. Then you can make a single face to glue on last of all.

8. **Using mathematics**

Here are some practical problems. There are several possible solutions. See how many you can think of. Make up similar problems to solve.

1   An explorer in unknown territory discovers a deep gorge. He needs to report on its width but it is too wide to get across to measure it. How can he estimate its width ?

2   He can see the bottom and wants to estimate its depth. How can he do this ?

3   On the other side of the gorge is a very tall unusual tree. How can he estimate its height ?

4   He has been travelling from his base camp in a north-easterly direction so he knows he has to go in a south-westerly direction to return to camp. Unfortunately, he has dropped his compass down the gorge. How can he find out which direction to go in ?

9. **The ellipse**

1   Draw a circle on graph paper, radius 10 units, centre at the origin. Find the y-coordinate of the point on the circle in the quadrant where x and y are positive, and $x = 1$. If the y-coordinate is b, mark with dots the points $(1, \frac{1}{2}b)$, $(1, -\frac{1}{2}b)$, $(-1, \frac{1}{2}b)$ and $(-1, -\frac{1}{2}b)$.
Repeat, finding the y-coordinates and halving them, for the points where $x = 2, 3$, etc. to 10, and also mark $(0, 5)$ and $(0, -5)$. Joint the points with a closed smooth curve, which is an ellipse.
You can draw different ellipses by taking different fractions of the y-coordinate, such as $0.7\,b$.

2   Take 2 points A and B, 10 cm apart, and fix the ends of a piece of string 15 cm long to these points. Hold the string tight with a pencil. Move the pencil, keeping the string tight. As the pencil moves it draws an ellipse.
Investigate for different lengths of string or different distances AB.

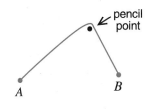

3   Show how you get an ellipse by taking a slanting slice of a cone or a cylinder. (Try slicing a candle.)
A torch throwing a circular beam of light onto a wall will give an elliptical beam if tilted. Are there other examples of ellipses occurring naturally ?

4   On tracing paper draw a circle radius 5 cm and mark dots about 0.4 cm apart all round the circumference. Mark a dot for point P 2.5 cm from the centre of the circle. Now fold the paper so that one dot lies on P. Make a firm crease.
Now make the next dot lie on P. Make another firm crease. Repeat for all dots in turn. (What curve would you get if you do the same starting with a point P outside the circle ?)

10. **Centres of a triangle**

It is easy to find the centre of an equilateral triangle because there is only one.
Investigate triangles of different shapes and find the following centres.
We are considering a triangle *ABC*.

1   *O*. Bisect *AB* and *BC*. These bisectors intersect at *O*. Show that the bisector of *AC*
will also pass through *O* ?

2   *I*. Bisect angles *A* and *B* (internally). These bisectors intersect at *I*. Show that the
bisector of angle *C* will also pass through *I* ?

3   *G*. Let the mid-points of *BC*, *CA* and *AB* be *D*, *E* and *F* respectively. Join *AD* and
BE. These lines intersect at *G*. Show on your drawing that *CF* also passes through *G*.
Can you discover any connection between the lengths of *AG* and *GD* (or *BG* and *GE*,
or *CG* and *GF*) ?

4   *H*. Draw the perpendicular line from *A* to *BC*, and the perpendicular line from *B* to
AC. These lines meet at *H*. Show on your drawing that the perpendicular line from
C to *AB* also passes through *H*.

5   Of the centres *O*, *I*, *G* and *H*, which centre is the incentre, the centre of the inscribed
circle ? Draw the inscribed circle of the triangle showing this centre.

6   Which centre is the circumcentre, the centre of the circumcircle ? Draw the
circumcircle of the triangle showing this centre.

7   Which centre is the centre of gravity (the balancing point) of the triangle ? Draw
triangles on thick cardboard, draw this centre on them, cut them out and try to
balance them at this point on the flat end of a pencil.

8   Find points *O*, *G* and *H* in the same triangle. What do you notice about these
points ?

9   **The 9-point circle**
In one diagram, repeat part **1** to find *O*, and draw all three bisectors. Repeat part **4** to
find *H*, and draw all three perpendiculars. Mark the mid-points of *AH*, *BH* and *CH*.
Find *N*, the mid-point of *OH*.
There is a circle, centre *N*, which passes through 9 special points of the triangle. Can
you decide which points it should pass through ? If so, find the required radius and
draw the circle.

11. **To find the day of the week for any date (1800–2099)**

By using this method you will be able to find the day of the week for any date without looking at a calendar for that year.

On which day of the week does your 18th birthday fall?

On which day of the week were you born?

On which day of the week does 1st January, 2001 fall?

Work out these and other dates.

e.g. 2nd September, 1995. This written as 2.9.95

You are going to write down 5 numbers, add them up, divide by 7 and find the remainder.

(a) Add the three numbers for day, month and year together.   106

(b) Double the number of the month.   18

(c) Write down the special number (see below)   2

(d) Divide the last two figures of the year by 4, ignoring any remainder.   23

(e) Write down the century number. (For years 1800–1899 this is 6, for 1900–1999 it is 4, for 2000–2099 it is 3.)

                                                                        4
                                                                      ───
                                                                      153

$153 \div 7$ gives remainder 6.

This remainder gives the day of the week, using this list.

Remainder	0	1	2	3	4	5	6
Day	Sun	Mon	Tues	Wed	Thur	Fri	Sat

So 2nd September, 1995 is a Saturday.

The special number is found by counting how many of the following list of imaginary dates would occur **after** the date you are using.

Feb 29,   Feb 30,   Feb 31,   Apl 31,   Jun 31,   Sep 31,   Nov 31.

(Do not count Feb 29 in a leap year as it is not an imaginary date.)

(In our example, after 2nd September there are 2 imaginary dates, Sep 31 and Nov 31, so the special number is 2.)

PUZZLE

62. Make 5 equal squares out of cardboard.
     Leave one square whole, and divide the
     other four into two pieces as shown.
     Rearrange the 9 pieces to make one large square.

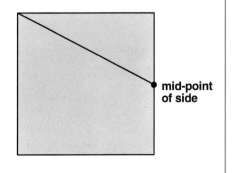

mid-point
of side

Formula checklist

This list should remind you of the more important formulae. There are some notes about learning formulae on page 433.

Indices

1. $a^m \times a^n =$
2. $a^m \div a^n =$
3. $(a^m)^n =$

Standard index form

4. The form of the number is

Variation

Formulae for:

5. y is directly proportional to x
6. y varies as the square of x
7. y is inversely proportional to x
8. y varies inversely as the square of x

9. The reciprocal of $x =$

Triangles

10. Sum of angles $=$
11. Exterior angle $=$

Quadrilaterals

12. Sum of angles $=$

Polygons

13 to 17. Interior angle and exterior angle of a regular polygon with:

13. 3 sides
14. 4 sides
15. 5 sides
16. 6 sides
17. 8 sides
18. Sum of exterior angles of a polygon $=$
19. Sum of interior angles of a polygon with n sides $=$

Lengths, areas and volumes

20. Perimeter of a rectangle $=$
21. Circumference of a circle $=$

Areas of:

22. Rectangle $=$
23. Square $=$
24. Triangle $=$
25. Parallelogram $=$
26. Trapezium $=$
27. Circle $=$

Volumes of

28. Cuboid $=$
29. Cube $=$
30. Prism, solid of uniform cross-section $=$
31. Cylinder $=$
32. Curved surface area of cylinder $=$

33. Pythagoras' theorem:

Similar figures

34. Scale factor =

Statistics

35. Mean of a set of numbers =
36. Mean of a frequency distribution =
37. Definition of the median:
38. Definition of the mode:
39. Range =
40. Interquartile range =

Probability

41. Probability of a successful outcome =
42. Probability (relative frequency) =

Mutually exclusive events

43. P(A or B) =

Independent events

44. P(A and B) =

Trig. in right-angled triangles

45. $\sin A$ =
46. $\cos A$ =
47. $\tan A$ =

48. Density =

49. Speed =
50. Average speed =

Graphs

51. Gradient of a line =
52. Gradient of the line $y = mx + c$ is
53. Point where $y = mx + c$ cuts the y-axis is

Sketch graphs of

54. $y = mx + c$
55. $y = x^2$
56. $y = x^3$
57. $y = \dfrac{1}{x}$

To the student: 6

The day before the examination

Get all your equipment ready:
Pen (and spare cartridges),
Pencil and sharpener,
Rubber,
Ruler,
Compasses, protractor, set square,
Calculator,
Watch.

For your calculator, buy new batteries and make sure they work. Spend a few minutes playing with your calculator to recall which functions you can get with the various keys. How do you find $\sqrt{40}$, $\sqrt[3]{64}$, 40^2, $\frac{1}{40}$, $\sin 40°$ and x where $\cos x° = 0.4$? Remove the instruction booklet which you must not take into the examination room.

Although there should be a clock in the examination room, you may not be able to see it from where you are sitting so it is advisable to wear your watch. Does it also need new batteries? If you have not got a watch, then borrow one or buy a cheap one.

You want to be comfortable in the exam room so plan to wear a jacket or pullover to keep you warm if it is cold, but which you can take off if you get too hot. (If it gets very stuffy during the exam, ask the invigilator if a window can be opened. If you are in a chilly draught, ask him if it can be closed.)

Check your exam timetable. If you think the exam is in the **afternoon**, check very carefully, because you will be too late if you turn up in the afternoon for an exam that actually took place that morning. Check with someone else in your class to make sure.

Have a last-minute glance at last year's paper or a practice paper. See what instructions were given on that. Plan ahead as to how you will allocate your time. Have a final look at your revision checklist and maybe do just a little more revision, but not too much, as this should be a time for relaxation. Get out into the fresh air and have some exercise. Then go to bed at a reasonable time.

The day of the examination

Get to the exam room in good time, with all your equipment, and have nothing on your desk or in your pockets which you are not supposed to have with you.

When the exam begins, make a note of the time shown on your own watch, and note the time it is due to end.

Check the instructions at the beginning of the paper so that you know whether you must answer all the questions or whether you have to make a choice from one section. Note any other important points.

Do not rush into the first question too quickly. Read it very carefully. Decide how to answer it, then do so. If you have to show your working, set it down neatly. You have plenty of time. It is so easy to make a mistake at this stage as you have not settled down, so do not be in too much of a rush.

When you have finished this question, and this applies to all the other questions as well, read the printed question again. Have you done what you were asked to do ? Have you answered all of it ? Is the answer reasonable ? (Should you check your calculations again ?) Is the answer given to the accuracy required, e.g. to 3 significant figures, and have you given the units, e.g. cm^2 ?

Continue answering questions carefully until you have done a few. Then check the time. If you are going very slowly it might be sensible to leave out any long questions so as to do a few quick ones at this stage. Remember it is the marks which count so spend the time on what will gain you the most marks.

If you cannot do a question, read it again carefully. What is it about ? Are you using all the information given ? Is there a diagram ? Is there any other information you could deduce from the diagram ? If there is not a diagram, would a sketch diagram help ? If so, draw one. What facts or formulae do you know about this topic ? Do they help ? If the question is in several parts, often an answer to an earlier part may be needed in working out a later part. Even if you cannot finish the question, put something down on paper because your attempt might be worth some marks and it cannot be marked if it is not written down. If you cannot do part (1) of a question but can do part (2), then do part (2) so that you will get the marks for that. You can always go back to thinking about part (1) later if you want to, and have the time. If you cannot get any further on any part of the question then abandon it and try a different one.

If the numbers in a question turn out to be complicated it is possible that you have made a simple mistake. Check that you have copied the numbers or expression correctly, and check the signs in your working.

Keep your writing clear. Show all necessary working with your answer as you cannot gain marks for it if it is in a jumbled mess at the bottom of the page. You can do rough work at the side of the page near the answer, and then cross it out if you wish, but cross it out neatly so that it can still be read, in case it is worth some marks.

Do not use white paint correction fluid to blot out your mistakes. Some Examination Boards do not allow you to use this, but even if allowed, it wastes time, and if you write over it the new writing might get soaked up and be illegible by the time your script has reached the examiner.

Once the examination is over, forget it, until the results come out. You have done your best and that is all that matters. We hope you will be satisfied with your final grade.
GOOD LUCK!

Index

Answers

Some answers have been given corrected to reasonable degrees of accuracy, depending on the questions. There may be variations in answers where questions involve drawings or graphs. Sometimes it will not be possible to give answers to the same degree of accuracy, depending on the scale used.

Page 3   **Exercise 1.1**

1. | 56 | 120 | 15 | 72 | 20 |
    | 24 | 15 | 6 | 0 | 106 |
    | 20 | 121 | 600 | 8 | 0 |
    | 60 | 8 | 12 | 13 | 144 |

2. | 8 | 3 | 11 | 6 | 3 |
    | 6 | 12 | 8 | 5 | 7 |
    | 8 | 10 | 12 | 7 | 9 |
    | 7 | 12 | 5 | 12 | 9 |

3. 1 3   4 0
    2 4   5 4
    3 2

4. 1 4   4 3
    2 8   5 19
    3 5

5. 1 15   5 250   8 12
    2 0   6 188   9 190
    3 19   7 36   10 36
    4 8000

6. 1 2   4 9, 10
    2 4   5 3, 4, 5
    3 5, 6

7. 1 4, 9   5 4, 12   8 8, 9
    2 5, 6   6 2, 3, 6   9 3, 8
    3 2, 50   7 3, 4, 5   10 7, 11
    4 1, 15

8. 1 4   4 106
    2 1024   5 105
    3 8

9. 1 8   2 4   3 10

Page 9   **Exercise 1.2**

1. 1 280   5 800 000   8 140 000
    2 71 000   6 240 000   9 300 000
    3 903 000   7 180 000   10 28 000
    4 4800

2. 1 700   5 300   8 400
    2 300   6 20   9 2
    3 6   7 30   10 250
    4 40

3. 1 36 180   5 21 438   8 10 545
    2 8683   6 14 256   9 72 197
    3 61 916   7 32 550   10 12 180
    4 9792

4. 1 38   5 9   8 13
    2 6   6 29   9 22
    3 31   7 17   10 34
    4 7

5. 1 52 r 4   4 15 r 10
    2 12 r 8   5 22 r 6
    3 12 r 33

6. 1 44.5   4 29.1
    2 43.4   5 30.4
    3 10.7

Page 12   **Exercise 1.3**

1. 23, 29

2. 1 31, 37   2 83, 89

3. **1** 16   **5** 4   **8** 88
    2 343   **6** 72   **9** 2700
    3 100 000 **7** 140   **10** 650
    4 11

4. **1** $2^4 \times 3$ **9** 2^6
    2 $3^2 \times 11$ **10** $2^2 \times 5^2$
    3 $2^2 \times 13$ **11** 3×13
    4 $2^2 \times 3 \times 5$ **12** $2^4 \times 5$
    5 $2^2 \times 3^2 \times 5$ **13** 11^2
    6 $2^3 \times 3$ **14** 3^4
    7 $2 \times 5 \times 7$ **15** $2 \times 3 \times 5^2$
    8 $2^5 \times 3$

5. **1** $3^2 \times 5^2$, 15   **4** 2^8, 16
    2 $2^2 \times 3^2 \times 7^2$, 42   **5** $3^2 \times 5^4$, 75
    3 $3^2 \times 11^2$, 33

6. **1** $2^2 \times 7$, 2^4, (1) 4, (2) 112
    2 2×5, $3^2 \times 5$, (1) 5, (2) 90
    3 $2 \times 3 \times 11$, $2^3 \times 11$, (1) 22, (2) 264
    4 $2 \times 3 \times 5 \times 7$, $2 \times 3^2 \times 5 \times 7$,
       (1) 210, (2) 630
    5 $2^4 \times 3^2$, $2^3 \times 3^3$, (1) 72, (2) 432

7. **1** 3^6 **5** 3^4 **8** 6^6
    2 5^3 **6** 2^3 **9** 3^{18}
    3 7^8 **7** 5^4 **10** 5^8
    4 2^{20}

8. **1** 81   **4** 91   **7** 81
    2 8   **5** 8   **8** 50
    3 37, 73 **6** 360

9. $2^6 \times 3^3$, 12

Page 17   Exercise 1.4

1. **1** 34, 40, 46. (Add 6)
    2 18, 21, 24. (Add 3)
    3 160, 320, 640. (Double)
    4 729, 2187, 6561. (Multiply by 3)
    5 -12, -15, -18. (Subtract 3)
    6 18, 24, 31. (Add 1 more each time)
    7 $\dfrac{1}{81}, \dfrac{1}{243}, \dfrac{1}{729}$. $\left(\text{Multiply by } \dfrac{1}{3}\right)$
    8 127, 255, 511. (Double and add 1)
    9 158, 318, 638. (Add 5, 10, 20, ...,
       doubling each time)
    10 720, 5040, 40 320. (Multiply by 2, 3, 4, ...)

2. **1** 12, 16, 20, 24, 28
    2 12, 9, 6, 3, 0
    3 12, 60, 300, 1500, 7500
    4 12, 6, 3, $1\frac{1}{2}$, $\frac{3}{4}$
    5 12, 13, 15, 18, 22

3. **1** 9, 14, 23   **4** 5, 9, 14
    2 18, 28, 46   **5** 11, 18, 29
    3 2, 3, 5

4. **1** 41, 55, 71   **4** 99, 148, 207
    2 37, 47, 58   **5** 80, 110, 145
    3 43, 60, 80

6. next 5 terms are 21, 34, 55, 89, 144

Page 19   Exercise 1.5

1. **1** 7   **8** 10   **15** -4
    2 3   **9** -9 **16** -8
    3 -1 **10** 3   **17** -3
    4 -6 **11** 0   **18** -4
    5 0   **12** 1   **19** 0
    6 -8 **13** 11   **20** 1
    7 -3 **14** 2

2. **1** -1 **5** 2   **9** -3
    2 -7 **6** -3 **10** 1
    3 -6 **7** -5 **11** 6
    4 0   **8** 7   **12** -9

3. **1** -16 **5** 3   **9** -9
    2 24   **6** 0   **10** 64
    3 -35 **7** 0   **11** -2
    4 -10 **8** 2   **12** -1

4. **1** -2 **5** -1 **9** 8
    2 -3 **6** -6 **10** 6
    3 -3 **7** -7 **11** -2
    4 9   **8** -1 **12** 0

5. **1** $-\frac{1}{2}$ **5** 0   **8** -1
    2 25   **6** 0   **9** $-\frac{1}{2}$
    3 -8 **7** -6 **10** -1
    4 1

6. **1** $-7°$ **4** $-8°$
    2 13 deg   **5** $-5°$
    3 15 deg

Page 21   Exercise 1.6

1. **1** 19   **4** 12
    2 16   **5** 16, 20
    3 20   **6** 8, 19

2. $2^3 \times 3^3 \times 5$; $a = 3$, $b = 3$, $c = 1$; 30

3. $378 = 2 \times 3^3 \times 7$, $441 = 3^2 \times 7^2$;
    1 21
    2 63
    3 $2 \times 3^3 \times 7^2$

4. **1** 60
   2 13
   3 17

8. $85^2 = 7225$

9. £244

10. £2772

11. 78

14. **1** £150   **3** £70
    2 £260   **4** £30

15. **1** +6   **5** +3   **8** −3
    2 +3   **6** −3   **9** 2
    3 −2   **7** 2   **10** 0
    4 −4

Page 24   Practice test 1

1. **1** 19, 23   **4** 27
   2 25   **5** 19, 25
   3 18, 27

2. $360 = 2^3 \times 3^2 \times 5$,
   $405 = 3^4 \times 5$,
   $145\,800 = 2^3 \times 3^6 \times 5^2$

3. **1** $7^2 \times 11$
   2 $7^3 \times 11^3 \times 13 \times 17$

4. **1** 1296
   2 64
   3 25 min

6. **1** 41, 48   **4** 29, 40
   2 −14, −18   **5** 2, 1
   3 12 500, 62 500

7. **1** risen 3 deg   **6** fallen 27 deg
   2 fallen 9 deg   **7** risen 10 deg
   3 risen 6 deg   **8** risen 3 deg
   4 risen 2 deg   **9** fallen 4 deg
   5 fallen 6 deg   **10** fallen 3 deg

8. **1** −8   **5** 2   **8** 49
   2 9   **6** 5   **9** 0
   3 63   **7** 9   **10** −8
   4 −5

Page 29   Exercise 2.1

1. **1** acute   **3** obtuse
   2 reflex   **4** reflex

2. **1** 25°   **2** 118°   **3** 72°

Page 32   Exercise 2.2

1. **1** $a = 136°, b = 78°, c = 50°, d = 96°$
   2 $e = 154°, f = 26°$
   3 $g = j = 110°, h = k = 70°$

2. **1** $a = b = 127°$
   2 $c = d = 29°$
   3 $e = 64°, f = 116°$

3. **1** $a = 160°$
   2 $b = 40°$
   3 $c = 35°, d = e = 145°$
   4 $f = 67°$
   5 $g = 54°$
   6 $h = 70°$

4. **1** $a = 80°$
   2 $b = 67°$
   3 $c = 125°, d = 55°, e = 40°$
   4 $f = h = 63°, g = 117°$

5. **1** $j = 60°, k = 50°, m = 70°$
   2 $n = 125°, p = 145°, q = 35°$

Page 37   Exercise 2.3

1. **1** $\angle A = 81°, \angle B = 55°, \angle C = 44°$
   2 $\angle A = 116°, \angle B = 37°, \angle C = 27°$

2. **1** $\angle A = 26°, \angle B = \angle C = 77°$
   2 $\angle A = \angle C = 18°, \angle B = 144°$

3. **1** $\angle C = 72°$ **4** $\angle C = 30°$
   2 $\angle B = 48°$ **5** $\angle C = 118°$
   3 $\angle A = 24°$

4. **1** $a = 30°$ **3** $c = 60°$
   2 $b = 38°$ **4** $d = 35°$

5. $\angle ABC = \angle ACB$
   1 74°   **3** 16°
   2 90°   **4** 32°

6. **1** 32°   **3** 64°
   2 64°   **4** 52°

Page 41   Exercise 2.4

1. $BC = 7.6$ cm, $\angle B = 34°, \angle C = 88°$

2. $\angle A = 58°, \angle B = 47°, \angle C = 75°$

3. $AC = 7.5$ cm, $\angle B = 43°, \angle C = 47°$

4. $AE = 4.5$ cm, $EC = 4.5$ cm

5. $AD = 4.7$ cm, $CD = 4.3$ cm

Page 42   Exercise 2.5

1. **1** 30°
    2 105°
    3 105°

2. **1** $a = b = 50°$, $c = d = 40°$
    2 $e = f = g = 20°$
    3 $h = j = 75°$, $k = 30°$
    4 $m = p = 40°$, $n = 100°$, $q = r = 70°$

3. $\angle A = 34°$, $x = 52$

4. **1** 70°
    2 35°
    3 110°

5. **1** 74°
    2 106°
    3 37°

6. $\angle ADE = 29°$, $\angle EAD = 27°$

7. $AC = 7.1$ cm

8. $\angle A = 104°$, $\angle B = \angle C = 38°$

Page 44   Practice test 2

1. $a = b = 74°, c = 106°$

2. $d = 117°, e = 63°$

3. $f = g = 38°$

4. $\angle ABC = \angle ACB$;
    $\angle ABC = \angle BCA = 68°$, $\angle ACD = 46°$,
    $\angle CDB = 90°$, $\angle BCD = 22°$

5. **3** 3

6. $\angle A = 69°$, $BD = 2.2$ cm, $DC = 4.4$ cm

Page 51   Exercise 3.1

1. **1** 7.61   **4** 10.02
    2 7   **5** 7.86
    3 0.63

2. **1** 20.96   **4** 9.09
    2 6.95   **5** 4.88
    3 0.37

3. **1** 15.48   **4** 9.42
    2 0.6   **5** 9.6
    3 5.6

4. **1** 0.97   **4** 2.2
    2 0.007   **5** 5.9
    3 0.16

5. **1** 13.2   **4** 2.7
    2 250   **5** 62
    3 1030

6. **1** 0.379   **4** 0.0031
    2 0.0015   **5** 0.17
    3 0.0213

7. **1** 0.072   **4** 0.63
    2 0.003   **5** 0.02
    3 0.012

8. **1** 8.792   **4** 0.24
    2 0.0798   **5** 0.001271
    3 198.38

9. **1** 39   **4** 300
    2 83   **5** 0.8
    3 31

10. **1** 0.75   **4** 0.37
    2 0.4   **5** 0.6
    3 0.7

11. **1** 29.712   **4** 4.680
    2 1.628   **5** 0.004
    3 202.916

12. **1** 29.7   **4** 4.68
    2 1.63   **5** 0.00353
    3 203

13. **1** 56 800   **4** 207
    2 83.0   **5** 1000
    3 253

14. **1** 2.86   **4** 0.97
    2 51.67   **5** 1.14
    3 0.09

15. **1** 0.67   **4** 0.17
    2 0.71   **5** 0.73
    3 0.44

16. 0.7, 0.75, 0.778, 0.8, 0.81

17. 60.9, 62.49, 62.5, 63.7, 63.72

18. 1

Page 57   Exercise 3.2

1. **1** 7.5   **5** 6   **8** 8
    2 12   **6** 51   **9** 18
    3 27   **7** 7   **10** 2
    4 4

2. 1 2769   5 10.9   8 22 054
   2 29   6 45 040   9 406
   3 5329   7 3003   10 307.72
   4 18

3. 1 170   4 6930   7 55.7
   2 0.000159   5 5.49   8 4.63
   3 1.27   6 0.194

4. 1 30 r 11   4 285 r 5
   2 35 r 22   5 6 r 40
   3 78 r 10

5. £10.20, £9.80

6. 24p

7. 52, 12p

8. £15.69

9. £55.80

10. £4227, £773

11. 60

12. 27, 34

13. 11, 12

14. 24.49

15. 15

Page 67   **Exercise 3.3**

1. 1 50   8 6000   15 36
   2 3000   9 64   16 52
   3 1000   10 31   17 560
   4 50   11 16   18 30
   5 365   12 135   19 5280
   6 4000   13 2000   20 1000
   7 880   14 150

2. 1 10.64 kg
   2 101.4°F
   3 1.25 kg (1250 g)
   4 4 ml

3. 1 750 g   5 1.6 m   8 78 mm
   2 12.6 cm   6 1.52 kg   9 120 cm
   3 260 cm   7 70 cl   10 3.04 tonnes
   4 0.4 ℓ

4. 1 7 cm
   2 $1\frac{1}{2}$ ins

5. 1 15 cm   4 2 tonnes
   2 2 kg (1.8 kg)   5 16 km
   3 45 ℓ

6. 1 3 yds (10 ft)   4 $7\frac{1}{2}$ miles
   2 10 lb (11 lb)   5 6 tons
   3 1 gall (7 pints)

7. 1 1.8   4 £30
   2 $3\frac{1}{2}$ kg, 35 kg   5 20
   3 72°

8. 10 ins

9. 12 lb

10. 864

11. 228 yd

12. 120 yd

13. 2004

14. 4.05, 14.00, 15.15, 18.05, 23.55;
1.10 am, 5.18 am, 10.30 am, 5.05 pm, 9.50 pm

15. 4 h 43 min

16. 4.05 pm

17. 1 29   4 29
   2 28   5 28
   3 29

18. 1 June
   2 September
   3 February

19. 5 h 10 min, 01.20

20. 40 100 km

Page 70   **Exercise 3.4**

1. 1 1800   5 1   8 300
   2 0.07   6 6   9 0.6
   3 36   7 7   10 100
   4 4.8

2. 2150

3. 0.4

4. 0.006

5. 28

6. 0.625

7. 0.054

8. 10.688

9. 1

10. $\frac{3}{40}$

11. 1   22.149
    2   0.0514
    3   81.6

12. 1   9877
    2   9876.52
    3   9880

13. 0.299, 0.3, 0.35

14. 1   343 000   4   54 600
    2   74.8   5   61.3
    3   3.07   6   24 400

15. 1   853   5   315   8   891
    2   26   6   334   9   20
    3   3147   7   22   10   52
    4   69 984

16. 10, 9

17. £5.62, 16p

18. 12 oz

19. 54 kg

20. 23, 25, 27

21. 32, 38

22. 11.4 cm

23. 1   60 g
    2   4 min
    3   30 m

24. 17 pieces, 24 cm

25. 250 g size

26. 50

27. £13.50

28. 1   £150
    2   £149.97

29. 40 min

30. 1   16.16, 25 min
    2   16.08, 36 min

31. 1   46°F, 8°C
    2   95°F
    3   20°C

Page 74   **Practice test 3**

1. 1   8   5   1050   8   9
   2   1.6   6   0.032   9   0.0018
   3   97   7   0.28   10   4.7
   4   4.3

2. $\frac{5}{8}$, $\frac{7}{10}$, $\frac{3}{4}$, $\frac{7}{9}$, $\frac{5}{6}$

3. 1   200 000   4   10
   2   40   5   9
   3   3600

4. 1   199 398   4   12
   2   45   5   8.8
   3   3721

5. 1   106.8   4   35.6
   2   28.4   5   47.2
   3   13.3

6. 31 r 2

7. 4.36

8. 1   2.38 kg   5   260 cm   8   5.12 m
   2   0.2 m   6   3100 g   9   32 ℓ
   3   5000 ml   7   2.8 cm   10   250 g
   4   120 mm

9. 6 g, 0.14 mm

10. 1   3.40 pm
    2   15.40

11. £37.80

12. 5

Page 79   **Exercise 4.1**

1. 112°

2. 85°

4. 1   parallelogram, rhombus, rectangle, square
   2   rhombus, square
   3   rectangle, square

5. 1   2   3   2
   2   2   4   4

6. 1 $a = c = 115°, b = 65°$
   2   $d = e = 45°, f = 90°$

7. 74°, 87°

8. 110°

9. 1   right-angled
   2   right-angled isosceles
   3   isosceles

10. **1** $\angle XCB, \angle XAD, \angle XDA$

11. **1** kite
    2 rhombus
    3 square

12. $AD = 5.4$ cm, trapezium

13. $AC = 6.9$ cm, $\angle ADC = 51°$, BD is axis of symmetry

14. $58°$

15. $\angle A = 141°$, $AD = 4.3$ cm

Page 85   Exercise 4.2

2. **1** $36°$ **2** $144°$

3. $162°$

4. 12

5. **1** $45°$ **2** 8

6. 36

7. $540°, 85°$

8. $720°, 147°$

9. $1080°, 135°$

10. $50°$

11. $\angle BCD = 108°, \angle BCP = 135°, a = 117°$

12. **1** isosceles trapezium **4** right-angled
    2 rectangle   **5** equilateral
    3 isosceles (obtuse angled)

Page 92   Exercise 4.3

1. **1** cuboid   **3** (triangular) prism
   2 cylinder   **4** cone

3. **1** 3   **2** 4

5. 2, 3, 5

6. 1, 3

Page 94   Exercise 4.4

1. **1** $84°$
   2 $48°$
   3 isosceles (acute-angled)

2. **1** $a = 85°$ **2** $b = 76°$

3. **1** both equal to DC
   2 isosceles
   3 $g = 90°, h = 60°, j = 15°, k = 45°$

4. $AB = 4.3$ cm, $AD = 8.0$ cm, $\angle DAB = 105°$

5. **1** parallelogram   **3** rectangle
   2 trapezium   **4** rhombus

6. **1** parallelogram   **3** rhombus
   2 rectangle   **4** square

7. $a = 30°, b = 75°, c = 150°$

8. **1** $120°$, hexagons
   2 $90°, 135°, 135°$; (square), octagons

9. **1** $108°$
   2 isosceles (obtuse-angled)
   3 $36°$
   4 $72°$
   5 isosceles trapezium
   6 rhombus

10. $140°$

11. $30°, 90°, 90°$

12. **1** $AD = 9.7$ cm   **2** $AB = 5.9$ cm

18. $F = 14, V = 24, E = 36$

Page 101   Practice test 4

1. **1** parallelogram, rectangle
   2 kite
   3 rhombus, square

2. $a = b = 52°, c = 104°, d = 49°, e = 79°$

3. $AC = BD = 7.1$ cm, angles at $X = 90°$

4. **1** $120°$
   2 $a = b = c = 60°$
   3 equilateral triangle
   4 rhombus

5. **1** $40°$
   2 $140°$
   3 $20°$

6. $F = 7, V = 7, E = 12$

7. E and G

Page 106   Exercise 5.1

1. **1** $\frac{2}{5}$ **4** $\frac{1}{4}$

   2 $\frac{1}{6}$ **5** $\frac{1}{3}$

   3 $\frac{2}{3}$

2. **1** 44, 9, 4, 7, 30, 12, 21, 26, 45, 48
    2 6, 33, 20, 8, 15, 9, 1, 7, 13, 25
    3 2, 7, 20, 25, 13, 11, 1, 6, 40, 9
    4 12, 4, 9, 2, 20, 3, 7, 15, 11, 40
    5 4, 10, 16, 6, 20, 40, 22, 60, 50, 12

3. **1** $\frac{2}{3}$ **5** $\frac{3}{10}$ **8** $\frac{7}{12}$

    2 $\frac{5}{6}$ **6** $\frac{2}{5}$ **9** $\frac{4}{9}$

    3 $\frac{1}{6}$ **7** $\frac{5}{8}$ **10** $\frac{3}{4}$

    4 $\frac{3}{10}$

4. **1** $\frac{14}{18}$ **4** $\frac{21}{24}$

    2 $\frac{12}{20}$ **5** $\frac{6}{20}$

    3 $\frac{15}{18}$

5. **1** $\frac{7}{4}$ **5** $\frac{23}{8}$ **8** $\frac{15}{2}$

    2 $\frac{7}{3}$ **6** $\frac{22}{5}$ **9** $\frac{10}{3}$

    3 $\frac{37}{10}$ **7** $\frac{9}{8}$ **10** $\frac{23}{10}$

    4 $\frac{11}{6}$

6. **1** $4\frac{3}{5}$ **5** $2\frac{3}{4}$ **8** $4\frac{1}{4}$

    2 $2\frac{5}{6}$ **6** $6\frac{2}{3}$ **9** $8\frac{1}{3}$

    3 $3\frac{1}{10}$ **7** $2\frac{3}{5}$ **10** $3\frac{1}{4}$

    4 $2\frac{5}{8}$

7. **1** $\frac{1}{3}$ **5** $\frac{3}{5}$ **8** $\frac{1}{9}$

    2 $\frac{2}{9}$ **6** $\frac{2}{3}$ **9** $\frac{1}{5}$

    3 $\frac{1}{6}$ **7** $\frac{1}{4}$ **10** $\frac{1}{3}$

    4 $\frac{3}{4}$

8. **1** £2.70   **5** 15 oz   **8** 4 ins
    2 8 ins   **6** 15°   **9** 9 lb
    3 60p   **7** 6 pints   **10** 2 ft 11 ins
    4 1 hour

9. **1** $\frac{5}{6}$ **4** $\frac{5}{6}$

    2 $\frac{1}{3}$ **5** $\frac{3}{4}$

    3 $\frac{2}{3}$

10. $\frac{1}{6}$

11. 150

Page 109   **Exercise 5.2**

1. **1** 3 : 8   **5** 2 : 1   **8** 5 : 8
    2 3 : 7   **6** 4 : 5   **9** 5 : 24
    3 3 : 2   **7** 5 : 12   **10** 3 : 10
    4 1 : 3

2. **1** 90p, £1.35   **4** £1.50, 25p
    2 56p, 98p   **5** £2.80, £1.20
    3 42p, 18p

3. **1** £450   **4** £7.50
    2 £67.50   **5** £27.50
    3 £160

4. 2.7 cm

5. 80p

6. 48°, 60°, 72°

7. 1 m³ sand, 2 m³ gravel

Page 113   **Exercise 5.3**

1. £7.70

2. 81 lb

3. £12

4. 16 days

5. 15 days

6. £300

7. £40

8. 28 m

9. 2 h

10. 30 weeks

11. 24 mph

12. £950

13. 10 lb

14. **1** 0.6 g/cm³
    2 3.86 kg
    3 25 000 cm³

15. 4.5 ℓ

16. **1** 70 km/h
    2 90 km
    3 20 min

17. 300 km/h

18. yes (average speed 45 mph)

19. 95 km/h

20. 3 h 48 min

Page 118   Exercise 5.4

1. **1** $\frac{9}{25}$ **4** $\frac{1}{30}$

   2 $\frac{9}{20}$ **5** $\frac{2}{3}$

   3 $\frac{7}{40}$

2. **1** 0.47   **4** 0.0625

   2 0.95   **5** 0.999

   3 0.225

3. **1** 75%   **4** $33\frac{1}{3}$%

   2 62.5%   **5** 87.5%

   3 15%

4. **1** 1.44 m   **4** 1.5 cm

   2 600 g   **5** £4.60

   3 5 min

5. **1** 72%   **4** $37\frac{1}{2}$%

   2 8%   **5** $66\frac{2}{3}$%

   3 60%

6. **1** £6.24   **4** £60

   2 £2.90   **5** £336

   3 £108

7. **1** 20%   **4** $22\frac{1}{2}$%

   2 $16\frac{2}{3}$%   **5** 20%

   3 12%

8. **1** £700   **3** 300 ml

   2 £4   **4** £9000

9. £28.20

10. £360, tax £63

11. **1** £180
    2 £60
    3 £18

12. **1** A
    2 C

13. 12%

14. 3.8%

Page 120   Exercise 5.5

1. Mr B $\frac{5}{12}$; Mr A won, 400 extra

2. 60 cows, $\frac{1}{4}$

3. 27

4. $\frac{2}{5}$

5. 180 gall

6. £500

7. A £240, B £300, C £360

8. £2437.50

9. £1600, £2800, £3600

10. 4.5 ℓ

11. 12 h

12. 49 min

13. £1155

14. 2

15. **1** 250 g
    2 5

16. £146.20, 48 h

17. £120.25

18. 0.8 g/cm^3

19. **1** 5 : 6
    2 6 : 5

20. **1** 48 mph
    2 36 mph
    3 38 miles/gall

21. 175 ml

22. **1** 50%, 25%, 20%, 10%, 5%, 1%
    2 $\frac{3}{10}$, $\frac{1}{3}$, $\frac{2}{5}$, $\frac{2}{3}$, $\frac{3}{4}$

23. 60%

24. £150, £100

25. £75

26. £90, £98.10; £188.10

27. £16

Page 124   Practice test 5

1. **1** $\frac{5}{6}$ **4** $3\frac{3}{5}$

   2 $\frac{15}{35}$ **5** $\frac{3}{10}$

   3 $\frac{24}{5}$ **6** £1.40

2. 126

3. 2.5 kg tin, 1 kg zinc

4. 42

5. 100 kg

6. 10 days

7. 64%

8. $\frac{1}{2}$ hour

9. 18 m^2/ℓ

10. £42.75

Page 126   Exercise A1

1. £2.50
2. 68 cm
3. £5.40
4. 36 ℓ
5. 18 days

6. 0.95
7. 53, 59
8. 11 kg
9. 4
10. £34

11. 110°
12. 2005
13. 80p
14. 3.23 pm
15. $\frac{3}{4}$

Page 127   Exercise A2

1. **1** 640
    2 260
    3 0.085
    4 5300
    5 0.52

2. **1** 3
    2 16 feet

3. 68°

4. 2

5. **1** sphere
    2 cylinder
    3 cone
    4 cuboid
    5 cube (or cuboid)

6. $AB = 5.8$ cm, $\angle ABC = 118°$, rhombus

7. £960, £1600, £2240

8. $\frac{3}{10}$, $\frac{3}{8}$, $\frac{1}{3}$, 38 %, 0.4

10. **1** 45°
    2 135°
    3 square

11. **1** 16.55
    2 7 h 13 min
    3 25p
    4 70 km/h

12. 79p

Page 129   Exercise A3

1. 3200

2. **1** −45°
    2 +90°
    3 180°
    4 −140°
    5 +62°

3. **1** 54 min
    2 8%

4. **1** 47
    2 15, 51
    3 47, 57
    4 34, 51
    5 27, 15

5. £60

6. **1** triangular prism
    2 cuboid
    3 pyramid with a square base

7. **1** 5.63
    2 3.23
    3 37.28
    4 0.10
    5 0.06

8. 48°

9. **1** 0.12
    2 0.0035
    3 1.4

10. £30.15

11. **1** trapezium
    2 parallelogram
    3 parallelogram
    4 rectangle
    5 rhombus

12. £250

Page 137   Example 2

$\frac{4}{9}$, $\frac{37}{90}$

Page 140   Example 5

1 week 9
2 weeks 1 and 2

Page 141   Exercise 6.1

1. frequencies in order starting with 44 matches: 1, 6, 8, 10, 12, 20, 3

2. $\frac{1}{4}$

4. food £15, transport £9.50, camp fee £7, extras £4.50

6. A 17, B 6, C 25, D 12; angles A 102°, B 36°, C 150°, D 72°

7. 5p; angles 191°, 61°, 43°, 29°, 11°, 7°, 18°

Page 148 Exercise 6.2

4. frequencies in order:
2, 10, 18, 20, 16, 9, total 75

5. frequencies in order:
4, 8, 8, 6, 3, 1

Page 149 Exercise 6.3

1. goals by home team, frequencies: 7, 16, 12, 4, 1, 2;
goals by away team, frequencies: 14, 10, 13, 3, 2;
total goals by home teams 66; total goals by away teams 53

3. **1** $\frac{2}{3}$
2 12 million cattle, 8 million sheep

4. 1p represented by $\frac{1}{2}°$;
angles in order: 220°, 86°, 36°, 18°

5. angles in order: 284°, 40°, 25°, 11°

6. angles in order: 108°, 50°, 29°, 25°, 18°, 130°

16. frequencies in order: 1, 5, 12, 16, 11, 4, 1

Page 153 Practice test 6

1. 640 workers

2. angles in order: 108°, 63°, 54°, 27°, 36°, 72°

4. frequencies in order: 2, 3, 5, 7, 6, 5, 2

Page 160 Exercise 7.1

1. **1** $5a$ pence **3** $(3e + 2f)$ pence
2 $120b$ (min) **4** $(100 - gh)$ pence

2. **1** $C = \dfrac{k^2}{100}$ **2** $e = \frac{1}{3}m$ **3** $m = \dfrac{n}{20}$

3. **1** c **8** d^2 **14** $3f$ **20** $2c^3$
2 0 **9** e^5 **15** $9g^2$ **21** $8d^2$
3 $8e$ **10** f^4 **16** $5h$ **22** $2ef$
4 $3g - 4h$ **11** $45a^2$ **17** $\dfrac{4m}{n}$ **23** $6a^2$
5 a^2 **12** $16bc$ **18** $1\frac{1}{2}$ **24** $9g^4h^6$
6 b^3 **13** $20e^3$ **19** $2ab$ **25** $4jk^2$
7 1

4. **1** a^7 **5** e^8 **8** $6h^7$
2 b^6 **6** f^6 **9** j
3 c^2 **7** 1 **10** $3k^4$
4 d^9

5. **1** $6a - 10$ **4** $5e^3 - 5e^2 + 10e$
2 $18b + 15c$ **5** $3f^2 - 54f + 12$
3 $4d^2 + 4d$

6. **1** $3a$ **5** $9e$ **8** $7h$
2 $-b$ **6** $-2f$ **9** $-3x$
3 $5c$ **7** 0 **10** $5x$
4 $-3d$

7. **1** $16xy$ **5** -1 **8** $\dfrac{1}{x}$
2 $-28xy$ **6** $-6xy$ **9** $4x^2$
3 $-\frac{2}{3}$ **7** $-24x^2$ **10** 0
4 $27x^2$

8. **1** $3a + 3b$ **6** $8p - 13q + r$
2 $c - 10d$ **7** $44 - 5s$
3 $8e - f$ **8** $x^2 - x - 6$
4 $-3g - 9h$ **9** $2x^2 - 9x + 4$
5 $j + 6k$ **10** $x - x^2$

9. **1** 23 **4** 3
2 34 **5** 100
3 50

10. **1** 2 **5** 52 **8** 24
2 10 **6** -2 **9** $-\frac{1}{2}$
3 5 **7** 18 **10** -22
4 -192

11. 3025

12. **1** 35 **2** -30

Page 164 Exercise 7.2

1. **1** $a = 21$ **5** $e = 7$ **8** $h = 22\frac{1}{2}$
2 $b = 19$ **6** $f = 7$ **9** $j = 5$
3 $c = 8$ **7** $g = 6$ **10** $k = 3$
4 $d = 140$

2. **1** $a = 3$ **5** $e = 10$ **8** $h = 13$
2 $b = 4$ **6** $f = 4$ **9** $j = 70$
3 $c = 5$ **7** $g = 26$ **10** $k = 8$
4 $d = 4$

3. **1** $x = 28$ **4** $x = \frac{3}{4}$
2 $x = -\frac{1}{6}$ **5** $x = 2$
3 $x = 10$

4. 8 years

5. **1** $x = 12$
2 $y = 24$
3 $z = 12$

Page 167   **Exercise 7.3**

1. **1** $x = 6$ **4** $x = 3$ or $x = 5$
    2 $x = 3$ **5** $x = 4$
    3 $x = 1$ or $x = 6$

2. **1** $x = 5$ **4** $x = 5$
    2 $x = 3$ **5** $x = 4$
    3 $x = 2$

3. **1** $x = 5.4$ **5** $x = 3.8$ **8** $x = 6.8$
    2 $x = 1.4$ **6** $x = 1.5$ **9** $x = 2.4$
    3 $x = 4.6$ **7** $x = 4.8$ **10** $x = 9.1$
    4 $x = 4.2$

4. Ann 16, Bobby 12 years old

5. 1.3 s

Page 169   **Exercise 7.4**

1. **1** 19, 23; $4n - 1$ **6** 217, 344; $n^3 + 1$
    2 12, 11; $17 - n$ **7** $-25, -35$;
                                          $25 - 10n$
    3 22, 25; $3n + 7$ **8** 30, 42; $n(n - 1)$
    4 75, 70; $100 - 5n$ **9** $\frac{5}{7}, \frac{6}{8}; \frac{n}{n + 2}$
    5 $\frac{1}{5}, \frac{1}{6}; \frac{1}{n}$ **10** 35, 46; $n^2 + 10$

2. **1** 2, 5, 8, 11   **5** 3, 8, 15, 24
    2 90, 80, 70, 60   **6** 3, 9, 27, 81
    3 2, 5, 10, 17   **7** $\frac{1}{2}, \frac{2}{3}, \frac{3}{4}, \frac{4}{5}$
    4 10, 100, 1000,   **8** 0, 7, 26, 63
         10 000

Page 169   **Exercise 7.5**

1. $\dfrac{100p}{q}$ pence

2. $\dfrac{2st}{5}$ min

3. $A = 60 + 25n$; £360

4. **1** $2a$ **4** 1
    2 0   **5** a
    3 a^2

5. **1** $20a^{13}$
    2 $3b^4$
    3 c

6. **1** $x - 1$ **4** $20 - 4x$
    2 $2x - 5y$ **5** $9x - 10$
    3 $9x - 13$

7. **1** 6   **5** $3\frac{1}{2}$ **8** 11
    2 0   **6** 12   **9** 6
    3 1   **7** $\frac{1}{6}$ **10** 120
    4 26

8. **1** 0   **4** 2
    2 -10 **5** 5
    3 8

9. $v = 0$

10. $E = 36$

11. **1** $x = 3$ **5** $x = -1\frac{1}{2}$ **8** $x = -10$
     2 $x = -7$ **6** $x = -1$ **9** $x = 7\frac{1}{2}$
     3 $x = -8$ **7** $x = 0$ **10** $x = \frac{1}{4}$
     4 $x = -\frac{2}{3}$

12. **1** $x = -3$ **4** $x = -1$
     2 $x = 15$ **5** $x = \frac{1}{3}$
     3 $x = -1\frac{3}{5}$

13. 7

14. **1** $x = 30$, 65°
     2 $x = 50$, equilateral triangle
     3 $x = 9$

15. $x = 4, y = 3$;
     $AB = DC = 11$ cm, $BC = AD = 15$ cm

16. 13 sides

17. breadth $= (110 - x)$ m; length $= 70$ m

18. $x = 2.4$

19. **1** 43, 51, 59; $8n + 3$
     2 32, 64, 128; 2^n
     3 5, 1, -3; $25 - 4n$

20. **1** 16, 25, 36; n^2
     2 30, 45, 63; $\frac{3}{2}n(n + 1)$
     3 13, 16, 19; $3n + 1$
     4 28, 34, 40; $6n + 4$
     5 20, 24, 28; $4n + 4$
     6 24, 35, 48; $(n + 1)^2 - 1$ or $n^2 + 2n$

Page 172   **Practice test 7**

1. £$\dfrac{k(y - x)}{100}$

2. $T = \frac{1}{3}c + \frac{1}{3}$

3. **1** $7a^3$
    2 $12a^6$
    3 $\frac{3}{4}$

4. $10x - y$

5. **1** $\frac{3}{5}$ **2** $-\frac{1}{3}$

6. **1** $x = 2$ **4** $x = 10$
    2 $x = 1\frac{1}{5}$ **5** $x = 5\frac{1}{3}$
    3 $x = -2$

7. $x = 11$, number $= 11$

8. **1** $x = 35$ **2** $x = 20$

9. **1** $x = 9$ **2** $x = 2.4$

10. **1** $-4, -7, -10; 11 - 3n$
    2 $\frac{5}{8}, \frac{6}{9}, \frac{7}{10}; \dfrac{n}{n + 3}$

Page 176   Exercise 8.1

1. **1** 11.2 cm   **4** 8.1 cm
    2 10 cm   **5** 4 cm
    3 2.2 cm

2. **1** $c = 15$ cm   **4** $b = 3.3$ cm
    2 $c = 6.7$ cm   **5** $b = 8.5$ cm
    3 $b = 7$ cm

3. $x = 10$ cm, $y = 8$ cm

4. **1** 11.0 cm   **2** 4.0 cm   **3** 5.0 cm

5. 5 cm

Page 179   Exercise 8.2

1. **1** 121 cm^2 **3** 77 cm^2
    2 48 cm^2 **4** 34 cm^2

2. 14.7 cm^2

3. **1** 8.5 cm   **2** 29.8 cm

4. 59 cm^2

5. **1** 120 cm^2 **2** $x = 15$

6. 81 cm^2

7. area 28 m^2, perimeter 22 m

8. 87 cm^2, 48 cm

9. $\triangle APS$ 3 cm^2, $\triangle BPQ$ 12 cm^2, $\triangle CQR$ 8 cm^2, $\triangle DRS$ 10 cm^2, $PQRS$ 31 cm^2

Page 182   Exercise 8.3

1. **1** 600 cm^3 **4** 45 cm^3
    2 125 cm^3 **5** 27 000 cm^3
    3 50 m^3

2. 450 m^3

3. **1** 21 cm^2 **2** 189 cm^3

4. **1** $7\frac{1}{2}$ m^2 **2** 30 m^3

5. 54 cm^2

6. 5 m

Page 184   Exercise 8.4

1. **1** circumference 88.0 cm, area 616 cm^2
    2 37.7 cm, 113 cm^2
    3 6.28 m, 3.14 m^2
    4 28.3 cm, 63.6 cm^2

2. **1** 198 cm^3 **3** 246 cm^3
    2 3770 cm^2 **4** 3140 cm^2

3. 7.73 cm^2

4. 58.3 m^2

5. $r = 3.6$ cm, area $= 40.7$ cm^2

6. 1290 cm^3

7. **1** square, by 0.517 cm
    2 circle, by 0.252 cm^2

Page 187   Exercise 8.5

1. **1** volume   **9** length
    2 length   **10** length
    3 area   **11** length
    4 length   **12** length
    5 area   **13** area
    6 volume   **14** length
    7 volume   **15** length
    8 area

2. **1** $\dfrac{pq}{r} + \sqrt{\pi r^2}$

    2 $\dfrac{3pqr}{\sqrt{p^2 + q^2}}$

    3 $\pi p^3 + 2q^2 r$

3. **1** Dimension 4, should be 3; $V = \pi r^2 h$

    2 Dimension 3, should be 1; $h = \dfrac{2A}{b}$

    3 Dimension 2, should be 1; $r = \sqrt{\dfrac{A}{\pi}}$

    4 Dimension 4, should be 3; $V = Ah$

    5 Dimension 1, should be 2; $S = 2\pi rh$

Page 188   **Exercise 8.6**

1. 39 m

2. 17 km

3. 25 feet

4. 4.9 m

5. $OP = 26$ cm, $AP = 16$ cm

6. **1, 3, 4,** (**5** is nearly right-angled)

7. **1**   27 m^2 **2**   £216

8. 1000 tiles, 42 boxes

9. 40 m^2

10. area = 84 cm^2, perimeter = 48 cm

11. **1**   25 cm   **3**   66 cm
    2   15 cm   **4**   234 cm^2

12. area = 24 cm^2 (approx.)

13. 2250 kg

14. **1**   50 m^2 **2**   500 m^3

15. 32 min

16. 27.6 tonnes

17. **1**   100 000 m^2 **2**   30 000 m^3

18. 324 cm^2

19. **1**   70 400 cm^2 **2**   7.04 m^2

20. **1**   15.9 m   **2**   5.64 m

21. 20.0 cm

22. **1**   length   **5**   length   **8**   none
    2   area   **6**   area   **9**   length
    3   none   **7**   length   **10**   length
    4   volume

Page 191   **Practice test 8**

1. **1**   5 cm   **2**   16 cm   **3**   21 cm

2. **1**   30 cm^2 **3**   36 cm^2
   2   21 cm^2 **4**   57 cm^2

3. **1**   150 cm^2 **2**   25 cm   **3**   12 cm

4. 180 cm^3

5. 35 m^2

6. 15 m^3

7. 1100 m

8. 385 cm^3, 12 tins

9. **1** $b + 2\pi r$
   2 $b^2 + \pi rh$
   3 $\frac{1}{3}b^3 + \pi r^2 h$

Page 194   **Example**

$ABCD$ is a parallelogram

Page 195   **Exercise 9.1**

1. $T\,(6, 4)$, $U\,(3, 5)$

3. **1**   24 unit^2
   2   6 unit^2, 4 unit^2
   3   14 unit^2

4. **1**   parallelogram; $E\left(4, 4\frac{1}{2}\right)$
   2 $J\,(-5, 7)$; 4 axes
   3   rhombus; $x = -4$, $y = -6$

5. **1**   line JKM; $y = x + 2$
   2   (2, 4)

Page 198   **Exercise 9.2**

1. y-values:
   1   1, 2, 3, 4, 5, 6
   2 $-5, -3, -1, 1, 3, 5$
   3   9, 8, 7, 6, 5, 4
   4   8, 6, 4, 2, 0, -2

2. y-values:
   1 $-4, -2, 0, 2, 4$
   2   3, $3\frac{1}{2}$, 4, $4\frac{1}{2}$, 5
   3   9, 6, 3, 0, -3

3. y-values: 16, 9, 4, 1, 0, 1, 4, 9, 16

4. y-values: 30, 20, 15, 12, 10, $7\frac{1}{2}$, 6

Page 200   **Exercise 9.3**

1. $C\,(8, 4, 0)$
   $F\,(8, 1, 6)$
   $G\,(8, 4, 6)$
   $H\,(2, 4, 6)$

2. $B\,(12, 4, 5)$
   $C\,(12, 7, 5)$
   $D\,(1, 7, 5)$
   $E\,(1, 4, 9)$
   $F\,(12, 4, 9)$
   $H\,(1, 7, 9)$

3. $B\,(9, -4, -2)$
   $C\,(9, 5, -2)$
   $D\,(-1, 5, -2)$
   $E\,(-1, -4, 4)$
   $F\,(9, -4, 4)$
   $G\,(9, 5, 4)$
   $H\,(-1, 5, 4)$

Page 201   Exercise 9.4

1.   **1** $y = \frac{1}{2}x$
     2 D (5, 5)
     3 $y = 5$

2. A and E, B and F, C and D

3. D $(-2, 0)$; parallelogram

4.   square, 10 unit^2

5.   **3** y-values: $-4, -2, 0, 2, 4$
     4 y-values: $12, 9, 6, 3, 0, -3$
     5 $(3.25, 2.25)$
     6 $(-2, 11)$

6. y-values: $-3, 0, 3, 6$

7. y-values: $8, 4.5, 2, 0.5, 0, 0.5, 2, 4.5, 8$

8. y-values: $9, 6, 4.5, 3, 2.25, 1.8, 1.5, 1.2, 1$

9. B (9, 3, 4)   10. C (6, 6, 5),
     C (9, 4, 4) F (6, 3, 17),
     D (2, 4, 4) G (6, 6, 17),
     E (2, 3, 7) H (2, 6, 17),
     F (9, 3, 7) AB 4 units,
     G (9, 4, 7) BC 3 units,
     H (2, 4, 7) AC 5 units,
                              CG 12 units,
                              $\angle ACG = 90°$
                              $AG = 13$ units

Page 204   Practice test 9

1.   parallelogram

2.   25 unit^2

3. y-values:
     1 $18, 14, 10, 6, 2, -2$
     2 $-14, -8, -2, 4, 10, 16$

4. y-values: $14, 7, 2, -1, -2, -1, 2, 7, 14$

5. A $(-8, -4, -3)$ E $(-8, -4, 4)$
     B $(7, -4, -3)$ F $(7, -4, 4)$
     C $(7, 9, -3)$ H $(-8, 9, 4)$
     D $(-8, 9, -3)$

Page 213   Exercise 10.3

1.   **1** $\frac{1}{6}$ **2** $\frac{1}{3}$

2.   **1** $\frac{1}{4}$ **2** $\frac{1}{2}$ **3** $\frac{3}{10}$

3.   **1** $\frac{1}{2}$ **2** $\frac{1}{6}$

4. $\frac{1}{8}$

5.   **1** $\frac{1}{13}$ **2** $\frac{1}{4}$ **3** $\frac{5}{26}$

6.   **1** $\frac{2}{11}$ **2** $\frac{4}{11}$ **3** $\frac{3}{11}$

7.   **1** $\frac{6}{25}$ **2** $\frac{1}{25}$ **3**   0

8.   **1** $\frac{4}{9}$ **2** $\frac{2}{9}$

9.   **1** $\frac{19}{36}$ **2** $\frac{1}{36}$ **3** $\frac{5}{36}$ **4** $\frac{3}{8}$

10. **1** $\frac{1}{4}$ **2** $\frac{4}{17}$

Page 216   Exercise 10.4

1.   **1**   1   **4** $\frac{1}{2}$
     2   0   **5** $\frac{1}{5}$
     3 $\frac{3}{20}$

2.   **1** $\frac{1}{16}$ **2** $\frac{3}{16}$ **3** $\frac{3}{16}$

3.   **1** $\frac{1}{12}$ **2** $\frac{1}{6}$ **3** $\frac{1}{6}$ **4** $\frac{1}{9}$

4.   **1** $\frac{1}{15}$ **2** $\frac{1}{5}$ **3** $\frac{1}{5}$

Page 217   Exercise 10.5

2.   **1**   0.24
     2   0.30
     3   0.58

3.   **1** $\frac{11}{25}$ **2** $\frac{3}{5}$ **3** $\frac{6}{25}$ **4** $\frac{3}{7}$

4.   **1** $\frac{1}{25}$ **2** $\frac{2}{25}$ **3** $\frac{1}{20}$, $\frac{1}{10}$

6.   **1**   A $\frac{1}{2}$, B $\frac{3}{8}$, C $\frac{3}{5}$, D $\frac{3}{7}$
     2   B
     3   C
     4   A
     5   C, D
     6   A, D
     7   B, D; $\frac{2}{5}$
     8   A, C; $\frac{8}{15}$

Page 218   Practice test 10

1.   **1** $\frac{1}{8}$ **2** $\frac{1}{2}$ **3** $\frac{3}{8}$

2.   **1** $\frac{3}{10}$ **2** $\frac{1}{5}$ **3** $\frac{1}{10}$

3.   **1** $\frac{1}{8}$ **2** $\frac{29}{200}$ **3** $\frac{7}{50}$

4.   **1** $\frac{4}{15}$ **2** $\frac{2}{15}$ **3** $\frac{1}{15}$

Page 220   **Exercise B1**

1. 7 years   6. $\frac{2}{3}$ 11. 54 cm^2

2. 20   7. 2   12. $\frac{1}{20}$

3. £8.91   8. 30 kg   13. 120°

4. 1500   9. 1 m   14. 12

5. 50°   10. $2 \times 3 \times 7$ 15. 60

Page 221   **Exercise B2**

1. £39

2. **1** 3600   **3** C
   2 B and D   **4** 14 000

3. **1** 150°
   2 15°
   3 45°

4. **1** 81, 121   **3** 32, 64   **5** $\frac{1}{6}, \frac{1}{7}$
   2 21, 28   **4** 65, 58

5. 32 min

6. $\frac{1}{2}$

7. **1** $x = -2\frac{1}{2}$ **4** $x = 10$
   2 $x = 8$ **5** $x = 2$
   3 $x = -\frac{4}{5}$

8. **1** $(-3, -3)$
   2 $(1, 5)$

9. wages £22 500, food £18 000, fuel £6000,
   extras £7500; new cost £56 730

10. 1 s and 9 s

11. **1** 125.44 cm^2
    2 yes, 25.44% larger

12. 3.5 m

Page 223   **Exercise B3**

1. 1000

2. missing figures in order:
   106, 24, 22, 27, 103, 31, 27, 127, 529
   1 Thursday   **2** £114.30

3. **1** $\frac{1}{6}$ **4** $\frac{7}{12}$
   2 $\frac{1}{3}$ **5** $\frac{6}{11}$
   3 $\frac{1}{6}$

4. **1** 5 cm
   2 132 cm^2
   3 60 cm^3

5. £6.85, £13.15

6. 2.7 cm

7. **1** x **2** x^6 **3** x^3

8. 65 km

9. **1** £25
   2 58.9%

10. **1** 116   **4** $n = 6$
    2 240   **5** $b = 6$
    3 $t = 7$

11. **1** $\frac{1}{6}$, 20
    2 $\frac{1}{13}$, 9
    3 12

12. $x = 100$; angles 105°, 75°, 105°, 75°;
    parallelogram

Page 236   **Exercise 11.1**

1. **1** £51.75
   2 31.9 dollars

2. 30 ℓ, 2.2 gallons

3. **1** £108   **2** $4\frac{1}{2}$ h

4. **1** 20 cm   **2** 20 s

Page 238   **Example 1**

walks: 6 km/h
cycles: $1\frac{1}{4}$ h, 27 km, 21.6 km/h
rests: 30 km from P
bus: 2.15 pm, $\frac{1}{2}$ hour, 60 km/h

Page 239   **Example 2**

17.5 m/s, 26 m/s

Page 240   **Exercise 11.2**

1. 30 km/h

2. **1** (1) and (4), 67 km/h
   2 (2), 33 km/h
   3 30 min

4. **1** 2.45 pm
   2 30 mph
   3 2.05 pm, 28 miles from A
   4 6 miles
   5 34 mph

5. **1** 20 min   **4** 10 min
    2 1 h 4 min   **5** 20 km/h
    3 2 km

6. **1** 20 km
    2 25 km/h, 18 min

7. **1** 22 m/s
    2 20 s, 105 s from the start

Page 246   Exercise 11.3

1. **1 B**   **3 D**
    2 A   **4 C**

5. **B**

Page 251   Exercise 11.4

1. Shop, A, B, C, F, G, D, Shop; 230 yd

2. **1** 4 or 8   **4** 2
    2 4   **5** 3
    3 6

Page 252   Exercise 11.5

1. **1** 47 km/h
    2 28 m/s

2. $70°F = 21°C$
    $80°C = 176°F$
    $98.4°F = 37°C$

3. 17 articles

4. **1** Mr B
    2 Mr A
    3 Mr C

5. 27°C

6. **1** 15 min
    2 28 km/h
    3 2 km

7. 3.00 pm, 120 km

8. **1** 7.5 m
    2 5.8 s

9. **1** 1125 m
    2 4.5 s and 25.5 s
    3 13 s

10. 39 m/s

12. **1** 6 am, 6 pm
    2 12 am, 12 noon, 12 am
    3 6 am

15. **1 C**   **3 B**
    2 A   **4 D**

16. yes (with 8 bridges)

19. yes for **2, 4**

Page 259   Practice test 11

1. **1** 570 pts
    2 £7.90

2. **1** $\frac{1}{2}$ hour   **4** 10 km
    2 15 km/h   **5** 16 km
    3 1.40 pm, 9 km   **6** 16 km/h

3. 9.51 am, 26 miles

4. 4.0 m/s

5. **1 D**   **3 B**
    2 A   **4 C**

6. yes: **1, 3, 4**

Page 264   Exercise 12.1

1. $x = 6, y = 2$ 7. $x = 3, y = 0$
2. $x = 3, y = -1$ 8. $x = -2, y = -1$
3. $x = 1\frac{1}{2}, y = 2\frac{1}{2}$ 9. $x = -3, y = -2$
4. $x = 2, y = -2$ 10. $x = \frac{1}{2}, y = -1\frac{1}{2}$
5. $x = 0, y = 6$ 11. $x = 11, y = 2$
6. $x = 11, y = -4$ 12. $x = 4, y = 1$

Page 266   Exercise 12.2

1. $x = 5, y = 3$ 7. $x = 2, y = -1$
2. $x = -2, y = 5$ 8. $x = 0, y = 1$
3. $x = 1\frac{1}{2}, y = -2\frac{1}{2}$ 9. $x = 13, y = 7$
4. $x = 7, y = 5$ 10. $x = 1, y = -4$
5. $x = -3, y = 2$ 11. $x = 9, y = 3$
6. $x = 2, y = 0$ 12. $x = -2, y = -2$

Page 269   Exercise 12.3

1. $x = 3, y = 1$ 11. $x = 1, y = \frac{1}{2}$
2. $x = 4, y = -2$ 12. $x = 5, y = 3$
3. $x = 2\frac{1}{2}, y = \frac{1}{2}$ 13. $x = 2\frac{1}{2}, y = -5$
4. $x = -1, y = 3$ 14. $x = -\frac{1}{2}, y = 0$
5. $x = 4, y = 7$ 15. $x = -2, y = 3$
6. $x = -2, y = -5$ 16. $x = 4, y = -3$
7. $x = 7, y = 2$ 17. $x = 0, y = -\frac{1}{2}$
8. $x = -1, y = -2$ 18. $x = 4, y = 1$
9. $x = -2, y = 4$ 19. $x = -1, y = \frac{1}{2}$
10. $x = -3, y = 2$ 20. $x = 8, y = -3$

21. $x = 4, y = -3$; $AB = CD = 11$ cm,
    $AD = BC = 15$ cm

22. tea 25p, coffee 35p

Page 270   Exercise 12.4

1. rose 25p, carnation 20p

2. $x = 40$, $y = 25$; $\angle ABD = \angle ACE = 70°$,
    $\angle CBD = 110°$

3. $x = 4$, $y = 3$; perimeter 39 cm

4. $a = 0.05$, $c = 5$

5. 6

6. 28 m at £20, 40 m at £16

7. $a = 3$, $b = -4$

8. **1** 8   **2** -1; $x = 3\frac{1}{2}$, $y = 4\frac{1}{2}$

Page 271   Practice test 12

1. 75 and 93

2. **1** $x = 5$, $y = -1$
    2 $x = 7$, $y = 4$
    3 $x = -1$, $y = 3$
    4 $x = 3\frac{1}{2}$, $y = -\frac{1}{2}$
    5 $x = 4$, $y = 11$

3. adult £1.60, child £1

Page 281   Exercise 13.2

1. **1** mean = 9   **4** mean = 40.7
        median = 8   median = 35
        range = 13   range = 76

    2 mean = 44   **5** mean = 1.9
        median = 39   median = 1.95
        range = 73   range = 0.7

    3 mean = 8
        median = 7
        range = 12

2. **1** median = 9   **3** median = $4\frac{1}{2}$
        mode = 12   mode = 5
        range = 9   range = 8

    2 median = 28
        mode = 27
        range = 8

3. **1** 64.4   **4** 3
    2 £917.40   **5** 2.9 kg
    3 2 h 1 min

4. **1** mean = 57 kg, median = 55 kg
    2 12 y 2 m
    3 164 g

5. 2.81; more in North-west

Page 285   Exercise 13.3

1. **1** 2.7   **2** 2   **3** 2
2. **1** 1.6   **2** 1   **3** 1
3. **1** 5.3   **2** 5.5   **3** 7
4. **1** 3.8   **2** 4   **3** 4

5. 30.7

6. 40.0 cm

7. **1** 12 – 14 marks
    2 11.1 marks

8. 4.0 min (3.98 min)

9. **1** 160 – 164 cm (159.5 – 164.5 cm)
    2 161.6 cm

10. **1** 15 – 19 cm (14.5 – 19.5 cm)
    2 17 cm
    3 17.3 cm

11. **1** 0 – 2 years
    2 5.6 years

Page 287   Exercise 13.4

8. frequencies in order: 2, 4, 7, 10, 14, 15, 8;
    mean = 6.8, median = 7, mode = 8

9. mean = 3.9, median = 4, mode = 3,
    probability = 0.6

10. **1** 6.5 cm, 9.5 cm; 8 cm
    2 13.8 cm

11. **1** 40   **4** 8.5 min
    2 30%   **5** 7.7 min
    3 8 – 9 min

12. frequencies: 3, 5, 4, 5, 5, 2, 1; 74.8

Page 291   Practice test 13

3. 1.9 faults

4. £95

5. **1** 0 – 10 min
    2 5 min
    3 17.8 min

Page 295   Exercise 14.1

2. **1** 4   **2** $\frac{1}{4}$

6. **1** $\frac{2}{3}$ **2** 48 cm

7. **1** 1.5 cm   **2** 66°

8. **1** 2.4   **2** 24 cm

Page 297   Exercise 14.2

1.   **1** $2:5$ **3**   yes
     2 $2:5$ **4** $2:5$

2.   **1** $9:5$; $x = 14.4$ cm, $y = 12.5$ cm
     2 $3:5$; $x = 44$ cm, $y = 10$ cm
     3 $7:3$; $x = 0.9$ cm, $y = 4.2$ cm
     4 $4:5$; $x = 20$ cm
     5 $5:8$; $x = 5.6$ cm

3.   **1** $3:5$; $d = 10.5$ cm
     2 $5:7$; $y = 21$ cm
     3 $7:5$; $x = 6$ cm, $y = 4.9$ cm
     4 $4:7$; $x = 2$ cm
     5 $5:2$; $x = 35$ cm, $y = 28$ cm

4. $3:4$

5.   **1** $2:3$
     2 $2:3$
     3   yes

Page 302   Exercise 14.3

1.   **1**   equiangular; $\dfrac{AB}{FD} = \dfrac{BC}{DE} = \dfrac{AC}{FE}$, $\angle A = \angle F$

     2   3 sides in proportion; $\dfrac{AB}{LK} = \dfrac{BC}{KM} = \dfrac{AC}{LM}$,

       $\angle A = \angle L$, $\angle B = \angle K$, $\angle C = \angle M$

     3   equiangular; $\dfrac{AB}{PQ} = \dfrac{BC}{QR} = \dfrac{AC}{PR}$, $\angle C = \angle R$

     4   2 sides in proportion and included angles equal;

       $\dfrac{AB}{TS} = \dfrac{BC}{SU} = \dfrac{AC}{TU}$, $\angle B = \angle S$, $\angle C = \angle U$

2.   **1**   2 sides in proportion and included angles equal
     2 $2:5$
     3 $\angle F$

3.   **1**   3 sides in proportion
     2 $\angle E$

4.   **1** $\frac{2}{3}$, $\frac{2}{3}$
     2   yes
     3 $\angle C$
     4 $2:3$

5.   **1**   equiangular
     2 $3:4$
     3 $3:4$
     4 3.6 cm

6.   2 sides in proportion and included angles equal; $\angle ACB = \angle DCE$, $\angle A = \angle D$, $\angle B = \angle E$; AB and ED are parallel

Page 305   Exercise 14.4

1. 3.5 km

2. 2 km

3. 8 cm by 5.4 cm

4. $1:250\,000$

5. $1:2000$, 3.3 cm

6. 200 m, 265 m, 1020 m

7. 87 m

8. 15 m

Page 306   Exercise 14.5

2.   **1** $4\frac{1}{2}$
     2 13.5 cm
     3 2 cm

3. 2

4.   **1** $5:6$
     2 $5:7$
     3   no

5. 6 cm

6.   **1** $2\frac{2}{3}$
     2 6.4 cm

7. 25 cm

8. 8 m, 12.5 m, 16 m; 1600 m^3

9.   **1** $\triangle AXD$, $\triangle CXB$
     2 $3:4$

10.   **1** $\triangle ABC$, $\triangle ADE$, $\triangle AFG$
      2 $3:4:6$
      3 C

11. 80 m

12. 12.8 m

13.   **1** 20 cm
      2   equiangular
      3 7.5 cm

14.   **1** $\triangle SAB$
      2 $\triangle DAB$, $\triangle BAT$ or $\triangle ABR$

15. 6.3 m

16. 1 5 m by 4 m
    2 3.5 m by 3 m
    3 3 m by 3 m
    4 20 m^2, £360

17. 90 m^2

18. 61 m

Page 310   Practice test 14

1. 16 cm by 12 cm

2. 6 : 7, 11.9 cm

3. 1 3 sides in proportion
   2 $\angle E$

4. 1 equiangular
   2 3 : 2
   3 4.5 cm

5. 1 : 50 000, 4.2 km

6. 1 30 cm by 24 cm
   2 3200 cm^3, 10 800 cm^3; 8 : 27

7. 480 m

Page 314   Exercise 15.1

1. 1 x is greater than 7
   2 x is less than or equal to 8
   3 x is less than 1
   4 x is greater than 1 and less than 4
   5 x is greater than or equal to -5

2. 1 $x < 6$ 4 $-3 < x < 10$
   2 $x \geqslant -2$ 5 $x \leqslant 5$
   3 $x > 0$

3. 1 $a < c < b$ 4 $a < b < c$
   2 $c < b < a$ 5 $b < c < a$
   3 $c < a < b$

4. 1 4, 5, 6   4 $-7, -6, -5$
   2 4, 5   5 0, 1, 2, 3, 4, 5
   3 $-2, -1, 0, 1, 2$

6. 1 $-2, -1, 0, 1, 2, 3, 4$
   2 $-4, -3, -2$
   3 0, 1, 2, 3, 4
   4 $-4, -3, -2, -1, 0, 1, 2, 3$
   5 no values
   6 $-3, -2, -1, 0, 1, 2, 3, 4$
   7 $-4, 3, 4$
   8 $-4, -3, -2, -1, 0, 1, 2, 3, 4$

7. 1 $x < 8$ 5 $x > 6$ 8 $x \geqslant -1$
   2 $x < -6$ 6 $x \leqslant \frac{3}{4}$ 9 $x > 1$
   3 $x \geqslant \frac{1}{2}$ 7 $x > 11\frac{1}{2}$ 10 $x \leqslant 5$
   4 $x \leqslant -4$

8. 1 $x < -6$ or $x > 6$
   2 $x < -1.5$ or $x > 1.5$
   3 $-10 \leqslant x \leqslant 10$
   4 $-1 < x < 1$
   5 $x \leqslant -\frac{1}{4}$ or $x \geqslant \frac{1}{4}$

9. 1 $-7 \leqslant x \leqslant 7$
   2 $x \leqslant -9$ or $x \geqslant 9$
   3 $-12 < x < 12$

10. 1 7, 8, 9, 10   3 9, 10
    2 1, 2, 3   4 6, 7, 8

11. 1 $9\frac{1}{4}$ 2 $7\frac{1}{3}$ 3 8, 9

12. $x \geqslant 2, y \geqslant 3, x + y \leqslant 9, 20x + 24y \leqslant 200$;
    5 lemons

Page 317   Example

1, 8, 27, 64, 125; cube numbers

Page 318   Exercise 15.2

1. 11.6, the mean

4. 1, 1, 2, 3, 5, 8, 13, 21, 34, 55, 89, 144;
   Fibonacci sequence

5. 1 $61 \to 62 \to 31 \to 32 \to 16 \to 8 \to 4 \to 2 \to 1$
   2 $92 \to 46 \to 23 \to 24 \to 12 \to 6 \to 3 \to 4 \to 2 \to 1$
   3 $149 \to 150 \to 75 \to 76 \to 38 \to 19 \to 20$
     $\to 10 \to 5 \to 6 \to 3 \to 4 \to 2 \to 1$

6. 1 2×20p
   2 20p, 10p, 5p, 2p
   3 2×2p

Page 322   Exercise 15.3

1. 1 $x \leqslant -5$ 2 $1 < x < 10$

2. 7

3. (1, 1), (1, 2), (1, 3), (1, 4), (2, 1), (2, 2), (3, 1)

4. 97

5. $0 \leqslant x \leqslant 5, \ 0 \leqslant y \leqslant 7, \ x + y \leqslant 10,$
   $50x + 20y \geqslant 300$; 5 coaches, 3 minibuses

6. 86°F, 25°C

8. **1** not prime; no, no, no, yes
   2 prime; no, no, no, no, no, no
   3 not prime; no, yes
   4 not prime; no, no, no, no, no, yes
   5 prime; no, no, no, no, no, no

9. **1** 120°   **2** 162°

10. **1** Luxembourg
    2 Belgium
    3 Denmark

11. **1** 0.618
    2 0.303

Page 327   Practice test 15

1. **1** $x \geq \frac{3}{4}$
   2 $x < 7$
   3 $-5 \leq x \leq 5$
   4 $x < -6$ or $x > 6$

2. $x \geq 2$, $y \geq 6$, $x + y \leq 10$;
   (dogs, elephants) = (2, 6), (2, 7), (2, 8), (3, 6), (3, 7), (4, 6); 4 dogs, 6 elephants, £24 profit

3. 1, 4, 9, 16, 25; square numbers

Page 328   Exercise C1

1. 6
2. 92
3. 3.5 kg
4. 50°
5. 30 m
6. 5
7. £117.50
8. 40
9. 37
10. 5
11. 14%
12. 6
13. 45 cm^2
14. 8
15. 7

Page 329   Exercise C2

1. **1** $x > -2\frac{3}{4}$ **2** $-3\frac{1}{2} < x < 4$

2. **1** January, 10.7 cm
   2 February, 2.7 cm
   3 April

3. area 616 cm^2, height 16.2 cm

4. $d = 68°$

5. **1** $x = 2.4$
   2 $x = 10$

6. **1** 165 ha
   2 120°
   3 $\frac{5}{12}$

8. $\frac{11}{50}$

9. 480 fr, £40

10. $x = 5$, $y = 1$;
    $AB = 7$ cm, $BC = 12$ cm, $AC = 9$ cm

11. **1** 48 min
    2 12 km/h
    3 15 km/h

12. frequencies in order: 6, 6, 7, 8, 3;
    modal class 16 − 20 h (15.5 − 20.5 h);
    mean 12.3 h

Page 331   Exercise C3

1. 25 cm

2. **1** 1   **5** 6   **8** 3
   2 3   **6** 4   **9** 5
   3 0   **7** 2   **10** 7
   4 an infinite
       number

3. 11

4. 3rd month

5. **1** $2^5 \times 3$
   2 360
   3 41, 43, 47

6. 54.2 m

7. B

8. **1** $\frac{1}{10}$ **2** $\frac{2}{5}$

10. **B**

11. the boy

Page 333   Exercise C4

1. **1** 4 : 7
   2 4 : 7

2. **1** $-6 \leq x \leq 6$
   2 $x \leq -5$ or $x \geq 5$

3. **1** frequencies in order: 5, 8, 11, 6
   2 8.0 cars/min
   3 7.9 cars/min

4. area 80 m^2, 16 000 m^3 to be removed

5. **1** $x = 5$, $y = 3$
   2 $x = 3$, $y = -2$

6. **1** 25.5 fr
   2 £5.90

7. **1** equilateral
   2 isosceles (obtuse-angled)
   3 right-angled

8. $\frac{25}{37}$

9. **1** 6 cm
    2 24 cm^2
    3 4.8 cm

10. **1** $x = 7$ **2** $x = 12$ **3** $x = 10$

11. 3

Page 346   Exercise 16.1

3. positive

4. negative

5. positive

6. negative

7. positive

8. positive correlation

9. positive correlation

Page 349   Exercise 16.2

1. 73
2. 30
3. 27
4. 21

5. 31
6. 17
7. 33
9. 57

Page 350   Exercise 16.3

1. **1** positive   **4** positive
    2 negative   **5** negative
    3 zero

2. £64 000

3. 72 kg

4. 41

6. 60

Page 352   Practice test 16

2. 1.67 m

3. 66

Page 358   Exercise 17.1

1. **1** 1   **5** 4   **8** 0.5
    2 350   **6** 100   **9** 600
    3 16   **7** 300   **10** 0.08
    4 0.63

2. **1** 13   **5** 500   **8** 600
    2 0.2   **6** 1200   **9** 6
    3 35   **7** 0.5   **10** 200
    4 10

3. **1** 13.3   **5** 482   **8** 640
    2 0.189   **6** 1016.4   **9** 6.6
    3 40   **7** 0.55   **10** 210
    4 10.46

4. **1** 3.248   **4** 39.69
    2 88.8   **5** 416.7
    3 2.3

5. **1** 8.80   **4** 6.91
    2 0.532   **5** 0.540
    3 0.0400

6. $M = 2.05$

7. £313.50

8. **1** 0.04$\dot{5}$
    2 0.0455
    3 0.045

9.   2, 0.5
        3, 0.$\dot{3}$, 0.333
        4, 0.25
        5, 0.2
        6, 0.1$\dot{6}$, 0.167
        7, 0.$\dot{1}$4285$\dot{7}$, 0.143
        8, 0.125
        9, 0.$\dot{1}$, 0.111
        10, 0.1
        11, 0.$\dot{0}\dot{9}$, 0.091

        12, 0.08$\dot{3}$, 0.083

    1 2, 4, 5, 8, 10
    2 3, 6, 9, 12
    3 11

Page 361   Exercise 17.2

1. **1** 55 kg, 65 kg   **4** 4.55 m, 4.65 m
    2 55.5 kg, 56.5 kg   **5** £650, £750
    3 245 ml, 255 ml

2. **1** metres   **4** metres
    2 grams   **5** cm
    3 litres

3. **1** 8.7 m   **5** 156.9 cm   **8** 5.44 kg
    2 280 g   **6** 4.1 ℓ   **9** 2500 ℓ
    3 4200 ℓ   **7** 5.0 m   **10** 47.0 s
    4 6 m

4. **1** 4.95 cm, 5.05 cm   **4** 59.5 ml, 60.5 ml
    2 195 g, 205 g   **5** £29.50, £30.50
    3 $2\frac{1}{2}$ min, $3\frac{1}{2}$ min

5. (possible answers)
    1 nearest cm; 1.615 m, 1.625 m
    2 nearest kg; 37.5 kg, 38.5 kg

Page 364   **Exercise 17.3**

1. **1** 5.06×10^2 **9** 3.45×10^{-1}
    2 2.187×10^3 **10** 2.08×10^{-2}
    3 1.507×10 **11** 9.307×10^4
    4 2.3×10^3 **12** 1.3×10^{-7}
    5 7×10^6 **13** 1.157×10
    6 2.7×10^{-2} **14** 1.157×10^{-1}
    7 5.1×10^{-4} **15** 9.9×10^{-3}
    8 6×10^{-6}

2. **1** 105   **9** 293
    2 96 000   **10** 1 100 000
    3 0.412   **11** 0.043
    4 5200   **12** 800 000
    5 0.0289   **13** 0.000203
    6 750 000   **14** 9900
    7 0.004   **15** 0.1072
    8 0.611

3. **1** 4.674×10^8 **7** 9.86×10^{-3}
    2 7.5×10 **8** 5.8×10
    3 2.209×10^7 **9** 3.481×10^{-5}
    4 2.2×10^3 **10** 2.5×10^{-7}
    5 3×10^{-2} **11** 1.6×10^{-6}
    6 2.64×10^3 **12** 8×10^{-2}

4. **1** $n = -3$
    2 $n = 3$

5. 7.35×10^{19} tonnes

Page 365   **Exercise 17.4**

1. **1** 30   **5** 75   **8** 160
    2 280 000   **6** 1200   **9** 37
    3 18   **7** 1000   **10** 13
    4 300

2. **1** 2   **5** 10   **8** 11.5
    2 300   **6** 30   **9** 30
    3 4   **7** 4.5   **10** 29
    4 4

3. **1** 1.89   **5** 9.5   **8** 13.2
    2 324.89   **6** 30   **9** 31.4
    3 3.84   **7** 4.5   **10** 30
    4 4.75

4. **1** 80.6   **5** 21   **8** 9
    2 1.7   **6** 770   **9** 3.6
    3 18   **7** 0.8   **10** 10
    4 3.6

5. **1** 7.61   **4** 32.718
    2 9.082   **5** 38 562.5
    3 37.2

6. 0.281

7. $v = 52.2$

8. **1** $s = 4.9$
    2 $A = 4.0$

9. $7500\,\ell$

10. $6.93\,\ell$

11. $s = 86.7$

12. 30, 0.0333   36, 0.0278
    31, 0.0323   37, 0.0270
    32, 0.03125   38, 0.0263
    33, 0.0303   39, 0.0256
    34, 0.0294   40, 0.025
    35, 0.0286

    1 32, 40   **3** 33
    2 30, 36   **4** 37

13. **1** tonnes   **4** km
    2 litres   **5** cm
    3 grams

14. (possible answers)
    nearest 5 min; $17\frac{1}{2}$ min, $22\frac{1}{2}$ min

15. **1** 6.5 cm   **5** 5.5 cm
    2 4.5 cm   **6** 3.5 cm
    3 22 cm   **7** 18 cm
    4 $29.25\,\text{cm}^2$ **8** $19.25\,\text{cm}^2$

16. **1** 1.5×10^4 **4** 5.276×10^{-1}
    2 3.64×10^2 **5** 2.32×10
    3 9.52×10^{-4}

17. **1** 1860   **4** 200 000
    2 0.00765   **5** 0.009
    3 12 609

18. 1.5×10^8 km

19. 8.99×10^{-5} g

20. 1.7×10^{10} tonnes

Page 368   **Practice test 17**

1. **1** 30 000   **5** 0.4   **8** 7
    2 14   **6** 90   **9** 11
    3 0.48   **7** 110   **10** 0.6
    4 36

2. **1** 20, 20.0   **4** 10, 10.0
    2 3, 3.06   **5** 40, 40.7
    3 16, 15.2

3. $W = 1.52$

4. **1** $0.01\dot{5}$
    2 0.0152
    3 0.015

5. 1 6.45 cm, 6.55 cm
    2 8.745 kg, 8.755 kg
    3 4.15 ℓ, 4.25 ℓ
    4 2 h 5 min, 2 h 15 min
    5 8 h $4\frac{1}{2}$ min, 8 h $5\frac{1}{2}$ min

6. 1 2.1×10^3 4 6.37×10^{-1}
    2 5.44×10^2 5 1.071×10
    3 1.8×10^{-3}

7. 1 126.5   4 678 000
    2 0.0238   5 5999
    3 0.7021

8. 7.5×10^{-5}

Page 374   Exercise 18.1

1. the perpendicular bisector of the line
    joining the rocks
2. a line parallel to the slide
3. an arc of a circle, centre at the top of the
    rope
4. a circle, centre at the centre of the fixed disc,
    radius 8 cm
5. $PA = 3.2$ cm
6. $PB = 3.6$ cm
9. 14 m

Page 376   Exercise 18.2

1. 1 $\begin{pmatrix} 3 \\ -2 \end{pmatrix}$ 2 $\begin{pmatrix} -1 \\ 5 \end{pmatrix}$ 3 $\begin{pmatrix} -2 \\ -3 \end{pmatrix}$

2. 1 $\mathbf{a} = \begin{pmatrix} 4 \\ 6 \end{pmatrix}$, $\mathbf{b} = \begin{pmatrix} 4 \\ 2 \end{pmatrix}$, $\mathbf{c} = \begin{pmatrix} 0 \\ -4 \end{pmatrix}$,

    $\mathbf{d} = \begin{pmatrix} -4 \\ 2 \end{pmatrix}$, $\mathbf{e} = \begin{pmatrix} 6 \\ -4 \end{pmatrix}$,

    $\mathbf{f} = \begin{pmatrix} -4 \\ 2 \end{pmatrix}$, $\mathbf{g} = \begin{pmatrix} 8 \\ 4 \end{pmatrix}$

    2 d, f   3 e   4 g

3. $\overrightarrow{AB} = \begin{pmatrix} 3 \\ 2 \end{pmatrix}$, $\overrightarrow{BC} = \begin{pmatrix} 1 \\ -4 \end{pmatrix}$,

    $DE = 2$ units

4. $\overrightarrow{AB} = \begin{pmatrix} 4 \\ 3 \end{pmatrix}$, $\overrightarrow{BC} = \begin{pmatrix} -4 \\ -5 \end{pmatrix}$,

    $\overrightarrow{AD} = \begin{pmatrix} -4 \\ -5 \end{pmatrix}$, $\overrightarrow{DC} = \begin{pmatrix} 4 \\ 3 \end{pmatrix}$

5. 1 $\overrightarrow{AB} = \begin{pmatrix} 4 \\ 1 \end{pmatrix}$, $\overrightarrow{BC} = \begin{pmatrix} 2 \\ 3 \end{pmatrix}$, A to $C = \begin{pmatrix} 6 \\ 4 \end{pmatrix}$

    2 $\overrightarrow{AB} = \begin{pmatrix} 1 \\ 3 \end{pmatrix}$, $\overrightarrow{BC} = \begin{pmatrix} 5 \\ -2 \end{pmatrix}$, A to $C = \begin{pmatrix} 6 \\ 1 \end{pmatrix}$

    3 $\overrightarrow{AB} = \begin{pmatrix} 4 \\ -2 \end{pmatrix}$, $\overrightarrow{BC} = \begin{pmatrix} 0 \\ 3 \end{pmatrix}$, A to $C = \begin{pmatrix} 4 \\ 1 \end{pmatrix}$

    4 $\overrightarrow{AB} = \begin{pmatrix} 5 \\ 1 \end{pmatrix}$, $\overrightarrow{BC} = \begin{pmatrix} -2 \\ 2 \end{pmatrix}$, A to $C = \begin{pmatrix} 3 \\ 3 \end{pmatrix}$

Page 380   Exercise 18.3

1. 1 028°   4 142°
    2 325°   5 227°
    3 250°

3. 1 208°   4 322°
    2 145°   5 047°
    3 070°

4. 123°

5. 1 225°   4 045°
    2 090°   5 270°
    3 315°

6. 1 260°   4 195°
    2 305°   5 121°
    3 080°

7. 1 119°   4 345°
    2 241°   5 029°
    3 074°

8. 1 B 065°, C 340°
    2 B 030°, C 112°
    3 118°
    4 321°
    5 from A 044°, from B 311°

9. 1 530 m, 066°   4 780 m, 083°
    2 1120 m, 096°   5 280 m, 209°
    3 1050 m, 290°

Page 383   Exercise 18.4

3. 420 m

5. 100 m

6. an arc of a circle, centre at the point C (where
    the wall meets the ground), radius 3 m

9. B (1, 5), C (5, 4); $\overrightarrow{CE} = \begin{pmatrix} 2 \\ 3 \end{pmatrix}$

10. 1 $\begin{pmatrix} -3 \\ -5 \end{pmatrix}$ 2 $\begin{pmatrix} 2 \\ -3 \end{pmatrix}$ 3 $\begin{pmatrix} -\frac{1}{2} \\ -4 \end{pmatrix}$

11. $A'(0, 6)$, $B'(-3, 4)$, $C'(-5, 0)$

12. $\begin{pmatrix} -34 \\ -42 \end{pmatrix}$

13. 298°, 1 : 200 000, 17.0 km, 254°

14. 1 040°
     2 6 km
     3 25 km

15. 313°, 2240 m

16. 242°, 25 km, 1 h 35 min

17. from A 39 km, from B 20 km

18. 1 N 70° W   4 S 70° E
     2 S 25° W   5 N 42° W
     3 N 53° E

Page 389   Practice test 18

2. 49 m

3. $\overrightarrow{AD} = \overrightarrow{BC} = \begin{pmatrix} -5 \\ -2 \end{pmatrix}$, parallelogram, $\begin{pmatrix} 2 \\ 4 \end{pmatrix}$

4. 1 $\overrightarrow{AB} = \begin{pmatrix} 5 \\ 0 \end{pmatrix}$, $\overrightarrow{AD} = \begin{pmatrix} 3 \\ 3 \end{pmatrix}$, B to $D = \begin{pmatrix} -2 \\ 3 \end{pmatrix}$

    2 $\overrightarrow{AB} = \begin{pmatrix} -1 \\ -2 \end{pmatrix}$, $\overrightarrow{AD} = \begin{pmatrix} 4 \\ -3 \end{pmatrix}$,

       B to $D = \begin{pmatrix} 5 \\ -1 \end{pmatrix}$

    3 $\overrightarrow{AB} = \begin{pmatrix} -1 \\ 2 \end{pmatrix}$, $\overrightarrow{AD} = \begin{pmatrix} 4 \\ -2 \end{pmatrix}$,

       B to $D = \begin{pmatrix} 5 \\ -4 \end{pmatrix}$

    4 $\overrightarrow{AB} = \begin{pmatrix} -4 \\ 0 \end{pmatrix}$, $\overrightarrow{AD} = \begin{pmatrix} 0 \\ -3 \end{pmatrix}$,

       B to $D = \begin{pmatrix} 4 \\ -3 \end{pmatrix}$

5. 338°

6. B to C 179 km, C to D 182 km, B to D 169 km

Page 396   Exercise 19.1

1. 1 2   3 3
    2 −1   4 −3

2. 1 0.4   4 −1.2
    2 1.1   5 0.7
    3 −0.2

3. 1 $y = 7 - x$
    2 $y = 2x - 5$
    3 $3y = x + 3$

4. $AB : -1$, $CD : 3$

5. 1 4, (0, −1)   4 −5, (0, 2)
    2 −1, (0, 3)   5 $\frac{1}{3}$, (0, 1)
    3 $\frac{1}{2}$, (0, 7)

7. 1 $y = 2 - 2x$ 4 $y = 2$
    2 $y = x + 2$ 5 $y = 2x$
    3 $y = 2 - x$ 6 $y = 2x + 2$

8. $y = 1.6x + 4$, $y = 32$ (approx.)

Page 399   Exercise 19.2

1. $x = 8$, $y = 2$

2. $x = 8$, $y = 6$

3. $x = -2$, $y = 5$

4. $x = 1.6$, $y = 3.7$

5. $x = 2$, $y = 0.5$

6. $x = 2.6$, $y = -0.2$

7. 1 $y = 2$, $x = 3$; $x = 2.7$, $y = 3.7$

8. $2x + y = 56$, $x + 2y = 64$; $x = 16$, $y = 24$;
    16 of 10p, 24 of 5p

Page 402   Exercise 19.3

5. 12 points

6. (−1, 3.5), (4, 1);
    isosceles (obtuse-angled) triangle

8. $1 \leqslant x \leqslant 5, 2 \leqslant y \leqslant 7, x + y \leqslant 9$

Page 403   Exercise 19.4

1. AB, DC gradient 1; BC, AD gradient $-\frac{2}{3}$

2. $-\frac{4}{3}$, $3y = 12 - 4x$

3. A (2, 0), $y = 4x - 8$

4. 14

5. gradient $\frac{1}{4}$, $(0, 1\frac{3}{4})$

6. $y = 2.1x + 32$, 157 (approx.)

7. $x = 2.8$, $y = 10.4$

8. 1 $P(0, -3)$, $R(0, 3\frac{1}{2})$
    2 $5\frac{1}{2}$ units
    3 $y = 2x - 3$, $x + 2y = 7$
    4 $T(2.6, 2.2)$
9. cost $(16x + 32y)$ pence; $x + y = 25$, $x + 2y = 40$, 10 packets of sweets, 15 bars of chocolate
11. $x > 3$, $y > 2$, $x + 2y < 11$
12. $x \geqslant 15$, $y \geqslant 5$, $x + y \leqslant 40$; $2x + y \leqslant 60$

Page 405   Practice test 19

1. $AB : \frac{1}{2}$, $CD : -3$, $EF : -\frac{1}{4}$, $GH : \frac{2}{5}$
2. $-8, -2, 13$; gradient 3; $(0, -2)$
3. 3.1, $c = 3.1\, d$ $(c = \pi d)$
4. $x = 4.3$, $y = -0.6$
5. $x \geqslant 4$, $y \geqslant 4$, $x + y \leqslant 10$, $2x + y \leqslant 15$; $(X, Y) : (4, 4), (4, 5), (4, 6), (5, 4), (5, 5)$; 4 Brand X, 6 Brand Y
6. $-2 \leqslant y \leqslant 0$, $y \leqslant 3x + 4$, $x \leqslant 0$

Page 409   Exercise 20.1

1. 1 $\frac{3}{11}$ 4 $\frac{2}{3}$
    2 $\frac{5}{7}$ 5 $\frac{3}{8}$
    3 $\frac{1}{4}$ 6 $\frac{1}{10}$

2. 1 $\frac{29}{6}$ 4 $\frac{47}{8}$
    2 $\frac{77}{10}$ 5 $\frac{22}{7}$
    3 $\frac{100}{11}$ 6 $\frac{42}{5}$

3. 1 $3\frac{7}{10}$ 4 $3\frac{7}{11}$
    2 $3\frac{1}{8}$ 5 $33\frac{1}{3}$
    3 $6\frac{1}{9}$ 6 $8\frac{3}{4}$

4. 1 $1\frac{1}{12}$ 5 $4\frac{3}{4}$ 8 $3\frac{1}{3}$
    2 $\frac{19}{24}$ 6 $7\frac{17}{24}$ 9 $4\frac{11}{20}$
    3 $4\frac{3}{10}$ 7 $5\frac{13}{18}$ 10 $5\frac{17}{24}$
    4 $5\frac{7}{40}$

5. 1 $\frac{11}{24}$ 5 $\frac{11}{20}$ 8 $\frac{2}{3}$
    2 $2\frac{1}{24}$ 6 $1\frac{1}{2}$ 9 $2\frac{4}{5}$
    3 $1\frac{7}{12}$ 7 $\frac{1}{9}$ 10 $3\frac{33}{40}$
    4 $1\frac{19}{36}$

6. 1 $\frac{1}{4}$ 5 $1\frac{1}{2}$ 8 $3\frac{3}{4}$
    2 $\frac{35}{48}$ 6 $\frac{3}{4}$ 9 $8\frac{1}{4}$
    3 $\frac{3}{4}$ 7 $11\frac{3}{7}$ 10 40
    4 $4\frac{1}{5}$

7. 1 $\frac{20}{21}$ 5 $\frac{5}{8}$ 8 $\frac{16}{21}$
    2 $\frac{9}{35}$ 6 $\frac{2}{5}$ 9 $\frac{10}{27}$
    3 $1\frac{1}{2}$ 7 $1\frac{9}{16}$ 10 $5\frac{1}{7}$
    4 4

8. 1 $5\frac{1}{12}$ 5 $2\frac{3}{5}$ 8 1
    2 $\frac{2}{3}$ 6 $\frac{1}{2}$ 9 $4\frac{11}{12}$
    3 $7\frac{1}{3}$ 7 2 10 $1\frac{1}{7}$
    4 8

9. 1 1 5 $25\frac{1}{6}$ 8 $2\frac{1}{5}$
    2 $3\frac{2}{3}$ 6 $\frac{1}{4}$ 9 $1\frac{13}{20}$
    3 $3\frac{1}{2}$ 7 $\frac{5}{16}$ 10 7
    4 3

10. $\frac{5}{12}$

11. £126

12. $\frac{13}{30}$

Page 414   Exercise 20.2

1. 1 $4a$
    2 $\dfrac{c}{9}$
    3 $\dfrac{5e^2}{3}$

2. 1 $\dfrac{13a}{24}$ 4 $\dfrac{d}{2}$
    2 $\dfrac{28b}{9}$ 5 $\dfrac{e}{6}$
    3 $\dfrac{11c}{10}$

3. 1 $\dfrac{2a}{3}$ 4 $\dfrac{3g}{2}$
    2 $\dfrac{2b}{5}$ 5 $\dfrac{5q^2}{3}$
    3 $\dfrac{ce}{15}$

4. **1** $x = 30$ **5** $x = 30$ **8** $x = -6$
    2 $x = 20$ **6** $x = -18$ **9** $x = \frac{1}{2}$
    3 $x = 13$ **7** $x = \frac{4}{5}$ **10** $x = 2\frac{1}{3}$
    4 $x = 12$

5. **1** $1\frac{1}{6}$ **5** $6\frac{1}{2}$ **8** $4\frac{11}{12}$
    2 0 **6** $\frac{3}{4}$ **9** $\frac{3}{8}$
    3 $\frac{7}{12}$ **7** 3 **10** $1\frac{1}{2}$
    4 $3\frac{1}{3}$

6. **1** $1\frac{5}{6}$ **2** $\frac{13}{36}$ **3** $\frac{2}{9}$

7. **1** 5   **4** 4
    2 10   **5** 3
    3 3

8. 2.4

9. 8

Page 415   **Exercise 20.3**

1. 32

2. $\frac{1}{20}$ s

3. £3

4. $5\frac{1}{2}$ ins

5. $3\frac{3}{4}$ ft

6. 360

7. $23\,\ell \left(22\frac{6}{7}\,\ell\right)$

8. $4\frac{1}{2}$ mph, $3\frac{3}{4}$ miles

9. 820

10. 15 miles, $\frac{5}{24}$

11. $9\frac{3}{8}$ ins

12. $13\frac{5}{8}$ ins by $9\frac{1}{2}$ ins

13. **1** $12xy$
    2 $\dfrac{7}{12xy}$
    3 $1\frac{1}{3}$

14. **1** $x = -8$
    2 $x = -15$
    3 $x = 4$

15. 36

16. **1** $\frac{1}{6}$ **2** $\frac{5}{6}$ **3** $\frac{1}{15}$

17. $\dfrac{360^\circ}{a}$, $\dfrac{360^\circ}{b}$, $\left(180 - \dfrac{360}{c}\right)^\circ$;
    $a = 4$, square

18. $3\frac{2}{7}$

19. $\frac{3}{5}$

20. **1** 8
    2 14

21. $y = 2$

22. $f = \frac{5}{12}$

23. $C = 200$

Page 418   **Practice test 20**

1. $5\frac{1}{4}$ ft

2. £750

3. £60.50

4. **1** $\dfrac{13a}{10}$ **2** $\dfrac{bc}{6}$

5. $x = -\frac{1}{3}$

6. 35

7. **1** 6   **2** 4

8. $s = 12$

9. $R = 12$

Page 420   **Exercise D1**

1. 20 cm   6. 13 y   11. £1
2. 25   7. 5   12. rhombus
3. 42   8. $\frac{1}{8}$ 13. $\frac{1}{6}$
4. $17\frac{1}{2}$ km   9. £12   14. 9
5. $-\frac{1}{2}$ 10. $1\frac{1}{2}$ h   15. £180

Page 421   **Exercise D2**

1. 40°, 60°, 100°, 160°

2. $2x^2$ cm²; $x = 3$; perimeter 41.0 cm

3. X £52.50, Y £37.50

4. 10.6 km

5. **1** $x = 8$ **2** $x = 2$

6. **1** $6\frac{7}{12}$ **4** $1\frac{2}{3}$
    2 $\frac{1}{2}$ **5** $5\frac{1}{2}$
    3 5

7. **1** 41
    2 66
    3 45

8. **1** 8
    2 1, 2, 3, 4, 5

9. **1** 1.9×10^3
    2 7.6×10^5

10. **1** 8 km/h
    2 30 km/h
    3 5.05 pm, 33 km from A

11. $x + y = 30$, $2x + y = 40$, 20 trainees

12. 4.45 min

Page 423   Exercise D3

1. mean 52 g, range 11 g

2. 8 amps

3. **1** 18°C, 4 am
    2 4 pm, 36°C

4. **1** 5 units
    2 $-1\frac{1}{3}$

5. **1** 20 ℓ
    2 £9.44
    3 £2.40

7. **1** pf (pence)
    2 $\frac{y}{x}$ pence
    3 $12 - x$, $x(12 - x)$
    4 $(x - 2)$ years
    5 £$(12x + 52y)$

8. **1** $2\frac{1}{3}$ **2** $7 : 3$

9. totals: R 16, S 10, T 23, U 11

10. 270 m

11. $x = 2$, $y = 1$

12. £52.56

Page 425   Exercise D4

1. **1** 100   **5** 1000   **8** 60
    2 1000   **6** 100   **9** 100
    3 60   **7** 1000   **10** 1 000 000
    4 1000

2. $\frac{1}{9}$

3. **1** $s = 14$
    2 0.88

4. 99°

6. $3 : 4$

7. orange 13p, lemon 20p

8. angles: 60, 90, 108, 120, 135, 140, 144;
    angle (7 sides) 129°

9. $\overrightarrow{OD} = \begin{pmatrix} 7 \\ 11 \end{pmatrix}$, $\overrightarrow{AD} = \begin{pmatrix} 6 \\ 8 \end{pmatrix}$, length 10 units

10. **1** prime; no, no, no, no, no, no
    2 not prime; no, yes
    3 prime; no, no, no, no, no, no
    4 not prime; no, no, no, no, yes
    5 not prime; no, no, no, no, no, yes

11. **1** 31.4 cm
    2 60°
    3 equilateral
    4 5 cm

12. £725, £75

Page 430   Exercise D5

4. **1** £49 945
    2 £53 243
    3 Freightliner, £3298
    4 Freightliner, 0.88 tons
    5 numbers in order:
         3099, 3432, 523, 510, 1254, 1220, 4880,
         5160; Truckmaster, 280 gallons
    6 337
    7 317
    8 30 330 miles
    9 28 530 miles
    10 1057 h
    11 957 h

Page 435   Exercise 21.1

1. **1** $\frac{9}{20}$ **2** $\frac{5}{8}$

2. **1** $\frac{3}{10}$ **2** $\frac{1}{2}$ **3** $\frac{7}{20}$

3. $\frac{3}{40}$

4. **1** $\frac{5}{12}$ **2** 49

5. **1** $\frac{3}{8}$ **2** $\frac{1}{4}$

6. **1** 0.35   **2** 0.45   **3** 0.05

7. **1** 0.2   **2** 0.3

Page 439   **Exercise 21.2**

1. $\frac{4}{25}$

2. **1** $\frac{4}{7}$ **2** $\frac{2}{7}$ **3** $\frac{8}{49}$

3. $\frac{1}{2}$

4. **1** $\frac{1}{25}$ **2** $\frac{1}{5}$

5. $\frac{1}{64}$

6. **1** $\frac{1}{10}$ **2** $\frac{1}{100}$

7. **1** $\frac{1}{16}$ **2** $\frac{1}{4}$

8. 0.0576

9. **1** $\frac{1}{10}$ **2** $\frac{1}{40}$

Page 443   **Exercise 21.3**

1. **1** $\frac{1}{25}$ **2** $\frac{8}{25}$ **3** $\frac{16}{25}$

2. **1** $\frac{1}{12}$ **2** $\frac{7}{12}$

3. 68%

4. **1** $\frac{125}{216}$ **2** $\frac{25}{72}$ **3** $\frac{5}{72}$ **4** $\frac{1}{216}$

5. **1** $\frac{27}{64}$ **2** $\frac{27}{64}$ **3** $\frac{9}{64}$ **4** $\frac{1}{64}$

Page 445   **Exercise 21.4**

1. **1** $\frac{8}{15}$ **2** $\frac{7}{15}$

2. **1** 0.01
    2 0.998
    3 0.83

3. **1** 0.06
    2 0.4
    3 0.7

4. **1** 0.18
    2 0.02
    3 0.2

5. **1** $\frac{1}{7}$ **2** $\frac{1}{42}$

6. **1** $\frac{8}{75}$ **2** $\frac{11}{25}$

7. **1** $\frac{1}{16}$ **2** $\frac{1}{676}$ **3** $\frac{15}{169}$

8. $\frac{3}{5}$

9. **1** $P(2) = P(12) = \frac{1}{36}$,

      $P(3) = P(11) = \frac{1}{18}$,

      $P(4) = P(10) = \frac{1}{12}$,

      $P(5) = P(9) \ = \frac{1}{9}$,

      $P(6) = P(8) \ = \frac{5}{36}$,

      $P(7) = \frac{1}{6}$

    2 7

    3 $\frac{1}{216}$

10. **1** 0.81   **2** 0.19

11. **1** $\frac{1}{25}$ **2** $\frac{8}{25}$

12. **1** $\frac{1}{16}$ **2** $\frac{9}{16}$ **3** $\frac{3}{8}$

13. **1** 0.3   **2** 0.343   **3** 0.441   **4** 0.784

14. **1** 0.54   **2** 0.375

15. **1** $\frac{1}{49}$ **5** $\frac{1}{2401}$
    2 $\frac{8}{49}$ **6** $\frac{9}{2401}$
    3 $\frac{25}{49}$ **7** $\frac{128}{2401}$
    4 $\frac{20}{49}$

Page 448   **Practice test 21**

1. $\frac{4}{15}$

2. **1** $\frac{11}{32}$ **2** $\frac{21}{32}$ **3** $\frac{63}{64}$

3. $\frac{1}{12}$

4. **1** $\frac{1}{12}$ **2** $\frac{1}{10}$ **3** $\frac{1}{120}$

5. **1** $\frac{2}{5}$ **2** $\frac{7}{15}$ **3** $\frac{2}{15}$

6. **1** $\frac{1}{4}$ **2** $\frac{7}{24}$

Page 451   Exercise 22.1

2. 1 $x^2 + 7x + 6$ 11 $3x^2 - 14xy - 24y^2$
    2 $x^2 - 10x + 21$ 12 $2x^2 + 3xy - 5y^2$
    3 $x^2 + 2x - 15$ 13 $9x^2 + 6xy + y^2$
    4 $x^2 + 8x + 16$ 14 $4x^2 + 8xy - 21y^2$
    5 $2x^2 + 7x + 5$ 15 $4x^2 + xy - 3y^2$
    6 $6x^2 - 7x - 5$ 16 $9x^2 + 12x + 4$
    7 $2x^2 - 5x + 3$ 17 $16x^2 - 9$
    8 $4x^2 - y^2$ 18 $4x^2 - 4xy + y^2$
    9 $60 + 11x - x^2$ 19 $x^2 - 16y^2$
    10 $x^2 - 2xy + y^2$ 20 $9x^2 + 3xy - 2y^2$

3. $3x^2 + 2x + 16$

Page 452   Exercise 22.2

1. 1 $5(2x - 3y)$ 11 $a^2(1 + a)$
    2 $3y(x - 4z)$ 12 $a(a + 2b - c)$
    3 $4\pi(a - b)$ 13 $7(7 + x^3)$
    4 $5(4abc + 2a - b + 5c)$ 14 $2\pi r(r + h)$
    5 $7xy(2x + 3y)$ 15 $xy(x - y)$
    6 $3(a + 2b + 4c)$ 16 $2(3c^2 - 2d^2)$
    7 $x(4x + 3)$ 17 $5e(e - 2f + 3g)$
    8 $a^2(a + b)$ 18 $4ax(a + 2x)$
    9 $y(y - 6)$ 19 $7x^2(3x - 2)$
    10 $x(2x^2 + y^2)$ 20 $t(t^2 + 3t + 1)$

2. 1 24.3   4 31.42
    2 169   5 6800
    3 9700

3. 628

4. $n + 2, n + 4, n + 6, n + 8$; $5n + 20$; $5(n + 4)$

Page 456   Exercise 22.3

1. 1 $x = \pm 12$ 6 $x = \pm 1.9$
    2 $x = 7$ 7 $x = 2.20$
    3 $x = \pm 0.24$ 8 $x = 1.01$
    4 $x = 49$ 9 $x = 0.81$
    5 $x = 216$ 10 $x = \pm 3.16$

2. 1 $x = \dfrac{c + b}{a}$ 4 $t = \sqrt{\dfrac{s}{5}}$

    2 $x = x = \sqrt{\dfrac{E}{3}}$ 5 $length = \dfrac{area}{breadth}$

    3 $x = \dfrac{v - u}{a}$ 6 $R = \dfrac{A - P}{P}$

7 $n = \dfrac{t + 360}{180}$ 9 $x = \dfrac{3y + 4}{2}$

8 $distance =$
   $speed \times time$ 10 $V = \sqrt{PR}$

3. 1 $h = \dfrac{S}{2\pi r}$ 3 $\dfrac{S}{2\pi r} = \dfrac{V}{\pi r^2}$

    2 $h = \dfrac{V}{\pi r^2}$ 4 $V = \dfrac{Sr}{2}$

4. 1 $x = 9a^2 - 2$
    2 $x = 34$
    3 $x = (3a - 2)^2, x = 16$

5. 1 $\ell = \dfrac{T^2 g}{4\pi^2}$

    2 $\ell = 1.01$

Page 458   Exercise 22.4

1. 2

2. $y = \frac{1}{4} x^2, 6\frac{1}{4}$

3. 9

4. 8

5. $y = 8x^3, 8000$

6. $\frac{1}{4}$

7. 125

8. 28

9. $y = \dfrac{90}{\sqrt{x}}, y = 11\frac{1}{4}$

10. 5 cm

11. 6.4 m^2

Page 459   Exercise 22.5

1. 1 $x^2 + 6x + 5$ 6 $6x^2 - x - 12$
    2 $x^2 - 8x + 12$ 7 $4x^2 - 20x + 25$
    3 $x^2 - 16$ 8 $x^2 - y^2$
    4 $x^2 + 6x + 9$ 9 $x^2 - 2xy - 15y^2$
    5 $3x^2 + 23x + 14$ 10 $4x^2 + 4xy - 15y^2$

2. area of $ABCD = (x + 4)^2$ cm^2
    area of triangles $= 8x$ cm^2
    area of $PQRS = (x^2 + 16)$ cm^2

3. $x = 20$, area $= 150$ cm^2

4. 0

5. **1** $7(2x - 3y)$ **6** $t(t + 1)$
    2 $3y(x + 3z)$ **7** $a(a + b - 2c)$
    3 $2\pi(a - b)$ **8** $3(3 + x^3)$
    4 $3(2a - b + 3c)$ **9** $2x(x + y)$
    5 $5x(3x - 5)$ **10** $2(2b - 1)$

6. **1** 35   **4**   15.3
    2 204   **5**   37
    3 31

7. $n(n + 1)$

8. **1** $x = \dfrac{c - ab}{a}$ **3** $x = \dfrac{5a}{3}$

    2 $x = \sqrt{a^2 - b^2}$ **4** $x = \dfrac{(b - 5)^2}{4}$

9. **1** $18\frac{3}{4}$ **2** $x = \sqrt{\dfrac{6V}{h}}$

10. **1** $c = \dfrac{b^2}{a}$ **2** $b = \sqrt{ac}$

11. **1** $(y = 0)$ **3**   55 m
    2 9 m   **4**   5 m

12. 6 kg

13. $2\frac{1}{2}$ h

14. 3 ohms

15. 12.5 tonnes

Page 462   Practice test 22

1. **1** $x^2 + 6x + 8$ **4** $x^2 - 100y^2$
    2 $x^2 + 14x + 49$ **5** $5x^2 - 22x - 48$
    3 $6x^2 - 13x + 6$

2. $x = 10$; square side 12 cm, rectangle 18 cm by
    8 cm

3. **1** $5(x + 3y)$ **4** $6(x^3 + 2)$
    2 $3x(x - 2)$ **5** $x(x^2 + y)$
    3 $4b(a - 3c)$

4. **1** $n = \dfrac{a - 360}{180}$ **4** $F = \dfrac{9C}{5} + 32$

    2 $r = \dfrac{s - a}{a}$ **5** $n = \dfrac{2s}{a + \ell}$

    3 $x = \dfrac{b^2}{4}$

5. **1** $R = \dfrac{100(A - P)}{P}$ **2** $R = 7\frac{1}{2}$

6. $y = \dfrac{36}{x^2}$, $y = 2\frac{1}{4}$

7. $W = 0.008\ell d^2$, 8.4 kg

Page 466   Exercise 23.1

1. **1** 2.74 cm
    2 4.60 cm
    3 5.47 cm

2. **1** 6.34 cm   **3**   12.7 cm
    2 3.71 cm   **4**   6.09 cm

3. **1** 6.95 cm
    2 3.28 cm
    3 2.66 cm

4. **1** 2.55 cm   **4**   5.07 cm   **7**   14.6 cm
    2 8.39 cm   **5**   7.47 cm   **8**   5.23 cm
    3 2.24 cm   **6**   8.67 cm   **9**   15.6 cm

5. 2.15 cm

6. 75 m

Page 469   Exercise 23.2

1. **1** 19.5°   **3**   26.7°
    2 33.7°   **4**   27.5°

2. **1** 45.6°
    2 48.2°
    3 36.9°

3. **1** $\angle A = 50.2°$, $\angle B = 39.8°$
    2 $\angle C = 53.1°$, $\angle A = 36.9°$
    3 $\angle B = 28.8°$, $\angle C = 61.2°$

4. **1** $\frac{8}{17}, \frac{15}{17}, \frac{8}{15}, \frac{15}{17}, \frac{8}{17}, \frac{15}{8}$

    2 $AB = 13$ cm; $\frac{12}{13}, \frac{5}{13}, \frac{12}{5}$

5. **1** 37.9°   **4**   40.5°
    2 53.1°   **5**   33.6°
    3 58.0°

6. 65°

7. 106°

8. **1** 11.8 cm   **2**   58.9 cm^2

Page 473   Exercise 23.3

1. 75 m

2. 17°

3. **1** 5.45 cm   **3**   22.8 cm^2
    2 8.39 cm   **4**   45.7 cm^2

4. **1** 90°   **3** 851 m
    2 293 m   **4** 277 m

5. 246 m

6. **1** 63 km   **2** 102 km

7. **1** 21 m
    2 45 m
    3 6.6°

8. 12.2 km, 260°

9. $AC = 6$ km, angle 7°

10. 32 m, 13°

Page 475   Practice test 23

1. 19.5 m

2. height = 9.51 cm, area = 47.6 cm^2

3. 201°

4. **1** 68.7°   **2** 42.6°

Page 481   Exercise 24.1

1. cum. freq. in order: 0, 2, 6, 16, 43, 60, 66, 74, 80
    3 59
    4 70, 51
    5 19

2. cum. freq: 0, 3, 13, 40, 73, 93, 99, 100
    3 63 kg
    4 71 kg, 54 kg
    5 17 kg

3. cum. freq: 0, 2, 12, 32, 47, 55, 60
    median 31 mm
    quartiles 35 mm, 28 mm
    interquartile range 7 mm

4. cum. freq: 0, 8, 55, 79, 96, 100
    median 19 min
    quartiles 28 min, 14 min
    interquartile range 14 min

5. cum. freq: 0, 6, 26, 66, 120, 165, 180
    median 44 000 km
    quartiles 53 000 km, 35 000 km
    interquartile range 18 000 km
    over 55 000 km, 21%

Page 483   Exercise 24.2

1. cum. freq: 0, 4, 13, 25, 44, 61, 72, 77, 80
    median 179 cm
    quartiles 182 cm, 175 cm
    interquartile range 7 cm

2. cum. freq: 0, 23, 51, 68, 79, 85, 90 (less than 17)
    median 12.8 years
    quartiles 14.0 years, 12.0 years
    interquartile range 2.0 years

3. cum. freq: 0, 7, 25, 56, 101, 161, 195, 200
    median 45 mph
    quartiles 49 mph, 39 mph
    interquartile range 10 mph

4. cum. freq: 0, 3, 11, 35, 56, 70, 72
    median 28.6 m
    quartiles 31.2 m, 26.4 m
    interquartile range 4.8 m

5. cum. freq: 0, 19, 47, 77, 96, 109, 118, 120
    median 4.9 years
    quartiles 7.4 years, 2.8 years
    interquartile range 4.6 years

6. cum. freq: 0, 6, 16, 33, 57, 72, 77, 80
    median 5.6 min
    quartiles 6.1 min, 5.1 min
    interquartile range 1.0 min
    longer: 17.5% of the workers

7. cum. freq: 0, 10, 22, 49, 86, 108, 120
    median £26
    quartiles £44, £13
    interquartile range £31

8. cum. freq. (men): 0, 13.7, 27.4, 44.2, 58.2,
    71.4, 82.1, 92.0, 97.7, 100
    (women): 0, 12.3, 24.7, 40.3, 53.5, 66.0, 76.4,
    87.0, 95.0, 100
    median: men 34 years, women 37 years
    quartiles: men 53 years, 18 years;
                women 59 years, 20 years
    interquartile range: men 35 years,
                          women 39 years

Page 485   Practice test 24

1. median 6.9 min
    quartiles 12.9 min, 2.8 min
    interquartile range 10.1 min

2. cum. freq. (A): 0, 1, 5, 10, 23, 38, 50, 56, 59, 60
    (B): (0), 0, 1, 3, 7, 12, 21, 34, 49, 60
    median A 55, B 77
    quartiles A 66, 44; B 87, 63
    interquartile range A 22, B 24

Page 490   Exercise 25.1

1. y-values: 64, 36, 16, 4, 0, 4, 16, 36, 64

2. y-values: 10, 4, 0, −2, $−2\frac{1}{4}$, −2, 0, 4, 10

3. y-values: -4, 3, 8, 11, 12, 11, 8, 3, -4; greatest value 12

4. y-values: 5, 0, -3, -4, -3, 0, 5; $(1, -4)$

5. y-values: 7, 1, -3, -5, -5, -3, 1, 7; $x = \frac{1}{2}$

6. y-values: 16, 9, 4, 1, $\frac{1}{4}$, 0, $\frac{1}{4}$, 1, 4, 9, 16

7. y-values: -48, -15, 0, 3, 0, -3, 15, 48

8. y-values: -27, -8, -1, $-\frac{1}{8}$, 0, $\frac{1}{8}$, 1, 8, 27

9. y-values: 10, 5, 3.3, 2.5, 2, 1.7, 1.3, 1, 0.5, 0.3, 0.3, 0.2, 0.1, 0.1

Page 493   Exercise 25.2

1. y-values: 7, 0, -5, -8, -9, -8, -5, 0, 7; least value -9

7.   **1** $y = x^2 - 4x + 4$
    2 $y = 4 - x^2$
    3 $y = 4x^2$

8. y-values: $-4\frac{1}{2}$, -6, -9, -18, 18, 9, 6, $4\frac{1}{2}$;

    when $x = 0.6$, $y = 30$; when $x = -0.6$, $y = -30$

9. $x^2 + 12x - 80 = 0$; 4.8 cm

10. $y = 3x^2$; y-values: 0, 300, 1200, 2700, 4800, 7500; 135 m by 45 m

11. $y = x^2(5 - x)$;
2.4 m by 2.4 m by 2.6 m or 4.1 m by 4.1 m by 0.9 m

Page 495   Practice test 25

1. y-values: -7, 0, 5, 8, 9, 8, 5, 0, -7; greatest value at $(1, 9)$

3.   **1** $y = \dfrac{x}{3}$ **3** $y = 3 - x$

    2 $y = 3x^2$ **4** $y = \dfrac{3}{x}$

4. $y = \dfrac{600}{x}$

Page 496   Exercise E1

1. $\frac{3}{4}$
2. 28
3. 30
4. 12
5. 2.7 kg
6. $(0, 5)$
7. 10 cm
8. $\frac{1}{3}$
9. 9
10. 8 kg
11. 8 cm
12. 20%
13. 10
14. 3 kg
15. 52 cm^2

Page 497   Exercise E2

1. $64°$

2. 5.2×10^{-3}

3.   **1**   48 g
    2 $47°C$

4.   **1** $a = \dfrac{v^2 - u^2}{2s}$

    2 $h = \dfrac{3V}{\pi r^2}$

    3 $r = \sqrt{\dfrac{S}{4\pi}}$

5. 110 ml for 92p

6. mean 2.06, median 2, mode 2

7.   **1**   **D**
    2   **A**

8.   **1** $y = -x$ **4** $y = -x + 3$
    2 $y = \frac{1}{2}x$ **5** $y = 2x + 1$
    3 $y = x - 1$

9. $DE = 13.5$ cm, $DF = 12$ cm

10.   **1** $\frac{1}{16}$ **2** $\frac{25}{72}$

11. $AC = 12$ cm; $\frac{4}{5}, \frac{3}{5}, \frac{4}{3}$

12. cum. freq: 0, 13.7, 27.4, 44.3, 58.3, 71.5, 82.2, 92.1, 97.8, 100;
median 34 years;
interquartile range 36 years;
over 65, 13%

Page 499   Exercise E3

1. 1 h 30 min

2. $39°$

3.   **1** $-\frac{2}{3}$ **2**   23   **3**   4

5.   **1**   0.8
    2   0.2

6. $\frac{1}{6}$, £240 000

7.   **1** $\frac{4}{7}$ **2** $\frac{2}{7}$

8. 25 576

9. 585 m

10. **1** $\sqrt{225} + \sqrt{64}$, by 6
    2 3^7, by 139
    3 43

11. **1** $A = 2x^2 + 4xh$
    2 110
    3 $h = \dfrac{A - 2x^2}{4x}$
    4 6 cm

12. cum. freq: 0, 14, 48, 70, 100, 118, 120;
    median 5.1 cm;
    interquartile range 4.4 cm

Page 502   Exercise E4

1. **1** 532   **4** 500
   2 0.035   **5** 9
   3 0.04

2. $-\frac{1}{2}$

3. 0.36

4. **1** 255°
   2 305°
   3 125°

5. 6 m

6. $x = 1.2$, $y = 0.8$

7. **1** **B**   **2** **D**   **3** **A**   **4** **C**

8. $x + y = 10$, $4y - x = 5$; $x = 7$, $y = 3$;
   $PQ = 21$ cm, $QR = 26$ cm, $PR = 13$ cm

9. 190 m

10. **1** $\frac{4}{15}$ **2** $\frac{1}{30}$ **3** $\frac{7}{15}$

11. **1** $0.01\dot{8}\dot{5}$
    2 0.019
    3 0.0185

12. y-values: -10, -2, 2, 5, 7.6, 10; $x = 2.4$ (2.45)

Page 504   Exercise E5

1. **1** $2\frac{2}{3}$ **2** 4   **3** $2\frac{3}{4}$

2. 36°

3. **1** $x = \dfrac{y - c}{m}$ **3** $x = \dfrac{b}{a + c}$
   2 $x = \dfrac{(y + 3)^2}{4}$ **4** $x = \sqrt{y - 4}$

4. 122°

5. **1** 12
   2 82

6. **1** 6   **3** 8.5
   2 7.5   **4** 12

8. C (18, 14, 0),
   F (18, 2, 15),
   G (18, 14, 15),
   H (2, 14, 15),
   $AC = 20$ units,
   $AG = 25$ units

9. $\overrightarrow{AB} = \overrightarrow{DC} = \begin{pmatrix} 2 \\ 4 \end{pmatrix}$,

   $\overrightarrow{BC} = \overrightarrow{DC} = \begin{pmatrix} -1 \\ -10 \end{pmatrix}$; parallelogram

10. $x \geqslant 3$, $y \geqslant 3$, $x + y \leqslant 12$, $2x + y \leqslant 16$

11. **1** $\frac{8}{15}$ **2** $\frac{7}{15}$ **3** 60

12. 71

Page 506   Exercise E6

1. **1** £187.20
   2 50 h

2. **1** $6x^5 + 2x^3$ **4** $6x^2 - 13xy - 5y^2$
   2 $x^2 - 8x + 7$ **5** $4x^2 + 4xy + y^2$
   3 $2x^2 + 11x + 15$

3. 1 : 2 000 000

4. $\frac{1}{6}$, $\frac{5}{9}$

5. $t + c = 180$, $2t + \frac{1}{2}c = 240$;
   table £100, chair £80

6. $x + y \leqslant 24$, $x \geqslant y$, $x \leqslant 3y$, $3y + x \geqslant 30$

7. cum. freq: 0, 2, 5, 19, 42, 86, 104, 109, 112;
   median 4.3%;
   interquartile range 1.6%;
   48 shares

8. 25%, 12.5%

9. **1** Pythagoras
   2 11 in (5, 11, 13) should be 12
   3 (13, 84, 85)

10. 6, 5.97

12. 50 s

Page 508   Exercise E7

1. **1** $2x(x + 4y)$
   2 $x(x - 12)$
   3 $4(3x^2 + 1)$

2. 69°

3. **1** 9 should be 10; triangular numbers;
   36, 45, 55
   2 22 should be 21; 55, 89, 144
   3 6 should be 8; 1000, yes
   4 66 should be 65; 44, 37, 30

5. **1** $\frac{1}{8}$ **2** $\frac{1}{4}$ **3** 0 **4** $2\frac{1}{3}$

6. yes **1, 3, 4**

7. **1** W
   2 Y
   3 X

9. y-values: 6, 1, -2, -3, -2, 1, 6

11. $x = 4.4$

12. £3.60